DATE DUE

SE 29 '95		
OC 21 '94		
OC 27 '95		
RENEW		
MR 8 '96		
MY 21 03		
AP 26 06		

DEMCO 38-296

GHOST TOWNS AND
MINING CAMPS OF CALIFORNIA

BOOKS BY REMI NADEAU

City-Makers
The Water Seekers
Ghost Towns and Mining Camps of California
Los Angeles: From Mission to Modern City
California: The New Society
Fort Laramie and the Sioux
The Real Joaquin Murieta
Stalin, Churchill and Roosevelt Divide Europe

Ghost Towns & Mining Camps of California

A HISTORY & GUIDE
BY REMI NADEAU

CREST PUBLISHERS, SANTA BARBARA, CALIFORNIA

COPYRIGHT © 1965 BY REMI NADEAU

Library of Congress Catalog Number 90-83223

PRINTED IN THE UNITED STATES OF AMERICA

Eighth Printing, 1990, Revised
ISBN 0-9627104-0-7 Softcover

Cover design by Michael Silverander
Maps by Robert S. Langstaff

Some of the material in this book was drawn from the following articles by Remi Nadeau: "Ho! For Kern River", Westways, November, 1951; "The Forty-eighters", Westways, March, 1958; "Where Fremont Dug Gold", Westways, November, 1958; "Joaquin — Hero, Villain or Myth?" Westways, January, 1963; "Go It, Washoe!" American Heritage, April, 1959.

Crest Publishers
P.O. Box 22614
Santa Barbara
CA 93121-2614

To Christine, Barbara and Remi

Acknowledgments

As I have been haunting ghost towns since childhood, the list of those to whom I am indebted for helping to shape this book is almost endless. My father and mother, Mr. and Mrs. Remi E. Nadeau, took me on old trails to abandoned towns as soon as I was old enough to travel. Both of them have visited most of the towns mentioned herein, including a few I have not seen. My wife, Margaret, was sporting enough to accompany me to Bodie and Aurora during our honeymoon in the Sierras, and has since bumped over many a sandy road to a lonely desert camp. Our children—Christine, Barbara, and Remi—have more than once fought their way through sagebrush to view a few crumbling walls.

In my own childhood I was fortunate enough to meet such mining camp authorities as W. A. Chalfant of Bishop, Jim Cain of Bodie, and John Delameter, formerly of Calico. Over many years since then I have drawn on the personal knowledge of Ed Shepherd and Mrs. Jack Gunn of Independence; Edward Elder of Lone Pine; Paul Hubbard, formerly of Randsburg; George Pipkin, formerly of Wildrose Station; Sewell "Pop" Lofink of China Lake; Douglas Mooers of Malibu (grandson of the discoverer of Randsburg); Mrs. J. S. Gorman of Moorpark; and W. J. Jenkins of Oakland. For special information I am indebted to Stephen Ginsburg of North Hollywood, an authority on Southern California ghost towns.

The most important source for the history of California mining towns is the body of letters, diaries, newspapers, reminiscences, and other original papers in various libraries and museums. Those institutions and persons most helpful over many years were the U.C.L.A. Library; Los Angeles County Museum Library; San Diego Public Library; Pasadena Public Library; Santa Monica Public Library; Inyo County Free Library at Independence, California; St. Joseph Public Library, St. Joseph, Missouri; Library of Congress, Washington, D.C.; History Room of the Wells Fargo Bank, San Francisco; American Antiquarian Society, Worcester, Massachusetts; Miss Mary Helen Peterson, Miss H. Elizabeth Martenis, William G. Wise, and Irwin Stein at the History Department of the Los Angeles Public Library; Miss Mary Isabel Fry and Dr. Edwin Carpenter at the Henry E. Huntington Library in San Marino; Frank Brezee and John Barr Tompkins at the Bancroft Library, University of California at Berkeley; Allan R. Ottley of the California State Library at Sacramento; James R. Koping of the Stockton Public Library; and Dorothy Cragen of the Eastern California Museum at Independence. I am also indebted to the *Inyo Register* of Bishop and to Donald Segerstrom of Sonora for permission to use their collections of mining town newspapers; to the office of the *Mariposa Gazette*; to Mr. and Mrs. Kenneth Robinson, Fred Richards, and Mrs. Sylvia Winslow of China Lake; and to two other ghost town buffs, E. D. Nadeau and Douglas Nadeau.

The drawings and photographs used as illustrations were all collected and selected by Robert A. Weinstein, of the Ward Ritchie Press.

Mr. Walter Clark, of the Research Laboratories, Eastman Kodak, was immensely helpful in providing very rare photographs of the American River mining camps in 1856.

Particularly gracious and helpful were The Henry E. Huntington Library, The California Historical Society, The Society of California Pioneers, The History Room of the Wells-Fargo Bank, The History Division of the Los Angeles County Museum, The California State Library, Title Insurance and Trust Co. of Los Angeles and San Diego, the George Eastman House, Eastern California Museum and the Bancroft Library.

Of especial assistance were Mr. Remi E. Nadeau, Dr. Edwin Carpenter, Mr. James De T. Abajian, Mrs. Helen Giffen, Mr. Douglas Mooers, Miss Irene Simpson, Miss Ruth I. Mahood, Mr. Allan R. Ottley, Mr. Joseph LaBarbera, Mr. Larry Booth, Mr. John Barr Tompkins, Mr. Beaumont Newhall and Dorothy Cragen. Both Mr. Burr Belden and Mr. Stephen Ginsburg have generously allowed the reproduction of certain rare photographs from their collections.

The photograph of the stamp mill at Panamint reproduced on page 177, credited to the *Westerners Brand Book No. 11*, is from the Russ Leadabrand Collection. The photograph on page 177 of Aurora, reproduced from the *Westerners Brand Book No. 11* was taken by Burton Frasher and is used through the courtesy of Burton Frasher Jr.

To stay within a reasonable scope it has been necessary to limit the towns covered to those originating as mining communities, and to eliminate those starting as agricultural, railroad, or oil centers. Generally, I have also restricted them to towns where metal—particularly gold, silver, and copper—was mined. Within these boundaries, I have tried to cover all those mining localities in California that were at one time large enough to be termed "towns," even though little might remain today.

Preface

If you want to find the essence of American character, study the people who made the Western mining frontier. For they left the restraints of society behind them and embarked on a desperate quest against the country's toughest natural obstacles. On such a background, the American spirit was painted in caricature — at its worst, and its best.

So this excursion through the Ghost Towns and Mining Camps of California is more than a collection of anecdote and story. It is a fragment of Americana which helps to explain the whole.

As for the towns themselves, many in this book are not ghostly, but are thriving communities included here because they are essential to the story and have their own atmosphere and relics of yesteryear. Many of the ghost towns have in the past been prey to vandals and looters. Today a more conservation-minded public tends to appreciate the charmed ruins and leaves them intact for others. The true ghost town buff follows the maxim, "Take nothing but photos, leave nothing but footprints."

Contents

Illustrations

PART I. THE DISCOVERY AND THE RUSH

TODAY'S *Mother Lode explorer should be cautioned on several possible misconceptions.*

First, the Gold Rush communities that have stayed alive and are presently well populated generally contain more old structures than the ghost towns. Occupied for generation upon generation, they were not allowed to fall into disrepair. So even though they don't appear in early-day dress, the old houses and stores are there if you can somehow get beneath the accretions of paint, stucco, and signboards. One way is to check the back of the main street buildings from a rear alley; there you will usually find the brick-arched windows, iron shutters, or rock walls that speak of the 1850s.

But these buildings were preserved with an eye to the practical, not the picturesque. If you are looking for the breath of antiquity you will want to seek the lovely ruins of towns that died. Many of them are on narrow (often dirt) roads heading into the Sierras east of Highway 49.

Yet one should remember that even these are not the living spirit of California mining camps, but their mortal remains. The air that hangs over these old scenes is one of sweet decay. They are fascinating, even romantic, but they give an opposite impression from the hellbent life that once surged through the same streets. To recapture such exciting pictures you have the rich opportunity to use your imagination.

Still another caution: Nearly all the oldest structures remaining in Mother Lode towns, dead or alive, date from the 1850s—generally from the middle and late '50s. The devastating fires that frequently swept the gold towns carried away the pioneer canvas, log, and board houses. Looking down most any main street, do not believe that you have caught hold of 1849. At best you are glimpsing the high tide of the gold boom in the maturing '50s. But after all, what more could be asked by any Gold Rush buff?

To help fill the gap of 1848 and '49, a narrative of events in these tumultuous years is provided in Part One.

*Daguerreotype of the saw mill at Coloma in which
James Marshall first discovered gold in 1848.*

Miners working placer deposits near original discovery site at Coloma, 1850-51.

Contemporary drawing showing a camp of Chinese miners in the early 1850's.

A group of young miners showing primitive equipment used in placer mining, 1853.

At Sardine Bar, miners turned the South Fork of the American River out of its bed to mine the gravel, 1856.

Daguerreotype portrait showing youthfulness of typical miner, 1849.

Miners going to their lunch at Cranwell's Bar, American River, 1856.

Wooden water wheels in river bed provide both water and power for washing out gold-bearing gravel, 1856.

Forest Hill, typical mountain mining community of the Sierras, 1856.

Chapter 1. "Gold! Boys, Gold!"

A PIECE OF YELLOW METAL. A little flake, shimmering in the water among the granite pebbles. Along the Sierra foothills millions like it lay in the stream beds, waiting to be discovered.

On a cold January morning in 1848, a tall, bewhiskered man —his eyes shaded by a slouch hat—is looking at this little flake. Through the quiet ripples it is plainly seen—shining and urgent—fairly dancing among its fellows.

The man stoops down, thrusts his hand into the icy water, seizes the flake. Sees another, takes it, too. Examines them closely. Can this be gold? Or iron pyrite—"fool's gold"? He sits down on the bank, hammers the first piece between two rocks. Under the blows the metal yields—spreads out, paper thin.

Back along the bank hurries James Marshall. Almost breathless, he arrives at a crude plank building—an unfinished sawmill. To the first workman he encounters Marshall shows the bright flakes in his hand.

"I have found it!" he declares, importantly.

The man looks up from his work, squints at the outstretched palm.

"What is it?"

"Gold!"

"Oh no!" is the dull answer, "that can't be."

His word doubted, Marshall replies with authority.

"I know it to be nothing else."

California's mighty treasure is unlocked, the giant oyster unhinged.

For centuries the Indians had seen and ignored it. For eighty years the Spanish, who knew gold when they saw it, occupied California without finding it. Franciscan missions rose and faded, Spanish rule was broken by Mexican revolution, and still the glittering booty lay undiscovered.

A trace had been found in Placerita Canyon, far to the south near the tiny pueblo of Los Angeles. A few other Southern

California canyons had yielded a few thousand dollars in gold. But compared to the fabulous mines of Mexico and Peru, this was nothing. To the Spanish, California was fit only for the production of cowhides and wine.

For twenty years a growing column of American trappers and traders had ventured across the massive Sierra into this Mexican province. Others had brought wagons and families, settling on the broad, rich valleys of the Pacific slope. Marshall himself was of this tribe—restless, dissatisfied, moving first to Oregon, then to California. All of them had passed by the very rivers that held the secret.

Still others—both Americans and Europeans—arrived by sailing vessel to take up land under the liberal policy of the Mexican governors. Typical was Captain John Augustus Sutter, a hearty Swiss who had come in 1839 by the roundabout route of Missouri and the Hawaiian Islands. From his thick-walled fort on the site of present-day Sacramento he ruled a veritable wilderness kingdom within Mexican California. His empire crept to the green Sierra slopes, knocking on the treasure house.

By 1846 the incoming foreigners had broken the Mexican dam. The United States was at war with Mexico, and Yankee squadrons descended on the California coast. After sharp fighting in the south, the province fell to the Americans. For months, while the war dragged on in Mexico, California was an occupied land—its future uncertain, its government the American military headquarters at Monterey.

At this unsettled moment Captain John Sutter chose to build a flour mill. To do so he needed lumber, and up in the pine-clad Sierra was an inexhaustible supply. In the summer of 1847 he sent a party of Indians and Americans into the wilderness to build a sawmill. Among the party were several Mormons, who had come to California in the American conquest. Leading the expedition was James Marshall—by trade, a wheelwright; by disposition, sullen, moody, excitable, a mystery to his closest companions.

In the wild, roaring South Fork of the American River, Marshall set up his camp. Locating the millsite inside a bend of the river, he dug a ditch that would divert a flow of water to drive the main wheel. And in that ditch, or tail race, he found gold on the morning of January 24, 1848.

Next morning, Marshall found more gold in the tail race. He and his companions tried it all by crude tests. At each experiment their hearts leaped higher.

Jim Marshall was now too agitated to think of anything but gold. He must hurry to Sutter with his discovery. Asking the men to keep the secret, he rode down the canyon on the 28th. That evening, in darkness and pouring rain, the anxious man arrived at the fort. There he and Sutter tested it; they found it to be what Sutter called "the finest kind of gold."

A few days later Sutter visited the discovery site and caught Marshall's enthusiasm. But he called the men around him and asked them to keep the secret for six weeks, so that he might finish his sawmill and flour mill before the excitement engulfed them all. To this they readily agreed. But while the men went back to work, Sutter and Marshall laid new plans. As partners, the discoverer and the landlord would reap the golden harvest. Urged on by Marshall, Sutter could see mountains of gold added to his empire.

Since the captain's original grant did not include the discovery site, the first step was to secure the land. Meeting with the local Indians, Sutter arranged to lease some ten or twelve square miles in return for clothing, farm implements and the promise to grind the native grain. He then returned to the fort and dispatched one of the mill hands, Charles Bennett, to Monterey. Sworn to secrecy, Bennett carried specimens of gold and a letter to the military governor, Col. Richard B. Mason. In it, Sutter asked for a pre-emption on the quarter section of land around the mill site. He and Marshall meant to control the gold fields with a double title.

Still, everything depended on secrecy. If the news escaped before Sutter's claim was confirmed, the treasure would lie open to every vagabond in California.

Then Sutter made his first mistake. Since the party at the mill needed provisions, he sent a wagonload by the Swiss teamster, Jacob Wittmer. When he returned to the fort he brought with him a sack of gold dust. That evening a few at the fort gathered in the blacksmith shop to see it tested. A yellow nugget was heated in the forge, then hammered on the anvil. Just as Marshall's original flake had done, it flattened under the blows—according to the nature of gold. Silence leaped into bedlam. Around the anvil the men danced—shouting, singing, laughing.

"Gold, gold, gold, it's gold, boys, it's gold!" chanted the loudest. "All of us will be rich! Three cheers for the gold!"

At this racket heads appeared at doorways all around the fort. Sutter himself stepped out of his room and motioned a friend to his side.

"My secret, I see, has been discovered," he said quietly, with a philosophic smile. "Since we expect to be rich, let's celebrate with a bottle of wine."

Down the Sacramento Valley in mid-February rode Sutter's secret emissary, Charles Bennett, carrying a land application to the governor. But he became instead a herald of gold to all he met, and a plague to Sutter. At the very first settlement—the board-walled village of Benicia—he poured forth the story. He showed the gold in the sprouting village of San Francisco. On down to Monterey pressed Bennett, spilling the news as he went. Into the adobe headquarters of Governor Richard B. Mason he stomped—presented Sutter's application and uncovered the gold. Mason refused the land application, but news of the gold discovery sprang through Monterey.

And so the beckoning cry resounded down the corridors of California. Gold was wealth, comfort, power. Now—almost for the first time—it could be won without a struggle. It lay in the Sierra canyons—shining and vibrant—to be picked up by the first arrivals.

This was the call, high and shrill, that broke on the frosty California air early in 1848. With the suddenness of a thunderclap, it killed a way of life, and brought forth another.

Up from Sutter's Fort in late February came the first modern Argonauts—three Mormon workmen heeding a message from a brother at the mill. At an exposed sand bar they struck far richer deposits than those in Marshall's tailrace. Back to the fort they went for supplies, and when they returned others trailed after them. Soon Mormon Island, as the sand bar was christened, became the first gold camp in California.

By this time the rumble of excitement was rising in San Francisco. The first miners were drifting in from the mountains, displaying bags of gold dust to curious street-corner crowds. Beginning in mid-March the two weekly newspapers gave modest notice. Word came that miners averaged $20 to $30 per day—ten times the prevailing workman's wage. By April San Francisco was stripped of pickaxes and crucibles as the first gold hunters headed for Sutter's Fort.

In April Marshall finished his mill and began turning out lumber. But it was a pitiful attempt at sane endeavor in a world gone mad. For within a few days came Sam Brannan, brought up from San Francisco by an urgent letter from partner George Smith at the Fort Sutter store. A confirmed opportunist, Brannan had an eye for gold in any form. He had brought a shipload of Mormon settlers to California in 1846, had founded the first newspaper in San Francisco the following year, and now operated between the bay and the fort as a merchant and trader. Shrewdly he surveyed the busy scenes at the mill and Mormon Island. Here was a rich discovery that all of California deserved to know. And as the whole country would come storming in, he would be on hand to sell the necessities of life—from blankets to shovels to whisky. Back down to the bay hurried Sam Brannan. In mid-May he was striding through the dirt streets of San Francisco, waving a quinine bottle full of yellow dust.

"Gold! Gold!" he bellowed like a town crier. "Gold from the American River!"

All at once the California Gold Rush was on. What had been an unhurried exodus now became a headlong stampede. Carpenters dropped their hammers, clerks closed their books, grocers locked their doors. With shovel and pick in hand, they headed for Sutter's Fort. At the presidio, Yankee soldiers deserted in a body, galloping off with the officers' horses. Across the bay and up the Sacramento scooted a fleet of sailing launches, jammed with Argonauts.

Day after day that procession of sails increased. San Francisco, so recently enjoying a building boom, was left deserted and silent. The new schoolhouse, first in the city, lost its teacher. Even the magistrates and members of the Town Council left their duties. The two newspaper editors, losing their subscribers and their printers, stopped publication and joined the throng. By the end of May not a workman was left in town save one blacksmith, who was feverishly turning out pickaxes at $5 to $10 each.

The strange contagion was also spreading to the ships anchored in the harbor. Over the sides went the crews, commandeering the life boats and sailing up the Sacramento River. One captain, pleading in vain for his men to stay, finally lowered a boat and went with them. A whaling ship sailed into Golden Gate, unaware of the discovery. Anchoring behind Sausalito in Whaleman's Harbor, the skipper sailed across the bay to San Francisco in a whale boat. There the few remaining inhabitants told him to move out quickly for the islands or lose his crew. But by the time he had returned and weighed anchor, his men had learned the news. When they found the ship heading out the Golden Gate they refused to go. The captain was forced to put into San Francisco, where the sailors gagged the night watch, took the whale boats and raced for the mines.

By the end of May all Northern California was afire. Ripened grain was left standing in the field unharvested. The spring cattle roundups were forgotten. In Sonoma, Benicia—every settlement in the north—houses and streets were deserted. From San Jose the jailor hurried up the road, taking his prisoners with him to dig for gold. At Carquinez Straits hundreds waited to be ferried across in two small sailboats and a few flimsy rowboats. The more impatient refused to wait, and swung eastward for the treacherous crossings of the San Joaquin.

"Along the whole route," as one Forty-eighter described it, "mills were lying idle, fields of wheat were open to cattle and horses, houses were vacant and farms going to waste."

Not until the end of May did the gold fever strike the provincial capital at Monterey. Unable to believe the wondrous stories, the local *Alcalde* (magistrate) sent a messenger to the mines to find the truth. On June 20 the rider pounded back into town, and was immediately surrounded by eager citizens. Dismounting, he pulled from his pockets some nuggets and passed them around. Next moment Monterey was thrown into a panic. Soldiers and sailors deserted their posts. One boarding-house keeper ran off without collecting the bills due from her lodgers.

"All were off for the mines," noted *Alcalde* Walter Colton in his diary, "some on horses, some on carts, and some on crutches, and one went in a litter."

Within three weeks every servant in town has disappeared, leaving the *Alcalde* and the Governor of California to shift for themselves in the kitchen—"grinding coffee, toasting a herring and peeling onions!" The American consul, Thomas O. Larkin, had already dashed off for the mines, and had immediately sent back for all the spare shovels, buckets, bowls, baskets, pans and tin cups in Monterey.

Down the coast sprang the contagion. By July 18 it reached Los Angeles, where eight American soldiers deserted and three military prisoners broke out of jail. They rode northward under a hail of bullets with a body of dragoons after them.

The story was the same in every coastal town, each of which had a company or more of the First Regiment of New York Volunteers, who were waiting to be mustered out of service and receive four months' back wages. Over 300 of them—one-third of the whole—deserted. The rest were mustered out in September and decamped immediately for the mines.

As early as June the news had flown beyond California. Members of the Mormon Battalion returning to Salt Lake after the Mexican War threw that young community into new excitement. But Brigham Young pronounced a warning against the California fever.

"If you elders of Israel want to go to the gold mines," he chided them, "go and be damned!"

Most of the Saints held to Brigham's counsel, though a few companies hitched up their teams and hurried to California.

"If they have a golden god in their hearts," he roared after them, "they had better stay where they are!"

Westward into the Pacific the word sailed, reaching Honolulu with the arrival of the schooner *Louise* on June 17. As ship after ship came in with wonderful tales and samples of the gold itself, the islanders caught the fever. Merchants found themselves so busy selling boots, shovels and pickaxes that they could hardly stop to count the money. Through the streets a frantic procession of boxes and bundles moved toward the wharves. On one vessel the captain and officers gave up their berths to the passengers, while others slept on the dining tables. Every ship sailing for San Francisco was crowded to the guards; one man shoved off into the Pacific in a whale boat, propelled only by a small sail and a pair of oars.

From the islands the schooner *Honolulu* carried the news to Oregon Territory, where American families were then carving new homes out of the wilderness. Catching the fever, the Oregonians dropped their plows, bade goodbye to wives and children, and headed southward. Throughout August pack trains were scurrying through the Willamette Valley for California. At Oregon City, Salem and other settlements, only women, children and old men were left to bring in the harvest. More than 2,000—two-thirds of the able-bodied men—left Oregon in 1848. Unable to muster a quorum, the Legislature was suspended. Both territorial newspapers stopped publication. The Attorney General, Commissary General, and judges of the territorial Supreme Court rushed off to California with pick and shovel.

Far to the south, sailing ships had also brought the news to the Pacific ports of South America by late summer of '48. Word sped through Peru of a "whole continent of gold." In Callao several vessels bound for other ports promptly set sail for California. One American schooner consigned to China turned her prow northward instead.

"Everybody here is almost crazy about it," wrote one Peruvian, "and numbers are preparing to leave Callao and pick up gold by basketfuls."

It was the same along the coast of Chile. Wrote a merchant of Valparaiso, "It is reported here that California is *all gold!*" So many clerks left Valparaiso that commerce came to a halt.

At the same time the news flew across the northern states of Mexico. Their own gold and silver mines in sad decline, the men of Sonora were ripe for the call. Soldiers, heads of government, men of wealth and position, all joined the throngs which left Tubac and Hermosillo in the fall of '48. In parties of fifty to a hundred they came, many with their entire families, their burros packed with provisions and mining tools.

Through the summer and fall the Forty-eighters swarmed across California's central plain and into the Sierra. Like some rag-tail army they came—motley, nondescript, wild-eyed. Onto the fertile plain of the Sacramento they descended—some of them breaking down fences, stealing horses, killing cattle as they chose. In their haste they left their campfires to burn along the road, setting the wheat fields aflame, so that the whole route from the bay to Sutter's Fort became a charred and smoldering waste. As they approached the mines every useful item was picked up and carried along like a leaf in the maelstrom. One landowner returned to his rancho at the junction of the Feather and Yuba Rivers to find the flooring torn up—the boards gone to make gold rockers for the mines. Upon Sutter's Fort the Argonauts fell like a horde of Goths.

"They stole the cattle and the horses," groaned Sutter, "they stole the bells from the Fort and the weights from the gates, they stole the hides, and they stole the barrels."

With one swoop the Forty-eighters conquered California—smashed its charming pastoral life, did what the invading American troops had never tried to do. The natives were almost left as bystanders in the onrushing stampede. In every pueblo they were the last to leave—and then only after the richness of the mines had been confirmed beyond doubt. In contrast to the restless Yankees they saw no point in rushing after gold when life was enjoyable enough in pastoral California. Were not the *fiesta* and the *fandango*, the roaring hearth and the welcome latch-string, paradise enough for any man? On his vast rancho bordering the north shore of San Francisco Bay, the aging Luis Peralta called his three boys about him while the world rushed past.

"My sons," he told them, gravely, "God has given this gold to the Americans. Had He desired us to have it, He would have given it to us ere now. Therefore, go not after it, but let others go. Plant your lands, and reap; these be your best gold fields. . . ."

But such wisdom was lost in this frenzied hour. Down upon the mines thundered the Forty-eighters. On almost every river where they sunk a pick, the happy miners had struck color. So much time was spent in following rumors of new strikes that most miners would have made more by remaining steadily in one spot. As fast as they explored every niche and corner of the treasure house, it yielded up more riches. A German struck a three-ounce nugget while digging a hole for a tent pole. An old man sitting on a rock was complaining of bad luck when a stranger suggested that he roll the stone over. This he did merely to humor the other—and discovered half a pound of gold! One soldier on furlough spent eight days in the mines and returned to duty at Monterey with more than five years' army wages.

So plentiful was the gold in '48 that the boys treated it recklessly, as though the supply was inexhaustible. Gold was taken so casually that it was freely loaned from one miner to another —sometimes to perfect strangers—in full confidence that it would be repaid. According to one story, a fellow was slow in returning six ounces to his tentmate, who dunned him for it at every meal. At the next reminder, the debtor rose abruptly from the table.

"Just wait ten minutes," he drawled, shouldering his pickaxe. "And *time* it."

Out into the night he stomped, and within the allotted time he was back with more than enough gold to settle the debt.

In the midst of such easy wealth, the mines were practically free of crime in '48. If a robber was caught his punishment was swift and sure. The boys dropped their picks, grabbed their rifles, formed a "miner's court" and tried him. If found guilty he was flogged or hanged, depending on the enormity of his crime. But through the first year in the mines, such justice was rarely invoked. Thousands of dollars were left in tents unguarded. A shovel or pick lying in a hole was the accepted sign of ownership, and no one thought of jumping the claim.

Yet California in '48 was no paradise. Gold digging was, in the words of one expert, "matter-of-fact, back-aching, wearisome work." Wages were not always high. When James Carson first arrived at Mormon Island he worked some fifty panfuls of dirt and recovered about fifty cents worth of gold. Complained another miner on the Stanislaus:

"I worked harder today than I ever did in my life, and all for what? Why, not more than twenty-five cents!"

Poor or rich, the Forty-eighter saw his pile diminish rapidly as he turned to buy the necessities of life at the wilderness stores of Sam Brannan, Charles Weber and other pioneer traders. Butter and cheese ran as high as $6 per pound. Blankets were $50 to $100. Shirts were $16, and were laundered but not ironed for $1 apiece. Horses were from $100 to $150 apiece, and since the miner could dig the price of a horse easier than he could feed and care for one, it was not unusual for him to pay this price for a mount, ride it to a new diggings, and then turn it loose.

Beset by hardships and extortionate prices, the miner adopted habits as rough and wild as his mountain surroundings. While carrying several thousand dollars on his person, he presented the most unwashed and beggarly appearance. He did manage to keep the Sabbath, but after his own fashion. Putting aside shovel and rocker, he spent Sunday washing his clothes, prospecting for new diggings, gambling away his week's earnings or drinking himself into a stupor. Living miles and sometimes continents away from home and family, he cast off civility with the ease of a snake shedding its skin. And although he remained honest in his dealings, he indulged in the most shameful dissipation whenever whisky found its way to the mines. Piles of bottles, purchased at $8 to $16 apiece, were commonplace sights in every populated gulch. One enterpriser hauled in a barrel of brandy and sold it by the wine glass, realizing $14,000. When a barrel of New England rum arrived on the Stanislaus the boys came running with every available container—cups, sauce pans and coffee pots—while one eager customer offered $10 to poke his straw in the bung.

Rivaling this pastime was the gaming table, which captured the miner's reckless spirit and most of his gold dust. Among the Sonorans gambling was a disease and a way of life. At their main camp on the Tuolumne, hundreds surged around the monte bank, frantically trying to lay their bets on the turn of a card. Throughout the mines poker was the favored game in '48. Bets ranged from one to six ounces, while one eyewitness reported a wager of thirty-six ounces, or $576. The pot was growing mightily in one game when a miner decided he needed more dust to see the last raise. Putting his pile aside, he calmly turned to a companion.

"Here, Jim," he remarked, "watch my pile until I go out and dig enough to call him."

Beginning in late summer the insufferable heat spread sickness through the mines, and the backwash of '48 began. Hordes of vagabonds descended upon Sutter's Fort, turning it into a carnival of humanity. To accommodate the traffic, Sutter had rented his stalls and shops to merchants, barkeepers and even a hotelman—so that the entire courtyard of the fort was filled with a sea of dishevelled miners, horses and wagons, piles of sacks and barrels, gaudy displays of merchandise. Here gambling and carousing raged around the clock as the wealth of the Sierra flowed in.

Nor had the high tide of gold-seekers yet appeared. Late in June Governor Mason headed for the mines to see for himself. There the miners crowded about to show their gold and tell fabulous tales of wealth. Returning to Monterey, Mason sent a letter to the War Department describing the gold excitement. There was enough gold in the new territory, he claimed, to pay for the Mexican War a hundred times over. On August 17 he sent it eastward in the hands of the trusted lieutenant, Lucien Loeser. With luck he would reach Washington in time to have the news incorporated in President James Polk's annual message to Congress.

Chapter 2. "Ho! for California!"

IN 1848 the American frontier stood at the great bend of the Missouri River, halted there by the forbidding plains and deserts that had been set aside for the Indians as their permanent hunting grounds. For a quarter century, however, trickles of population had spilled westward—traders to Santa Fe; pioneer settlers to Texas, Oregon and Upper California; and most recently, Mormon colonists to Salt Lake. Because the war with Mexico had suddenly brought much of this territory under American rule, the California emigration of 1849 was expected to be greater than usual. But there was no reason to believe that the frontier was ready to make another major advance.

By the early fall of '48 the fantastic story of California gold was spreading through the United States. Since August the first rumors had appeared in Atlantic newspapers. Since October letters from various officials in California had kindled a flame of interest. Excitement was beginning to rise when President James K. Polk confirmed the importance of the discovery in his message to Congress on December 5. To substantiate his words, he submitted the official report from Governor Mason.

Such confirmation, printed in newspapers throughout the country, was like a torch to the tinder. Lingering skepticism gave way to complete credulity. In every home, on every street corner, California was the overriding topic. Horace Greeley's New York *Tribune* cried out exultantly: "We are on the brink of the Age of Gold."

Through December, January and February, the nation was a scene of feverish preparation. Either as individuals or in hastily-formed "California mining associations," an army of gold hunters gathered provisions for the great trek. In store windows and newspaper ads, every conceivable commodity was labeled with the magic word "California." There were "California hats," "California pistols," even "California pork and beans." On doors and counters the posted notice "G. T. C." meant only one thing: "Gone to California."

Nearly everyone, in fact, had a friend or relative who had announced his departure—an act which immediately made him a home town hero. Almost all expected to return, wealthy and admired by all, within a year.

Since the overland passage was impossible in winter, the first Argonauts chose the ocean routes. For the first time, an important advance of the American frontier was spearheaded by sea, and led by those farthest East. As the California companies arrived at the coast, every port from Boston to New Orleans was overrun. Ticket offices were jammed; at the docks, a horde of Argonauts pleaded to be taken aboard the ships. Skippers and mates were so anxious to get off that they shipped as ordinary seamen, rather than wait for their own vessels to be outfitted. The ships were jammed with "Californians" who lined the railings like some guerrilla army about to invade a hostile shore. Rifles and shotguns were slung from their backs; revolvers and Bowie knives hung from their belts. At their sides were shovels, picks, gold pans and various "gold-sifting machines."

At length, with cheer upon cheer from relatives on the wharf, the ships would cast off—sometimes accompanied by the booming of a deck cannon. But as they stood out into the Atlantic, the spirit of hilarity was over. Heavy wintry seas and the fearful tossing of the deck sent every passenger to the rails. Could all the gold in California be worth such misery?

But once the landlubbers got their sea legs, the California fever seized them once more. Standing before the mast, they took the salt spray in their faces and conjured visions of California gold.

The quickest way to the mines was *via* the Isthmus of Panama, and since monthly postal service was just being established to California over this route, the earliest emigrants rode the mail steamers. Chugging across the Caribbean Sea, the paddlewheelers landed their passengers in eight or ten days at the miserable village of Chagres, on the Atlantic side of the Isthmus. From here they pushed on up the Chagres River in canoes, propelled along by native polesmen. Through tropical forests they rode, past chattering monkeys and parakeets. A thousand miles from the states, the Isthmian jungle resounded to "O Susannah!" as the Argonauts taught the words of this Gold Rush theme song to the canoemen.

After some forty miles they stopped at one of two primitive outposts, Gorgona or Cruces. From these points, roads led over the divide to the Pacific port of Panama. Though little more than a day's muleback ride, this was the toughest stretch of the entire trip. The Cruces road had been paved years before by the Spanish gold traders, but since the South American revolutions the traffic had vanished and the road was in bad repair. Great gullies cut across it, forcing a laborious descent into defiles so narrow that when a pack mule fell, it was impossible to raise him without removing the load. While the Argonauts stepped over the bodies of dead mules, vultures flapped out of the way, to return after the party had passed. As one Argonaut described the road, "It is only fit to be traveled by a mountain deer or goat. . . ."

In the evening the mule trains descended into the drowsy city of Panama, which sprawled by the Pacific in quiet decay. With the great days of the South American gold trade long past, she was now suddenly aroused to play the way station on another golden trek. The lusty Americans came upon her like some raucous storm—clattering through her streets, filling her hotels, crowding her fandango halls.

But in Panama their headlong rush abruptly halted. There were not enough ships to take them up the Pacific. By the spring of '49, 3,000 angry Americans idled in this unhealthy, vice-ridden city, their money wasting away in hotel bills and gambling losses. By October they were in a state of delirium. The arrival of a steamer was heralded by shooting of guns, shouting in the streets, and a wholesale stampede to the landing—followed by a nightlong celebration by the fortunate ticket-holders. When two new steamers were put into service, the Americans stormed the ticket office by the hundreds, breaking windows, collapsing the balustrade on the stairs, and finally fighting their way back into the street—hats crushed, clothing torn, hands clutching a precious ticket to California.

Similar problems were encountered by other emigrants crossing the continent above Panama. A few parties packed across Nicaragua, the Isthmus of Tehuantepec, and various other routes across Mexico. Except for the uncertainty of ship passage on the Pacific side, some of these proved to be simpler and safer than the beaten paths.

But the most popular sea route was the voyage round the Horn, which took from four to nine months, depending largely on the winds. In 1849 more than 15,000 Argonauts shipped *via* the Cape in what became known as the California Fleet. On this 15,000-mile trip, monotony was the chief enemy. In mid-Atlantic a sailing vessel might lie becalmed for days or even weeks while the passengers wore heavily on each other's nerves. All day long, the passengers were on deck playing whist or backgammon on the tops of barrels. Every school of porpoise was the signal for frantic unlimbering of fishing gear. Pistols were fired at sea birds and sharks, or in celebration of Independence Day or the crossing of the Equator—at any possible excuse.

As time wore on, more ingenious pastimes were devised: auction sales, debates, kangaroo courts, cotillion dances with half the men dressed as women. For such a diversion there was no lack of accompanying music. More than one ship had a complete band, which strolled along the deck blaring forth with "Yankee Doodle," "Home Sweet Home," and the inevitable "O Susannah!"

In the early spring of '49 the California army descended upon Rio de Janiero and the smaller port of St. Catherine's Island further down the Brazilian coast. Some arrived in time to participate in the pre-Lenten carnival. Most came afterward, when the streets were shrouded in silence and decorum. In this situation the hilarious Yankees made themselves conspicuous. There were riotous parties every night at the hotels. Soldiers patrolling the corners after the curfew hour challenged the revelers as they passed down the street, but the words "Americanos—amigos!" became the accepted password.

The same unruly spirit wore hard on the captains of the California Fleet. Years of sea adventure never schooled them to manage this wild cargo. The passengers insisted on climbing aloft in the rigging to help the crew. When the ship was becalmed they jumped overboard for a swim and a bath. Many of them consumed fearful quantities of rum and brandy, making it nearly impossible to keep the sailors sober.

On every ship a group of sturdy, God-fearing passengers worked against this carnival atmosphere. Church services were held on deck every Sunday. On one ship a temperance pledge was circulated the day after each new orgy. But the pious passengers noted with sadness the continuing rise of drinking and profanity.

Most of all, the Californians complained. They complained about the slow passage, the water supply, and especially the food. One distraught captain warned them he would put into the nearest port and have them thrown in irons for mutinous language. Another threatened to put them on short rations unless they stopped complaining.

"I never heard such grumbling," he observed, "even from whalemen."

Real troubles awaited the Californians as they approached the Horn. Once the vessels turned full under Tierra del Fuego, the raging Cape storms were upon them. Snow and sleet whitened the rigging; mountain-high seas broke against the bow, sending foaming waves over the deck, tossing the ship until its lee rail dipped the surface. Below, crockery and hardware flew in all directions. Passengers tried to sleep while holding tight to their bunks, lest they be plunged out of bed onto the brine-washed floor. Some of them prayed for the first time in their lives.

Off Tierra del Fuego the brig *Colorado* fought to keep from being blown onto the rocks. At the height of the storm the tops of the masts were broken off, dangling crazily above the deck. Robbed of its balance, the ship lurched uncontrolled before the storm. Wave after wave broke upon the helpless vessel. Water poured below decks, where the wretched passengers were frantically manning the buckets. Above the storm they heard the dread cry: "The ship is sinking!" The captain, haggard and dripping, came into the dining saloon.

"We can do nothing more," he told the stricken faces; "if it is God's will we shall be saved."

California gold was nothing in this sickening instant. But the ship stayed afloat until dawn, when the passengers found themselves clear of the rocky shore. The crew was cleaning the broken rigging from the battle-scarred deck. They were sailing westward under a fair wind.

Up the Pacific pressed the Californians—for the first time pointing toward the land of gold. Catching the southeast trades, they fairly flew up the Chilean coast. A few ships pushed on without stopping; more than one Argonaut traveled from New York to San Francisco without ever seeing the mainland. But most vessels were forced by water shortage to put into the Chilean ports—perhaps to pest-ridden Talcahuano or the more inviting Valparaiso—where for the first time they heard later news of the California mines.

Fired anew with tales of gold, they stood out to sea again, drawing halfway to the Hawaiian Islands in their quest for an eastward wind that would blow them into San Francisco. For weeks they lay becalmed in the horse latitudes, with California scarcely a four-day run before them.

But at last, with a wind filling the sails, the ships scooted for California. With spirits bursting, all hands paraded the deck in their finest clothes, ready for the arrival. Pistols were inspected, tools sharpened for the descent upon the gold fields.

Throughout the summer of 1849 the California Fleet straggled through the rock-bound Golden Gate and into San Francisco harbor. The vanguard arrived in June; at the high point in mid-September they were coming in at the rate of ten per day. As each new ship glided among the "forest of masts" that filled the harbor, the Argonauts could hardly contain themselves. So frantic was the crew of the ship *Hopewell* that she rammed into two vessels and stove her own side.

"I expect," announced one eager arrival, "to be worth a thousand in a few days."

Since March of '49, the overland army had been assembling for the second wave of the great migration. From as far East as the Appalachians they came, taking passage on the river steamboats or driving their teams across country, converging on the point where the Missouri River leaves its westward course and bends sharply to the north. Here, the frontier town of Independence was the traditional outfitting place for westward travel. Overtaking it in popularity was St. Joseph, situated eighty miles upstream. A third outpost was Kanesville, established by the Mormons two years before at Council Bluffs, Iowa. Those who took the perilous southern route *via* the Arkansas River and Santa Fe generally outfitted at Fort Smith, Arkansas.

To these jumping-off places every steamer brought another mass of gold hunters, who filled the hotels or camped on the outskirts of town. The main streets were jammed with emigrant teams, produce wagons, auction sales, horse and mule markets. Blacksmith and harness shops were besieged with customers. Daguerreotype studios did a thriving business in "accurate likenesses" to send home to the loved ones. General stores advertised all manner of "California fixins." At night the gaming tables were crowded; many a well-intentioned Argonaut reached the end of his westward march in the muddy alley behind an Independence saloon.

Outside of town where the wagon trains were forming, the men were drawing up the rules of organization that would guide them across the plains. The laws were harsh and uncompromising—dictated by the hazardous journey ahead. Among the typical provisions: "Members shall not be allowed to quarrel among themselves, nor shall any member be allowed to drink intoxicating liquors, gamble, use profane language, or labor on the Sabbath." Nearly every constitution sealed the bargain with a mutual vow: "If any member of this company shall be so unfortunate as to lose their teams or provisions, we pledge ourselves that we will not leave them on the plains to suffer but will take care of the unfortunate."

So with high spirits the great army gathered itself and plunged across the Missouri. All the way from St. Jo up to Council Bluffs, ferries were operating to carry the wagons to the opposite shore. With wheels creaking and chains rattling, the teams fell into line across the prairie—the white-canvassed wagons standing like a squadron of sails against the horizon. Beyond the point where the Independence and St. Joseph trails converged, eight thousand vehicles formed a continuous line across the plain.

Along the shallow Platte they rolled, across the green prairies of what would later be the states of Nebraska and Wyoming. This was Indian country, and every Argonaut expected to fight for his scalp. But in '49 most Plains Indians were more of a nuisance than an actual threat. Descending on a wagon camp at supper time, they would crowd about the campfire, getting in the cook's way and hinting for an invitation to dinner. At night they would creep into the wagon corral and run off with food, equipment and livestock.

This was also buffalo country, and the adventurers were eager for the chase. More than one old bull, panicked by his pursuers, charged through a wagon camp, scattering pots and pans, stampeding the stock and drawing a fusillade of shots. By the end of May dead buffalo lined the trail, many of them killed more for sport than necessity. At night the roasting of buffalo was the signal for a general feast. Neighboring campers were invited in, and someone was sure to produce a fiddle for a "hoe down," carried off with much clapping and yelling.

But each day as the teams were yoked up and turned into the trail, the overland route took its toll in hardship. Wagons had been piled so high with goods that the animals were wearing themselves out on the easiest stretch of the road. By the time the trains reached Fort Kearney the men were throwing away excess baggage by the armful. Chairs, stoves, trunks and other luxuries went first. Then boots, quilts, sides of bacon, bags of salt—even firearms. All the way to Fort Laramie the overland trail was paved with provisions, trappings and pieces of wood sawed off the wagons.

Too late most Argonauts lightened their loads. Their animals were already sore and jaded from the overpowering weight. Many were dying in the harness, and soon the trail was marked by the carcasses of oxen and mules.

By contrast, trains of pack mules were hurrying past the wagons without difficulty. Impressed by this example, many Argonauts cut up their wagons into pack saddles and pressed on by mule train. They soon found themselves at the head of the migration.

From Fort Laramie west the going became tougher. The grass was shorter and scarcer; exhausted animals were further weakened by lack of food. The rivers were swifter and deeper; although crude ferries were doing a bustling business at every crossing, they were used for wagons only. Animals and men jumped into the current and paddled fiercely for the other shore. Most of these landsmen were no swimmers. More of them died by drowning than any other cause.

Sickness, too, was prevalent among the Argonauts, for the

rigors of the trail weakened the hardiest of them. Cholera followed them from the settlements. Pneumonia took its toll; drenched by prairie storms, they often slept in their wet clothes. Accidental gunshot wounds were not infrequent, for the Argonauts were armed to the hilt with rifles and pistols. Not all wounds were accidental; as misery heightened and tempers grew short, conflict was inevitable.

One by one the high avowals of their company constitutions were forgotten in the overwhelming realities of the trail. At first the assembled companies voted whether to travel on Sundays; later they pushed on through the Sabbath as a matter of course. Loyalty to one's own company was lost in the headlong race to California. Men moved from one wagon train to another if they thought they could gain speed, until the entire trail was one common community on wheels.

Beyond the Continental Divide, crossed by most emigrants at historic South Pass, lay the final test. Some swung southward to Fort Bridger and to welcome asylum in the new Mormon settlement at Salt Lake. Others pushed directly westward over Sublette's Cut-off, dropping into Bear River Valley by lowering wagons with ropes down the cliffs.

Either way, the terror of the Great Salt Desert lay ahead. Over this sterile route the wisest men carried grass along for their animals, hiring an Indian or half-breed guide to show the way and warn against poisonous water holes.

Animals were dying in great numbers now. Indians skulked along the trail, shooting arrows into the oxen so as to retrieve them for beef after they were abandoned. Partial relief was offered by the winding Humboldt River. But beyond it lay fifty miles of waterless desert before reaching the cool streams flowing out of the Sierra.

Through this barren inferno the gold fever was forgotten; survival was everything. One emigrant counted 100 wagons and 500 animals left along the trail. Those who reached water first carried some back to relieve others who had fallen along the way.

"I gave an old man a drink from my canteen," wrote one diarist, "which seemed to have done him more good than a purse of gold."

Still worse was the route to the south taken by those reaching Salt Lake too late to cross the Sierra before the snows. Among these was Louis Nusbaumer, a German-American who spent Christmas day in the southwestern desert throwing away his worldly possessions to lighten the load. With three oxen packed with food, he and his companion pushed across alkali wastes in the vicinity of Death Valley. Nearly crazed with thirst, the doughty German tried to drink salt water at a desert spring. Overtaking a wagon party which had a supply of water, he offered to exchange his coat and two shirts for a drink. The man in charge refused. But when the latter had to abandon an ox, Louis and his friend shot the animal and caught its blood in a drinking cup.

Compared to the desert passage, the Sierra crossing was almost anti-climax. It was laborious, especially for wagon parties, but in these soaring granite peaks was ample water, and relief from merciless heat. Through several gaps in the mountains, ranging from Goose Lake down to Carson Pass, the emigrants poured over the crest and down the western slope.

As the early arrivals brought tales of suffering on the trail, California moved quickly to claim its own. From San Francisco to the mines, the people poured $100,000 into a relief fund for the emigrants. Military authorities sent parties loaded with provisions and fresh animals over the Sierra. To the stragglers foundering in the desert, these merciful troopers were God-sent. Women and children were mounted on the fastest animals and escorted into the settlements. By the end of October the migration of 1849 was safely in.

Then down the broad and fertile Sacramento Valley they rolled, past ranch houses, herds of horses and cattle. Here, once more, was civilization—however primitive and remote. Into riotous Sacramento City they thronged, meeting their seaborne comrades who had arrived by launch and schooner up the river from San Francisco. Some never got to the settlements, but with shovel and gold pan had struck color on the upper reaches of the Feather and Yuba Rivers.

The rush of '49 was over. For many it was hard disappointment. Back-breaking work and an ounce of gold per day were the miner's lot in '49, with diminishing fortune in the years that followed. But by sheer force of energy the Forty-niners tore the American frontier loose from its Missouri River moorings, and sent it leaping to the Pacific; gave the West Coast a powerful momentum that has never faded; and showed a world of kings and dictators that individuals, acting on their own, could make history.

PART II. THE CENTRAL MINES

HISTORY'S *greatest gold rush brought more than population to California. Within a few tumultuous years it brought steamboats, railroads, telegraph lines, commerce, finance, agriculture, industry—all the trappings of civilization. But in the first years after Jim Marshall's discovery, life was simple, primitive, and in many ways charmingly naïve. Civilized men, flung suddenly into a wilderness, had to start a new society from scratch.*

Mostly, this act in the California drama took place in what was called the Central Mines. Here the Mother Lode was first tapped; here was the earliest stamping ground of the Forty-eighters—those who preceded the deluge of 'Forty-nine. Here is the effective birthplace of American society in California.

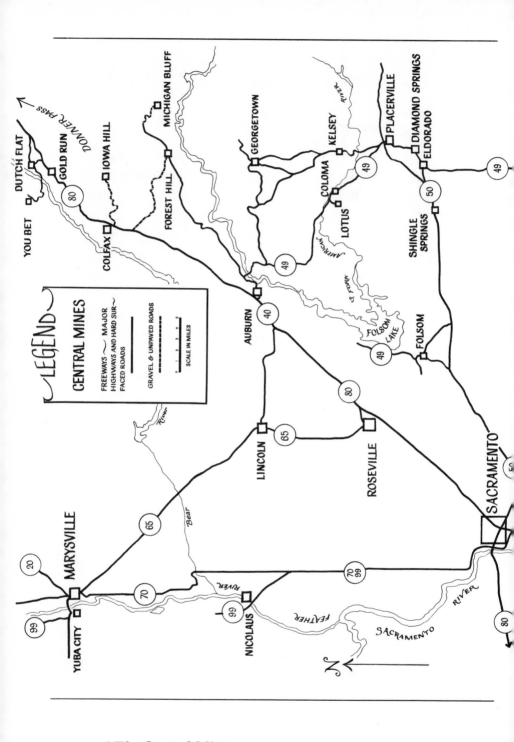

*Rocker designed for separating gold from gravel
in use by young miner.*

*Miners demonstrating the long tom for a photographer
on a Sunday afternoon near Auburn, 1852.*

Woman visitor from Sacramento or San Francisco watches Auburn miners operating double long tom, 1852.

Chinese and American miners operating sluice box at Auburn, 1852.

*Typical construction of Sierra mountain town
at Yank's Station (Meyers).*

*Early railroad town of Cisco shows the bustle of
mountain freighting traffic.*

Panama straws, sailors' jackets, and tall beaver hats. A great confusion of dress was always in evidence at the mines, 1856.

The Central Mines / 41

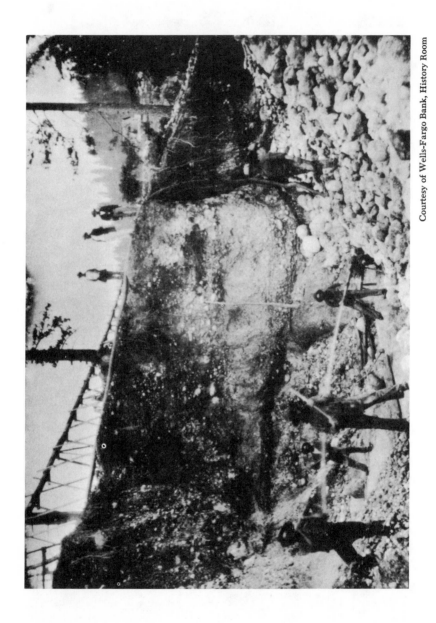

Miners using hydraulic monitor at Michigan Bluff, 1854.

Chapter 3. Coloma: Where Gold Began

IN THE FIRST WEEKS of the rush, Sutter's vanity exceeded his caution. One had but to announce himself as a titled dignitary, and the hospitable Swiss would accompany the whole party to the millsite on the South Fork of the American.

"These gentlemen have come to see the gold mines, Mr. Marshall," he would proudly declare on arrival. And Marshall, making no attempt to hide his displeasure at the interlopers, gave them the same treatment he gave to all the rest who inquired about the gold.

"You'll find it anywhere you've a mind to dig for it down there," he snapped, jerking his arm in the direction of the river.

Following Marshall's whimsy, the tenderfeet were almost sure to strike color wherever they happened to turn the earth. Word soon spread that the famed discoverer had an uncanny sense in finding gold. Men followed him everywhere, knocked on his cabin door at all hours, begging him to lift his finger and point the way. In desperation he turned more into his lonely self, tried to shut out the multitude that was crowding in upon him.

At first the gold-seekers settled along the banks of the South Fork, between Sutter's Mill and Mormon Island. Scarcely a stone's throw from the discovery site sprang the town of Coloma, first important mining town in the Gold Rush. Shunning the initial tent-and-canvas phase that would mark the birth of other mining towns, Coloma sprang full grown from lumber cut at Sutter's Mill (and sold at $500 a thousand feet). By the summer of 1848 Coloma had about three hundred frame buildings and a big hotel under construction. Along the main street they bore the false fronts and wooden awnings which set the style in mining camps for the next half century.

The remote boom town also established the tradition of outrageous prices. Almost any commodity—flour, pork, sugar, coffee—sold at the flat rate of a dollar a pound. Shovels and picks were at least $50 each, butcher knives between $10 and $25, boots $25 to $50 a pair, wool shirts $50 each. The Sierra

Indians were bewildered by the white man's frenzied interest in the yellow metal, and at one point on the South Fork were giving a handful of gold dust for a cotton handkerchief or shirt.

In Coloma one woman took in laundering at a dollar an item. When her husband came back from the mines after four weeks' work, she laughed at his hard-earned pile. In the same time she had earned double the amount washing shirts.

Since coin was scarce in the remote Sierras, gold dust quickly became Coloma's currency—with a pinch of dust supposed to equal one dollar. One South Fork storekeeper insisted on doing the pinching himself; wetting his thumb and forefinger, he would plunge his hand in the miner's sack and come out with from four to eight dollars' worth. But in early '48 gold was so plentiful that the miners passed this off as a huge joke.

One day a popular miner died on the South Fork, and the boys resolved to give him a proper funeral. The grave was dug in a flat nearby, and the ceremony was performed by a one-time preacher who had given up the Gospel for the call of gold. When he launched into a long prayer some of the boys grew restless and began fingering the dirt from the grave. They found it "lousy with gold." In a moment the ex-preacher sensed the distraction and opened one eye.

"Boys, what's that?" One glimpse was enough. "Gold, by God!"

Solemnly raising his hand, he dismissed the congregation and led the rush for pick and pan. As for the body of the deceased miner, it was later consigned to ground that was more hallowed—and less rich.

By June there were two thousand men in and around Coloma. The creak and rattle of their rockers provided a constant tune from dawn to dusk.

It was soon apparent that Marshall's chance discovery was far from the richest. Mountaineers who visited Sutter's Mill remembered similar ground elsewhere and went back to make their own strikes. Up and down the river new ground was abandoned when it no longer yielded two or three ounces per day.

As elsewhere in the mines of 1848, the Coloma region knew almost no crime. Tools and equipment were left lying about without the slightest fear of robbery. At Mormon Island one mining party piled all its equipment and provisions in an open place, leaving them unguarded and unmolested for days at a time.

The few cases of outlawry were summarily dealt with by traditional miners' justice. In the summer of 1848 one rascal stole a sack of gold; when captured, he refused in spite of threats to tell where it was hidden. The miners gave him thirty lashes, but still he defied them. Exasperated, they tried more subtle torture. He was tied to a tree with his back laid bare to the mosquitoes which abounded on the South Fork in July. After three hours of this attention, he surrendered.

"Untie me," he moaned, "I will tell."

"Tell first," was the miners' demand. And while some of them shooed the insects off his back, others followed his directions and found the gold. Then they washed his back, cut him loose and helped him dress. That was frontier justice.

But while the first year of gold has been called "the Age of Innocence," 1849 was different. With the flood tide of the gold rush came a motley crew of cutthroats and thieves. Miners' courts were improvised to cope with the crime wave, and since there was a scarcity of jails, punishment often included such grim procedures as ear-cropping and branding. Whisky flowed freely in the courtrooms, with the bill customarily paid by the defendant.

But Coloma's hectic days were numbered. She had won her population and excitement on the strength of Marshall's original discovery, not on inherent wealth. Richer localities up and down the Mother Lode were soon drawing the restless gold hunters. In late 1851 a visitor called Coloma "the dullest mining town in the whole country."

By 1870 Coloma—once the home of 10,000 miners—was reduced to two hundred residents. It was a place of quiet serenity, of flower gardens and shaded lanes. The throbbing pulse of a stormier hour returned only once a day—when the Concord stage whirled in and lurched to a stop at the Wells Fargo office.

As for Marshall, his life paralleled that of his discovery spot. Unwilling to join in the headlong rush he had launched, he

Coloma: Where Gold Began / 45

tried to capitalize on his now-famous name. At first he exacted half the earnings of the Mormon diggers at the sawmill. When this failed he went up the South Fork of the American with another prospector to make a new strike. Three miles northward they picked up a cupful of gold from a sand bar.

"Now, James," said his companion, "suppose we divide this gold."

"No," returned Marshall, abruptly, "I don't divide. You are a hired man."

"That ends our contract," cried the other.

And the lonely Marshall went his way, holding himself above the miner's lot by virtue of his discovery, and gaining nothing.

A similar fate met John Sutter. Joining the gold-seekers, he stumbled through the Sierra foothills with his little army of Indian diggers. But the doughty Swiss was no better at mining gold than keeping its secret. On the South Fork of the American his camp was invaded by a wave of miners who quickly stripped the diggings. Sutter then moved his caravan south of the Cosumnes River and founded a new camp—Sutter Creek. Here gold clinked into his coffers until several saloons were established nearby. Then, according to his own account, the workers drank and gambled away their day's earnings, forcing him to give up and break camp.

But the master himself was example for the slave. On the day of departure, with the entire outfit packed up and ready to mount, Sutter was too inebriated to climb aboard his mule. Instead he swayed unsteadily before the whole company, regaling the Indians with his military triumphs in Switzerland.

Unsaddling, the party remained for three more days until the jolly captain was ready to move. Then, with a flourish, the comic caravan of John Sutter jolted its way out of Sutter Creek and out of the California mines.

Marshall and Sutter—tragic pair! Having put the roaring flood in motion, they were spewed like driftwood upon the shore. Unequal to their historic role, they became silent and disgruntled bystanders in a world gone mad.

COLOMA. The discovery site is a state park, with appropriate historical markers and an extensive museum. The principal point of interest is the replica of John Sutter's original sawmill, whose tailrace was the site of the gold discovery.

One of the old stone buildings is the Coloma jail, built in the early 1850s. Two well-preserved brick buildings are the Robert Bell Store, built around 1856, and Bekeart's Store, dating from 1853. The Wan Lee store, and another operated by one of his Chinese countrymen, Wah Hop, are also preserved from the 1850's.

Among the frame buildings in the area, some were originally built of lumber from Sutter's sawmill. Also standing are the Emmanuel Episcopal Church, built in 1856, and St. John's Catholic Church, the first of that faith in the Mother Lode.

On the hill overlooking the town are the grave and statue of James Marshall. Near the statue is a restoration of Marshall's cabin, where he lived at the time of the discovery and for some twenty years afterward.

LOTUS. Here are the remains of a small town, originally named Marshall after the gold discoverer, and then Uniontown. Still standing are the Adam Lohry store and home, constructed in 1859.

KELSEY. At this little settlement, first known as Kelsey's Diggings, James Marshall spent his last days. A restored frame cabin stands where he operated a blacksmith and carpenter shop. Among other buildings is Tom Allan's saloon, frequented by Marshall.

GEORGETOWN. Well worth the trip for a confirmed ghost-town enthusiast is Georgetown, one of the nostalgic spots in the Central Mines. Originally bearing the remarkable name of Growlersburg, Georgetown was ravaged in 1856 by a fire that swept away all its earliest buildings except the Masonic Hall. Rebuilt almost entirely of brick, the town has a number of structures dating to the late '50s, including the former Wells

Fargo office and the old Balser House, which served first as a hotel, then a theater, and later as a lodge meeting house. Georgetown is one of the few sizable settlements still breathing the atmosphere of the Gold Rush—principally because it is off the beaten track of Highway 49.

Chapter 4. Placerville: Hangtown & Horace Greeley

NO SERIOUS VISITOR is allowed to leave Placerville without hearing two stories—how it got its early name of Hangtown, and how Horace Greeley arrived after his wild stage ride over the Sierra. But these are only a part, and a small one at that, of the heritage of rare old Placerville. Its narrow and winding streets, nestled in a pine-clad fold of the Sierra foothills, saw the ebb and flow of California history for two uproarious decades. It was, by turns, the first big gold camp after the discovery at Coloma; the hell-roaring gateway to California for the overland Argonauts; and depot for the stampede back across the Sierras to the Comstock Lode.

Its story began in June of '48, when Indians carried word along the forks of the American of a new placer that was yielding six ounces ($96) per man per day. In a twinkling another stampede was on to the new camp below the South Fork. Over hill and across canyon tumbled the boys, leaving rich diggings behind for the rumor of something richer. Within a week the old placers were depopulated and close to a thousand were crowding into the new ground. After the river level fell in midsummer the men were forced to carry their ore several hundred yards to water. But even with this time-consuming delay they still made two to four ounces per day. Frequently someone would strike a *bonanza*, or rich pocket, and others would scramble in shoulder to shoulder, many reaping several hundred dollars in a day.

Through the summer of '48 Dry Diggings, as it was called, was the great rendezvous for all the Argonauts—be they American backwoodsmen, native Californians, or deserters from army and navy. Ragged, dirty, bewhiskered—they were yet, in the words of one, "the happiest set of men on earth."

By autumn it was a thriving camp, composed first of tents and log cabins, then of board and shingle stores, muddy streets and surging traffic. By the winter of 1849 gold was still plentiful, but not plentiful enough to prevent the rise of crime. In January five men broke into a gambler's room and while one of them held a pistol at his head, rifled his belongings. They were immediately captured, tried by a vigilance court of two hundred irate miners, and given thirty-five lashes each. Then three of them were charged with robbery and attempted murder on the Stanislaus River. A miner's jury found them guilty again.

"What shall be done with them?" demanded the acting judge.

"Hang them!" someone shouted. And though one miner mounted a stump and pleaded against lynch law, the three men were placed in a wagon, driven under a tree on the main street, and each fitted with a noose. At a signal, the wagon was driven out from under them.

Since this was the first recorded lynching on the Mother Lode, the place quickly got its second name—Hangtown.

The event and the name had a civilizing influence. Bad men were on their good behavior in this strict camp. And as the mines prospered, the town went metropolitan. Regular stages arrived in 1851, bringing passengers to several hotels which offered such luxuries as tablecloths and silver service. In fact, the place was becoming famous abroad for other things besides lynch law. An imaginative cook put together eggs, bacon, oysters and other grease-loving ingredients in what became known as a "Hangtown Fry." The concoction appealed to hardy stomachs, and was soon a celebrated dish up and down the Mother Lode. Leading restaurants in San Francisco had to put it on the menu to satisfy visiting miners.

As whole families moved in to replace the strictly male population, Hangtown became positively genteel. It got so the young ladies parading along the streets in their fine hoop skirts were unapproachable. "They're dreadful shy of Forty-niners, turn their noses up at miners," ran a rousing Gold Rush song called "Hangtown Gals." And when Hangtown acquired a temperance league and a Methodist church, the seal was placed on her lawless days. Agitation began for a less morbid name.

Besides, the hangman's tree was no longer the town's most distinctive feature. Gold had been discovered in the neighboring creek, and on the approaches to town groups of men were working feverishly at the business of placer mining. Standing barefooted in icy mountain water, they were shoveling sand into long toms, the trough-like contraptions which separated the gold. In fact, one eager prospector struck pay dirt in the center of town, and the boys descended on it with pick and shovel. A visitor found parties of energetic miners digging holes and operating long toms right in the middle of Main Street and even in some of the houses.

"There was a continual noise and clatter," he reported, "as mud, dirt, stones and water were thrown about in all directions."

Yes, old Hangtown had changed, and the people began clamoring for a more fitting name—Placerville. In 1850 the Legislature gave it the new title, though the disagreeable "Hangtown" persisted in popular usage for some years. But as Placerville it was incorporated in 1854, and as Placerville it supplanted Coloma as the seat of El Dorado County three years later.

By this time the placers that had given it a name were fading, but the town lived high through the '50s as the roistering terminus of the Overland Trail. Earliest gold hunters had gone over Truckee Pass and into California by way of the Yuba and Feather Rivers. But in the early '50s most of the wagons dropped below Lake Tahoe, down the South Fork of the American River and into Placerville.

Through the high tide of the Gold Rush, this was the hoped-for haven after a 2300 mile trek across the American desert and over the lofty Sierras. One weary wagon train, with its chains jingling and mules snorting as they had every day since leaving the bend of the Missouri, was drawing near Placerville when an almost-forgotten noise split the air. A rooster had crowed! Without a signal, the wagons halted and the astonished men let out a yell. Here, at last, was civilization.

The town at the end of that covered wagon trail was not a pretentious sight. One arrival called it "one long straggling street of clapboard houses and log cabins." Through this narrow thoroughfare, blocked with miner's diggings and knee-deep mud puddles, sloshed bearded Argonauts, six-horse stages, plodding ox and mule teams. The only paving was a litter of "old boots, hats, and shirts, old sardine boxes, empty tins of preserved oysters, empty bottles, worn-out pots and kettles, old ham-bones, broken picks and shovels . . . ."

The unique institution of the town was its general stores, which served as combination saloon, grocer's, hardware shop and social hall. Behind the counter, which was also a bar, were stacked whisky bottles, canned fish, bottled pickles, and every conceivable item. And prices? An ounce of gold dust ($16) bought a pound of gun powder, a chicken or a bottle of champagne. Business was thriving, but conducted with pure informality. The storekeeper customarily sat with miners at a rude table, playing seven-up for "the drinks."

In snowy weather, a customer could comfortably spend a whole day in one of these retreats, provided his credit was good. Witness, for example, the story told by one page of a daybook from an old Placerville store: "Mr. Boyer 6.25—2 drinks, .50; 1 ditto; .25; 1 lug tobacco, .50; 2 drinks, .50 ½ pie, .50; 1 drink, .25; 5 drinks, 1.25; ¼ pie, .25; 1 drink, .25; ½ pie, .50; 2 drinks, .50; 1 ditto, .25; 1 drink, .25." There is no record of a final necessity: 1 stretcher.

Probably it was such a grocery store as this that Mark Hopkins started in 1849; here he launched on a career which made him one of the Big Four rail builders, the first to span the Sierras with tracks. The one item which the stores did not carry was meat; this was handled exclusively by butchers, and one of these was Philip D. Armour, who began here his upward climb in the meat packing business. Still another Placerville pioneer was John M. Studebaker, who made wheelbarrows for the miners and saved the $4000 with which he started his wagon-building business in South Bend, Indiana. Today, sleek Studebakers roll over Placerville streets once trod by the original, one-wheel model.

Meanwhile Placerville was taking on a permanent air. Stone

and brick buildings were lining her winding streets. A decline in mining and a devastating fire gave Placerville a double blow in 1856, but her greatest days were yet to come. It was in June, 1857, that Jared B. Crandall, one of California's stagecoach kings, drove his Concord out of Placerville and into the Sierra pines. In the next few days, accompanied by directors of his company, he prodded his six horses over rocky ledges and steep ravines, across Johnson Pass and down into the Mormon village of Genoa, in what would later be Nevada Territory. Then they fought their way back, to be hilariously greeted at Placerville by a shouting, shooting crowd.

It was the first stage over the Sierras between California and the Carson Valley. While state officials talked of surveys and road appropriations, Crandall had proven that the route was feasible—with no road but the primitive emigrant trail. After that, Crandall's stages ran biweekly over the great barrier, soon connecting with another stage line spanning the Utah desert to bring California into direct communication with the Atlantic. Placerville was a major milestone on the path of empire.

But the line had its disadvantages. Those six-horse stages careened along precipitous mountain roads that defied gravity and paled the tenderfoot passenger. In winter the coaches were withdrawn, leaving it to that intrepid postman, Snowshoe Thompson, to carry the mail between Placerville and the Carson Valley.

But by 1859 the route was becoming almost civilized. Such furious whips as Hank Monk would take their coaches through in several hours, with never a quiver, though perhaps they had brushed death a dozen times. In that year, along came Horace Greeley, America's great publisher and crusader, who was just then interested in a transcontinental Western railroad. On the bouncing stage ride from Missouri he'd already been spilled on the prairie when a herd of buffalo stampeded the stage horses and overturned the coach; dumped into the Laramie River when the vehicle capsized again; plunged once more into the Sweetwater River, where he lost a trunk full of manuscripts; and generally shaken up and beaten down by the incessant bumping and swaying of a three-week stage ride.

At the foot of the Sierras he encountered the incomparable

Hank Monk, whose coach promptly whirled him out of the desert and into the clouds. Over hair-tingling Sierra roads lurched the stage, as Horace himself said, "just as fast as four wild California horses, whom two men could scarcely harness, could draw it." When they clattered into Placerville, a dishevelled and discomposed Greeley emerged from the coach and before the crowd could capture him, made his way to the Carey House bar. The Placerville crowd that had turned out for a grand welcome found him there, and escorted him to a waiting banquet table. There, in response to ringing toasts, the poor man arose—not from a chair, according to press accounts, but from a couch. Whether or not he said so then, he later admitted:

"I cannot conscientiously recommend the route I have traveled to summer tourists in quest of pleasure, but it is a balm for many bruises to know that I am at last in California."

This much is fact. But Placerville, delighted at this priceless joke on Horace, blew it into something more. Within a few months every journalist and storyteller who came to California was repeating it—with embellishments. Artemus Ward, the great prankster of the 19th Century, passed through Placerville shortly after and dressed up the story like this:

When Greeley was put aboard Monk's stagecoach, the driver was ordered to deliver him in Placerville for a speaking engagement at seven o'clock. Off dashed the coach with such furious speed and fearful bouncing that Greeley soon decided he wasn't in such a hurry, after all.

"Sir," he told Monk out the window, "I don't care if we don't get there at seven!"

"I have got my orders," retorted the driver, and urged the horses to a faster pace. Finally Horace poked his head out again.

"I don't care," he pleaded, "if we don't get there at all."

"I've got my orders," shouted Hank, and went madly on. Then a jarring bump sent Greeley's head crashing through the roof of the coach. "Keep your seat, Horace," ordered the unruffled Hank Monk.

Just outside of Placerville, a welcoming committee, complete with brass band, stopped the stage to take Greeley and carry him in honor to the city, but Hank whipped up the team and scattered the crowd with the cry, "I've got my orders!"

When Mark Twain came along in 1861, he first heard the story from a stage driver at the Platte River. Out of Denver a passenger related it in identical words. A cavalry sergeant from Fort Bridger repeated the exact yarn, followed by a Mormon preacher who got on at Salt Lake. Along the Carson River they picked up a half-dead wanderer who launched into the same story.

Mark Twain then rebelled. "Suffering stranger," he warned, "proceed at your peril." The man stopped, but as Twain claimed, "In trying to retain the anecdote in his system he strained himself and died in our arms."

Over his next six years in California and Nevada the humorist heard that "deathless incident 81 or 82 times"—from drivers and passengers, Chinese and Indians, flavored with every aroma including "whisky, brandy, beer, cologne, sozodont, tobacco, garlic, onions, grasshoppers. . . ." Mark Twain has been spared the thousands of retellings since then, and today any Placerville patriot believes that Horace Greeley came whirling into town on Hank Monk's stage with his head sticking through the top.

It was in the same year of Greeley's trip that Placerville swung into its final, furious hour.

The fabulous Comstock Lode had been discovered in the Washoe country (soon to be part of the new state of Nevada). As the tide of humanity swung back over the Sierra, Placerville became the main outfitting point for the Washoe silver mines. It was suddenly so overwhelmed with business that there were not enough wagons or mules in the countryside to keep the stampede moving. The hills above town were piled with boxes of merchandise while their owners vainly offered fantastic freight fees for hauling them over the Sierra. Stagecoaches and mule trains were booked up days in advance. Streets and hotels, saloons and restaurants, were thronged with a noisy crowd of expectant millionaires.

Recharged by the Nevada excitement, Placerville even aspired to become a railroad center when work began on the "Placerville and Sacramento Valley Railroad." But the rails stopped at Shingle Springs a few miles short of town, and the rival Central Pacific line of the Big Four pushed on over the Sierras. After 1867 Placerville lost her traffic to the railroaders.

But the quaint old camp, its streets still following the original mule paths, thrives today as the center of a lumber, mineral and vineyard country. And the town which once changed its name to Placerville out of civic pride, today insists on telling everybody (for the same reason) that its name used to be Hangtown.

POINTS OF INTEREST

PLACERVILLE. Modern Placerville is charmingly nestled in the Sierra foothills, with the distinctive atmosphere of a true mountain town. But though many of its buildings date from the golden era, most of them are camouflaged with plaster, paint, and advertising signs. Some old buildings are identifiable including the city hall and the judicial court, built in 1857 and 1862, respectively, and several church edifices built in the 1860s.

EL DORADO. Once called Mud Springs, El Dorado was founded as a way station at the foot of the Carson Pass emigrant route. In the 1850s it boomed as a mining camp. Until recently it was one of the most picturesque ruins in the Mother Lode, but the line of abandoned stone buildings was torn down in 1956, and only a few walls remain.

DIAMOND SPRINGS. Among the few remaining structures in this once-flourishing camp are the Wells Fargo office, Louis Lepetit's store, and the Odd Fellow's Hall, all built in the 1850s.

SHINGLE SPRINGS. This quaint town began as a stopping place on the road from Sacramento to Placerville, then blossomed as a mining town when gold was discovered nearby in 1850. The Wells Fargo office and what was originally called the Shingle Springs House both date from the 1850s, while the original Planter's Hotel was built in 1861.

Chapter 5. Auburn: Three-Story Town

THERE IS A PLEASANT LEGEND that Auburn was never one of the wild towns of the Mother Lode. Unlike her raucous neighbors, she was at least moderate in her sins.

Perhaps this harmless tale grows out of her sylvan setting. Could this quaint and rustic place, nestled in the tree-shaded Sierra foothills, have been a rendezvous of bad men and a scene of violence? Or maybe it is her innocent name, recalling her English namesake of Goldsmith's lines: "Sweet Auburn! loveliest village of the plain."

Auburn today is California's unique "three story town." At the lower level is the scene of her first gold strike in May, 1848, when hundreds of miners poured in from the discovery site at Sutter's Mill and points south. Known at first as Rich Dry Diggings, the new locality produced as much as $1500 a day for a lucky few. Of this original site little is left today save some half-hidden foundations.

By 1850 Auburn numbered 1500 persons, and the more permanent gold town mushroomed on its second location a little farther up the hill. Town lots were laid out around a Spanish-style plaza, with one parcel to go to each citizen. One "sooner," an enterprising barkeeper, moved in on one of the choicest lots and started his building. The aroused populace held a mass meeting and sent a rider to the county seat at Nicolaus for an injunction. By the time he got back the crisis was over. The building was finished and the barkeep was placating everybody with free drinks.

It is this middle location around the plaza that is Auburn's picturesque "Old Town." On its narrow and winding streets stand oldtime buildings of false fronts and wooden canopies. Some are ghosts, some are occupied; only a few go back to the 1850s. But all of them carry the frontier flavor which makes "Old Town" Auburn one of the most colorful of Sierra mining camps.

Less than half a mile higher lies the modern city—as lively and progressive a town as California boasts. As the seat of Placer County, she is the capital of a territory rich in agricultural and mining products. From her highest point a panoramic view of the American River Valley is unsurpassed. Quiet and orderly is the modern town of Auburn. But in her younger days?

Auburn's first lynching occurred on Christmas Day, 1850, when one citizen killed another and gave himself up to the sheriff. An outraged mob captured him, tried him by miners' court and hung him to an oak tree handily situated in the middle of town. Despite this grim lesson, another Auburnite committed murder soon after—resulting in another seizure, another rump court, another lynching. But, of course, Auburn was a quiet town.

In the spring of 1850 Auburn decided that she ought to be the seat of Sutter County, which then included much of Northern California. So she secured an election on the issue, in rivalry with the existing county seat of Nicolaus. To the polls inside her biggest general store she brought not only Auburnites, but voters from as far away as Coloma, in El Dorado County. With the lure of free "refreshments," she captured a majority larger than the county's whole population. This so impressed her rivals that next year when the new Placer County was formed, she remained the seat of government without a contest.

Auburn was, after all, a quiet and orderly town.

Then in 1855 California's Gold Rush struck the rocks in a financial panic. Surface mining had passed its peak, and for months the lagging gold supply had forced the banks to withdraw money from circulation to meet the needs of business. California was vulnerable to the slightest financial setback. It came in January, 1855, when the St. Louis bank of Page and Bacon Company closed its doors. As soon as the news reached California a run was started on the San Francisco branch. By February 23rd nearly all the banks in the state had locked their doors. Californians were clamoring for their funds. In Auburn's neighboring towns of Nevada City, Coloma, Placerville and Sacramento the crowds collected outside the banks and discussed how they could recover their deposits. But what happened in Auburn? An armed crew forced the bankers to open the safe and pass out the money to the depositors. On the whole, though, Auburn was a quiet town.

Outlawry came early to Placer County. By April, 1852, the gold country's first important stage holdup occurred a few miles north of Auburn near Illinoistown. Reelfoot Williams and his gang stopped a coach and made off with $7500 from the express box. A posse from Marysville caught up with them on the Yuba River and in a short battle put the Williams gang out of business. Throughout the middle 1850s two bandits ranged through the mines—and made the country around Auburn their general headquarters. One of these was "Rattlesnake Dick" Barter, who won his wicked name not from personal ferocity but because he first settled at Rattlesnake Bar. Dick had been an honest miner until he was twice falsely accused of thefts. Each time he was exonerated. But with his reputation smirched, he changed his name, left Rattlesnake Bar and settled in the northern town of Shasta.

Before long a former neighbor came through camp and, catching sight of Dick, dealt him another foul blow by telling of his suspect character. At this final injustice, Dick broke down and took to the road to fulfill his reputation. One night near Shasta he robbed a lone traveler and vanished with the melodramatic news that he was "Rattlesnake Dick, the Pirate of the Placers."

Quickly Dick returned to the Auburn country and took up the highwayman's trade in earnest. For six years he plundered the highroads from Nevada City to Folsom. Many times he was captured and lodged in the local calaboose to await trial, but as many times the slippery outlaw made his escape. One chronicler insists that "he broke out of every jail in Placer and Nevada Counties."

Such a character was, of course, out of place in staid and sedate Auburn.

Once Dick and a companion showed themselves on the streets of Nevada City and calmly took seats on the southbound stage. Hearing this news, a deputy sheriff of Placer County decided to carry the burlesque still further by waylaying the stage at Harmon Hill. But the two bandits were unimpressed, and boldly demanded to see the officer's warrant. When he stopped to produce it, they sent a bullet barrage through the stage windows. The deputy bravely returned the fire with a one-shot derringer. No one was hurt, and before the officer could reload the robbers coolly left the stage and with some rude remarks, bade the bewildered deputy goodbye.

In the end, Dick carried his boldness too far. One night in July, 1859, he and a fellow bandit rode openly through the main street of Auburn. The town could not let this insult pass, and a three-man posse caught up with the pair before they had gone a mile. The leader called on them to halt.

"Who are you, and what do you want?" Dick demanded, and ended the brief conversation with a blast of gunfire. One posseman was killed, but the other two fired back. Dick lurched in the saddle, then righted himself and rode off with his comrade. He didn't go far. Next morning his body was found by the roadside and carried back into town on the Auburn stage.

This was an unusually exciting moment in a camp which was always quiet and orderly.

A very different type from Rattlesnake Dick was Auburn's second bad man, Tom Bell. A doctor by profession, Bell tried to make a living in the gold country as a miner and then as a gambler. Failing in these, he methodically decided on armed robbery as the more promising pursuit. Tom Bell was like that —calm, calculating, daring, a sort of intellectual bandit.

The brains he brought to the highwayman's profession were not enough to keep him out of jail after his first escapade in 1855. But he soon broke loose from the state prison and took the road again—this time at the head of a sizable band of desperadoes.

For more than a year Tom Bell terrorized the roads in and around Auburn. At least three highway taverns were his secret hideouts, the proprietors tipping him off on the departures of well-heeled guests.

In August, 1856, Tom Bell heard of a $100,000 gold shipment on the Camptonville stage, and resolved to make holdup history. This was a mistake. His gang got nothing for their pains but a running fight with the guard and passengers. And all the law in Northern California rallied to track him down.

The Placer County Sheriff caught up with the gang at an inn near Auburn, but during the battle Bell got away. With a remnant of his band he left the mines and hid out near Firebaugh's Ferry, on the San Joaquin River. There he was surprised by a posse, taken without a fight and hung without ceremony.

It looked as though life in quiet Auburn might be duller than ever.

Then in May, 1858, six bandits halted the Auburn stage and seized over $21,000 from the Wells Fargo chest. Soon afterwards at Yankee Jim's, Auburn's nearest neighbor, robbers made off with another express box. Just beyond Yankee Jim's near Forest Hill, a squad of six or seven men pulled another holdup early in 1859.

The Auburn country was a mighty poor risk for Wells Fargo, but it was painfully quiet.

Meanwhile, the Iron Horse had invaded California and was heading Auburn's way. Theodore Judah, the man who surveyed the Central Pacific crossing of the Sierras, had launched his original Sacramento Valley Railroad. Construction began in February, 1855, and a year later trains began operating from Sacramento to Folsom.

When the line stalled at this point, the eager Auburn people were not to be denied their railroad. They founded another line and had trains running into Auburn by October, 1862.

But this little Gold Rush railroad was left behind in the bigger race for a transcontinental connection. In 1863 the Central Pacific, owned by the Big Four firm of Stanford, Crocker, Huntington and Hopkins, started still a third line from Sacramento toward Auburn—and the challenging Sierras. Four months later the original Sacramento Valley Railroad resumed construction beyond Folsom toward Auburn. California's first big railroad race was on.

Auburn itself came into the drama when Central Pacific rails reached the town in June, 1864. This was a death blow to Auburn's own little railroad. But the Sacramento Valley line bought up the corpse and began ripping up the valuable rails for use on its own route.

At this, both Auburn and the Central Pacific stepped in. First they got an injunction against destroying the track, but the Sacramento Valley officials were able to dodge the server. Then a Placer County deputy arrived at the disputed roadbed with a posse and a warrant for the superintendent's arrest. Where could that gentleman be found, he asked.

"He's up in the cabin car ahead," answered a foreman. "Better take all your boys with you—he's an ornery cuss!"

So the deputy and all his men walked into the designated car —and a neat trap. The foreman locked the door and signaled to the locomotive. The train steamed out of Placer County and out of the deputy's jurisdiction.

From then on the contest was a grim railroad war. Each side got reinforcements, and guarded its work camps with armed sentries. Prisoners captured by the Central Pacific forces were thrown in the Auburn jail. But the next time a sheriff's posse tried to interfere with the Sacramento Valley crews, the railroad was ready with its own warrant—secured from a friendly justice of the peace. The deputies were packed off to another jail, charged with carrying concealed weapons and disturbing the peace!

When one of the victims escaped and rode into Auburn with this news, the town virtually exploded. Local militia, the intrepid Auburn Grays, marched over to the railroad and fell upon the work gang with fixed bayonets. After an almost bloodless skirmish, the railroaders surrendered. The Auburnites marched them triumphantly off to the town jail.

In the end it was not Auburn blades but the bankruptcy courts that defeated the Sacramento Valley line and sealed a Central Pacific victory. The railroad of the Big Four went on over the mountains to span the continent with iron.

And Auburn went along her quiet, uneventful way.

Auburn is, of course, only a part of the Placer County tradition. This is the land of the ridiculous place names—most of them now unmarked sites and all of them monuments to the Forty-niner's sense of humor. Here were Shirt Tail Canyon, You Bet, Last Chance, Deadman's Bar, Rattlesnake Bar, Frytown, Ground Hog's Glory, Milk Punch Bar, Drunkard's Bar, Humbug Bar, Ladies' Canyon, Miller's Defeat, Devil's Basin and Hell's Delight.

Yes, the rugged spirit of '49 lies over the Auburn country. But it's powerfully quiet and law abiding—and always has been.

AUBURN. The lower or "old" section remains one of the best-preserved and most picturesque of Mother Lode ghost towns, with its Spanish-type plaza, its firehouse surmounted by a quaint bell tower, and its row of false-front buildings climbing staunchly up the hill. Among the latter is the office of the *Placer Herald*, founded in 1852 and one of the oldest continuously published newspapers in California.

From Highway 49 below Auburn a spectacular road winds eastward into the mountains to three camps worth visiting by the dedicated Mother Lode enthusiast:

YANKEE JIM'S. Once a large mining town, Yankee Jim's is marked today by a few old buildings in a delightfully shaded dell.

FOREST HILL. While lumbering is today the chief activity in this area, the real spirit of the Gold Rush hangs over this remote and fairly well preserved town in the Sierra pines.

MICHIGAN BLUFF. Unlike Forest Hill, Michigan Bluff is a ghost town. Once the center of vast hydraulic mining operations, it is marked today by a few frame and stone buildings.

Paralleling the North Fork of the American River, U.S. Highway 40 runs north from Auburn to other historic spots:

COLFAX. Not a mining town, Colfax was founded and remained as a railroad shipping point. It was named for Schuyler Colfax, who was elected Vice President on the ticket with General U. S. Grant in the election of 1868.

GOLD RUN. Only a few remains stand to show the site of this once-prosperous hydraulic mining town.

DUTCH FLAT. Located a short way off Highway 40, Dutch Flat was originally named for two Germans who settled here in 1851. Like a treasured heirloom, the sloping town has been preserved against the ravages of fire, storm, and commercialism that have spoiled other Mother Lode gems. Its name became a household word in California during the 1860s, when Charles Crocker and his partners of the Central Pacific built their transcontinental railroad across the Sierras over the "Dutch Flat Route."

PART III. THE SOUTHERN MINES

Reached mainly *through the San Joaquin River port of Stockton, the Southern Mines had a distinctive character of their own. They nestled along Sierra foothills dotted with oak and piñon—a pastoral setting so characteristic of California. On the first visit one may be disappointed not to find them farther up in the forested mountains, where mines ought to be.*

But they retain other rewards not found in most American mining districts. The plazas, the overhanging balconies, the occasional iron grillwork show a strong cosmopolitan influence. Among the earliest arrivals were native Californians, Mexicans, Chileans, Frenchmen, Italians, and Chinese. The Southern Mines had their fandango halls, their bull-and-bear fights—and their grim racial clashes.

Partly because of this rich and varied heritage, the Southern Mines have had a penchant for legend that is reminiscent of the Old World. Combined with the American weakness for exaggeration, this has created a mature body of folklore that survives all the arrows of spoilsport historians.

Thus the visitor in search of history must often dig through layers of fable. He will learn to discount the number of men executed from each of numerous Hangman's Trees. He will learn to downgrade the peak population figures claimed by towns now represented by a broken stone wall and a gas pump.

Yet the traveler through the Southern Mines is struck by the sheer number of communities. Now one of the least populated in California, this region once teemed with young men in a hurry. One realizes that big things happened here.

So it is not surprising that a mythology would spring up among people with an epic period behind them. To these inheritors of a Golden Age, the men of the Gold Rush have become giants.

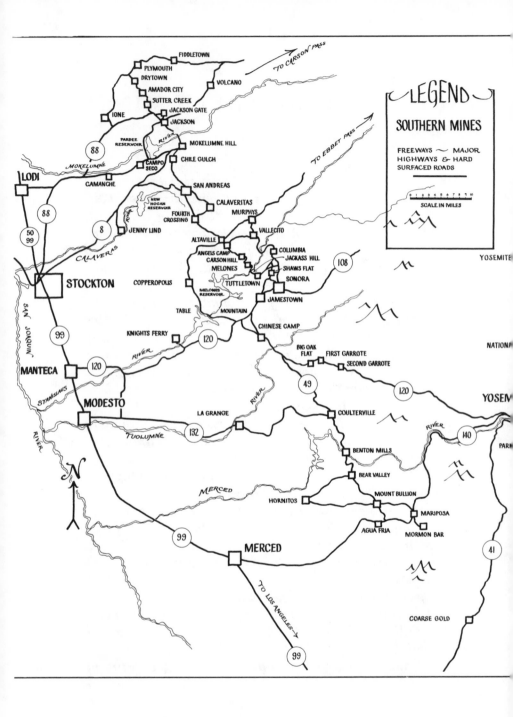

Daguerreotype showing the narrow and crowded main street of Fiddletown, 1850-51.

The Southern Mines / 65

*Group of miners at Sutter Creek (3rd man from right wears a
Mexican War Army shako on his head), 1851.*

Placer mining by Chinese using sluice boxes, about 1856.

*Jenny Lind, example of board and shingle mining
community in the oak-dotted hills of Calaveras County.*

*Early miners cabin construction, using hand-felled
High Sierra timber.*

*Rare portrait, believed to be of George Angel,
founder of Angel's Camp.*

Busy center of Jackson, one of the larger communities among the Southern mines.

Iron shutters and false fronts characterize legendary Angel's Camp.

Natty boulevardier, Charles E. Bolton, committed 28 stage holdups under the name of Black Bart.

Chapter 6. Volcano and the Amador Mines

THE BEST OF MOTHER LODE GHOST TOWNS lie off the beaten path, and near the top of the list is Volcano. From Jackson in Amador County, a good road takes you twelve miles to what is left of one of the rousing camps of the Gold Rush. And what is left fairly breathes the flavor of Forty-nine.

First of all, this was the land of contradictory names. Contrary to miners' belief, there were no volcanoes at Volcano. Fiddletown was supposedly named for the numbers of Missouri fiddlers who took turns playing a tune while their partners mined the stream; but a visitor of 1850 reported that "not a fiddler was to be had in Fiddletown." And Drytown had, in its heyday, twenty-six saloons. Of course, there were other local names which were only too true: Helltown, Hogtown, Loafer Flat, Bedbug, Whisky Slide, Murderer's Gulch.

Despite its remoteness, Volcano was the first real excitement of the Amador country. Troops who had come to California in the American conquest were the first Argonauts on the ground, giving the place its original name of Soldier Gulch. They found placers and clay beds so rich that the early comers averaged $100 per day. By 1849, gold-seekers were pouring into the new camp. Finding rocks and crags which resembled volcanic craters, they mistakenly gave it the name of Volcano.

But the wilderness camp was born to trouble. Sierra Indians, having discovered the value of white man's gold, were also mining in Volcano. Natives and intruders got along well enough until the summer of 1849. One day an American missed his pick, and claimed the Indians had stolen it. The chief, anxious to preserve peace, told a group of miners that if the pick was in the Indian camp, he would bring it back. When he ran off to fulfill the mission, an American rifle cracked and brought him down. Rod Stowell, a former Texas ranger, had mistaken the Indian's move and was too quick on the trigger.

Volcano's peace was broken, and the outraged Indians prepared for war. To cover their own blunder, the Americans who had precipitated the trouble announced to their comrades that the Indians had attacked them and murdered one. At this, the whites armed themselves and stormed the Indian stronghold. The natives were driven out, but not without leaving at least one American dead on the Volcano trail. This was the end of the Volcano War—except that when its citizens discovered that the Stowell group had lied about the cause of the trouble, they ran the rogues out of camp.

The finale was typical of Volcano's light respect for legalities. In the first state elections of 1849, territorial officials neglected to notify Volcano. But Bayard Taylor, news correspondent for Horace Greeley's New York *Tribune*, visited the town in the same month and carried with him some political messages from candidates in Mokelumne Hill. The Volcano boys concluded that he was an official who had come to call an election, and insisted on it even after Taylor pleaded that he was a reporter. So he consulted with the Alcalde (a combination mayor, sheriff and judge), and recommended an election procedure. They not only followed this out scrupulously, but finding a candidate on the ballot with the name of Taylor, mistook him for their visitor and gave him a unanimous vote.

"Had I known this fact sooner," noted Bayard Taylor, "I might have been tempted to run for Alcalde, at least."

The majesty of government was just as carelessly dismissed throughout the Amador country. Justice was less a matter of due process than of mob decision. At Sutter Creek a gambler stabbed a man, and was immediately tried by miners' court; he was given seventy-five lashes while the victim still lived, but was hanged next day when the man died—a double punishment which seemed perfectly reasonable to Sutter Creek. When a stabbing occurred in Volcano, the boys lynched the supposed culprit within half an hour.

In Fiddletown, $9,000 was taken from the Wells Fargo office, and five men were arrested for the crime for the good and sufficient reason that they had bad reputations. Lacking evidence, the boys sought to produce some by taking out three of the prisoners and hoisting them by the neck until they confessed. But with much hoisting the score stood: no confessions, no evidence, and after the Sheriff arrived from Jackson, no prisoners.

Fiddletown, in fact, was quite at home outside the law. Before Amador County was established, it somehow managed to reside in a no-man's land between El Dorado and Calaveras counties. It was perfectly willing to vote with El Dorado, but at tax collecting time it stood squarely behind its geographic barriers. Fiddletown, too, produced a classic in courtroom procedure. When a witness exhausted the court with his outlandish story, the judge took care of the situation:

"I declare court adjourned. This man is a damned liar. Court is in session."

Things were much the same in Amador City. Justice of the Peace for 1854 was Henry Lark, a horse-trader who held court in the Magnolia Saloon. He was playing seven-up with the bartender one day when Sheriff Jim Wall hauled in a man accused of stealing meat from his neighbor. The Sheriff knew better than to break up the game.

"Here judge, give me your hand while you settle this business."

"Git, and don't bother me!" answered the magistrate, who was evidently winning. But at the end of the hand he managed to change places with the sheriff. Throwing his leg over the table, he scrutinized the prisoner.

"Well, what you got to say for yourself?"

"I beg," interrupted the barkeep, engrossed in his cards.

"I'll see you damned first," retorted the sheriff.

"Sheriff, keep silence in the court," shouted the judge. A moment of quiet, as Justice Lark resumed his questioning.

"Cut the kerds, Barkeep."

"Run 'em."

"I was only borrowin' the meat, your Honor."

"No, you don't, Mr. Wall; put your little old jack on that ace!"

"Either this court or that game must adjourn if you don't make less noise!"

"One moment, Judge; count your game, Wall."

"High, jack, game."

"Silence in court!"

More quiet, while the judge continued the examination. At

the next shout from the bar he jumped up, furious, but caught a glimpse of the barkeeper's hand.

"Wall," said the justice, "I'll bet you five dollars you're beaten."

"Done! Come down with the cash."

The prisoner—quietly remembering a previous appointment—vanished.

"Fraud and cheating!" screamed Justice Lark. "I fine you both ten dollars for contempt of court."

* * *

If Amador County played loose with the law, its isolation was partly to blame. For the first two years of the Gold Rush, its traffic moved along trails by foot or horseback. When a stage coach service finally reached the town in 1854, it had a dubious reception. Down-stages carrying out gold shipments were apt to encounter masked men who took professional interest in the Wells Fargo box. It was soon noticed that they were remarkably adept at guessing which coaches carried the loot, and the suspicion was raised that they just might be getting inside help. Unable to catch the robbers, Wells Fargo finally took the hint and pulled out of Volcano. That ungrateful camp could shift for itself.

Meanwhile, the rest of Amador had taken more permanent root with the discovery of rich quartz veins. First strike was made at Amador City in February 1851 by a Baptist preacher; an indirect descendant of this and neighboring mines is the famous Keystone, one of the most fabulous gold producers of California. Quartz leads were also discovered at Sutter Creek in 1851, and the next year in Fiddletown. Together with the lode mines of Jackson, these produced the real gold boom of Amador County.

Despite its provincial name, Fiddletown became an important point on the Mother Lode. As late as the 1860s it was a trading outpost for surrounding camps. Bret Harte publicized it with his "An Episode of Fiddletown." But by 1878 its citizens could no longer see the joke in its priceless name, and changed it to the miserable title, Oleta. After half a century they came to their senses, and today its entrance sign announces, almost impudently, that this is Fiddletown.

As for Volcano, it lay largely outside the quartz belt. By 1855 it was resorting to hydraulic mining, and was showing signs of wear. But if Volcano died early, its remains have outlasted those of other camps down on the traveled highway. Volcano is still Volcano, though its erupting days are over.

POINTS OF INTEREST

VOLCANO. One authority has called Volcano "the most picturesque of all the Mother Lode towns." Considering only the unrestored ghost towns, it probably has the most buildings still standing. First among these is the St. George Hotel, which the newcomer faces upon entering town. Built in 1854, it is still in operation. Among the other buildings, all of them well marked, are the Adams Express office, the Wells Fargo building, the Odd Fellows and Masonic Hall, and those two essential institutions of any self-respecting Gold Rush town, the jail and the brewery. On a hill overlooking Volcano is the Methodist Church, where Thomas Starr King preached as part of his tour to support the Union cause during the Civil War.

FIDDLETOWN. Another well-preserved community off the beaten track, Fiddletown has a number of adobe, brick, and stone buildings of early vintage.

SUTTER CREEK. One of the most picturesque towns located on Highway 49, Sutter Creek is decorated with old balconies over the sidewalks, and has not been spoiled with an over-abundance of modern signs.

AMADOR CITY. Among a number of remaining buildings, most of them abandoned, are the Amador Hotel, the Imperial Hotel, the Amador Mercantile Building, and the headquarters of the old Keystone Mine (now converted to an inn).

DRYTOWN. A few brick buildings dating from the 1850s are still standing in this once-flourishing town.

Chapter 7. Mok Hill & Its Feudin' Twin, Jackson

IF CALIFORNIANS ARE INCORRIGIBLE hometown boosters, they can lay the original blame on the exuberant citizens of the Gold Rush camps. And the finest examples of this local bombast were the neighboring (and feuding) towns of Mokelumne Hill and Jackson, in the heart of the Southern Mines.

From the beginning these two camps were headed for trouble out of conflict of character. Mok Hill, as it was called, was the northernmost of the camps with a cosmopolitan flavor. Here were large colonies of Frenchmen, native Californians, Mexicans and Chileans; here flourished the fandango hall and the bull-and-bear fight. Jackson had its mixed population, but it definitely bore the American stamp.

In lawlessness the camps were also rivals. In both places the man who was robbed looked to his own gun rather than to the law for justice; and if he shot one of the offenders there was no thought of a trial. Mokelumne had at least two lynchings and, according to one report, five killings in one week. Jackson was supposed to have hanged ten to fifteen men, depending on varying estimates, from the same execution tree.

When the Gold Rush began, Mok Hill got a head start on its neighbor. Discovered in August 1848, it was a thriving, canvas-tented camp within a year. Jackson, in fact, was founded as a way station on the road from Sacramento to Mokelumne Hill; by the end of 1849 its population was only some sixty persons. But as rich diggings were uncovered along Jackson Creek, the camp flourished in its own right.

Then trouble began. Calaveras County (which then included Jackson) was formed in 1850, and the county seat was won by the nearby camp of Double Springs. Since it had only one building, Jackson and Mok Hill considered this a deliberate insult. So in July, 1851, an election was held to relocate the county seat. Mokelumne, still having the larger population, naturally won—or at least that was the result reported by the county clerk, Colonel Collyer.

But the Jackson men were not through. Three of them rode

down to Double Springs and invited everybody in the Court-house (which also served as saloon) to drink to the new county seat, Mok Hill. This suggestion could hardly be ignored, even by Col. Collyer. And while everybody was toasting, one Jackson man grabbed the official records from a nearby table, threw them in a wagon and dashed off to the new seat of Calaveras County. By the time the county clerk arrived, one Judge Smith had recounted the ballots and declared Jackson the winner. This was county government, Gold Rush style.

Col. Collyer accepted the situation and set up office in Jackson. But when he was defeated at the next election, he adopted the Jackson system and locked up the ballots. Judge Smith thereupon broke into his desk, counted the votes and declared Collyer the loser. The Colonel then made the mistake of promising to shoot Judge Smith on sight, and lost out a third time in a contest of bullets.

Meanwhile, Jackson's triumph as the county seat lasted only nine months. In April, 1852, Mokelumne Hill won a second election, and possession of the crucial records. Jackson and neighboring camps then walked out of Calaveras and formed their own Amador County—with Jackson as the official seat. As for Mokelumne, it finally relinquished the seat of Calaveras County in 1866 to the more permanent community of San Andreas. This time Jackson had no objections.

The miners did not always take their elections seriously. When California applied for admission to the Union in 1849, a convention assembled at Monterey and framed a state constitution. With characteristic audacity, California held an election in November, 1849, for ratifying the Constitution and choosing state officers—before Congress had fairly begun to debate the question of admission. At Mok Hill, as elsewhere in California, election day was rainy and miserable. Despite the momentous occasion, few citizens stirred out of their tents until noon. Finally the Alcalde appointed two inspectors and set up the polls in the camp's largest tent—a saloon. Observing the scene was the 19th century journalist and author, Bayard Taylor, who noted that the inspectors were seated "behind the counter, in close proximity to the glasses and bottles, the calls for which were quite as frequent as the votes."

Mok Hill & Its Feudin' Twin, Jackson / 79

Since most citizens knew neither Constitution nor candidates, their judgment was limited. A candidate named Fair received a number of votes on the strength of his auspicious name. Another lost about twenty votes for having previously appeared on the river wearing a stovepipe hat. Admitted one voter:

"When I left home I was determined to go it blind. I went it blind in coming to California, and I'm not going to stop now. I voted for the Constitution, and I've never seen the Constitution. I voted for all the candidates, and I don't know a damned one of them. I'm going it blind all through, I am."

Mokelumne's unanimous vote in favor of the Constitution was representative of the California balloting. As it happened, the 1849 Constitution has been recognized as one of the most admirable documents of its kind.

This gambler's spirit was characteristic of miners in the Mokelumne-Jackson region, if not in the whole Mother Lode. In Mok Hill, a Negro miner arrived and asked some of the boys where to dig. They pointed out, by way of a practical joke, a hill that had already been combed over and pronounced barren. A week later he was back on the street, loaded down with gold. And the boys promptly stampeded to their "barren" hill.

The same thing happened to three young Germans in Jackson. They were directed to some mine tailings—rock that had already been worked over. Within a few days they had earned $700, having dug down through the tailings to a rich vein beneath.

These chance strikes, according to an early Mok Hill citizen, were not the exceptions. The reason so many miners failed, he insisted, was that they were trying to go by some sensible geologic theory. Such men "would be baffled at every turn," for the irregular distribution of mineral in the Mother Lode defied geology. One miner named Clarke was famed for his rich discoveries. He once fell down a steep hill, got to poking around at the bottom with his knife, and made a million-dollar strike. The secret of Clarke's success, concluded the Mokelumne chronicler, "was that he had no theory. . . ."

With such diggings under foot, most miners fell easy prey to the gambling tables of Mok Hill and Jackson. If they lost their pile on Saturday night, they could dig another next week. It also made them connoisseurs of the most expensive food and drink. "It was no unusual thing," reported Bayard Taylor, "to see a company of these men, who had never before had a thought of luxury beyond a good beefsteak and a glass of whiskey, drinking their champagne at ten dollars a bottle, and eating their tongue and sardines, or warming in the smoky camp-kettle their tin canisters of turtle soup and lobster salad."

Such epicurean tastes were especially costly in a land where prices were topsy-turvy. At the "Brandy and Sugar" Hotel in Jackson, a slice of bread was $1.00. Buttered, $2.00. In Mokelumne, board for mules was comparable: barley was $1 a quart and grass $1 a handful.

Prices like these are the chief reason why many, if not most, of the fortunes made in the Gold Rush came not from mining, but from trading. In 1849, a man named Fash so succeeded in cornering the commerce of Mokelumne Hill that the camp acquired the nickname, "Fashville." His operation of the only store in camp and the only mule team from the outside world was merely the beginning of his accomplishments. One of Fash's most lucrative assets was a big sheet-iron stove, on which a miner could cook any item at a $1.00 fee. Fash's specialty was apple pie, which sold fast at $2.00 each. One day he ran out of apples, but having a heavy stock of beans on hand, produced a bean pie and sold it as a "novel and delicate luxury." Poker games were the fashion at Fash's place, subject to the house rule that whenever somebody won a pot with four-of-a-kind, he had to order drinks for everybody. Fash's muleteers brought in Mok Hill mail as a free service, until he hung out a new sign: "Fash's Letter Express." After that, letters were $2.00 apiece.

The Hillites, as they were called, might overlook such business tactics, but the mining profession had strict moral rules. One of these was that no man could mine his claim with slave labor. Near Mokelumne Hill a Chilean named Dr. Concha was working his mine with a force of peons; what was more, he staked a number of claims in their names. This did not please the American miners, who may also be suspected of opposing Chilean miners in general. When the report reached Mokelumne Hill that Dr. Concha's men had driven a party of Americans off some rich ground, the trouble exploded into the "Chilean War."

The American miners met on "the Hill" and passed a resolution banishing Chileans from the diggings. Dr. Concha in turn went down to Stockton and secured a warrant for the arrest of the Americans. Some sixty of his men marched into Mok Hill in December 1849, killed two miners and made off with thirteen prisoners. At this, the Mokelumne miners rose in arms, and a company of Rangers was hurriedly sent from Stockton.

But before the night was over the prisoners had struggled free and captured the Chilean band. The new captives were brought into Mokelumne for trial; three were hanged and others given lesser punishment. The Chilean War was over, but the resentment it kindled reached from California to South America.

Nor was this the only battle between Yankees and foreigners at Mok Hill. On a nearby knoll, a group of Frenchmen were working an exceedingly rich claim. When some American miners tried to seize the property, the French dug in for a fight and planted a Tricolor banner in their midst. At this provocation, several hundred Yankee miners assembled and stormed the fort, carrying off a fortune in high-grade ore. The whole act of piracy went unpunished, and was soon dignified with the name "French War"—another monument to the primitive side of Gold Rush California.

But Mok Hill had its refinements. Late in 1851 the Hillites established a theatre—complete with candles for footlights and genteel-looking miners for the female roles. One young actor was eager to show his talents at tragedy, and was given the lead in Richard III. But the Mok Hill boys took the role less seriously. When Richard rushed to the front of the stage, sank to his knees and shouted, "My kingdom for a horse!"—a Mexican burro that had been smuggled under the stage answered with a fearful braying. In the confusion, a stagehand raised the footlights and a candle caught Richard in the nose. While the house roared, the outraged king rushed from the scene and his talents were lost forever to the tragic stage.

Such was the riotous spirit of Mok Hill and Jackson in the Golden Fifties. Mokelumne, a thriving camp when Jackson was still unborn, now remains as a near-ghost town on Highway 49. But Jackson, spurred by the development of such famous mines as the Argonaut and the Kennedy, outlived its rival and stands today as one of the busiest towns in the Mother Lode. And tempers have cooled since the days when county seats were won by the town with the fastest buckboard.

POINTS OF INTEREST

MOKELUMNE HILL. Until recent years, Mok Hill presented to the passerby one of the most delightful examples of Gold Rush architecture. But a devastating fire along Highway 49 has changed that. One now has to drop down into the side streets to get the town's real flavor and explore its historic buildings, most of which are well marked. Prominent among them are the remains of the old Hemminghoffen-Suesdorf Brewery. A hill overlooking town is known as French Hill, where the Americans stormed the fort of the beleaguered Frenchmen.

CHILE GULCH. South of Mokelumne Hill along Highway 49 is the site, now obliterated, of the so-called Chilean War.

JACKSON. Unlike Mokelumne Hill, Jackson is a lively and well-populated town. Many more old buildings are preserved, though usually camouflaged behind modern dress. Among the objects of interest are the Amador County Courthouse of 1854 vintage, the National Hotel, the Wells Fargo office, and a museum housed in an 1858 building.

JACKSON GATE. Principal landmark remaining at this outpost north of Jackson is the store of the Chichizola family, said to date from 1850. The huge wheels, plainly visible from the road between Jackson Gate and Martell, were not installed there until 1912. They were used in conveying tailings from the Kennedy Mine.

Mok Hill and Its Feudin' Twin, Jackson / 83

DOUBLE SPRINGS. Once the seat of Calaveras County, Double Springs is marked today by two historic structures—the old Wheat mansion, built in 1860; and behind it, part of the frame house that served as Calaveras County's first court house.

Chapter 8. Calaveras: Jumping Frog Country

ONE SPOT in the heart of the Southern Mines is general headquarters for California folklore—from Joaquin Murieta and Black Bart to Bret Harte and Mark Twain. Here lie the twin capitals of the Jumping Frog Country, Angel's Camp and San Andreas.

It was not from spotless virtue that the roaring camp of Angel's got its name. Its founder was George Angel, who had come to California as a soldier during the Mexican War. When news of the gold strike at Sutter's Mill reached Monterey, he was one of some ninety men who struck out for the Sierras. They reached Calaveritas Creek in May, 1848, and Angel himself built a trading post on what came to be called Angel's Creek. Within a year the hills at Angel's Camp were "dotted with tents," in the words of one observer, "and the creeks filled with human beings to such a degree that it seemed as if a day's work of the mass would not leave a stone unturned in them." Four years later the population reached 4500, and Angel's was one of the hubs of the Mother Lode.

Meanwhile, the rival camp of San Andreas had sprung up a few miles away. Founded in 1848 by Mexican prospectors, it was one of the earliest to suffer from the racial clashes that rocked the Mother Lode. When the richness of San Andreas became known, American miners poured in and drove many of the Mexicans out. At least one of the San Andreas victims, according to legend, struck back.

The story goes that Joaquin Murrieta was living near town when a gang of Americans descended on his place. They hung his brother for a crime he didn't commit, ravished his sweetheart and horse-whipped Joaquin for good measure. Swearing vengeance, the proud youth took the outlaw trail and formed a band of cut-throats to prey on American settlements up and down the Mother Lode. All of the twenty-one murderers of his brother were brought to justice—nineteen by Joaquin's own hand. Between 1851 and '53 he was in and out of nearly every camp in the Southern Mines, robbing where he chose, laughing at the law, taking from the rich and giving to the poor—all in true Robin Hood tradition.

At least this is the version in the popular literature on Joaquin. Probably no American bandit—not even Jesse James—has been more widely chronicled. Joaquin is the subject of more than two dozen biographies, counting all the separate editions—eleven of them in Spanish; two novels; two epic poems; one play; one motion picture; and almost countless newspaper serials, magazine articles, and separate book chapters. Scarcely a town in the Southern Mines of the gold country fails to claim some landmark as a favorite haunt of Joaquin.

Beginning in the 1930s, Francis P. Farquhar and Joseph Henry Jackson applied literary scholarship to the Murrieta biographies, tracing all of them in a direct line of descent back to an original story by John Rollin Ridge published in 1854. Most of the rest were piratings, or piratings of piratings, usually with added layers of fancy. As for the original version, Jackson called it "as preposterous a fiction as any the Dime Libraries ever invented. . . ."

Although alert scholarship had exposed the Murrieta fiction, it hardly proved there were no facts to be had. Was there a Joaquin, and if so, what is his real story?

The public nature of Joaquin's exploits would suggest contemporary newspapers as the best hunting ground. From these sources—often providing two or three supporting reports of the same episodes—there emerges a Joaquin who terrorized Amador, Calaveras, and probably Mariposa Counties for just two months—January to early March, 1853.

On January 23 a Mexican suspected of horse stealing was captured by two Americans at Bay State Ranch near San Andreas. But he was rescued at gun point by three other Mexican riders. Reinforced from San Andreas, a party of five Americans pursued the outlaws to the vicinity of Calaveritas Creek; but when they overtook their quarry near the top of a hill south of San Andreas, they found the Mexicans had increased to twelve. The gang promptly rode down upon their pursuers, firing as they came. The Americans, exhausting their ammunition in a short battle, returned to San Andreas. The Mexicans proceeded to a place called Yackee Camp, two miles south of San Andreas, where they shot at any Americans they found. Killing one man, they pushed on to a nearby quartz mill and murdered two more Americans before going into hiding.

At this outrage—the first recorded appearance of Joaquin and his band—the whole Calaveras community was aroused. Mass meetings were held in San Andreas and Double Springs; resolutions were passed ordering the Mexican population to leave the county; parties were stationed at the ferries on the Stanislaus and the Calaveras; and the region in between was scoured for the outlaws. Three Mexicans supposed to have been part of Joaquin's gang were taken at various places and hanged without ceremony. Bands of Americans drove the Mexican population from San Andreas and the upper Calaveras River. Reported the Stockton newspaper, "If an American meets a Mexican, he takes his horse, his arms, and bids him leave."

For two weeks, while posses patrolled Calaveras County, Joaquin and his band remained hidden. By the first week in February the region was too hot for comfort; one of the gang, said to be Joaquin's brother, was captured and hanged at Angel's Camp. Joaquin and his men headed north. At Winter's Bar they forced the ferryman to carry them across the Mokelumne River; then they rode around Jackson, robbing as they went, through the present Amador County.

On February 8 they attacked a Chinese camp near Big Bar on the Cosumnes River, massacring six persons and making off with $6,000. Near Fiddletown three of the band were surprised by a posse on February 12 and were forced to decamp with a single horse—two men riding and the other running behind hanging to the animal's tail. When the latter was wounded, one of the riders changed places with him. Shortly afterward the horse was shot, but with their usual resourcefulness the bandits managed to escape in the brush. Doubling southward, they killed three Chinese and one American near Jackson.

With these atrocities, northern Calaveras County (now Amador County) rose in fury. Mass meetings at Jackson and Mokelumne Hill dispatched posses in pursuit. Wrote one correspondent, "Woe to the Mexicans if they are caught." One unfortunate was taken on the Mokelumne River and hanged at Jackson without trial. When Joaquin's band robbed a German traveler north of Jackson, a posse of twenty men rode out of town and encountered four of the bandits, including Joaquin himself, near a chaparral-covered hill. One outlaw was killed and Joaquin wounded in the cheek—which could account for later descriptions of him specifying a scar on the right cheek. But the bandits scrambled into the chaparral, which as one witness wrote, was "so thick even a dog canot git through it."

Overnight the besiegers tried to surround the mountain and sent for reinforcements. By the morning of February 17 some fifty Americans and a hundred Indians had gathered, spurred on by a local reward of $1,000 offered for Joaquin's head. But once again the fugitives made their escape. Stealing horses and saddles, they rode south and crossed the Mokelumne River— on a stolen boat, according to one report. At a Chinese camp near Rich Bar on the Calaveras River they killed three persons, wounded five more, and corralled and robbed the rest (one report said the victims totalled 200 persons, and the haul $30,000).

Riding northward to Forman's Ranch, near the Mokelumne River, the bandits were surprised there by a posse early in the morning of February 22. But they escaped under a hail of bullets, with one of their number wounded in the hand. While their pursuers followed only ten minutes behind, they descended on another Chinese camp, killed three, mortally wounded five others, and rode off with several thousand dollars.

All next day they flew ahead of their pursuers, plundering Chinese camps along the way. Just before dark, as the posse later reported, "we saw them about three quarters of a mile distant, robbing some Chinamen. They turned and saw us advancing, but they stirred not an inch until we were within half a mile of them, when they mounted their horses and rode off at the speed of the wind. . . . We attempted pursuit, but our horses were worn out. . . ."

With this catalogue of butchery in two weeks' time, Joaquin made himself the terror of the Southern Mines, and the sensation of California. More than ever the settlers were panicked; at least two posses were in the field, and citizens of the Cosumnes River collected $1,000 reward for Joaquin. The Chinese, who had suffered the brunt of Joaquin's ferocity, were leaving their isolated camps and congregating in the large settlements for protection. The *Calaveras Chronicle* reported: "It is to be regretted that, so insecure is life now considered in this county, in consequence of the recent outrages, that there is a perceptible falling off in the population."

A few days after his last daring escape on February 22, Joaquin was reported in the town of Hornitos, in Mariposa County —apparently having left Calaveras for good. With his usual bravado he was playing monte in a saloon and drinking freely until his comrades dragged him away for fear the authorities might take him. About March 4 all of the stock at the ranch of an American near Quartzburg, Mariposa County, were run off by a band of Mexicans. The determined owner, one Prescot, tracked them into Hornitos, found them in a tent, and collected seven or eight Americans to surround and capture them. Entering the tent with a light, Prescot and a companion had seized one man when they were met with a fusillade of bullets which wounded them both. While the rest of the Americans opened fire, the fugitives escaped unharmed in the dark. It was widely reported that this was Joaquin and his band.

On May 17 the Governor signed a bill authorizing Captain Harry Love, a former Mexican War express rider and California peace officer, to raise a company of twenty rangers and bring Joaquin to justice. The rest of the story is comparatively well known. On July 25 Love's rangers came upon a band of Mexicans in the San Joaquin Valley near the mouth of Arroyo Cantua, north of the present town of Coalinga. In the fight that followed the rangers killed the leader (supposedly Joaquin) and also a man identified as Manuel "Three-Fingered Jack" Garcia, well known in California as a brigand and cutthroat.

To prove they had actually killed Joaquin, the rangers

brought back the leader's head and Three-Fingered Jack's deformed hand preserved in a keg of brandy. In Mariposa County and other parts of the state, Love sought out seventeen persons supposed to know the bandit and secured affidavits that this was indeed the head of Joaquin. The grisly trophies were put on display at Stockton, then in San Francisco, where the curious paid $1.00 admission.

No sooner had the head been placed on exhibit than some persons claiming to have known the bandit said it was not Joaquin's. Curiously, the head was never taken to Calaveras County, the one area where a number of people had actually seen the outlaw.

Whether he was killed by Love's rangers or whether he went into permanent hiding, the fact remains that there was a bandit named Joaquin. He was not very much like the bandit described by Ridge and subsequent biographers. Yet he was not, as scholar Joseph Henry Jackson believed, "manufactured, practically out of whole cloth. . . ." For two months he and his band ravaged the Southern Mines and killed approximately twenty people—perhaps more. In that flash of time he was the biggest news in Calaveras County.

For the Mother Lode traveler, one lesson to be drawn is that particular landmarks pointed out as the haunts of Joaquin should be appreciated only as legend, as yet unsupported by historical evidence. But contemporary sources at least bear witness that he probably visited San Andreas, Campo Seco, and Lancha Plana in Calaveras County; Drytown, Jackson Gate, and Fiddletown in Amador County; and Quartzburg and Hornitos in Mariposa County.

A far more durable bandit was Black Bart, in whom San Andreas also takes a proprietary interest, since it was the scene of his trial and conviction. When it came to pure robbery, both in quantity and quality, Black Bart was assuredly the prince of California bandits. To be sure, he was somewhat late getting started; Bart robbed his first stage in 1875. But for the next eight years, armed only with a shotgun and a stern voice, this bold highwayman stopped no less than twenty-eight stages.

Bart was no ordinary ruffian. He planned and executed his robberies with careful research and admirable finesse. He always worked alone, though he sometimes mounted a battery of broomsticks over a rock beside the road to impress stage-drivers with his imaginary confederates. He always left the passengers alone, and on one occasion is supposed to have returned to an excited lady her proffered purse.

Bart ranged as far North as the Oregon border, but it was the stage drivers of the gold country who most often heard his stentorian command, "Throw down that box!" He left no clues, except in two early robberies when he placed a tantalizing bit of poetry in the empty Wells Fargo chest, signed by "Black Bart, the PO8." Two stanzas gave a hint of Bart's character, but not his identity:

> *"I've labored long and hard for bread*
> *for honor and for riches*
> *But on my corns too long yove tred*
> *You fine haired ——— —— ————*
> *Let come what will I'll try it on*
> *My condition cant be worse*
> *and if thers money in that Box*
> *Tis munny in my purse."*

By the time this colorful scoundrel had perpetrated twenty-seven successful holdups, he had California sheriffs, Wells Fargo detectives and the U. S. Postal authorities in a high lather. But every enterprise has its bad days, especially highway robbery. On November 3, 1883, the Sonora stage rolled westward toward the Calaveras town of Copperopolis. At the bottom of Funk Hill the lone passenger, a young boy with a rifle, got out to do some hunting; the driver agreed to pick him up on the other side of the hill. As the laboring team neared the top, out sprang Black Bart with leveled shotgun.

This time he ran into trouble. The Wells Fargo chest was bolted to the floor of the coach. To gain time in opening it, Bart ordered the driver to take the horses on over the hill out of sight. But there the driver came upon the boy and his gun. He came back over the hill just as Bart was making off with the loot, sent him a volley of three shots and hit him.

The wounded Bart escaped, but in the confusion he left behind a handkerchief—with its tell-tale laundry mark. Wells Fargo detectives traced it to the apartment of Charles Bolton, San Francisco. There they arrested a dapper little man who had been leading a double life as San Francisco boulevardier and Mother Lode stage robber. Those fine haired —————— ——————, whoever they were, had the last laugh, after all.

Black Bart was taken to San Andreas, seat of Calaveras County, and tried for his last holdup. It was the biggest excitement in the town since the first gold rush. The trial was cut short when Bart pleaded guilty, but he tried to make up for that by delivering a long courtroom speech. The outlaw served a few years at San Quentin, and then faded from history. It was small punishment for twenty-eight robberies, but then Bart had never fired a shot. Besides, he had been uncommonly polite.

It was in the area from Angel's Camp south to Table Mountain that Bret Harte spent two months on the Mother Lode in 1855. Here most of his identifiable story settings were laid, and here alone does he show real familiarity with gold country geography. In this Calaveras country that chivalrous old reprobate, Colonel Starbottle, held forth. And in Angel's itself were laid such stories as *Mrs. Skaggs' Husband* and *The Bell Ringer of Angel's*.

Still, Bret Harte arrived too late to capture the Gold Rush spirit in his Mother Lode stories. As one critic puts it, "The flavor of decay hangs about his mining towns; they are just the places which he might have seen in Calaveras in 1855."

Even later came Mark Twain, who described the Angel's of 1865 as a "decayed mining camp." True, he got a poor first impression from boarding a week at the local French restaurant, which served a straight fare of chili beans and "bad, weak coffee" for every meal. On the first day Twain's companion, Jim Gillis, called the waiter and told him he had made a mistake. They had ordered coffee. "This is day-before-yesterday's dishwater."

A few days later Mark Twain made a momentous entry in his notebook: "Coleman with his jumping frog—bet a stranger $50—Stranger had no frog and C. got him one:—In the meantime stranger filled C's frog full of shot and he couldn't jump. The stranger's frog won." Coleman later became Jim Smiley, and this fragmentary anecdote—probably related by the bartender at the Angel's Hotel—became Mark Twain's first famous story, *The Celebrated Jumping Frog of Calaveras County*.

First published in *Clapp's Saturday Press*, it was reprinted across the country and even translated into French. This latter effort dealt such a horrifying blow to the picturesque Western dialect of the *Jumping Frog* that Mark Twain later retaliated by translating it literally back into English. Such phrases as, "Well, I don't see no p'ints about that frog that's any better'n any other frog," became, "Eh bien! I no saw not that that frog had nothing of better than each frog." This, said Twain, was sheer martyrdom.

In any case, the *Jumping Frog* made Mark Twain famous, and immortalized Angel's Camp. In return, the town each spring honors Mark Twain, his story and the Gold Rush days in general with a three-day festival climaxed by a Jumping Frog contest—one of the biggest community celebrations in California.

POINTS OF INTEREST

SAN ANDREAS. Though some old buildings were sacrificed in widening the highway through town, other winding streets in the hillside business district are redolent with antiquity. As in other large Mother Lode towns, a good starting point for an historical tour is the local museum, located here in the Chamber of Commerce building.

CAMPO SECO. The old Adams Express building, a number of rock walls, and a few adobe houses are the main features of this once-lively town, located on a dirt road west of San Andreas.

CAMANCHE. This nostalgic community on the North Fork of the Mokelumne River still exhibits several old structures of dressed stone.

JENNY LIND. Named in a burst of enthusiasm for the Swedish Nightingale, this ghost camp is marked by the remains of Sinclair's adobe store and the Rosenberg building, made of sandstone.

All along the lower reaches of the Mokelumne, as on most other rivers flowing out of the Mother Lode, the visitor sees mile upon mile of rock piles—the residue of dredge mining that occurred over many decades.

FOURTH CROSSING. Halfway between San Andreas and Altaville on Highway 49 is Fourth Crossing, a once-popular stage stop. Biographers believe it was here that Bret Harte tried his luck at panning gold.

CALAVERITAS. On a dirt road southeast of San Andreas are the remains of Calaveritas, once populated by Mexican placer miners. Its adobe walls are gradually mouldering under the elements.

ALTAVILLE. Prominent among the landmarks of Altaville are the Prince Hotel; the Demarest foundry; the Prince and Garibardi store, built in 1857; and a brick grammar school serving Altaville children from 1858 to 1950.

ANGEL'S CAMP. The chief point of interest is the Angels Hotel, where bartender Ben Coon is supposed to have related the Jumping Frog story to Mark Twain. The large waterwheel seen on entering town from the south was once employed to operate an arrastre, or ore-grinding mill.

COPPEROPOLIS. Founded as a staging center, Copperopolis boomed as a focal point of the copper craze that seized California in the 1860s. Dating from that period, most of its remaining buildings were constructed of brick brought from the then-fading town of Columbia.

VALLECITO. Among the landmarks in this quaint settlement are the old Wells Fargo office (1854) and, across the street, remains of the Wells Fargo stables, which were built in 1851 before the company was founded. On another street is the stone Cuneo Building, also dating from 1851.

MURPHY'S. The lore of the Gold Rush runs strong in Murphy's, easily one of the best-preserved towns on the Lode.

Named for the founding brothers, Daniel and John Murphy, this out-of-the-way camp thrived first as a placer mining center and later as gateway to the Calaveras Grove of Sequoia Giant trees. In the Murphy's (or Mitchler) Hotel, built in 1855 as the Sperry Hotel, one may still see in old register books the signatures of Mark Twain, Henry Ward Beecher, Ulysses S. Grant, Black Bart and one "Old Dan the Guide," from "God Knows Where." In the doorway are bullet holes from an early-day gunfight.

Other historic buildings are the Jones Apothecary Shop, the Traver building, Victorene Compere's Store, and the Catholic and Congregational churches—all well marked and dating from the Gold Rush.

Chapter 9. Columbia: Gem of the Southern Mines

EVEN IN THE GOLD RUSH, Columbia held a special place in California's heart. With her red brick face, wrought iron trimmings and myriad shade trees, she was the gaudy showplace of the Mother Lode. To the boys she was like a beautiful, if slightly tarnished, woman—the toast of the mines.

A century has not dimmed Columbia's reputation. Though the throbbing life which once surged through her streets is gone, she is today the ghost town supreme to Californians. Since 1945, when the crumbled camp was made a historical state park, they have been restoring her faded charm as a monument to California's golden era.

Columbia was not quite a Forty-niner camp. Nearby Sonora was born in the summer of 1848, but two winters passed before prospectors struck the Columbia treasure. On March 27, 1850, a party headed by Dr. Thaddeus Hildreth found gold in a dry gulch; in the next two days they took out thirty pounds of gold (worth some $4680) and started one of the biggest stampedes of the Gold Rush. Since the discovery spot lay in the heart of the teeming Southern Mines, it mushroomed overnight. Within a month, according to reports, population jumped from zero to 5,000—one of the most tumultuous rushes on record.

Out of this explosive beginning sprang a town which astounded California with its headlong growth. By 1852 she still wore a board-and-canvas look, but she contained no less than four banks, three express offices, eight hotels, a daguerreotype parlor, seventeen general stores, two fire companies, forty saloons, numerous fandango houses, forty-three faro tables with a combined capital approaching $2 million—and withal such badly-needed institutions as three churches, a Sunday school, two bookstores, a temperance group and a choral society.

Outside communication was provided by pony riders of the "Chain Lightning Express," covering the thirty miles from Knight's Ferry in the less-than-lightning time of three hours. Eight stages brought passengers from the nearest connection at Sonora. And in the height of the boom, the four miles between the twin cities was solidly lined with miners' shanties.

For all her roughness, Columbia believed in culture. She had three theatres, including a Chinese version with forty Oriental actors. Most elaborate was the Exchange, where Edwin Booth played Richard III. In this festooned emporium, its stage decorated by a pine sapling growing up through the boards, William and Caroline Chapman delighted Columbia audiences night after night. The whooping miners flung gold purses to the players on opening night until the stage was literally covered; threw so much silver coinage on succeeding nights that they created a shortage in town for several months; and finally escorted the Chapmans in triumph to their next engagement in Sonora.

Irrepressible Columbia never did things halfway. When word reached camp that the first woman was arriving, the boys dropped their shovels, decorated Main Street with arches, took the brass band and marched down to Sonora several thousand strong to provide an escort.

Like other Sierra camps, Columbia put decent women on a marble pedestal. Word got around that Big Annie, a notorious madame, had pushed the town schoolmarm into the street. The outraged fire boys dragged their machine to Annie's place and washed the old girl out of the building. Columbia chivalry could do no more.

The town's first chance for a big celebration came on Independence Day, 1851. Sonora, still the metropolis of the Southern Mines, had just been laid waste by fire, and all of Tuolumne County gathered at Columbia for the Fourth. The town seized the opportunity with fervor. From every roof waved the stars and stripes, with others hung across Main Street. There was, according to one eye-witness, "a continual discharge of revolvers, and a vast expenditure of powder and squids and crackers, together with an unlimited consumption of brandy."

But this was merely the informal phase of celebration. The official event was launched with a grand parade consisting of: the Columbia brass band; the teachers and pupils of the town school, who sang hymns whenever the musicians "had blown themselves out of breath"; 100 or more Masons in full regalia; a long cavalcade of horsemen, including "whoever could get a four-legged animal to carry him," with "horses, mules and jackasses" thrown in together; a hook-and-ladder brigade; several hundred miners walking in pairs, each dragging a wheelbarrow containing pick, shovel, frying pan, coffee-pot and tin cup—symbols of mining life; and finally another gang pulling a long tom on wheels, while several pretended to be operating it with much flourish of shovels. All of this was greeted with shouting, cheering, and cat-calling from the sidelines.

The whole procession wound up at the town arena, which usually served for bull-and-bear fights. Here, while the band appropriately played "Hail, Columbia," the celebrants took their seats for the solemn program, consisting of the reading of the Declaration of Independence and the Fourth of July oration. This was delivered in rousing fashion by Tuolumne County's rising politician, James W. Coffroth, whom an observer described as "a pale-faced, chubby-cheeked young gentleman, with very white and extensive shirt-collars." The fledgeling spellbinder covered everything from Plymouth Rock to George III, until his restless audience raised some very unceremonious shouts—"Gaas, gaas!" Then, after Columbia's chorus of dinner bells had called the boys to a meal, the festivities were capped by the Latin touch—a bull fight.

It would take more than a crowd's insult to down James Wood Coffroth, a man of unbounded optimism, good cheer and personal ambition. Known as "Columbia's favorite son," he was described as the "jolliest, freest, readiest man that ever faced a California audience . . . the typical politician of early-day California."

Arriving in the mines the previous year at the age of twenty-one, Coffroth had applied for work at the Sonora *Herald* office with the modest acknowledgement that he was a "Philadelphia editor." They had him busy writing poetry and editorials, both of which he finished off with fantastic rhetoric.

Finally several irate gamblers invaded the *Herald* office on a question of editorial policy, and one of the bullets barely missed the editorial writer. Coffroth took up law.

By the end of '51 young Coffroth had settled in the booming Columbia camp, a promising attorney with an impromptu legal education. He quickly got himself elected to the state Assembly, then to the Senate. His rise was not hindered by a fine flair for publicity. In 1855 he challenged a man to a duel for slandering his character to a lady and "interference in my private affairs"; the other refused, but Coffroth got his satisfaction in the liberal amounts of free newspaper space. Yet it was said of him that he "never had a personal enemy," and his easy-going humor was famous. When he was boomed for governor, Coffroth said that his reason for running was that he wanted to pardon his many friends in the state prison.

Coffroth had no intention of letting all this personal talent go to waste. He threw it into the stream of Columbia history whenever occasion offered. His first opportunity to sway events came when a knifing scrape stirred Columbia in November, 1853. Pete Nicholas, an Austrian miner, had drunk himself into a fighting mood when he encountered John Parote, a citizen of nearby Pine Log, in a Main Street store. Pete grabbed Parote, who tried to struggle free; he struck his assailant and fell back over a sugar sack, pulling Nicholas with him. Pete produced a knife and stabbed his victim, who fell back unconscious. Pete was arrested and held prisoner to await trial.

This episode was a familiar story in rough-and-tumble Columbia, but now her citizens decided it was too familiar. Besides, the men of Pine Log marched into town ready to wreak justice in the name of their friend, Parote. Next morning Columbia calmly ate breakfast and then proceeded to drag Pete from the care of the town constable and down the street to a waiting tree. Just as the victim was about to be swung off his feet, the constable and his deputy climbed into the tree to cut the rope. Under their weight the limb broke, dropping everything to the ground. The crowd was equally determined, and brushing aside the officer, took the helpless prisoner to another tree.

At this timely moment appeared James Coffroth. Nicholas was his friend, and he hoped to stall the mob till the sheriff arrived. Gaining attention, he launched his speech. He was, said Coffroth, also anxious that justice be done. The murderer ought to be hanged—at this the boys nodded agreement.

"But for the everlasting honor of our glorious republic," added the speaker, "let all things be done decently and in order. . . . As a matter of course Nicholas will be hanged. . . . But for the credit of Columbia give the man a trial."

Coffroth's strategy worked. Before he had finished the sheriff arrived from Sonora, moved through the crowd organizing his deputies, and finally addressed the boys.

"Gentlemen, you will excuse me, but this man is going to the Sonora jail, there to await his trial by law. I am going to take him there."

The gentlemen thought different, and swarmed forward to grab the prisoner. But the sheriff's deputies held firm, and the mob was stopped at last. While the angry men cursed Coffroth and the sheriff, Nicholas was hauled off to Sonora. The following February he was tried and sentenced to hang. It looked as though Coffroth's promise would be fulfilled.

But by this time Pete had another lawyer who was as cunning as Coffroth. He knew that the entire state was then absorbed in the problem of choosing a permanent state capital. The legislature at Benicia was flooded with petitions from San Jose, Sacramento and other towns scrambling for the honor. Not to be outdone, the boys of Pine Log got up a petition to make their camp the state capital and circulated it throughout the county. After it had gained 10,000 signatures, Pete's lawyer saw it on a store counter in Columbia one day and quietly stuffed it in his pocket. Back in his office, he tore off the original heading and substituted a plea for commutation of Pete's death sentence. Then he sent it off by pony rider to Governor John Bigler at Benicia.

Mr. Bigler had never heard of Pete Nicholas, but he did recognize 10,000 votes when he saw them. He didn't know that some of the very names on the petition were those of the men who had helped fix the noose around Pete's neck. Any man who had the confidence of 10,000 neighbors, he decided, couldn't be all bad. The governor commuted Pete's sentence to ten years' imprisonment—a term which was later reduced to four.

Columbia was cheated of justice, but she went along with the joke. In fact, she embellished it into an even more fantastic legend which still persists in California. Columbia, it is solemnly declared on a Main Street historical marker, missed becoming the state capital by two votes.

As the decade of the '50s faded, so did Columbia's golden treasure. Shouldering pick and blankets, the boys answered the call of richer stakes. By 1867 an observer reported "almost total desertion" of the once fabulous town.

POINTS OF INTEREST

COLUMBIA. First visiting point in this wonderful outdoor museum of the Gold Rush is the office of the State Division of Beaches and Parks. Here you can obtain guide literature and directions from a park ranger. In addition to such historic sights as the jail, the churches, and O'Fallon's theater, a number of old buildings are operated as stores catering to tourist fancies. Refreshments and meals are also served in authentic buildings with early-day interior atmosphere. Columbia is, hopefully, only the most developed example of other historic communities to be restored by the state parks system.

CARSON HILL. Little remains of this once-bustling town on Highway 49 south of Angel's, but it bears noting as the source of the largest gold nugget—195 pounds troy weight—found in California.

JACKASS HILL. A short distance north of Tuttletown is the turnoff to Jackass Hill, a popular camping spot for packers to the mines. Some 200 donkeys were tethered here at one time. On the site is a cabin (now restored and opened to the public) in which Mark Twain spent five months in the winter of 1864-65. The Hill was also the scene of mining excitement in the early 1850s.

TUTTLETOWN. Only important point of interest remaining in this settlement is the rock building that once housed Swerer's store, where Mark Twain was a customer.

SHAW'S FLAT. A few interesting walls remain to show the site of Shaw's Flat, one of several near-vanished towns on the roads between Columbia and Sonora.

Chapter 10. Sonora: Queen of the Southern Mines

"SONORA IS A FAST PLACE and no mistake," wrote a citizen of 1851. "We have more gamblers, more drunkards, more ugly, bad women, and larger lumps of gold, and more of them, than any other place of similar dimensions within Uncle Sam's dominions."

In its Gold Rush heydey, Sonora was a city of superlatives. With a permanent population of 5,000, it was the biggest in the Southern Mines. With a total yield of over $600,000,000 from Tuolumne County mines, it was also the richest. And with an average of around one unpunished murder a week, it was certainly the wildest.

Though more than sixty miles south of the discovery site at Coloma, Sonora was one of the first Mother Lode camps. Among the original Forty-Eighters were Mexicans from the state of Sonora. As early as August they found rich placers on the Stanislaus and Tuolumne Rivers, and settled what came to be called the Sonorian Camp.

It proved a fabulous treasure. The gold was coarse and nuggets were frequent. In the first months, men were taking out several ounces apiece daily.

This kind of news traveled fast. By early 1849, Sonora was

no longer a Mexican camp. American miners jammed the decks of river steamers to Stockton, then raised a continuous cloud of dust on the trail to the new diggings. At night, camp-fires lighted the road all the way from Stockton to Sonora. By the end of 1849 there were over 10,000 Mexicans and 4,000 Americans and Europeans in the Sonora district.

From then on, the town was the most cosmopolitan center in the mines. Its streets were lined with a conglomeration of Spanish-type adobes, with their overhanging balconies, and American frame buildings of high false fronts. Its saloons and gambling dens were lavishly decorated with crystal chande-liers and sexy paintings; entertainment varied from brass bands to strolling guitarists to a lady piano-player "in black velvet who sings in Italian." On Sunday, a day reserved for merry-making, the visitor could take in anything from a bull-fight to a circus.

From the moment the Forty-niners arrived, Sonora's day of peace and plenty was over. The lusty Americans, convinced of a divine right to dominate the continent, had just had their belief confirmed by the Mexican War. California was theirs, and they had no intention of letting the best mines fall to Mexicans, whether from Sonora or California. There followed a shameful campaign of abuse against the "foreigners."

At first the Mexicans gave up their claims without a fight, but in July, 1849, 1,500 more of them reached the Tuolumne diggings. In the clash that followed, Sonora was the storm cen-ter. Many of the persecuted Mexicans took to outlawry and preyed on their tormentors. Within one month twelve mur-ders were committed in and around Sonora.

This explosive situation was capped in June, 1850, when the state Legislature passed a law requiring a $30 tax from all foreign miners—an open jab at the Mexican population.

When the collector arived in Sonora to levy his iniquitous tax, the fireworks began. Thousands of Mexicans in the district held meetings, denounced the tax, and swore to defy the author-ities. At this, the Americans armed themselves and marched into Sonora, where they organized a rifle company and set up a night patrol in the streets. Mexican guerrillas stepped up their raids; miners slept with their gold dust under their pillows, but even then thieves dared to rob them. The men camping on the hillside above town took turns standing watch through the night.

"No man dreams of travelling without the pistol and the knife," said the Sonora *Herald*.

On July 10, in the midst of this tension, miners at a nearby camp discovered three Indians and a Mexican burning the bodies of two Americans. Concluding that the four were the murderers, the enraged men marched them into Sonora and turned the town into a frenzy.

While the prisoners were given a preliminary hearing, hundreds of angry citizens gathered at the courthouse. The accused were abruptly snatched away and borne to a tree on a nearby hill. Here the mob selected a jury, help a rump court, and found the four guilty. Ropes were quickly looped around their necks and the Mexican was already swinging in the air when four county officials broke through the crowd and halted the lynching. In a moment Sheriff George Work and a deputy were backing them up with leveled revolvers. The miners grudgingly parted ranks and allowed the four to be taken to jail.

Four days later, while Sonora still seethed, a rumor ran through town that a number of Mexican guerrillas—allies of the prisoners—were camped several miles away. The Sheriff then struck out with twenty armed riders and came back with no less than 110 Mexican prisoners—all murder suspects. They were herded into a corral to await examination. Next day, when the four original captives were to be tried, a thousand more miners marched into town from the hills to make the confusion complete.

That afternoon the courthouse was packed with armed citizens for the opening of the trial. In that anxious moment a pistol went off accidentally. Pandemonium took over. A hundred guns were out and the shooting was general. The courthouse instantly disgorged its contents by every door and window. Out of the buildings in Sonora's streets men came running with revolver and rifle, some of them shooting at several Mexican bystanders.

Amid the dust and smoke, the District Attorney mounted a stump in the street and pleaded for order. When the crisis had passed, the only bloodshed was found to be the wounded wrist of the original shooter.

Somewhat sheepishly, the Sonora crowd settled down to wait out the trial. Finally it was determined that the four prisoners had found the two bodies several days after the murder, and had been cremating them according to their religious custom— as an act of charity. As for the 110 Mexicans in the corral, they were each examined, exonerated, and in the words of the presiding judge, sent "joyfully homeward." Most of them having arrived at the mines only a few days before, they gained a rather negative first impression.

But Sonora's temper still raged. With rumors reaching town of more murders, a mass meeting was held July 20—attended by several thousand armed miners. Lacking any murder suspects, they vented their anger on Mexicans in general. Resolutions were passed ordering all foreigners to get out of Tuolumne County in fifteen days, and furthermore, to give up their firearms. They might avoid either penalty by getting a permit from a committee of three Americans in each camp, who would decide which foreigners were "persons engaged in permanent business and of respectable characters."

For several days after this fanatical outburst, Sonora was an armed camp. At night guards stood watch at the edges of town to meet a surprise attack. The banishment order was actually enforced in a few outlying camps, but most harassed Mexicans needed no invitation to leave. Two hundred of them, all with pack burros and some with families, passed through Sonora on their way back to Mexico—a sorrowful and disillusioned company.

By September, with three-fourths of the Mexicans gone, Sonora was a dead town. With its population shrunk from five thousand to three thousand, it lapsed into hard times. The Sonora *Herald* suspended for lack of patronage, and one citizen noted with relief that in six weeks "there have been only two men shot in our streets."

In 1851 the foreign miners tax was repealed, and Mexicans felt a measure of safety in Tuolumne County. But Sonora's big boom had been killed by mobocracy at its worst.

Still, the Queen of the Southern Mines was not downed this

easily. Center of a galaxy of lesser mining camps, she was soon gaining a degree of refinement which set her apart from her rougher neighbors. In Sonora the traveler could get decent lodging in several clean hotels, could even enjoy that almost forgotten luxury, ice cream. With snow regularly packed in on mules from the higher mountains, even the drinks were iced.

On Sundays, the population, miners and all, turned out in its best attire. The most striking item of dress was a bright silk neckerchief—usually red—which was tied loosely over the chest and hung over one shoulder. Some local dandies had their broad-brimmed hats decked with feathers, flowers, or squirrels' tails. Many tried to outdo each other with fancy whisker styles; some beards were braided and coiled up "like a twist of tobacco," while others were separated into three tails which reached to the belt. One extremist divided his long beard in two and tied it in a big bow under his chin, where it served as a necktie.

The reason for all this foppery in the midst of the Gold Rush was obvious enough. In yard after yard on Sonora's residential streets, clotheslines were now hung with dresses and petticoats.

"Time was," observed the Sonora *Herald* in July, 1852, "when the presence of virtuous women in the mines was a thing wished for, not enjoyed."

Even this was not the most striking evidence of Sonora's orderliness, according to one visitor who had traveled the length of the Mother Lode. When he saw a policeman collar a disorderly drunk and march him sternly off to jail, he knew he had reached civilization.

The magistrate of old Sonora was a priceless character, Major Richard C. Barry—a veteran of the Texas war of independence and the Mexican War. A stocky, red-faced frontiersman, Barry became Justice of the Peace in 1850 and brought Sonora a certain amount of order—but no law. Ignorant, prejudiced, bull-headed, and inordinately proud, Barry was the legal dictator of Tuolumne County. His surviving docket, kept on scraps of paper, records the most amazing justice court ever operating under the United States Constitution. Take the case of Jesus Ramirez, who was charged with no less an offense than stealing a mule from the Sheriff, George Work. Reported Justice Barry:

"George swares the Mule in question is hisn and I believe so to on heering the caze I found Jesus Ramirez guilty of feloaniusly and against the law made and provided and the dignity of the people of Sonora steeling the aforesade mare Mule sentensed him to pay the costs of Coort 10 dolars, and fined him a 100 dolars more as a terrour to all evel dooers. Jesus Ramirez not having any munney to pay with I rooled that George Work shuld pay the costs of Court, as well as the fine. . . ."

For some reason, this admirable arrangement brought protest:

"H. P. Barber, the lawyer for George Work in solently told me there were no law fur me to rool so I told him that I didn't care a damn for his book law, that I was the Law myself. He jawed back so I told him to shetup but he wouldn't so I fined him 50 dolars, and comited to gaol for 5 days for contempt of Coort in bringing my rooling and dississions into disreputableness and as a warning to unrooly citizens not to contredict this Coort."

Sonora's days of frontier justice are gone, but unlike most gold camps of the Southern Mines, she is still a thriving city—the center of a mining, lumbering and orchard country.

POINTS OF INTEREST

SONORA. With its many old buildings and its narrow streets that wind among its many hills, Sonora is one of the most picturesque of Mother Lode towns. Among the structures having some historic significance are several churches, including St. James Episcopal, which dates from 1859. Nowhere is the visitor more rewarded by a walk along the residential streets, where one is charmed both by the well-kept Victorian homes and by the unhurried, neighborly ways of their inhabitants.

JAMESTOWN. The covered balcony architecture typical of the best-preserved Mother Lode towns is never more boldly displayed than in Jamestown, which still carries the look of the California mining frontier. Though many of the prominent frame buildings are of a more recent vintage, a number of brick, stone, and adobe structures date from the 1850s.

KNIGHT'S FERRY. On Highway 120 west of Jamestown is Knight's Ferry, where William Knight started the first ferry over the Stanislaus River on the road from Stockton to Sonora. The present covered bridge, one of the few remaining in California, dates from 1862. Other points of interest are the remains of the flour mill, saw mill, and woolen mill located west of the bridge. Another is the old Dent House, where Ulysses S. Grant visited his brother-in-law in 1854. Knight's Ferry was also the center of placer mining along the lower river, and was the seat of Stanislaus County from 1862 to '72.

CHINESE CAMP. The thick growth of "Trees of Heaven" planted by its Oriental pioneers tends to obscure at first glance the number of well-preserved old buildings in Chinese Camp. They include the Wells Fargo building, the U.S. Post Office, St. Francis Xavier Catholic Church, and Rosenbloom's Store. Despite its name, Chinese Camp was equally well populated by Americans and Europeans at its heyday in the 1850s.

TABLE MOUNTAIN. The plain at the foot of this mesa, located north of Chinese Camp, is supposed to be the field where some 2,000 Chinese staged a battle with spears, knives, tridents, and a few muskets on the morning of September 16, 1856. After several hours of combat the casualties were four killed and four wounded.

BIG OAK FLAT. The northernmost approach from the Mother Lode to Yosemite National Park takes its name from this once-substantial town. Among several rock structures still standing, the best is the old Odd Fellows Hall. As for the Big Oak Flat Road to Yosemite, it's an interesting drive, but don't take it if you're in a hurry.

SECOND GARROTE. Here are two examples of how the many Mother Lode myths are born.

In a two-story house located here lived two men whose careers paralleled those in Bret Harte's famous tale, "Tennessee's Partner"; speculation that they were the actual source of the story has been embellished to the point where the house has been claimed as the one-time home of Bret Harte.

At the edge of this tiny hamlet is a Hangman's Tree where, it is solemnly reported, sixty men were executed.

No firsthand historical evidence has been advanced to support either of these two notions. That something sordid actually occurred here is at least hinted by the name—"garrote" being a Spanish word for "strangle." Yes, there is also a First Garrote two miles down the road.

Chapter 11. Mariposa: Mother Lode Outpost

THERE IS NOTHING ghostly about the Mother Lode town of Mariposa. American tourists passing through it on the road to Yosemite are unaware that this was a flourishing camp before white men entered the famous valley. For Mariposa today is a community of neon signs and automobiles and busy stores. Ghost towns, perhaps, at nearby Hornitos, Mt. Bullion and Bear Valley—but not Mariposa.

From the beginning this locality has dared to be different. Situated at the extreme southern end of the Mother Lode, it was one of the few camps founded on a Spanish rancho. And it was here that miners first abandoned placer mining in the stream beds and struck pick in the actual Mother Lode.

The big man of old Mariposa was that California immortal, Col. John C. Frémont. After playing his part in the conquest of the territory during the Mexican War, Frémont decided to settle down near San Francisco Bay. In 1847 he sent $3000 to the American consul and asked that he buy a certain ranch near San José. What he got was Rancho Las Mariposas, known as the Mariposa or Butterfly. It was a mammoth tract of 45,000 acres in what was then a wild and worthless region. Frémont angrily demanded either the San José ranch or his $3000. He got neither.

Two years later, Frémont's cast-off rancho turned out to be the richest one in California. The tumultuous wave of fortune-seekers which descended on the Mother Lode in the spring of 1849 spread as far south as Mariposa—and found placer gold.

In August prospectors uncovered the fabulous Mariposa vein—
a section of the vast Mother Lode—and began hard rock mining.

Frémont complained no more. Next month he was in San
Francisco waving rock samples and boasting of Mariposa's
treasure.

This was exciting news for gold-mad Californians. The unknown quartz ledge which they knew had yielded the rich
gravel of Sierra streams had now been discovered! A bigger
quartz strike was soon to be made at Grass Valley in the Northern Mines, but this was Mariposa's hour.

Down to this southernmost outpost came the gold hunters—
afoot, horseback, or by wagon and team. From San Francisco
they took steamer for Stockton on the San Joaquin, then pushed
on by trail for Mariposa. From the mines they passed through
Angel's Camp and Sonora, crossed the Tuolumne and Merced
Rivers to reach the diggings.

It made no difference that this was Frémont's land. The new
Mariposans founded their town on the frontier institution,
"squatter's rights." But Frémont was less worried about the
townsite than the mining claims. Since his rancho was one of
those "floating grants" without definite boundaries, gold seekers were freely staking out ground and claiming that it was
outside Frémont's territory. They charged instead that Frémont arbitrarily extended his borders to cover every new strike.
It was the one big point at which Spanish titles clashed with
the Gold Rush.

Mariposa's ore was so rich that claim-jumping had been a
favorite pastime from the start. Around March, 1850, a party
of Missourians drove ox teams into Mariposa flat, took up
claims on the creek, and seized the property of the nearest
neighbors. The victims then went upstream and secured the
services of the newly-elected peace officer—a tall and robust
Kentuckian. He first went down and tried to reason with the
claim-jumpers, who defied him in appropriate language.

Next morning the Kentuckian was back—this time with
ninety armed miners anxious for excitement. Before he could
restrain them, they jumped into the holes and threw the Missourians' tools across the flat. Then, while the officer tried to

calm them, they told the interlopers to get out of camp or see all their equipment wrecked. With mighty oaths the Missourians yoked up their animals and drove off. Justice in the California mines was sometimes crude, but usually effective.

Meanwhile, Mariposa was stricken with worse troubles than claim-jumping. Rumors reached the settlement that Indians of the Sierra foothills were planning to drive out the American intruders. One of the leaders at Mariposa was James D. Savage, who operated trading posts on Mariposa Creek and the Fresno River. On a trip to San Francisco he took with him an Indian chief, in order to impress him with the strength of the whites and the folly of attacking them. When they returned, Savage found the Indians already on the warpath. A party of whites had been murdered near Mariposa. Other Argonauts were forced to pay tribute in order to pass through unmolested. Savage hurriedly called a conference of Indians in front of his store and warned them of the dreadful consequences of a war on the Americans.

"A chief who has returned with me," he concluded, "from the place where the white men are so numerous can tell you that what I have said is true."

But the chief's part was unrehearsed. He stepped up and astonished Savage by telling his tribesmen that if they would unite in a war, "all the gold diggers could be driven from the country." At this the Indians gathered around in ready approval while one chief solemnly pronounced, "My people are now ready to begin a war against the white gold diggers."

Savage could hardly take time to kick himself for his blunder. He pulled out of Mariposa with a warning to the miners of imminent attack. In quick succession the Indians pillaged his Fresno River store and two other Mariposa County trading posts.

Hurriedly the Americans formed a company and retaliated by surprising a large Indian village near the North Fork of the San Joaquin. While the victims ran out of their burning wigwams, the Americans shot twenty-four of them, including the chief. With this merciless blow, the shooting phase of the Mariposa Indian War was ended.

But meanwhile the whole state feared a general Indian uprising. The governor called for a volunteer militia to take the field, and most of the men in Mariposa County joined up. Electing James Savage as their major, they formed the famous Mariposa Battalion. Early in 1851 Savage led his men through winter snows to track down the remaining tribes and make an enforced peace. They rounded up the Indians, but they also penetrated far enough into the Sierras to find a breath-taking valley of towering cliffs and magnificent waterfalls. And so the Mariposa Battalion's historic fame lies not so much in its Indian fighting, but in the effective discovery of Yosemite.

Beginning in the mid-'50s, the Mariposa country was torn by new strife over Frémont's rancho. Since the exact boundaries of his grant were undetermined, Frémont had them surveyed to include Mariposa, Bear Valley, and much of the richest mining property. Men who had worked this ground for years while the ownership was unsettled were now outraged. In 1857 one group, the Merced Mining Company, "jumped" Frémont's Black Drift and Josephine Mines. Shunning violence, he counterattacked with a lawsuit.

Irresistably, The Butterfly was leading him further into the financial woods. And while the lawyers fought in court, the Merced outfit cast covetous eyes on Frémont's third and last mine, the Pine Tree.

Into this tense situation the explorer brought his wife and family in the summer of 1858. Settling in a cottage behind Bear Valley, the group consisted of Jessie, her three children and several young friends. While Frémont busied himself with his mine, Jessie and the others made up a gay and carefree company, riding horseback by day, holding sprightly conversation in the evenings. For the cultivated Jessie it was an adventurous contrast to the drawing rooms of Washington and Paris.

Within a few weeks this idyllic life was rudely shattered by the hard realities of the Gold Rush. In the small hours of July 9, more than fifty Merced Company men rode grimly through Bear Valley and pressed on for the Pine Tree Mine. This time Frémont was ready for them. Working deep within the blackness were six well-armed men. When the Merced party swooped down upon the entrance, these defenders held the advantage of position. With boulders and mining equipment they threw up breastworks inside the tunnel mouth. Barrels of gunpowder were rolled into place. Before they would give up the mine, hollered the Frémonters, they would blow up the entrance!

Balked by this stubborn handful, the Merced army turned to new strategy. The main force camped on the level ground before the tunnel entrance. Guards were posted higher up the mountainside at the Black Drift, which connected with the Pine Tree workings deep inside the earth. Others were stationed at every trail to cut off outside communication. They would lay siege to Frémont's mine.

Before dawn word of the attack reached Frémont at his ranch house. Outraged, he still kept his soldier's cool head. While Jessie and the family slept, he held a council of war with his lieutenants. The veteran warrior was almost enjoying the challenge.

"They'll find," he snapped with a satisfied smile, "they have jumped the wrong man."

Mustering some twenty-seven men, Frémont promptly besieged the besiegers. His force was soon guarding the Pine Tree road behind the Merced men, cutting off their line of supply. Though outnumbered two to one, Frémont's men announced they were "prepared to die sooner than yield a single hair."

And so the silent war began—each side overawing the other. Sheriff Crippin of Mariposa County arrived and ordered the Merced men to disperse. Openly ignored, he rode off to Mariposa and returned later with a handful of warrants. Only four men surrendered. When the Sheriff rode back into town with this pitiful haul, the *Mariposa Gazette* demanded that he raise a citizen's posse.

"Unless it be done," cried the editor, "all law-loving people might as well leave the county at once."

The realistic Frémont had already abandoned hope of local help. He was sending messengers to the Governor in Sacramento, calling for the state militia. But the Merceders guarded every ford and pass. As Frémont's riders galloped out, they were as quickly intercepted.

In this situation, the young people of Frémont's cottage were eager to act. One of them, a young Englishman named Douglas

Fox, rode into the brush and managed to elude the enemy sentries. At Coulterville he roused help; other riders pounded across San Joaquin Valley to Stockton, where telegraph lines hummed with Frémont's message to the Governor.

But until a reply could arrive, the desperate siege continued. After four days the Merceders tried another tactic. To Frémont's ranch they sent a letter, offering to pull out if he would remove his own men from the mine and leave it in charge of a neutral committee until the lawsuit was settled. Next day Frémont's defiant refusal was read aloud to the sullen Merced crowd.

"The demand you make upon me," he declared, "is contrary to all my sense of justice and what is due to my own honor."

Warned also that the Governor had been notified, the Merceders now stirred themselves to action. Since the Pine Tree opening was well guarded by Frémont's men, it was resolved to take them from behind through the connecting chambers of the Black Drift. But on the night of the assault the Colonel's outside force overheard the plan. A towering, broad-shouldered Frémonter, weighted down with fighting equipment, appeared out of the brush and deliberately walked past the Merceders to the mouth of the Pine Tree.

"Sandy," he shouted, "look out for the Black Drift!"

With a chorus of clicks, a battery of Merced rifles cocked for action. The man's bold move had caught the enemy off guard. But slowly he moved back across the clearing and disappeared in the underbrush. The Merceders still could not fire the first shot.

Desperate, they now switched to a final strategem. Frémont's wife and family were sheltered a few miles away. Threaten the ranch house, and the Colonel would surely divert his forces to the rescue. Then the Pine Tree would fall into Merced hands.

Next day a messenger came to Jessie Frémont's door, giving her and the family twenty-four hours to flee before the ranch would be burned. But far from alarming the Colonel, brave Jessie sent back a note, stalling for time. A few hours later, before the plotters could carry out their threat, a messenger from Sacramento was pounding up the trail to the Pine Tree. To the Merced men in the clearing, the Governor's command was terse and pointed: Disperse, or he would send in the militia.

Their attack already foiled by the courage of the Frémonters, the Merced men were ready to quit. For five days they had held a bear by the tail. The Governor's order now gave them a graceful means of letting go. Back over the Pine Tree trail rode the Merced army. They had, indeed, jumped the wrong man.

The ordeal was too much for Jessie. Frémont did his best to make Bear Valley a gracious home. Among the distinguished visitors they entertained in the following months were Horace Greeley and Richard Henry Dana. But the charm of the place had been broken. In the spring of 1859 Frémont bought Jessie a home in San Francisco. And although he won his lawsuit against the Merced Company, the Colonel himself was soon to leave Mariposa forever. No businessman, he found himself in financial troubles that cost him control of the rancho in 1861. Before he turned his back on The Butterfly, it had cost him the best years of his life.

POINTS OF INTEREST

MARIPOSA. At this gateway to Yosemite stands one of the prize landmarks of the Mother Lode, the Mariposa County Courthouse. Built in 1854, it is the oldest continuously used county courthouse in California, and one of the few made of wood. This New England style edifice, looking more like a country church than a courthouse, was the scene of the litigation over Frémont's Pine Tree Mine.

Several other reminders of Mariposa's early days remain. On the main street stands the brick office of Frémont's company. Facing it across the street is the quaint Schlageter Hotel, with its broad wooden balcony. On the hill to the south of town is the old jail, made of granite blocks from the intrusion which halts the Mother Lode vein two miles south of town.

MORMON BAR. Two miles southeast of Mariposa is Mormon Bar, technically the lowermost camp on the Mother Lode. Founded by Mormons in 1849, it is marked today only by some crumbling adobe walls hidden among the trees and boulders on the east bank of Mariposa Creek.

AGUA FRIA. Seat of Mariposa County from 1850 to '54, this mining camp is revealed only by a historical marker and a few rock foundations.

COARSEGOLD. Proving that some spurs of the Mother Lode extended below Mariposa County is the small settlement of Coarsegold, founded by Texans in 1849. First and largest among a number of Madera County placer camps, Coarsegold later became a center of hard rock mining.

HORNITOS. The tough reputation for the Mariposa district goes to Hornitos, which was founded by outcasts who were run out of the neighboring town of Quartzburg for the crime of being Mexicans. They formed their own community at Hornitos, which soon outgrew Quartzburg. Today Hornitos lives on as one of the best preserved ghost towns in the Mother Lode, while Quartzburg is all but forgotten.

In its heyday Hornitos was a wide-open camp whose streets were lined with fandango halls, bars, and gambling dens. One visitor of 1857 was walking past the sidewalk gaming tables when two players flashed knives at each other. The dealer then covered them with his pistol and suggested with evident logic that they could go somewhere else and finish the dispute without interrupting his game. Followed by a crowd, the pair adjourned to a nearby lot and fell upon each other with their knives.

Soon one of them staggered back covered with vicious wounds, tossed down a glass of brandy, and retook his seat at the card table. Despite this show of bravado, he was soon buried with his opponent in what the visitor called "Dead Man's Gulch."

This was Hornitos in the roaring Fifties. Today its turbulent spirit still lingers in the ruins of the old Wells Fargo office, the store where the firm of D. Ghirardelli got its start in 1855, and other buildings of stone and adobe—nearly all with the iron doors and shutters characteristic of Mother Lode towns.

LA GRANGE. Founded as a mining camp in 1852, La Grange lived on as a commercial center and was for several years the seat of Stanislaus County. A few old structures still stand in this quaint village. For a time Bret Harte taught school at La Grange, and it is the probable setting for several of his short stories.

THE FRÉMONT COUNTRY. Driving north from Mariposa on Highway 49, one comes immediately into what might be called California's Frémont Country.

First locality is Mt. Bullion, named for Jesse Benton Frémont's father, Senator Thomas H. Benton, who was nicknamed "Old Bullion" for his campaign to maintain hard currency.

Next is Mt. Ophir, where the remains of an early private mint are prominent among a number of interesting stone foundations.

Most important of the Frémont communities is Bear Valley, founded by the explorer as a company town for the operation of his mines. Here are several old buildings of the 1850s, including one of several Trabucco "chain stores" operated in Mariposa County's Gold Rush days.

North of Bear Valley, a dirt road turns off to the left and doubles back to the mouth of Frémont's Pine Tree Mine, scene of siege and counter-siege. Finally, where the highway crosses the Merced River are the remains of Benton Mills, where Frémont dammed the river and milled his ore. These, too, he named for Thomas Hart Benton.

COULTERVILLE. Among the oak-dotted hills so typical of the Southern Mines, and roughly halfway from Jamestown to Mariposa on Highway 49, lies the remnant of Coulterville. A number of widely scattered landmarks survive—the Jeffrey Hotel, the inevitable Wells Fargo office, the Wagoner Store, two Bruschi stores, and the town jail.

PART IV. THE NORTHERN MINES

CALIFORNIA's *Northern Mines were served by stagecoaches from the Feather River port of Marysville, as well as from Sacramento City itself. Often the Central Mines, located on the forks of the American River, were included by popular usage with the Northern Diggings. In any case, the latter extended northward to the Feather River, and they took in some of the finest scenery in California.*

Here the gold towns, whether living or deserted, nestle in the most charming and often astounding spots—on the slopes of mountains, in the bottom of steep canyons, alongside turbulent rivers. They are like the gold and silver camps of Colorado, and from a distance some of them—with their gleaming church spires—resemble forest-bound hamlets of middle Europe.

Also occasionally included among the Northern Mines is a whole empire of camps in the upper end of California's Coast Range. Founded between 1849 and '51, they represent a second rush within the bigger stampede to California from 1848 to '53.

If California ever had any frontier, it was this untamed country north and west of Sacramento Valley. For a time, to paraphrase an old Texas saying, there was no law north of the Pit River, no God north of the Trinity.

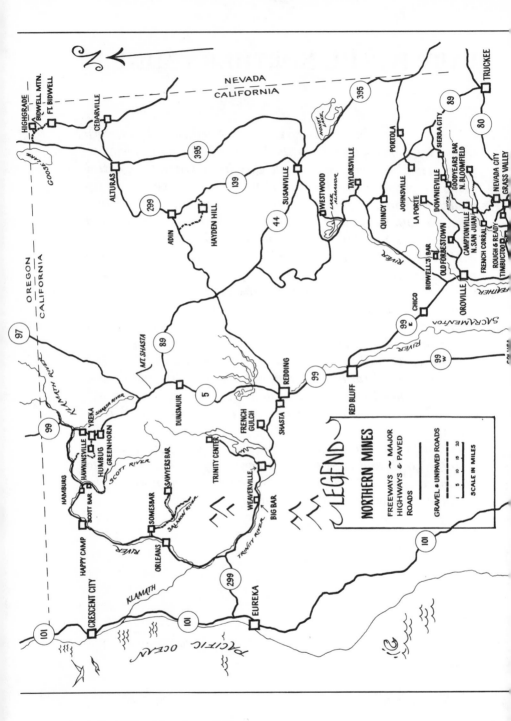

Home office of the Coyote and Deer Creek Water Co., Nevada City, 1852.

Courtesy of California State Library

Elbow room was rare in the mines when a rich pocket was found, 1851.

The backbreaking hand labor of moving tons of rock is temporarily suspended for the pleasure of the visiting daguerreotypists, 1851.

*Grass Valley's first celebrity—internationally famous
entertainer Lola Montez.*

Courtesy of California State Library

Gold is where you find it—best at your doorstep, Sugar Loaf Hill, Nevada City, 1852.

No gold-bearing stream could escape the swift appearing sluice boxes, Nevada City, 1852.

The Northern Mines / 125

*Johnsville, a latter-day gold town of the 1870's, remains
a gem of the Northern mines.*

Chapter 12. Grass Valley: Miner's Mining Town

LEAST GHOSTLY OF ANY TOWN on the Mother Lode is Grass Valley, which is still called the greatest mining city in the Far West. A place named Butte, Montana, may dispute this. But Grass Valley is at least the biggest mining town in California. A century ago it was the eighth largest city in the state —bigger than Los Angeles, San Diego and Oakland.

Unlike most mining camps, Grass Valley never really had a decline and fall. Even in the depression, its streets and hotel lobbies were bustling with mining men. One traveler of 1933 pronounced Grass Valley the one city in the United States where you had to wire ahead for hotel reservations. In more than a century of mining, the place has turned out upwards of $100 million in gold. Its Empire and Idaho-Maryland mines are still the second and third deepest gold mines (after the Homestake of South Dakota) in the world.

Grass Valley is, moreover, the point which sparked the big shift from placer to quartz mining in California. Situated a scant thirty-three miles north of the discovery site at Coloma, the Grass Valley streams were virtually ignored in the first two Gold Rush years. A handful of men had worked the creeks since 1848, but neither placer mining nor obscurity was to be Grass Valley's lot.

Half the camps in the West were, according to tradition, discovered while a prospector was chasing after his straying burro. But Grass Valley rose before the day of jackass prospectors, and in her case the animal was a cow. One day in October, 1850, a miner named George Knight followed his wayward bossy as far as the pine-covered slope of Gold Hill. There he stubbed his toe on a piece of quartz. In the custom of all true miners, he scrutinized his providential find—and promptly forgot about his cow. Back at his cabin he pounded the rock into dust and panned out a bright showing of gold.

Immediately the original Grass Valley miners hurried up the

hillsides. One of them found a small boulder worth $500. That was enough. The big rush to Grass Valley, and to the new business of shaft mining, was on.

Knight's discovery was not the first quartz mine in California. Lode mining, as contrasted to placer mining in the stream beds, had begun a year earlier at Mariposa, in the Southern Mines. But the Grass Valley strike can be called the effective discovery. It started the boom in shaft mining which eventually supplanted the placer workings.

Scarcely four miles away Nevada City, a flourishing placer town, suddenly went quartz mad. From all over the Mother Lode, miners hurried to Grass Valley by the hundreds. Demand for ore-crushing tools was so great that within a week all the hammers and anvils for twenty miles around were lugged into camp. Every pharmacy from Sacramento to San Francisco was relieved of its mortar and pestle. They all went to Grass Valley.

Soon came more elaborate machinery. Mexican miners, who knew about quartz mining, built arrastres—by which the ore was ground by millstones turned with one-mule power. Then came the stamp mills, which were simply gigantic, multi-barreled mortars and pestles operated by steam engine. They were not invented in Grass Valley, but were developed here to a fine point. By 1853, with its placer beds faltering, California was turning wholeheartedly to the job of tapping the underground source of gold.

It was at Grass Valley, too, that mining stock promotion was first perfected. The town was equally at home digging gold with shovels or stock certificates. The stock frenzy grew so uproarious that one newspaper burlesqued the whole business by advertising the "Munchausen Quartz Rock Mining and Crushing Company," with a Board of Directors including P. T. Barnum and Robinson Crusoe. Grass Valley was the original spot where one could apply Mark Twain's definition of a mine: "a hole in the ground owned by a liar."

But Grass Valley was never a phoney. In seven years' time Knight's original Gold Hill mine produced $4,000,000. Through the 1850s dozens of other mines were opened, yielding millions more. By 1853 Grass Valley was a city of 3,000, the bustling center of several daily stage lines, a hospitable town with a reputation for good hotels in a region where these were an oddity.

Hardrock mines—requiring capital, machinery and steady payrolls—had given Grass Valley a permanent air in contrast to the boom-and-bust placer towns. It was one of the first cities on the Mother Lode to temper its rough male population with an influx of wives and families. The civilizing effect was remarkable. Numerous churches—several of them still in use— were built in the 1850s. And it was one of the first mining camps to have a legitimate theater, even though it was fitted up in the Alta Saloon. Complete with footlights and orchestra, the "Grass Valley Theater" company played every night to a packed, exuberant house.

Though Grass Valley might have been partly refined, it was never quiet. In the early 1850s, one visitor strolled down the street on a Sunday morning and heard in close succession a streetside Church sermon, a mule auction, a street vendor selling tea, a drunken sailor singing Auld Lang Syne and a sidewalk dance by two Swiss girls to the tune of hand organ and tambourine. All this was in addition to the clank and clatter of the stamp mills which rang in the ears of Grass Valley night and day.

In September, 1855, the thriving city was struck flat. An incendiarist kindled its wooden walls, and in two hours its entire 300 buildings were devoured in a furious blaze. With roofs crashing about them, the people rushed into the streets and made for the hillsides. It was known as the "million dollar fire"—probably the worst in the Mother Lode. But with their belongings and property wiped out, the Grass Valley people started anew before the ashes cooled. Next morning the Wells Fargo agent rolled a portable shack up against his only surviving asset—a brick vault. With the ground still hot under him, he tacked up a sign and opened for business. Spurred by this example, the town turned to the job of rebuilding; soon a city of brick walls and iron shutters rose from the ruins. Modernized versions of these buildings, dating from 1855, are seen along Grass Valley's streets today.

The spirited town could hardly let this disaster pass without trying to catch its author. An innocent but disreputable citizen was seized and accused of the crime. An angry crowd gathered, and one bloodthirsty character demanded an immediate lynching. After all, he argued seriously, Grass Valley couldn't afford to let neighboring Nevada City, which had already had a hanging, run off with all the honors. This precious reasoning, which probably appealed to a certain element, was argued down. The man was set free after a trial.

But while there is no record of a lynching in Grass Valley, the town was far from dull. There's a story, for example, of a late poker game in the bar of the Peckham Hotel. A crowd gathered as the stakes mounted, and one of the onlookers was a rough-looking pioneer known as Old Mississippi. All at once an argument began. The players grabbed for the pot. A free-for-all fight followed, in which Old Mississippi was knocked to the floor. When things quieted down he propped himself on his elbow, exhibited a bloody face, and asked:

"I reckon there's been a row here, boys—hain't there?—is anybody hurt?"

With its dander up, Grass Valley was ready for anything. In the wet winter of 1852-53, roads from Sacramento were choked with mud and Grass Valley was almost isolated. Supplies were scarce, and what food there was sold at fantastic prices. So the embittered townsmen acted; they held a Hunger Convention at Beatty's Hotel. Awful maledictions were hurled at the "soulless speculators" in San Francisco who were cornering the food market. "We will," they resolved, "go to San Francisco and obtain the necessary supplies—peaceably if we can, forcibly if we must."

In this ugly mood, 100 men made ready to descend on the Bay City—until the question of financing the expedition came up. With this sobering thought the meeting adjourned, and the boys cooled their wrath until the weather cleared and new supplies arrived. Grass Valley would let San Francisco off, this time.

Rough and refined, primitive and civilized, Grass Valley was a city of violent contrasts which could only have been born of the California Gold Rush. But while it thought it had seen everything, Grass Valley was hardly prepared for the coming of Lola Montez.

The incomparable Lola, Countess of Landsfeldt, would have disrupted things anywhere. Dancer, actress, adventuress—she was the mistress of a king and the toast of mid-Century Europe. Born in Ireland, she had crashed the London stage as an exotic Spanish dancer with the assumed name, Lola Montez. From then on her life was a whirl of sensations, pretense and trouble. Ludwig I of Bavaria became infatuated with her, and bestowing the title of Countess of Landsfeldt, made her his mistress. For a time the fiery Lola was the power behind the throne—and not a particularly evil power, at that.

Then came the revolution of 1848, and while a student mob stormed the palace, Lola appeared in the window drinking champagne. Leaving Bavaria, she settled for a time in Paris. Here she is supposed to have given soirées which included such names as George Sand, Alexander Dumas and Victor Hugo.

In 1851 she came to America—probably for several reasons. For one, she had picked up two husbands in her travels, and faced a bigamy rap in London. Second, she was now past thirty and her charms were not increasing. Perhaps enthusiastic American audiences would be more appreciative.

New York, Philadelphia and Boston greeted her effusively, but the excitement soon wore thin. Her celebrated Spider Dance, in which she released a skirtful of cork-and-rubber spiders at the climactic moment, naturally aroused interest. But while Lola was vivacious, she was not a brilliant dancer, and her acting was less than inspired. Her attraction lay in her striking beauty—particularly the flowing black hair and flashing eyes.

Still, Lola had been disappointed by her American reception. She craved above all things to be the center of attraction, even if this meant notoriety. She resolved next to go to California, where the rousing miners would surely do her justice. She invaded San Francisco with much fanfare in May, 1853.

But the Bay City was already taking on a sophisticated air. While the audiences went wild, the critics sniffed at Lola's performances. By way of a dramatic exit, she took another husband and went to Sacramento. Here she was charivareed one night by a raucous mob, which she faced from the balcony with fierce epithets: "Cowards, low blackguards, cringing dogs and lazy fellows!" A few days later a local editor slurred her dancing ability, and she challenged him to a duel—either with pistols or with the choice of two pills in a box (one of them deadly poison). But even this did not greatly impress Sacramento.

All of which explains why Lola, seeking an appreciative audience somewhere, wound up next in Grass Valley. With her husband and her reputation, she descended on Grass Valley in the fall of 1853 and scandalized the good ladies of the town. Settling in a house which is still the most prided landmark of the city, she kept Grass Valley in a state of confusion for nearly two years. Her idiosyncrasies were the talk of the town—and of all California. She frequently strolled the streets, dressed in low-cut gowns and smoking a cigar. And she raised two grizzly bear cubs, which were kept chained in the front yard.

Grass Valley had a large European, and particularly French, population. So Lola also revived her Parisian hobby, the salon. Every evening her parlor was crowded with young blades of the town—holding sprightly conversation, drinking champagne and flirting with Lola. Her husband was obviously in the way, and she got rid of him. Besides, he had killed one of her pet grizzlies for biting him in the leg.

But Lola had her tender side. Among her neighbors was the Crabtree family, and little Lotta Crabtree was permitted to spend time with Lola, learning to sing and dance. It was the beginning of a stage career which was to win the acclaim of California and the nation. Lotta, the opposite of Lola in girlish innocence, was to outshine her teacher.

Lola might have got along with Grass Valley, but she could not keep out of the limelight. When a preacher condemned her spider dance, she went around to his house, knocked on the door, and went through the whole dance before his astonished eyes. Later the local newspaper offended her, so she horse-whipped the editor.

By 1855 Lola's antics were wearing hard in Grass Valley, and she was off for a new gold rush in Australia. Six years later she died in poverty in New York—an event which sentimental

California noted with more generosity than it did her personal appearance.

GRASS VALLEY. Rebuilt of brick after the fire of 1855, the center of modern Grass Valley contains many buildings more than a century old. But to breathe the true charm of yesteryear, one must get away from the remodelings that have disguised the business houses and explore Grass Valley's side streets. Among the sights here is the home of Lola Montez, at the corner of Mill and Walsh Streets.

ROUGH-AND-READY. Located west of Grass Valley on Highway 20, this once-thriving Gold Rush town survives chiefly through its picturesque title, which was the nickname of General Zachary Taylor. The founding group that arrived in 1849 was headed by an officer who had served under Taylor in the Mexican War. Since "Old Rough and Ready" had recently been inaugurated President of the United States, it was natural to christen the new town after him.

TIMBUCTOO. Another flourishing town of the '50s was Timbuctoo, which is now marked only by the shell of the Wells Fargo office.

FRENCH CORRAL. Somewhat better preserved is French Corral, on a road winding from Highway 20 north to Highway 49. Enjoying both a placer boom and a hydraulic mining boom, this town was lively from 1849 to the 1880s.

Chapter 13. Nevada City: Gold Metropolis

CALIFORNIANS have always delighted in labeling towns, regardless of size, with the dignified title of "city." Granddaddy of these honored places—and incidentally one of the most deserving—is Nevada City, in the heart of the Northern Mines. With true California modesty her citizens acknowledge:

That she was the biggest mining camp in California;

That she was named long before the state of Nevada;

That the four miles separating her from the sister city of Grass Valley are the most heavily traveled in the state.

At least two of these claims are amply justified. In her heyday during the middle Fifties, Nevada City was easily the biggest town in the mines. With a population of 10,000 she was outdistanced only by San Francisco and Sacramento.

First prospected by James Marshall in 1848, the place was named Nevada City two years later in honor of the Sierra Nevada Mountains. In 1861 when the territory of Nevada was organized, the people of Nevada City sharply objected on the ground that they had first claim to the name. Congress was unimpressed, and Nevada City has been strenuously explaining her origin ever since.

As to the third claim, such thoroughfares as Wilshire Blvd. and Highway 101 may take issue. Suffice to say that in Gold Rush days, at least, this route bore more traffic than any other four miles in the state. And considering the procession of ox and mule teams, stage coaches, burro trains and cattle herds that raised dust on this road, it was probably as dangerous as any modern highway.

From the first, Nevada City was never quite like her neighbors. Her miners were not absorbed in the usual placer mining, but found richer rewards in the ancient river deposits nearby. These were mined with small shafts known as coyote holes, which became so famous that a main thoroughfare in Nevada City was called Coyote Street. With early-comers reaping as much as $6000 per day, Argonauts flocked in by the thousands. Mining laws were non-existent and claim disputes were rife, but one old-timer had his own solution. A newcomer found him at work one day and opened conversation. The pioneer was noncommittal until he was asked the boundaries of his claim. Straightening up, he pointed to his gun leaning against a tree.

"D'ye see that rifle there, stranger?"

"Yes."

"Well, jist as fur as that rifle carries, up and down this ravine, I claim—and no further."

This was not the only case of gunpoint mining law in Nevada City. Eager treasure-hunters were driving a shaft in the main street when a storekeeper called a halt. The men went ahead, answering that there was no law against it.

"Then I'll make a law," concluded the merchant, leveling a revolver. The pertinence of this statute was immediately acknowledged.

In the city's first two years, hardrock mining was a curiosity. One early arrival reported that the men of his camp had a good laugh over the busy efforts of nearby miners, who were actually "digging up the rock for a foot or more down." But after the big quartz discovery at Grass Valley in October, 1850, Nevada City's hardrock ledges took on sudden luster. The frenzy which marked this new rush is shown in one miner's tale of Nevada City's first mining suit. Charles Ferguson and a partner returned from a trip to find two men had jumped their claim. When the interlopers ordered them off, they stood ground and began sinking a shaft. At this the jumpers brought suit and somehow won their case. A sheriff's posse was called in to eject Ferguson and his partner, who were busy washing the ore through their long tom. Ferguson tried to stall by arguing but the possemen shut off the water and picked up the long tom.

"As the water ran off," Ferguson later recalled, "I saw the yellow gold glittering in the box. I seized hold of it and carried it off bodily about fifty yards farther, although at any ordinary time it would have taken two men to do it, but the sight that I had seen gave me for the moment superhuman strength—the gold was so thick in the wet mass in the box that it looked like yellow pudding."

Scooping up the richest of it in a tin dish, he sunk it out of sight in a pool of water. He was panning out the rest when one of the jumpers came up and saw what was left. Disappointed, the man soon sold the claim for $100 to a buyer who turned it back to Ferguson.

Although claim jumping was a major sport, Nevada City was fairly civilized for a mining camp. Beginning in 1851 whole families arrived in town, and henceforth the presence of decent women had a sobering effect. Though miners might be used to the company of saloon girls, they treated a virtuous woman with near reverence. Recalled one Nevada City pioneer:

"Every miner seemed to consider himself her sworn guardian, policeman and protector, and the slightest dishonorable word, action or look of any miner or other person would have been met with a rebuke he would remember so long as he lived. If, perchance, he survived the chastisement."

By 1850 Nevada City consisted of some 250 buildings ("frame houses, dingy old canvas booths and log cabins") extending along the bottom of a ravine. She was hardly a metropolis, but she did have one cultural jewel—a theater. This barn-like building, situated on Main Street, was the first playhouse in the Sierras, and one of the most famous on the Lode. Here Edwin Booth trod the boards in the hectic Fifties, and here *Richard III* was performed for spectators who delighted in "hooting, yelling, whistling and stamping their feet."

Isolated as she was, Nevada City early became a great staging center for the Yuba River camps, the Sierra summit and points northeast. By 1851 Nevada City stages ran out of Sacramento several times a day—carrying express at the rate of $2.50 a letter. A traveler of that year describes the confused scene at stage departure time in Sacramento. The entire street was jammed with coaches and horses, prospective passengers and their baggage, and frantic "runners" who were drumming up business for their respective lines.

"All aboard for Nevada City," shouts one. "Who's agoin'? Only three seats—the last chance today for Nevada City—take you there in five hours. Who's there for Nevada City?"

Sighting a man who reveals some indecision, the runner descends on him without mercy.

"Nevada City, sir? This way—just in time!"

Grabbing the man's arm, he hustles him through the crowd and is boosting him into the Nevada City stage when the victim manages to declare that he wants to go to Coloma. Unmoved, the runner holds tight and shouts for one of his fellows.

"Oh, Bill! Oh, Bill! Where the devil are you?"

"Hullo!" answers Bill.

"Here's a man for Coloma!"

And runner No. 1 clutches his quarry by the arm until runner No. 2 arrives to claim him. The whole thing, concludes the observer, was ridiculous. "Apparently, if a hundred men wanted to go anywhere, it required a hundred more to dispatch them. There was certainly no danger of anyone being left behind." In fact, the chances were that an innocent passerby would suddenly find himself bound for Nevada City and points north.

This was scarcely the only hazard on roads in the Northern Mines. Nevada City highways, especially that four-mile route between the town and Grass Valley, were the especial haunt of road agents. In May, 1858, the Auburn stage was just outside Nevada City when five bandits stepped into the road. The passengers prepared for a thorough fleecing—all except a Nevada City bank messenger, carrying a sizable load of gold dust. He drew his pistol, with no other effect than to bring a remonstrance from one of the robbers to "be careful." At this, the unruffled bank man agreed that there was really nothing to fight about, that all the treasure was in a Wells Fargo chest on the next stage. After a cursory search, the outlaws let the first stage go, and robbed stage No. 2 of $21,000. The clever bank agent felt bad about getting off at Wells Fargo's expense, but after all, business was business.

The arch-bandit of Nevada City did not appear until the mid-Sixties, when a character bearing the alias of Jack Williams invaded the highroads. At first he concentrated on lone travelers. One night he stood on the road from You Bet to Nevada City and stopped no less than six men in a row. Another time he and his gang chased a recalcitrant victim all the way into Grass Valley, where they sent two shots at his disappearing heels.

In May, 1866, they opened business with the express lines. First, the stage from North San Juan was stopped three miles above Nevada City, and its two Chinese passengers robbed despite furious protest. But when they came to the Wells Fargo box, the robbers found the treasure stored safely in an inner chest made of chilled iron. The stubborn object could not be broken. The stage clattered on with Wells Fargo triumphant.

But Jack Williams had a one-track mind. A few mornings

later his men were on the road again, stopping the north-bound stage at the summit north of Nevada City. This time they had two sledges, a crowbar, a portable blacksmith's kit and a can of giant powder. They would get that gold, they said, or blast the coach into the Yuba River.

While passengers watched, they went grimly to work and on the second explosion, blew open the box. Jack Williams heaved the gold sack over his shoulder, passed a flask of brandy among the passengers as an act of courtesy, and made off with his two companions.

Nevada City was broadminded, but this effrontery almost at her gates was unforgivable. A six-man posse headed by the Sheriff of Nevada County swung out of town and pushed into the brush in pursuit. Unaccountably, five of them left the trail while a sixth man pushed on alone. This was Steve Venard, packing a formidable fifteen-shot Henry rifle.

Crossing the South Yuba, he suddenly came face to face with his quarry. Two of them were already aiming at Steve when he opened fire. His first shot found Jack Williams' heart, the second pierced the head of another, and a few moments later a fourth shot brought down the last bandit. It was a busy day's work for deputy Venard and his Henry rifle. By early afternoon the chest had been returned to Wells Fargo and Nevada City's face had been saved.

Graced as she was with fine women, a theater, and other marks of culture, Nevada City was not a particularly rough town. "There were but very few cases tried before Judge Lynch," recalled an early resident, "only three cases of shooting, and those poor shots." She did indulge, however, in the more genteel method of slaughter—dueling.

Late in 1851 a sailing man named George Dibble got into an argument with one E. B. Lundy, a Canadian known chiefly as a son of the owner of Lundy's Lane, where a War of 1812 battle was fought. Dibble called Lundy a liar and then challenged him. Lundy was a sure shot—the survivor of several previous duels. He tried to avoid the encounter, and on the day before the meeting shot the wick off a candle in an attempt to dissuade his challenger. But Dibble was intent on getting "satisfaction." For the duel he adopted the dubious strategy of drawing Lundy's fire and then shooting him at leisure. This was a mistake. Lundy's first shot struck home. Dibble walked off the field and died.

There were other duels less tragic. Two rival doctors quarreling in a saloon resorted to arms, fired five shots each while the roomful of men scrambled for cover, satisfied their honor without inflicting a scratch, and celebrated with another drink. A third duel looked completely tragic when one contestant fell covered with blood—until the blood proved to be currant jelly loaded in the two pistols by local pranksters.

Nevada City, dubbed a "laughing camp" by one chronicler, has never taken things too seriously. Unless, of course, you ask whether she was named for the state of Nevada. . . .

POINTS OF INTEREST

NEVADA CITY. At least as well preserved as Grass Valley, Nevada City has been called "the most charming of all the major Gold Rush cities." While the many old buildings on the main street have been modernized, stepping into the parallel avenues to the north puts you at once into the storied past. For a sightseeing tour the place to start is the Nevada County Historical Museum housed in the No. 1 firehouse. From here you will be directed to the pioneer assay office, the National Hotel, the historic churches, and the remaining buildings of a once-populous Chinatown. But beyond individual landmarks, the winding, tree-shaded streets themselves, with their Victorian trimmings of another age, make Nevada City what another chronicler has called "a story-book town."

NORTH SAN JUAN. Once called San Juan, this delightful old town had the "North" added to its name in 1857, when the U.S. Postal Service wanted to remove the confusion with the San Juan in San Benito County. It was not a Spanish-type community, but with its remaining brick buildings and touches of iron grillwork it bears a resemblance to some of the towns in the Southern Mines.

NORTH BLOOMFIELD. Like North San Juan, this locality was once thriving with the business of hydraulic mining,

which has left such fantastic erosion along the entire San Juan
Ridge. Some early frame and stone structures remain in this
appealing, tree-shaded settlement.

Chapter 14. Downieville
and the Yuba River Camps

THE BRAWLING, tempestuous Yuba River, with its equally
unruly tributaries, hurtles out of the Sierra Nevada and then
glides easily into the Feather River at Marysville. Into this remote country, containing some of the most incomparable
mountain scenery in California, came a horde of miners in
mid-19th Century. But they scarcely saw the native beauty;
they simply saw the Yuba streams as sources of gold, the mountains as obstacles in the quest.

Gold was first discovered on the Yuba in June, 1848, at
Rose's Bar, 18 miles east of Marysville. As eager prospectors
worked up the river and its branches, they founded new camps
—Bullard's Bar, Foster's Bar, Goodyear's Bar and Downieville.
All of these were located at spots where the streams had
changed their course enough to reveal sand bars rich with gold.

By the early '50s, miners were so thick along the North Fork
that, according to the story, a piece of news could be carried
by word of mouth the whole 70 miles from Downieville to
Marysville in 15 minutes. The accuracy of the dispatch, by the
time it reached its destination, was not guaranteed.

Metropolis of the Yuba mines was, and still is, Downieville.
In the fall of 1849, William Downie, a Scotsman with a flair
for leadership, headed up the North Fork with a party consisting of an Irishman, an Indian, a Hawaiian and ten Negroes.
At the present site of Downieville they struck rich gold, built a
log cabin and settled down to wait out the winter.

Things went well in this far-off outpost until the holiday
season. A serious question then arose over whether the party
should drink its only bottle of brandy on Christmas or on New
Year's. For several days the boys argued heatedly and earnestly

on this point of etiquette, finally settling on Christmas. On the appointed day, they made a punch of brandy, nutmeg and hot water, and then launched the celebration with toasts to sweethearts, wives and country. At the height of the festivities, Downie, who was by then going under the title of Major, decided that the occasion required a formal observance. He climbed to the roof of the cabin with an American flag in one hand and a pistol in the other.

"I made a short speech," the Major recalled, "waved the flag and fired a few shots and finished up by giving three cheers for the American Constitution."

This somewhat unorthodox celebration of the first Christmas on the North Yuba set the tone for the roaring Gold Rush town of Downieville. It specialized in festivities of any kind, particularly the Fourth of July. And in its heyday, it was hardly a rewarding field for temperance workers. Major Downie records that in this cold and rugged country, any miner who abstained was considered either "a crank or a suspicious character." Bottles were opened not by drawing the cork but by the quicker method of breaking off the neck. In earliest days when Downieville had only one saloon, any celebrant who stood a round of drinks for the house paid the flat price of one ounce of gold ($16). If there weren't enough men in the bar to fill out an ounce's worth, someone went out and rounded up neighbors and passers-by.

One of Downieville's first justices of the peace was a saloonkeeper. In 1850, a man was brought before him for stealing a pair of boots. Finding him guilty, the justice ruled that he return the property and, as a fine, stand the drinks for the crowd. The hilarious court then adjourned to the bar and proceeded to make the most of the opportunity. So, after several rounds, did the prisoner. In the midst of the orgy he disappeared, leaving the saloonkeeper-justice to stand the fine.

Downieville could appreciate this kind of joke. One day a greenhorn approached the claim of miner Jack Smith, who immediately dropped his work and began poking in the trunk of a pine tree. Palming a gold nugget, he pretended to pull it out of the bark. The astonished newcomer then began working the bark himself.

"No, you don't!" put in Jack. "This is my tree." The stranger tackled another pine nearby, but without success.

"Maybe you are too near the ground," advised the miner. "Some of them are 'top-reefers', as we call them here; try about 20 feet higher up."

So the greenhorn shinnied up the tree. At Jack's urging, he kept climbing higher. Finally when the man was well out on a high limb busily searching for gold, Jack could hold himself no longer. Howling with glee, he ran off to tell the boys, while the greenhorn wondered what demon had suddenly seized his new-found friend.

Downieville's greatest hoax was pulled by a store clerk named William Slater, a fast-talking character who had somehow earned the trust of the miners. In 1850, Downieville had neither roads nor express service, and its chief problem was to market its golden treasure. Slater had once remarked that a man who knew where to go in San Francisco could sell gold for $22 an ounce. So when it came time for someone to "go below" with the camp's collective savings, the boys chose William Slater. They were so grateful for this service that when he left with $25,000 in gold dust and nuggets, they generously told him to keep for himself $2 for each ounce.

That was the last Downieville ever saw of William Slater. He passed through San Francisco and was seen at the Isthmus of Panama by a traveler who later turned up in Downieville. Slater, the new arrival reported, had strongly recommended that he come to the North Yuba camp and meet its jolly citizens. They were in no mood to return the compliment.

In that same year, Downieville began to lose its isolation. Sam Langton, who was to become one of the stagecoach kings of the Mother Lode, started a pony express from Marysville to Downieville. Pack trains began operating over the same route, bringing in scarce provisions that sold for outrageous prices in the mountain-bound camp.

But the jagged country still made the Downieville trail a distinct adventure. One traveler wrote thus of a particularly rough section: "At last, after a great deal of scrambling and climbing, my shins barked, my clothes nearly torn off my back, and my eyes half scratched out by the bushes. . . . I considered

that I had got over the worst of it." In another spot the precipitous trail was too narrow for man or beast to pass one another.
Down-traffic had to cling to the upper bank while the up-traffic
passed by.

"The mules," reported the observer, "understood their own
rights perfectly well. Those loaded with cargo kept sturdily
to the trail, while the empty mules scrambled up the bank,
where they stood still till the others had passed. It not infre-
quently happened, however, that a loaded mule got crowded
off the trail. . . . This was always the last journey the poor mule
ever performed."

Above Downieville, the trail was worse. Along one narrow
section there was a sheer 80-foot drop to the rocky stream below. Hikers could only pass at certain places, and then only by
holding on to one another. At one spot even this path was
broken by a gap of several yards, which the miners had bridged
with a thin pine log. As you teetered on this support, with one
foot stepping on the cliff itself, you could look down between
your legs and see sharp rocks, "strongly suggestive of sudden
death."

Despite its alpine location, Downieville had a population of
several thousand by 1851. Completely surrounded by mountains, its single street barely found room between the hillside
and the river. It boasted a newspaper, a theater, several hotels.
Though everything had to be packed in by muleback, the saloons were as elegantly decorated as any on the Mother Lode.
There was a notable absence, however, of plate glass mirrors.

Quaint and peaceful-looking, like a "toy village" when seen
from afar, the Downieville of the '50s bore a veneer of refinement. In its restaurants, as one visitor observed, "men in red
flannel shirts, with bare arms, spread a napkin over their muddy knees, and studied the bill of fare for half an hour before
they could make up their minds what to order for dinner." But
its exuberant, rougher side made itself apparent at every
opportunity.

Downieville's first Independence Day, 1850, was celebrated
with a rousing spree which including a knifing and a public
horsewhipping. The event of 1851 was marked by another carnival which ended in the worst tragedy of Downieville's his-

tory. Late that night, one Joe Cannon reeled his way homeward with several companions, and accidentally fell through the doorway of a house. In this dwelling lived a Spanish-American and his paramour, Juanita, a beautiful woman who was favorably known among the miners. Before the two were aroused, Cannon's companions pulled him outside and the group continued its unsteady way. Next morning Cannon passed by and stopped to apologize. Apparently the more he said the more infuriated the Spanish couple became. Finally Juanita grabbed a knife and plunged it into his side, killing him instantly.

When the news of this act spread up and down the river, the angered miners assembled in Downieville, seized the hapless pair, chose a popular court and held a trial. The man was acquitted but Juanita was found guilty and sentenced to be hung. The mob improvised a gallows by the river and performed the deed—only a few hours after the knifing episode.

The news that Downieville had hanged a woman immediately spread throughout California. Her citizens were shocked that lynch law had come to this shameful extremity. Popular tribunals had been accepted as a stern necessity in a lawless region; vigilantism was, in fact, the order of the day in 1851. Blame for this final crime was not Downieville's alone, but also that of a California citizenry which had embraced mob justice. The state recoiled at the Juanita incident, and for the next five years, at least, Californians relied more on established legal processes than on "Judge Lynch."

By 1855, Downieville resolved to have a quiet Fourth of July. Miss Sarah Pellet, a noted temperance lecturer, was on her way up the Yuba River, and was engaged for the principal oration. In anticipation of this splendid diversion, the boys launched a veritable reform crusade and joined the Sons of Temperance Society by the hundreds. Downieville saloons were all but deserted.

The festive day arrived, and thousands of miners assembled in town. The boys were so anxious to hear Miss Pellet that when another speaker waxed exceedingly long, they fired a volley of pistol shots in the air to shut him up. This in turn led to a duel between the orator and one of his tormentors, with double-barreled shotguns as weapons. The erstwhile speaker was killed, Miss Pellet left town, and Downieville's saloons reaped the result of a fallen crusade.

DOWNIEVILLE. Probably the most charming of the Gold Rush towns in the Northern Mines, Downieville and its sister towns of the Yuba River are fully worth the drive up the last lap of Highway 49. For the beginning of your Downieville tour, start at the Pioneer Museum, and don't overlook the quaint neighborhood streets that wind along the steep hillsides.

CAMPTONVILLE. While this lower Yuba town was once a thriving gold camp, repeated fires destroyed its old buildings. Today's houses are of relatively late construction.

GOODYEAR'S BAR. Below Downieville a short way off Highway 49 lies what is left of Goodyear's Bar, named for two Goodyear brothers who were among the founders in the summer of 1849. What the site lacks (it has only a few wooden structures) in historic interest, it compensates for in exhilarating mountain scenery.

SIERRA CITY. Founded in 1850, Sierra City was one of the best preserved of all Mother Lode towns until a fire damaged it in recent years. But it is still worth the exciting thirteen-mile drive up the turbulent North Fork of the Yuba from Downieville. The Busch Building, perhaps the most prominent of its landmarks, does not date from the Gold Rush, but from the early 1870s.

JOHNSVILLE. North of Sierra City and a few miles west of Highway Alternate 40 is Johnsville, the epitome of the wooden frontier town popularized in Western movies. Though Johnsville retains some earmarks characteristic of the Gold Rush towns — overhanging balconies and a quaint belltower — it was actually founded in the 1870s. Also known as Jamison, it is partly restored by the State Division of Beaches and Parks.

Downieville and the Yuba River Camps / 145

Chapter 15. Feather River: Canyon Country

NOWHERE is the proverb, "Gold is where you find it," better applied than in the Feather River country. There is no other explanation why thousands of men invaded this remote and rugged region a century ago. To reach their goal they braved raging torrents, precipitous trails, merciless weather. When they arrived they carved precarious townsites between river and canyon walls, and proceeded to lead a life as wild and untamed as their surroundings.

The Feather River discoveries were not completely accidental. Though fully 90 miles north of the original discovery site at Sutter's Mill, the lower Feather mines were opened as early as July, 1848. John Bidwell, the frontiersman who had led one of the first two emigrant trains into California in 1841, had a ranch on Chico Creek; a few weeks after Marshall's strike, Bidwell visited the Sutter mill and found the sand bar reminiscent of his Feather River country.

Back he went to the Feather, panning its shores as he traveled. Only a few miles above the present Marysville, he found light gold. By the time he reached the region of the river's three main forks, the gold was so rich that he went no farther. At this spot on the Middle Fork rose Bidwell's Bar, first of the rough and wealthy Feather River camps.

Then in the winter of 1849-'50, one Thomas Stoddard came into the young camp of Downieville with tales of a fabulous Gold Lake, which he had discovered in the Sierra fastnesses. When he had leaned over to drink from its water, he had seen at its bottom nothing less than boulders of pure gold!

That was enough for the boys of Downieville, and of the whole Northern Mines, for that matter. Could the estimable Stoddard find this Gold Lake again? He thought he could, but everything would have to wait until the spring thaws. By May, 1850, when Stoddard led a stealthy, 25-man party out of Downieville on the momentous quest, it was followed by a thousand Argonauts.

For days they scrambled over the unbroken country of the upper Feather watershed. When the Gold Lake remained unfound, Stoddard grew hesitant. They had, he said, taken the wrong "divide." His followers were furious.

"If you've deceived us," growled one, "we'll blow the top of your damn'd head off."

At this point the miners held a meeting, and reported to Stoddard that if he did not produce his Gold Lake within 24 hours, he would be strung up to the handiest pine tree. At this sobering promise, Stoddard forgot about Gold Lake and took the first opportunity to decamp. Back to Downieville trudged an angered, sheepish crew. Never again did Stoddard dare show himself in the California mines.

But his Gold Lake proved the first of the breed of lost mine legends which produced real strikes as a by-product. Three Germans straggling back from the Gold Lake stampede cut across into the North Fork of the Feather River. On the east branch of this stream they found shining gold particles lodged in rock crevices. Within four days they are said to have taken out $36,000 worth of pure gold.

When this news reached the camps around Bidwell's Bar, a second rush set in for the upper Feather country. A party of 100 reached the discovery site, found a big gold nugget, washed $285 from a single panful, and decided this was the right spot. By the end of July, 1850, several hundred men had arrived to found the well-named camp of Rich Bar. Soon after were discovered the equally-fabulous localities of Smith Bar, Indian Bar and Missouri Bar. This rugged treasure-house, teeming with thousands of gold-hunters, became the northern outpost of the Mother Lode.

Meanwhile, the lower Feather diggings had been booming since Bidwell's first discovery. A few miles west of Bidwell's Bar, Ophir City sprang up in 1850. Later its name was changed to Oroville, the one Feather River camp still thriving today. North of Oroville the Feather enters its craggy, steep-walled canyon, and for this reason the town became as much a transportation center as a mining camp. From Marysville, head of steam navigation on the Feather, stages and mule teams brought passengers and cargo as far as Oroville and Bidwell's

Bar. From there, pack trains carried freight 53 miles along the tempestuous North Fork to the Rich Bar diggings.

Just getting to the end of wagon navigation at Bidwell's Bar, however, was a real adventure. As far as Marysville, at the junction of the Feather and Yuba Rivers, travel was civilized enough on board the gilded steamboats. Unless, of course, rival captains took to racing and sent the pressure gauges above the safety limits—at which time crews, boat and passengers were liable to be exploded sky high.

Above Marysville, an eyewitness account of travel hazards is provided by a New England lady named "Dame Shirley" Clappe, who journeyed to Rich Bar with her husband in 1851. The northbound stagecoach, as she described it, was "the most excruciatingly springless wagon that it has ever been my lot to be victimized in. . . ." The first 30 miles were smooth and scenic, but 10 miles below Bidwell's the road took to the mountains and ran along a harrowing precipice. Shirley was too petrified to scream.

"It seemed to me," she wrote later, "should the horses deviate a hairbreadth from their usual track, we must be dashed into eternity."

"Wall," said the driver when that stretch had been safely passed, "I guess yer the furst woman that ever rode over that 'ere hill without hollerin.'"

North of Bidwell's, Dame Shirley and her husband proceeded on muleback, twice losing their way before looking down upon the rude camp of Rich Bar. The last five miles into town were so steep and precarious that riders dismounted and led their animals; but despite warnings, the plucky Shirley rode her mule all the way and arrived safely—after falling off only once.

The early Feather River camps were as primitive as the trail. In '51 Oroville was so insignificant that Dame Shirley failed to mention it. At Bidwell's Bar "there was nothing to sleep in but a tent, and nothing to sleep on but the ground, and the air was black with the fleas hopping about in every direction . . . " But by the mid-'50s the rich diggings of the lower Feather had made Bidwell's a city of 2,000—complete with a newspaper, three daily stages and the first suspension bridge in California.

By '56 Oroville had surpassed its neighbor; wrote one citizen: "Coaches are rattling through our street at all hours of the day and night." Early next year the *Gazelle*, a bantam-sized stern-wheeler, pushed up the Feather all the way to Oroville. For three months in that high-water year other steamboats arrived, making Oroville one of the few California mining towns ever reached by water.

But on the upper river, Rich Bar and its neighbors never got beyond the shanty stage. Dame Shirley described the camp as a single street with about 40 nondescript structures—tents, "plank hovels," log cabins and one unique edifice "formed of pine boughs and covered with old calico shirts." Only two-story building in town was the imposing Empire Hotel, a picturesque union of wood and canvas which Shirley called "just such a piece of carpentering as a child of two years old, gifted with the strength of a man, would produce." But because all materials had to be freighted from Marysville at 40 cents a pound, "this impertinent apology for a house" cost $8,000 to build.

Social life on the upper Feather was even less attractive to a cultured New England woman of the 1850s. As she put it, "there are no newspapers, no churches, lectures, concerts or theaters; no fresh books; no shopping, calling, nor gossipy little tea-drinking; no parties, no balls, no picnics, no tableaux, no daily mail (we have an express once a month), no promenades, no rides or drives; no vegetables but potatoes and onions, no milk, no eggs, no *nothing*."

As in other Mother Lode camps, the boys accepted this stern existence with exemplary fortitude—at first. In fact, when the first gamblers imported two painted ladies as a proper orna-ment to the camp (building for them what later became the Empire Hotel), the boys were shocked. Within a few weeks the tainted pair were forced to leave town by public opinion—and this at a time when they were the only females on the upper Feather. Crushed at this ingratitude, the gamblers sold their $8,000 investment to a hotelkeeper for a few hundred dollars.

But Rich Bar's honor was not long preserved. The gamblers soon recouped their losses many times over, and their numbers multiplied. Despite seemingly prohibitive freight rates, whisky was packed into the North Fork camps in enormous quantities.

Though the miners treated Dame Shirley with near-reverence, she could not help being horrified to witness constant gambling, carousing, swearing and fighting. The Feather River mines had outgrown their age of innocence.

If anything, Rich Bar was more strenuously intemperate than other Gold Rush camps. A newcomer pulling in at three in the morning found the revelry in full swing at the hotel bar.

"It strikes me," he confessed to the proprietor, "your customers are rather late tonight."

"It's a little late this morning perhaps for night before last," admitted the host, "but for last night, why bless you, it's only just in the shank of the evening!"

Dame Shirley herself describes a three-week "saturnalia" in nearby Indian Bar, where she and her husband moved in the fall of '51. In the following winter, life on the far-off Feather began to pall on the restless miners. As the holidays approached they made extensive preparations—consisting chiefly of hauling in frightful quantities of brandy and champagne. They started out on Christmas Eve with an oyster-and-champagne supper and an all-night dance. For the next three weeks Indian Bar was on the warpath. Almost every day a boat-load of celebrants capsized in the river; being too numb to get panicky, none of the victims drowned. Any citizen who withheld from the bacchanal was arrested by a kangaroo court and sentenced to "treat the crowd." Finally the marathon ended from sheer exhaustion—not of the revelers, but of the brandy.

Such excess living on the Feather usually led to violence, and July, 1852, was particularly explosive. On Independence Day the ladies (four in number) and gentlemen of the upper Feather were enjoying an elegant dinner at the hotel when a fight erupted in the barroom below and two men rushed into the dining room with "blood-bespattered shirt bosoms." One lady fainted, and the festivities faltered.

A week later Dame Shirley and several friends went for a quiet walk in the forest and were returning laden with wild flowers when "a perfectly deafening volley of shouts and yells" rose from the camp. It marked the beginning of a battle between Americans and Mexicans which ended in the banishment of six of the latter.

Then a few days afterward Shirley was chatting amiably with two ladies at the door of her cabin when three or four hundred men suddenly rushed by with much shouting to the scene of the latest attempted killing. In all, three weeks in July produced what Shirley detailed as "murders, fearful accidents, bloody deaths, a mob, whippings, a hanging, an attempt at suicide, and a fatal duel." The North Feather in the early '50s was not noted for charm and serenity.

The Feather River camps lived hard and died early. Late in 1852 the fluming companies which had turned the river to work its gravel bed failed to find paying deposits. Almost overnight, Rich Bar and its neighbors were abandoned. Downstream, Bidwell's Bar was pronounced "another deserted village" by 1856. Except for the city of Oroville, little is left to mark the once-flourishing Feather River mines. In the North Fork of the Feather, even the scenery itself is marred by man-made dams, powerlines, a highway and a railroad. And though Rich Bar alone is said to have produced $3,000,000, no one has yet found the lake with boulders of gold.

POINTS OF INTEREST

OROVILLE. This is now the busy center for construction of the Oroville Dam, keystone of the Feather River Project and the tallest dam in the world. The city's historic gold days are recalled in several old landmarks and three museums, including a Chinese temple dating from the 1850s.

BIDWELL'S BAR. Little is left at Bidwell's Bar beyond the historic suspension bridge constructed in the 1850s.

CHEROKEE. Atop Table Mountain thirteen miles north of Oroville on state Highway 70 is the ghost town of Cherokee. Among its interesting sights are a museum in an old hotel and a well-kept cemetery. Much in evidence are scenes of early gold placer and hydraulic mining.

FORBESTOWN. On a dirt road east of Oroville lies the abandoned camp of Forbestown, started by B. F. Forbes in 1850. For many years a thriving gold town, Forbestown is marked today by crumbling rock foundations, wooden and stone walls, and piles of used lumber and other flotsam common to ghost camps. Located in a pine forest, it is a picturesque and inviting ruin.

LA PORTE. Known as Rabbit Creek in the 1850s, La Porte was the scene of hydraulic mining and also of some of the earliest ski sports in the world; as early as the 1860s miners raced each other down the slopes on homemade skis. Almost depopulated except for a few inhabitants, La Porte has a number of old brick ruins and stone foundations reminiscent of its golden hour.

SUSANVILLE. In 1855 a prospecting party led by the celebrated mountain man, Peter Lassen, discovered gold in Honey Lake Valley. On the site of Susanville an inn had already been established on one of the Sierra emigrant routes by Isaac Roop, who named the town after his daughter. Beginning in 1856 Roop, Lassen, and a number of other early settlers established the Territory of Nataqua, which included parts of both California and what was later Nevada. Afterward, when the Territory of Nevada was created in 1861, the Honey Lakers tried to maintain to California tax collectors that they were situated within the new territorial boundaries. Roop's cabin was requisitioned for a determined stand and called Fort Defiance. On February 15, 1863, a posse headed by the Sheriff of Plumas County held a pitched battle with the secessionists entrenched in the fort. But when the boundary line was surveyed, Susanville was discovered to be in California for sure. The Honey Lakers consoled themselves by seceding from Plumas County and establishing their own Lassen County.

Today Susanville is a busy center of agriculture, stock raising, lumbering, and vacationing. Still standing on Weatherlow Street is Isaac Roop's cabin, an interesting museum of California's "Little Confederacy."

Chapter 16. Old Shasta: Gateway to Gold

"THE LONGEST ROW of brick buildings in California"— that was the boast of Old Shasta, whose ghost now nestles in the quiet hills six miles west of Redding. Such superlatives are typical of a town whose turbulent history and violent contrasts fire the imagination. Once the biggest settlement between Sacramento and the Oregon border, Shasta now has only a handful of faithful residents.

Shasta was, first of all, a gold town. Near here the first California gold discovery outside the Mother Lode was made by Major Pierson B. Reading, the state's earliest permanent white settler north of Red Bluff. Just where he found it is in dispute— both Shasta and Trinity Counties claiming the honor. But around July, 1848, at a place called Reading's Bar, he and a crew of Indians began taking out gold at the rate of $832 per day.

Shasta's own gold discovery came in the spring of 1849, sparking California's second gold rush. Through the summer of '49, Argonauts from Oregon and the Mother Lode poured into this mushrooming camp. Known first as Reading's Springs, it was a tent city of more than 500 persons by October.

Rich as it was, Shasta was the most isolated town in California during 1849. An old mule trail blazed by the Hudson's Bay Company was all that connected it with Sacramento, 188 miles to the south. Pack trains and a few hardy teamsters carried supplies over this route at the stiff charge of $800 to $1000 a ton. At this rate, it looked like a cold and hungry winter for Shasta's pioneers.

Their fears were confirmed when the rains came. This was the wet winter which flooded Northern California and made the streets of Sacramento a thoroughfare for ferries and at least one steamboat. Shasta, dreading both flood and isolation, was seized with panic. Many people sold their goods at sacrifice prices (20 cents a pound for flour) and struck out for the settlements. Soon Shasta was cut off when the swollen Sacramento River halted all traffic at the Colusa crossing.

Now the wily merchants who had bought up Shasta's meager supplies at panic prices made the most of the situation. Flour soared to $2.25 per pound, tacks to $1.50 per dozen. Shasta had been caught in the dizzy economics of California's Gold Rush.

After this experience, Shasta became transportation-conscious. By 1851 a new road was built up the Sacramento Valley, and the first stagecoach rolled into the bustling camp. At the same time, new gold discoveries in the Trinity and Siskiyou mountains had increased the northward traffic. Shasta stood at the gateway to this golden empire, the point where the road ended and the trail began.

For Californians traveling from the Mother Lode to the new diggings, Shasta became a link in a unique and colorful transportation hookup. From Sacramento you took a sternwheeler up the river to the head of steam navigation at Colusa—or in high water, as far as Red Bluff. Then you took a stage for Shasta, known as "the head of 'Whoa navigation.' " Then you rode saddleback over the rocky trail to Weaverville and points northwest. It was a route unhampered by luxury in any form.

Henceforth, Shasta flourished more as a trans-shipping center than a gold camp. By 1857, four stages from the South and three mule trains from the North raised dust into Shasta every day. The fastest mode of communication was the stagecoach, carrying passengers, mail and express packages. It was a highly specialized vehicle, distinguished from others by the leather thoroughbraces which supported the carriage and took up the shocks of the road for both horses and passengers. The favorite model was the elegant Concord coach, shipped all the way from New Hampshire around Cape Horn to California. Considered the last word in horse transportation, it carried nine passengers inside and from six to eight on top. Rival stages from Colusa to Shasta carried travelers through in just over 12 hours—at the alarming rate of thirteen miles per hour.

While the six-horse stage was built for speed, the eight- and ten-mule freight teams specialized in tonnage. Plodding along at three miles an hour, they would cover the Colusa-Shasta route in around eight days. In mountain country the lead pair usually wore a bow of team bells over the collars, as a warning to head-on traffic coming around a blind bend. In contrast to the stage driver's box seat and six reins, the muleskinner rode astride the near wheeler and controlled the team by a single jerkline running through harness rings to the leaders. In her palmiest days, Shasta's streets were jammed with a hundred such teams every day.

At local wholesale houses, goods were unloaded and placed in saddle boxes for the most primitive transportation of all—pack mules. In trains of around 120 mules each, supplies moved on over bumpy, precipitous trails to Weaverville, Scott's Bar, Yreka and the Oregon settlements. As this means of transport had been employed in Mexico for some 300 years, operations were in the hands of hardened Mexican muleteers. Though each animal was limited to around 300 pounds, no cargo was impossible for the mule trains. Crates of squawking chickens, stamp mill machinery, dismantled pianos, printing presses—all swayed and jostled over Trinity trails to the tramp of hoofs and the Spanish oaths of the muleteers.

Accidents were common by this crude conveyance. Whisky Creek, located just beyond Shasta, got its name when a barrel of whisky fell from a mule pack and spilled into the stream—causing a sudden rush of thirsty miners to the water's edge.

Over this same route beyond the head of "Whoa navigation," express was carried by pony rider. Competition was so furious between the rival lines of Wells Fargo and Adams & Company that Shasta witnessed many a pony express race.

The most celebrated race began December 28, 1853, when a steamer brought an important message into San Francisco Bay. Since there was no telegraph connection with Portland, Oregon, the two lines sent pony riders hurrying northward with the news. Wells Fargo was leading when the scurrying hoofs passed through Marysville. Below Tehama the Adams messenger flew ahead.

At the Sacramento River crossing, rider Bill Lowden took the saddle for Adams over the last sixty miles to Shasta. He had just finished fording the river when the Wells Fargo man reached the opposite bank. Lowden hurried on, alerting each station with a whistle as he approached. Then the keeper would ride down the road leading a fresh mount at a gallop. Lowden, carrying his 54-lb. saddlebags, would switch horses without touching the ground and spur onward.

Some 35 miles below Shasta, Lowden struck a snag. He whirled up to Prairie House to find the Adams agent in a fist-fight with the Wells Fargo keeper, and his relief mount running loose. This didn't slow down Bill Lowden. He caught up with the fresh horse, jumped to the ground, grabbed him by the tail and sprang into the saddle with one leap. Then he pulled the express bags from his old horse and pressed on.

"I lost about one minute here," Lowden later apologized. But the Adams man flew into Shasta so far ahead of his rival that Wells Fargo conceded the rest of the race to Portland. Lowden had changed horses nineteen times and touched the ground only once, bringing the express to Shasta at an average speed of twenty-three miles an hour. Adams agreed to overlook the delay at Prairie House, and paid Bill Lowden $2000 for his epic ride.

Through this reckless, roaring era, Shasta rode the crest of prosperity. Between 1852 and '57 she numbered several thousand citizens—one of the fifteen biggest cities in California. In the surrounding placer bars—bearing such picturesque names as Mad Mule Canyon, Salt Pork Ridge, Gambler's Gulch, Piety Hill, Grizzly Gulch, and Jackass Flat—gold nuggets were numerous and miners were earning from $16 to $200 a day. From the Trinity and Siskiyou mines, pack trains were bringing in as much as $100,000 worth of gold every week.

In the earliest days, Shasta was a town of frame buildings, made of yellow pine lumber lined with cotton cloth. Fire struck this veritable tinder box on June 14, 1853, and in thirty-three minutes the whole business section went up in cinders.

But Shasta in her prime was too tough to burn out. In the next four years a fireproof Shasta rose from the ashes. With twenty-eight new structures, she was claiming the longest row of brick buildings in California. Prosperity returned in full force, and it was Shasta that provided the first shipment of gold received at the San Francisco Mint.

The golden treasure flowing through this thriving camp was not overlooked by California's knights of the road. Among the first of such gentry to arrive were five members of Rattlesnake Dick's gang, who were fascinated by a shipment of $80,000 worth of gold being packed over Trinity Mountain in the summer of '56. Since pack mules over the route were plainly branded and easily identified if stolen, Dick himself was to meet the gang with fresh animals for carrying off the loot.

At an abrupt bend in the trail, the robbers descended on the pack train and quickly overpowered the muleteers, whom they tied to trees. Then they unloaded the gold and hurried off to a secret hiding place.

But Rattlesnake Dick failed to show up with the new mules, and was, in fact, resting in the Auburn jail on a charge of mule stealing. After several days' wait, one of the outlaws grew restless and was killed in a fracas with the leader. The remaining four buried half the gold and lugged the rest across Sacramento Valley to the Mother Lode country. But on the road near Auburn a Wells Fargo posse was waiting for them. In the fight that followed, the leader was killed and the other three captured. Half the loot was recovered, but the other $40,000 hidden on Trinity Mountain stands high in the lore of California's buried treasure.

The failure of this robbery, one of the biggest in the Gold Rush, couldn't scare out other Shasta outlaws. In the late 1860s, a Shasta County barber named John Allen branched out into the horsetrading business—using other people's horses. When a posse caught up with him long enough to deliver a hail of buckshot, one of the men claimed a hit; he said it sounded like shooting a bird on a sheet-iron roof. John Allen got away, but his barbering days were over.

"Sheet-Iron Jack" finally carried his boldness too far when he rode openly into Shasta for an evening's entertainment. In a drunken brawl he shot an opponent and was promptly packed off to jail. Sentenced to two years in San Quentin, he was hustled out of Shasta on the next downstage. But at the outskirts of town, two robbers opened fire on the coach and then retreated into the brush. Infuriated at this competition, Jack leaned out the window and filled the air with epithets.

Jack soon escaped, and in November 1876, he and two companions robbed two Shasta stages and one Yreka stage. This triple blow was Jack's last important escapade. He was caught by the sheriff and sent back to San Quentin.

But long before this final flicker of excitement, Old Shasta's light had dimmed. In 1857, her citizens, anxious to prevent coastal ports from gaining the Weaverville trade, had extended the wagon road into the interior. By 1859, wheeled traffic was rolling to Weaverville in one direction and the Oregon border in another. Shasta kept her trade, but she was no longer the bustling head of "Whoa navigation."

Then in 1872, Shasta was shunted off the route of travel when the California & Oregon Railroad reached the new town of Redding. Six years later Shasta's gold placers were worked out, and by 1888, the fading city of brick relinquished the county seat to Redding. After that it was a ghost—one of the proudest and stateliest in California.

POINTS OF INTEREST

SHASTA. One of the truly romantic ruins among California ghost towns, Shasta has been improved as a State Historical Monument. Its famous rows of brick buildings, once fallen into ruin, have been partly restored. Among the outstanding landmarks are a museum, the courthouse and jail, and the Masonic Hall.

FRENCH GULCH. Much of interest remains, including an industrious population, in this gold town of the 1850s, which still exhibits several brick buildings dating from wilder times.

Chapter 17. Weaverville: Northwest Outpost

CALIFORNIA has mining camps that are better preserved, more active, and more ghostly, but none more quaint than Weaverville. Mountainbound in the·crown of the Trinity Alps, this remote gold town is quiet, ageless, almost drowsy. But its tree-shaded streets and century-old buildings carry the unmistakable flavor of the roaring '50s.

The first strike at this remote spot below Trinity River was made in 1849 by William Weaver, a Mississippi-born frontiersman. Next year the town sprang up bearing his name; by 1852 it was the riotous capital of the Coast Range diggings, with 40 wooden buildings and a population of 1200.

But to mine gold was one thing; to get it marketed and haul

in the trappings of civilization was another. By 1851, connection with the outside world was improved with construction of a wagon road up the Sacramento Valley as far as Shasta, and development of ports at Humboldt Bay. But all goods still had to be packed by mule train 40 miles from the valley or 100 miles from the coast. With freight rates at forbidding levels, prices were outrageous and luxuries rare at Weaverville.

Life was rugged enough in summer months, but in the hard winter of 1852-3, Weaverville was completely marooned. Snow was so deep that it crushed the roofs of houses. For a whole week there was nothing to eat in town but barley. Many residents escaped on snowshoes and the rest were thinking about it when the first thaws came.

There was a more formidable danger in the Trinity Alps. Resentful at the white man's invasion of their mountain domain, the Digger Indians raided pack trains and isolated camps, killing horses and sometimes the miners as well. One early resident tells how a stranger stopped at his camp one night, and next morning found nothing left of his mule but the carcass. Soon another newcomer came along, and they warned him about his mule. So he slept with the animal's tether rope tied to his wrist and his pistol within reach. In the morning the rope was undisturbed, but the Indians had gotten the man's mule, his pistol and his blanket.

This running war between whites and Indians came to a climax in May, 1852, when a band of warriors killed the butcher of Weaverville while he was driving a herd of cattle. With the whole Trinity country aroused, a Sheriff's posse trailed the Indians to their village and massacred over a hundred—all but two or three children. This barbarous act was enough to cow the rest of the Trinity Indians. In the fall of '52 the local chief came into Weaverville and, in ceremonies attended by at least a thousand miners, signed a peace treaty.

But the backwoods camp was not freed of troubles. Being wealthy, isolated, and short on such civilizing influences as women and churches, Weaverville in the early '50s was one of the wildest towns in the mines. One citizen of 1852 wrote home that society "is decidedly bad—gambling, drinking and fighting being the amusements of the miners in their leisure hours. Saturday night is usually celebrated by such hideous yells and occasionally a volley from their revolvers, which makes it rather dangerous to be standing around." A few months later he added: "Nothing fatal has taken place since my last letter but there have been some awfully close shaves. One man has been shot through the cravat, one through the hat and one in the arm. The Weaverville Hotel has been sacked and fistfights without number have come off, but as nobody has been killed nothing has been done."

Law counted for so little that one saloonkeeper openly defied the Trinity County Sheriff. On July 4, 1852, the officer came to take possession of the establishment on a creditor's attachment. The proprietor and his mistress drove him out at gunpoint. Soon the Sheriff was back with a small posse, and while all Weaverville crowded about, went inside. The defending pair raised their revolvers.

"If you shoot you are a dead man," warned the officer.

Next moment a volley shook the building, and the Sheriff was struck in the groin. The crowd pushed outside, while the combatants fought it out. After 15 or 20 shots the side of the law won a unanimous victory. One citizen drew a stern conclusion on the state of Weaverville society: "Sunday these two persons were killed; yesterday buried; and today almost forgotten."

Weaverville meant to uphold the majesty of the law, even if it took a lynching to do it. In the fall of 1852 an accused murderer was brought into town. The local judge admitted that the prisoner could not be tried until the next court session three months off. Everybody knew the camp had no jail.

The answer to this problem came quick. The man was tried and found guilty by an impromptu miner's court. A second question arose over the time of execution. The majority of the crowd attending voted to wait 10 days, but one group held out for a hanging next morning. An argument grew hot and pistols were drawn. Said one witness: "I thought for some time that half a dozen more lives would be lost in discussing this point." But at last the guns were put away and the 10-day period accepted peacefully. After all, Weaverville had to stand for law and order.

A few months later Weaverville got its jail, and after disastrous fires had made wood give way to brick, the place gained a more permanent look. By June of '53 Weaverville had over 2000 people, 14 stores, four hotels, four gambling houses, and 14 barrooms. It was in the mid-'50s, too, that Weaverville was struck with the spiral staircase craze. Main Street buildings were graced at one time with no less than seven outside spiral stairs, all of them made of iron in local blacksmith shops. Only three remain, but they give Weaverville a picturesque distinction among California mining towns.

High society came to Weaverville as early as 1852. With some 32 "respectable ladies" in the district, the citizens decided to hold a New Year's Eve Ball. The dance drew a crowd of miners who insisted on appearing in "store clothes"—dress coat, white vest, boiled shirt and polished boots. Since there weren't enough formal outfits in Weaverville to go around, they were passed among the miners, who would wear them for an hour or so and then retire from the dance floor and lend them to another. "It went off first-rate," reported one celebrant. "I was afraid there would be a row of some kind but everyone behaved themselves with propriety. . . ."

After that beginning, Weaverville was a social-minded camp. The following Fourth of July it held not one ball, but two. Such events were so rare in the California mines that four ladies of Shasta rode 40 miles on muleback over rough mountain trails to attend.

By 1856 Weaverville was becoming positively refined. It had a theater, a schoolhouse, church, Sunday school, and naturally enough—a dancing class. Trained for such intricate steps as the waltz and the schottische, the miners were ready for even greater social triumphs. The next Fourth they held a magnificent ball at Chauncey's Hotel two miles out of town, danced till sunrise and horseraced back to Weaverville. Social notes from an eyewitness:

"Miss Burbank's horse fell going about 2.40, through an old bed of a stream. She went about 15 feet over his head and landed in a soft muddy place, with all her ball fixin's on. Some gents along with her washed off the thickest of the mud and got her in a buggy. Mrs. Todd broke down the seat in a wagon and created considerable confusion as she weighs about 200. . . . Taking it all together it was the greatest affair of its kind that has ever come off here. . . ."

But Weaverville could still have its stormy moments. Most famous of these was provided by its large population of Chinese, who were a familiar part of the California Gold Rush scene. With their patient methods they could make a living at gold mining in ground abandoned or worked over by Americans. In its heyday Weaverville contained several hundred Chinese, who generally kept to themselves and settled their own quarrels. According to some accounts they were divided into two "companies"—one from Canton and the other from Hong Kong.

In the summer of 1854 they fell into an argument and made ready for war. The town blacksmiths were rushed with orders for spears, pikes and tridents. One munitions maker, obviously an opportunist, agreed to make 100 spears for the Canton Party at $1.50 each; within an hour the Hong Kongs won him over with an order for 200 spears; an hour later the Cantons secured his services with a bid of 300 spears at $2.50 each.

But no matter; all the blacksmiths and merchants in town were busy. For the next few days both sides were marching, drilling and parading the streets with tin helmets, iron shields, home-made bombs, pikes, and squirt guns containing some foul liquid. With morbid anticipation the miners made no attempt to prevent a clash, but awaited it as a choice diversion.

Everything seemed to happen in Weaverville on July 4, and the Chinese war was no exception. On the appointed day the belligerents took up their positions in a field one mile from town. The Sheriff arrived to stop the battle, but 2000 American spectators interfered. The Chinese, they said, had gone to a lot of trouble for this event, and many of the Americans had come a long way to see it. Wouldn't it be a shame for the Sheriff to stop it all now? So the peace officer stepped aside.

Meanwhile, the two parties had been running through maneuvers with much beating of gongs and tooting of horns. Said one observer, "Now they would halt, with their poles upright looking like a forest of trees. Then lowering the points of their spears, with awful yells, they would run two or three hundred yards. Then stop, the front rank dropping on one knee, forming a perfect rampart of spears and shields."

Finally, the leader of the Hong Kongs rolled up his pant-legs, struck his sword on his shield and shouted a signal. The army, some 150-strong, charged across a gulley and into the blades of the enemy. The Cantons fell back. Then their reserves came up on the left flank. But by a prearranged plot with the Hong Kongs, some of the Americans drove them back. The Canton army then fled, leaving the Hong Kongs in possession of the field.

By this time the festive spirit of the occasion had turned sour. Eight Chinese and one American lay dead, with six to eight wounded. Most Americans were disgusted that some of their own people had taken sides in the battle.

Thus ended Weaverville's Chinese war, one of the curiosa of the Gold Rush. "We thought that the whole thing would be a farce," summarized one American, "but their coolness and courage surprised us and the play turned into a tragedy at the close."

Until the late '50s, Weaverville wavered between reckless-ness and refinement. Even its "respectable ladies" and its fancy balls could not dull the rough edge of the mining camp. When the sheet music for the latest song hit was sent to one resident from his sister in New England, he wrote back: "I received the music all right but there is only one piano in town and that is unfortunately in a house of ill-fame."

By 1858 Weaverville shed its isolation when a wagon road was built from Shasta to replace the rugged mule trail. For several decades it continued to thrive as a gold camp. Today, with its iron-shuttered buildings and spiral stairs, Weaverville has lost its rough edge but not its atmosphere.

POINTS OF INTEREST

WEAVERVILLE. A living museum of California's golden days, Weaverville is one of the most delightful mountain towns in the state. A number of brick and adobe buildings date from the late 1850s. Among them are the office of one of the oldest newspapers in California; an historical museum; and a Chinese Joss House (temple) preserved as a State Historical Monument.

BIG BAR. One of many camps by this name in the gold diggings, Big Bar is located on the road from Weaverville to Eureka, through some of the thrilling scenery of the Trinity Alps.

TRINITY CENTER. Founded in the early 1850s, Trinity Center is located on the road running from Weaverville along the northwest side of Trinity Reservoir. Though mining has declined, Trinity Center has outlasted many other neighboring camps long since forgotten.

Chapter 18. Yreka
and the Klamath Camps

TODAY, California's scenic Klamath country is a picture of peace and serenity. But then, things have changed in a hundred years. When the land was new in the gold-struck 1850s, life was as raw and rugged as the Klamath Mountains—and a lot less permanent. Indian attacks, stage robberies, shootings— these were the hazards of travel and residence in old-time Siskiyou County.

This far north region got a slow start—for mining country. Argonaut wagon trains came over the Siskiyous and along the base of towering Mount Shasta as early as June, 1849—but found no gold. By 1850 gold-hunters trudging overland from Oregon were testing the Klamath River bars. They made the big discovery in March, 1851. After camping on what later became Yreka Flats, some Oregonians pulled stakes one morning and moved on. Abraham Thompson let his mules graze by the trail, and as one of them pulled up a tuft of grass, noticed yellow flecks in the roots. Quickly he panned out some of the dirt —and at sight of the coarse gold he ran after his friends.

"Come back! I've struck it!"

That was the beginning of the big rush to the north border. Within six weeks 2000 men had left the Mother Lode and flocked into Thompson's Dry Diggings. By late spring the new town of log cabins and brush wickiups got a second name. If you walked a short distance out of camp you could see far to the south the magnificent peak that dominates the Siskiyou country—Mount Shasta, or, as the miners called it, Shasta Butte. So the town became Shasta Butte City.

But this sounded too much like that of the earlier camp, Shasta City, 100 miles southward. One day some of the boys were sitting about trying to think of a new name. The county clerk had an inspiration, and approached a nearby group of Indians.

"What do you call the mountain?" he inquired, pointing to Shasta.

"I-e-ka—'the white'," they answered.

By the time a citizen rode south to record the new name at the state capital, it had been corrupted to Yreka. So the boys succeeded in keeping a name for Shasta, or so they thought, and they would pounce on anyone who dared suggest that Yreka sounded too much like Eureka, the port city on the northern coast.

Yreka soon became the metropolis of the far north country. By 1852 it had an estimated 5000 population, some fifty store buildings and a bursting energy. Its citizens wore guns as a matter of course. First building in town was a saloon, with a bar duly sandbagged and bullet-proofed for protection of the bartender. Behind another bar, a newcomer noticed a revolver "cocked and capped" for instant action.

Legal process in such a country was less than formal. One of the remarkable judges of California's gold days was Yreka's George C. Vail, whose decisions were wholly unencumbered by legal training. But what he lacked in law, he made up in audacity and common sense.

A young Oregonian came into his court and charged that an employer was skipping town without paying him for an entire winter's work. Vail promptly left the bench and took two constables in pursuit. On the road from Yreka they overtook the accused and hauled him back to court. He acknowledged the debt, but said he had no money. This did not disturb Judge Vail.

"Constable," he ordered coolly, "take that man and stand

Yreka and the Klamath Camps / 165

him on his head; then shake him well, and listen if you can hear anything drop."

Next moment the defendant was tried and found guilty. From his pockets fell a bag of gold dust in the amount of $2000. Out of this came the plaintiff's pay and an ounce of gold each for the two constables and judge—as "court costs." Then the culprit, having been placed right side up, was freed.

By 1854 Yreka's lawlessness was wearing hard on a small core of civilized residents. The few ladies in town decided to build a church—feeling, as one of them put it, "an imperative need of some influence other than the saloon and gaming table." Such a cause, pushed by persuasive femininity, captured the enthusiasm of the boys. Gallantly they contributed a fortune in gold dust, and prepared for quieter days. A Union Church, joined by Protestant and Catholic alike, was raised on the Plaza.

When it was almost finished, the ladies held a dedication supper inside. Just as the Sheriff, in the place of honor, stood ready to slice the viands, the good assemblage was startled by a volley of shots. A man flung open the door.

"Sheriff, come quick! The Greenhorns are storming the jail!"

Now the Greenhorns were miners of nearby Greenhorn Creek, who had clashed with the Yreka Flats Ditch Association over water rights. One of them had been jailed for cutting the Yreka ditch, and they were now in the process of liberating him—forcibly. The Sheriff and every man in the church dashed outside and joined battle.

"Many ladies ran out in excitement and curiosity," recorded one churchwoman, "but hearing a fusillade of shooting, mingled with the uproar of angry voices, speedily retreated."

Some minutes later the churchmen trudged back to the supper table. The Greenhorns had succeeded in rescuing their man. Casualties included one dead and several wounded. Apologies to the ladies were made and accepted. There was a general feeling that the Gospel was arriving none too soon.

Early-day Yreka might be crude, but it was not all bad. Up and down the nearby creeks, the honest miner plied his trade with rocker and long tom, living a simple, outdoor life. The poet, Joaquin Miller, on an early morning stroll in the Yreka diggings, leaves this impression:

"Now the smoke from the low chimneys of the log cabins began to rise and curl through the cool, clear air on every hand, and the miners to come out at the low doors; great hairy, bearded, six-foot giants, hatless and half-dressed. They stretched themselves in the sweet, frosty air, shouting to each other in a sort of savage banter, washed their hands and faces in the gold pans that stood by the door, and then entered their cabins, to partake of the eternal beans and bacon and coffee, and coffee and bacon and beans."

If the Yreka country was primitive, its transportation was still worse. For the first few years, travel to Yreka was by horseback and mule train from Shasta, 100 miles southward, although Oregonians managed to get a few wagons over the Siskiyou Mountains. The trail was rough and precipitous, with such other inconveniences as bandits and hostile Indians.

In fact, Shasta Valley holds distinction as the scene of the first organized road agentry in California. By October, 1851, one Charlie Smith was leading an outlaw gang numbering as high as 30 men. On the 23rd four robbers disguised as Indians surprised two miners a few miles south of Yreka. But the intended victims opened fire, and were reinforced by another party of travelers who drove the bandits off.

Then in 1856 a stage road was pushed through to Yreka by the roundabout Pit River route. The Sacramento *Union* called the route "a terrible rough one," and one traveler complained of miserable lodging houses where arrivals waded "through mud and slush to find a dirty wash basin, dirtier towels and 'yaller' soap, or no soap at all." And for meals the tired passengers got "half-cooked beans, heavy bread, stale butter, and bread pudding."

Meanwhile, the Pit River Indians were not agreeable to the white man's invasion. Travel along the route was constantly interrupted by their depredations. By late August, 1856, they ventured to make the first Indian attack on a California stagecoach. Driver Jared Robbins, alone on the downstage south of Yreka, was a few miles below the Pit River ferry when a war party jumped his stage. He was hit in the first volley of arrows, but whipping up the team, he flew onward for the next station —seventeen miles away.

Down that rutted and winding road careened stage and team, with Indian riders swarming around like enraged hornets. Arrows struck both Robbins and his horses, but it was the bumpy road which brought down the first casualty. Jolted and pounded unmercifully, the coach broke down and overturned in the middle of an open meadow. By the time the Indians reached the wreck, Robbins was on his way again—riding one horse and leading the rest. More pounding pursuit and more savage arrows, but at the end of that seventeen-mile race Robbins flew into the safety of the stage station—wounded but very much alive.

After that the Pit River route was left to daredevils and the Indians. In 1857, work was begun on a new stage road north from Shasta City in the Coast Range. By 1860 the road was completed through Scott River to Yreka. Travelers could board stage for the Siskiyou country with a fair expectation of arriving with their scalps.

But the new route was not neglected by California's masked gentry. By the middle 1870s, with the Iron Horse supplanting the stagecoach on the state's main arteries, highwaymen turned to the long, rugged and rewarding road between Shasta City and Jacksonville, Oregon. On this route in 1876, robbers stopped no less than five stages, one of them carrying the Western transportation king and owner of the line, Ben Holladay. Of his twenty-eight robberies, arch-bandit Black Bart honored the Yreka stages seven times. When President Rutherford B. Hayes and General William T. Sherman passed through Yreka in 1880, they received a proper welcome, but the crowd was meager. Most of the male population was off in the Siskiyous chasing stage robbers.

Still it was the unrelenting Indian who was the main danger for early-day Siskiyou settlers. The discoverers of Scott's Bar were driven out by Klamath Indians in 1850. By 1852 the Shastas, Modocs and Pit River Indians were all on the warpath. When the Modocs massacred an emigrant train, the whites organized a volunteer company and combed the north country. Failing to flush the quarry, they resorted to treachery.

The Indians were invited to peace talks, and deliberately murdered.

This foul deed crippled Modoc strength, though Indian raids continued throughout the '50s. In 1873 the final chapter of the pathetic story was written when U.S. troops were called upon to put the remnant of the Modocs back on their reservation in southern Oregon. Led by the audacious Captain Jack, the Indians entrenched themselves in California's impregnable Lava Beds and held off as many as a thousand soldiers for three months. Then they played the white man's game and slew the opposing general in a truce conference. In the end Captain Jack was finally caught through the perfidy of some of his own warriors, and hanged according to white man's law.

Peace had come to the Siskiyou country, but the era of the gold placers had already seen its halcyon days. Shasta Valley people turned to farming and ranching. When the railroad invaded Siskiyou in 1887 it shunned Yreka by eight miles, but her citizens countered by spanning the gap with their own line, the Yreka Western Railroad. The modern Highway 99 passes through the city to assure its commercial position; today Yreka is one of the few California mining towns to survive on something else than gold. As for lofty I-e-ka, she still looks down from the clouds with the same benign tolerance that she showed to the Forty-niners.

POINTS OF INTEREST

YREKA. Except for the matter of size, one might say of Yreka today what a visitor of a century ago called it: "a rather pretty little place." Seat of Siskiyou County, Yreka is today as appealing and as busy as it was in the Gold Rush. Some of the old buildings still stand as a link with the past. An interesting exhibit of gold samples is on display at the Hall of Records. Remains of the water ditch that Yreka miners dug for more than 90 miles from Shasta River may still be seen paralleling Highway 99 to the west.

GREENHORN. Two miles below Yreka is the location of Greenhorn, where only a few frame buildings remain.

Yreka and the Klamath Camps / 169

HAWKINSVILLE. Located north of Yreka, Hawkinsville dates from the early 1850s. Some frame houses and a church mark the site.

HUMBUG CITY. Founded in 1851, Humbug is situated some ten miles northwest of Yreka. Little remains of the town, but the evidence of intensive mining operations still abounds in the vicinity.

SAWYER'S BAR. In the middle of the Salmon Mountains to the west of Yreka is Sawyer's Bar, once the biggest of several camps on the Salmon River and its forks. The principal old landmark is an early-day wooden Catholic church.

SOMES BAR. Near the mouth of the Salmon is Somes Bar, founded as a mining camp in the Gold Rush and now a center for fishing and camping.

THE KLAMATH RIVER TOWNS. Like the Salmon, the Upper Klamath and its tributaries were more populated in the hectic '50s than they are today. Most of the camps lived hard and died young. In 1863 a traveler found them either deserted or in rapid decay, with most of the buildings abandoned.

Traveling along the Klamath west of Highway 99, one may turn south at the mouth of Scott River to the deserted camp of Scott's Bar, located in a deep and awesome gorge. Founded by John Scott in 1850, the site contains a number of tumbledown structures and foundations to show the activity that once livened this remote canyon.

Further west on the Klamath is Hamburg, today "a wide place in the road," in the gold days a flourishing town. Happy Camp was another sizable settlement in the 1850s, but has lived on as an outfitting point for fishermen and packers going into the remote Marble and Salmon mountains.

For twenty years (1855-75) Orleans Bar on the Klamath River was the seat of Klamath County, and relinquished the honor only when the county was broken up and redivided with other counties.

HAYDEN HILL. In northern Lassen County, sixteen miles south of Adin, lies the old mining town of Hayden Hill. Its mines, producing mostly gold and some silver, had a very long production record in both the 19th and 20th centuries.

HIGH GRADE. In 1905 gold was discovered by a sheepherder in the rugged Warner Mountains, at the extreme northeast corner of California. The town of High Grade boomed first in the summer of 1905 and became the object of a still bigger stampede in the fall of 1909 and the spring of 1910. Its remains are located three miles northwest of Mount Bidwell near the dirt road from New Pine Creek to Fort Bidwell.

PART V. THE SAGEBRUSH CAMPS OF EASTERN CALIFORNIA

The LINK *between California's Gold Rush towns and her desert mining camps was the stampede back over the Sierras to the Washoe mines in 1859 and the early '60s. At the very moment when the Mother Lode was declining, the Comstock Lode was discovered in the Washoe country—what would soon become the state of Nevada. The grand army of veteran miners trooped back over the old route of a decade earlier—perhaps feeling foolish that they had hurried past such a bonanza in the rush of '49.*

Once in the sagebrush they remained to follow new strikes in Nevada and California throughout the 1860s and '70s. The lessons learned in placering the Sierra streambeds were useless now. The boys had to learn something about ores, both gold and silver, and where to look for them. Instead of earning a living standing knee-deep in icy water shoveling sand into a sluice box, the typical miner now spent his time trudging over the hot desert trying to find a rich claim that he could sell to a mine developer. Then he would live high in the nearest mining town until his money ran out. Undaunted, he would pile pick, shovel, and provisions on his burro and head back into the sage-brush.

So the men who coped with too much water in the Sierras now had to learn how to get along with too little. The log-cabin miner became the jackass prospector, and he made the transition because hardihood was his stock in trade. When he and his fellows first crossed back over the Sierras to the desert in the Washoe rush of a century ago, one early Comstocker welcomed them with a salute that became a prophecy: "Let no man speak disparagingly of these men. Let no one sneer at the ragged miners. They are the pioneers in a great era. . . ."

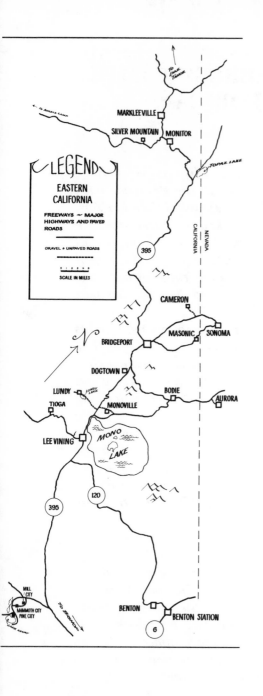

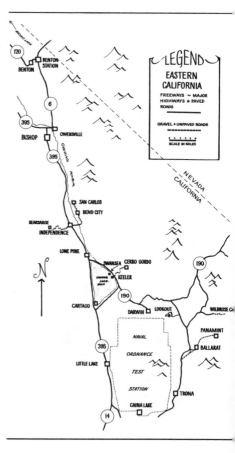

Down-canyon view of Cerro Gordo, leading silver producer of the 1870's.

Sitting on a mountain top, the silver mining town
of Lookout flourished in the late 1870's.

Rich ore was packed by mule-back to these Modoc furnaces
at Lookout owned by Senator George Hearst.

*Pack burros bring wood for the furnaces of Senator Stewart's
twenty-stamp mill, built at Panamint in 1875.*

*Before the boundary line was surveyed, Aurora, Nevada,
was the county seat of Mono County, California.*

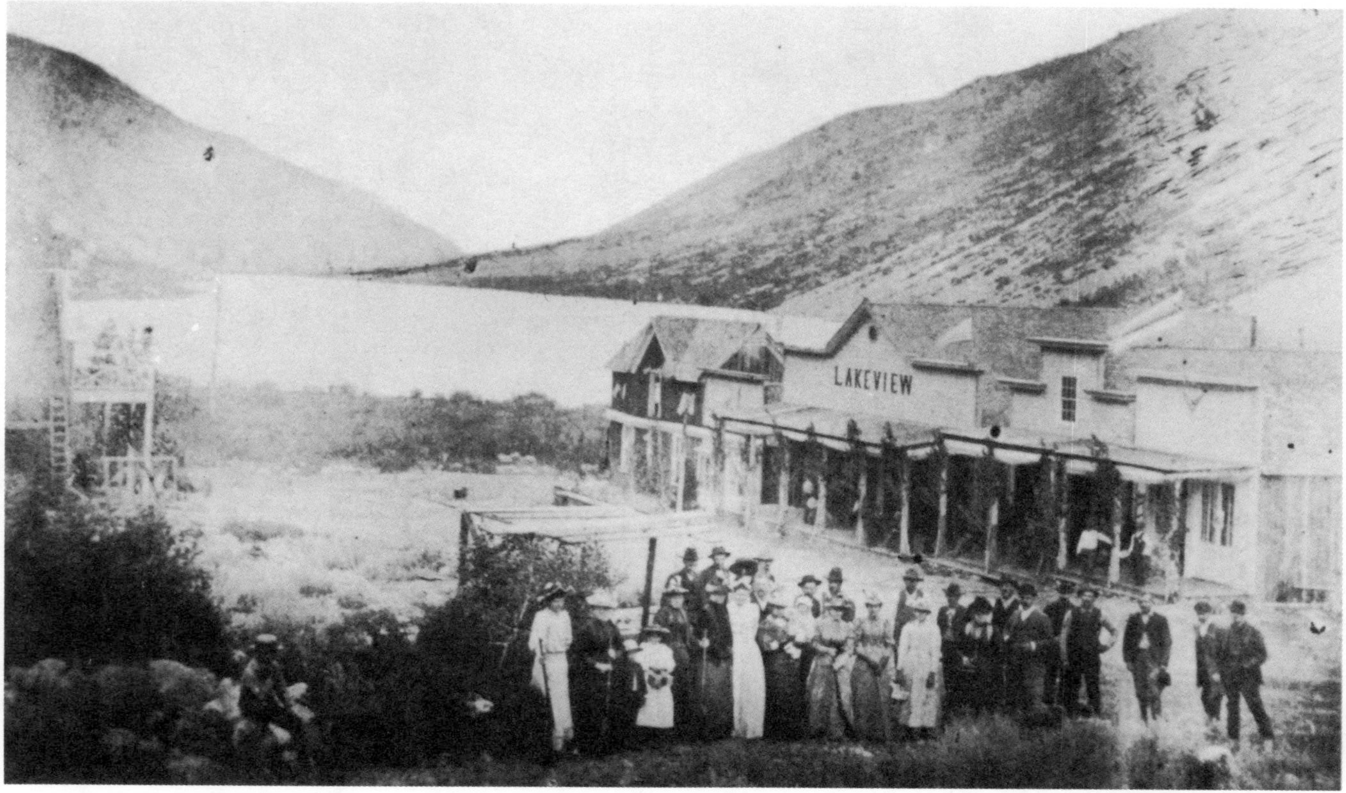

Courtesy of Stephen Ginsburg

The massive flywheel for this forty-stamp mill at Mammoth was hauled by mule-team all the way up from Mojave in 1879.

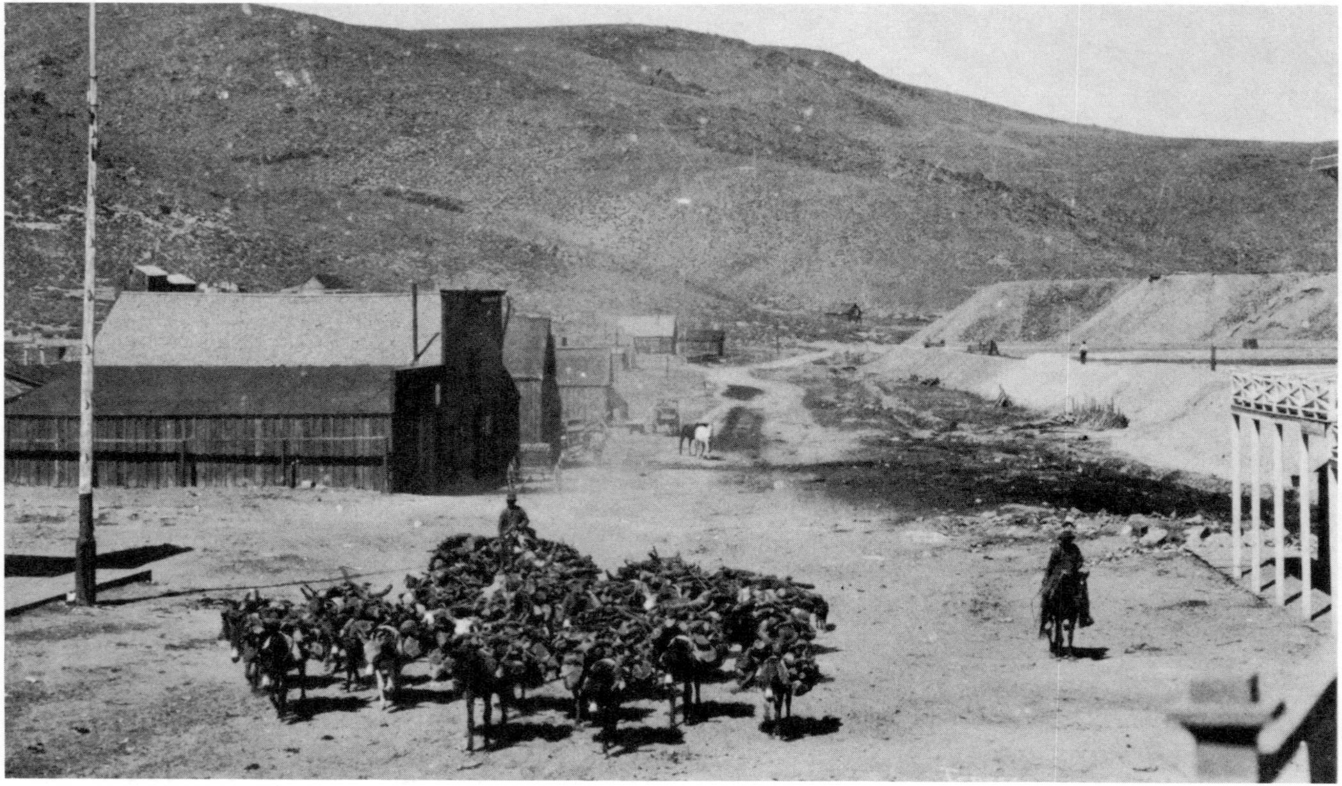

Courtesy of Los Angeles County Museum

Riding the near wheeler, a teamster guides his freight-laden, ten-horse team into Bodie.

Bodie citizenry turn out in Sunday best for Independence Day Celebration.

Chapter 19. The Rush in Reverse

INTO THE MOUNTAIN-BOUND MINING CAMP of Grass Valley, California, rode a weary traveler late in June 1859. He had jogged more than 150 miles over the massive Sierra Nevadas from the Washoe country—what would soon be called the Comstock Lode. With him, mostly as a curiosity, he carried some odd-looking chunks of gold-bearing ore.

Next day Melville Atwood, the local assayer, tested the rock. What he discovered made him doubt his own calculations. For besides the gold content, which ran nearly $1,000 to the ton, the specimens contained a much higher value in silver—over $3,000 per ton!

What was more, the stranger confided, over in Washoe the discoverers were extracting the gold and throwing the rest away! Since California's big strike more than a decade earlier, prospectors had not even thought of looking for anything but gold! In fact, an earlier assay of Washoe ore in Nevada City had failed to reveal the silver.

Within hours of Atwood's assay, the neighboring towns of Grass Valley and Nevada City were boiling with excitement. First to learn the news was Judge James Walsh, an old hand in California mining and a friend of the ore-bearing stranger from Washoe. Near midnight he banged frantically on the door of another friend. Quickly they piled provisions on a mule, mounted horse and spurred out of Grass Valley. Not far behind them clambered a desperate party in pursuit—one traveling on borrowed money, another on a borrowed horse. Within two days a clattering column was surging through the pine-forested Sierra—some on horseback, some afoot, all bent forward like hounds on the scent.

By the summer of 1859 Washoe ore was being shipped back over the Sierra—ore so rich that it could be carried 160 miles by muleback and another 80 miles by steamer, and could then be smelted in San Francisco at a fantastic profit. By October the growing shipments were attracting attention as they passed through California's mining region. Early arrivals in Washoe were writing back that the mines were the richest in the country. California newspapers were quoting assay figures of thousands of dollars per ton. Before long, bars of Washoe silver were hauled through the streets of San Francisco and displayed in bank windows before the eyes of gathering crowds. All at once California rang with a new cry: Silver in Washoe!

In fact, only silver could have excited the Californians in 1859. For too long they had followed the call of gold. As the placers had declined in the mid-50s, they had been quick to heed each rumored strike. But against the cry of silver these stalwarts had no immunity. When it burst upon them in the fall of 1859, they were especially vulnerable. It had been a long summer, and in Sierra canyons the placer and hydraulic mines were idle for lack of water. At the end of September one Sacramento man estimated a thousand unemployed were roaming the town. "Never before," he wrote, "have I seen so many people looking for work and can't get it."

To this restless crew the silver call was like a trumpet blast. All at once mules, horses, flour, picks and shovels were in fevered requisition. "From the crack of day to the shades of night," exclaimed one San Franciscan, "nothing is heard but Washoe." It made no difference that the new strike was located in the very desert through which most of them had suffered on their way to California. They could only agree that it was "Forty-nine all over again!"

With "Washoe!" thundering like a battle cry, the rabble army converged on the Sierra passes. The favorite route was up the American River canyon; at its foot lay Placerville, which was suddenly overrun with silver-seekers. One of them was the journalist, J. Ross Browne, who later described his attempt to get a night's sleep in a Placerville hotel room. People were rushing through the corridors all night, he wrote, "in and out of every room, banging the doors after them, calling for boots, carpet-sacks, cards, cock-tails, and toddies; while amidst the ceaseless din arose ever anon that potent cry of 'Washoe!' . . . ."

In this breathless spirit California marched to the Comstock Lode. And as the line of glory-hunters moved through Placerville's streets each morning—clattering with shovels, picks and wash pans—there rose from the throats of bystanders the inevitable shout, "Go it, Washoe!"

Up into the pines the adventurers thronged, making an un-broken line of men, mules and wagons from Sacramento Valley over the mountains to Carson Valley. As the stagecoach whirled around blind bends, the passengers found themselves looking hundreds of feet downward to the churning American River while the wheels dusted the brink. In the steepest stretches they walked and sometimes pushed as the teams struggled upward. Those who hiked or rode muleback suffered worse—slogging in the ruts of freight wagons, jumping out of the trail to avoid being knocked down when a pack train brushed relentlessly past.

Among the worst hazards on the trail were the wayside taverns, where the travelers piled in on one another in frantic quest for board and bed. Typical was Dirty Mike's, where one paid for the privilege of sleeping on the floor in company with numerous other flea-bitten vagabonds, in a room whose only fixtures were a piece of looking glass fastened to the window casing and a common comb and toothbrush dangling by strings nearby. Best stopping place on the route was Strawberry Flat, where hundreds of travelers congregated each night, flooding the barroom and jostling each other for a place near the dining room door. J. Ross Browne thus described the evening meal:

At the first tinkle of the bell the door was burst open with a tremendous crash, and for a moment no battle-scene in Water-loo . . . could have equalled the terrific onslaught of the gallant troops of Strawberry. The whole house actually tottered and trembled at the concussion, as if shaken by an earthquake. Long before the main body had assaulted the table the din of arms was heard above the general uproar: the deafening clatter of plates, knives, and forks, and the dreadful battle-cry of "Waiter! Waiter! Pork and beans! Coffee, waiter! Beefsteak! . . . quick, waiter, for God's sake!"

Next morning, after a night's sleep in a room with 250 com-panions and a bracing wash at the horse trough, the silver-hunter was on his way. At Genoa, first settlement reached on the east side of the Sierra, accommodations were even more formidable. Lodgers were packed like stowaways—two and three in a bunk, the unfortunate ones curling up on saloon floors, behind store counters, between packing boxes and even on the tops of nail kegs. At the booming new town of Carson City, last stop before the mines, one weary arrival ate a hearty meal and then told the hotel keeper he was ready to be shown to his room. "Just imagine my surprise," he wrote, "when the landlord informed me that he had no place for me to sleep but on the floor, that is, if I had blankets. . . ."

Early in November a storm struck the Sierra, covering it with the snow and ice that had already brought tragedy to many California-bound emigrants in previous years. But this only deterred the faint-hearted and the sane. While commercial traffic was halted, the most frantic rainbow hunters floundered upward in the snow, resting at the highest outposts until the weather cleared enough for them to push over the summit. One storm after another raked the Sierra in one of the fiercest winters on record. Snow drifted as deep as 50 feet in the upper canyons. Numberless animals and a few men met death in blizzards and avalanches, but still the most daring pressed on —driven by visions of Washoe silver.

As the spring thaw approached, all of California seemed to rally at the foot of the Sierra. The winter's isolation had left the Comstock so short of supplies that prices were soaring, and between rival freight packers there was a breakneck race to be first across with whisky and other "necessities." As early as February they laid blankets in the snow for their animals to walk on, taking them up behind the train as it advanced and spreading them on the path ahead. Imaginative freighters tried sleighs, but these were stalled at the frequent patches of windswept granite. Mule trains were the only resort—taking not only merchandise, but offering to deliver passengers in Washoe at $30 per head. By early March even the stages were running again, but passengers had to walk much of the way, holding the coach to keep it from rolling down the mountainside. Above Strawberry Flat they trudged on by foot, braving fierce winds and shoveling a path before them across the summit.

With the first days of spring the Washoe trail was a continuous scar of slush and mud through the Sierra snow. A traveler called it "nothing but one trough of mire from two to three feet deep . . ." Adding further obstruction were the broken wagons, abandoned boxes and dead animals that literally lined the trail for the entire hundred miles across the mountains.

Worse hazards stalked the other Sierra routes opened to accommodate the tide. From California's Northern Mines the adventurers stormed up the tempestuous Yuba River, joined a mule train at Downieville and bent onward along narrow trails that hung hundreds of feet above the foaming river. From the Southern Mines they ventured through giant redwood groves and over Ebbet Pass to the Carson River. Near the summit of this remote passage the stampeders encountered more than rough trail. Two of them stayed up all night waving firebrands to protect a load of bacon from three grizzly bears which, as one man recalled, "were grumbling and gnashing their teeth."

By April some 150 Californians were arriving in the Washoe country every day. Estimates of its population reached 10,000 in the spring of 1860, with thousands more on the way. Those remaining in California were investing every spare cent in Washoe mining stocks. "The Washoe mania has operated very much against us here," wrote one San Francisco merchant, "diverting men and money from the legitimate channels."

Early in May a savage Indian uprising in the Washoe country knocked the remaining steam out of the first rush. But such setbacks could not down the Lode, which was basically sound to the extent of an estimated one-third of a billion dollars. The tide to the Comstock rose again in the summer of 1860 and ran heavily until '63. Its riches helped to finance the Union side of the Civil War. Through the 1860s and '70s its wealth was the first fact of economics on the Pacific Coast. For the rest of the century its legend inspired the countless prospectors who combed the Great Basin looking for "another Comstock."

Chapter 20. Cerro Gordo: L.A.'s Comstock

MOTORISTS driving through Owens Valley, on the east side of the Sierras, sometimes catch a glint of light high in the Inyo Range on the opposite side of Owens Lake. This is reflected sunlight from a window at the old mining camp of Cerro Gordo, which looks down on the valley below from its mountainside perch some 9000 feet high.

From this abandoned town, now reached by eight miles of steep and winding dirt road, once flowed as much as $13,000,-000 in silver and lead bullion. Between 1868 and 1875 its thriving trade helped to spur a furious boom in the young city of Los Angeles. In its day, Cerro Gordo's traffic was fought for by railroad kings and freightmasters, by every rival trading center from Los Angeles to Visalia. Deserted today, it stands as the greatest silver and lead producer in California history.

Discovered by Mexican prospectors in 1865, Cerro Gordo belongs to the era of the Comstock and the silver craze. It languished virtually unknown in remote Owens Valley until 1867, when one of its Spanish-speaking pioneers rode into Virginia City, gleefully displaying chunks of rich silver ore.

After that the rush was on. Into the new camp on the brow of the Inyo Mountains came a stream of adventurers—miners, teamsters, merchants, gamblers. One of the first arrivals was M. W. Belshaw, a mining engineer from San Francisco. A shrewd and audacious operator, Belshaw quickly recognized that Cerro Gordo was a treasure house, and that it could be controlled by the man who controlled its smelters. Hurriedly he bought an interest in the Union Mine, the one reliable source of the lead ore needed in the smelting process. Then he hauled in machinery for a smelter, built a toll road over the only feasible route into town, and piped water from the only adequate springs nearby. Belshaw was not the man to leave a stone unturned.

Joining him as an owner of the Union Mine was Victor Beaudry, a French Canadian who operated a store at Cerro Gordo. The two would dominate the history of Cerro Gordo for the next decade.

By the fall of 1868 Belshaw and Beaudry were producing silver-lead bullion at a faster rate than the United States had ever seen. The metal bars, each weighing eighty-five pounds and shaped like a long loaf of bread, posed a real shipping problem from this remote camp on the wrong side of California. To haul their output they secured the mule-team freighter, Remi

Nadeau—the writer's great, great grandfather. For the next eleven years—except for a few months in 1872-73—his jingling mule teams hauled the silver-lead shipments of Cerro Gordo.

In the earliest days the wagons rolled for 220 miles around the north side of Owens Lake, southward past Little Lake and across the Mojave Desert, and through Los Angeles to San Pedro. There they were transferred to paddlewheel steamboats for the 400-mile ride up the coast to San Francisco, where a refinery had been specially built for the purpose. The lead went to a local shot tower, the silver to the U.S. Mint. Any excess bullion was shipped around the Horn to the refineries of Swansea, Wales.

Sparked by Belshaw's energy, Cerro Gordo suddenly blossomed from a shanty camp to a full-fledged mining town sprawling up the slope of Buena Vista Peak. Through her rutted streets surged a motley parade of men and animals. Ten- and twelve-mule teams hauled bullion down the precipitous "Yellow Grade" on the first leg of the three-weeks' journey to the coast, and brought back provender and merchandise—everything from baled hay to billiard tables. An unending procession of pack burros carried in water, charcoal and pinon timbers for the furnaces and mines. By 1870 two six-horse coaches rolled in every day from Owens Valley, where they connected with stage lines to Virginia City, San Francisco, and Los Angeles.

Such feverish activity was always accompanied by lawlessness in Western mining camps—and Cerro Gordo had more than its share. Through the early '70s it was as famous for its shootings as for its silver riches. "Cerro Gordo is a prolific source of the 'man for breakfast' order of items," was the wry comment of an Owens Valley editor at news of the third shooting scrape in two days.

An ambitious young doctor arrived in town, only to leave the same night without his baggage. To the first man he met down the Yellow Grade, he frankly declared himself: "My friend, I came here to buy a stock of drugs and practice medicine, but damn me if I want an interest in a shooting gallery!"

Not that Cerro Gordo had no law. One night a pile of wooden

poles was stolen—an unforgivable crime in this lumber-shy camp. One inoffensive citizen was dragged before the Justice of the Peace as a suspect. Not a speck of evidence could be found against him, but the worthy magistrate had a duty to perform.

"You may not have stolen the poles," he admitted, "but there has been poles stolen, and I must make an example of somebody, so I fine you twenty-five dollars."

Most of Cerro Gordo's violence was traceable to two establishments, one at each end of town, which were generously termed "dance halls." The object of more than one fatal argument was a charming girl known as "The Fenian," the reigning belle of Cerro Gordo. Possessing a ferocious temper and a weakness for whisky, she was often less than ladylike. While on a sojourn to Los Angeles she beat up a man for calling her an Irish dog, broke an Italian boy's harp for refusing to play an Irish song, and returned to Cerro Gordo by request of the L.A. authorities. One night while staggering among the cabins on the side of Buena Vista Mountain she lost her footing and fell through a roof, causing the Chinese card-players beneath to flee the shack in terror.

By the fall of 1871 the more civic-minded citizens of Cerro Gordo decided to break the evil influence of the gay-gartered troupe led by The Fenian. The honest miner, thought these reformers, must abandon the quick-time of the harp and fiddle for more cultural, high-minded pursuits.

So the "Cerro Gordo Social Union," a literary and debating society, was founded. The largest hall in town was rented for the meetings, and the boys eagerly took up the new diversion. Week after week the debaters played to a full house, the girls found their dance floors deserted, and the club's founders congratulated each other on their success.

Enthusiasm was at its highest one night during a stormy political contest. The town's chief orator was condemning his opponents with such vehemence that he had to pause for a long breath of air. At that moment the sweet strains of the harp and fiddle drifted in the windows.

As one man, the crowd abruptly rose and made for the door. To the nearest dance hall they resolutely marched, while the speaker harangued empty benches. The one man remaining was the club's secretary, who was nursing a lame foot. The Cerro Gordo Social Union had met its inevitable fate.

Excitement also stalked the Cerro Gordo stage road, though most holdups were on the Mojave Desert at a safe distance from town. California's famed bandidos, Tiburcio Vasquez and Cleovaro Chavez, stopped the Cerro Gordo stage in 1874 at Coyote Holes, near the foot of Walker Pass. On the box beside the driver was none other than M. W. Belshaw, who was relieved of a silver watch, $20 in gold and a pair of new boots.

But in 1875 two other robbers rode boldly up the Yellow Grade and sacked Belshaw's toll house, almost within sight of Cerro Gordo. Two weeks later they returned and robbed the upstage two miles below town, making off with the Wells Fargo chest and the U.S. mailbag.

At this outrage, a formidable posse whirled down the Yellow Grade and scoured desert trails for the intruders. When the evil pair held up a freight station and boasted that they would kill Belshaw and Beaudry on sight, word passed through Owens Valley that the bullion kings had Cerro Gordo fortified against attack. But before matters grew worse, one of the outlaws was killed and the other fled to Mexico.

Though a lawless and remote camp, Cerro Gordo nevertheless cut a wide swath in California commerce. Nevada's Comstock Lode, pouring hundreds of millions into the wealth of San Francisco, was then towering over the other Western mining districts. But Cerro Gordo was the Comstock for another California city—Los Angeles. The coming of the bullion teams to Southern California in 1868 had happily coincided with a new influx of farmers. They found a ready-made market for their products—wine, corn and other items for Owens Valley miners, hay and barley for the freight mules. By 1870 all the surplus barley grown in Los Angeles County was consumed by Remi Nadeau's bullion teams.

"To this city," said the Los Angeles *News*, "the Owens River trade is invaluable. What Los Angeles is, is mainly due to it."

Other towns, notably Visalia, Santa Barbara, and Ventura, were quick to bid for the trade. For a few months in 1872-73 Bakersfield drew the traffic, only to lose it again to Los Angeles.

By early 1875 the Southern Pacific had reached past Bakersfield to the foot of the Tehachapis—settling for good the direction of Cerro Gordo traffic. Los Angeles enterprisers tried to build their own railroad to Owens Valley and hold the trade, but before it was well started Nadeau's bullion teams were connecting with the S.P. railhead.

So steady was Cerro Gordo's production that for years the freight wagons were unable to catch up with the furnace output. More teams were put on the road, the teams themselves were augmented with more mules and wagons, but the metal bars kept piling up at the source. In 1872, a small steamboat, the *Bessie Brady*, began hauling the bullion across Owens Lake to speed the process. But this merely transferred the piles from Cerro Gordo to the south shore of the lake.

During the Bakersfield debacle, 30,000 ingots had accumulated in Owens Valley, and passing miners were building them into temporary cabins. But in 1873 Nadeau insisted that Belshaw and Beaudry join him in financing a new firm, the Cerro Gordo Freighting Company. He built new stations and began dispatching teams on an almost hourly basis like a stage line. Within a few months, using eighty teams of sixteen mules and three wagons each, the freighters cleared the furnace output for the first time.

Meanwhile, Belshaw and Beaudry had been fighting to keep their iron control of Cerro Gordo. Since 1869 another company had been operating a smelter at Owens Lake on ore brought down from Cerro Gordo. Belshaw's first reaction was to let his toll road fall into such neglect that the Owens Lake Company could scarcely bring enough ore to the furnace. It answered by trying to build another road, but found it impossible to get around the strategic canyon occupied by Belshaw's toll house. Then when it took the issue to the County Supervisors, Belshaw got himself voted a member at the next election.

But there was more than one way to fight the bullion king. Allies of the Owens Lake Company bought the San Felipe Mine, which held a conflicting claim to Belshaw and Beaudry's great Union Mine. But they countered by acquiring the San Felipe mortgage, foreclosing, and buying the property at Sheriff's sale. So great was Belshaw's power in Owens Valley that when a

San Felipe man arrived from San Francisco to pay off the indebtedness within the six months allowed by law, the undersheriff refused to take his money.

Believing themselves secure, the bullion kings now told the Owens Lake Company that they "owned the whole hill," and ordered it to quit working its mines. The rival outfit then financed a lawsuit to claim ownership of Belshaw and Beaudry's property. During the "big trial" in 1873, an armed clash was barely averted when Belshaw's miners halted an inspection of the disputed property by force.

Finally the decision went to the San Felipe group, but Belshaw and Beaudry kept the issue in the courts for over two years until their enemies settled for a minor interest in the Union Mine.

By this time the Union's fabulous treasure was failing. In December 1876 Belshaw shut down his furnace, and the following year a severe fire dealt the company a final blow. Cerro Gordo was all but deserted when the last mule team carried a load of bullion down the Yellow Grade in October, 1879.

Since then, more than one new company has tried to strike a new fortune on Buena Vista Peak. Around 1915 a bucket tramway was built to carry ore down the side of the Inyo Range to a narrow gage railroad which had its terminus at Owens Lake. But today Cerro Gordo is a dead camp, with only a few empty buildings remaining to remind visitors of a day when it was L.A.'s Comstock.

.

POINTS OF INTEREST

CERRO GORDO. From the little village of Keeler on the east shore of Owens dry lake, a dirt road heads up into the Inyo Range and Cerro Gordo. The last two-thirds of the eight-mile trip are steep and winding.

Until recently, in the heat of summer, your engine was apt to boil before you reached the town, particularly if you had been experiencing a tailwind on the upward climb. However, the road has been much improved.

As you enter town, the remains of Victor Beaudry's smelter,

and part of the chimney, are standing on your left. In the middle of town is the two-story American Hotel, built in 1871. Thanks to restoration work led by the town's current owner, Jody Stewart, this and other buildings have been preserved. These include what is thought to be Victor Beaudry's General Store. Over the divide at the head of San Lucas Canyon, which heads northeastward into Saline Valley, is the rock furnace of the Owens Lake Company, its shale chimney built for convenience up the face of the slope. Dominating the town are the rebuilt workings of the Union Mine, while the canyon sides above town are still pocked with the remains of the half-caves, half-shacks where the miners once lived. Even over the Buena Vista Peak, the ground is still pitted with craters marking the caved-in mouths of old mines which the visitor would do well to avoid for safety's sake.

SWANSEA. This small locality was the headquarters of Belshaw's rival, the Owens Lake Company. Situated near the old shoreline of Owens Lake a short distance north of Keeler, it is marked today only by the crumbled remains of the brick smelter.

DARWIN. South of Owens Lake in the Coso Range, rich silver-lead deposits were discovered late in October 1874. By the year's end the town of Darwin—named for an early explorer of the region, Dr. Darwin French—had sprung up at the foot of Mount Ophir. One of the first arrivals was Victor Beaudry, who made haste to buy a nearby spring, lay pipes into Darwin and become "water king" of the new camp. Following him were several hundred stampeders from Cerro Gordo and another current Inyo County mining camp, Panamint. More adventurers from the tough Nevada towns of Pioche, Columbus, and Eureka arrived with a sharp eye for claims not held by right of shotgun. Claim holders soon moved out of town and lived in tents on their locations to hold them against the covetous newcomers.

By the end of 1875 Darwin boasted two smelters, some twenty operating mines, 200 frame houses and more than 700 citizens. Every day two Cerro Gordo Freighting Company teams, each equipped with sixteen mules, pulled out of Darwin loaded with silver, skirting Owens Lake to reach the old Cerro Gordo bullion trail at Olancha. Lola Travis took her flock of girls from Cerro Gordo and started a dance hall in Darwin. Heading the fifteen saloons was the Centennial, complete with cut-glass chandeliers and a billiard table advertised as "of the same pattern as used in the Palace Hotel in San Francisco."

Darwin reached its peak in 1876 with five furnaces and more than a thousand inhabitants. The town's wealth was not overlooked by California's fraternity of highwaymen, who robbed the Darwin stages repeatedly in 1875 and '76.

Darwin's decline began in August of 1876 when the Defiance smelter, largest in town, shut down temporarily. An exodus began which rose to a stampede when Bodie and Mammoth City beckoned two years later. Darwin's light would not flicker out, however, without a labor dispute in 1878, wherein the disagreement turned into a general shooting match by all hands.

Today the ghost of Darwin is a collection of rude shacks—few if any of them traceable to the 1870s. In the late 1940s the Anaconda Copper Company revived mining on Mount Ophir, and Darwin provided two-thirds of California's lead output. But the Defiance smelter, with its scattered and rusted machinery, remains the one recognizable landmark of the old town.

OLD COSO. In March 1860 an exploration party from California's Central Valley discovered gold deposits in the Coso Range between Little Lake and what is now Darwin. Reports of the first comers created a modest rush and a new town. Through the summer of 1860 the excitement mounted; the Visalia *Delta* reported, "Parties are leaving almost daily for the mines." Coso was going strong throughout the early 1860s, and when the easiest ores were skimmed by the Americans, Mexican miners experienced in working gold mines arrived in numbers. Through the 1870s Coso was a live camp, though it never numbered more than a few hundred.

Located about seven miles southwest of Darwin, Old Coso is inside the Naval Ordnance Test Station firing range, and therefore inaccessible to the public. Eleven rock houses, using adobe for mortar, are still standing, while others remain in nearby canyons. Some other foundations, Mexican arrastres, and rusted machinery help to mark this century-old ghost town.

CIVIL WAR TOWNS OF OWENS VALLEY

Beginning in 1862 prospectors braved Indian hostilities to make new discoveries in Owens Valley. The first was San Carlos, started in the fall of '62 a few miles north of the present-day Independence, on the east side of Owens River. Two others founded in 1863 were Bend City, three miles south of San Carlos, and Owensville, situated to the north near the present locality of Laws. All were largely adobe or stone walls, which have all but disappeared today. Though they numbered several hundred people between them, they were handicapped by remoteness from the nearest head of "Whoa navigation." Closest stage depots were Visalia in San Joaquin Valley and Aurora in Nevada; from either place you rented a horse and rode on for Owens Valley.

For some two years the excitement lasted. The streets of San Carlos, Bend City, and Owensville rang with the hubbub of mule teams, and occasionally with the staccato of pistol shots. Agitation was begun for a new county seat east of the Sierra and south of Mono County. But by the time it was created by the Legislature in 1866, the mining camps had faded and the farming center of Independence became the seat of Inyo County.

KEARSARGE. In 1863 Secessionists in Owens Valley named their mine (later the Alabama Hills) after the rebel raider, the *Alabama*. In June the U.S.S. *Kearsarge* defeated and sank the *Alabama* off the coast of France. Several Union men, prospecting in the Sierra during the fall of 1864, gave their retort to the Southerners by naming their claim the Kearsarge Mine. Through the mid-1860s the remote camp of Kearsarge flourished; a 40-stamp mill and a number of log cabins were built on the west side of Kearsarge Peak. On March 1, 1867, it came to an abrupt end when a snow avalanche destroyed most of the buildings. That night the population of Kearsarge moved down to Owens Valley. Mining activity continued, but although good ores were worked, the mine never paid for itself and was finally deserted.

Chapter 21. Panamint: A California Legend

A FEW MINING CAMPS stand out beyond their historical context as part of Western folklore: Bodie, Deadwood, Tombstone, and, not least, Panamint. Two books have been written about this fabulous ghost town; one a novel, *The Parson of Panamint*; the other a history with frank excursions into the unhistoric, *Silver Stampede*. Panamint is a necessary fragment of the California legend.

Yet this camp rose and fell in the slight space of three years. Its population never exceeded 2000. As a mineral producer it was a dead loss. And few Californians have any idea where its ghost is located.

The Panamint of history was the California echo of Nevada's Big Bonanza. In 1873 the West Coast was caught in the frenzy over the new silver strike in the Comstock's Con Virginia and California mines. Their owners—Fair, Mackay, Flood and O'Brien—had suddenly become the Bonanza Kings of Western mining. With wild optimism ruling the day, any new silver discovery was hailed as a potential Comstock.

It was on this crisp tinder that the Panamint spark fell. In January of '73, three prospectors poking through the canyons of the Mojave Desert struck silver in the Panamint Range, the western wall of Death Valley. Rock samples showed astounding values ranging from $300 to $3000 per ton. But the discovery was made at the head of Surprise Canyon in remote Panamint Valley, 200 miles from the coast. To translate this kind of ore into cash required two things: transportation and capital.

For more than a year the first Panaminters spent more energy pursuing these two necessities than in digging silver. Finally, in the spring of 1874, they found both. The Los Angeles Chamber of Commerce raised money and built a wagon road to Panamint Valley. Capital was provided by the two Nevada Senators, John P. Jones and William M. Stewart.

Panamint's name suddenly skyrocketed from the fame of these two investors. Stewart was the leading lawyer on the Comstock, the man who had written the Nevada Constitution and literally fathered the 36th state. Jones was a mine superintendent who had gained fame as hero of the terrible Yellow Jacket fire of 1869. More recently he had won new popularity among Nevada miners by outsmarting the California banking interests which had dominated Comstock finance. Knowing of a rich new lead in the Crown Point Mine, he quietly bought up its mining stock and made himself one of Nevada's silver kings.

When the West Coast heard of the latest interest of these "Silver Senators," the stampede to Panamint was on. Through the summer and fall of 1874 desert roads were choked with silver seekers bound for Surprise Canyon. By November no less than seven stages a week were carrying the crowds into Panamint from the direction of Virginia City, San Francisco, Los Angeles and San Bernardino.

In the bottom of Surprise Canyon a rude town was rising from the handiest materials—stone shanties, log cabins built of pinon pines and even frame buildings made from lumber hauled in by mule team at $250 per thousand feet. Of the fifty structures that lined the mile-long street, there were six general stores offering goods at prices ranging from $2 per dozen eggs to $200 per ton of hay; at least twelve saloons, led by the Oriental, whose elegant furnishings were advertised as "the finest on the Coast outside of San Francisco;" a Bank of Panamint; a brewery; a meat market (whose wagon also served as the town hearse); and the office of a small but virile newspaper, the Panamint *News*. The sides of the canyon were dotted with the cabins, tents and caves of the miners, but were too steep to permit wheeled traffic. The mule teams, ox trains and stages kept to the main street, which was made livelier by showers of rock from the hills whenever a new blast was set off in the mines.

Panamint was just about as far from law and order as a California town could get, and so were her citizens. Among them was Ned Reddy, proprietor of the Independent Saloon, who had already killed two men in Owens Valley, supposedly in self-defense. Owner of the Oriental Saloon was Dave Neagle, who had arrived after a shooting scrape in Pioche, Nevada; later, as bodyguard to Justice Stephen Field, he would put a violent end to the violent career of Judge David S. Terry.

But Panamint's quickest gunman was Jim Bruce, professional gambler. The claim that Panamint's Boot Hill was his private cemetery was not quite fair. But two Panaminters did bite the dust before his ready trigger. One of them burst in on him in the boudoir of one of the camp's madames, and was promptly chastened with lead. Another prospector had a shooting argument with Bruce in front of the Bank of Panamint and came out second best. A witness to this second duel was one of the founding fathers, Senator Stewart, who discreetly took refuge behind a stone wall while bullets swept the main street.

It remained for two Nevada stage robbers, John Small and John McDonald, to bring the Robin Hood element to Panamint. Living in nearby Wildrose Canyon, they swaggered Panamint's streets unmolested by the law. On one occasion they journeyed to Nevada, robbed the Eureka stage and wounded the messenger, then returned to their Panamint hideout with the loot.

It was this outlaw pair that sold Senator Stewart one of his biggest Panamint mines. According to his reminiscences, they hung about while his giant stamp mill was being built, inquiring pointedly when he would begin shipping bullion. Finally on June 29, 1875, the great monster was fired up and the twenty stamps began grinding up the ore. When the first silver bullion was tapped from the smelter, the bad men were on hand, armed with six-shooters and sheepish grins.

But the crafty Stewart was ready for them. Out of his smelter rolled silver ingots weighing from four to five hundred pounds each. The bandits abruptly lost their smiles.

"Do you think it's right to play that game on *us?*" one of them demanded with injured pride. "And after we sold you the mine, too. Why, we can't haul away one of those boulders!"

It was Stewart's turn to grin.

"You can't expect *me* to be sorry for you, can you?"

So, while the hard-hearted Senator watched, the robbers

tried to lift one of the silver pigs. It remained stubbornly in place. Then they got a pack mule and tried to heave the thing on his back. With no stomach for the venture, the animal bucked furiously until the men gave up. What was the use of making off with these impossible objects, anyway? Only Stewart's company could cash them in.

For months Small and McDonald had to suffer the torture of watching these silver balls leaving Panamint regularly by Remi Nadeau's mule teams, lurching down Surprise Canyon and across Panamint Valley. Before the cargo could reach Los Angeles and the steamboats which would carry it to the San Francisco mint, it had to traverse 200 miles of lonely desert under no protection but an unarmed driver. But there was nothing Small and McDonald could do about it. The insult was so deflating that on April 20, 1876, they robbed a general store of $2300 and left Panamint for good.

But while Stewart was opening production in Panamint, his Senator partner was on the coast rounding out the enterprise on a grand scale. If Panamint was to be another Comstock, it needed a railroad. And so in September, 1874, John P. Jones rode into Los Angeles and put up $220,000 toward a proposed line from tidewater to the silver country—the Los Angeles and Independence Railroad. Then he visited Santa Monica Bay and bought up three-fourths of the Rancho Santa Monica y San Vicente as a sea-going outlet for his tracks. What was more, Jones contacted the Eastern railroad magnate, Jay Gould, and suggested linking up with his Union Pacific line for a transcontinental connection. Gould agreed informally to meet him halfway, and the Panamint venture became national news.

All this did not suit the Big Four directors of the Southern Pacific—Stanford, Crocker, Huntington and Hopkins. They had their eyes on the Panamint traffic, and were miffed when Jones carefully avoided a connection with their Southern California rails. Worse still would be any linkup which would introduce a competing transcontinental line into California. To the Big Four, such a challenge meant action.

The strategic spot in Jones' master plan was Cajon Pass, where a Los Angeles and Independence survey party had already made preliminary explorations. On January 7, 1875, a band of Southern Pacific men rode into the Cajon to drive their stakes and take possession. But the L.A. & I. had an alert construction engineer—young Joseph U. Crawford. Getting wind of the S.P. move, he took his own crew and headed for the pass the same day. Somewhere along the sandy bottom of Cajon Creek they passed the rival S.P. gang. Knowing the ground from his previous reconnaissance, Crawford rode straight for Toll-gate Canyon—the one spot too narrow for more than one railroad. His men were driving stakes and running lines when the Southern Pacific men arrived. Jones' railroad had won the first round.

Then Huntington of the Southern Pacific tried to stop the upstart railroad with an act of Congress. On January 8 a bill was introduced to give the S.P. an exclusive right-of-way through Cajon Pass. But the Los Angeles people heard of it and deluged Congress with such outraged protest that it dropped the scheme. Huntington soon had to calm his alarmed partners. "I do not think they will hurt us much," he wrote. "I will ventilate their safe harbor."

But Jones had only begun to fight. In July he founded the town of Santa Monica with a grand auction sale of lots. By December the L.A. & I. rails had reached from the bay 14 miles to Los Angeles. And in Cajon Pass his men were digging a tunnel which would give access to the Mojave Desert—and Panamint.

Then things began to happen which deflated Jones' dream. A financial panic swept California and took with it the leading Los Angeles bank, thus hurting stock sales for the L.A. & I. In the accompanying crash of Comstock mining securities, Jones was badly crippled. Then some of the most promising Panamint mines started running out of ore. In the spring of 1876 Jones and Stewart shut down their mill while their miners explored for more raw material. The Panamint venture had suddenly stalled.

Out of Surprise Canyon now trudged a disconsolate horde— miners, stock promoters, merchants with their goods, even the Panamint *News* editor with his hand press and type cases. Nights in Panamint's roaring saloons suddenly went still. Town lots that had sold as high as $1000 could not be given away. By May, 1877, the last company mines were closed and Panamint was a dead camp. Today the reckless miners who once inhabited these hillsides are replaced by jackrabbits and ground squirrels. And the shouts of revelry that used to burst from saloon doors now find echo only in the rustle of wind through the sagebrush on Main Street.

POINTS OF INTEREST

BALLARAT. Taking the road to Death Valley through Trona, the traveler crosses the Slate Range into Panamint Valley. A short side road to the east brings one to Ballarat, a ghost town dating from the 1890s, when gold was discovered in the canyons south of Panamint. Named for the famed Australian gold center, this camp served for several decades as a hell-roaring oasis for Mojave Desert prospectors. Today it is marked by a number of picturesque adobe walls that are crumbling under the elements.

PANAMINT. From Ballarat the visitor continues on a dirt road up the great alluvial fan at the mouth of Surprise Canyon. If conditions are favorable, you can get to the mouth of the canyon before having to proceed for the last few miles on foot. Though cloudbursts have left little of the Panamint that was, the camp still displays many stone walls, a frame house, the brick stamp mill, and a bucket tramway which furnished it with ore from a leading mine.

LOOKOUT. Beginning in 1875 the camp of Lookout flourished in the Argus Range. It was connected by pack trail with its neighboring mines, the Minnietta and Modoc (the latter owned by Senator George Hearst, father of William Randolph Hearst).

Today's tourists find a remnant of this silver boom in the rock charcoal kilns of Wildrose Canyon in the Panamint Range; their product was hauled by Remi Nadeau's mule teams across Panamint Valley for the smelters of the Modoc and Minnietta.

For the traveler of today the Modoc and Minnietta may be reached by driving west on a dirt road from the main north-south highway through Panamint Valley. The Minnietta is located on the south side of Lookout Mountain, while the Modoc is in a deep canyon about a mile away on the east side of the mountain, and requires a short but steep hike from the end of the road. Reaching Lookout is even wilder, since it is perched on top of the mountain above the mines. It requires either a hike of about three miles up an old mule trail from the Modoc, or a roundabout drive via the back of the mountain if you have a jeep. Located on the north slope of eastern Lookout Mountain, it exhibits the remains of some forty buildings in various stages of decay, including half-a-dozen with all the walls still standing.

MILLSPAUGH. South of Maturango Peak on the western slope of the Argus Range is the site of Millspaugh, a short-lived camp that flared just after the turn of the century during the Tonopah-Goldfield era. Almost nothing is left at the location, which could be reached by dirt road from China Lake through Mountain Springs Canyon to Etcheron Valley, then by a dubious and unpredictable road about two-and-a-half miles east of Carricut Dry Lake into the Argus Mountains. But the site is within the Naval Ordnance Test Station range, which is closed to public travel.

Chapter 22. Bodie: Badman's Roost

"AS SOON AS the local talent get to thinking they're tough," a Comstock undertaker once complained, "they go to try it out in Bodie and Bodie undertakers get the job of burying them."

No doubt about it, Bodie was a bad town. It was gloriously rich; it was remote; and its boom in the late '70s was timed to draw a horde of adventurers from Virginia City and other fading Nevada camps. This combination gave meaning to the standard Western phrase, "Bad man from Bodie." One arrival of 1879 noted six fatal shooting scrapes during his first week in town. The daily *Bodie Standard* of September 5, 1880, mentioned three shootings and two stage holdups—apparently an ordinary day's work. A little girl, whose family was leaving the neighboring town of Aurora for the new camp, ended her nightly prayer with: "Goodbye, God; we're going to Bodie!"

According to legend, Bodie owes its discovery to a wounded rabbit and its name to a signpainter's mistake. In 1858 Waterman "Bill" Body, an adventurous Dutchman from New York state, crossed the Sierras from the Mother Lode to reach a new strike at Monoville, a now-forgotten camp near the shore of Mono Lake. The following July, while riding past the townsite of Bodie, he shot and wounded a rabbit. In trying to dig it out of a hole, he discovered something else—gold.

Body never lived to reap the rewards, for he died in a snowstorm while trying to reach his cabin a few months later. But his discovery sparked a mining boom in the Mono country. In August, 1860, the rousing town of Aurora was founded across the border in Nevada. Here it was that a painter is said to have changed Body's name in putting up the sign "Bodie Public Stables." At any rate, Bodie it has been since the early 1860s.

But while Aurora burned brightly during the Civil War, Bodie slumbered. In 1864 one visitor found less than twenty frame and adobe houses in town. Then in the middle '70s two partners paid $950 for what came to be known as the Standard Mine. They barely grubbed out an existence until another accident gave Bodie its tumultuous rebirth. A sudden cave-in exposed a fabulous ore body. The pair took out $37,000 in gold and silver before they sold the mine in 1876 for $65,000.

Meanwhile, the nearby Bodie Mine was languishing—its stock passing at 25 cents a share. Unknown to the owners, the miners had discovered a new vein which skyrocketed its real value. Mysteriously, Bodie Mine stock began to rise. Before its original promoters could buy it back, it had soared to $55 per share. Miners who had taken stock in lieu of wages earned $880 a day; a Chinese launderer came off with $55 for cleaning a shirt. In a month, Bodie yielded $600,000 in ore.

This news shook the West like an alarm bell in the fall of 1877. Miners who had stampeded to every strike from the Mother Lode to Pikes Peak now turned their feet toward Bodie. By February, 1878, the new camp was so overrun that one arrival wrote of the difficulty in finding "even a place to spread one's blankets." Chilling winds, snowstorms and 9000 feet altitude made Bodie a miserable place.

But on they came. By the end of the '78 rush, Bodie had over a hundred buildings of familiar false fronts and wooden awnings, and some three thousand heavy-booted, wide-hatted adventurers. Through her bustling streets moved horsemen and pack burros; twenty-mule freight wagons from as far as Mojave on the Southern Pacific Railroad and Wadsworth on the Central Pacific; and daily and weekly stagecoaches from Carson City, Sonora, Mammoth City and Owens Valley.

In its heyday between 1878 and 1881, Bodie ran full blast round the clock, both above and below ground. Underneath, in the shafts of the Standard, the Bodie, and nearly thirty other mines on the side of famed Bodie Bluff, a total of $25,000,000 was being recovered in gold and silver ore. On top, fortunes were also passing across the bars and gaming tables of the hell-roaring Bonanza, Rifle Club, Champion, and the dozen or so other saloons which graced the main street. At its height Bodie boasted two banks, three breweries, half-a-dozen hotels, a sizable red light district, four daily newspapers, a well-populated Boot Hill, a volunteer fire brigade, and what was claimed as the West's biggest Chinatown after San Francisco's. The boys liked to insist that Bodie had "the widest streets of any Western mining town, the wickedest men, and the worst climate out-of-doors."

From the beginning of its big revival, Bodie was tough and proud of it. One of the earliest and most popular sports was claim-jumping. To settle one dispute in August, 1879, the adjacent Owyhee and Jupiter Mines hired professional gunmen and joined battle in earnest. From two makeshift forts the rival corps carried on an exchange of fire for two days. Then the Jupiter forces tried strategy. One group jumped into the open to draw Owyhee fire while another gained a commanding position on higher ground. With bullets coming through their roof, the Owyhees still managed to hold out until several hundred armed members of the Bodie Miners Union marched up and halted the fight. Each side had lost one man, but it was the Jupiter superintendent and five of his men who were arrested. Their sentence by a vigilante court: twenty-four hours to get out of town. It is said that the Jupiter boss swaggered around Bodie insulting various citizens until the last hour, then jumped in a buggy and wheeled out of town at top speed.

Apparently the original "Bad man from Bodie" was one "Rough and Tumble Jack," who was described by a Nevada newspaper as "one of the roughest and toughest customers ever known." In January, 1878, he was boasting of his physical prowess in a main street bar, claiming to be the undisputed "chief" of Bodie. He went outside with one challenger, and the two coolly drew guns at a distance of two feet and unloaded them at each other. Back into the bar reeled Rough and Tumble Jack. The other, with one arm shattered, reloaded his gun by holding it between his knees. A moment later Jack got a second dose which proved sufficient to end the career of Bodie's first bad man.

After that shootings—usually unpunished—were weekly and sometimes daily occurrences. The camp's better citizens stood the bombardment until New Year's Eve, 1879, when one celebrant objected to another dancing with his wife, and got a fatal bullet for his effort. This was too much, even for Bodie. A vigilance committee took the culprit from his jail cell, hustled him down Bodie's main street to the scene of the crime, and hung him on a makeshift gallows. The one voice raised against the affair was that of a former Attorney General of Nevada. He took the hint and rode out of town, however, after one of the vigilantes cried, "Get a rope and we'll hang you!"

Not that Bodie meant to flout the law. A hearing was held on the lynching—with the jury including the leader of the vigilantes and the one who had applied the noose! As for the original shooting: "Case dismissed, as the defendant was taken out and hanged by a mob."

Bodie's one lynching had no noticeable effect on its bad men. In fact, they soon turned their attention to the Concord stages which rocked out of town every day groaning with gold and silver bullion. The cliff-lined canyon through which it passed between Bodie and Aurora was made to order for banditry. During 1880 enterprising road agents stopped the Bodie stage no less than six times. On two days they robbed the upstage, then waited for the downstage and robbed it, too.

Wells Fargo Express was getting its fill. It soon began putting on two or more guards when a heavy consignment was shipped, transferring stage passengers to a light wagon which followed at a safe distance through the canyon. Before the last double holdup the company brought in its crack shotgun messenger, Mike Tovey—a Canadian who was shy of manner but not of nerve. On the afternoon of September 5, while Bodie still buzzed with news of the morning holdup, Tovey and a second guard rode the downstage while the passenger wagon brought up the rear. Near the scene of the first robbery, Tovey got out and walked ahead. Undaunted by this precaution, two robbers fired a volley at the guard. He then retreated to the stage and cut loose at the advancing enemy with a shotgun. One bandit was killed outright and the other was frightened away. But while Tovey went to a nearby house to get a wounded arm dressed, the surviving robber came back and rode off with Wells Fargo's treasure chest.

Successes of the road agents failed to make a dent in Bodie's high prosperity. No extravagance was too great, no celebration too extreme, for this riotous camp. In 1879 someone remembered that old Bill Body's remains lay down the canyon in an unmarked grave. "Poor old Body!" said the boys. Nothing was too good for the town's noble founder! A search was launched forthwith, and his bones were brought back in triumph. For days they were on public exhibit, subject to handling and close scrutiny by every civic-minded citizen. On November 1, 1879, amidst much speech-making (and doubtless elbow-bending) Bill Body's bones were laid to rest in Boot Hill.

What, then, of a suitable monument to Bodie's founder? For months the camp waited while an elaborate headstone was ordered and hauled in by twenty-mule team. But when it arrived the month was September, 1881, and Bodie was stunned by news of President Garfield's death by assassination. Nothing was too good for the nation's martyred President! The monument was erected as a memorial, and Bill Body's bones remained in a transplanted, but still forgotten grave. Bodie's heart was big, but it was not always constant.

Meanwhile, boisterous Bodie was about to gain the ultimate

feature of all top-notch mining camps—a railroad. Since 1880 the narrow-gauge Carson and Colorado, a branch of the Virginia and Truckee, had been inching southward across Nevada sands. In its march toward California's Owens Valley it would come no nearer to Bodie than some forty miles. This plan was hardly acceptable in that proud camp. Accordingly another branch was begun in the spring of 1881 to connect Bodie with Benton, a mining town situated next to the Carson and Colorado route. Practical purpose of the road was to supply Bodie's deep-growing mines with timbers from fresh forests south of Mono Lake. But its name was the Bodie and Benton, and the owners also aimed to make rail connection with the outside world.

When the boys found that Chinese laborers were being imported for the work, their enthusiasm suddenly dimmed. Since the 1850s, intolerance of Chinese had been rife on the Coast, particularly since they were a source of cheap labor. At a rousing meeting in the Miners Union Hall, the boys resolved to carry out the popular slogan, "the Chinese must go!" A rough and not altogether sober mob, traveling by wagon, horseback, and foot, moved toward the work camp east of Mono Lake.

But messengers for the railroad had ridden ahead with the warning. Immediately the Chinese were placed in boats and carried to an island in the middle of Mono Lake. When the Bodie bad men arrived, they found the camp deserted and their intended victims protected by several miles of inhospitable brine. The unholy crusade thereupon collapsed. For the next full day the ragged army was dragging back into town, somewhat sobered after a forty-mile round trip. Thereafter the Mono fiasco was a moot subject in Bodie.

As for the railroad, its Chinese workmen went back on the job undisturbed. By November, 1881, they completed 31½ miles to the Mono timber stands, which is as far as the road ever got. Over its rugged grades, sometimes as steep as six percent, soon chugged a quartet of quaint little engines with quaint little names—"Mono," "Inyo," "Yolo," and "Como."

Bodie had its railroad, but its halcyon days were numbered. When a rumor reached the Mono County Supervisors that Bodie's mines might falter, they promptly decided that there was no time to lose in building the new courthouse at Bridgeport, the county seat. With a stiff six-and-a-half percent tax levied on all property (chief of which was Bodie's Standard Mine), they erected the new building in 1881. The elegant Victorian structure, carefully maintained ever since, stands today as probably the most picturesque county courthouse in California—a monument to the Standard Mine.

By 1882 Bodie's noontide had passed, and the boys were soon deserting her for new silver strikes in Arizona and Colorado. After Bodie mining stocks crashed the following year, the town faded fast. The Standard was merged with the Bodie in 1887 and continued to run intermittently, but the truth was that the camp's underground treasure was largely exhausted. It was the old familiar saga—a rich strike, an uproarious stampede, an hour of frenzied triumph, and afterward the shell of a town standing in ghostly silence.

One man who would not believe that the camp was dead was Jim Cain, an original arrival of the late '70s. Living in Bodie with his family, he gradually bought up the mines and buildings until he virtually owned the town. For years he opened the Bank of Bodie every day at 10 a.m.—when the only possible customers were the ground squirrels which scampered across the grass on the main street. When surfaced highways brought Bodie within the reach of motorists in the 1920s, old Jim Cain showed off his ghost town to wondering tourists, always assuring them that Bodie would come back.

POINTS OF INTEREST

BODIE. Until 1932, when a fire swept away two-thirds of the business district, this was probably the best preserved wooden ghost town in the Far West. Enough buildings remain, including the Miners Union Hall, the Protestant Church, the Fire House, and several former saloons, to make Bodie well worth the thirteen-mile side trip from Highway 395 south of Bridgeport. The many deserted houses on the side streets, plus the sizable cemetery on the hill to the northwest, testify that this was once a populous town. The workings of the Standard Mine, located on the slope of Bodie Bluff, are fenced off from sightseers because of the danger of falling down one of the many shafts in the area.

The State Division of Beaches and Parks now maintains the townsite as a State Historical Monument, and rangers are available to answer questions about this ghost town prototype. With their help, Bodie will be preserved from further decay. Today, from her warped board walks to her sagging false fronts, Bodie still keeps her reckless and truculent air.

MASONIC. A mile north of Bridgeport, a dirt road branches northeastward through Rock Spring Canyon to Sonoma in Nevada. On the way is the small camp of Masonic, nine miles from pavement in California, seven miles from pavement in Nevada. While the district had previously been prospected for a number of years, the first big discovery was not made until 1902, and substantial production of gold ore began in 1907. Located in three clusters of population along the road on the north slope of Masonic Mountain, the town still has a number of cabins standing. The Nevada approach is best.

CAMERON. This old gold camp, which was at its height in 1882-3, is located twelve miles north of Bridgeport via Highway 22 and four miles west on a poor and unpredictable dirt road through part of Frying Pan Canyon. Almost nothing remains standing. Other nearby camps, even more obscure today, are Star City, located a mile-and-a-half northwest of Cameron by trail; Clinton, three miles north of Cameron near the mouth of Ferris Canyon (also accessible by trail); and Belfort, located in Boulder Flat about two-and-a-half miles west of Star City by trail.

DOGTOWN. On Highway 395, six-tenths of a mile south of the dirt turnoff to Bodie, one reaches the nearest auto point to Dogtown, located a few hundred yards off the road. In 1857 Mormons found gold here and started the first mining excitement in Mono County. Fortune-seekers came in from the Mother Lode and founded a town that today is marked by little more than piles of sand placered in Dogtown Creek.

MONOVILLE. Near the foot of the Conway Grade, a big canyon to the east reveals the general site of Monoville, where gold was discovered by a miner from Dogtown in 1859. A small rush from the Southern Mines set in over Mono and Sonora Passes, bringing seven hundred men to Monoville within a few months. The town never became big and boisterous like some of its neighbors, but the excitement led to demands by the new population for another county separate from Calaveras County. As a result, Mono County was created in 1861. However, the population dwindled to 430 by the census of 1870, and Mono County had to wait for the Bodie stampede to regain a respectable population. Little remains to show the site of Monoville excepting the Sinnamon Cut, where a golden fortune was mined by hydraulic monitors.

AURORA. The dedicated ghost towner will want to attempt a fourteen-mile drive on a generally-bad road east of Bodie to the historic old town of Aurora. Located inside Nevada, Aurora could conceivably be classed among California mining camps, since it was the seat of Mono County until a boundary survey proved it to be outside of California. Founded in 1860, Aurora had two newspapers, a population of several thousand, and a dramatic vigilance committee episode. The town is completely deserted, and would still be in excellent condition but for the work of commercial operators who were allowed to haul most of the bricks away. Even the old cemetery, dating to Civil War days, has been desecrated by souvenir hunters. They have stolen the gravestones and headboards of loved ones whose children and grandchildren still live in California and Nevada.

Chapter 23. Mammoth: Timberline Treasure

LOST MINES hold a fond place in Western tradition, and California has contributed more than its share. Of these, none has surpassed the famous "Lost Cement Mine," which sent a small army of prospectors combing the Mono country for over two decades. They never fulfilled their quest, but in the process they founded several roaring camps in the High Sierra and opened up a scenic wonderland—Mammoth Lakes.

Like most legends, the story of the Lost Cement Mine has several versions. Mark Twain's account, recorded in *Roughing It*, is as good as any. In the early '50s three German brothers joined the Gold Rush and reached the Sierra somewhere in the Mono country. While resting in a canyon they found a vein of cement "shot full of lumps of dull yellow metal." It was two-thirds pure gold! Loading themselves with rock samples, they covered up the vein, made a map of the location and struck on again over the mountains. Two of them died on the gruelling trek, and the third reached the Mother Lode settlements so worn out that he never ventured back to find his mine. But he gave his map and the samples to a miner named Whiteman, who journeyed over the mountains and spent the rest of his life searching for the cement mine.

Mark Twain came to Nevada's Esmeralda mines, across the state border from the Mono country, in the early 1860s. In the mining camp of Aurora he got "one accidental glimpse" of Whiteman, who displayed a chunk of cement given him by the German. "Lumps of virgin gold," said Mark, "were as thick in it as raisins in a slice of fruit cake."

From time to time, word went through town that Whiteman had appeared—in disguise, of course—and the camp would be thrown into a frenzy. The universal object was to follow the miner and his map to the lost mine. Wrote Mark: "I have known it reported at eleven at night, in a large mining-camp, that Whiteman had just passed through, and in two hours the streets, so quiet before, would be swarming with men and animals. Every individual would be trying to be very secret, but yet venturing to whisper to just one neighbor that W. had passed through. And long before daylight—this in the dead of winter—the stampede would be complete, the camp deserted, and the whole population gone chasing after W."

This, if we may believe Mark Twain, was the state of mind in the border country south of Lake Tahoe in the '60s and '70s.

In June, 1877, a group led by James A. Parker discovered a wide ledge of silver-gold ore on Gold or Red Mountain east of

Lake Mary. According to custom, they announced it as "the largest bonanza outside of Virginia City." By August, a Comstock company had optioned it for $40,000, and before mountain snows melted in the spring of 1878, had sent in a crew of miners and ordered a 40-stamp mill.

This kind of news sent a miner's heart leaping, and the stampede was on. From the mining camp of Benton, on the route between Owens Valley and Bodie, a wagon road was hurriedly built to the Mammoth mines. Another branch was constructed from Bishop Creek to the lake country by J. L. C. Sherwin, and the famous highway switchbacks over the toughest part of this route are still known as the Sherwin Grade. By April, 1878, an upper Owens Valley resident described the passing traffic: "Men bound for the lake district . . . pass through here daily. Some go afoot, others horseback while a few navigate by vehicles."

One of the earliest to arrive was General George S. Dodge, a noted California mining investor. Owners of one of the mines showed him their property, offered ore samples and quoted assay figures. Dodge sat down on a pine stump in the main street and looked up a thousand feet to the Mammoth outcroppings. "I don't want to know how rich they are," he answered. "They'll do for a deal anyhow."

With this bold optimism, General Dodge bought the mine for $30,000 in cash and mining stock, giving another spurt to the Mammoth boom. For the next two years the district rode high on California's wave of mining excitement. In the spring of 1878, lots were occupied and fenced for a mile up the single street, with at least 20 log houses under construction. By 1879, it had two newspapers, two breweries, six hotels, six general stores and twenty-two saloons. A thousand people had arrived, and town lots of 25-foot frontage were selling at $1500.

In April, 1879, the Mammoth mine reached ore which was said to be "half gold," and excitement raged still higher. Mammoth Mine stock jumped from $3 to $15 a share. Reported one newcomer:

"The main street here is a jam of men and teams coming in from all parts and loaded with every conceivable article."

Travel into this remote camp was by three methods, each

from a different direction. Freight arrived by twenty-mule team over a wearisome trek of 220 miles from Mojave, on the Southern Pacific Railroad. Passengers came by a tri-weekly coach from Benton, which connected with stages from Nevada's Carson City, 150 miles away. Californians who cared to rough it by a more direct route could leave the stage at Fresno Flats (now Oakhurst), south of Yosemite, and take the saddle train 55 miles over the ridge of the Sierra. This approach was not recommended for those with bad nerves or a short temper.

But for at least four months of the year, Mammoth was completely snowbound. In this grim season most houses were buried in snow, with entry made by burrowing down to the front door. All travel was by skis, which the Mammothites called "snowshoes." There were no horses in camp, and as one resident put it, "we couldn't use them if they were here."

To add to this handicap, Mammoth was dogged with bad luck. In hauling in machinery for the stamp mill, the huge boiler offered the toughest problem. It was carried by rail from San Francisco to Mojave, then carefully transferred to one of Nadeau's twenty-mule team freight wagons. Then for 10 or 12 days it was pulled across the Mojave Desert and through Owens Valley.

Finally, the plodding animals reached the Sherwin Grade— a day's haul from Mammoth City. As they labored upward to the tune of cracking blacksnake and jingling chains, the wagon toppled over and the boiler crashed into the canyon below. No amount of straining and swearing could haul the stubborn object back up to the road, and at last report it lay there still.

Mammoth finished its stamp mill—after further delay. But an even bigger problem was getting the ore from the mine down the dizzy 3500-foot decline to the mill. The miners built a trestle, which blew down in the first heavy wind. Next came a chute lined with sheet-iron, but the first carload smashed it to splinters. Then they erected a covered tramway; on the starting ride, the car jumped the track at the first curve and cracked up. The structure was remodeled, but soon a car got out of control on an icy track and almost killed the brakeman. Mule power was installed on a more level section of the route, but another Sierra breeze blew the mule from the track. After that it was reported that mountain storms were slowing production. Apparently the reason was that whenever a wind rose in the canyon the mule laid down until it passed.

Under such misfortunes, the Mammoth company had spent some $385,000 by early 1880, and had produced an estimated $200,000 in silver and gold. This was less than satisfactory to the stockholders, and the whole works shut down for good. A snowshoe army marched out of Mammoth, and by the spring break-up, the camp was deserted. Nobody has yet found the mine with gold as thick as raisins in a fruit cake.

POINTS OF INTEREST

MAMMOTH CITY. At first glance, little remains of Mammoth City as one drives down the old Mammoth Road from Twin Lakes. But high on the side of Gold Mountain one can see the tailings of the Mammoth Mine. Beyond the willow thicket that lines the road are the remains of a small mill built by a later investor in the 1890s. Alongside the road on the south are two log cabins, both of them containing a few of the cut nails (along with many wire nails of later vintage) that indicate construction prior to about 1885-90. On the north side of the road are the real remains of the town. Among the pines and up the slope, hidden by thick manzanita, are many stone foundations and a few stone walls. Only a hike among these ruins can give any idea of the real size of Mammoth City in its heyday.

PINE CITY. Unrecognizable today, Pine City was situated alongside Lake Mary near the junction of the Lake George and Lake Mary roads.

MILL CITY. About half-a-mile below Mammoth City, the road winds among the pines and goes by a camp ground on the left. Entering the campground and driving to its southwestern corner, one may go a little farther among some summer houses before the road ends. A short walk on a plain trail beyond this point brings one into a clearing—the site of Mill City.

Dominating the scene are the remains of the Mammoth Mining Company's forty-stamp mill, including the stone foundation and a huge flywheel perhaps twenty feet in diameter. Clearly painted on the wheel in two places are the letters: "M.M. Co., Care of C.G.F. Co., Mojave." This forwarding address marked there by a Southern Pacific Railroad freight agent may be translated: "Mammoth Mining Company, Care of Cerro Gordo Freighting Company, Mojave"—the latter being the freighting outfit operated by Remi Nadeau, with headquarters at Mojave after the Southern Pacific line was finished from San Francisco to Los Angeles. Among the aspens and pines on the hill above the millsite are the sunken foundations of other houses that made up Mill City.

BENTON. A silver camp, Benton dates from the 1860s and played an important role in Mono County mining life during the bonanza heyday of Bodie and Mammoth. From Bishop, take U.S. Highway 6 north for thirty-four miles to Benton Station, once a depot on the old Carson and Colorado Railroad from Nevada. Then turn west four miles to Benton itself, now a sleepy village in striking contrast to its turbulent past. Still remaining are a few historic buildings and the cemetery, which can be pointed out to the visitor from the town's general store.

LUNDY. In 1879, gold was discovered near the west end of Lundy Lake, a few miles from Mono Lake, in what became the Homer Mining District. Here sprang the mining camp of Lundy, famous for its timberline mines, snow avalanches and a hilarious newspaper, the *Homer Mining Index.*

The latter was edited by a character known as "Lying Jim Townsend," said to have been the inspiration for Bret Harte's *Truthful James.* He specialized in puffing up the size of the town for the benefit of British mine investors. Lundy was small, even for the Sierra camps, but the *Mining Index* carried ads for two banks, a railroad timetable and writeups of gay first nights at the theater.

But there was nothing imaginary about Lundy's snowslides. Two resolute miners had their cabin buried by avalanches in two successive winters. Six feet of snow fell on Lundy in March, 1882, starting a whole series of slides. One mountain of snow dropped several thousand feet and covered three cabins, whose occupants were later rescued. Another miner lay in bed one night worrying over warnings from friends in town; he rose and started for Lundy, and was scarcely out of the way when a snowslide buried his shack.

Located at the west end of Lundy Lake, the old camp today includes several old stone and frame buildings—a few of early vintage—and a number of rock foundations. The May Lundy Mine, which is said to have produced $2,000,000 in gold before it was shut down in 1898, may be seen high up on the mountainside to the south.

TIOGA (Bennettville). Near the top on the west side of Mt. Excelsior, north of Tioga Pass, is the Sierra ghost town of Tioga or Bennettville. Its mining history dates to 1860, when the first silver claim was made by some adventurer who strayed off the beaten paths of the California Gold Rush. In 1878 the Tioga Mining District was organized, eastern capital was soon forthcoming, and a crude town sprang up at an altitude of nearly 12,000 feet.

But though the silver ore was there for the taking, the trick was to get it refined and transported from its remote Sierra perch. Milling machinery was sledded in from Lundy to the east. A road was built over the Sierra from the Southern Mines. A long tunnel was driven to tap the silver ledge. But the eastern capital ran out and in July 1884 the whole operation was shut down. Picks were left in the tunnel and miners' plates abandoned at the table in the mess hall. Tioga was a mining town that never mined an ounce of silver. But it did spark the first road over Tioga Pass—one that was later taken over by the National Park Service for the benefit of vacationers bound to Tuolumne Meadows.

SILVER MOUNTAIN. One of the first real strikes made in the High Sierra was at Silver Mountain, located east of Ebbet Pass near the headwaters of the Carson River. In 1863, when the main Silver Mountain discovery was made, the Comstock boom was at its height and California was ready to believe any new silver strike a potential bonanza. Miners from the Mother Lode stampeded over the old Ebbet Pass emigrant road, paralleling the Stanislaus River. Soon stages began running from the Southern Mines as far as Silver Valley, west of the summit, whence a saddle train carried passengers the remaining miles to Silver Mountain.

"As we descend the canyon from the summit," wrote an early arrival of August, 1863, "suddenly a bright new town bursts into view. There are perhaps forty houses, all new. . . . This log shanty has a sign up, *Variety Store;* the next, a board shanty the size of a hogpen, is *Wholesale & Retail Grocery;* that shanty without a window, with a canvas door, has a large sign of *Law Office;* and so on to the end. . . . Tunnels and drifts are being sunk, and every few minutes the booming sound of a blast comes to the ear like a distant leisurely bombardment."

In these first days the camp was seized with silver fever. Hundreds of miners were "scampering like a nest of disturbed ants"; mining terms—"lode," "indications," "rich rock"—were heard on all sides; speculation was raging in town lots. "Nearly everyone," observed the visitor, "is, in his belief, in the incipient stage of immense wealth."

Despite such bursting confidence, Silver Mountain never rivaled Virginia City. But together with the neighboring camp of Monitor, it drew enough population to form the new county of Alpine in 1864. By 1875, the county seat had shifted from Silver Mountain to Markleeville, and the old camp was deserted by the mid-'80s.

Today the remains of Silver Mountain lie along the bank of Silver Creek on a remote dirt road a few miles south of Markleeville. The most substantial ruins are the old jail and the home of Lord Lewis Chalmers, an English mine developer who threw in his lot with Silver Mountain in her palmiest days. Also intact is the old Alpine County courthouse, but its present location is at Markleeville, where it was moved from Silver Mountain in the 1880s.

MONITOR. Six miles southeast of Markleeville, Highway 89 goes eastward over Monitor Pass to meet U.S. Highway 395.

On Monitor Creek west of the pass is a locality called Loope on the maps, but is actually the site of the old mining town of Monitor. Flourishing throughout the 1860s and '70s, Monitor was big enough to support a weekly newspaper, the *Alpine Miner*. Today practically nothing is left of the old camp. Two miles up Loope Canyon is the site of Mogul, another mining town of the same period. The mines of the Monitor-Mogul district produced silver and copper, with some gold.

PART VI. GHOST CAMPS
OF THE SOUTH

THE MINING TOWNS of *Southern California, not to be confused with the Southern Mines of the Mother Lode, spanned almost the entire mineral era of California. In fact, from the first Kern River excitement in 1854 to the Death Valley camps of the early 1900s, they covered nearly the whole period of the nation's mining frontier.*

Moreover, they were located in scattered spots throughout the region—in the southern Sierras, the Sierra Madres, the Colorado and Mojave Deserts—even in the Coast Range, which was singularly barren through most of California. They simply proved, again, that "gold is where you find it."

For these reasons the Southern California camps fall into no neat category. But in their entirety they represent the whole saga of Western gold and silver mining. Most of them rose and fell like a flash flood in a desert canyon. More than in the North, they are today abandoned—all except a very few such as Julian that turned to other activities.

Due to neglect and the ravages of wind, sun, and rainstorm, most of them are nearly obliterated. In the pinon pines and the sagebrush of Southern California, cracked and rusted ruins remain as monuments to the jackass prospector—the man with sand in his boots and the sun in his eyes.

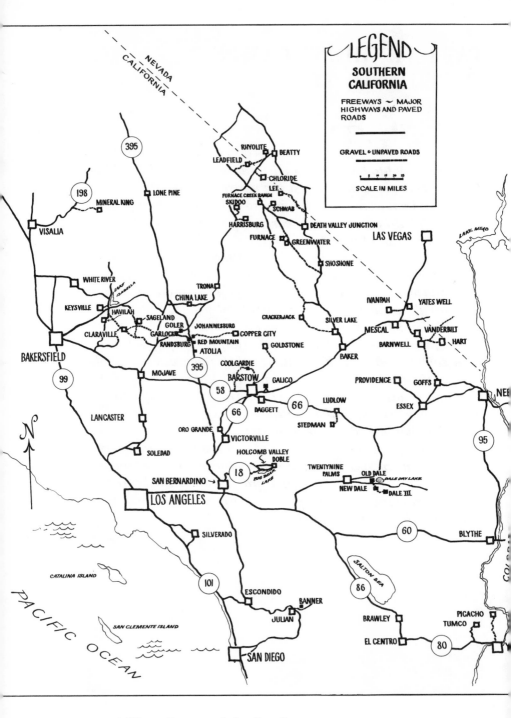

Long mule-team loading ore at the Silver King Mine, Calico, in the 1880's.

Sprawling on the side of Rand Mountain in the 1890's, Randsburg was Southern California's biggest gold strike.

Randsburg miners had champagne tastes and champagne pockets to match. Helping to celebrate Flag Day in 1896 is the discoverer of the Yellow Aster Mine, F. M. Mooers, fourth from left.

*In 1907 all roads led to Skidoo—California's
last big gold rush.*

*Lonely, desolate Borate, center of the Calico Mountain
borax excitement of the late 1880's.*

*From birth to death in 10 short years was the fate of Skidoo
—Southern California's Coloma of the early 1900's.*

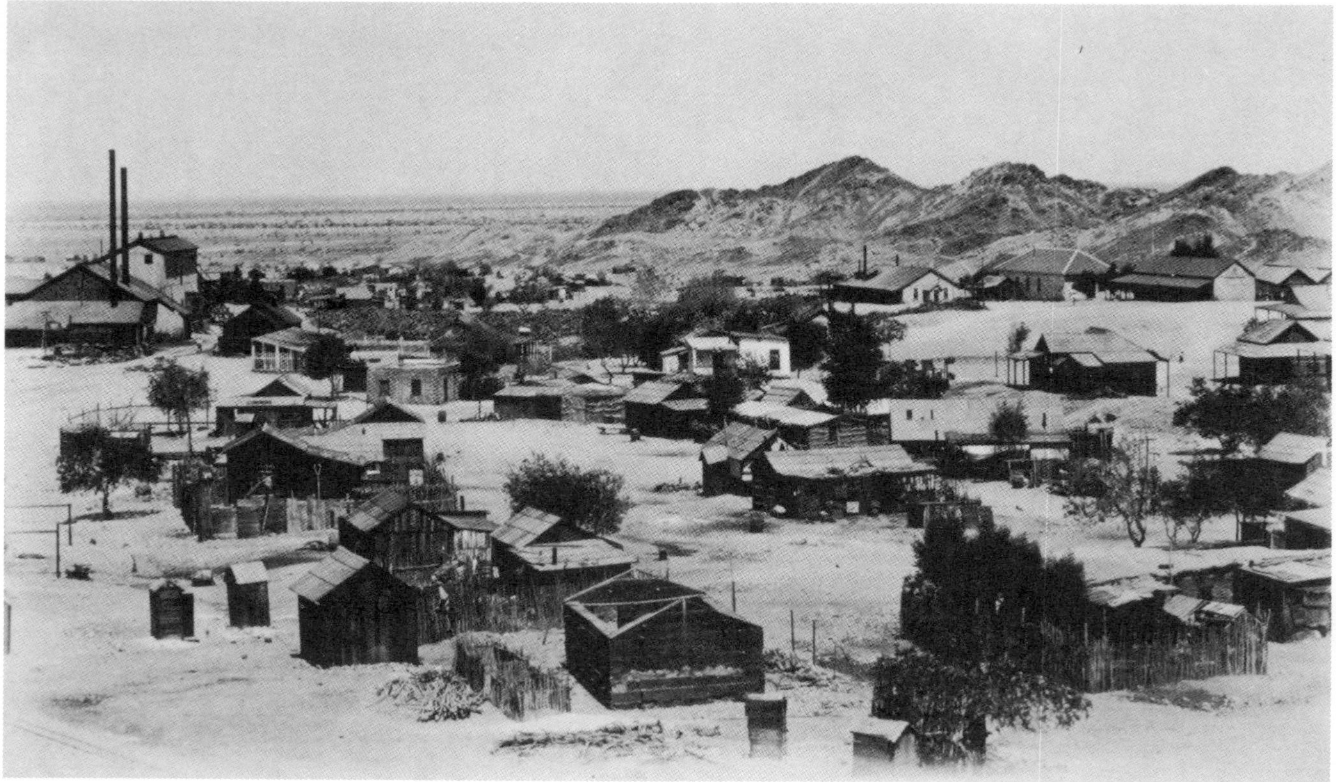

Courtesy of Title Insurance & Trust Co.

Chapter 24. The Kern River Camps

LITTLE REMAINS in the Kern River country to show for the early days of gold. Much of what there was is now under water backed up by Isabella Dam, southern anchor in the Central Valley Project. But the sites of the old camps of Keysville and Havilah are still accessible over bumpy dirt roads for the true California ghost town hunter.

Today the Kern County empire, with its capital at Bakersfield, is made up largely of cotton and oil. But in the gold era the valley was a worthless plain, and population in the thousands inhabited the mountain section of Kern River and its South Fork. For the Kern was really Southern California's first mining rush. In one brief moment it was the biggest mining news in a state that was gloriously and proudly gold-crazy.

It all began in the summer of 1854, when California was suffering the first setback after the high tide of the Gold Rush. The placers were failing, the shift to quartz mining had only begun, and depression was creeping over the state. Southern California, which had boomed as the supplier of beef cattle for the mines, was returning to the pre-Yankee spirit of *poco tiempo*.

At this receptive moment came the cry of gold from Kern River. A party of Argonauts had found it near the junction of the Kern and its South Fork. By August 130 men were on the ground, taking out from $10 to $25 apiece per day. One of them picked up a 2½-pound nugget. As if this news was not enough, the report passed through the Mother Lode that a Mexican from Kern River had flourished a bag of nuggets on the streets of Mariposa and told his listeners of hills "yellow with outcroppings."

Quickly, Southern California editors seized on Kern River as proof of the mineral wealth which they had long claimed for the neglected South. In December the matter was settled when an Angeleno wrote from Kern River that "there is no doubt of there being a plenty of gold here. . . . The only difficulty is that we have no provisions."

Provisions? L.A.'s merchants saw their signal. Here was the

end of Southern California's doldrums. A second Gold Rush—and Los Angeles was to be its San Francisco!

In 1854 there was no wagon road directly North from Los Angeles. This didn't stop the Angelenos. The dynamic Phineas Banning, local stage and freight king, drove a coach out of Los Angeles to prove the route was feasible. The first obstacle was the formidable Fremont Pass, just beyond San Fernando Valley. Here his passengers got out and walked while Banning's horses fought their way to the top. Down the other side plunged a rugged brush-covered gulch at a near-perpendicular angle.

Against the pleas of his comrades, Banning urged his team over the edge with the retort that a driver who couldn't negotiate that hill "should confine himself to ox teaming in the valley." Over they toppled, crashing headlong at the bottom of the pass. Feverishly the passengers scrambled down and pulled Banning from the wreckage.

"Didn't I tell you?" beamed the stageman. "A beautiful descent, far less difficult than I had anticipated."

In this spirit, Los Angeles got through to Kern River. Her merchants raised money to fix the worst spots in a new road which led over Fremont Pass, up San Francisquito Canyon, past the Army fort at Tejon Pass, and as far as the mouth of Kern River Canyon as it emerges into San Joaquin Valley. From this point a pack trail led through the rugged Kern River gorge for the last thirty miles to the mines. By early February, 1855, Banning was sending regular six-horse stages and ten-mule freight wagons to Kern River. Accompanying them were two express lines and a virtual horde of gold seekers.

For Southern California had now caught the fever. Raising dust through the streets of Santa Barbara, Los Angeles and San Bernardino were miners and storekeepers, wagon trains and pack burros, herds of cattle and bands of sheep.

"Picks, pork, shovels, hard bread and pans are at a premium," wrote a Santa Barbara citizen.

"Our public houses are crowded with strangers," said the Los Angeles *Star*, "although every kind of conveyance is called into requisition to get to the diggings."

"Through the entire distance," observed one Argonaut, "one cannot lose sight of men, teams and cattle."

By early March the editor of the Los Angeles *Southern Californian* lost his head in the frenzy.

"Stop the Press!" he wrote. "Glorious News from Kern River! Bring out the Big Guns! There are a thousand gulches rich with gold and room for ten thousand miners."

Northern California kept its head until steamers from the South began bringing news of the mining craze. On February 12 the *Goliah* reached San Francisco with word the miners were making up to $50 per day. Over 2000 men were on the ground and more were on the way from as far as Sonora, Mexico.

The skeptical North could hold itself no longer. Next day the *Goliah* pulled out of San Francisco jammed with rainbow hunters. A party of riders left the Bay the same day by the overland route. By early March river steamers—some of them decked with huge signs, "Kern River"—were puffing out of Sacramento and other northern points loaded to the guards. Then they descended on Stockton, head of navigation on the San Joaquin. Into this bustling center—her streets and stores suddenly alive with men—converged steamboats, freight wagons and stagecoaches. It was '49 all over again. "Ho! for Kern River!" shouted the men of '55. "Kern River or Bust!"

South from Stockton the crowds took a wagon road that entered the Sierras by way of White River and came to an end at Posey Flat. In the last thirty miles over Greenhorn Mountain they pressed on by foot or horseback.

Life in this new Kern country of rocky hills and scrub junipers followed the Mother Lode pattern. At the main settlement of "Forks of the Kern," miners slept in tents, worked all day carrying ore to be washed at the river in their long toms, paid exorbitant prices for food and tools. Living far from ordered society, the miners observed no law but their own consciences. One storekeeper was shot and killed, according to the report, "because he refused to sell a man a pair of pants on credit." When foreign miners—French, Spaniards and Mexicans—arrived, the hostile Americans refused to let them stake out the best ground.

But by early spring it was apparent that nobody was going to gain a fortune on Kern River. Gold was there, though not in quantities which made the trip worthwhile. Denouncing the whole excitement as a Los Angeles promotion scheme, disheartened miners drifted back into the settlements and dampened the Kern River fever. By May only a few hundred men remained where as many as five thousand had crowded in scarcely a month before. One eyewitness summed up the dismal scene: "Provisions, tools, bad whisky and vicious rattlesnakes . . . in all directions."

The Los Angeles papers tried to bolster the gold boom by fairly pleading with the miners to stay on the Kern. "Two or even one dollar per day," said the *Star*, "is far better employment than to come back here and loaf around our grog shops." But it was no use; Southern California's dream of mining glory had vanished. The Kern River "humbug" became a laughing stock in the Northern gold fields. A stray horse wandering through Sacramento had a derisive sign tied to his rear: "Bound for Kern River."

Still, the Kern country's golden days were not over. A rich ledge which was one of the sources of the gold placers had been discovered in a side ravine by one Captain Richard Keys as early as 1854. Near his Keys Mine grew a rustic frontier town named Keysville, first American community in what is now Kern County. Without formal streets, its rough wooden stores were scattered at random over the shallow hillslope, while miners' cabins dotted the mountainside above. Through the late '50s this was one of the most remote settlements in California—110 miles to the nearest town of Visalia in one direction, 140 miles to Los Angeles in another. Most supplies came in over the northern route, and were packed over Greenhorn Mountain until 1856. The first wagons on the trail from Posey Flat had to follow the ridges and canyon bottoms while one teamster went ahead and chopped down trees with an axe. Teams were doubled going up the steepest mountains, while wagons were held back on the downhill run by dragging trees behind. First wagon to arrive in the Kern mining country was lowered by rope down the mountainside into Keysville. One visitor called it "the hardest wagon road I have ever seen that was much traveled."

In 1856 this far-off settlement found itself in the midst of an

Indian war. The tribes of San Joaquin Valley had taken the warpath, and most of Keysville's able-bodied men rode out to help put down the uprising. Just over Greenhorn Mountain a party of miners killed five Indians in cold blood; the infuriated natives then proclaimed war on all the whites in the Southern Sierras—of which Keysville was the chief settlement. Around May 1 its people heard that some five hundred Indians had gathered at the mouth of the Kern for an assault on the town.

Keysville was thrown into panic. With most of her men away, she was left with only sixty defenders. Wielding picks and shovels, they hurriedly dug an earth "fort" on a prominent knoll near the lower edge of town. To the commander of Fort Tejon and the Los Angeles sheriff they sent riders in quest of arms, ammunition and reinforcements.

"We have fortified ourselves and will defend ourselves if they make an appearance," ran one message.

From Fort Tejon came a troop of cavalry, which found no Indians on the Kern, but came on anyway and occupied Keysville. In Los Angeles the citizens held a meeting to raise a rescue company, but before they could act the Indian scare had subsided.

In April 1863, when Indian fighting was intense in Owens Valley, a relief company of cavalry was sent over Walker Pass. On the way the troopers stopped at Keysville and learned that a party of Indians was encamped several miles to the north. Advancing in the dark, they surrounded and captured the village, separated thirty-five of the grown males, and then coolly murdered them. It later turned out that the victims of this foul massacre were peaceable Indians who had refused to war against the whites. Reported the captain, proudly, "Not a soldier injured."

As early as 1860 Kern mining was branching out beyond Keysville. A miner bearing the unenviable name of "Lovely" Rogers struck out from Keysville on a prospecting trip and lost his mule. In the tradition of half the mining strikes in the West, he found the animal in a remote canyon, picked up a rock to throw at him, and found it was rich in gold. His discovery led to development of the famed Big Blue Mine and the new Kern River town of Quartzburg.

The newest Kern camp grew in wealth and wickedness until the temperance element gained power and turned the town dry. Saloonkeepers thereupon moved a mile down the river and founded their own town—with the obvious name of Whisky Flat. In 1864 the new camp made a concession to respectability by changing its name to Kernville. Through the early 1860s these rival towns were the center of population in the Kern country.

Into this backwoods center in 1864 came the genial showman, Asbury Harpending, a Confederate sympathizer in search of refuge. From Kernville he pushed on with three companions into the Tehachapi Mountains south of the river. In this wild country they made a rich new strike, organized a mining district and named their camp Havilah—after the locality in Genesis "where there is gold."

This pine-shaded camp promptly boomed in the fashion of Kern mining excitements. Men flocked in by the hundreds, town lots sold as high as $20 a front foot, pack trains and stage coaches were arriving regularly from Kernville and Los Angeles.

From the beginning Havilah was known as a hotbed of secessionists, of whom Harpending later claimed to be the leader. Suspicion against the place grew so strong in California that a troop of cavalry was sent from San Joaquin Valley to bring Havilah into line.

But the camp was warned of the invasion and laid its own strategy. When the bluecoats reached the outskirts of town, they were immediately surrounded by a small army of well-heeled miners. Harpending, according to his own account, then stepped forward and, with a mock salute, told the officer in charge that they were "just in time for breakfast."

Heeding his sense of discretion, the officer thereupon accepted the offer, and that was the end of Havilah's troubles.

In fact, by the end of the Civil War the Kern mining community was demanding its place under the California sun. In 1866 Kern County was formed, with Havilah as the seat of government. Through the early 1870s the influx of real mining capital kept the Kern camps thriving. Havilah boasted two newspapers, while Kernville and Quartzburg supported nearly a dozen stamp mills. In 1875 one of Nevada's silver senators, John P. Jones, came through and in his familiar offhand manner bought up the Big Blue and most of the neighboring mines. Then he built a tremendous eighty-stamp quartz mill, and for several years the Kern camps hummed with full production. But fire blackened the Big Blue installations in 1883, and the heyday of Kern River mining was over.

POINTS OF INTEREST

Much of the cradle of Kern County settlement—including the original townsites of Kernville and Quartzburg—is under water at the bottom of Lake Isabella.

KEYSVILLE. Reached by a dirt road, this pioneer mining camp of Kern County is marked only by half-a-dozen houses of comparatively recent vintage. But on a small knoll at the lower edge of town the visitor may still see the outlines of the circular trench and shoulder-high breastworks of the fort built to defend Keysville against Indians. In a gulch to the north of town is the entrance to the Keys Mine, discovered in 1854.

HAVILAH. The pioneer cemetery is the only important old landmark remaining at what was once the seat of Kern County.

CLARAVILLE. Near the base of Piute Mountain, reached by dirt roads from several directions, is the site of Claraville, founded early in 1866. While no building of early date remains on the actual site of Claraville, there are many rock foundations and boards with cut nails hidden from view among the sagebrush on the north side of the road just west of Landers Meadow. Beyond where the road crosses Kelso Creek, the pine-covered slopes to the north are pocked with the remains of mining shafts, and there is a well-defined ditch dug by the miners to carry snow water to their workings for a long distance along the contour of the mountainside.

SAGELAND. Of somewhat later vintage is Sageland, located just north of Kelso Valley and marked today by two or three houses that do not date to its pioneer days. Across a hillside to the northwest are the remains of old ore workings, while on a ridge to the northeast is the original cemetery. Here a number of weathered picket boards, with the typical carved points of the Victorian cemetery fence, are scattered about in somewhat pathetic reminiscence of lives long departed. The cut nails abounding on the knoll date it at least as far back as the 1880's.

MINERAL KING. North of the Kern country, tucked in a sharp indentation of the Sequoia National Park boundary, is Mineral King, a mining camp of the 1870s. From the main highway entering Sequoia, a dirt road branches east at Hammond and follows along the East Fork of the Kaweah River. Crossing the river at Oak Grove, it hugs the north side of the canyon, crosses a spur of the park boundary, and after twenty-five tortuous miles arrives at Mineral King in the Sequoia National Game Refuge.

In 1873 a party of spiritualists discovered silver here and founded the town. Two years later the toll road was built and a modest rush of miners followed. But the deposits were never rich, and an end to the mining era was written by a snowslide that buried part of the workings in 1888.

Today Mineral King is a resort for summer homes and a starting-point for pack trips in the Sierra country. On the old road four miles short of Mineral King is another old camp, Silver City, which also has a pack station and summer homes.

WHITE RIVER. The little village of White River, ten miles east of Delano, was founded as a gold camp in the 1850s. First called Dogtown, it soon went by the wonderful name of Tailholt, which was later changed to the more respectable title of White River. Among the points of interest are two cemeteries —one north of the river for regular citizens, and a small one south of the river for the town toughs who died violently.

Chapter 25. Julian City: Southland Bonanza

EARLY-DAY CALIFORNIA had hundreds of rancho grants and hundreds of gold mines, but the two claims clashed at only two points. One was on Colonel Frémont's Mariposa Rancho, near Yosemite. The other was at San Diego County's one mining bonanza, Julian City.

San Diego in 1870 was a town with a magnificent harbor, a delightful climate, and little else. California's earliest settlement, it had watched with envy the spectacular rise of Northern California cities during the Gold Rush.

Then in 1867 Alonzo Horton arrived and took charge. Near the old San Diego community clustering beneath the mission, he subdivided an entirely new town, and placed San Diego on the high tide of a Southern California boom.

Meanwhile, placer mining on a small scale had been started in the late 1850s high in the San Diego Mountains, west of the old Santa Ysabel chapel. In January, 1869, the first trace of gold was discovered on the ranch lands of Mike Julian, a former San Diegan. This activity was not lost on San Diego newspaper editors, who had long claimed that golden treasure in the mountains behind the city only waited exploration.

This was the situation early in 1870, when several prospecting parties were combing the San Diego Mountains. On February 20 a party including N. C. Bickers was camped on the Julian lands. Since this was Sunday, they were taking their leisure. Bickers was returning to camp from a walk when he accidentally kicked over a piece of quartz. According to miner's habit he picked it up, and saw specks of free gold. Excitedly he raced back to his friends, but the consensus was that nothing could be done about it on the Sabbath. One disciplinarian even refused to look at the rock on Sunday.

But next day, in the teeth of a rainstorm, the prospectors descended on Bickers' discovery. On Tuesday, February 22, they took out half a ton of the rich ore. Convinced that they had a mine, they consulted their calendar and christened it the George Washington.

At first the miners of the Julian country tried to keep the secret. The new owners of the Cuyamaca Rancho, lying to the South, were trying to confirm their boundaries with a survey. If they heard of the gold discovery, they might try to "float" their grant northward to include the mines.

But one miner broadcast the story. The Julian men held a meeting to decide their course. They first went to the Cuyamaca surveyor and asked him where he was finding the boundary. He was noncommittal. Then, since the news was out, they decided to make the most of it. Down to San Diego went Bickers and a companion, carrying nearly a ton of rock samples. Part of it was left in a San Diego show window, and the rest shipped to San Francisco for refining.

Within minutes the streets of San Diego fairly hummed. Reported the San Diego *Bulletin*: "The news flew like wildfire, and soon the whole town was agog to learn the particulars." Quick estimates put the value of the ore between $50 and $10,000 to the ton. At this, many San Diegans struck out at once, pausing only long enough to get provisions, tools, and directions.

In San Francisco the excitement was almost as intense. Results of the ore tests showed values from $75 to $200 per ton. The *Alta California*, usually conservative where mining discoveries were concerned, published a glowing letter from a gold-struck San Diegan. That was enough. On only twelve hours' notice, the steamer *Oriflamme* churned out of the Golden Gate jammed to the rails with 150 Argonauts. At San Diego most of them stopped long enough to inquire the route to the diggings.

This was the Julian rush, California's big mining excitement of 1870. From Northern California the gold-hunters came by sea. From the Southland, they converged along roads through Los Angeles and San Bernardino. San Diego, convinced at last that gold prosperity had reached its door, prepared to harvest the mining trade. It started a line of stages to the mines via Poway and Ramona (fare, $8), and began building a new road to shorten the distance to 44 miles. Los Angeles, sending freight teams and stages to the diggings, loomed as a competitor.

"There will be an immense crowd of gold seekers," the Los Angeles *News* told its readers. "They must naturally be skinned. Fellow citizens, let us prepare to do the skinning."

Center of excitement, however, was the Julian mine. Within days of the George Washington strike, a town named after Mike Julian was laid out, and lots were selling at from $50 to $180 apiece. By mid-March, 800 gold seekers were on the ground. Wrote one:

"The people here are positively wild. Such a thing as a sober thought is unknown. The rumor comes that Tom, Dick, or Harry has 'struck it' and forthwith the whole camp rushes pell mell for the 'new diggin's.' People don't sleep here at all (or if they do they are more lucky than I). All night long the ferocious prospectors make the hills resound with their stories of the day's adventures. Talk of Babel!"

At first, Julian was a tent city, with a handful of log cabins. Then, as lumber arrived by mule team from San Diego, frame buildings rose along the main street. Two stamp mills were under construction, preparing to work rich ores from such mines as the Washington, Golden Chariot, Ready Relief, Stonewall and—of all names—Lady's Leg.

But this booming camp had its troubles. Rains and chilling weather made life miserable for the treasure-hunters, most of whom slept on the ground and cooked by campfire. The first April wind blew down every tent and knocked over the general store. "Gunn's express matter," reported one resident, "was distributed among the hills and gulches gratis."

Then there were the bad men. By June, 1870, Julian City had two shooting scrapes and a Vigilance Court. An *hombre* named Trask shot a Chinese citizen for pure entertainment, and then had to ride for the brush under a hail of bullets from Julian's outraged population.

Late in April the Julianites began to notice an unusual amount of missing horses. One Bob Crawford, whose reputation as a horse thief had accompanied him from Montana, was discovered with a stolen saddle. The miners formed a Vigilance Committee, took Crawford to the nearest tree and hoisted him up to a limb "once or twice." Under this gentle persuasion he confessed to stealing both saddle and horses and was promptly banished from camp. Before it adjourned, the committee resolved "to hang the first man who shall commit a murder here." The threat was not invoked until 1874, when an Indian was hanged for attacking a woman near Julian.

Still, Julian City was not a lawless town. Its greatest test came when a few landowners tried to jump the whole mining camp. There was talk of gunplay, but the Julian men chose to fight it out in the courts.

The Rancho Cuyamaca, one of the last Mexican grants in California, had been given in 1845 to Augustin Olvera, the Spanish pioneer for whom Olvera Street in Los Angeles is named. In the early 1850s a U.S. Land Commission took up the task of settling all California property titles. It rejected Olvera's claim, for the reason that he submitted no map, no boundary description and no clue to show where in San Diego County his rancho existed.

Olvera then appealed, and won the second round in the Southern California District Court. The government next appealed the case to Washington but failed to press the suit until it was too late. In the 1860s drought and poor markets forced most Southern California ranchos into the hands of mortgage-holders, and Cuyamaca was no exception. The new owners got the title suit dismissed and asked for an official boundary survey of their property.

It was in the midst of this survey that the Julian gold strike was made. True to the miners' fears, the Cuyamaca people moved in. Within a few weeks of the discovery, two of them appeared in Julian and announced that the mines were on Cuyamaca land. They were willing to let the men continue exploration, and if the mines proved permanent they would settle for a royalty on all ores.

This demand threw the hustling camp into sudden paralysis. Work on the main stamp mill was halted; word was dispatched to San Francisco to stop delivery of the machinery. The men left their mines, called a meeting in Julian, and sent a delegation to the Cuyamaca people asking the terms. They got them: royalty figures which left the miners less than half the returns after paying milling costs on the ore.

As one man put it, this amounted to a "prohibition." The miners resolved to fight, and at another mass meeting attended by more than 500, picked a delegation to seek help in San Diego.

Incensed at this threat to its new mining trade, the harbor city responded with a huge meeting of its own on May 28, 1870. For the first time San Diegans heard details of the conflict. They learned that the Cuyamaca people had presented a letter supposedly written in 1846 by General Ortega, then owner of the neighboring Santa Ysabel Rancho, saying that his property was bounded on the south by the Cuyamaca. This evidence was too little and too late, said one aroused speaker.

"But if the Ortega letter is to guide the surveyor," he concluded, "and the Santa Ysabel Rancho forms one of the boundaries of the grant, then the mines will be gobbled up by the land-sharks. . . ."

San Diego promised to help, but another setback came when the surveyors reported in favor of the Cuyamaca claim. The miners, fired for battle, took the case to court. For years they held their stand, financing the litigation through the yield from the mines. Still, the steam had been knocked out of the Julian stampede. In 1873 the town made a strong bid for the county seat, but its population probably never exceeded a thousand. When the Tombstone excitement flared in the late '70s, most of Julian's remaining population packed off for Arizona. By 1887 it was a quiet village of two stores and a tri-weekly mail.

Then the few miners who had remained won their reward. The boundary case was settled, and the northern Cuyamaca line was established seven miles south of Julian City. The town, together with its neighboring community of Banner, gained new life. By 1890 four quartz mills were running and a fifth was under construction. Six years later there were a thousand men in the district and Julian City boasted hotels, churches and schools.

But by this time a new attraction had invaded the Julian country. The pleasant valley had become a stockman's range, supporting some 16,000 horses and cattle and about 10,000 sheep. Pioneer farmers arrived, and soon Julian became known for choice apples, pears and honey. Though its gold production reached an estimated total of $5,000,000, Julian is today a reformed mining camp with an agricultural basis—and a clear title. As for San Diego, it got its commerce and its population —but never another mining frenzy like Julian.

POINTS OF INTEREST

JULIAN. No ghost town, Julian today breathes the spirit of its gold days in its bustling streets, with the difference that mule teams and stage coaches are replaced by autos and pick-up trucks. Frame buildings of false fronts and wooden awnings complete the nostalgic look of this authentic old gold camp.

BANNER. Six miles east of Julian on Highway 78 is the location of Banner, a companion camp to Julian. Its discovery dates to February, 1871, but very little remains at its original site on a public campground under the shadow of Volcan Mountain.

CUYAMACA. Another camp of the Julian-Banner era is Cuyamaca, once located nine miles south of Julian on Highway 79.

PICACHO. In Imperial County, up the Colorado some twenty-five miles from Yuma, is the site of Picacho, located on the California bank in one of the few sections where the river flows from west to east. Mexicans located the first placers here in 1862, and a pueblo of Spanish atmosphere—complete with bullfights and fiestas—flourished in the early years. Later, the Picacho Mine and other deposits were opened in the hills near Picacho Peak. With construction of big stamp mills, the town became a center of hardrock mining and took on an American character. A five-mile railroad was built connecting the Picacho Mine with one of the mills. Today Picacho has been largely obliterated by floods, although a rock house remains. In many places the roadbed of the old railroad is still visible.

TUMCO. At the turn of the century Tumco (also known as Hedges) boomed as a mining town in the Cargo Muchacho Mountains that border Imperial Valley on the east. Today, a few walls and some mining structures are still to be seen at the townsite. Take a dirt road at Ogilby Station on the Southern Pacific Railroad, go two miles northwest paralleling the railroad, then branch north on a road that leads into the hills for three-and-a-half miles to Tumco.

SILVERADO. One of the few mining towns in coastal Southern California is Silverado, easily reached by paved road in the Santa Ana Mountains of northeastern Orange County. A boom town in 1878, it flourished until 1881. Today Silverado Canyon is lined with homes, and there is little or no evidence of the old mining town.

SOLEDAD. Beginning in the 1860s a small gold-mining town existed in Soledad Canyon, north of Los Angeles. Only assured earlyday remains are some evidences of mining activity on the hillsides across the canyon from Ravenna Station.

Chapter 26. Calico: Model Ghost Town

AT LEAST one desert camp—Calico—is apt to be more famous as a ghost than it ever was in real life. For Walter Knott, of Knott's Berry Farm, champion collector of Californiana, has added Calico to his treasury of keepsakes. Now restored, it is a mining town made to order for tourists.

Calico first leaped onto the California stage in 1881—just in time to take up where the fading camp of Bodie left off. Two prospectors first located the famed Silver King Mine in April, but the ore was mediocre. Then in June a third miner associated with the others climbed to the top of the ledge, stuck his knife into the ore, and found it was like "cutting into a lead bullet." Feverishly he scrambled down and raced back to camp.

"Look here," he shouted to his partners, "pure horn silver!"

Soon Silver King ore was in a San Francisco smelter, where it returned a value of $400 to $500 per ton. Later shipments included chunks of pure silver the size of two fists. When this news struck the California mining world, the stampede was on. Busy gateway to the mines was San Bernardino, where, as one observer put it, "everybody in town was carrying specimens in his pockets."

"The road from this town to the mine is alive with men and teams," he added. "There is now more travel through the Cajon than ever before."

On a narrow shelf of land below the King mine sprang the new town, which at first consisted of two stores, one boarding house, two assay offices, and the remarkable combination of boot and shoe shop with adjoining bar. But within a year the camp was bursting with 2,000 men and a long, single street lined with canvas and adobe buildings—the latter wearing the characteristic pink hue of the Calico hills.

In the rugged canyons behind the town appeared new mines of picturesque names—Dragon, Snow Bird, Four Aces, Burning Moscow and Jersey Lily (named for the currently-popular Lily Langtry). From these mines a line of twenty-mule teams hauled ore through the streets of Calico on their way to the nearby mill at Oro Grande, an earlier mining camp located on the Mojave River.

In those first flush days Calico's optimism had no limits. One newcomer recalled that judging by talk in the restaurants, "half the diners were wealthy men to whom a few thousands of dollars were a mere bagatelle. While we ate, mills and roads were planned, railroads laid out and new camps started as though such things were mere incidents of the day's work."

Calico was clearly named for the hills at its back; their kaleidoscopic hues of green and rose had already earned the name of "Calico Mountains." But at least one version of the town's christening deserves repeating. A notable "man about town in Calico" was Joe Joiner, whose outstanding attire included a swallow-tail coat and a beard which hung to his knees. When "Buena Vista" or some other fine-sounding Spanish name was suggested, Joe rebelled.

"It ain't gonna be no Boona Vista, nor nothin' o' the sort!" he snorted. "Look at the colors in them rocks! I say call her Calico!"

Joe may have named the town, but his fun-loving neighbors had the last word. They were especially attracted to those magnificent whiskers, which were said to be such an "awful nuisance" when the wind blew that Joe wore 'em in braids or stuffed 'em in his trousers. One night Joe lingered too long at the brass rail and on his way home fell asleep in the main street. As one of the Calico muleskinners described it, Joe Joiner awoke next morning to find that the boys had cut off "the haw side of his beard" and the "gee-tail of his coat"—a humiliation which thereafter kept the "man about town" off the camp's main street.

But Calico had an ample supply of characters. One of the first was irrepressible John Overshiner, who came up from San

Diego to found the town's newspaper. Its name, the Calico *Print*, was as inspired as that of another mining camp newspaper, the Tombstone *Epitaph*. In fact, when the *Epitaph* commented that the Calico *Print* smacked of petticoats, Overshiner was equal to the challenge: "It overshines a graveyard inscription, anyhow."

Another prize Calico native was Bill Harpold, who kept an abominable hotel known as the Hyena House, which consisted of barrel staves on the outside and holes-in-the-rocks on the inside. When the Calico stage rolled in, Bill was on hand with a wheelbarrow and the commanding yell: "Here y'are, gentlemen! Right this way for Hyena House, best hotel in all Calico!" Bill's breakfasts were simple and straightforward: chili beans and whisky. When Hyena House caved in after a storm, Bill was unconcerned as he dragged out his two guests. He was sorry, he said, for the leaky roof.

Calico's best-loved character was Dorsey, a black and white shepherd which earned fame as the only four-legged mail carrier in the United States. For three years Dorsey delivered Uncle Sam's cargo from Calico to the nearby Bismarck mines. He was usually a playful dog, but once the mail sacks were on his back Dorsey was strictly business. Touching him was considered tampering with the U.S. mails. Dorsey's master, a Bismarck miner, once refused a $500 offer with the reply, "I'd sooner sell a grandson."

Tradition has it that Calico was never a tough town, and the story goes that there was only one killing in the first two years. Editor Overshiner insisted that "there are no more orderly and law abiding people living anywhere than in Calico."

If so, Calico had a powerful lot of bad luck. It was probably the only mining town in California where the brothels were in the middle of the business district, rather than on the outskirts. They were undisturbed until they started robbing the patrons, one of whom was bold enough to protest and bring down the full force of the law.

And was Calico particularly gun shy? Early in 1885 a dispute arose over the famous Occidental Mine, which was so rich that ore under $100 per ton was thrown away. Opposing sides, armed with rifles and shotguns, squared off for a battle royal.

At the last moment the deputy sheriff arrived and won a grudging agreement to settle the case in court.

Ordinarily, law and order were less triumphant. Whenever things got especially dull in Calico—which was seldom—the town roughs marched over to the east end and raided Chinatown. Life was hectic for Calico's Oriental population until the year the Chinese decided to fight back. At the next invasion, they counterattacked with laundry paddles and hot irons, forcing the raiders into ignominious retreat. Thereafter, Chinatown was unmolested.

But Calico's roughs had plenty of diversion. Their idea of an April Fool's joke was to stuff a dummy and then shoot it full of holes in a mock battle on Main Street. The "shooting spirit" fairly penetrated the Calico community. In the mid-'80s its residents seized a sudden fad for fencing vacant lots. One stranger came upon some young boys driving stakes and stretching wire near the edge of town, and asked what they were doing.

"Fencing in a lot," was the stout answer.

"But you boys are not of age and you can't hold any real estate."

"You bet we can," retorted one. "If anybody tries to jump my lot, I'll shoot him!"

By 1885 Calico began to look almost civilized. It had a schoolhouse, church services, temperance lectures, a literary society, even a dancing school. The social triumph of the year came on May 1, when the Calico ladies held their "May Day Ball and Ice Cream and Strawberry Festival" in the town hall. Gay events included a maypole dance, crowning of a queen of the May and other good fun until two in the morning. At that time James Patterson, superintendent of the Occidental Mine, was called outside. He and two friends appeared on the front steps to be greeted by a shower of raw eggs, with maybe a brickbat thrown in. Some uninvited guests from a rival mine were expressing their disappointment, Calico style.

This naturally called for war. Patterson and friends drew their guns and fired away. The attackers retreated—except one, who dashed up the steps and ran right through the May Day Ball and Ice Cream and Strawberry Festival. Right behind him sprinted an Occidental man, shooting at his quarry while the party was thrown into panic and several women fainted. Nobody was hurt, but by the time the deputy sheriff arrived, the festival was over. Most of Calico thought that this was going a mite too far. Growled the Calico *Print:* "a disgraceful and outrageous assault." It might have passed on the Fourth of July, but on May Day—!

Calico had already had a new spurt to its boom when the Iron Horse came by its front door. As the Santa Fe Railroad reached across Arizona to the California border, the Southern Pacific moved to block entry. It started a new line from Mojave to Needles on the Colorado River, and the construction train passed a few miles south of Calico by mid-1882. To the camp this meant a sizable drop in shipping costs, and the mines were soon disgorging lower-grade ores that were previously ignored. At the nearest point on the railroad grew the town of Daggett, bustling depot for Calico. For years Daggett, its streets filled with twenty-mule teams, was the busiest and toughest whistle stop on the Mojave Desert. Crowded with gamblers and bunco artists, it was modestly called "the worst place between Mojave and New York." Meanwhile, the stampede to Calico was renewed—this time by rail.

"Every day people were arriving on the trains from both east and west," wrote one visitor; "others came along via the ties; and across the desert from Cajon Pass straggled a long procession. . . . Some were in wagons with their scant household goods, and others on foot, unencumbered by any earthly possession beyond blankets and canteens."

From Daggett, train passengers were whisked onward by the Calico Stage Line, which advertised "a new, Light-running, Easy-riding Concord Coach." It also gave special assurance to the timid: "Children and nervous persons taken forcibly and effectually."

Calico was still flush with silver when a new kind of boom struck camp. Borax had been found in the Calico Mountains as early as 1883, but it was several years later that huge ledges of a more valuable product—calcium borate—were discovered in the hills just east of Calico town. By 1898 a railroad was built between Daggett and the Calico Mountains to tap the deposits, and the district eventually turned out almost as much wealth in borax as it did in silver.

Through the 1890s, however, Calico went into its silver decline. By the turn of the century the price of silver had dropped from $1.31 to 63 cents, and Calico's great days were over. Today it enjoys a third boom in the tourist business—but it's a mining town without paying mines, without miners and without May Day balls that turn into shooting scrapes.

POINTS OF INTEREST

CALICO. When the writer first visited Calico in the late 1930s it consisted of a number of adobe walls and roofless buildings made of the dark pink soil typical of the Calico Mountains. Today it has been restored as a commercial enterprise by the operators of Knott's Berry Farm, and is an interesting family attraction.

Center for the borax excitement in the Calico Mountains was Borate, whose site can be reached by leaving Highway 91 four miles east of Yermo, going north on a dirt road for another four miles, then turning east on a dim and dubious road into the mountains for about three miles.

ORO GRANDE. This small community on the Mojave River, now marked chiefly by a large cement plant, began in 1878 when gold was discovered in the Old Silver Mountains and Granite Mountains. Like Calico, it boomed in the early 1880s.

COOLGARDIE. One of the few placer districts on the desert, Coolgardie was discovered about 1900 and enjoyed a short rush of miners. The desolate site is located 19 miles north of Barstow.

GOLDSTONE. While its mining history goes back to 1881, the Goldstone district boomed with the gold discovery of December 1915. Within a few months it was practically covered with claims. A few structures remain in various stages of collapse at the townsite south of Goldstone Lake and thirty-three miles northeast of Barstow.

VICTORVILLE. First called Mormon Crossing, Victorville was a mining town in the early 1880s, even before it was a railroad town.

STEDMAN. In some reddish hills eight miles south of Ludlow (on the Santa Fe Railroad) are a few frame headworks which are shown on maps as the Pacific Mine. These deposits were first discovered about 1898 by John Suter, roadmaster for that section of the railroad, while searching for a source of water to serve the trains. The town that sprang up was first called Rochester, then Stedman. A railroad going by the impressive name of Ludlow and Southern was built the eight miles from Ludlow to Stedman between 1899 and 1901. The Bagdad Chase Mine, located just south of the town, produced more than half the total recorded gold production of San Bernardino County. Recently, vandals destroyed the remaining buildings in Stedman, but it is still worth the easy drive south of Ludlow.

THE HOLCOMB VALLEY CAMPS. In the next valley north of Big Bear Lake, high in the San Bernardino Mountains, "Uncle Billy" Holcomb discovered gold in May 1860. Within weeks a rush of miners came by way of the Santa Ana River headwaters and over the top of the mountains by mule path.

Another road was soon built from the Cajon Pass summit along the rim of the Mojave Desert to reach the west end of Holcomb Valley. Today the site is best reached by the Polique Canyon Road, which heads northwest from Fawnskin at the north shore of Big Bear Lake. Through Holcomb Valley the visitor finds scattered old log or frame buildings. Some of them are marked by the Forest Service signs and—as shown by their cut nails—date at least to the 1880s.

Biggest town in the district was Belleville, which sprouted about half a mile east of the present Holcomb Public Campground and in the vicinity of the well-marked Hang Man's Tree. The site is indicated only by piles of rubbish and an old arrastre.

During the Civil War, Holcomb Valley was a secessionist stronghold. Terrorized by the rebels, Union men were afraid to express their sentiments. In July 1861 one person was killed and several wounded in a shooting affray between Unionists and secessionists. The Unionists sent word to San Francisco for troops, and one of them hastened there by stage to make a personal plea. Four companies of infantry and a detachment of cavalry were quickly dispatched, and according to one Holcomb Valley Unionist, "the troops barely got here in time." For the rest of the war, Holcomb Valley continued to erupt with rebel conspiracy, and was a notorious rallying point for parties escaping to the Confederacy.

DOBLE. East of Holcomb Valley is the Doble Mine, once owned by the Comstock bonanza king, E. J. "Lucky" Baldwin. Flourishing in the 1870s, it was worked off and on until the machinery was taken away in 1951. West of the mine is the old mill site, while below the mine toward Baldwin Lake is the location of the small town of Doble, now almost obliterated.

PALM CITY (TWENTY-NINE PALMS). Beginning in 1873 Twenty-Nine Palms (then often called Palm City) became the supply center for a number of mines in the hills northeast of the Little San Bernardino Mountains.

DALE. Located near the Pinto Mountains nineteen miles east of Twenty-Nine Palms, gold mines at Old Dale were first discovered in the early 1880s. It came into prominence with discovery of the Virginia Dale Mine in 1885, and was active until the turn of the century. At that time most of the activity was transferred a few miles away to New Dale, six miles southeast overlooking the Pinto Basin. Dale the Third was situated on a nearby ridge. All three localities were virtually abandoned by 1916, although there was a small revival of activity at New Dale in the 1930s. A few rock walls and frame houses remain at the sites, particularly at what has been termed Dale the Third.

PROVIDENCE. Evidence of early mining activity abounds in the Providence Mountains, located in the eastern Mojave Desert between the Santa Fe and Union Pacific railroad lines. Richest mine of all was the Bonanza King, discovered in the 1870s and extensively developed in the 1880s. According to one report, it produced nearly $1,000,000 in eighteen months alone.

Here stands the town of Providence—mainly a company town for the Bonanza King Mine, though serving as a commercial center for the Silver King and other mines in the Providence Mountains. A comparatively well-preserved desert ghost town, it was built largely of white softstone sawed from a nearby ledge. The old stamp mill and a number of buildings still stand in various stages of decomposition to mark the town and its main street.

Providence may be reached by a twenty-five mile road (surfaced for about twelve miles) that goes northwest from Essex on Highway 66 to Mitchell Caverns State Park. A little less than twenty miles from Essex, a sign marked 7IL Ranch indicates a branch road going north that ends at Providence and the Bonanza King Mine. The last mile or more may be in disrepair, but like other desert roads may be negotiated by very slow driving and perhaps some occasional shovel work.

HART. Northeast of Essex on the Santa Fe line is Goffs, where a dirt road heads north thirty-seven miles to an agricultural ghost town called Barnwell. From here a dirt road goes east nine miles to the Castle Mountains and the townsite of Hart, located less than five miles from the Nevada border. Gold was discovered here about 1907, in the same general excitement that swept the desert after Tonopah and Goldfield, but only a few ruins remain of the little town of Hart.

Chapter 27. Randsburg:
Gay 90's Stampede

EXCEPT IN COLORADO, the West's mining excitements seemed to have faded by the 1890s. In the California and Nevada deserts, exhaustion of underground treasure and the poor price of silver brought mining stagnation. To cap it all, a depression seized the nation in 1893 and made the Gay Nineties less than gay.

Then came Randsburg. Together with its neighbor camps

springing up in the Mojave Desert, it broke the spell for California mining. Of the thousands who stampeded to the side of Rand Mountain, few made their fortune. But they had the time of their lives in California's one big mining boom of the 1890s.

First strike of the new gold diggings came in 1893 at Goler, between Red Rock Canyon and Randsburg. This was enough to create a town, a stage line from Mojave, and an eager population which prospected the nearby hills. Next year two miners found placer gold on the slope of Rand Mountain. One of them, Frederic M. Mooers, took two others back to the spot in the spring of 1895 to find the source of this surface color. Near the top of the mountain they broke a chunk off a rock outcropping and found it heavy with gold.

"Boys, we needn't look any further," shouted Mooers; "we've struck it rich."

The jubilant miners located their first claims on April 25, labeling them with the one name, Rand Mine—after the famous gold district opened a decade earlier in Transvaal, South Africa. When stock promoters began putting the Rand label on everything they sold, the name was changed to Yellow Aster —the big mine of Randsburg.

Meanwhile, the first rush for the Rand had begun. From Mojave to Panamint Valley, desert prospectors flocked to the new ground. But with a fortune under foot, Mooers and his partners were too broke to develop it. They almost sold half the mine to one newcomer, but soon the wife of one of them—a San Bernardino woman doctor named Rose Burcham—arrived to halt any talk of sale. Next, a mining expert showed up, examined the ground, and clinched the case.

"Boys, you have a good thing," he told them. "Get a 100-stamp mill and shovel in the entire mountain, for it's all ore."

Randsburg would eventually get its 100-stamp mill, making it one of the few mining booms to enrich the discoverers. From the beginning, in fact, this was a "poor man's camp." Locators of the Butte Mine were so destitute that they would have had to break camp the next day out of sheer hunger. As it was, they had to grind out enough gold dust from the first ore to raise the $1.60 fee for recording the claim.

For a full year the Randsburg boom was strictly local. Mojave prospectors continued to locate new mines, and to give them such picturesque names as Big Norse, King Solomon, Monkey Wrench, Minnehaha, Bully Boy, Napoleon and Gold Coin. By the end of 1895 the camp still contained only thirteen buildings—some of them part canvas.

But in the summer of '96, miner Si Drouillard found the St. Elmo Mine more than five miles east of the Rand Mine on the open desert. Added to the growing roster of rich lodes, it showed that the Rand deposits comprised "one of nature's great treasure houses." Randsburg's big rush was on.

From out of Southern California and Nevada came a horde of fortune-seekers in the fall of '96 and winter of '97. Randsburg mushroomed to some 300 buildings and tents, its population to some 2,500 by early 1897—with forty or fifty more arriving every day. Through its surging streets walked Argonauts from as far off as Australia and South Africa. Under foot, they believed, was another Comstock Lode.

The Randsburg stampede converged along two general routes. From San Bernardino and points east, gold hunters took the Santa Fe Railroad through Barstow to the nearest station, Kramer. Over the last twenty-eight miles to Randsburg, three stages a day delivered Randsburg's population.

From Los Angeles the Argonauts rode the Southern Pacific to Mojave, then took one of the four daily stages for the mines. Just below Red Rock Canyon the coaches veered eastward through Garlock, adding an extra pair to the four-horse team for the sandy, uphill pull into Randsburg. Wrote one passenger:

"All along the road from Mojave to Randsburg we passed dozens of team and freighting wagons, some of the latter having sixteen horses; also three or four stages returning to Mojave, many private conveyances, burro prospecting outfits, and miners and tenderfeet, with packs on their backs, going on foot to the new El Dorado."

Another newcomer described his stagecoach companions: "miscellaneous load of capitalists, carpenters, prospectors, miners, drummers [traveling salesmen], fakers, newspaper correspondents, and perhaps a traveling company of barnstormers."

When the stageload rocked into camp, Randsburg's welcome was exuberant and typical. The whole population turned out to greet newcomers, and to line up at the post office for mail. In the crowd, according to one arrival, were "sturdy Cornishmen from the mines, tramp-like prospectors from the hills and desert, keen dealers in mines that others have found, gamblers, actors, mule-punchers, and the general riff-raff that gathers whenever gold clinks and moral restraints are lax. The deputy sheriff is there," the eyewitness continues, "with a fierce black mustache, a slouchy sombrero, a long, black frock coat, high boots, and protruding pistol. There are women in the crowd, but the most prominent are not the most worthy."

Randsburg was rowdy, but not particularly lawless. By March of '97 it had witnessed three or four shooting scrapes. A band of toughs, proudly calling itself the "Dirty Dozen," tried to run things in true mining camp style. At this, peaceable Randsburgers formed a Citizens' Committee "to enforce the laws," and posted a pointed notice.

"Ten Deputy Constables have been appointed," it warned, "and any riotous and threatening conduct will be suppressed and punished."

The Dirty Dozen were properly cowed, and though Randsburg flourished in the farthest corner of huge Kern County, it shunned a tough reputation. Good clean fun, however, was something else again. Randsburg was quick to acquire a brass band, a volunteer fire company, an Orpheus Theater—and a full complement of saloons. In her streets, complete with boardwalks and false fronts in the best mining camp tradition, the entire population met every night in social confab. It was the custom for everybody, whether imbibing or not, to make the rounds of the bars and dance halls each evening and mix with the crowd.

With Randsburg it was anything for a joke or a celebration. Its riotous Fourths of July included sack races, grand balls— and dynamite salutes which rattled every building in camp. Once a stage driver, swinging an empty coach through town, turned too short at the end of the street and overturned the vehicle. When a wise-cracking bystander bet him drinks for the crowd that he couldn't do it twice, the driver wheeled down the street and capsized his stage again. The boys were just as prompt to collect the bet.

By 1897 Randsburg mining was big business. The neighboring town of Johannesburg had been founded over the divide a mile away. The Yellow Aster Mine had yielded its owners $250,000 in ore, catapulting them from prospectors to mining magnates. Most of this had been hauled by twenty-mule team to the stamp mill at Garlock, but by '97 both Randsburg and "Joburg" had small mills of their own. The first of Randsburg's $8 million gold yield was on its way.

At the same time Randsburg was rising to that upper class of mining camps gifted with a railroad. From the Santa Fe line at Kramer, tracklayers were spiking steel across the desert for the standard-gauge Randsburg Railroad. When the Iron Horse reached Rand Mountain, the giant ore bodies would find their proper market, and Randsburg its proper place as a second Comstock.

On December 23, 1897, the rail crews laid track over the hill into Johannesburg. This naturally called for a celebration, Randsburg style. That afternoon, all of Joburg and half the population of Randsburg turned out to cheer the first Iron Horse. Finally the expected train chugged over the hill and stopped in the midst of the shouting crowd.

"The locomotive blew a long blast," described one eyewitness, "and everything that could make a noise chimed in."

But the Rand District had just begun to celebrate. "Tonight," wrote a news correspondent, "the two towns of Randsburg and Johannesburg are painting things vermilion." It was an understatement. Just before midnight, in the midst of the carnival, fire broke out in a gasoline storehouse at Randsburg. The fire company swiftly arrived with its new "chemical engine." It was greeted by exploding drums of gas and oil which sent burning liquid to other buildings hundreds of feet away.

"The fire was a magnificent spectacle," said one gleeful celebrant. "'The black smoke, intermingled with flame, rolled up hundreds of feet, to fall back in showers of sparks on the roofs of adjoining buildings. Each explosion of oil added to the terror of the situation, and red-hot drums flew through the air in all directions, but, miraculously, no one was killed."

Randsburg was equal to the moment. Despite explosions which knocked several men down, the Randsburgers joined their firemen in attacking the blaze. They blew up several structures in the path of the flames, and checked the fire before it had consumed more than three buildings. Randsburg went home, but it was not through celebrating. Next night the firemen held their Christmas Eve ball, with proceeds going to pay for their new engine which had received a premature baptism of fire.

The fire boys, in fact, had only begun to fight. Less than a month later, in the early morning of January 19, flames broke out in the Mojave Saloon and spread rapidly up Rand Street. The close-packed wooden buildings kindled like tinder, and soon the town was spouting smoke 1,000 feet high. The St. Elmo, main hotel in town, was consumed early, the guests escaping only with their clothes.

"Men, women and children filled the streets," recorded one citizen. "Everybody near the fire was intent on saving their houses or furniture."

The one hope of rescuing part of the town was to keep the flames from jumping Broadway. When the Broadway Hotel was threatened men climbed to the roofs of nearby buildings and tore loose burning boards with their bare hands. Two or three fell from exhaustion before the fire was controlled. But half of Randsburg lay in smoking cinder.

All of this was part of mining camp life, and Randsburg turned cheerfully to the job of rebuilding. Less than five months later another fire took care of the other half.

Yet it would take more than fires to down the Rand District. Randsburg's gold output had scarcely begun to fade when rich deposits of tungsten were found on Rand Mountain. The nearby town of Atolia was born, and the whole Rand District boomed again.

Then in 1919, discovery of the Big Silver Mine near Atolia gave the district its third mining excitement. Here was founded the silver town of Red Mountain, "where every night is Saturday night, and Saturday night is the Fourth of July." Today the Rand District is quieter, but the old-timers will tell you it's just resting between booms.

GOLER. At Goler Canyon in the east end of the El Paso Mountains the rough camp of Goler flourished from 1893 to the Rand discovery in 1895. Little but miners' diggings mark the site today.

GARLOCK. Located on the present Southern Pacific line that skirts the southern slope of the El Paso Mountains, Garlock was founded in the fall of 1895 when an eight-stamp mill was installed there to work ores from Rand Mountain and other nearby districts. By 1899 it was a fairly sizable town with several hundred population and a number of frame buildings along its main street. Today little is left except the railroad siding.

RANDSBURG. One of the best-preserved mining towns on the desert, Randsburg still gives evidence of its once-large size. A relatively few inhabitants operate a handful of enterprises on the main street, while up the canyon to the south are the giant workings of the Yellow Aster Mine. Starting place for visitors is the Desert Museum.

Throughout this district, old mine shafts—complete with ladders and sometimes with windlasses—beckon the inquisitive explorer. But dropping a rock down the hole often reveals a startling depth. The best advice is to be careful of your ground near the mouth of mines, trust no old timbers, and stay out of the shafts.

JOHANNESBURG. Founded shortly after Randsburg, "Joburg" was smaller and less rambunctious. But it did boast a railroad, which continued to operate until it was shut down and the rails removed in the early 1930s. So many houses of more recent vintage have been built, and so many pioneer buildings torn down, that Joburg today gives little impression of its boom era.

ATOLIA. In 1905 rich tungsten ore was discovered five miles southeast of Randsburg, and by 1907 the town of Atolia was founded there. The demand for tungsten during World War I created a boom which sent Atolia's population to 2,000 by 1915.

Randsburg: Gay 90's Stampede / 259

RED MOUNTAIN. Less than a mile south of Joburg is Red Mountain, which was born with the rich silver strike of 1919 that became known as the Big Silver Mine. One of the richest silver deposits in California, the Big Silver produced more than $7,000,000 in its first four years. The town of Red Mountain, first called Osdick after two brothers who owned a stamp mill nearby, was for many years the rip-roaring trading center for miners and prospectors who came in from miles around.

COPPER CITY. A "city" only by virtue of Western generosity, this camp was located in the 1880s and was busy during the Rand excitement of the 1890s. The site, which contains no remains, is situated on the south side of a range of hills southeast of Pilot Knob—a twenty-six-mile drive on a dirt road east of Atolia. It is inside a Naval Ordnance Test Station range and is out-of-bounds to the public.

Chapter 28. The Death Valley Camps

POPULATION FOR MOST of California has always zoomed steadily upward, but Death Valley's census reached its peak at the century's turn. Between 1905 and '08, several thousand miners, promoters, gamblers, prostitutes, and other fragments of humanity poured into this "white heart of the Mojave" and then poured out again. Overnight were born the wild and raucous camps of Greenwater, Harrisburg, and—of all names—Skidoo. Then, as though blown by a hot desert wind, they faded—leaving nothing but great piles of tin cans and empty bottles.

This was the tail end of the West's last big gold rush. It started in the early 1900s, when the riotous Nevada towns of Tonopah and Goldfield aroused the mining world by producing a cool $250,000,000. It drew near to Death Valley when the Mojave Desert's greatest prospector, Shorty Harris, made his Bullfrog strike in August, 1904. On the barren hills just inside the Nevada border sprang Rhyolite, which brought seven thousand people and two railroads racing across the desert.

From Rhyolite the excitement leaped to California and the very rim of Death Valley. Arthur Kunze, a miner who had strayed south from Tonopah, had already found promising copper ore in the Black Mountains near the southern end of the valley. But Nevada was then wild over gold, and Death Valley was considered too remote to make a copper mine pay. Kunze and his partners spent two years trying to sell their claims. But by the spring of 1906 Rhyolite and its railroads brought the valley closer to civilization. Kunze sold out to various mining magnates, among them Charles M. Schwab, president of Bethlehem Steel.

In those days, the Schwab touch was all that was needed to launch a new stampede. And when Nevada heard that one of Kunze's partners had sold his share for $40,000 cash, the rush to Death Valley was on.

Out of Goldfield stormed a host of men—by horseback, foot, and chugging auto. Over the last miles this motley crew came up a ravine so steep and gruelling in the desert sun that it earned the grim name of Dead Horse Canyon. Within a month a thousand adventurers were on the ground looking for copper —and excitement. In less than five months, claim stakes and rock monuments peppered the ridge of the Black Mountains for thirty miles.

Thus was born Greenwater, farthest outpost of the desert mining frenzy in the 1900s. Her saga will forever serve to show what can be done by the combination of two ingredients— excitement and publicity. Before 1906 there was nothing on these brush-covered slopes but a dismal spring whose water was an unappetizing green. Within a year Greenwater had two thousand people, a $100,000 bank, two newspapers, a magazine glorying in the name of Death Valley *Chuckwalla*, and a boundless future. It was, claimed the boys, "the world's biggest copper deposit." When it attracted mining capital from Butte, Montana, the copper center of the world, they knew it would be "bigger than Butte."

This kind of city would certainly need room for growth. At first the camp lay in a ravine near the main claims, but this hardly afforded room for another Butte. So after Christmas of 1906 the whole camp pulled stakes and moved two miles to the new Greenwater, on a broad slope just east of Death Valley's rim. Over the rugged route marched a procession of miners and merchants, carrying their possessions with them and looking like refugees from a desert cloudburst. Along the road an enterprising barkeeper dropped his inventory and began catering to the parade. So did a Greenwater butcher. Pausing for a shot or a steak, the trekkers pushed on with new zest.

"Saloons and boarding-houses, stores and brokerage firms are doing business on the run," wrote one observer, "and trying to be on both sides of the mountain at the same time. . . . Those who remain in the old camp are walking two miles to the new to get their eggs for breakfast. Those who journeyed to the new are walking two miles to the old to get their mail. . . ."

All this was a mere lark for wild and reckless Greenwater. Though technically out of bounds, it followed the wide open tradition of Nevada camps. Gambling was illegal in California, but at Greenwater faro, roulette and poker roared round the clock. So did the other customary mining camp vices.

But while the copper camp had no peace officers during most of its career, it had a form of miner's justice. Greenwater could tolerate a lot, but as in other desert camps, it was sometimes necessary for a citizens' committee to collar a particularly obstreperous character and hand him a canteen. This was a silent but effective invitation to start walking. When four robbers were caught in Greenwater they were ordered to be on the street at nine the next morning. At the appointed hour, Greenwater's entire body politic met them and served notice that they had half an hour to settle matters before their departure. One optimist asked for an hour, but was soon convinced that he could make it on time if he tried. Within the half hour the four outcasts and their canteens were heading toward Dead Horse Canyon.

Greenwater was stern, but it could also be sentimental—on occasion. When Billy, one of the town hangers-on, died in a bout with Demon Rum, Greenwater resolved to bury him in style. For the padding of the coffin one saloonkeeper offered the packing from a barrel of bottle beer. Another contributed some respectable street clothes for Billy's last public appearance. On the night before the service, the improvised mortuary was vis-

ited by the belle of the camp, Tiger Lil. She surveyed the undertaker's work and was especially pleased at the way he had
placed Billy's right hand on the chest—"just the way he held a
poker hand." Still, something was missing . . .

Next day Greenwater turned out in its best attire and followed the hearse over a bumpy half mile to the town cemetery.
Tiger Lil rode beside the driver, taking a particular interest in
the proceedings. A young man who had studied for the ministry performed the service, and his wife closed the ceremony by
singing "Nearer My God to Thee."

Those who had seen the open coffin knew the secret: close to
his vest Billy's fingers held a poker hand. The cards? Tiger Lil
had sent him off in style with five aces.

By mid 1907 Greenwater was on the crest of its boom. From
the nearest railroad thirty-five miles away lurched one of the
earliest auto stages in the West—the Death Valley Chug Line.
The fearless driver on this hair-raising ride was Alkali Bill;
according to the Greenwater *Times*, "he generally goes out
empty and comes back loaded." Greenwater was, in fact, the
first mining area in California reached by auto—and when you
got there gasoline was a dollar a gallon.

Among the other luxuries in this parched country was water.
Hauled in from wells thirty miles away, it sold as high as
twelve cents a gallon retail. Mule teams freighting in water
drank up half their cargo en route. With water this scarce, fire
was the dread of Greenwater. When flames broke out in the
office of the Greenwater *Miner*, its editors had to let it burn to
the ground; water to put it out would have cost more than the
plant was worth.

Meanwhile, other discoveries were contributing to Death
Valley's big mining boom. In the summer of 1905 Shorty Harris left Rhyolite, the Nevada town sprung from his gold discovery. In a drunken spree he had sold his original Bullfrog claim
for $900, and had promptly dissipated that as well—according
to the custom of desert prospectors. Now he headed across Death
Valley in search of a new strike.

On the way he met Pete Aguerreberry, another famed
Death Valley prospector. What happened next is in dispute;
each man claims he made the discovery. But one of them found

an outcropping of high grade at what is now Harrisburg Flats, next to Emigrant Canyon.

"They beat me out of Bullfrog," shouted Shorty, "but now I'm going to show 'em."

"You take one side and I'll take the other," said Pete.

So the two miners followed the outcrop up the mountainside, putting up locations for themselves and some friends. That night when they met other prospectors at Wildrose Springs, the secret was out. The rush came so fast it caught the discoverers by surprise. Pete Aguerreberry had to go down to Ballarat, the gold camp in the south end of Panamint Valley. When he got back a few days later, the flats were overrun with gold-seekers; his own claim stakes had been pulled up and men were occupying the ground. Shorty Harris was also away, but Pete lost no time in identifying himself as French Pete, the discoverer.

"Before I would let anybody take it away from me," he boomed, "I would fight and either leave my bones or another man's on the ground."

His listeners pulled up their stakes and Pete put back his.

Harrisburg, as the camp came to be called, was never a big excitement. Its population got no further than three hundred. But it led to the discovery of the one Death Valley camp which paid for itself. In the rush to Harrisburg, two miners were going up Emigrant Canyon and got lost in a fog—one of the few recorded on the Mojave Desert. They strayed up the side of Tucki Mountain, north of Harrisburg Flats, and made the gold strike which founded the town of Skidoo.

One of them was Harry Ramsey, famous in the mining world as one who had grubstaked the discoverers of Goldfield. Ramsey and his partner now sold out to Bob Montgomery, who had owned the main mine in Rhyolite, for the sum of $60,000. Then Charles M. Schwab invested some money in Montgomery's mine. When these big movements were broadcast, all roads led to Skidoo.

"Follow Schwab to Skidoo, the New Gold Camp of 1907," advertised one mining stock company.

Winter and summer, the gold hunters trekked out of Rhyolite and across Death Valley. It was then that Stovepipe Wells sprang up as a stopping place on the weary route. In the summer of 1907, at least sixteen men died trying to cross the blistering valley on the way to Skidoo.

There are two versions on just how Skidoo got its wonderful name. One is that it was first discovered on the 23rd of the month—calling to someone's mind the popular remark which then covered any situation—"Twenty-three Skidoo" (meaning "beat it"). The other is that Bob Montgomery announced he would bring water into camp from Telescope Peak, twenty-three miles away—causing the same wisecrack.

In any case, Skidoo it was, and the new camp promptly gained a bank, a newspaper, a red light district, a row of saloons, seven hundred citizens, and a telephone line all the way across Death Valley to Rhyolite.

Skidoovians, as they were called, were somewhat touchy about murder, there being no jail in camp. One rough character, a saloonkeeper named Joe Simpson, had recently shot up a hotel in Independence while on his way to Skidoo. In April, 1908, he went on a prolonged jag; running out of money, he decided to get it by the direct process of robbing the bank. But when he presented his gun at the teller's window, he was overpowered by several men and thrown out by the manager, Jim Arnold. Sometime later Joe got another gun and went storming back into the bank.

"Have you got anything against me, Jim?" he demanded.

"No, Joe, I've got nothing against you."

"Yes, you have," Joe insisted dramatically, "your end has come—prepare to die."

He thereupon shot Arnold in the chest—a mortal wound. The constable came running up and wrestled with Simpson, who was wildly emptying his gun. He was placed under guard, but three days later the aroused Skidoovians took action. Overpowering the officer, they took Simpson and hanged him to a telephone pole. Skidoo was so excited that night over the big event—the first lynching in California mines for years—that one man claimed he was awakened and told the news twenty-three times. "I was surprised every time," he added. One of the town ne'er-do-wells, hearing of it, skidooed out of camp. He was reported still running when he passed Stovepipe Wells next morning.

No one thought of punishing the lynchers. Said the coroner's jury, "He died by strangulation by persons unknown." Headlined the Skidoo *News*, "MURDERER LYNCHED WITH GENERAL APPROVAL." As for the rest of California, it sent out news photographers who reached remote Skidoo somewhat late. Joe was already buried. But Skidoo was not a town to hide its light under a bushel. Joe was obligingly dug up and rehung for the benefit of the press cameras.

Skidoo, like Greenwater, had already been waning fast since the panic of autumn, 1907. Investment money suddenly disappeared, and without more capital coming in, the Death Valley camps collapsed. Greenwater's death was abrupt and complete; her mines had run out of ore at two hundred feet. Practically the only shipments ever made were rock from the claim monuments—hauled away in the camp's dying hour. This was the end of California's "second Butte."

Skidoo was harder to kill. For another decade it continued to yield gold and silver ore—perhaps as much as $3,000,000. But when the pipeline to Telescope Peak was sold for metal in World War I, Skidoo died of thirst.

Death Valley mining flared again in 1926, when the quack promoter, C. C. Julian, founded the town of Leadfield, at the head of Titus Canyon. But Julian was even then under investigation by state officials. Like Greenwater before it, Leadfield mined more stockholder's pockets than mountains.

POINTS OF INTEREST

GREENWATER. To reach the site of Greenwater, take the road from Furnace Creek toward Shoshone, turning southwest at a dirt road 5.8 miles south of the turnoff to Dante's View. The town was located 1.8 miles along this dirt road; little is there now but some stone foundations among the sagebrush. If you want to see the ghost of Greenwater, don't go to its site. The lumber of its shacks was hauled to the little Amargosa River town of Shoshone.

FURNACE. A contemporary of Greenwater was the copper camp of Furnace, located 1.4 miles on a dirt road paralleling the Greenwater road and branching from the Furnace Creek-Shoshone road 2.8 miles south of the Dante's View turnoff.

SCHWAB. Two miles east of Furnace Creek Junction, a bad dirt road goes nine miles up Echo Canyon to the site of Schwab, a small camp dating from the Greenwater era and named for the noted financier. A few tumbledown houses remain.

LEE. Another small town of the same period was Lee, which was located in the Funeral Mountains just inside the California border. Its site, which contains only a few remains, may be reached by driving north from Death Valley Junction to a point half-a-mile inside Nevada. There a dirt road turns west and goes in and out of California and Nevada for twenty-one miles to what was once Lee. It is hardly worth the trip, as the road gradually worsens and becomes negotiable only for jeep-type traffic.

RHYOLITE. Not a California town, but nevertheless a "must" for the Death Valley tourist, is Rhyolite—one of the big excitements of the Tonopah-Goldfield boom. Once served by two railroads, Rhyolite is deserted today and fast vanishing under the desert elements. The bottle house and the railroad station are among the principal points of interest.

CHLORIDE CITY. Still another camp of the Rhyolite gold boom is Chloride City, located in a small basin in the Funeral Range. From a point on the Rhyolite road 2.6 miles west of the Nevada border, take a dirt road southeast 4.7 miles; then turn right (south) on a short branch that leads into the little valley and townsite. A few buildings associated with the Chloride Cliff Mine remain.

LEADFIELD. C. C. Julian's old town at the top of Titus Canyon is reached by a dirt road branching from Nevada Highway 58 about 2.4 miles west of the Rhyolite turnoff. Leadfield is 14.5 miles along this road, and while the remains are not imposing the drive is made additionally worthwhile by the rugged desert scenery on down Titus Canyon. The road is one-way only, and should not be attempted without first inquiring about conditions at ranger headquarters in Death Valley.

HARRISBURG. Just over a mile north of Emigrant Pass in the Panamint Range, a dirt road goes 1.8 miles east to the site of Harrisburg, where practically nothing exists today. An additional five mile drive takes one to Aguerreberry Point, the best view of Death Valley from the west.

SKIDOO. Little more than two miles north of the Harrisburg road, another winds seven miles to the site of Skidoo, where little is left but the cemetery, the remains of the stamp mill, and several mines.

SILVER LAKE. Just over eight miles north of Baker, the traveler drives through some fascinating adobe walls that stir the imagination. These are the remains of Silver Lake, a town on the old Tonopah and Tidewater Railroad. Flourishing in 1910, it served as a center for many mines in the nearby mountains.

CRACKERJACK. From Silver Lake a dirt road leads west twenty-four miles to Avawatz Pass, which divides the Avawatz Mountains. West of the road going north through the pass, and about two miles southwest of Cave Springs, are the scant remains of Crackerjack. This gold camp reached its height in 1907-8 and was deserted by 1918.

IVANPAH. In 1867 three prospectors struck silver on the east slope of Clark Mountain, which is north of Mountain Pass and Interstate Highway 15, just west of the Nevada border. Little came of the discovery until Mat Palen made a big new silver strike in 1872. For a time Ivanpah was talked about in every camp from the Sierras to the Colorado River, and stampeders descended on the place from all directions. The camp produced at least $4,000,000 before it died in 1885.

Today Ivanpah may be reached by taking the overpass at Yates Well, just south of Ivanpah Dry Lake, and going west a short distance on a paved road. Here you intersect a dirt road (it was once the main paved highway, but has been covered with sand). Turn north for two miles to a dirt road leading west through the sagebrush up the alluvial slope toward Clark Mountain. After eleven miles, turn left and park next to a cattle corral and two cottonwood trees. Walk west across a ravine and you find yourself in a shallow canyon that was the site of Ivanpah. The remains of two mills, a smelter, and about a dozen rock and adobe buildings are easily found.

VANDERBILT. Southeast from Mountain Pass is Ivanpah Station or South Ivanpah (not to be confused with the old mining camp of Ivanpah) on the Union Pacific line. By driving east about four miles on an old railroad bed (the tracks have been torn up) into the New York Mountains, you reach the old camp of Vanderbilt. The gold and silver mines here were discovered in the 1870s and reached a peak of activity in the 1890s. A number of frame buildings remain to make this an interesting ghost town.

MESCAL. This old silver town was launched in 1887, and is located one mile south of Interstate 15 on a dirt road just west of Mountain Pass.

Post Script:
Other California Mining Towns

CAMBRIA. Started as a mining town during California's copper craze of 1863, Cambria was later a center for quicksilver mining in the Santa Lucia Range. It is located on California Highway 1 between Morrow Bay and San Simeon.

KLAU. This mining town on a road from Cambria to Paso Robles was the center for several quicksilver mines dating from the 1870s.

LOS BURROS AND GORDA. On the coast side of the Santa Lucia Range west of Jolon, in Monterey County, is a small gold mining district first worked by the Spanish. Activity began in earnest with the discovery of the Last Chance Mine on Alder Creek in 1887. Two very small settlements—Los Burros and Gorda—were reported active as late as 1916.

NEW IDRIA. First operated in 1850, the famous New Idria Mine of San Benito County is second only to New Almaden in the production of California quicksilver. Named for the Idria quicksilver district in Austria, the mine and the town are located in the Diablo Range sixty-six miles southeast of Hollister by paved road.

NEW ALMADEN. Fourteen miles south of San Jose on the east side of the Santa Cruz Mountains are the oldest mine and mining town in California—New Almaden—named for the famed Almaden quicksilver center in Spain. First extracted by the Indians for warpaint and other uses, the cinnabar deposits were known to the Spanish-speaking Californians as early as 1824. The mine was officially located by Andres Castillero in 1845—first as a silver and gold mine, and then for its more important content, quicksilver. But the mine soon became the prize in a celebrated dispute that rocked the courts for many years. The issue was intensified when California's Gold Rush put a premium on quicksilver for its value in smelting gold-bearing ores.

One of the longest producers among American mines, New Almaden has turned out a sizable proportion of the nation's quicksilver. The remaining relics of older times are a tumble-down schoolhouse, a powder magazine, and some old cemeteries (largely vandalized).

THE MOUNT DIABLO COAL TOWNS. For some thirty years beginning in the mid-1850s, a number of coal mining towns—Somersville, Nortonville, Judsonville, and Stewartville—flourished on the northeast approach to Mt. Diablo in Contra Costa County. But when they closed in the 1880s most of the buildings were torn up and transported elsewhere.

Bibliography

NEWSPAPERS

Auburn *Placer Herald*, Jan.-Mar., 1853

Aurora *Esmeralda Union*, Nov. 23, 1867-Sept. 12, 1868

Bakersfield *Kern County Courier*, Jan. 21, 1871-Sept. 9, 1876; *Southern Californian*, July 3, 1873-July 1876; *Kern County Gazette*, Nov. 13, 1875-Oct. 14, 1876

Bishop Creek *Times*, Nov. 1, 1881-Feb. 1882

Bodie *Standard*, Sept. 5, 1880

Boston *California Bulletin*, Mar. 6, Apr. 5, 19, 1849

Calico *Print*, Oct. 10, 1886

Columbia *Gazette*, Feb. 12-Mar. 5, 1853, Mar. 15, 1856

Darwin *Coso Mining News*, Nov. 6, 1875-Nov. 10, 1877 (incomplete)

Downieville *Mountain Echo*, June 19, 1852-June 1853

Grass Valley *National*, Oct. 5, 1853 (Extra)

Havilah *Miner*, June 29, 1872-May 1874

Honolulu *Polynesian*, June 24-Nov. 4, 1848; *Sandwich Island News*, June 22-Oct. 5, 1848

Independence (Calif.) *Inyo Independent*, July 9, 1870-Feb. 1882

Julian *Sentinel*, May 9-16, 1890, July 23-Dec. 1891

Kanesville (Council Bluffs, Ia.) *Frontier Guardian*, Feb.-June 1849

London *Times*, Dec. 22, 1848-Jan. 15, 1849

Los Angeles *News* (scattered issues), Apr. 1866-Nov. 1872; *Southern Californian*, July 20, 1854-June 20, 1855; *Star*, June 1853-July 1856, June 1868-Jan. 1871, Apr. 1874-Dec. 1875

Mariposa *Chronicle*, Jan. 20, 1854; *Democrat*, Aug. 5, 1856; *Gazette*, July 14, 1858

Marysville *Herald*, Aug. 6-Dec. 1850

Mokelumne Hill *Calaveras Chronicle*, Mar. 19-26, 1853

New Orleans *Picayune*, Jan. 26-Feb. 21, 1849

New York *Tribune*, Nov. 25, 1848-Jan. 15, 1849

Panama *Star*, Mar. 17, Nov. 10, 1849

Panamint *News*, Nov. 26, 1874-May 18, 1875 (inc.)

Philadelphia *Public Ledger*, Dec. 1, 1848-Jan. 11, 1849

Quincy *Prospector*, Mar. 3-Nov. 17, 1855

Randsburg *Miner*, July 2, 1898, Mar. 17, 1900 (copies)

Rhyolite *Herald*, Feb. 8, 1907

Sacramento *Placer Times*, Apr. 28, 1849-June 7, 1850; *Union*, Jan.-Mar. 1853, July-Oct. 1859, Mar.-Oct. 1860

St. Joseph (Mo.) *Gazette*, Ap.-June 1849; *Adventure*, Mar. 16-Ap. 20, 1849

Salt Lake City *Deseret News*, June 29, July 6, 1850

San Bernardino *Argus*, Sept. 14, 1874-Feb. 8, 1875 (inc.); *Guardian*, Mar. 21, 1874-May 22, 1875; *Telegram*, June 1881-May 1885

San Diego *Bulletin*, Sept. 1869-Dec. 2, 1871 (inc.); *Union*, Dec. 30, 1869-1871 (inc.)

San Francisco *Alta California*, Feb. 1849-Dec. 1850, Dec. 1852-Aug. 1853, July-Oct. 1859, Ap.-Oct. 1860; *Bulletin*, Oct. 13-31, 1859, Jan.-Ap. 2, 1860; *The Californian*, Mar. 15-Aug. 14, 1848; *The California Star*, Mar. 18-June 10, 1848; *The California Star and Californian*, Nov. 18-Dec. 9, 1848; *Call*, July-Oct. 1859, Mar.-Oct. 1860; *Herald*, Ap. 18, May 9, 1853; *Pacific News*, Aug. 1849-Jan. 1850.

Santa Barbara *Gazette*, May 24, 1855-Dec. 1856

Silver Mountain *Silver Miner*, June 30, 1868

Sonora *Herald*, July 4-13, 27, Dec. 28, 1850-Feb. 1, 1851.

Stockton *San Joaquin Republican*, May 14, 1851-Aug. 1853; *Times*, Mar. 1850-Ap. 1851, Dec. 1852-Aug. 1853

Visalia *Delta*, Nov. 20, 1867-June 27, 1872.

Weaverville *Trinity Journal*, Oct. 16, 1858

LETTERS, DIARIES, MEMOIRS *(manuscript)*

Baker, Isaac W., *Journals, 1849-52.* Bancroft Library, Berkeley

Bertheau, Cesar, *Journal of Voyage, 1849.* State Library, Sacramento

Blake, Seth B., *Diary 1849-50.* Sac.
Bradford, John S., *Diary, 1849, Illinois to California.* Sac.
Buffum, Joseph Curtis, *Diary, 1847-55.* Sac.
Carder, James B., *Journal on board the ship Hopewell, 1849.* Bancroft
Chamberlin, William E., *Diary, April 11-Aug. 20, 1849.* Sac.
Child, Sophia A., *Correspondence, 1849-51.* Ban.
Clark, Sterling B. F., *Diary, Crossing the Plains, 1849.* Sac.
Counts, George, *Copy of Diary March 23-May 4, 1849.* Ban.
Crackbon, Joseph, *Narrative of a Voyage from Boston to Calif., 1849.* Sac.
Dimmick, Kimball Hale, *Diary, San Francisco April 16-Oct. 26, 1848.* Huntington Library, San Marino
Dwinnelle, John Whipple, *Diary, 1849.* Ban.
Emerson, William Henry, *The Diary of, 1849.* Sac.
Farrar, Jarvis G., *Diary of, 1849-1852.* Sac.
Fitch, John R., *Letters and journal, 1848-52.* Hunt.
Fletcher, Warren, *Papers, including journal, Jan. 2-July 15, 1849.* Ban.
Gould, Charles, *Diary as member of Boston and Newton Ass'n, 1849.* Ban.
Hall, O. J. *The Diary of a '49er.* Sac.
Hittell, John S., *Letters concerning the discovery . . . at Sutter's Mill.* Ban.
Hyde, Henry Hovy, Jr., *Journal of a Voyage . . . 1849.* Sac.

Jordan, Dr. David, *Diary, 1849, from Ohio to Calif.* Sac.
Josselyn, Amos P., *Journal of, 1849.* Sac.
Kirkpatrick, Charles A., *Journal of, 1849.* Ban.
Larkin, Thomas O. *Letters and papers, June 1-Sept. 10, 1848.* Ban.
Lindsay, Tipton, *A Journal of a trip to Calif., 1849.* Ban.
McCrackan, John, *Letters of, 1849-53.* Ban.
Meredith, Griffith, *Journal from N.Y. in 1849 via Cape Horn to S.F.* Sac.
Miller, Reuben G. *Journal, 1849.* Hunt.
Nusbaumer, Louis, *Adventures of a Trip to the Gold fields, 1849-50.* Sac.
Reynolds, W. P., *Letter, S.F., Dec. 27, 1848.* Hunt.
Richardson, Henry P., *Letter, S.F., July 9, 1848.* In Stearns Papers, Hunt.
Rogers, John Page, *Five Letters to Wife while en route from Oregon and in the Mines, Sept. 23, 1848-Jan. 3, 1849.* Sac.
Smith, Azariah, *Diary, Sutter's Mill, Jan.-April 1848.* Photostat at Ban.
Snow, Joseph Chester, *Diary and Papers, 1849-53.* Ban.
Taylor, Augustus F., *Diary 1849, of a trip to Calif.* Ban.
Taylor, John, *Journal of a voyage, N.Y. to S.F., 1849.* Ban.
Tuttle, Charles Albion, *Correspondence with his wife and misc. papers.* Ban.
Winchester, Jonas, *Letters from a Gold Hunter, Feb. 27-Dec. 8, 1849.* Sac.

LETTERS, DIARIES, MEMOIRS (*Published*)

Ayers, Col. James J., *Gold and Sunshine.* Boston, 1922
Bari, Valeska (ed.), *The Course of Empire.* N. Y., 1931
Bell, Horace, *Reminiscences of a Ranger.* Los Angeles, 1881
Bidwell, John, *Echoes of the Past.* Ed., Milo M. Quaife, Chicago, 1922
Bigler, Henry W.., "*Diary of, in 1847 and 1848*," Overland, Sept. 1887; "*Reminiscence of Gold Discovery,*" Q. of Soc. Calif. Pioneers, S.F., Vol. 1, No. 3
Borthwick, J. D., *Three Years in California.* Edinburgh & London, 1857
Brewer, William H., *Up and Down California in 1860-64.* New Haven, 1930
Brooks, J. T., *Four Months Among the Gold Finders.* London & N.Y., 1849
Browne, J. Ross, *A Peep at Washoe and Washoe Revisited.* Balboa Island,

1959
Bruff, J. Goldsborough, *Gold Rush,* 2 Vols. N.Y., 1944
Buck, Franklin A., *A Yankee Trader in the Gold Rush.* Boston, 1930
Buffum, E. Gould, *Six Months in the Gold Mines.* Phila., 1850
Burnett, Peter H., *Recollections and Opinions of an Old Pioneer.* N.Y., 1880
Carson, J. H., *Early Recollections of the Mines.* Stockton, 1852
Christman, Enos, *One Man's Gold,* Ed. by Florence M. Christman. N.Y., 1930
Clappe, Louise A. K. S., *California in 1851.* S.F., 1933
Cordua, Theodor, "*Memoirs,*" Ed. and Trans. by E. D. Gudde, California Historical Society Quarterly, Vol. 12, No. 4
Coke, Henry John, *A Ride over the*

Rocky Mountains. London, 1852

Colton, Rev. Walter, *Three Years in California.* New York, 1850

Crosby, Elisha O., *Memoirs,* Ed. by Charles A. Barker. San Marino, 1945

Delano, Alonzo, *Life on the Plains and at the Diggings.* Auburn & Buffalo, 1854

Downie, William, *Hunting for Gold.* S.F., 1893

Eaton, Henry G., "Bodie Was a Swell Town!" L. A. Times Sun. Mag., July 31, 1932

Ferguson, Charles D., *The California Gold Fields.* Oakland, 1948

Frémont, Elizabeth Benton, *Recollections.* N.Y., 1912

Frémont, Jesse Benton, *Far West Sketches.* Boston, 1890

Gerstaeker, Friedrich, *California Gold Mines.* Oakland, 1946

Gillis, William R., *Gold Rush Days with Mark Twain.* N.Y., 1930

Greeley, Horace, *An Overland Journey.* N.Y., 1860

Gregson, Mrs. Eliza and James, *The Gregson Memoirs.* S.F., 1940

Gwin, William M., "Memoirs." California Hist. Soc. Quarterly, Vol. 19

Hafen, LeRoy R., *Journals of the Forty-Niners.* Glendale, 1954

Hancock, Samuel, *The Narrative of Samuel Hancock, 1845-60.* N.Y., 1927

Harpending, Asbury, *The Great Diamond Hoax.* S.F., 1913

Hollingsworth, John McHenry, *The Journal of, 1846-49.* S.F., 1923

Ingalls, John, *California Letters.* Worcester, Mass., 1938

Johnson, Theodore T., *Sights in the Gold Region.* N.Y., 1849

Keller, George A., *A Trip Across the Plains.* Oakland, 1855

Kelly, William, *An Excursion to California,* 2 vols. London, 1851

Leinhard, Heinrich, *A Pioneer at Sutter's Fort, 1846-50.* Trans. and ed. by Marguerite Eyer Wilbur. Los Angeles, 1941

Leuba, Edmond, "A Frenchman in the Panamints," Calif. Hist. Soc. Q., v. 17, Sept., 1938

Lynch, James, *With Stevenson to California.* San Luis Obispo, 1896

Lyman, Chester S., *Around the Horn to the Sandwich Islands and California, 1845-50,* Ed. by F. J. Taggart. New Haven, 1924; "*Letters of, Sept.-Nov. 1848,* in S.F.," Cal. Hist. Soc. Q. June 1934

Marryatt, Frank, *Mountains and Molehills.* N.Y., 1855

Marshall, James, "The Discovery of Gold in California," Hutching's California Magazine, Nov. 1857

Megquier, Mary Jane, *Apron Full of Gold,* Ed. by Robert G. Cleland, San Marino, 1949

Mellen, Herman F., "Reminiscences of Old Calico," Historical Society of Southern California Quarterly, June-Sept.-Dec., 1952

Miller, Joaquin, *California Diary, 1855-57,* Ed. John S. Richards. Seattle, 1936

Moerenhout, Jacques Antoine, *The Inside Story of the Gold Rush,* Trans. and ed. by Abraham P. Nasatir. S.F., 1935

Pritchard, James A., *Overland Diary,* Ed. by Dale L. Morgan. Denver, 1959

Revere, Joseph Warren, *A Tour of Duty in California.* N.Y., 1849

Royce, Sarah, *A Frontier Lady.* New Haven, 1932

Russ, Carolyn Hale, *The Log of a Forty-Niner.* Boston, 1923

Ryan, William R., *Personal Adventures in . . . California.* London, 1852

San Felipe Mining Co. *vs.* Belshaw et al. Calif. Supreme Court Records, v. 289

Sawyer, Lorenzo, *Way Sketches.* N.Y., 1926

Shaw, Reuben Cole, *Across the Plains in '49.* Farmland, Indiana, 1896

Sherman, William T., *Memoirs,* Vol. 1. N.Y., 1891

Stewart, William M., *Reminiscences of,* Ed. by G. R. Brown. N.Y. and Wash., 1908

Sutter, John A., *New Helvetia Diary, 1845-48,* S.F., 1939; *Sutter's Own Story,* Ed. by E. G. Gudde, N.Y., 1936; *The Diary of,* S.F., 1932; "The Discovery of Gold in California," Hutchings' California Magazine, vol. 4, No. 5, Nov., 1857

Taylor, Bayard, *Eldorado,* 2 vols. N.Y., 1850

Thornton, J. Quinn, *California in 1848,* 2 vols. N.Y., 1849

Twain, Mark, *Roughing It.* Hartford, 1872

War Dept., U.S., *The War of the Rebellion,* v. 50, Parts 1 and 2. Wash., 1899

Wells, Fargo & Co., Scrapbook, *Posters and other papers relating to Robberies, 1871-75; Robber's Record,* S.F., 1885 (includes reports of detectives James B. Hume and John Thacker, 1870-1885).

Bancroft, Hubert Howe, *History of California*, v. 6 & 7, S.F., 1888 & 1890; *California Pastoral*, v. 34 of *Works*, S.F., 1888; *California Inter Pocula*, v. 35, S.F., 1888; *Popular Tribunals*, v. 36 & 37, S.F., 1887; *History of Oregon*, v. 2, S.F., 1888

Beattie, George W. and Helen P., *Heritage of the Valley*. Pasadena, 1939

Browne, J. Ross, *Report on Mineral Resources of the U.S.* Wash., 1867

Bucklee, Edna Bryan, *The Saga of Old Tuolumne*. N.Y., 1935

Cain, Ella M., *The Story of Bodie*. S.F. & Sonora, 1956; *The Story of Early Mono County*. S.F., 1961

California State Division of Mines, *Annual Reports of the State Mineralogist*. Sacramento, 1882-1918; 1954-56.

Caruthers, William, *Loafing Along Death Valley Trails*. Ontario, Calif., 1951

Chalfant, Willie A., *The Story of Inyo*, Chicago, 1922; *Outposts of Civilization*, Boston, 1928; *Tales of the Pioneers*, Stanford, 1942; *Gold, Guns, and Ghost Towns*, Stanford, 1947; "Cerro Gordo," Hist. Soc. of So. Calif. Pubs., v. 22, 1940

Coy, Owen C., *Gold Days*. L.A., 1929

Dane, George Ezra, in collab. with Beatrice Dane, *Ghost Town*. N.Y., 1941

Davis, Sam P. (ed.) *The History of Nevada*. Reno and L.A., 1913

Dryer, Marjorie, "Old Dale Diggings," Westways, Oct. 1957

Dudley, Aaron, and Fickewirth, Alvin, "Ghost Town of the Mojave," Westways, Nov. 1941

Fairfield, Asa Merrill, *Fairfield's Pioneer History of Lassen Co.*, S.F., 1916

Fisk, O. J., "Ghosts of Greenwater," Westways, Nov., 1940

Glasscock, C. B., *Gold in Them Hills*, Indianapolis, 1932; *A Golden Highway*, Indianapolis, 1934; *Here's Death Valley*, N.Y., 1940

Greene, Charles L., "The California Rand," Overland, May, 1897

Gudde, Edwin G., *California Place Names*, Berkeley, 1960

Guinn, James M., "The Sonoran Immigration," Hist. Soc. of So. Calif. Pubs., v. 8, 1909-10

Holland, Henrietta, "George Washington's Birthday, 1870," Westways, Feb. 1948

Hoover, Mildred B., Rensch, Hero E. and Ethel G., *Historic Spots in California*, Revised by Ruth Teiser. Stanford, 1948

Hungerford, Edward, *Wells Fargo*, N.Y., 1949

Hunt, Rockwell D., *John Bidwell*. Caldwell, Idaho, 1942

Jackson, Joseph Henry, *Anybody's Gold*, N.Y., 1941; *Bad Company*, N.Y., 1949

Jenkins, Olaf P., *Geologic Guidebook Along Highway 49*. S.F., 1948

Johnston, Philip, "Epitaph for Ivanpah," Westways, Jan. 1942

Kneiss, Gilbert H., *Bonanza Railroads*, Stanford, 1954

Land of Sunshine, "Randsburg, the Great New Mining Camp of So. Calif.," March, 1897

Lord, Eliot, *Comstock Mining and Miners*. Wash., 1883

Page, Elizabeth, *Wagons West*. N.Y., 1930

Parsons, George F., *The Life and Adventures of James W. Marshall*. S.F., 1935

Rickard, Thomas A., *The Romance of Mining*, Toronto, 1945

Rourke, Constance, *Troupers of the Gold Coast*. N.Y., 1928

Royce, Josiah, *California*. Cambridge, Mass., 1886

Russell, C. P., "The Bodie that Was," Touring Topics, Nov. 1929; "Early Mining Excitements East of Yosemite," Sierra Club Bull., v. 13, no. 1.

Shinn, Charles H., *Mining Camps*, N.Y., 1885; *Story of the Mine*, N.Y., 1896

Sunset, Editors of, *Gold Rush Country*. Menlo Park, Calif., 1957 & 1963

Thompson, David G., *The Mojave Desert Region: A Geographic, Geologic, and Hydrologic Reconnaissance*. Wash., 1922

Tinsley, H. G., "A Desert Mining Town," Harper's Weekly, March 6, 1897

Walker, Franklin D., *San Francisco's Literary Frontier*. N.Y., 1939

Wilson, Neill C., *Treasure Express: Epic Days of Wells Fargo*. N.Y., 1936

Winther, Oscar O., *Express and Stagecoach Days in California*, Stanford, 1936; *Via Western Express and Stagecoach*, Stanford, 1945

Wynn, Marcia Rittenhouse, *Desert Bonanza*. Culver City, Calif., 1949

Index

2847

Armenia, Azerbaijan, and Georgia
country studies

Federal Research Division
Library of Congress
Edited by
Glenn E. Curtis
Research Completed
March 1994

On the cover: Cultural artifacts from Georgia (upper
left) and Azerbaijan (right), and folk costume from
Armenia

First Edition, First Printing, 1995.

Library of Congress Cataloging-in-Publication Data

Armenia, Azerbaijan, and Georgia : country studies / Fed-
eral Research Division, Library of Congress ; edited by
Glenn E. Curtis.—1st ed.
    p. cm.—(Area handbook series, ISSN 1057–5294)
(DA Pam ; 550–111)
  "Research completed March 1994."
  Includes bibliographical references (pp. 257–68) and
index.
  ISBN 0–8444–0848–4
  1. Transcaucasia—Handbooks, manuals, etc. I. Curtis,
Glenn E. (Glenn Eldon), 1946– . II. Library of Congress.
Federal Research Division. III. Series. IV. Series:
DA Pam ; 550–111.
DK509.A727 1995   94–45459
947'.9–dc20   CIP

Headquarters, Department of the Army
DA Pam 550–111

Reprinted without alteration on recycled acid-free paper

Bernan
Lanham, Maryland
May 1995

Foreword

This volume is one in a continuing series of books prepared by the Federal Research Division of the Library of Congress under the Country Studies/Area Handbook Program sponsored by the Department of the Army. The last two pages of this book list the other published studies.

Most books in the series deal with a particular foreign country, describing and analyzing its political, economic, social, and national security systems and institutions, and examining the interrelationships of those systems and the ways they are shaped by cultural factors. Each study is written by a multidisciplinary team of social scientists. The authors seek to provide a basic understanding of the observed society, striving for a dynamic rather than a static portrayal. Particular attention is devoted to the people who make up the society, their origins, dominant beliefs and values, their common interests and the issues on which they are divided, the nature and extent of their involvement with national institutions, and their attitudes toward each other and toward their social system and political order.

The books represent the analysis of the authors and should not be construed as an expression of an official United States government position, policy, or decision. The authors have sought to adhere to accepted standards of scholarly objectivity. Corrections, additions, and suggestions for changes from readers will be welcomed for use in future editions.

Louis R. Mortimer
Chief
Federal Research Division
Library of Congress
Washington, D.C. 20540–5220

Acknowledgments

The authors are indebted to numerous individuals and organizations who gave their time, research materials, and expertise on affairs in the nations of the Transcaucasus to provide data, perspective, and material support for this volume.

The collection of accurate and current information was assisted greatly by the contributions of Professor Stephen Jones of Mount Holyoke College, Dee Ann Holisky, Betty Blair of *Azerbaijan International*, and Joseph Masih of the Armenian Assembly of America. The authors acknowledge the generosity of individuals and public and private agencies—including *Azerbaijan International*, the Embassy of Azerbaijan, and the White House Photo Office—who allowed their photographs to be used in this study.

Thanks also go to Ralph K. Benesch, who oversees the Country Studies/Area Handbook Program for the Department of the Army. In addition, the authors appreciate the advice and guidance of Sandra W. Meditz, Federal Research Division coordinator of the handbook series. Special thanks go to Marilyn L. Majeska, who supervised editing; Andrea T. Merrill, who managed production; David P. Cabitto, who designed the book cover and the illustrations on the title page of each chapter, provided graphics support, and, together with Thomas D. Hall, prepared the maps; and Helen Fedor, who obtained and organized the photographs. The following individuals are gratefully acknowledged as well: Vincent Ercolano, who edited the chapters; Barbara Edgerton and Izella Watson, who did the word processing; Catherine Schwartzstein, who performed the final prepublication editorial review; Joan C. Cook, who compiled the index; and Stephen C. Cranton and David P. Cabitto, who prepared the camera-ready copy.

Contents

List of Figures

Preface

At the end of 1991, the formal liquidation of the Soviet Union was the surprisingly swift result of partially hidden decrepitude and centrifugal forces within that empire. Of the fifteen "new" states that emerged from the process, many had been independent political entities at some time in the past. Aside from their coverage in the 1991 *Soviet Union: A Country Study,* none had received individual treatment in this series, however. *Armenia, Azerbaijan, and Georgia: Country Studies* is the first in a new subseries describing the fifteen post-Soviet republics, both as they existed before and during the Soviet era and as they have developed since 1991. This volume covers Armenia, Azerbaijan, and Georgia, the three small nations grouped around the Caucasus mountain range east of the Black Sea.

The marked relaxation of information restrictions, which began in the late 1980s and accelerated after 1991, allows the reporting of nearly complete data on every aspect of life in the three countries. Scholarly articles and periodical reports have been especially helpful in accounting for the years of independence in the 1990s. The authors have described the historical, political, and social backgrounds of the countries as the background for their current portraits. In each case, the authors' goal was to provide a compact, accessible, and objective treatment of five main topics: historical background, the society and its environment, the economy, government and politics, and national security.

In all cases, personal names have been transliterated from the vernacular languages according to standard practice. Place-names are rendered in the form approved by the United States Board on Geographic Names, when available. Because in many cases the board had not yet applied vernacular tables in transliterating official place-names at the time of printing, the most recent Soviet-era forms have been used in this volume. Conventional international variants, such as Moscow, are used when appropriate. Organizations commonly known by their acronyms (such as IMF—International Monetary Fund) are introduced by their full names. Autonomous republics and autonomous regions, such as the Nakhichevan Autonomous Republic, the South Ossetian Autonomous Region, and the Abkhazian Autonomous Republic, are introduced in their full form (before 1991 these also included the phrase "Soviet Socialist"), and subsequently referred to by shorter forms (Nakhichevan, South Ossetia, and Abkhazia, respectively).

Measurements are given in the metric system; a conversion table is provided in the Appendix. A chronology is provided at the beginning of the book, combining significant historical events of the three countries. To amplify points in the text of the chapters, tables in the Appendix provide statistics on aspects of the societies and the economies of the countries.

The body of the text reflects information available as of March 1994. Certain other portions of the text, however, have been updated. The Introduction discusses significant events and trends that have occurred since the completion of research; the Country Profiles include updated information as available; and the Bibliography lists recently published sources thought to be particularly helpful to the reader.

Table A. Chronology of Important Events

Period	Description
EARLY HISTORY	
95–55 B.C	Armenian Empire reaches greatest size and influence under Tigran the Great.
66 B.C.	Romans complete conquest of Caucasus Mountains region, including Georgian kingdom of Kartli-Iberia.
30 B.C.	Romans conquer Armenian Empire.
A.D. 100–300	Romans annex Azerbaijan and name it Albania.
ca. 310	Tiridates III accepts Christianity for the Armenian people.
330	King Marian III of Kartli-Iberia accepts Christianity for the Georgian people.
FIFTH–SEVENTH CENTURIES	First golden age of Armenian culture.
ca. 600	Four centuries of Arab control of Azerbaijan begin, introducing Islam in seventh century.
645	Arabs capture Tbilisi.
653	Byzantine Empire cedes Armenia to Arabs.
NINTH–TENTH CENTURIES	
806	Arabs install Bagratid family to govern Armenia.
813	Armenian prince Ashot I begins 1,000 years of rule in Georgia by Bagratid Dynasty.
862–977	Second golden age of Armenian culture, under Ashot I and Ashot III.
ELEVENTH–FOURTEENTH CENTURIES	Byzantine Greeks invade Armenia from west, Seljuk Turks from east; Turkish groups wrest political control of Azerbaijan from Arabs, introducing Turkish language and culture.
1099–1125	David IV the Builder establishes expanded Georgian Empire and begins golden age of Georgia.

Period	Description
1000–late 1200s	Golden age of Azerbaijani literature and architecture.
1100s–1300s	Cilician Armenian and Georgian armies aid European armies in Crusades to limit Muslim control of Holy Land.
1200–1400	Mongols twice invade Azerbaijan, establishing temporary dynasties.
1375	Cilician Armenia conquered by Mamluk Turks.
1386	Timur (Tamerlane) sacks Tbilisi, ending Georgian Empire
FIFTEENTH CENTURY	Most of modern Armenia, Azerbaijan, and Georgia become part of Ottoman Empire.
SIXTEENTH CENTURY	
1501	Azerbaijani Safavid Dynasty begins rule by Persian Empire.
1553	Ottoman Turks and Persians divide Georgia between them.
EIGHTEENTH CENTURY	
ca. 1700	Russia begins moving into northern Azerbaijan as Persian Empire weakens.
1762	Herekle II reunites eastern Georgian regions in kingdom of Kartli-Kakhetia.
NINETEENTH CENTURY	
1801	After Herekle II's appeal for aid, Russian Empire abolishes Bagratid Dynasty and begins annexation of Georgia.
1811	Georgian Orthodox Church loses autocephalous status in Russification process.
1813	Treaty of Gulistan officially divides Azerbaijan into Russian (northern) and Persian (southern) spheres.
1828	Treaty of Turkmanchay awards Nakhichevan and area around Erevan to Russia, strengthening Russian control of Transcaucasus and beginning period of modernization and security.
1872	Oil industry established around Baku, beginning rapid expansion.

Period	Description
1878	"Armenian question" emerges at Congress of Berlin; disposition of Armenia becomes ongoing European issue.
1891	First Armenian revolutionary party formed.
1895	Massacre of 300,000 Armenian subjects by Ottoman Turks.

TWENTIETH CENTURY

Period	Description
ca. 1900	Radical political organizations begin to form in Azerbaijan.
1908	Young Turks take over government of Ottoman Empire with reform agenda, supported by Armenian population.
1915	Young Turks massacre 600,000 to 2 million Armenians; most survivors leave eastern Anatolia.
1917	Armenia, Azerbaijan, and Georgia form independent Transcaucasian federation. Tsar Nicholas II abdicates Russian throne; Bolsheviks take power in Russia.
1918	Independent Armenian, Azerbaijani, and Georgian states emerge from defeat of Ottoman Empire in World War I.
1920	Red Army invades Azerbaijan and forces Armenia to accept communist-dominated government.
1921	Red Army invades Georgia and drives out Zhordania government.
1922	Transcaucasian Soviet Federated Socialist Republic combines Armenia, Azerbaijan, and Georgia as single republic within Soviet Union.
1936	Armenia, Azerbaijan, and Georgia become separate republics within Soviet Union.
1936–37	Purges under political commissar Lavrenti Beria reach their peak in Armenia, Azerbaijan, and Georgia.
1943	Autonomy restored to Georgian Orthodox Church.
1946	Western powers force Soviet Union to abandon Autonomous Government of Azerbaijan, formed in 1945 after Soviet occupation of northern Iran.
1959	Nikita S. Khrushchev purges Azerbaijani Communist Party.

Period	Description
1969	Heydar Aliyev named head of Azerbaijani Communist Party.
ca. 1970	Zviad Gamsakhurdia begins organizing dissident Georgian nationalists.
1972	Eduard Shevardnadze named first secretary of Georgian Communist Party.
1974	Moscow installs regime of Karen Demirchian in Armenia to end party corruption; regime later removed for corruption.
1978	Mass demonstrations prevent Moscow from making Russian an official language of Georgia.
1982	Aliyev of Azerbaijan named full member of Politburo of Communist Party of the Soviet Union.
1985	Shevardnadze named minister of foreign affairs of Soviet Union and leaves post as first secretary of Georgian Communist Party.
Late 1980s	Mikhail S. Gorbachev initiates policies of *glasnost* and *perestroika* throughout Soviet Union.
1988	Armenian nationalist movement revived by Karabakh and corruption concerns.
February	Nagorno-Karabakh government votes to unify that autonomous region of Azerbaijan with Armenia.
December	Disastrous earthquake in northern Armenia heavily damages Leninakan (now Gyumri).
1989 April	Soviet troops kill Georgian civilian demonstrators in Tbilisi, radicalizing Georgian public opinion.
Spring	Mass demonstrations in Armenia achieve release of Karabakh Committee arrested by Soviets to quell nationalist movement.
September	Azerbaijan begins blockade of Armenian fuel and supply lines over Karabakh issue.
Fall	Azerbaijani opposition parties lead mass protests against Soviet rule; national sovereignty officially proclaimed.
November	Nagorno-Karabakh National Council declares unification of Nagorno-Karabakh with Armenia.
1990 January	Moscow sends troops to Azerbaijan, nominally to stem violence

Period	Description
	against Armenians over Karabakh
Spring	Levon Ter-Petrosian of Armenian Pannational Movement chosen chairman of Armenian Supreme Soviet.
October	In first multiparty election held in Georgia, Gamsakhurdia's oppositionist party crushes communists; Gamsakhurdia named president.
1991 January	Georgian forces invade South Ossetia in response to independence movement there; fighting continues all year; Soviet troops invade Azerbaijan, ostensibly to halt anti-Armenian pogroms.
April	After referendum approval, Georgian parliament declares Georgia independent of Soviet Union.
May	Gamsakhurdia becomes first president of Georgia, elected directly in multiparty election.
August	Attempted coup against Gorbachev in Moscow fails.
September	Armenian voters approve national independence.
October	Azerbaijani referendum declares Azerbaijan independent of Soviet Union; Ter-Petrosian elected president of Armenia.
December	Armenians in Nagorno-Karabakh declare independent state as fighting there continues; Soviet Union officially dissolved.
1992 January	Gamsakhurdia driven from Georgia into exile by opposition forces.
March	Shevardnadze returns to Tbilisi and forms new government.
Spring	Armenian forces occupy Lachin corridor linking Nagorno-Karabakh to Armenia.
June	Abulfaz Elchibey elected president of Azerbaijan and forms first postcommunist government there.
July	Cease-fire mediated by Russia's President Yeltsin in South Ossetia.
October	Parliamentary election held in Georgia; Shevardnazde receives overwhelming support.
Fall	Fighting begins between Abkhazian independence forces and Georgian forces; large-scale refugee displacement continues through next two years.

Period	Description
1993 June	Military coup deposes Elchibey in Azerbaijan; Aliyev returns to power.
Fall	Multilateral negotiations seek settlement of Karabakh conflict, without result; fighting, blockade, and international negotiation continue into 1994.
October	Shevardnadze responds to deterioration of Georgian military position by having Georgia join Commonwealth of Independent States, thus gaining Russian military support; Aliyev elected president of Azerbaijan.

Introduction

THE THREE REPUBLICS of Transcaucasia—Armenia, Azerbaijan, and Georgia—were included in the Soviet Union in the early 1920s after their inhabitants had passed through long and varied periods as separate nations and as parts of neighboring empires, most recently the Russian Empire. By the time the Soviet Union dissolved at the end of 1991, the three republics had regained their independence, but their economic weakness and the turmoil surrounding them jeopardized that independence almost immediately. By 1994 Russia had regained substantial influence in the region by arbitrating disputes and by judiciously inserting peacekeeping troops. Geographically isolated, the three nations gained some Western economic support in the early 1990s, but in 1994 the leaders of all three asserted that national survival depended chiefly on diverting resources from military applications to restructuring economic and social institutions.

Location at the meeting point of southeastern Europe with the western border of Asia greatly influenced the histories of the three national groups forming the present-day Transcaucasian republics (see fig. 1; fig. 2). Especially between the twelfth and the twentieth centuries, their peoples were subject to invasion and control by the Ottoman, Persian, and Russian empires. But, with the formation of the twentieth-century states named for them, the Armenian, Azerbaijani, and Georgian peoples as a whole underwent different degrees of displacement and played quite different roles. For example, the Republic of Azerbaijan that emerged from the Soviet Union in 1991 contains only 5.8 million of the world's estimated 19 million Azerbaijanis, with most of the balance living in Iran, across a southern border fixed by Persia and Russia in the nineteenth century. At the same time, slightly more than half the world's 6.3 million Armenians are widely scattered outside the borders of the Republic of Armenia as a result of a centuries-long diaspora and step-by-step reduction of their national territory. In contrast, the great majority of the world's Georgian population lives in the Republic of Georgia (together with ethnic minorities constituting about 30 percent of the republic's population), after having experienced centuries of foreign domination but little forcible alteration of national boundaries.

The starting points and the outside influences that formed the three cultures also were quite different. In pre-Christian times, Georgia's location along the Black Sea opened it to cultural influence from Greece. During the same period, Armenia was settled by tribes from southeastern Europe, and Azerbaijan was settled by Asiatic Medes, Persians, and Scythians. In Azerbaijan, Persian cultural influence dominated in the formative period of the first millennium B.C. In the early fourth century, kings of Armenia and Georgia accepted Christianity after extensive contact with the proselytizing early Christians at the eastern end of the Mediterranean. Following their conversion, Georgians remained tied by religion to the Roman Empire and later the Byzantine Empire centered at Constantinople. Although Armenian Christianity broke with Byzantine Orthodoxy very early, Byzantine occupation of Armenian territory enhanced the influence of Greek culture on Armenians in the Middle Ages.

In Azerbaijan, the Zoroastrian religion, a legacy of the early Persian influence there, was supplanted in the seventh century by the Muslim faith introduced by conquering Arabs. Conquest and occupation by the Turks added centuries of Turkic influence, which remains a primary element of secular Azerbaijani culture, notably in language and the arts. In the twentieth century, Islam remains the prevalent religion of Azerbaijan, with about three-quarters of the population adhering to the Shia (see Glossary) branch.

Golden ages of peace and independence enabled the three civilizations to individualize their forms of art and literature before 1300, and all have retained unique characteristics that arose during those eras. The Armenian, Azerbaijani, and Georgian languages also grew in different directions: Armenian developed from a combination of Indo-European and non-Indo-European language stock, with an alphabet based on the Greek; Azerbaijani, akin to Turkish and originating in Central Asia, now uses the Roman alphabet after periods of official usage of the Arabic and Cyrillic alphabets; and Georgian, unrelated to any major world language, uses a Greek-based alphabet quite different from the Armenian.

Beginning in the eighteenth century, the Russian Empire constantly probed the Caucasus region for possible expansion toward the Black Sea and the Caspian Sea. These efforts engaged Russia in a series of wars with the Persian and Ottoman empires, both of which by that time were decaying from within. By 1828 Russia had annexed or had been awarded by treaty all of present-day Azerbaijan and Georgia and most of present-day Armenia. (At that time, much of the Armenian population remained across the border in the Ottoman Empire.)

Except for about two years of unstable independence following World War I, the Transcaucasus countries remained under Russian, and later Soviet, control until 1991. As part of the Soviet Union from 1922 to 1991, they underwent approximately the same degree of economic and political regimentation as the other constituent republics of the union (until 1936 the Transcaucasian Soviet Federated Socialist Republic included all three countries). The Sovietization process included intensive industrialization, collectivization of agriculture, and large-scale shifts of the rural work force to industrial centers, as well as expanded and standardized systems for education, health care, and social welfare. Although industries came under uniform state direction, private farms in the three republics, especially in Georgia, remained important agriculturally because of the inefficiency of collective farms.

The achievement of independence in 1991 left the three republics with inefficient and often crumbling remains of the Soviet-era state systems. In the years that followed, political, military, and financial chaos prevented reforms from being implemented in most areas. Land redistribution proceeded rapidly in Armenia and Georgia, although agricultural inputs often remained under state control. In contrast, in 1994 Azerbaijan still depended mainly on collective farms. Education and health institutions remained substantially the same centralized suppliers as they had in the Soviet era, but availability of educational and medical materials and personnel dropped sharply after 1991. The military conflict in Azerbaijan's Nagorno-Karabakh Autonomous Region put enormous stress on the health and social welfare systems of combatants Armenia and Azerbaijan, and Azerbaijan's blockade of Armenia, which began in 1989, caused acute shortages of all types of materials (see fig. 3).

The relationship of Russia to the former Soviet republics in the Transcaucasus caused increasing international concern in the transition years. The presence of Russian peacekeeping troops between Georgian and Abkhazian separatist forces remained an irritant to Georgian nationalists and an indication that Russia intended to intervene in that part of the world

Figure 3. Nagorno-Karabakh, 1994

when opportunities arose. Russian nationalists saw such intervention as an opportunity to recapture nearby parts of the old Soviet empire. In the fall of 1994, in spite of strong nationalist resistance in each of the Transcaucasus countries, Russia was poised to improve its economic and military influence in Armenia and Azerbaijan, as it had in Georgia, if its mediation activities in Nagorno-Karabakh bore fruit.

The countries of Transcaucasia each inherited large state-owned enterprises specializing in products assigned by the Soviet system: military electronics and chemicals in Armenia, petroleum-based and textile industries in Azerbaijan, and chemicals, machine tools, and metallurgy in Georgia. As in most of the nations in the former Soviet sphere, redistribution and revitalization of such enterprises proved a formidable obstacle to economic growth and foreign investment in Armenia, Azerbaijan, and Georgia. Efforts at enterprise privatization were hindered by the stresses of prolonged military engagements, the staying power of underground economies that had defied control under communist and postcommunist governments, the lack of commercial expertise, and the lack of a legal infrastructure on which to base new business relationships. As a result, in 1994 the governments were left with oversized, inefficient, and often bankrupt heavy industries whose operation was vital to provide jobs and to revive the national economies. At the same time, small private enterprises were growing rapidly, especially in Armenia and Georgia.

In the early 1990s, the Caucasus took its place among the regions of the world having violent post-Cold War ethnic conflict. Several wars broke out in the region once Soviet authority ceased holding the lid on disagreements that had been fermenting for decades. (Joseph V. Stalin's forcible relocation of ethnic groups after redrawing the region's political map was a chief source of the friction of the 1990s.) Thus, the three republics devoted critical resources to military campaigns in a period when the need for internal restructuring was paramount.

In Georgia, minority separatist movements—primarily on the part of the Ossetians and the Abkhaz, both given intermittent encouragement by the Soviet regime over the years—demanded fuller recognition in the new order of the early 1990s. Asserting its newly gained national prerogatives, Georgia responded with military attempts to restrain separatism forcibly. A year-long battle in South Ossetia, initiated by Zviad Gamsakhurdia, post-Soviet Georgia's ultranationalist first president, reached an uneasy peace in mid-1992. Early in 1992, however, the violent eviction of Gamsakhurdia from the presidency added another opponent of Georgian unity as the exiled Gamsakhurdia gathered his forces across the border.

In mid-1992 Georgian paramilitary troops entered the Abkhazian Autonomous Republic of Georgia, beginning a new conflict that in 1993 threatened to break apart the country. When Georgian troops were driven from Abkhazia in September 1993, Georgia's President Eduard Shevardnadze was able to gain Russian military aid to prevent the collapse of the country. In mid-1994 an uneasy cease-fire was in force; Abkhazian forces controlled their entire region, but no negotiated settlement had been reached. Life in Georgia had stabilized, but no permanent answers had been found to ethnic claims and counterclaims.

For Armenia and Azerbaijan, the center of nationalist self-expression in this period was the Nagorno-Karabakh Autonomous Region of Azerbaijan. After the Armenian majority there declared unification with Armenia in 1988, ethnic conflict broke out in both republics, leaving many Armenians and Azerbaijanis dead. For the next six years, battles raged between Armenian and Azerbaijani regular forces and between Armenian militias from Nagorno-Karabakh ("mountainous Karabakh" in Russian) and foreign mercenaries, killing thousands in and around Karabakh and causing massive refugee movements in both directions. Armenian military forces, better supplied and better organized, generally gained ground in the conflict, but the sides were evened as Armenia itself was devastated by six years of Azerbaijani blockades. In 1993 and early 1994, international mediation efforts were stymied by the intransigence of the two sides and by competition between Russia and the Conference on Security and Cooperation in Europe (CSCE—see Glossary) for the role of chief peace negotiator.

Armenia

Armenia, in the twentieth century the smallest of the three republics in size and population, has undergone the greatest change in the location of its indigenous population. After occupying eastern Anatolia (now eastern Turkey) for nearly 2,000 years, the Armenian population of the Ottoman Empire was extinguished or driven out by 1915, adding to a diaspora that had begun centuries earlier. After 1915 only the eastern population, in and around Erevan, remained in its original location. In the Soviet era, Armenians preserved their cultural traditions, both in Armenia and abroad. The Armenian people's strong sense of unity has been reinforced by periodic threats to their existence. When Armenia, Azerbaijan, and Georgia gained their independence in 1991, Armenia possessed the fewest natural and man-made resources upon which to build a new state. Fertile agricultural areas are relatively small, transportation is limited by the country's landlocked position and mountainous terrain (and, beginning in 1989, by the Azerbaijani blockade), and the material base for industry is not broad. A high percentage of cropland requires irrigation, and disorganized land privatization has delayed the benefits that should result from reducing state agricultural control. Although harvests were bountiful in 1993, gaps in support systems for transport and food processing prevented urban populations from benefiting.

The intensive industrialization of Armenia between the world wars was accomplished within the controlled barter system of the Soviet republics, not within a separate economic unit. The specialized industrial roles assigned Armenia in the Soviet system offered little of value to the world markets from which the republic had been protected until 1991. Since 1991 Armenia has sought to reorient its Soviet-era scientific-research, military electronics, and chemicals infrastructures to satisfy new demands, and international financial assistance has been forthcoming. In the meantime, basic items of Armenian manufacture, such as textiles, shoes, and carpets, have remained exportable. However, the extreme paucity of energy sources—little coal, natural gas, or petroleum is extracted in Armenia—always has been a severe limitation to industry. And about 30 percent of the existing industrial infrastructure was lost in the earthquake of 1988. Desperate crises arose throughout society when Azerbaijan strangled energy imports that had provided over 90 percent of Armenia's energy. Every winter of the early 1990s brought more difficult conditions, especially for urban Armenians.

In the early 1990s, the Armenian economy was also stressed by direct support of Karabakh self-determination. Karabakh received massive shipments of food and other materials through the Lachin corridor that Karabakh Armenian forces had opened across southwestern Azerbaijan. Although Karabakh sent electricity to Armenia in return, the balance of trade was over two to one in favor of Karabakh, and Armenian credits covered most of Karabakh's budget deficits. Meanwhile, Armenia remained a command rather than a free-market economy to ensure that the military received adequate economic support.

In addition to the Karabakh conflict, wage, price, and social welfare conditions have caused substantial social unrest since independence. The dram (for value of the dram—see Glossary), the national currency introduced in 1992, underwent almost immediate devaluation as the national banking system tried to stabilize international exchange rates. Accordingly, in 1993 prices rose to an average of 130 percent of wages, which the government indexed through that year. The scarcity of many commodities, caused by the blockade, also pushed prices higher. In the first post-Soviet years, and especially in 1993, plant closings and the energy crisis caused unemployment to more than double. At the same time, the standard of living of the average Armenian deteriorated; by 1993 an estimated 90 percent of the population was living below the official poverty line.

Armenia's first steps toward democracy were uneven. Upon declaring independence, Armenia adapted the political system, set forth in its Soviet-style 1978 constitution, to the short-term requirements of governance. The chief executive would be the chairman of Armenia's Supreme Soviet, which was the chief legislative body of the new republic—but in independent Armenia the legislature and the executive branch would no longer merely rubber-stamp policy decisions handed down from Moscow.

The inherited Soviet system was used in the expectation that a new constitution would prescribe Western-style institutions in the near future. However, between 1992 and 1994 consensus was not reached between factions backing a strong executive and those backing a strong legislature.

At the center of the dispute over the constitution was Levon Ter-Petrosian, president (through late 1994) of post-Soviet Armenia. Beginning in 1991, Ter-Petrosian responded to the twin threats of political chaos and military defeat at the hands of Azerbaijan by accumulating extraordinary executive powers. His chief opposition, a faction that was radically nationalist but held few seats in the fragmented Supreme Soviet, sought to build coalitions to cut the president's power, then to finalize such a move in a constitution calling for a strong legislature. As they had on other legislation, however, the chaotic deliberations of parliament yielded no decision. Ter-Petrosian was able to continue his pragmatic approach to domestic policy, privatizing the economy whenever possible, and to continue his moderate, sometimes conciliatory, tone on the Karabakh issue.

Beginning in 1991, Armenia's foreign policy also was dictated by the Karabakh conflict. After independence, Russian troops continued serving as border guards and in other capacities that Armenia's new national army could not fill. Armenia, a charter member of the Russian-sponsored Commonwealth of Independent States (CIS—see Glossary), forged security agreements with CIS member states and took an active part in the organization. After 1991 Russia remained Armenia's foremost trading partner, supplying the country with fuel. As the Karabakh conflict evolved, Armenia took a more favorable position toward Russian leadership of peace negotiations than did Azerbaijan.

The dissolution of the Soviet Union made possible closer relations with Armenia's traditional enemy Turkey, whose membership in the North Atlantic Treaty Organization (NATO—see Glossary) had put it on the opposite side in the Cold War. In the Karabakh conflict, Turkey sided with Islamic Azerbaijan, blocking pipeline deliveries to Armenia through its territory. Most important, Turkey withheld acknowledgment of the 1915 massacre, without which no Armenian government could permit a rapprochement. Nevertheless, tentative contacts continued throughout the early 1990s.

In spite of pressure from nationalist factions, the Ter-Petrosian government held that Armenia should not unilaterally annex Karabakh and that the citizens of Karabakh had a right to self-determination (presumably meaning either independence or union with Armenia). Although Ter-Petrosian maintained contact with Azerbaijan's President Heydar Aliyev, and Armenia officially accepted the terms of several peace proposals, recriminations for the failure of peace talks flew from both sides in 1993.

The United States and the countries of the European Union (EU) have aided independent Armenia in several ways, although the West has criticized Armenian incursions into Azerbaijani territory. Humanitarian aid, most of it from the United States, played a large role between 1991 and 1994 in Armenia's survival through the winters of the blockade. Armenia successively pursued aid from the European Bank for Reconstruction and Development, the International Monetary Fund (IMF—see Glossary), and the World Bank (see Glossary). Two categories of assistance, humanitarian and technical, were offered through those lenders. Included was aid for recovery from the 1988 earthquake, whose destructive effects were still being felt in Armenia's industry and transportation infrastructure as of late 1994.

After the Soviet Union collapsed, Armenia's national security continued to depend heavily on the Russian military. The officer corps of the new national army created in 1992 included many Armenian former officers of the Soviet army, and Russian institutes trained new Armenian officers. Two Russian divisions were transferred to Armenian control, but another division remained under full Russian control on Armenian soil.

Internal security was problematic in the transitional years. The Ministry of Internal Affairs, responsible for internal security agencies, remained outside regular government control, as it had been in the Soviet period. This arrangement led to corruption, abuses of power, and public cynicism, a state of affairs that was especially serious because the main internal security agency acted as the nation's regular police force. The distraction of the Karabakh crisis combined with security lapses to stimulate a rapid rise in crime in the early 1990s. The political situation was also complicated by charges of abuse of power exchanged by high government officials in relation to security problems.

By the spring of 1994, Armenians had survived a fourth winter of acute shortages, and Armenian forces in Karabakh had survived the large-scale winter offensive that Azerbaijan launched in December 1993. In May 1994, a flurry of diplomatic activity by Russia and the CIS, stimulated by the new round of fighting, produced a cease-fire that held, with some violations, through the summer. A lasting treaty was delayed, however, by persistent disagreement over the nationality of peacekeeping forces that would occupy Azerbaijan. Azerbaijan resisted the return of Russian troops to its territory, while the Russian plan called for at least half the forces to be Russian. On both diplomatic and economic fronts, new signs of stability caused guarded optimism in Armenia in the fall of 1994.

The failure of the CSCE peace plan, which Azerbaijan supported, had caused that country to mount an all-out, human-wave offensive in December 1993 and January 1994, which initially pushed back Armenian defensive lines in Karabakh and regained some lost territory. When the offensive stalled in February, Russia's minister of defense, Pavel Grachev, negotiated a cease-fire, which enabled Russia to supplant the CSCE as the primary peace negotiator. Intensive Russian-sponsored talks continued through the spring, although Azerbaijan mounted air strikes on Karabakh as late as April. In May 1994, Armenia, Azerbaijan, and Nagorno-Karabakh signed the CIS-sponsored Bishkek Protocol, calling for a cease-fire and the beginning of troop withdrawals. In July the defense ministers of the three jurisdictions officially extended the cease-fire, signaling that all parties were moving toward some combination of the Russian and the CSCE peace plans. In September the exchange of Armenian and Azerbaijani prisoners of war began.

Under these conditions, Russia was able to intensify its three-way diplomatic gambit in the Transcaucasus, steadily erasing Armenians' memory of airborne Soviet forces landing unannounced as a show of strength in 1991. In the first half of 1994, Armenia moved closer to Russia on several fronts. A February treaty established bilateral barter of vital resources. In March Russia agreed to joint operation of the Armenian Atomic Power Station at Metsamor, whose scheduled 1995 reopening is a vital element in easing the country's energy crisis. Also in March, Armenia replaced its mission in Moscow with a full embassy. In June the Armenian parliament approved the addition of airborne troops to the Russian garrison at Gyumri near the Turkish border. Then in July, Russia extended 100 billion rubles (about US$35 million at that time) for reactivation of the Metsamor station, and Armenia signed a US$250 million contract with Russia for Armenia to process precious metals and gems supplied by Russia. In addition, Armenia consistently favored the Russian peace plan for Nagorno-Karabakh, in opposition to Azerbaijan's insistence on reviving the CSCE plan that prescribed international monitors rather than combat troops (most of whom would be Russian) on Azerbaijani soil.

Armenia was active on other diplomatic fronts as well in 1994. President Ter-Petrosian made official visits to Britain's Prime Minister John Major in February (preceding Azerbaijan's Heydar Aliyev by a few weeks when the outcome of the last large-scale campaign in the Karabakh conflict remained in doubt) and to President William J. Clinton in the United States in August. Clinton promised more active United States support for peace negotiations, and an exchange of military attachés was set. While in Washington, Ter-Petrosian expressed interest in joining the NATO Partnership for Peace, in which Azerbaijan had gained membership three months earlier.

Relations with Turkey remained cool, however. In 1994 Turkey continued its blockade of Armenia in support of Azerbaijan and accused Armenia of fostering rebel activity by Kurdish groups in eastern Turkey; it reiterated its denial of responsibility for the 1915 massacre of Armenians in the Ottoman Empire. In June these policies prompted Armenia to approve the security agreement with Russia that stationed Russian airborne troops in Armenia near the Turkish border. In July Armenia firmly refused Turkey's offer to send peacekeeping forces to Nagorno-Karabakh. Thus, Armenia became an important player in the continuing contest between Russia and Turkey for influence in the Black Sea and Caucasus regions. Armenians considered the official commemoration by Israel and Russia of the 1915 Armenian massacre a significant advancement in the country's international position.

Early in 1994, Armenia's relations with Georgia worsened after Azerbaijani terrorists in Georgia again sabotaged the natural gas pipeline supplying Armenia through Georgia. Delayed rail delivery to Armenia of goods arriving in Georgian ports also caused friction. Underlying these stresses were Georgia's unreliable transport system and its failure to prevent violent acts on Georgian territory. Pipeline and railroad sabotage incidents continued through mid-1994.

The domestic political front remained heated in 1994. As the parliamentary elections of 1995 approached, Ter-Petrosian's centrist Armenian Pannational Movement (APM), which dominated political life after 1991, had lost ground to the right and the left because Armenians were losing patience with economic hardship. Opposition newspapers and citizens' groups, which Ter-Petrosian refused to outlaw, continued their accusations of official corruption and their calls for the resignation of the Ter-Petrosian government early in the year. Then, in mid-1994 the opposition accelerated its activity by mounting antigovernment street demonstrations of up to 50,000 protesters.

In the protracted struggle over a new constitution, the opposition intensified rhetoric supporting a document built around a strong legislature rather than the strong-executive version supported by Ter-Petrosian. By the fall of 1994, little progress had been made even on the method of deciding this critical issue. While opposition parties called for a constitutional assembly, the president offered to hold a national referendum, following which he would resign if defeated.

Economic conditions were also a primary issue for the opposition. The value of the dram, pegged at 14.5 to the United States dollar when it was established in November 1993, had plummeted to 390 to the dollar by May 1994. In September a major overhaul of Armenia's financial system was under way, aimed at establishing official interest rates and a national credit system, controlling inflation, opening a securities market, regulating currency exchange, and licensing lending institutions. In the overall plan, the Central Bank of Armenia and the Erevan Stock Exchange assumed central roles in redirecting the flow of resources toward production of consumer goods. And government budgeting began diverting funds from military to civilian production support, a step advertised as the beginning of the transition from a command to a market economy. This process included the resumption of privatization of state enterprises, which had ceased in mid-1992, including full privatization of small businesses and cautious partial privatization of larger ones. In mid-1994 the value of the dram stabilized, and industrial production increased somewhat. As another winter approached, however, the amount of goods and food available to the average consumer remained at or below subsistence level, and social unrest threatened to increase.

In September Armenia negotiated terms for the resumption of natural gas deliveries from its chief supplier, Turkmenistan, which had threatened a complete cutoff because of outstanding debts. Under the current agreement, all purchases of Turkmen gas were destined for electric power generation in Armenia. Also in September, the IMF offered favorable interest rates on a loan of US$800 million if Armenia raised consumer taxes and removed controls on bread prices. Armenian officials resisted those conditions because they would further erode living conditions.

Thus in mid-1994 Armenia, blessed with strong leadership and support from abroad but cursed with a poor geopolitical position and few natural resources, was desperate for peace after the Karabakh Armenians had virtually won their war for self-determination. With many elements of post-Soviet economic reform in place, a steady flow of assistance from the West, and an end to the Karabakh conflict in sight, Armenia looked forward to a new era of development.

Azerbaijan

Azerbaijan, the easternmost and largest of the Transcaucasus states in size and in population, has the richest combination of agricultural and industrial resources of the three states. But Azerbaijan's quest for reform has been hindered by the limited contact it had with Western institutions and cultures before the Soviet era began in 1922.

Although Azerbaijan normally is included in the three-part grouping of the Transcaucasus countries (and was so defined politically between 1922 and 1936), it has more in common culturally with the Central Asian republics east of the Caspian Sea than with Armenia and Georgia. The common link with the latter states is the Caucasus mountain range, which defines the topography of the northern and western parts of Azerbaijan. A unique aspect of Azerbaijan's political geography is the enclave of the Nakhichevan Autonomous Republic, created by the Soviet Union in 1924 in the area between Armenia and Iran and separated from the rest of Azerbaijan by Armenian territory. In 1924 the Soviet Union also created the Nagorno-Karabakh Autonomous Region within Azerbaijan, an enclave whose population was about 94 percent Armenian at that time and remained about 75 percent Armenian in the late 1980s.

Beginning in the last years of the Soviet Union and extending into the 1990s, the drive for independence by Nagorno-Karabakh's Armenian majority was an issue of conflict between Armenia, which insisted on self-determination for its fellow Armenians, and Azerbaijan, which cited historical acceptance of its sovereignty whatever the region's ethnic composition. By 1991 the independence struggle was an issue of de facto war between Azerbaijan and the Karabakh Armenians, who by 1993 controlled all of Karabakh and much of adjoining Azerbaijan.

The population of Azerbaijan, already 83 percent Azerbaijani before independence, became even more homogeneous as members of the two principal minorities, Armenians and Russians, emigrated in the early 1990s and as thousands of Azerbaijanis immigrated from neighboring Armenia. The heavily urbanized population of Azerbaijan is concentrated around the cities of Baku, Gyandzha, and Sumgait.

Like the other former Soviet republics, Azerbaijan began in 1991 to seek the right combination of indigenous and "borrowed" qualities to replace the awkwardly imposed economic and political imprint of the Soviet era. And, like Armenia and Georgia, Azerbaijan faced the complications of internal political disruption and military crisis in the first years of this process.

For more than 100 years, Azerbaijan's economy has been dominated by petroleum extraction and processing. In the Soviet system, Azerbaijan's delegated role had evolved from supplying crude oil to supplying oil-extraction equipment, as Siberian oil fields came to dominate the Soviet market and as Caspian oil fields were allowed to deteriorate. Although exploited oil deposits were greatly depleted in the Soviet period, the economy still depends heavily on industries linked to oil. The country also depends heavily on trade with Russia and other former Soviet republics. Azerbaijan's overall industrial production dropped in the early 1990s, although not as drastically as that of Armenia and Georgia. The end of Soviet-supported trade connections and the closing of inefficient factories caused unemployment to rise and industrial productivity to fall an estimated 26 percent in 1992; acute inflation caused a major economic crisis in 1993.

Azerbaijan did not restructure its agriculture as quickly as did Armenia and Georgia; inefficient Soviet methods continued to hamper production, and the role of private initiative remained small. Agriculture in Azerbaijan also was hampered by the conflict in Nagorno-Karabakh, which was an important source of fruits, grain, grapes, and livestock. As much as 70 percent of Azerbaijan's arable land was occupied by military forces at some stage of the conflict.

In spite of these setbacks, Azerbaijan's economy remains the healthiest among the three republics, largely because unexploited oil and natural gas deposits are plentiful (although output declined in the early 1990s) and because ample electric-power generating plants are in operation. Azerbaijan has been able to attract Western investment in its oil industry in the post-Soviet years, although Russia remains a key oil customer and investor. In 1993 the former Soviet republics remained Azerbaijan's most important trading partners, and state bureaucracies still controlled most foreign trade. Political instability in Baku, however, continued to discourage Turkey, a natural trading partner, from expanding commercial relations.

The political situation of Azerbaijan was extremely volatile in the first years of independence. With performance in Nagorno-Karabakh rather than achievement of economic and political reform as their chief criterion, Azerbaijanis deposed presidents in 1992 and 1993, then returned former communist party boss Heydar Aliyev to power. In 1992, in the country's first and only free election, the people had chosen Abulfaz

Elchibey, leader of the Azerbaijani Popular Front (APF), as president. Meanwhile, the Azerbaijani Communist Party, formally disbanded in 1991, retained positions of political and economic power and was key in the coup that returned Aliyev to power in June 1993. Former communists dominated policy making in the government Aliyev formed after his rubber-stamp election as president the following October. However, the APF remained a formidable opposition force, especially critical of any sign of weakness on the Nagorno-Karabakh issue.

During the transition period, the only national legislative body was the Melli-Majlis (National Council), a fifty-member interim assembly that came under the domination of former communists and, by virtue of postponing parliamentary elections indefinitely, continued to retain its power in late 1994. Aliyev promised a new constitution and democratic rule, but he prolonged his dictatorial powers on the pretext of the continuing military emergency. Work on a new constitution was begun in 1992, but the Nagorno-Karabakh conflict and political turmoil delayed its completion; meanwhile, elements of the 1978 constitution (based on the 1977 constitution of the Soviet Union) remain the highest law of the land, supplemented only by provisions of the 1991 Act of Independence.

Azerbaijan's post-Soviet foreign policy attempted to balance the interests of three stronger, often mutually hostile, neighbors—Iran, Russia, and Turkey—while using those nations' interests in regional peace to help resolve the Karabakh conflict. The Elchibey regime of 1992–93 leaned toward Turkey, which it saw as the best mediator in Karabakh. Armenia took advantage of this strategy, however, to form closer ties with Russia, whose economic assistance it needed desperately. Beginning in 1993, Aliyev sought to rekindle relations with Russia and Iran, believing that Russia could negotiate a positive settlement in Karabakh. Relations with Turkey were carefully maintained, however.

Beginning in 1991, Azerbaijan's external national security was breached by the incursion of the Armenian separatist forces of Karabakh militias and reinforcements from Armenia. Azerbaijan's main strategy in this early period was to blockade landlocked Armenia's supply lines and to rely for national defense on the Russian 4th Army, which remained in Azerbaijan in 1991. Clashes between Russian troops and Azerbaijani civilians in 1991 and the collapse of the Soviet Union, however, led Russia to a rapid commitment for withdrawal of troops and equipment, which was completed in mid-1993.

Under those circumstances, a new, limited national armed force was planned in 1992, and, as had been done in Armenia, the government appealed to Azerbaijani veterans of the Soviet army to defend their homeland. But the force took shape slowly, and outside assistance—mercenaries and foreign training officers—were summoned to stem the Armenian advance that threatened all of southern Azerbaijan. In 1993 continued military failures brought reports of mass desertion and subsequent large-scale recruitment of teenage boys, as well as wholesale changes in the national defense establishment.

In the early 1990s, the domestic and international confusion bred by the Karabakh conflict increased customs violations, white-collar crime, and threats to the populace by criminal bands. The role of Azerbaijanis in the international drug market expanded noticeably. In 1993 the Aliyev government responded to these problems with a major reform of the Ministry of Internal Affairs, which had been plagued by corruption and incompetence, but experts agreed that positive results required a more stable overall atmosphere.

In December 1993, Azerbaijan launched a major surprise attack on all fronts in Karabakh, using newly drafted personnel in wave attacks, with air support. The attack initially overwhelmed Armenian positions in the north and south but ultimately was unsuccessful. An estimated 8,000 Azerbaijani troops died in the two-month campaign, which Armenian authorities described as Azerbaijan's best-planned offensive of the conflict.

When the winter offensive failed, Aliyev began using diplomatic channels to seek peace terms acceptable to his constituents, involving Russia as little as possible. Already in March, the chairman of the Azerbaijani parliament had initiated a private meeting with his opposite number from Armenia, an event hailed in the Azerbaijani press as a major Azerbaijani peace initiative. Official visits by Aliyev to Ankara and London early in 1994 yielded little additional support for Azerbaijan's position. (Turkey remained suspicious of Aliyev's communist background.)

At this point, Azerbaijan reasserted its support for the CSCE peace plan, which would use international monitors rather than military forces to enforce the cease-fire in Karabakh. Perhaps with the goal of avoiding further military losses, Aliyev approved in May the provisional cease-fire conditions of the

Bishkek Protocol, sponsored by the CIS. That agreement, which softened Azerbaijan's position on recognizing the sovereignty of Nagorno-Karabakh, was subsequently the basis for terms of a true armistice.

Azerbaijan's official position on armistice conditions remained unchanged, however, during the negotiations of the summer and fall of 1994, in the face of Armenia's insistence that only an armed peacekeeping force (inevitably Russian) could prevent new outbreaks of fighting. During that period, sporadic Azerbaijani attacks tended to confirm Armenia's judgment. At the same time, Aliyev urged that his countrymen take a more conciliatory position toward Russia. Aliyev argued that the Soviet Union, not Russia, had sent the troops who had killed Azerbaijanis when they arrived to keep peace with Armenia in 1990 and that Azerbaijan could profit from exploiting rather than rejecting the remaining ties between the two countries.

In May Aliyev signed the NATO Partnership for Peace agreement, giving Azerbaijan the associate status that NATO had offered to East European nations and the former republics of the Soviet Union in late 1993. The same month, Aliyev received a mid-level United States delegation charged with discussing diplomatic support for the Nagorno-Karabakh peace process, Caspian Sea oil exploration by United States firms, and bilateral trade agreements.

In July Aliyev extended his diplomacy to the Muslim world, visiting Saudi Arabia and Iran in an effort to balance his diplomatic contacts with the West. Iran was especially important because of its proximity to Karabakh and its interest in ending the conflict on its border. Iran responded to offers of economic cooperation by insisting that any agreement must await a peace treaty between Azerbaijan and Armenia.

In the fall of 1994, a seventeen-point peace agreement was drafted, but major issues remained unresolved. Azerbaijani concerns centered on withdrawal of Armenian forces from Azerbaijani territory and conditions that would permit Azerbaijani refugees to return home. (An estimated 1 million Azerbaijanis had fled to other parts of Azerbaijan or Iran from occupied territory.) The top priorities for Armenia were ensuring security for Armenians in Karabakh and defining the status of the region prior to the withdrawal of forces.

A second result of the failed winter offensive of 1993–94 was a new crackdown by the Aliyev government on dissident activity. Early in 1994, censors in the Main Administration for Protecting State Secrets in the Press sharply increased censorship of material criticizing the regime, and the government cut the supply of paper and printing plates to opposition newspapers. In May a confrontation between Aliyev loyalists and opponents in the Melli-Majlis resulted in arrests of opposition leaders and reduction in the number of members required for a quorum to pass presidential proposals.

The issue behind the May dispute was Aliyev's handling of the Karabakh peace process. A variety of opposition parties and organizations claimed that the Bishkek Protocol had betrayed Azerbaijan by recognizing the sovereignty of Nagorno-Karabakh. A new coalition, the National Resistance Movement, was formed immediately after the May confrontation in the Melli-Majlis. The movement's two principles were opposition to reintroduction of Russian forces in Azerbaijan and opposition to Aliyev's "dictatorship." By the end of the summer, however, the movement had drawn closer to Aliyev's position on the first point, and the announcement of long-delayed parliamentary elections to be held in the summer of 1995 aimed to defuse charges of dictatorship. Draft election legislation called for replacing the "temporary" Melli-Majlis with a 150-seat legislature in 1995.

In October 1994, a military coup, supported by Prime Minister Suret Huseynov, failed to topple Aliyev. Aliyev responded by declaring a two-month state of emergency, banning demonstrations, and taking military control of key positions. Huseynov, who had signed the Bishkek Protocol as Azerbaijan's representative, was dismissed.

Price and wage levels continued to reduce the standard of living in Azerbaijan in 1994. Between mid-1993 and mid-1994, prices increased by an average of about sixteen times; from November 1993 to July 1994, the state-established minimum wage more than doubled. To speed conversion to a market economy, the ministries of finance and economics submitted plans in July to combine state-run enterprises in forms more suitable for privatization. Land privatization has proceeded cautiously because of strong political support for maintaining the Soviet-era state-farm system. In mid-1994 about 1 percent of arable land was in private hands, the bureaucratic process for obtaining private land remained long and cumbersome, and state allocation of equipment to private farmers was meager.

Meanwhile, in 1994 currency-exchange activity increased dramatically in Azerbaijani banks, bringing more foreign currency into the country. The ruble remained the most widely used foreign unit in 1994. In June, at the insistence of the IMF and the World Bank, the National Bank of Azerbaijan stopped issuing credit that lacked monetary backing, a practice that had fueled inflation and destabilized the economy.

The main hope for Azerbaijan's economic recovery lies in reviving exploitation of offshore oil deposits in the Caspian Sea. By 1993 these deposits had attracted strong interest among British, Norwegian, Russian, Turkish, and United States firms. Within a consortium of such firms, Russia would likely have a 10 percent share and provide the pipeline and the main port (Novorossiysk on the Black Sea) for export of Azerbaijan's oil. An agreement signed in September 1994 included United States, British, Turkish, Russian, and Azerbaijani oil companies.

In the early 1990s, the development of Azerbaijan's foreign trade was skewed by the refusal of eighteen nations, including the United States, Canada, Israel, India, and the Republic of Korea (South Korea), to import products from Azerbaijan as long as the blockade of Armenia continued. At the same time, many of those countries sold significant amounts of goods in Azerbaijan. Overall, in the first half of 1994 one-third of Azerbaijan's imports came from the "far abroad" (all non-CIS trading partners), and 46 percent of its exports went outside the CIS. In that period, total imports exceeded total exports by US$140 million. At the same time, the strongest long-term commercial ties within the CIS were with Kazakhstan, Russia, Turkmenistan, and Ukraine.

Like Armenia, Azerbaijan was able to improve internal conditions only marginally while awaiting the relief of a final peace settlement in Karabakh. Unlike either of its Transcaucasus neighbors, however, Azerbaijan had the prospect of major large-scale Western investment once investment conditions improved. Combined with potential oil earnings, diplomatic approaches by President Aliyev in 1994 to a number of foreign countries, including all of Azerbaijan's neighbors, seemed to offer it a much-improved postwar international position. A great deal depended, however, on the smooth surrender of wartime emergency powers by the Aliyev government and on accelerating the stalled development of a market economy.

Georgia

Georgia possesses the advantages of a subtropical Black Sea coastline and a rich mixture of Western and Eastern cultural elements. A combination of topographical and national idiosyncracies has preserved that cultural blend, whose chief impetus was the Georgian golden age of the twelfth and early thirteenth centuries, during long periods of occupation by foreign empires. Perhaps the most vivid result of this cultural independence is the Georgian language, unrelated to any other major tongue and largely unaffected by the languages of conquering peoples—at least until the massive influx of technical loanwords at the end of the twentieth century.

Since independence, Georgia has had difficulty establishing solid political institutions. This difficulty has been caused by the distractions of continuing military crises and by the chronic indecision of policy makers about the country's proper long-term goals and the strategy to reach them. Also, like the other Transcaucasus states, Georgia lacks experience with the democratic institutions that are now its political ideal; rubber-stamp passage of Moscow's agenda is quite different from creation of a legislative program useful to an emerging nation.

As in Azerbaijan, Georgia's most pressing problem has been ethnic separatism within the country's borders. Despite Georgia's modest size, throughout history all manifestations of a Georgian nation have included ethnic minorities that have conflicted with, or simply ignored, central power. Even in the golden age, when a central ruling power commanded the most widespread loyalty, King David the Builder was called "King of the Abkhaz, the Kartvelians, the Ran, the Kakhetians, and the Armenians." In the twentieth century, arbitrary rearrangement of ethnic boundaries by the Soviet regime resulted in the sharpening of various nationalist claims after Soviet power finally disappeared. Thus, in 1991 the South Ossetians of Georgia demanded union with the Ossetians across the Russian border, and in 1992 the Abkhaz of Georgia demanded recognition as an independent nation, despite their minority status in the region of Georgia they inhabited.

As in Armenia and Azerbaijan, influential, intensely nationalist factions pushed hard for unqualified military success in the struggle for separatist territory. And, as in the other Transcaucasus nations, those factions were frustrated by military and geopolitical reality: in Georgia's case, an ineffective Georgian army required assistance from Russia, the imperialist neighbor against whom nationalists had sharpened their teeth only three years earlier, to save the nation from fragmentation. At the end of 1993, Russia seemingly had settled into a long-term role of peacekeeping and occupation between Georgian and Abkhazian forces.

The most unsettling internal crisis was the failed presidency of Zviad Gamsakhurdia, once a respected human rights advocate and the undisputed leader of Georgia's nationalist opposition as the collapse of the Soviet Union became imminent. In 1991 Gamsakhurdia's dictatorial and paranoid regime, followed by the bloody process of unseating him, gave Georgia a lasting reputation for instability that damaged prospects for foreign investment and for participation in international organizations.

The failure of the one-year Gamsakhurdia regime necessitated a new political beginning that coincided with the establishment of Eduard Shevardnadze as head of state in early 1992. Easily the most popular politician in Georgia and facing chronically fragmented opposition in parliament, Shevardnadze acquired substantial "temporary" executive powers as he maneuvered to maintain national unity. At the same time, his hesitation to imitate Gamsakhurdia's grab for power often left a vacuum that was filled by quarreling splinter parties with widely varied agendas. Shevardnadze preserved parts of his reform program by forming temporary coalitions that dissolved when a contentious issue appeared. Despite numerous calls for his resignation, and despite rampant government corruption and frequent shifts in his cabinet between 1992 and 1994, there were no other serious contenders for Shevardnadze's position as of late 1994.

Shevardnadze also used familiarity with the world of diplomacy to reestablish international contacts, gain sympathy for Georgia's struggle to remain unified, and seek economic ties wherever they might be available. Unlike Armenia and Azerbaijan, Georgia did not arouse particular loyalty or hostility among any group of nations. In the first years of independence, Shevardnadze made special overtures to Russia, Turkey, and the United States and attempted to balance Georgia's approach to Armenia and Azerbaijan, its feuding neighbors in the Transcaucasus.

The collapse of the Soviet Union changed Georgia's economic position significantly, although industrial production already was declining in the last Soviet years. In the Soviet system, Georgia's assignment was mainly to supply the union with agricultural products, metal products, and the foreign currency collected by Georgian tourist attractions. This specialization made Georgia dependent on other Soviet republics for a wide range of products that were unavailable after 1991. Neither diversification nor meaningful privatization was possible, however, under the constant upheaval and energy shortages of the early 1990s. In addition, powerful organized criminal groups gained control of large segments of the national economy, including the export trade.

After the January 1992 fall of Gamsakhurdia's xenophobic regime, the maintenance of internal peace and unity was a critical national security issue. Although some progress was made in establishing a national armed force in 1994, paramilitary organizations—the Mkhedrioni (horsemen) and the National Guard—remained influential military forces in the fall of 1994. The small size and the poor organization of those groups had forced the request for Russian troop assistance in late 1993, which in turn renewed the national security dilemma of occupation by foreign troops. Meanwhile, civilian internal security forces, of which Shevardnadze took personal control in 1993, gained only partial victories over the crime wave that accompanied Georgia's post-Soviet upheavals. A series of reorganizations in security agencies failed to improve the protection of individuals against random crime or of the economic system against organized groups.

Through most of 1994, the Abkhazian conflict was more diplomatic than military. In spite of periodic hostilities, the uneasy truce line held along the Inguri River in far northwestern Georgia (in the campaign of October 1993, Georgian forces had been pushed out of all of Abkhazia except the far northern corner). The role of the 3,000 Russian peacekeepers on the border, and their relationship with United Nations (UN) observers, was recognized by a resolution of the UN Security Council in July. Throughout that period, the issue of the return of as many as 300,000 Georgian refugees to Abkhazia was the main sticking point of negotiations. The Abkhaz saw the influx of so many Georgians as a danger to their sovereignty, which Georgia did not recognize, and the refugees' plight as a bargaining chip to induce further Georgian withdrawal. No settlement was likely before the refugee issue was resolved. Meanwhile, supporting the refugees placed additional stress on Georgian society.

A legal basis for the presence of Russian troops in Georgia had been established in a status-of-forces treaty between the two nations in January 1994. The treaty prescribed the authority and operating conditions of the Group of Russian Troops in the Caucasus (GRTC), which was characterized as on Georgian territory for a "transitional period." In the summer of 1994, high-level bilateral talks covered Georgian-Russian military cooperation and further integration of CIS forces.

The Georgian economy continued to struggle in 1994, showing only isolated signs of progress. At the beginning of the year, state monopolies were reaffirmed in vital industries such as tea and food processing and electric power. By May, however, after prodding from the IMF, Shevardnadze began issuing decrees that eased privatization conditions. This policy spurred a noticeable acceleration of privatization in the summer of 1994. When the new stimulus began, about 23 percent of state enterprises had been privatized, and only thirty-nine joint-stock companies had formed out of the more than 900 large firms designated for that type of conversion. A voucher system for collecting private investment funds, delayed by a shortage of hard currency, finally began operating. But the state economic bureaucracy, entrenched since the Soviet era, was able to slow the privatization process when dispersal of economic power threatened its privileged position in 1994.

Between mid-1993 and mid-1994, prices rose by an average of 300 percent, and inflation severely eroded the government-guaranteed minimum wage. (In August the minimum wage, which was stipulated in coupons [for value of the coupon—see Glossary], equaled US$0.33 per month.) Often wages were withheld for months because of the currency shortage. In September the government raised price standards sharply for basic food items, transportation, fuel, and services. Lump-sum payments to all citizens, designed to offset this cost, failed to reach many, prompting new calls for Shevardnadze's resignation. Under those conditions, most Georgians were supported by a vast network of unofficial economic activities.

In mid-1994 unemployment was estimated unofficially at 1.5 million people, nearly 50 percent of Georgia's working-age population. The exchange rate of the Georgian coupon stabilized in early 1994 after many months of high inflation, but by that time the coupon had been virtually displaced in private transactions by the ruble and the dollar. The national financial system remained chaotic—especially in tax collection, customs, and import-export operations. The first major state bank was privatized in the summer of 1994. In August parliament approved a major reform program for social welfare, pricing, and the financial system.

In July 1994, a Georgian-Russian conference on economic cooperation discussed transnational corporations and concluded some contracts for joint economic activities, but most Russian investors demanded stronger legal guarantees for their risks. Numerous Western firms established small joint ventures in 1994, but the most critical investment project under discussion sought to exploit the substantial oil deposits that had been located by recent Australian, British, Georgian, and United States explorations in the Black Sea shelf near Batumi and Poti. A first step in foreign involvement, an oil refinery near Tbilisi, received funding in July, but the Western firms demanded major reform of commercial legislation before expanding their participation.

Georgia experienced a major energy crisis in the winter of 1993–94; following the crisis, in mid-1994 Turkmenistan drastically reduced natural gas supplies because of unpaid debts. Some fuel aid was expected for the winter of 1994–95 from Azerbaijan, the EU, Iran, and Turkey. The output of the domestic oil industry increased sharply in mid-1994. As winter approached, Georgia also offered Turkmenistan new assurances of payment in return for resumption of natural gas delivery.

Georgia's communications system, a chronically weak infrastructure link that also had discouraged foreign investment, began integration into world systems in early 1994 when the country joined international postal, satellite, and electronic communications organizations. Joint enterprises with Australian, French, German, Turkish, and United States communications companies allowed the upgrading of the national telephone system and installation of fiber-optic cables.

In the first half of 1994, the most frequent topic of government debate was the role of Russian troops in Abkhazia. By that time, opposition nationalist parties had accepted the Russian presence but rejected Abkhazian delays in allowing the return of refugees and Shevardnadze's tolerance of those delays. In May Shevardnadze overcame parliament's objections to new concessions to the Abkhaz by threatening to resign. The new agreement passed, and opposition leaders muted their demands for Shevardnadze's ouster in the belief that Russia was seeking to replace him with someone more favorable to Russian intervention. Nevertheless, in the fall of 1994 few Georgian refugees had returned to Abkhazia.

Shevardnadze's exercise of extraordinary executive powers remained a hot issue in parliament. One faction called for reduced powers in the name of democracy, but another claimed that a still stronger executive was needed to enforce order. In a July poll, 48 percent of respondents said the government was obstructing the mass media. Although the 1992 state of emergency continued to restrict dissemination of information, the Georgian media consistently presented various opposition views. Likewise, the Zviadists, Gamsakhurdia's supporters, although banned from radio and television, continued to hold rallies under the leadership of a young radical, Irakli Tsereteli.

In 1994 the government took steps to improve the internal security situation. In the latest of a long series of organizational and leadership shuffles, Shevardnadze replaced the Emergency Committee, which had been headed by former Mkhedrioni leader Jaba Ioseliani, with the Emergency Coordinating Commission, headed by Shevardnadze, and gave the commission a vague mandate to coordinate economic, political, defense, and law-enforcement matters. Ioseliani, whose command of the Mkhedrioni still gave him great influence, became a deputy head of the commission.

Shevardnadze's attempt to form a new, one-battalion Georgian army was delayed throughout the first half of 1994. The Ministry of Defense continued drafting potential soldiers (a very high percentage of whom evaded recruitment) for the Georgian armed forces and streamlining its organization. In September the national budget had not yet allocated wages, and sources of rations and equipment had not been identified—mainly because parliament had not passed the necessary legislation. Ministry of Defense plans called for the country's remaining state farms to be designated for direct military supply, as was the practice in the Soviet era. The disposition of existing paramilitary forces remained undecided as of late 1994.

The intelligence service had been reorganized in late 1993 to include elite troops mandated to fight drug smuggling and organized crime. In the spring of 1994, new agencies were formed in the State Security Service to investigate fiscal crimes and to combat terrorism. And in August 1994, the Ministry of Internal Affairs announced a major new drive against organized crime and drug traffickers throughout Georgia. Parliament and local jurisdictions offered indifferent support, however.

In 1994 Georgia began solving some of its most critical problems—laying a political base for a market economy, solidifying to a degree Shevardnadze's position as head of state, stabilizing inflation, and avoiding large-scale military conflict. But long-term stability will depend on comprehensive reform of the entire economy, eradication of the corruption that has pervaded both government and economic institutions, redirection of resources from the Abkhazian conflict into a civilian infrastructure suitable for international trade (and for major loans from international lenders), and, ultimately, finding political leaders besides Shevardnadze who are capable of focusing Georgians' attention on building a nation, rather than on advancing local interests. All those factors will influence the other major imponderable: Russia's long-term economic and political influence in Georgia, which increased greatly in late 1993 and in the first half of 1994.

October 18, 1994

*   *   *

In the months following preparation of this manuscript, a number of significant events occurred in the three countries of the Transcaucasus. Cease-fires in two major conflicts, between Abkhazia and Georgia and between Armenia and Nagorno-Karabakh on one side and Azerbaijan on the other, remained in effect despite periodic hostilities. Although the two sets of peace talks continued to encounter fundamental differences, signs of compromise emerged from both in the first months of 1995, with the assistance of international mediators. All three countries continued efforts to stabilize their economies, reduce crime, and normalize political systems distorted by lengthy states of emergency.

At the beginning of 1995, Armenia had made the most progress toward economic recovery and political stability, although its population suffered another winter of privation because of Azerbaijan's fuel blockade. In December a summit of the Organisation for Security and Cooperation in Europe (OSCE, formerly the CSCE) had succeeded in merging OSCE and Russian peace efforts on Nagorno-Karabakh for the first time in an accord signed in Budapest. Russia was expected to become the head of the OSCE Minsk Group, which had been negotiating on behalf of Western Europe for the previous two years. In return, Russia accepted OSCE oversight of peacekeeping in the conflict zone. Armenia's President Ter-Petrosian reported the opening of three defense plants and full staffing of the Armenian Army in 1994, improving Armenia's national security position.

In November 1994, the World Bank announced loans to Armenia of US$265 million for infrastructural, agricultural, and energy applications. The bank cited Armenia's new reform program to control inflation and expand the private sector, together with the first increase in Armenia's gross national product (GNP—see Glossary) since independence, as the reasons for this investment. In December the reform package went into effect. Expected to improve the standing of President Ter-Petrosian's embattled government, the reform included substantial reduction of the government's budget deficit, which had caused many workers to go unpaid and others, including teachers, to accept barely subsistence wages. The second major reform measure was ending government subsidies for basic staples, including bread and utilities—a stringency measure highly unpopular in the short term but calculated to attract more international assistance. The price of bread rose by ten times as soon as the new law went into effect. In late 1994 and early 1995, Armenia also continued reestablishing commercial ties with Iran by signing a series of three economic treaties covering taxation, free trade, and capital investments. Beginning in 1992, commercial activity between the two countries had doubled annually, and the pace was expected to accelerate markedly in 1995.

Although the Armenian government's preparations for another winter of hardship under the Azerbaijani blockade were more extensive than in previous years, conditions for the average Armenian were barely better than the year before. In the winter of 1994–95, Armenia's chronic fuel shortage, and the rising social unrest caused by it, were relieved somewhat by a new fuel agreement with Georgia and Turkmenistan. The pact provided for substantial increases in delivery of Turkmen natural gas through the Georgian pipeline. Although this mea-

1

sure increased the daily electricity ration from one hour to two hours, long-term fuel increases depended on additional negotiations and on the payment of Armenia's substantial debt to Turkmenistan. In January the State Duma, the lower house of Russia's parliament, was considering a major grant of credit to Armenia, which would be used in reopening the Armenian Atomic Power Station at Metsamor. The arrangement would be a major step in solidifying economic ties with Russia, which also has given technical assistance for the plant.

According to Armenian Ministry of Industry figures, 40 percent of the country's 1994 industrial output, worth a total of US$147 million, was sold for hard currency. Among the main customers were Iran, Syria, the United Arab Emirates, Cyprus, Belgium, and several North African countries. Although machine-building industries did not work at full capacity in 1994 because of a reduced market in Russia, industry was buoyed by the resumption of full production at the Nairit Chemical Plant after several years of shutdown. Nairit was expected to produce goods worth US$60 million per month in 1995.

Armenia's state commission for privatization began voucher distribution to the public in October 1994. At that point, vouchers for ten enterprises were available, with another fifty due for consideration in February 1995. High profitability was the chief criterion for listing enterprises for privatization. The Nairit plant and the Armenian Electrical Machine Plant, Armenia's largest and most profitable industrial facilities, were converted to private joint-stock enterprises in January 1995.

In Azerbaijan, hopes for economic improvement continued to depend on foreign investment in offshore oil deposits in the Caspian Sea. Those hopes were subdued somewhat by disagreements over the September 1994 agreement of Western, Russian, and Iranian oil interests to aid Socar, Azerbaijan's state oil company, to develop offshore deposits in the Caspian Sea.

Throughout the last months of 1994, Russia insisted that its 10 percent share of the new deal was unfair on the grounds that all Caspian countries should have equal access to Caspian resources. Russia also continued strong opposition to a new pipeline through Iran to Turkey, which the Western partners favored. The Western firms were dismayed by Azerbaijan's offer of a share of its oil deal to Iran, by the political uncertainty that seemed to escalate in Azerbaijan after the oil deal was signed, and by the rapid deterioration of existing Caspian fields, many of which were deserted in early 1995. Experts agreed that world oil prices would play an important role in Azerbaijan's profit from the agreement.

In December 1994, Russia's military occupation of its separatist Chechen Autonomous Republic (Chechnya) closed the main rail line from Russia, the chief trade route to other CIS republics and elsewhere. Replacement trade routes were sought through Iran, Turkey, and the United Arab Emirates. At the same time, hyperinflation continued, spurred by full liberalization of prices to conform with IMF credit requirements. The 1995 budget deficit equaled 20 percent of the gross domestic product (GDP—see Glossary). Foreign credit, especially loans from Turkey, was being used to provide food and social services—needs exacerbated by the continuing influx of Karabakh refugees. Economic reform, meanwhile, was delayed by more immediate concerns. Most industries were operating at about 25 percent of capacity during the winter of 1994–95.

In the last months of 1994, Russia struggled to maintain influence in Azerbaijan. Its position was threatened by approval of the multinational Caspian oil deal in September and by the Azerbaijani perception that the West was restraining Armenian aggression in Karabakh. In November President Aliyev met with Russia's President Boris N. Yeltsin, who offered 300,000 tons of Russian grain and the reopening of Russian railroad lines in an apparent effort to increase Russia's influence throughout the Transcaucasus. Azerbaijani opposition parties, led by the Azerbaijani Popular Front (APF), continued to predict that Aliyev's overtures to Russia would return Russia to a dominant position in Azerbaijani political and economic affairs. Experts predicted, however, that Russia would continue to play a vital economic role; at the end of 1994, about 60 percent of Azerbaijan's trade turnover involved Russia.

In early 1995, the issue of Nagorno-Karabakh's status continued to stymie the peace talks jointly sponsored in Moscow by the OSCE and Russia under the Budapest agreement of November 1994. Although Azerbaijan had signed several agreements with Nagorno-Karabakh as a full participant, the extent of the region's autonomy remained a key issue, as did the terms of the liberation of Azerbaijan's Lachin and Shusha regions from Armenian occupation. The Azerbaijani position was that the principals of the negotiations were Armenia and Azerbaijan, with the respective Armenian and Azerbaijani communities in Nagorno-Karabakh as "interested parties." (At the end of 1994, an estimated 126,000 Armenians and 37,000 Azerbaijanis remained in the region.) Azerbaijan lodged an official protest against Russian insistence that the Karabakh Armenians constituted a third principal. In February presidents Aliyev and Ter-Petrosian met with presidents Nursultan Nazarbayev of Kazakhstan and Shevardnadze of Georgia in Moscow and expressed optimism that the nine-month cease-fire would hold until complete settlement could be reached. Nazarbayev and the presidents of Russia and Ukraine offered to be guarantors of stability in Nagorno-Karabakh if Azerbaijan would guarantee the region's borders.

After the unsuccessful coup against him by Prime Minister Suret Huseynov in October 1994, Azerbaijan's President Heydar Aliyev maintained his position. Despite loud opposition from the APF and other parties, Aliyev appeared to occupy a strong position at the beginning of 1995. In early 1995, friction developed between Aliyev and Rusul Guliyev, speaker of the Melli-Majlis, each accusing the other of responsibility for worsening socioeconomic conditions. Former president Abulfaz Elchibey remained a vocal critic of Aliyev and had a substantial following in the APF.

In Georgia, the unresolved conflict with the Abkhazian Autonomous Republic remained the most important issue. The repatriation of Georgian refugees to Abkhazia, a process conducted very slowly by Abkhazian authorities in the early autumn of 1994, ended completely between November 1994 and January 1995. Opposition parties in Georgia, especially the National Liberation Front led by former prime minister Tengiz Sigua, increased their pressure on the government to take action, likening Abkhazia to Russia's secessionist Chechen Autonomous Republic, which Russia invaded in December 1994. (In fact, the official position of the Shevardnadze government supported the Russian move, both because of the parallel with Abkhazia and because of the need for continued Russian military monitoring of the cease-fire.) In January an attempted march of 1,400 armed Georgian refugees into Abkhazia was halted by Georgian government troops, and organizer Tengiz Kitovani, former minister of defense, was arrested for having organized the group. Although the UN adopted resolutions in January condemning the Abkhazian refugee policy, UN officials saw little hope of a rapid change in the situation in 1995.

The issue of human rights continued to dog the Shevardnadze administration in late 1994 and early 1995. In February

1995, the Free Media Association of Georgia, which included most of the country's largest independent newspapers, officially protested police oppression and confiscation of newspapers. Newspaper production had already been restricted since the beginning of winter because of Georgia's acute energy shortage.

The Georgian political world was shocked by the assassination in December 1994 of Gia Chanturia, leader of the moderate opposition National Democratic Party and one of the country's most popular politicians. Responsibility for the act was not established. Chanturia's death escalated calls for resignation of the Cabinet of Ministers, an outcome made more likely by the parliament's failure to pass Shevardnadze's proposed 1995 budget and by continued factionalism within the cabinet.

An important emerging figure was Minister of Defense Vardiko Nadibaidze, an army general entrusted in 1994 with developing a professional Georgian military force that would reduce reliance on outside forces (such as Russia's) to protect national security. At the end of 1994, Georgian forces were estimated at 15,000 ground troops, 3,000 air and air defense personnel, and 1,500 to 2,000 in the coastal defense force.

Economic reform continued unevenly under the direction of Vice Premier for Economics Temur Basilia. By design, inflation and prices continued to rise in the last months of 1994, and rubles and dollars remained the chief currency instead of the Georgian coupon. In a November 1994 poll, one-third of respondents said they spent their entire income on food. Distribution of privatization vouchers among the population was scheduled to begin in mid-1995. In November 1994, more than 1,500 enterprises had been privatized, most of them classified as commercial or service establishments. A group of Western and Japanese donors pledged a minimum of US$274 million in credits to Georgia in 1995, with another US$162 million available pending "visible success" in economic reform.

In Geneva, peace talks between the Georgian government and the Abkhazian Autonomous Republic reached the eighteen-month mark; the major points of disagreement continued to be the political status of Abkhazia and the repatriation of Georgian refugees. The Abkhazian delegation insisted on equal status with Georgia in a new confederation. The Russian and UN mediators proposed a federal legislature and joint agencies for foreign policy, foreign trade, taxation, energy, communications, and human rights, providing Abkhazia substantially more autonomy than it had had when Georgia became independent but leaving open the question of relative power within such a system. In early February 1995, preliminary accord was reached on several points of the mediators' proposal.

As 1995 began, prospects for stability in the Transcaucasus were marginally better than they had been since the three countries achieved independence in 1991. Much depended on continued strong leadership from presidents Aliyev, Shevardnadze, and Ter-Petrosian, on a peaceful environment across the borders in Russia and Iran, and on free access to the natural resources needed to restart the respective national economies.

February 28, 1995 Glenn E. Curtis

Chapter 1. Armenia

Armenian folk costume

Country

Formal Name: Republic of Armenia.

Short Form: Armenia.

Term for Citizens: Armenian(s).

Capital: Erevan.

Date of Independence: September 23, 1991.

Geography

Size: Approximately 29,800 square kilometers.

Topography: Dominated by Lesser Caucasus range, running across north and then turning southeast to Iran. Armenian Plateau to southwest of mountains. Plateau, major feature of central Armenia, slopes gradually downward into Aras River valley, which forms border with Turkey to west and Iran to south.

Climate: Mountains preclude influence from nearby seas; temperature and precipitation generally determined by elevation: colder and wetter in higher elevations (north and northeast). In central plateau, wide temperature variation between winter and summer.

Society

Population: By official 1994 estimate, population 3,521,517; in 1994 annual growth rate about 1.1 percent; 1991 population density 112.6 persons per square kilometer.

Ethnic Groups: In 1989 census, Armenians 93.7 percent, Azerbaijanis 2.6 percent, Kurds 1.7 percent, and Russians 1.6 percent.

NOTE—The Country Profile contains updated information as available.

Languages: Official state language Armenian, spoken by 96 percent of population. Russian first language of 2 percent, second language for about 40 percent of population.

Religion: Approximately 94 percent of population belongs to Armenian Apostolic Church. Other religions include Russian Orthodox, Roman Catholic, Protestant denominations, and Islam.

Education and Literacy: Education compulsory through secondary school. Literacy estimated at 100 percent. In early 1990s, substantial changes, begun in previous centralized Soviet system, emphasized national heritage.

Health: Nominal continuation of Soviet-era guarantee of universal care, but health care system deteriorated under stress of independence and Nagorno-Karabakh conflict. Severe shortage of basic medical supplies in early 1990s, and many clinics and hospitals closed.

Economy

Gross National Product (GNP): Estimated at US$2.7 billion in 1992, or US$780 per capita. In 1992 growth rate –46 percent. Economic growth crippled after 1989 by Azerbaijani blockade of fuel and other materials and by demands of Nagorno-Karabakh conflict.

Agriculture: After privatization in 1990, assumed larger share of economy; most land privately owned by 1993. Farms small but relatively productive. Main crops grains, potatoes, vegetables, grapes, berries, cotton, sugar beets, tobacco, figs, and olives.

Industry and Mining: Dominant light manufacturing products include footwear, woven clothing, and carpets. Nonferrous metallurgy, machine building, electronics, petrochemicals, fertilizers, and building materials most important heavy industries. Mining resource base broad, including copper, molybdenum, gold, silver, and iron ore, but little developed.

Energy: Nearly all energy supplied from abroad, causing severe shortage under blockade of early 1990s. Natural gas, delivered from Turkmenistan via Georgia pipeline, frequently blocked. Hydroelectric plants main domestic source; natural gas supply from Russia intermittent because of pipeline damage.

Exports: In 1990 worth US$2.1 billion. Principal items textiles, shoes, carpets, machines, chemical products, processed foods, and metal products. Postcommunist export markets shifted toward Turkey and Iran, but traditional ties with Russia and Eastern Europe remained. License controls eased in 1992. Total export trade, severely constricted by blockade, about US$135.6 million in 1993.

Imports: In 1990 worth US$2.8 billion. Principal items light industrial products, industrial raw materials, fuels, and energy. Principal import suppliers Russia, Turkmenistan, Belarus, Ukraine, and Kazakhstan. Nearly all energy and much food imported.

Balance of Payments: Estimated in 1992 as US$137 million deficit.

Exchange Rate: Dram introduced November 1993, to become exclusive national currency early 1994. May 1994 rate about 390 drams per US$1. Second national unit, luma (100 to the dram), introduced February 1994.

Inflation: Dram devalued as Russian ruble devalued, early 1994, against United States dollar. Prices raised in steep periodic increments, including 30 percent rise March 1994. Prices in 1993 rose 130 percent as fast as wages.

Fiscal Year: Calendar year.

Fiscal Policy: Highly centralized government system, with no regional authority. Indexation of salaries and prices and currency devaluation used to balance supply and demand. Taxes added and changed 1992–93 to improve national income.

Transportation and Telecommunications

Highways: In 1991 about 11,300 kilometers of roads, of which 10,500 hard-surface.

Railroads: In 1992 total mainline track about 825 kilometers, none of which standard gauge. International lines to Azerbaijan, Georgia, Iran, and Turkey. Service disrupted in early 1990s.

Civil Aviation: Ten usable airports, six with hard-surface runways. Zvartnots Airport, near Erevan, only airport accommodating large jets. State Airlines Company of Armenia national airline.

Inland Waterways: None.

Ports: None.

Pipelines: Natural gas pipeline 900 kilometers in 1991; service disrupted in early 1990s.

Telecommunications: Direct-dial telephone system with 200 circuits and international service in 1991. Radio and television controlled by State Committee for Television and Radio Broadcasting. Armenian and Russian television broadcasts available to 100 percent of population via International Telecommunications Satellite Organization (Intelsat) satellite. Thirteen radio stations broadcast domestically in Armenian, Kurdish, and Russian.

Government and Politics

Government: National government with most administrative powers. Thirty-seven districts with local legislative and executive organs. National legislature unicameral Supreme Soviet of 248 members. Highest executive organ, Council of Ministers, appointed by president with consent of prime minister, who is named by president with consent of parliament. Presidency, given broad emergency powers during Nagorno-Karabakh conflict, most powerful government office. Legislative process cumbersome and fragmented, delaying passage of new constitution and other vital legislation. As of 1994, reform of Soviet-era judicial system awaited new constitution.

Politics: Since independence in 1991, presidency, most ministries, and parliamentary plurality held by members of Armenian Pannational Movement. Main opposition parties Liberal Democratic Party and Armenian Revolutionary Federation. First multiparty election 1991. Many minority parties represented in parliament, with coalitions on specific issues.

Foreign Relations: In early 1990s, foreign policy determined strongly by Nagorno-Karabakh conflict with Azerbaijan. Some rapprochement with traditional enemies Turkey and Iran.

Limited relations established with Western Europe. Close ties with Russia and accords with other members of the Commonwealth of Independent States. Worldwide Armenian diaspora facilitates foreign support.

International Agreements and Memberships: Member of United Nations, International Monetary Fund, World Bank, European Bank for Reconstruction and Development, and Conference on Security and Cooperation in Europe.

National Security

Armed Forces: Armenian Army divided into army, air force, and air defense forces; total forces about 50,000, including reserves. In 1994 about 20,000 active troops, including border guards and internal security troops, supplied mainly by conscription. About 2,000 troops in air force and 2,000 in air defense forces. Reserve call-up available in crisis, although reserve support weaker in postcommunist era. One Russian division remained in Armenia in 1994.

Major Military Units: National army formed in 1992 to emphasize maneuverability and response to attack. Highest organizational level brigade, each with 1,500 to 2,500 troops and divided into three or four battalions. Air defense forces reinvigorated and new military aviation program established in early 1990s. Most of two Russian motorized divisions transferred to Armenian control in 1992. Much equipment obtained from Russian units formerly stationed in Armenia.

Military Budget: Estimated in 1992 at US$33.8 million.

Internal Security: Run by State Administration for National Security. Border troops supplemented by Russian forces along Iranian and Turkish borders. Militia used as regular police force of somewhat over 1,000 troops; duties include drug detection. Some units of former Committee for State Security (KGB) function under Armenian control.

Figure 4. Armenia, 1994

ARMENIAN CIVILIZATION HAD its beginnings in the sixth century B.C. In the centuries following, the Armenians withstood invasions and nomadic migrations, creating a unique culture that blended Iranian social and political structures with Hellenic—and later Christian—literary traditions. For two millennia, independent Armenian states existed sporadically in the region between the northeastern corner of the Mediterranean Sea and the Caucasus Mountains, until the last medieval state was destroyed in the fourteenth century. A landlocked country in modern times, Armenia was the smallest Soviet republic from 1920 until the dissolution of the Soviet Union in 1991 (see fig. 4). The future of an independent Armenia is clouded by limited natural resources and the prospect that the military struggle to unite the Armenians of Azerbaijan's Nagorno-Karabakh Autonomous Region with the Republic of Armenia will be a long one.

Historical Background

The Armenians are an ancient people who speak an Indo-European language and have traditionally inhabited the border regions common to modern Armenia, Iran, and Turkey. They call themselves *hai* (from the name of Hayk, a legendary hero) and their country Haiastan. Their neighbors to the north, the Georgians, call them *somekhi*, but most of the rest of the world follows the usage of the ancient Greeks and refers to them as Armenians, a term derived according to legend from the Armen tribe. Thus the Russian word is *armianin*, and the Turkish is *ermeni*.

The Ancient Period

People first settled what is now Armenia in about 6000 B.C. The first major state in the region was the kingdom of Urartu, which appeared around Lake Van in the thirteenth century B.C. and reached its peak in the ninth century B.C. Shortly after the fall of Urartu to the Assyrians, the Indo-European-speaking proto-Armenians migrated, probably from the west, onto the Armenian Plateau and mingled with the local people of the Hurrian civilization, which at that time extended into Anatolia (present-day Asian Turkey) from its center in Mesopotamia. Greek historians first mentioned the

Armenians in the mid-sixth century B.C. Ruled for many centuries by the Persians, Armenia became a buffer state between the Greeks and Romans to the west and the Persians and Arabs of the Middle East. It reached its greatest size and influence under King Tigran II, also known as Tigranes or Tigran the Great (r. 95–55 B.C.). During his reign, Armenia stretched from the Mediterranean Sea northeast to the Mtkvari River (called the Kura in Azerbaijan) in present-day Georgia (see fig. 5). Tigran and his son, Artavazd II, made Armenia a center of Hellenic culture during their reigns.

By 30 B.C., Rome conquered the Armenian Empire, and for the next 200 years Armenia often was a pawn of the Romans in campaigns against their Central Asian enemies, the Parthians. However, a new dynasty, the Arsacids, took power in Armenia in A.D. 53 under the Parthian king, Tiridates I, who defeated Roman forces in A.D. 62. Rome's Emperor Nero then conciliated the Parthians by personally crowning Tiridates king of Armenia. For much of its subsequent history, Armenia was not united under a single sovereign but was usually divided between empires and among local Armenian rulers.

Early Christianity

After contact with centers of early Christianity at Antioch and Edessa, Armenia accepted Christianity as its state religion in A.D. 306 (the traditional date—the actual date may have been as late as A.D. 314), following miracles said to have been performed by Saint Gregory the Illuminator, son of a Parthian nobleman. Thus Armenians claim that Tiridates III (A.D. 238–314) was the first ruler to officially Christianize his people, his conversion predating the conventional date (A.D. 312) of Constantine the Great's legalization of Christianity on behalf of the Roman Empire.

Early in the fifth century A.D., Saint Mesrop, also known as Mashtots, devised an alphabet for the Armenian language, and religious and historical works began to appear as part of the effort to consolidate the influence of Christianity. For the next two centuries, political unrest paralleled the exceptional development of literary and religious life that became known as the first golden age of Armenia. In several administrative forms, Armenia remained part of the Byzantine Empire until the mid-seventh century. In A.D. 653, the empire, finding the region difficult to govern, ceded Armenia to the Arabs. In A.D. 806, the Arabs established the noble Bagratid family as governors, and later kings, of a semiautonomous Armenian state.

The Middle Ages

Particularly under Bagratid kings Ashot I (also known as Ashot the Great or Ashot V, r. A.D. 862–90) and Ashot III (r. A.D. 952–77), a flourishing of art and literature accompanied a second golden age of Armenian history. The relative prosperity of other kingdoms in the region enabled the Armenians to develop their culture while remaining segmented among jurisdictions of varying degrees of autonomy granted by the Arabs. Then, after eleventh-century invasions from the west by the Byzantine Greeks and from the east by the Seljuk Turks, the independent kingdoms in Armenia proper collapsed, and a new Armenian state, the kingdom of Lesser Armenia, formed in Cilicia along the northeasternmost shore of the Mediterranean Sea. As an ally of the kingdoms set up by the European armies of the Crusades, Cilician Armenia fought against the rising Muslim threat on behalf of the Christian nations of Europe until internal rebellions and court intrigue brought its downfall, at the hands of the Central Asian Mamluk Turks in 1375. Cilician Armenia left notable monuments of art, literature, theology, and jurisprudence. It also served as the door through which Armenians began emigrating to points west, notably Cyprus, Marseilles, Cairo, Venice, and even Holland.

The Mamluks controlled Cilician Armenia until the Ottoman Turks conquered the region in the sixteenth century. Meanwhile, the Ottoman Turks and the Persians divided Caucasian Armenia to the northeast between the sixteenth and eighteenth centuries. The Persians dominated the area of modern Armenia, around Lake Sevan and the city of Erevan. From the fifteenth century until the early twentieth century, most Armenians were ruled by the Ottoman Turks through the *millet* (see Glossary) system, which recognized the ecclesiastical authority of the Armenian Apostolic Church over the Armenian people.

Between Russia and Turkey

Beginning in the eighteenth century, the Russian Empire played a growing role in determining the fate of the Armenians, although those in Anatolia remained under Turkish control, with tragic consequences that would endure well into the twentieth century.

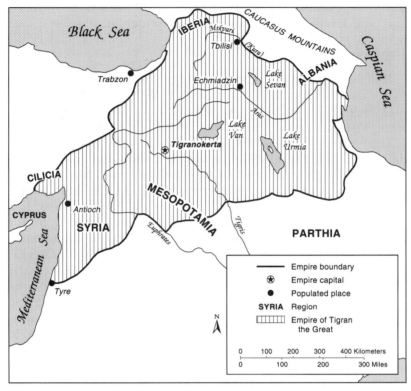

Source: Based on information from David Marshall Lang, *Armenia: Cradle of Civilization*, London, 1980, 132.

Figure 5. The Empire of Tigran the Great, ca. 65 B.C.

Russian Influence Expands

In the eighteenth century, Transcaucasia (the region including the Greater Caucasus mountain range as well as the lands to the south and west) became the object of a military-political struggle among three empires: Ottoman Turkey, tsarist Russia, and Safavid Persia. In 1828 Russia defeated Persia and annexed the area around Erevan, bringing thousands of Armenians into the Russian Empire. In the next half-century, three related processes began to intensify the political and national consciousness of the ethnic and religious communities of the Caucasus region: the imposition of tsarist rule; the rise of a market and capitalist economy; and the emergence of secular national intelligentsias. Tsarism brought Armenians from Russia and from the former Persian provinces under a single legal order. The tsarist system also brought relative peace and security by fostering commerce and industry, the growth of towns, and the building of railroads, thus gradually ending the isolation of many villages.

In the mid-nineteenth century, a major movement toward centralization and reform, called the Tanzimat, swept through the Ottoman Empire, whose authority had been eroded by corruption and delegation of control to local fiefdoms. Armenian subjects benefited somewhat from these reforms; for instance, in 1863 a special Armenian constitution was granted. When the reform movement was ended in the 1870s by reactionary factions, however, Ottoman policy toward subject nationalities became less tolerant, and the situation of the Armenians in the empire began to deteriorate rapidly.

National Self-Awareness

The Armenians themselves changed dramatically in the mid-nineteenth century. An intellectual awakening influenced by Western and Russian ideas, a new interest in Armenian history, and an increase in social interaction created a sense of secular nationality among many Armenians. Instead of conceiving of themselves solely as a religious community, Armenians— especially the urban middle class—began to feel closer kinship with Christian Europe and greater alienation from the Muslim peoples among whom they lived.

Lacking faith in reform within the empire, Armenian leaders began to appeal to the European powers for assistance. In 1878 Armenian delegates appeared at the Congress of Berlin, where the European powers were negotiating the disposition of Ottoman territories. Although Armenian requests for European protection went largely unanswered in Berlin, the "Armenian question" became a point of contention in the complex European diplomacy of the late nineteenth century, with Russia and Britain acting as the chief sponsors of Armenian interests on various issues.

The Armenian independence movement began as agitation on behalf of liberal democracy by writers, journalists, and teachers. But by the last decade of the nineteenth century, moderate nationalist intellectuals had been pushed aside by younger, more radical socialists. Armenian revolutionary parties, founded in the early 1890s in Russia and Europe, sent their cadres to organize in Turkey. Because of the self-destruction of one major party, the Social Democratic

Hnchaks, and the relative isolation of the liberals and the "internationalist" Social Democrats in the cities of Transcaucasia, the more nationalist of the socialist parties, the Armenian Revolutionary Federation (ARF, also known as the Dashnak, a shortened form of its Armenian name), emerged by the early twentieth century as the only real contender for Armenian loyalties. The ARF favored Armenian autonomy in both the Russian and the Ottoman empires rather than full independence for an Armenia in which Russian- and Ottoman-held components would be unified.

In the last decades of the nineteenth century, the Armenians' tendency toward Europeanization antagonized Turkish officials and encouraged their view that Armenians were a foreign, subversive element in the sultan's realm. By 1890 the rapid growth of the Kurdish population in Anatolia, combined with the immigration of Muslims from the Balkans and the Caucasus, had made the Armenian population of Anatolia an increasingly endangered minority. In 1895 Ottoman suspicion of the westernized Armenian population led to the massacre of 300,000 Armenians by special order of the Ottoman government.

Meanwhile, on the other side of the Russian border, Armenian churches and schools were closed and church property was confiscated in 1903. Tatars massacred Armenians in several towns and cities in 1905, and fifty-two Armenian nationalist leaders in Russia were tried en masse for underground activities in 1912.

The Young Turks

The Armenian population that remained in the Ottoman Empire after the 1895 massacre supported the 1908 revolution of the Committee of Union and Progress, better known as the Young Turks, who promised liberal treatment of ethnic minorities. However, after its revolution succeeded, the Young Turk government plotted elimination of the Armenians, who were a significant obstacle to the regime's evolving nationalist agenda.

In the early stages of World War I, Russian armies advanced on Turkey from the north, and the British attempted an invasion from the Mediterranean. Citing the threat of internal rebellion, the Ottoman government ordered large-scale roundups, deportations, and systematic torture and murder of Armenians beginning in the spring of 1915. Estimates vary from 600,000 to 2 million deaths out of the prewar population of about 3 million Armenians. By 1917 fewer than 200,000 Armenians remained in Turkey.

Whatever the exact dimensions of the genocide, Armenians suffered a demographic disaster that shifted the center of the Armenian population from the heartland of historical Armenia to the relatively safer eastern regions held by the Russians. Tens of thousands of refugees fled to the Caucasus with the retreating Russian armies, and the cities of Baku and Tbilisi filled with Armenians from Turkey. Ethnic tensions rose in Transcaucasia as the new immigrants added to the pressures on the limited resources of the collapsing Russian Empire.

World War I and Its Consequences

As was the case for most of Europe, World War I changed Armenia's geopolitical situation. The war also precipitated an ethnic disaster of rare magnitude and brought the Armenians who remained in their native territory into a new type of empire.

Postwar Realignment

Between 1915 and 1917, Russia occupied virtually the entire Armenian part of the Ottoman Empire. Then in October 1917, the Bolshevik victory in Russia ended that country's involvement in World War I, and Russian troops left the Caucasus. In the vacuum that remained, the Armenians first joined a Transcaucasian federation with Azerbaijan and Georgia, both of which, however, soon proved to be unreliable partners. The danger posed by the territorial ambitions of the Ottoman Turks and the Azerbaijanis finally united the Caucasian Armenian population in support of the ARF program for autonomy. In May 1918, an independent Armenian republic was declared; its armies continued to fight on the Allied side south of the Caucasus until the Ottoman Empire surrendered in October 1918. The independent republic endured from May 1918 to December 1920. In the new government, ARF leaders R.I. Kachazuni and A.I. Khatisian became prime minister and foreign minister, respectively.

The Republic of Armenia included the northeastern part of present-day eastern Turkey, west along the Black Sea coast past Trabzon and southwest past Lake Van. But Armenia's precarious independence was threatened from within by the terrible economic conditions that followed the war in the former Ottoman Empire and, by 1920, by the territorial ambitions of Soviet

Russia and the nationalist Turks under Kemal Atatürk. Atatürk had rehabilitated Turkey rapidly under a new democratic system, but the ruling party still hoped to create a larger state by taking territory in western Armenia from which Armenians had been driven. In defending its independence, the Republic of Armenia waited in vain, however, for the material and military aid promised at the Paris Peace Conference in 1919. The Allies' memories of the 1915 massacre faded as war weariness and isolationism dominated their foreign policy.

In agreeing to the 1920 Treaty of Sèvres, the World War I Allies and Turkey recognized Armenian independence; as part of the treaty, Armenia received some disputed territory in what had been the Ottoman Empire. However, most of western Armenia remained in Turkish hands. Eastern Armenia, ravaged by warfare, migration, and disease, had an Armenian population of only 720,000 by 1920. Caught between the advancing Turks and the Red Army, which had already occupied neighboring Azerbaijan, in November 1920 the ARF government made a political agreement with the communists to enter a coalition government. The Treaty of Aleksandropol', signed by this government with Turkey in 1920, returned Armenia's northern Kars district to Turkey and repudiated the existence of Armenian populations in newly expanded Turkey.

Into the Soviet Union

In 1922 Armenia was combined with Azerbaijan and Georgia to form the Transcaucasian Soviet Federated Socialist Republic (TSFSR), which was a single republic of the Soviet Union until the federation was dissolved and each part given republic status in 1936. When the TSFSR was formed, the new Soviet government in the Armenian capital of Erevan ruled over a shrunken country with a devastated economy and few resources with which to feed the populace and rebuild itself. In integrating their republic into the newly forming Soviet Union, Armenian communists surrendered the sovereignty that the independent republic had enjoyed briefly. Although it eliminated rival political parties and restricted the range of public expression, the new government promoted Armenian culture and education, invited artists and intellectuals from abroad to return to Armenia, and managed to create an environment of greater security and material well-being than Armenians had known since the outbreak of World War I.

*Folk dancers celebrating Armenian Independence Day
(May 28, 1918) in Erevan
Courtesy Azarian Churukian*

The Communist Era

During the rule of Joseph V. Stalin (in power 1926–53), Armenian society and its economy were changed dramatically by Moscow policy makers. In a period of twenty-five years, Armenia was industrialized and educated under strictly prescribed conditions, and nationalism was harshly suppressed. After Stalin's death, Moscow allowed greater expression of national feeling, but the corruption endemic in communist rule continued until the very end in 1991. The last years of communism also brought disillusionment in what had been one of the most loyal republics in the Soviet Union until the late 1980s.

Stalinist Restructuring

Stalin's radical restructuring of the Soviet economic and political systems at the end of the 1920s ended the brief period of moderate rule and mixed economy under what was known as the New Economic Policy (see Modern Economic History, this ch.). Under Stalin the Communist Party of Armenia (CPA) used police terror to strengthen its political hold on the population and suppress all expressions of nationalism. At the height of the Great Terror orchestrated by Stalin in 1936–37, the ranks of CPA leaders and intellectuals were decimated by Lavrenti Beria, political commissar for the Transcaucasian republics.

Stalin's enforced social and economic engineering improved literacy and education and built communications and industrial infrastructures where virtually none had existed in tsarist times. As they emerged from the Stalin era in the 1950s, Armenians were more mobile, better educated, and ready to benefit from the less repressive policies of Stalin's successor, Nikita S. Khrushchev (in power 1953–64). The years of industrialization had promoted an upward social mobility through which peasants became workers; workers became foremen or managers; and managers became party and state officials.

Communism after Stalin

After Stalin's death in 1953, Moscow granted the republic more autonomy in decision making, which meant that the local communist elite increased its power and became entrenched in Armenian politics in the 1950s and 1960s. Although overt political opposition remained tightly restricted, expressions of moderate nationalism were viewed with greater tolerance. Statues of Armenian national heroes were erected, including one of Saint Vartan, the fifth-century defender of Armenian Christianity.

Even as Armenia continued its transformation from a basically agrarian nation to an industrial, urban society—by the early 1980s, only a third of Armenians lived in the countryside—the ruling elite remained largely unchanged. As a result, corruption and favoritism spread, and an illegal "second economy" of black markets and bribery flourished. In 1974 Moscow sent a young engineer, Karen Demirchian, to Erevan to clean up the old party apparatus, but the new party chief soon accommodated himself to the corrupt political system he had inherited.

The New Nationalism

Three issues combined by 1988 to stimulate a broad-based Armenian nationalist movement. First, the urbanization and industrialization of Armenia had brought severe ecological problems, the most threatening of which was posed by a nuclear power plant at Metsamor, west of Erevan. Second, many Armenians were angered by the pervasive corruption and arrogance of the communist elite, which had become entrenched as a privileged ruling class. Third and most immediate, Armenians were increasingly concerned about the status of Nagorno-Karabakh, an autonomous region of Azerbaijan having nearly 200,000 Armenians living under Azerbaijani rule, isolated from mainstream Armenian culture.

Control of Nagorno-Karabakh (the conventional geographic term is based on the Russian for the phrase "mountainous Karabakh") had been contested by the briefly independent republics of Armenia and Azerbaijan after World War I. In 1924 the Soviet government designated the region an autonomous region under Azerbaijani jurisdiction within the TSFSR. At the time, 94.4 percent of the estimated 131,500 people in the district were Armenian. Between 1923 and 1979, the Armenian population of the enclave dropped by about 1,000, comprising only about 76 percent of the population by the end of the period. In the same period, the Azerbaijani population quintupled to 37,000, or nearly 24 percent of the region's population. Armenians feared that their demographic decline in Nagorno-Karabakh would replicate the fate of another historically Armenian region, Nakhichevan, which the Soviet Union had designated an autonomous republic under Azerbaijani administration in 1924. In Nakhichevan the number of Armenians had declined from about 15,600 (15 percent of the total) in 1926 to about 3,000 (1.4 percent of the total) in 1979, while in the same period immigration and a higher birth rate had increased the Azerbaijani population from about 85,400 (85 percent) to 230,000, or nearly 96 percent of the total.

In addition to fearing the loss of their numerical superiority, Armenians in Nagorno-Karabakh resented restrictions on the development of the Armenian language and culture in the region. Although the Armenians generally lived better than Azerbaijanis in neighboring districts, their standard of living was not as high as that of their countrymen in Armenia. Hostile to the Azerbaijanis, whom they blamed for their social and cultural problems, the vast majority of Karabakh Armenians preferred to learn Russian rather than Azerbaijani, the language of Azerbaijan. As early as the 1960s, clashes occurred between the Karabakh Armenians and the Azerbaijanis, and Armenian intellectuals petitioned Moscow for redress of their situation in Nagorno-Karabakh.

A series of escalating attacks and reprisals between the two sides began in early 1988. Taking advantage of the greater freedom introduced by the *glasnost* (see Glossary) and *perestroika* (see Glossary) policies of Soviet leader Mikhail S. Gorbachev (in power 1985–91) in the late 1980s, Armenians held mass demonstrations in favor of uniting Nagorno-Karabakh with Armenia. In response to rumored Armenian demands, Azerbaijanis began fleeing the region. A two-day rampage in the industrial town of Sumgait, northwest of Baku, resulted in the deaths of more than 100 Armenians. During 1988, while Moscow hesitated to take decisive action, Armenians grew increasingly disillusioned with Gorbachev's programs, and Azerbaijanis sought to protect their interests by organizing a powerful anti-Armenian nationalist movement.

Nagorno-Karabakh and Independence

The conflict in Nagorno-Karabakh (often called simply Karabakh) served as a catalyst for nationalist movements following the precipitous decline of the Soviet Union in the late 1980s (see fig. 3). In the early 1990s, the struggle defied all negotiating efforts of the West and Russia.

Karabakh as a National Issue

The protests of the Armenians of Nagorno-Karabakh against Azerbaijani rule began in the spirit of *perestroika*, but the movement evolved quickly into a political organization, the Karabakh Committee, a broad anticommunist coalition for democracy and national sovereignty. In the confusion following the earthquake that devastated northern Armenia in December 1988, Soviet authorities tried to stem the growing opposition to their rule by arresting the leaders of the committee. The attempt by the CPA to rule in Armenia without support from Armenian nationalists only worsened the political crisis. In March 1989, many voters boycotted the general elections for the Soviet Union's Congress of People's Deputies. Massive demonstrations were held to demand the release of the members of the committee, and, in the elections to the Armenian Supreme Soviet, the legislative body of the republic, in May, Armenians chose delegates identified with the Karabakh cause. At that time, the flag of independent Armenia was flown for the first time since 1920. The release of the Karabakh Committee followed the 1989 election; for the next six months, the nationalist movement and the Armenian communist leadership worked as uncomfortable allies on the Karabakh issue.

Gorbachev's 1989 proposal for enhanced autonomy for Nagorno-Karabakh within Azerbaijan satisfied neither Armenians nor Azerbaijanis, and a long and inconclusive conflict erupted between the two peoples. In September 1989, Azerbaijan began an economic blockade of Armenia's vital fuel and supply lines through its territory, which until that time had carried about 90 percent of Armenia's imports from the other Soviet republics. In June 1989, numerous unofficial nationalist organizations joined together to form the Armenian Pannational Movement (APM), to which the Armenian government granted official recognition.

The Karabakh Crisis Escalates, 1989

The Azerbaijani-Armenian conflict escalated steadily in the summer and fall of 1989. Both the APM and the newly formed Azerbaijani Popular Front (APF) called for abolition of the Special Administrative Committee that Gorbachev had established to manage Nagorno-Karabakh. The Armenians held to their position that the region must become part of Armenia, and radical Azerbaijanis called for abolition of Karabakh autonomy. As hundreds of thousands of Azerbaijanis demonstrated in Baku, their government further restricted the flow of goods and fuel into Karabakh and Armenia. In August 1989, Karabakh Armenians responded by electing their own National Council, which declared the secession of Karabakh from Azerbaijan and its merger with Armenia. The Armenian Supreme Soviet then declared the Karabakh National Council the sole legitimate representative of the Karabakh people. The Azerbaijani Supreme Soviet responded by abrogating the autonomy of both Karabakh and Nakhichevan.

Although the declarations and counter-declarations of mid-1989 were ultimately declared invalid by the Supreme Soviet of the Soviet Union, and although both Armenia and Azerbaijan continued to be governed by communist parties, neither republic was willing to obey Moscow's directives on the Karabakh issue. In November 1989, in frustration at its inability to bring the parties together, the Supreme Soviet of the Soviet Union abolished the Special Administrative Committee and returned direct control of Karabakh to Azerbaijan. Rejecting Moscow's decision, the Armenian Supreme Soviet declared Karabakh a part of Armenia in December 1989.

After more than two years of the Karabakh conflict, Armenia had gone from being one of the most loyal Soviet republics to complete loss of confidence in Moscow. Gorbachev's unwillingness to grant Karabakh to Armenia and his failure to end the blockade convinced Armenians that the Kremlin considered it politically advantageous to back the more numerous Muslims. Even the invasion of Azerbaijan by Soviet troops in January 1990, ostensibly to stop pogroms against Armenians in Baku, failed to dampen the growing anti-Soviet mood among Armenians (see Within the Soviet Union, ch. 2).

A New Political Climate

The resignation of Suren Harutiunian as first secretary of the CPA in April 1990 and the triumph of the APM in the elections of the spring and summer of 1990 signaled the end of the old party elite and the rise of a new Armenian political class that had matured during the two years of tensions over Karabakh. The newly elected Armenian parliament (which retained the Soviet-era name Supreme Soviet or Supreme Council) chose Levon Ter-Petrosian instead of the new CPA first secretary as its chairman, and hence as head of state of the republic.

With the APM in power and the communists in opposition, the transition from Soviet-style government to an independent democratic state began in earnest. The new government faced a nearly complete collapse of order in the republic. Buildings were seized by armed men in Erevan, and several independent militia groups operated in Erevan as well as on the Azerbaijani frontier. Frustrated by the Azerbaijani blockade and determined to defend their republic and Karabakh, members of Armenia's Fidain (whose name was taken from an Arabic term literally meaning "one who sacrifices himself " and recalling the Armenian freedom fighters of the turn of the century) raided arsenals and police stations to arm themselves for the coming battles. In July Gorbachev demanded immediate disarmament of the Armenian militias and threatened military intervention if they did not comply. In response, Ter-Petrosian's government itself disarmed the independent militias and restored order in Erevan.

On August 23, 1990, Armenia formally declared its intention to become sovereign and independent, with Nagorno-Karabakh an integral part of what now would be known as the Republic of Armenia rather than the Armenian Soviet Socialist Republic. The Armenian nation was defined broadly to include not only those living in the territory of the republic but also the worldwide Armenian émigré population.

In redefining Armenian national interests, the government acknowledged—but temporarily put aside—the painful question of Armenian genocide, having in mind improved relations with traditional enemies Turkey and Iran. This policy prompted strong criticism from extreme nationalist groups that wanted to recover territory lost to Turkey in World War I. The CPA was also vehemently critical.

Independence

In January 1991, the Armenian Supreme Soviet decided not to participate in Gorbachev's planned referendum on preserving the Soviet Union. In March the parliament announced that, instead, the republic would hold its own referendum in September, in compliance with the procedure outlined in the Soviet constitution for a republic to secede. Although literal compliance would mean that Armenia would not be fully independent for five years after the referendum, Moscow soon moved to change Armenia's course. Without notifying the Armenian government, Moscow sent paratroopers to the republic in early May, ostensibly to protect Soviet defense installations in Armenia. Ter-Petrosian's official statement in reaction characterized the move as a virtual declaration of war by the Soviet Union.

In August 1991, when a self-proclaimed emergency committee attempted to overthrow Gorbachev and take control in Moscow, the Armenian government refused to sanction its actions. Fearing an extension of the Soviet incursion of May, Ter-Petrosian approached the Moscow coup very cautiously. The republic's Defense Committee secretly resolved to have the Armenian armed forces go underground and wage guerrilla warfare. Ter-Petrosian, who believed that Gorbachev's personal blunders, indecisiveness, and concessions to conservative communists were to blame for the coup, was overjoyed when the conservatives were defeated. But the coup itself convinced Armenians of the need to move out of the Soviet Union as rapidly as possible, and it validated Ter-Petrosian's refusal to participate in the revival of the Soviet Union advocated by Gorbachev.

Within two months of the coup, Armenians went to the polls twice. In September 1991, over 99 percent of voters approved the republic's commitment to independence. The immediate aftermath of that vote was the Armenian Supreme Soviet's declaration of full independence, on September 23, in disregard of the constitution's restraints on secession. Then in October, Ter-Petrosian was elected overwhelmingly as president of the republic. He now had a popular mandate to carry out his vision of Armenian independence and self-sufficiency.

As political changes occurred within the republic, armed conflict continued in Nagorno-Karabakh during 1991. Armenia officially denied supporting the "Nagorno-Karabakh defense forces" that were pushing Azerbaijani forces out of the region; Armenia also accused the Soviet Union of supporting Azerbaijan as punishment for Armenia's failure to sign Gorbachev's new Union Treaty. In turn, Azerbaijan called Armenia an aggressor state whose national policy included annexation of Azerbaijani territory.

Postindependence Armenia

Two immediate tasks facing independent Armenia were rebuilding its devastated economy and strengthening its fledgling democratic institutions. But the escalating war in Nagorno-Karabakh and the effective blockade of the republic by the Azerbaijanis led to a total collapse of the economy. By early 1993, the government seemed helpless before mounting economic and political problems. The last remaining oil and gas pipelines through neighboring Georgia, which itself was being torn by civil and interethnic war, were blown up by saboteurs. To survive the cold, Armenians in Erevan cut down the city's trees, and plans were made to start up the nuclear power plant at Metsamor. In February 1993, demonstrations called for the resignation of the government, but Ter-Petrosian responded by naming a new cabinet headed by Hrant Bagratian.

While economic and political conditions deteriorated within Armenia, the military position of the Armenians in the Karabakh struggle improved dramatically. Various peace negotiations sponsored by Iran, Russia, Turkey, and a nine-nation group from the Conference on Security and Cooperation in Europe (CSCE—see Glossary) had begun in 1991 and sporadically had yielded cease-fires that were violated almost immediately. In the spring of 1992, while the Azerbaijani communists and the nationalist Azerbaijani Popular Front fought for control in Baku, Karabakh Armenian forces occupied most of Nagorno-Karabakh, took the old capital, Shusha, and drove a corridor through the Kurdish area around Lachin to link

Nagorno-Karabakh with Armenia. But the immediate result of this victory was the collapse of Russian-sponsored peace negotiations with Azerbaijan and the continuation of the war.

Beginning a counteroffensive in early summer, the Azerbaijanis recaptured some territory and created thousands of new refugees by expelling Armenians from the villages they took. In midsummer this new phase of the conflict stimulated a CSCE-sponsored peace conference, but Armenia stymied progress by demanding for the first time that Nagorno-Karabakh be entirely separate from Azerbaijan.

By the end of 1992, the sides were bogged down in a bloody stalemate. After clearing Azerbaijani forces from Nagorno-Karabakh and the territory between Karabakh and Armenia, Armenian troops also advanced deep into Azerbaijan proper— a move that brought condemnation from the United Nations (UN) Security Council and panic in Iran, on whose borders Armenian troops had arrived. In the first half of 1993, the Karabakh Armenians gained more Azerbaijani territory, against disorganized opposition. Azerbaijani resistance was weakened by the confusion surrounding a military coup that toppled the APF government in Baku and returned former communist party boss Heydar Aliyev to power.

The coup reinvigorated Russian efforts to negotiate a peace under the complex terms of the three parties to the conflict: the governments of Armenia and Azerbaijan, and the increasingly independent and assertive Karabakh Armenians. CSCE peace proposals were uniformly rejected during this period. Although Russia seemed poised for a triumph of crisis diplomacy on its borders, constant negotiations in the second half of 1993 produced only intermittent cease-fires. At the end of 1993, the Karabakh Armenians were able to negotiate with the presidents of Azerbaijan and Russia from a position of power: they retained full control of Nagorno-Karabakh and substantial parts of Azerbaijan proper (see After Communist Rule, ch. 2).

Physical Environment

Armenia is located in southern Transcaucasia, the region southwest of Russia between the Black Sea and the Caspian Sea. Modern Armenia occupies part of historical Armenia, whose ancient centers were in the valley of the Aras River and the region around Lake Van in Turkey. Armenia is bordered on the north by Georgia, on the east by Azerbaijan, on the south by Iran, on the southwest by the Nakhichevan Autonomous Republic of Azerbaijan, and on the west by Turkey (see fig. 1).

Topography and Drainage

Twenty-five million years ago, a geological upheaval pushed up the earth's crust to form the Armenian Plateau, creating the complex topography of modern Armenia (see fig. 2). The Lesser Caucasus range extends through northern Armenia, runs southeast between Lake Sevan and Azerbaijan, then passes roughly along the Armenian-Azerbaijani border to Iran. Thus situated, the mountains make travel from north to south difficult. Geological turmoil continues in the form of devastating earthquakes, which have plagued Armenia. In December 1988, the second largest city in the republic, Leninakan (now Gyumri), was heavily damaged by a massive quake that killed more than 25,000 people.

About half of Armenia's area of approximately 29,800 square kilometers has an elevation of at least 2,000 meters, and only 3 percent of the country lies below 650 meters. The lowest points are in the valleys of the Aras River and the Debet River in the far north, which have elevations of 380 and 430 meters, respectively. Elevations in the Lesser Caucasus vary between 2,640 and 3,280 meters. To the southwest of the range is the Armenian Plateau, which slopes southwestward toward the Aras River on the Turkish border. The plateau is masked by intermediate mountain ranges and extinct volcanoes. The largest of these, Mount Aragats, 4,430 meters high, is also the highest point in Armenia. Most of the population lives in the western and northwestern parts of the country, where the two major cities, Erevan and Gyumri (which was called Aleksandropol' during the tsarist period), are located.

The valleys of the Debet and Akstafa rivers form the chief routes into Armenia from the north as they pass through the mountains. Lake Sevan, 72.5 kilometers across at its widest point and 376 kilometers long, is by far the largest lake. It lies 2,070 meters above sea level on the plateau. Terrain is most rugged in the extreme southeast, which is drained by the Bargushat River, and most moderate in the Aras River valley to the extreme southwest. Most of Armenia is drained by the Aras or its tributary, the Razdan, which flows from Lake Sevan. The Aras forms most of Armenia's border with Turkey and Iran as well as the border between Azerbaijan's adjacent Nakhichevan Autonomous Republic and Iran.

*Damage to apartment buildings in Leninakan (present-day
Gyumri) caused by 1988 earthquake
Courtesy John Filson*

Climate

Temperatures in Armenia generally depend upon elevation.
Mountain formations block the moderating climatic influences
of the Mediterranean Sea and the Black Sea, creating wide sea-
sonal variations. On the Armenian Plateau, the mean midwinter temperature is 0°C, and the mean midsummer temperature
exceeds 25°C. Average precipitation ranges from 250 millimeters per year in the lower Aras River valley to 800 millimeters at
the highest altitudes. Despite the harshness of winter in most
parts, the fertility of the plateau's volcanic soil made Armenia
one of the world's earliest sites of agricultural activity.

Environmental Problems

A broad public discussion of environmental problems
began in the mid-1980s, when the first "green" groups formed
in opposition to Erevan's intense industrial air pollution and to
nuclear power generation in the wake of the 1986 reactor
explosion at Chernobyl'. Environmental issues helped form the
basis of the nationalist independence movement when environmental demonstrations subsequently merged with those for
other political causes in the late 1980s.

In the postcommunist era, Armenia faces the same massive environmental cleanup that confronts the other former Soviet republics as they emerge from the centralized planning system's disastrous approach to resource management. By 1980 the infrequency of sightings of Mount Ararat, which looms about sixty kilometers across the Turkish border, became a symbol of worsening air pollution in Erevan.

In independent Armenia, environmental issues divide society (and scientists) sharply into those who fear "environmental time bombs" and those who view resumption of pollution-prone industrial operations as the only means of improving the country's economy. In the early 1990s, the latter group blamed Armenia's economic woes on the role played by the former in closing major industries.

In 1994 three national environmental laws were in effect: the Law on Environmental Protection, the Basic Law on the Environment, and the Law on Mineral Resources. The Council of Ministers, Armenia's cabinet, includes a minister of the environment. However, no comprehensive environmental protection program has emerged, and decisions on environmental policy have been made on an ad hoc basis.

Environmental conditions in Armenia have been worsened by the Azerbaijani blockade of supplies and electricity from outside. Under blockade conditions, the winters of 1991–92, 1992–93, and 1993–94 brought enormous hardship to a population lacking heat and electric power. (The large-scale felling of trees for fuel during the winters of the blockade has created another environmental crisis.) The results of the blockade and the failure of diplomatic efforts to lift it led the government to propose reconstruction of the Armenian Atomic Power Station at Metsamor, which was closed after the 1988 earthquake because of its location in an earthquake-prone area and which had the same safety problems as reactors listed as dangerous in Bulgaria, Russia, and Slovakia. After heated debates over start-up continued through 1993, French and Russian nuclear consultants declared operating conditions basically safe. Continuation of the blockade into 1994 gave added urgency to the decision (see Energy, this ch.).

Another environmental concern is a significant drop in Lake Sevan's water level because of drawdowns for irrigation and the diversion of water to hydroelectric plants to compensate for the electric power lost through the inactivity of the nuclear plant at Metsamor. This crisis was addressed in 1992–93 by construction of a tunnel to divert water into the lake from the Arpa River. Engineers estimated that once the project is finished, the tunnel will allow 500 million cubic meters of water to be drawn from the lake annually, while maintaining a constant water level. The Ministry of the Environment reported that the lake's water level had dropped by fifty centimeters in 1993. Experts said that this drop brought the level to within twenty-seven centimeters of the critical point where flora and fauna would be endangered.

Among major industrial centers closed to curtail pollution were the Nairit Chemical Plant, the Alaverdy Metallurgical Plant, and the Vanadzor Chemical Combine. Economic requirements triumphed over environmental considerations when the Soviet-era Nairit plant was reopened in January 1992 after being closed in 1989 because of the massive air pollution it caused. Newly independent Armenia needed the income from foreign sales of Nairit rubber and chemical products, many of which had been assigned exclusively to that plant under the Soviet system and were still unavailable elsewhere to the former Soviet republics in the early 1990s. Up-to-date environmental safety technology and adherence to international standards were promised at Nairit when the decision to resume production was announced.

Population and Ethnic Composition

The forces of history have wrought dramatic changes on the boundaries of the various Armenian states; the population's size and the ethnic makeup of those states have also been strongly affected. In the twentieth century, particularly significant changes resulted from Turkish efforts to exterminate Armenians during World War I and from the large-scale emigration of Azerbaijanis from Armenia in the early 1990s.

Population Characteristics

The origins of the Armenian people are obscure. According to ancient Armenian writers, their people descend from Noah's son Japheth. A branch of the Indo-Europeans, the Armenians are linked ethnically to the Phrygians, who migrated from Thrace in southeastern Europe into Asia Minor late in the second millennium B.C., and to the residents of the kingdom of Urartu, with whom the Armenians came into contact around 800 B.C. after arriving in Asia Minor from the West. Although ethnologists disagree about the precise timing and elements of this ethnic combination (and even about the origin of the term *Armenian*), it is generally agreed that the modern Armenians have been a distinct ethnic group centered in eastern Anatolia since at least 600 B.C.

In the nineteenth century, the Armenians were the most urban of the Transcaucasian peoples, but they were also the most dispersed. A merchant middle class was the most powerful social group among the Armenians, although the church and secular intellectuals also provided leadership. Armenians pioneered exploitation of the oil deposits in and around Baku, and the economic growth of the ancient Georgian capital, Tbilisi, was largely an enterprise of Armenian merchants and small industrialists.

The massacres and displacements that occurred between 1895 and 1915 removed nearly all the Armenian population in the Turkish part of historical Armenia. In 1965 the Soviet Union estimated that 3.2 million Armenians lived in all its republics. The Turkish census the same year showed only 33,000 Armenians in Turkey, most of them concentrated in the far west in Istanbul. In 1988 Armenia's population declined by 176,000, reversing a trend over the previous decade, in which average population growth was 1.5 percent per year. According to the 1989 census, the population of Armenia was about 3,288,000, an increase of 8 percent from the 1979 census figure. An official estimate in 1991 put the population at 3,354,000, an increase of 2 percent since 1989. In 1989 Armenians were the eighth largest nationality in the former Soviet Union, totaling 4,627,000. At that time, only about two-thirds of the Armenians in the Soviet Union lived in Armenia. Some 11.5 percent lived in Russia, 9.4 percent in Georgia, 8.4 percent in Azerbaijan, and the remaining 4 percent in the other republics. In recent years, Armenian refugees from Azerbaijan, Georgia, Russia, and the Central Asian republics have settled in Armenia, compounding an already severe housing shortage. The number of Armenians living in other countries, primarily France, Iran, Lebanon, Syria, and the United States, has been estimated at between 3 million and 9 million.

In 1991 Armenia's population density, 112.6 persons per square kilometer, was second only to that of Moldavia (now Moldova) among the Soviet republics. About 68 percent of the population lives in urban areas and 32 percent in rural areas. In 1990 Armenia's capital, Erevan, had a population of 1.2 million, or about 37 percent of the population of the republic; the

View of Erevan
Courtesy A. James Firth, United States Department of Agriculture

second largest city, Leninakan, had 123,000 residents. The twelfth largest city in the former Soviet Union, Erevan is the second largest in the Caucasus region, after Tbilisi.

In 1979 Armenian families residing in Armenia averaged 4.5 persons, including an average of 4.3 for urban families and 4.8 average for rural families. This average was larger than those of the Baltic, Georgian, Moldavian, and predominantly Slavic republics of the Soviet Union but less than the family averages of the Soviet Muslim republics. In 1989 average life expectancy was 71.9 years (69.0 years for males and 74.7 years for females). The birth rate was 21.6 live births per 1,000 population; the death rate was 6.0 per 1,000.

Ethnic Minorities

Ethnically the most homogeneous of the Soviet republics, Armenia had few problems with ethnic minorities during the Soviet period. According to the last Soviet census, conducted in 1989, Armenians made up 93.3 percent of Armenia's population, Azerbaijanis 2.6 percent, Russians 1.6 percent, and Muslim Kurds and Yezidi (Christian Kurds) together 1.7 percent. Fewer than 30,000 others, including Greeks and Ukrainians, lived in the republic in 1989. During the Soviet period, the

31

Figure 6. Ethnic Groups in Armenia

republic's largest non-Armenian group was the Azerbaijanis. By 1989, however, almost all of the Azerbaijanis, who had numbered 161,000 in 1979, either had been expelled or had emigrated from Armenia (see fig. 6). The figure for the 1989 census included 77,000 Azerbaijanis who had returned to their native country but were still considered residents of Armenia.

Language, Religion, and Culture

Through the centuries, Armenians have conscientiously retained the unique qualities of their language and art forms, incorporating influences from surrounding societies without sacrificing distinctive national characteristics. Religion also has been a strong unifying force and has played a political role as well.

Language

The Armenian language is a separate Indo-European tongue sharing some phonetic and grammatical features with other Caucasian languages, such as Georgian. The Iranian languages contributed many loanwords related to cultural subjects; the majority of the Armenian word stock shows no connection with other existing languages, however, and some experts believe it derives from extinct non-Indo-European languages. The distinct alphabet of thirty-eight letters, derived from the Greek alphabet, has existed since the early fifth century A.D. Classical Armenian (*grabar*) is used today only in the Armenian Apostolic Church as a liturgical language. Modern spoken Armenian is divided into a number of dialects, the most important of which are the eastern dialect (used in Armenia, the rest of Transcaucasia, and Iran) and the western dialect (used extensively in Turkey and among Western émigrés). The two major dialects differ in some vocabulary, pronunciation, grammar, and orthography.

In the Soviet period, schools in Armenia taught in both Armenian and Russian; in a republic where over 95 percent of the people claimed Armenian as their native language, almost all of the urban population and much of the rural population knew at least some Russian. At the end of the Soviet period, 91.6 percent of Armenians throughout the Soviet Union considered Armenian to be their native language, and 47.1 percent of Armenians were fluent in Russian.

Religion

Mostly Christians since the early fourth century A.D., the Armenians claim to represent the first state to adopt Christianity as an official religion. The independent Armenian church considers its founders to have been the apostles Bartholomew and Thaddeus and officially calls itself the Armenian Apostolic Church. (It is also referred to as the Armenian Orthodox Church or the Gregorian Church.) The conversion of Armenia by Saint Gregory the Illuminator occurred by about A.D. 314, although the traditional date is A.D. 306. Armenian Christians then remained under the powerful combined religious and political jurisdiction of the Roman Empire until the sixth century. At that point, the Armenian church asserted its independence by breaking with the Byzantine doctrine of Christ's dual (divine and earthly) nature, which had been expressed officially by the Council of Chalcedon in A.D. 451.

Since the schism, the Armenian Apostolic Church has been in communion only with the monophysite churches (those believing that the human and divine natures of Christ constitute a unity) of Egypt, Syria, and Ethiopia. Rather than embrace the monophysite doctrine, however, the Armenian church holds that Christ had both a divine and a human nature, inseparably combined in a complete humanity that was animated by a rational soul.

Although the Armenian Apostolic Church often is identified with the Eastern Orthodox churches of Eastern Europe, Russia, and Georgia, the Armenian church has been juridically and theologically independent since the early Middle Ages. As a national church, it has played a vital role in maintaining Armenian culture, through the preservation and expansion of written traditions and as a cultural focus for Armenians scattered around the world. In the long periods when Armenians did not have a state of their own, their church was both a political and a spiritual leader, and religion was at the center of the Armenian national self-image. Under the *millet* system by which the Ottoman Empire ruled subject peoples, the patriarch of Constantinople was recognized as the head of the Armenian community, and the Russian Empire treated the catholicos, the titular head of the Armenian Apostolic Church, as the most important representative of the Armenian people.

The Armenian Apostolic Church is headed by Vazgen I, supreme catholicos of all Armenians, who resides in the holy city of Echmiadzin, west of Erevan. The membership of the church is split between a majority that recognizes the supreme catholicos without qualification and a minority that recognizes the catholicos of Cilicia, whose seat is at Antilyas in Lebanon. Closely affiliated with the Armenian Revolutionary Federation (ARF), the minority branch of the church was hostile to any accommodation with communist regimes while Armenia was under Soviet rule. Both branches of the church have been closely identified with the movement for national independence, however. A split occurred within the United States membership of the Armenian Apostolic Church in 1933, when ARF sympathizers assassinated the Armenian archbishop of New York. Two factions remained distinct in the United States in the early 1990s.

Two additional patriarchates in Jerusalem and Istanbul lack the status of full catholicates. Three dioceses are located in other former Soviet republics, and twenty bishoprics function in other countries. Total church membership was estimated at 4 million in 1993. The Armenian Orthodox Academy and one seminary provide religious training.

About 94 percent of the population of Armenia belongs to the Armenian Apostolic Church. Small Roman Catholic and Protestant communities also exist in Armenia. Catholic missionaries began converting Armenians in the Ottoman and Persian empires in the early modern era, and American Protestant missionaries were active in the nineteenth century. The Kurdish population, which totaled 56,000 in 1993, is mostly Muslim but also includes many Christians. Kurds now constitute the largest Muslim group in Armenia because most Azerbaijani Muslims emigrated in the early 1990s. A Russian Orthodox community also exists.

The Armenian Diaspora

Beginning in the eleventh century, a long series of invasions, migrations, conversions, deportations, and massacres reduced Armenians to a minority population in their historic homeland on the Armenian Plateau. Under these conditions, a large-scale Armenian diaspora of merchants, clerics, and intellectuals reached cities in Russia, Poland, Western Europe, and India. Most Armenians remaining in historical Armenia under the Ottoman Empire in the fifteenth century survived as peasant farmers in eastern Anatolia, but others resettled in Constantinople, Smyrna, and other cities in the empire. There they became artisans, moneylenders, and traders. In the nineteenth century, the political uncertainties that beset the Ottoman Empire prompted further insecurity in the Armenian population. Finally, the Young Turk government either massacred or forcibly removed the vast majority of Armenians from the eastern Anatolian provinces in 1915 (see Between Russia and Turkey, this ch.).

Today about half the world's Armenians live outside Armenia. Armenian communities have emerged in the Middle East, Russia, Poland, Western Europe, India, and North America, where Armenians have gained a reputation for their skill in crafts and in business. Although accurate statistics are not available, the Armenian diaspora is about equally divided between the 1.5 million Armenians in the other republics of the former

Soviet Union and a similar number in the rest of the world. The postcommunist Republic of Armenia has officially defined the Armenian nation to include the far-flung diaspora, a policy in accord with the feelings of many diaspora Armenians.

A common theme in Armenian discourse is the need to preserve the culture and heritage of the Armenian people through education and mobilization of younger members of the community. In this task, the Republic of Armenia enjoys the enthusiastic support of the international Armenian community, which sees a new opportunity to impart information to the rest of the world about Armenian culture—and especially to rectify perceived inattention to the tragedy of 1915.

The Armenian diaspora maintains its coherence through the church, political parties (despite their mutual hostilities), charitable organizations, and a network of newspapers published in Armenian and other languages. Armenian émigrés in the United States have endowed eight university professorships in Armenian studies. With the reemergence of an independent Armenia, diaspora Armenians have established industries, a technical university, exchange programs, and medical clinics in Armenia. Several prominent diaspora Armenians have served in the Armenian government.

Culture

The international Armenian community remains loyal to strong cultural traditions, many of which have enriched the societies into which Armenians emigrated. Cultural tradition has been a means of maintaining a sense of national unity among widely dispersed groups of Armenians.

Literature and the Arts

The Armenians became active in literature and many art forms at a very early point in their civilization. Urartian metalworking and architecture have been traced back to about 1000 B.C. The beginning of truly national art is usually fixed at the onset of the Christian era. The three great artistic periods coincided with times of independence or semi-independence: from the fifth to the seventh century; the Bagratid golden age of the ninth and tenth centuries; and the era of the kingdom of Lesser Armenia in the twelfth to fourteenth centuries.

Of especially high quality in the earlier periods were work in gold and bronze, as well as temples, military fortifications, and aqueducts. In the early Christian era, classical church architecture was adapted in a series of cathedrals. The circular domes typical of Armenian churches were copied in Western Europe and in Ottoman Turkey. The best example of the distinctive architectural sculpture used to adorn such churches is the early tenth-century Church of the Holy Cross on an island in Lake Van. The architecture of contemporary Erevan is distinguished by the use of pinkish tufa stone and a combination of traditional Armenian and Russian styles.

Armenian painting is generally considered to have originated with the illumination of religious manuscripts that thrived from the ninth to the seventeenth century. Armenian painters in Cilicia and elsewhere enriched Byzantine and Western formulas with their unique use of color and their inclusion of Oriental themes acquired from the Mongols. Many unique Armenian illuminated manuscripts remain in museums in the West.

The nineteenth century saw a blooming of Armenian painting. Artists from that period, such as the portrait painter Hacop Hovnatanian and the seascape artist Ivan Aivazovsky, continue to enjoy international reputations. Notable figures of the twentieth century have included the unorthodox Alexander Bazhbeuk-Melikian, who lived a persecuted existence in Tbilisi, and the émigré surrealist Arshile Gorky (pseudonym of Vosdanik Adoian), who greatly influenced a generation of young American artists in New York. Other émigré painters in various countries have continued the tradition as well.

The Armenian literary tradition began early in the fifth century A.D. with religious tracts and histories of the Armenians. The most important of these were written by Agathangelos, Egishe, Movses Khorenatsi, and Pavstos Buzand. A secular literature developed in the early modern period, and in the eighteenth century Armenian Catholic monks of the Mekhitarist order began publishing ancient texts, modern histories, grammars, and literature. In the nineteenth century, Armenians developed their own journalism and public theater. Khachatur Abovian wrote the first Armenian novel, *Verk Haiastani* (The Wounds of Armenia), in the early 1840s. Armenian literature and drama often depict struggles against religious and ethnic oppression and the aspirations of Armenians for security and self-expression.

National Traditions

Major Armenian holidays commemorate both religious and

historical events. Besides Christmas and Easter, the most important holidays are Vartanants, the day marking the fifth-century defense of Christianity against the Persians, and April 24, which commemorates the 1915 genocide of the Armenians in Turkey.

At times of celebration, Armenians enjoy traditional circle dances and distinctive national music. Their music and their cuisine are similar to those of other Middle Eastern peoples. A typical Armenian meal might include lamb, rice pilaf, eggplant, yogurt, and a sweet dessert such as *paklava* (baklava). Armenians pride themselves on their close family ties, hospitality, and reverence for their national language and culture, an appreciation that is passed from one generation to the next.

Education, Health, and Welfare

In the first years of independence, Armenia made uneven progress in establishing systems to meet its national requirements in social services. Education, held in particular esteem in Armenian culture, changed fastest of the social services, while health and welfare services attempted to maintain the basic state-planned structure of the Soviet era.

Education

A literacy rate of 100 percent was reported as early as 1960. In the communist era, Armenian education followed the standard Soviet model of complete state control (from Moscow) of curricula and teaching methods and close integration of education activities with other aspects of society, such as politics, culture, and the economy. As in the Soviet period, primary and secondary school education in Armenia is free, and completion of secondary school is compulsory. In the early 1990s, Armenia made substantial changes to the centralized and regimented Soviet system. Because at least 98 percent of students in higher education were Armenian, curricula began to emphasize Armenian history and culture. Armenian became the dominant language of instruction, and many schools that had taught in Russian closed by the end of 1991. Russian was still widely taught, however, as a second language.

In the 1990–91 school year, the estimated 1,307 primary and secondary schools were attended by 608,800 students. Another seventy specialized secondary institutions had 45,900 students, and 68,400 students were enrolled in a total of ten postsecondary institutions that included universities. In addition, 35 per-

*Men playing checkers at old-age home in Erevan
Courtesy A. James Firth, United States Department of Agriculture*

cent of eligible children attended preschools. In the 1988–89 school year, 301 students per 10,000 population were in specialized secondary or higher education, a figure slightly lower than the Soviet average. In 1989 some 58 percent of Armenians over age fifteen had completed their secondary education, and 14 percent had a higher education. In 1992 Armenia's largest institution of higher learning, Erevan State University, had eighteen departments, including ones for social sciences, sciences, and law. Its faculty numbered about 1,300 and its student population about 10,000. The Erevan Architecture and Civil Engineering Institute was founded in 1989. Eight other institutions of higher learning, all located in Erevan, teach agriculture, fine arts and theater, economics, music, applied science and technology, medicine, pedagogy and foreign languages, and veterinary medicine.

Health

The social and economic upheavals that followed the earthquake of 1988 combined with the political collapse of the Soviet Union to create a catastrophic public health situation in Armenia. According to Soviet statistics published between 1989 and 1991, the incidence of tuberculosis, viral hepatitis, and cancer were among the lowest in the Soviet republics (see table 2, Appendix). In 1990 the rates of infant mortality and maternal mortality, 17.1 and 34.6 per 1,000 population, respectively, were also among the lowest rates in the Soviet Union.

The level of medical care declined rapidly in the late 1980s and the early 1990s, however, largely because of the Azerbaijani blockade and the additional stress caused by war casualties. Even in 1990, Armenia ranked lowest among the republics in hospital beds per 1,000 population and exactly matched the Soviet Union average for doctors per 1,000 population. Before 1991 Armenia had acquired stocks of medical supplies and equipment, thanks largely to the Western aid projects that followed the 1988 earthquake. By 1992, however, the trade blockade had made the supply of such basic items as surgical gloves, syringes, and chlorine for water purification unreliable. In the escalating medical crisis that resulted from this vulnerability, elderly people and newborns were particularly at risk; in late 1992 and early 1993, healthy infants reportedly were dying in hospitals because of the cold and the lack of adequate equipment.

In December 1992, President Ter-Petrosian declared Armenia a disaster area and appealed to the UN Security Council to focus on the crisis in the republic. Government officials estimated that without emergency humanitarian aid some 30,000 people would die. Early in 1993, the United States launched Operation Winter Rescue to send needed assistance to Armenia. In June Project Hope sent US$3.9 million worth of medicine from the United States. From mid-1992 to mid-1993, United States medical assistance totaled US$20 million.

All hospitals in Armenia are under the jurisdiction of the Ministry of Health or the Erevan Health Department. In 1993 about 29,900 hospital beds were available. Hospitals generally had surgical, physical therapy, pediatric, obstetric/gynecological, and infectious disease wards. But according to reports, by 1993 more than half the hospitals in Armenia had ceased functioning because electricity, heat, or supplies were lacking.

Thirty-seven polyclinics serve the rural areas, which have no comprehensive health centers; such clinics are each designated to provide basic medical services to about 10,000 people. Sixty-two outpatient centers specialize in child or adult medicine in urban areas. Immunizations against certain diseases are given to most infants before they are one year old: in 1991 some 95 percent of infants were immunized against poliomyelitis, 88 percent against diphtheria, and 86 percent against pertussis.

Between 1986 and 1994, two cases of acquired immune deficiency syndrome (AIDS) were reported in Armenia: one foreigner who was subsequently deported, and one Armenian who contracted the disease in Tanzania and was treated in Armenia. Experts believe that the Azerbaijani blockade has acted to limit the incidence of AIDS. Although no AIDS clinics are operating, some research has been conducted. In 1992 Armenian scientists announced the discovery of a possible treatment compound.

Social Welfare

The social safety net also weakened drastically in the first years of independence. Beginning in 1989, a large share of national expenditures on welfare services went to the victims of the earthquake. In the early 1990s, Armenia nominally retained the Soviet-era system of social services (retirement, survivor, and disability pensions; allowances to the parents of newborn children; sick and maternity leave; unemployment compensation; and food subsidies). In the early 1990s, however, acute budget shortages brought severe cuts in almost all the social welfare programs of the Soviet era and their replacement by intermittent foreign aid programs. The Ministry of Labor and Social Security allocates social benefits and charitable aid from outside the country. In 1993 only 35 percent of those officially considered unemployed received jobless benefits (see Labor and the Standard of Living, this ch.).

The Economy

In 1991, Armenia's last year as a Soviet republic, national income fell 12 percent from the previous year, and per capita gross national product (GNP—see Glossary) was 4,920 rubles, just 68 percent of the national average for the Soviet Union. In large part because of the earthquake of 1988, the Azerbaijani blockade that began in 1989, and the collapse of the internal trading system of the Soviet Union, the Armenian economy of the early 1990s remained far below its 1980 production levels. In the first two years of independence (1992–93), inflation was extremely high, productivity and national income dropped dramatically, and the national budget ran large deficits.

Modern Economic History

At the beginning of the twentieth century, the territory of present-day Armenia was a backward agricultural region with some copper mining and cognac production. From 1914 through 1921, Caucasian Armenia suffered from war, revolution, the influx of refugees from Turkish Armenia, disease, hunger, and economic misery. About 200,000 people died in 1919 alone. At that point, only American relief efforts saved Armenia from total collapse.

The first Soviet Armenian government regulated economic activity stringently, nationalizing all economic enterprises, requisitioning grain from peasants, and suppressing most private market activity. This first experiment in state control ended with the advent of Soviet leader Vladimir I. Lenin's New Economic Policy (NEP) of 1921–27. This policy continued state control of the large enterprises and banks, but peasants could market much of their grain, and small businesses could function. In Armenia the NEP years brought partial recovery from the economic disaster of the post-World War I period. By 1926 agricultural production in Armenia had reached nearly three-quarters of its prewar level.

By the end of the 1920s, Stalin's regime had revoked the NEP and established a state monopoly on all economic activity. Once this occurred, the main goal of Soviet economic policy in Armenia was to turn a predominantly agrarian and rural republic into an industrial and urban one. Among other restrictions, peasants now were forced to sell nearly all their output to state procurement agencies rather than at the market. From the 1930s through the 1960s, an industrial infrastructure was constructed. Besides hydroelectric plants and canals, roads were built and gas pipelines were laid to bring fuel and food from Azerbaijan and Russia.

The Stalinist command economy, in which market forces were suppressed and all orders for production and distribution came from state authorities, survived in all its essential features until the fall of the Soviet government in 1991. In the early stages of the communist economic revolution, Armenia underwent a fundamental transformation into a "proletarian" society. Between 1929 and 1939, the percentage of Armenia's work force categorized as industrial workers grew from 13 percent to 31 percent. By 1935 industry supplied 62 percent of Armenia's economic production. Highly integrated and sheltered within the artificial barter economy of the Soviet system from the

American University of Armenia, formerly Communist Party
Higher School, Erevan
Courtesy Monica O'Keefe, United States Information Agency

1930s until the end of the communist era, the Armenian econ-omy showed few signs of self-sufficiency at any time during that period. In 1988 Armenia produced only 0.9 percent of the net material product (NMP—see Glossary) of the Soviet Union (1.2 percent of industry, 0.7 percent of agriculture). The republic retained 1.4 percent of total state budget revenue, delivered 63.7 percent of its NMP to other republics, and exported only 1.4 percent of what it produced to markets out-side the Soviet Union.

Armenian industry was especially dependent on the Soviet military-industrial complex. About 40 percent of all enterprises in the republic were devoted to defense, and some factories lost 60 to 80 percent of their business in the last years of the Soviet Union, when massive cuts were made in national defense expenditures. As the republic's economy faces the prospect of competing in world markets in the mid-1990s, the greatest liabilities of Armenian industry are its outdated equip-ment and infrastructure and the pollution emitted by many of the country's heavy industrial plants (see Environmental Prob-lems, this ch.).

Natural Resources

Although Armenia was one of the first places where humans smelted iron, copper is the most important raw material mined there today. Deposits of zinc, molybdenum, gold, silver, bauxite, obsidian, and semiprecious stones, as well as marble, granite, and other building materials, are also present. Significant expansion is believed possible in the exploitation of most of those materials, which until the mid-1990s had been largely untouched. Some oil deposits have been identified, but the complex geology of the region makes recovery difficult and expensive. In 1993 an American expedition tentatively identified further deposits of natural gas and oil, but exploitation was not expected for several years.

Agriculture

Armenia has 486,000 hectares of arable land, about 16 percent of the country's total area. In 1991 Armenia imported about 65 percent of its food. About 10 percent of the work force, which is predominantly urban, is employed in agriculture, which in 1991 provided 25.7 percent of the country's NMP. In 1990 Armenia became the first Soviet republic to pass a land privatization law, and from that time Armenian farmland shifted into the private sector at a faster rate than in any other republic. However, the rapidity and disorganization of land reallocation led to disputes and dissatisfaction among the peasants receiving land. Especially problematic were allocation of water rights and distribution of basic materials and equipment. Related enterprises such as food processing and hothouse operations often remained in state hands, reducing the advantages of private landholding.

By 1992 privatization of the state and collective farms, which had dominated Armenian agriculture in the Soviet period, had put 63 percent of cultivated fields, 80 percent of orchards, and 91 percent of vineyards in the hands of private farmers. The program yielded a 15 percent increase in agricultural output between 1990 and 1991. In 1993 the government ended restrictions on the transfer of private land, a step expected to increase substantially the average size (and hence the efficiency) of private plots. At the end of 1993, an estimated 300,000 small farms (one to five hectares) were operating. In that year, harvests were bountiful despite the high cost of inputs; only the disastrous state of Armenia's transportation infrastructure prevented relief of food shortages in urban centers (see Transportation and Telecommunications, this ch.).

Agriculture is carried out mainly in the valleys and on the mountainsides of Armenia's uneven terrain, with the highest mountain pastures used for livestock grazing. Fertile volcanic soil allows cultivation of wheat and barley as well as pasturage for sheep, goats, and horses. With the help of irrigation, figs, pomegranates, cotton, apricots, and olives also are grown in the limited subtropical conditions of the Aras River valley and in the valleys north of Erevan, where the richest farmland is found. Armenia also produces peaches, walnuts, and quinces, and its cognac enjoys a worldwide reputation.

Irrigation is required for most crops, and the building of canals and a system of irrigation was among the first major state projects of the Soviet republic in the 1920s. By the 1960s, arable land had been extended by 20 percent, compared with pre-Soviet times. Most farms had electricity by the early 1960s, and machinery was commonplace. In the Soviet era, women made up most of the agricultural work force; a large percentage of the younger men had responded to the Soviet industrialization campaign by migrating to urban centers. In 1989 farms were operating about 13,400 tractors and 1,900 grain and cotton combines.

The principal agricultural products are grains (mostly wheat and barley), potatoes, vegetables, grapes, berries, cotton, sugar beets, tobacco, figs, and olives. In 1989 Armenia produced 200,000 tons of grain, 266,000 tons of potatoes, 485,000 tons of vegetables, 117,000 tons of sugar beets, 170,000 tons of fruit, 119,000 tons of grapes, 105,000 tons of meat, 491,000 tons of milk, and 561,000 tons of eggs.

Industry

The most important elements of Armenian heavy industry are metalworking, machinery manufacture, electronics, and the production of chemicals, petrochemicals, fertilizers, and building materials (see table 3, Appendix). In 1993, with the aid of British and Russian specialists, a chemical combine was designed to streamline production and marketing of Armenia's chemical products, which had been among the republic's most profitable outputs in the Soviet system. In the later Soviet period, the country became known for its high-quality scientific research, particularly in computer science, nuclear and elementary particle physics, and astrophysics. An estimated 30 percent of Armenia's industrial production infrastructure was destroyed or damaged by the earthquake of 1988.

In the Soviet period, Armenian industry contributed trucks, tires, elevators, electronics, and instruments to the union economy, but several of the plants in those sectors also were lost in 1988. In the years of the Azerbaijani blockade, heavy industrial production has declined sharply because the supply of fuels and electricity has been limited and the price of raw materials has become prohibitive.

Armenian plants were an important part of the Soviet military-industrial complex, producing a variety of equipment. In the early 1990s, the Armenian Ministry of Defense attempted to re-establish agreements with the defense establishments of Russia and other member countries of the Commonwealth of Independent States (CIS—see Glossary). Such a move would enable Armenia to resume production of sophisticated electronic air defense components, which would significantly bolster the domestic economy.

Armenia's most important light consumer products are knitted clothing and hosiery, canned goods, aluminum foil for food packaging, and shoes. Most durable consumer goods are imported (see table 4, Appendix). In 1993 production of consumer products declined even more sharply than other sectors. Food imports increased dramatically to compensate for a 58 percent drop in domestic food processing from 1991 to 1992.

Overall industrial production in 1993 was about 60 percent of that in 1992, but the percentage rose steadily through 1993 after a very slow beginning. Food production for 1993, however, was only 50 percent of the 1992 amount, retail sales were 58 percent, and paid services to the population were 32 percent.

Energy

In 1990 Armenia produced less than 1 percent of its energy requirement, which was filled by imports from Russia (50 percent) and other republics of the Soviet Union. In the late Soviet era, Armenia had a share in the Joint Transcaucasian Power Grid, but that arrangement and short-term supply agreements with Azerbaijan ended with the Nagorno-Karabakh conflict. The 1988 earthquake destroyed the largest nonnuclear thermoelectric plant; the two remaining plants are located south of Erevan and near Razdan, northeast of Erevan.

Woman feeding chickens in a rural village
Courtesy Aline Taroyan

Hydroelectric plants provide 30 percent of domestic electricity, but the output of the largest producer, the Razdan Hydroelectric Plant, was cut drastically because of its negative effect on the water level of its source, Lake Sevan. By early 1994, however, a fifth hydroelectric generating unit was under construction, with international funding, to help alleviate the energy shortage. Planners are also considering construction of two medium-sized hydroelectric stations on the Dzoraget and Debet rivers in the far north, or 300 to 450 small stations on lakes. The obstacle to such plans is the high cost of importing technology.

In the early 1990s, severe shortages of energy led to blackouts, periodic shutdowns of the subway system, inadequate heating of urban buildings, and the further decline of industry. Schools, institutes, and universities were closed through the winters of 1991–92 and 1992–93.

In the 1980s, Soviet planners had attempted to improve Armenia's power generation capacity by building the Armenian Atomic Power Station at Metsamor. However, that station's two reactors were shut down after the 1988 earthquake to avoid future earthquake damage that might cause an environmental catastrophe. The heat and power crisis caused by the Azer-

47

baijani blockade instituted in 1989 caused the government to reconsider use of Metsamor, despite the station's location in earthquake-prone northern Armenia and the possibility of a terrorist attack that could release large amounts of radiation.

In 1993 Metsamor had an estimated capacity to provide 20 percent of Armenia's energy requirements. Plans were made for startup of one of the two reactors by 1995 after careful equipment testing and international technical assistance—with the provision that the plant would remain closed if alternative sources of power could relieve the acute shortage of the prior three years.

In 1993 the delivery of electric power to industrial consumers was cut to one-third of the 1992 level. Under continued blockade conditions, the winter of 1993–94 brought acute shortages of coal, heating oil, and kerosene to heat homes and city apartment buildings and to keep industries running. Significant deposits of high-quality coal have been identified in Armenia, with holdings estimated at 100 million tons. But exploitation would require massive deforestation, a consequence that is considered environmentally prohibitive. In September 1993, Turkmenistan agreed to deliver 8.5 million cubic meters of natural gas per day during the winter, as well as kerosene and diesel fuel in 1994. (Turkmenistan was already an important fuel supplier to postcommunist Armenia.) Although Georgia guaranteed full cooperation in maintaining gas delivery through its pipeline into Armenia, in 1993 explosions on the line interrupted the flow twelve times. Azerbaijani groups in Georgia were assumed to be responsible for the bombings.

Postcommunist Economic Reform

When Mikhail S. Gorbachev began advocating economic reform in the late 1980s, Armenians introduced elements of the free market and privatization into their economic system. Cooperatives were set up in the service sector, particularly in restaurants—although substantial resistance came from the CPA and other groups that had enjoyed privileged positions in the old economy. In the late 1980s, much of the Armenian economy already was operating either semi-officially or illegally, with widespread corruption and bribery. The so-called mafia, made up of interconnected groups of powerful officials and their relatives and friends, sabotaged the efforts of reformers to create a lawful market system. When the December 1988 earthquake brought millions of dollars of foreign aid to the

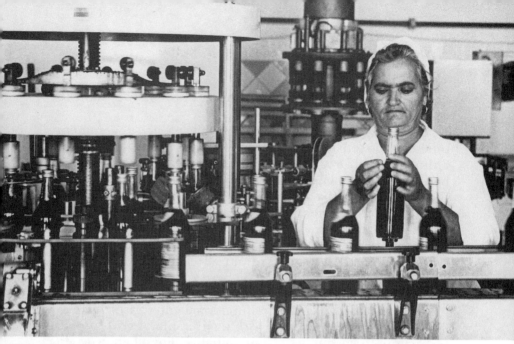

Woman working in a cognac factory, Erevan
Woman working in a shoe repair shop, Erevan
Courtesy Aline Taroyan

devastated regions of Armenia, much of the money went to corrupt and criminal elements.

Beginning in 1991, the democratically elected government pushed vigorously for privatization and market relations, although its efforts were frustrated by the old ways of doing business in Armenia, the Azerbaijani blockade, and the costs of the Nagorno-Karabakh conflict. In 1992 the Law on the Program of Privatization and Destatization of Incompletely Constructed Facilities established a state privatization committee, with members from all political parties. In mid-1993 the committee announced a two-year privatization program, whose first stage would be privatization of 30 percent of state enterprises, mostly services and light industries. The remaining 70 percent, including many bankrupt, nonfunctional enterprises, were to be privatized in a later stage with a minimum of government restriction, to encourage private initiative. For all enterprises, the workers would receive 20 percent of their firm's property free of charge; 30 percent would be distributed to all citizens by means of vouchers; and the remaining 50 percent was to be distributed by the government, with preference given to members of the labor organization. A major problem of this system, however, is the lack of supporting legislation covering foreign investment protection, bankruptcy, monopoly policy, and consumer protection.

In the first postcommunist years, efforts to interest foreign investors in joint enterprises were only moderately successful because of the blockade and the energy shortage. Only in late 1993 was a department of foreign investments established in the Ministry of Economics, to spread information about Armenian investment opportunities and improve the legal infrastructure for investment activity. A specific goal of this agency is creating a market for scientific and technical intellectual property.

A few Armenians living abroad made large-scale investments. Besides a toy factory and construction projects, diaspora Armenians built a cold storage plant (which in its first years had little produce to store) and established the American University of Armenia in Erevan to teach the techniques necessary to run a market economy.

Armenia was admitted to the International Monetary Fund (IMF—see Glossary) in May 1992 and to the World Bank (see Glossary) in September. A year later, the government complained that those organizations were holding back financial assistance and announced its intention to move toward fuller price liberalization and the removal of all tariffs, quotas, and restrictions on foreign trade. Although privatization had slowed because of the catastrophic collapse of the economy, Prime Minister Hrant Bagratian informed United States officials in the fall of 1993 that plans had been made to embark on a renewed privatization program by the end of the year.

Labor and the Standard of Living

The abrupt termination of economic relations with many former Soviet republics, each concerned with its own immediate needs, forced reduction of the work force and plant closings in Armenia. In the years following, the effects of the Nagorno-Karabakh conflict continued and exacerbated the trend. In 1991 some 39 percent of the active work force was employed in industry and construction; 21 percent in the arts, education, and health; 19 percent in agriculture and forestry; 7 percent in transportation and communications; and 6 percent in commerce and food services (see table 5, Appendix).

About 96,000 persons were officially classified as unemployed in September 1993, a 55 percent increase since the beginning of the year. Another 150,000 workers were expected to apply for government support grants before the end of 1993.

About 800,000 Armenians (approximately one-quarter of the population) were homeless in 1991. Especially hard-hit by unemployment was the highly skilled work force that had been employed in the Soviet military-industrial complex until that sector of the economy was severely cut in the late 1980s. Conversion of plants to civilian production progressed slowly in the early 1990s; according to one estimate, 120,000 jobs were lost during this process.

In 1988 the Armenian living standard was slightly lower than that of the Soviet Union as a whole. The per capita consumption by Armenians was 12 percent below the average for Soviet republics. Average daily nutritional consumption was 2,932 calories, of which 45 percent was grains and potatoes (see table 6, Appendix).

After the fall of the Soviet Union, living standards in Armenia fell precipitously. By the end of 1993, the decrease in production, shortages of food and fuel, and hyperinflation had reduced the living standard of an estimated 90 percent of Armenians to below the official poverty line. In the winter of 1993–94, average monthly income was enough to pay for rent and public transportation, plus either ten eggs or 300 grams of butter. Fish and bread, still under price controls, were the only affordable staple foods. Average per capita housing space in 1993 was fifteen square meters.

The National Financial Structure

The various aspects of Armenia's financial system were reformed or replaced piecemeal in the early 1990s, with the national cash flow severely restricted by the strangulation of foreign trade and diversions to support military operations and emergency humanitarian needs (see table 7, Appendix).

Banking

Banking reforms in Armenia moved somewhat more slowly than in other former Soviet republics. In late 1991, the specialized state banks of the Soviet system were converted into joint-stock commercial banks, and some new commercial banks were formed. But the State Bank of Armenia (Gosbank Armenia) and the Bank for Foreign Economic Affairs remained official branches of central state banks in Moscow. The consequence was diminished local control over monetary policy.

A new Central Bank of Armenia was not fully established until early 1994, and even then the bank was not entirely free of state control. The global financial community considers the bank's independence vital to normalization of Armenia's international financial dealings, along with stabilization of the dram (for value of the dram—see Glossary), the national currency established in 1993, and regularization of the dispersal of state pension allowances. In 1993 official exchange rates for the dram were as much as 100 percent more than black-market rates, which economists consider the more accurate value. Because of a shortage of hard currency in 1993, banks tried to restrict sales of hard currency that would further diminish the exchange value of the dram.

The National Budget

The tax base of the 1992 budget was to include a new value-added tax (VAT—see Glossary), several excise taxes, and a revised system of enterprise and personal income taxes. Hard-currency export earnings were to be taxed at 25 percent. The fastest-growing expenditure categories were national defense and allowances to citizens to mitigate the effects of price liberalization. The 1992 budget called for a cut of about 45 percent in real expenditures(equivalent to a nominal increase of 155 percent), which would still leave a deficit of 1.2 billion rubles, or 11 percent of total expenditures. Budgets were extremely difficult to plan because of the Azerbaijani blockade and the unpredictable inflation rate.

Price Policy

In mid-1990 the government introduced a three-stage price reform program, implementation of which was severely hindered by the contraction of the national economy. The purpose of the first stage was to improve agricultural production incentives by raising government procurement prices for staple products. The second stage raised wholesale prices and tariffs to bring them closer to world market levels and to stimulate price negotiations. The third stage fixed prices (usually at increases of 300 to 500 percent) for food, medicine, utilities, and transportation, but it freed the prices of most other items. Experts believed that prices would not reach true equilibrium until the end of shortages caused by the blockade.

Between December 1992 and September 1993, annual price increases for various goods and services ranged from nearly 600 to over 1,200 percent. Whereas the average monthly increase for all expenditures in 1993 was 23 percent, the rate fell considerably in the second half of the year. By the summer of 1993, monthly increases had fallen below 17 percent.

Transportation and Telecommunications

Armenia's mountainous topography, landlocked location, and antagonistic neighbors have made movement of goods and maintenance of a transportation system difficult. Despite these problems, however, the country's air, rail, and highway networks serve the nation's needs adequately. Domestic movement of goods is occasionally hampered by poor maintenance of roads. In addition, since independence in 1991, movement of goods across international borders has frequently been disrupted because many of the country's important rail and highway links with the outside world pass through Azerbaijan. Beginning in 1989, complete stoppage of international trade across this border led to escalating food and fuel shortages in Armenia.

In 1991 Armenia had 11,300 kilometers of roads, of which about 10,500 kilometers were paved. Most roads radiate from

Figure 7. Transportation System of Armenia, 1994

Erevan, and in the western part of the country four-lane highways connect major cities (see fig. 7). The main route for international travel of passengers and goods before the start of the
conflict with Azerbaijan was Route M24, which leads northeast
out of Erevan to connect with Route M27, the principal east-
west highway across the Caucasus Mountains. Other major
highways extend southeast from the capital to southern Armenia and to Azerbaijan's Nakhichevan Autonomous Republic
and west to the populated areas of western Armenia and to the
Turkish border.

In 1992 Armenia had about 100,000 state-owned vehicles
(automobiles, trucks, taxis, and buses). Observers noted, how-

ever, that at any given time about one-third of these vehicles were inoperable because of poor maintenance and unavailability of spare parts. Average vehicle age in 1992 was 6.5 years.

Armenia had 825 kilometers of mainline railroad track in 1992, excluding several small industrial lines. Most lines are 1.520-meter broad gauge, and the principal routes are electrified. The rail system is roughly configured like a " Y " and has lines radiating from a central point just south of Erevan. The northeast branch roughly parallels Route M24 to Azerbaijan. About 85 percent of all goods used in Armenia are imported by rail, and before the conflict with Azerbaijan, most came via this rail line. Closure of the line at the international border during the early 1990s has caused severe disruption to the Armenian economy. The southern branch of the line extends south toward the Turkish border, where it turns southeast into Nakhichevan. The war with Azerbaijan has stopped service on this segment of the rail system as well.

In 1994 the last operative portion of the country's rail lines was the northwest branch of the "Y," which winds through the populated areas of northwestern Armenia before crossing into Georgia. A short spur of this line at Gyumri connects with the Turkish rail system. However, a difference in gauge with the Turkish system means that goods crossing the Turkish border must undergo a time-consuming reloading process.

In 1991 Armenia Railways, the state-owned rail system, operated with 100 electric and eighty diesel locomotives. Delays in the delivery of spare parts from Russia have been a nagging problem in the maintenance of the system. Cannibalization of rolling stock to obtain parts has severely reduced service.

Erevan's new subway system was still largely under construction in the early 1990s. In 1994 nine stations had opened on the first ten-kilometer section of heavy-rail line. This first line connected Erevan's industrial area with the downtown area and the main rail station. Work on an additional four kilometers was slowed by the 1988 earthquake. Plans called for an eventual system of forty-seven kilometers organized into three lines.

Armenia's principal airport, Zvartnots, is about seven kilometers from downtown Erevan. With a runway approximately 2,700 kilometers long, the airport can handle airplanes as large as the Russian Tu-154 and IL–86 or the Boeing 727. In 1993 the airport handled about 34,000 tons of freight. The State Airlines Company of Armenia, the new state-run airline, provides direct or nonstop service to about a dozen cities of the former Soviet

Union, as well as to Paris. The Russian and Romanian national airlines also provide regular international air service into Erevan. Since the beginning of the conflict with Azerbaijan, fuel shortages have curtailed expansion of passenger and cargo service, however. Several other airports elsewhere in Armenia have paved runways, but most are used for minor freight transport. Although air cargo has the potential to relieve the effects of the Azerbaijani blockade of land routes, efforts to fly in aviation kerosene were frustrated in 1993 by corruption in the Main Administration for Aviation and by high prices charged by Russian suppliers.

Armenia's one major natural gas pipeline branches off the main Transcaucasian line that runs from Russia through Georgia to Baku. The Armenian spur begins in western Azerbaijan and reaches its main terminus in Erevan. In all, Armenia has 900 kilometers of natural gas pipeline. Armenia imports most of its fuel and, before the conflict with Azerbaijan, imported 80 percent of its fuel from Azerbaijan via the pipeline or in rail tanker cars. Like Armenia's rail and highway links, the pipeline from Azerbaijan has been closed by the Azerbaijani blockade.

In 1991 the American Telephone and Telegraph Company installed 200 long-distance circuits in Armenia, which gave the republic the capacity, available elsewhere in the former Soviet Union only in Moscow, to receive direct-dial international calls. Radio and television are controlled by the State Committee for Television and Radio Broadcasting. Ten AM and three FM radio stations broadcast from Erevan, Kamo, and Sisian. Broadcasts are in Armenian, Kurdish, and Russian to points within Armenia, and in those languages plus Arabic, English, French, Persian, Spanish, and Turkish to points outside the country. The single television station broadcasts in Armenian and Russian. According to Soviet statistics of the late 1980s, between 90 and 95 percent of Armenian homes had radios or televisions. No statistics are available for the blockade years, but experts believe that under blockade conditions substantially fewer Armenians have had regular access to broadcast information.

Foreign Trade

In the Soviet period, Armenia traded almost solely with the union's other republics. A foreign trade organization (FTO) controlled each product group, and exports by each Armenian enterprise were determined by the State Planning Committee (commonly known by its Russian acronym, Gosplan) in Moscow. Enterprises had no control over the size or destination of shipments of their products. Together with Estonia and Tajikistan, Armenia had the highest level of imports among the Soviet republics. Its exports consisted mostly of semifinished goods that needed processing in other republics.

In the years since the breakup of the Soviet Union, Armenia's economy has been hurt by the need to import much of its food and almost all of its oil and gas. In 1989 the FTO monopoly was removed, allowing enterprises to seek their own buyers and sellers abroad. In 1992 the government removed most state controls over foreign trade. Export licensing continued to protect enterprises from fraud and to enforce domestic market quotas. In the early 1990s, most of Armenia's exports went to Russia, Eastern Europe, and various developing countries (see table 8, Appendix). By January 1992, Armenia had signed bilateral trade protocols with most of the former Soviet republics. To ensure flexibility in the face of future price liberalization, prices were to be set in direct negotiation between enterprises. Enterprises were not strictly bound by protocols signed by their respective governments, although quotas remained a possibility. At this stage, all payments were to be in rubles.

In 1990 Armenia's largest sources of export income were light industrial products (mostly knit clothing, shoes, and carpets), machines and metal products, processed foods, and chemical products. The highest total expenditures on imports were for light industrial products, processed foods, chemical products, energy and fuels, and unprocessed agricultural products. In 1990 Armenia showed a trade deficit of 869 million rubles in industrial goods and a deficit of 278 million rubles in agricultural goods.

In April 1992, Armenia became the first former Soviet republic to sign a comprehensive bilateral trade agreement with the United States and the first to receive most-favored-nation status. Canada soon followed in granting Armenia similar status. In planning future trade, Armenia expected to rely heavily on foreign markets for products from its newly organized complex of chemical enterprises, for which demand was identified in the former Soviet republics, Eastern Europe, Iran, Syria, Turkey, Argentina, and Australia.

Government and Politics

The Republic of Armenia declared its sovereignty on August 23, 1990, and became an independent state a year later, on September 23, 1991. In October 1991, Levon Ter-Petrosian, who had been elected democratically as chairman of the Armenian Supreme Soviet under the Soviet system in 1990, was chosen president of the republic in a six-candidate election. As of early 1994, Armenia was a reasonably stable democratic state, although its party structure was fractious and its legislative branch ineffectual. Because no consensus could be reached on a new constitution, a standoff between parliament and the president remained unresolved in early 1994.

Parliament

The 248 members of Armenia's unicameral parliament (Geraguin khorhurt in Armenian, officially retaining the term "Supreme Soviet" from the communist era) are elected for five-year terms and meet for six months each year. The prime minister and the Council of Ministers, which together constitute the executive branch of the government, are chosen from parliament. Although half the members of parliament (124) must be present for a quorum, a majority of the votes of the entire body (125) is needed to pass laws. In the early 1990s, because more than 160 members were rarely present and the ruling party did not have a majority in the body, the parliament was proving unable to act decisively on major legislative issues. Moreover, a two-thirds majority of the parliament (165) is needed to override a presidential veto. In the absence of a constitution, however, the parliament has issued laws regulating the relations and powers of the branches of government.

The Presidium, the parliament's executive body, administers parliament when it is not in session. The Presidium is made up of the president of the republic (whose title is also chairman of parliament), two deputies, the secretary of the parliament, and the twelve chairmen of the permanent parliamentary committees. Often laws are initiated by the president of the republic, sent to the Presidium for review, and then passed on to appropriate committees before being reviewed and voted upon by the whole parliament. (Besides permanent committees, the parliament can create temporary committees to deal with specific issues.)

Once parliament passes a law, the president of the republic, who also may participate in parliamentary debates, must sign or veto within two weeks. In early 1994, parliament had not yet passed legislation replacing Soviet-era laws in several major areas: criminal and civil codes, administrative violations, marriage and family, labor rights and practices, land tenure, and housing.

The Presidency

As it has developed in the 1990s, the Armenian presidency is the most powerful position in government. More than a ceremonial head of state, the president is the most active proposer of new legislation, the chief architect of foreign and military policy, and, during Armenia's prolonged state of national emergency, the unchallenged center of government power in many areas.

Levon Ter-Petrosian, a former philologist and a founding member of the Karabakh Committee, became the first president of independent Armenia in 1991. Ter-Petrosian has occupied the political center of Armenian politics as the single most important politician in the country and the principal advocate of moderate policies in the face of nationalist emotionalism. The parliamentary plurality that Ter-Petrosian's party, the Armenian Pannational Movement (APM), enjoyed at the formation of the republic in 1991 enhanced presidential authority at the expense of parliament, where the majority of seats were divided among many parties. Beginning in 1992, Ter-Petrosian took several controversial unilateral actions on major issues, which brought accusations of abuse of power.

State Administrative Bodies

The Council of Ministers, which performs the everyday activities of the executive branch of government, is presided over by the prime minister, who reports directly to the president and to parliament. The prime minister is named by the president but must be approved by parliament. The members of the council are appointed by joint decision of the president and the prime minister.

The Council of Ministers underwent a series of changes in the early 1990s as Ter-Petrosian sought a prime minister with whom he could work effectively. As a result, four men occupied that position between 1991 and 1993. The principal source of friction within government circles is factional disagreement about the appropriate elements and pace of economic reform. In the first years of independence, most of the members of the council have belonged to the APM. In 1994 the Council of Ministers included the following ministries: agriculture, architecture and urban planning, communications, construction, culture, defense, economics, education, energy and fuel, environment, finance, food and state procurement, foreign affairs, health, higher education and science, industry, internal affairs, justice, labor and social security, light industry, national security, natural resources, trade, and transportation.

In addition to the regular ministries, state ministries coordinate the activities of ministries having overlapping jurisdictions. State ministers rank higher than regular ministers. In 1994 there were six state ministries: agriculture, construction, energy and fuel, humanitarian assistance, military affairs, and science and culture. State agencies have responsibilities similar to those of ministries, but they are appointed by and report directly to the president. Seven state agencies were operating in 1994.

The Judiciary

With no constitution in place, the structure of the new Armenian judiciary remains unformalized. Most judges are holdovers from the Soviet period, and the power to appoint judges has not been decided between the legislative and executive branches. Appointment and training of new judges are high priorities in replacing the Soviet judicial system with an independent judiciary.

District courts are the courts of first instance. Their judges are named by the president and confirmed by the parliament. The Supreme Court, whose chief justice is nominated by the president and elected by a simple majority of parliament, provides intermediate and final appellate review of cases. The court includes a three-member criminal chamber and a three-member civil chamber for intermediate review and an eleven-member presidium for final review. The full, thirty-two-member court provides plenary appellate review.

The general prosecutor is nominated by the president and elected by parliament. The general prosecutor's office moves cases from lower to higher courts, oversees investigations, prosecutes federal cases, and has a broad mandate to monitor the activities of all state and legal entities and individual citizens. The general prosecutor appoints district attorneys, the chief legal officers at the district level.

The Constitution

As of early 1994, adoption of a constitution for the Republic of Armenia remained a controversial and unresolved project.

In the meantime, the 1978 constitution, a replica of the Soviet Union's 1977 document, remained in effect except in cases where specific legislation superseded it. At the end of 1992, the president and the APM parliamentary delegates presented a draft constitution. They put forward a revised version in March 1993. Then, after nearly a year's work, a bloc of six opposition parties led by the Armenian Revolutionary Federation (ARF) presented an alternative constitution in January 1994 that would expand the parliament's power, limit that of the president, expand the authority of local government, allow Armenians everywhere to participate in governing the republic, and seek international recognition of the 1915 massacre. As 1994 began, observers expected a long struggle before parliament adopted a final version.

Local Government

The republic is divided into thirty-seven districts, or *gavarner*, each of which has a legislative and administrative branch replicating the national structures. Pending adoption of a new constitution prescribing a division of power, however, all major decisions are made by the central government and are merely implemented by the district administrations.

Political Parties

During Armenia's seventy years as a Soviet republic, only one party, the Communist Party of Armenia (CPA), was allowed legal status. As a branch of the Communist Party of the Soviet Union, it ruled under the direct orders of the leadership in Moscow. Following the collapse of communist authority, two major parties and dozens of minor ones competed for popularity along with the remnants of the CPA.

In the years following independence, the most vocal and powerful opposition party was the Armenian Revolutionary Federation (ARF). Founded in 1890, the ARF was the ruling party in the Republic of Armenia in 1918–20; forbidden under the communist regimes, the ARF built a strong support network in the Armenian diaspora. When the party again became legal in 1991, its foreign supporters enabled it to gain influence in Armenia out of proportion to its estimated membership of 40,000. With a platform calling for a coalition government, greater power for the parliament at the expense of the executive, and a strong social welfare program, the ARF gained eighteen seats in the 1992 parliamentary election.

The Liberal Democratic Party (LDP), founded in 1921, calls for privatizing the economy and rapidly establishing all possible conditions for a free-market economy. It also backs a strong system of state social welfare and recognition of Nagorno-Karabakh's independence. The LDP had seventeen seats in parliament in 1994.

Former dissident Pariur Hairikian heads the National Self-Determination Union, which has called for a coalition government based on proportional representation of each party. With only one seat in parliament, the union takes a radical-right position on most issues. Extreme nationalist parties with racist ideologies also have small followings. Most opposition parties have been critical of Ter-Petrosian's Nagorno-Karabakh policy; in 1992 they formed the so-called National Alliance to coordinate their foreign policy positions. Because of parliament's institutional weakness, oppositionists frequently have organized massive public rallies demanding the president's resignation.

In the first years of independence, the ruling elite came primarily from the Armenian Pannational Movement (APM), the umbrella organization that grew out of the Karabakh movement. In the 1992 parliamentary election, the APM gained fifty-five seats, easily giving it a plurality but leaving it vulnerable when opposition coalitions formed on individual issues. The next largest delegation, that of the ARF, had twelve seats. In 1993 the failure of Ter-Petrosian's government to bring the Karabakh conflict to an end, its own willingness to compromise on the Karabakh question, and the daily grind of fuel and food shortages reduced the popularity of the ruling nationalist movement.

Human Rights

In April 1991, Armenia signed the International Covenant of Civil and Political Rights and accepted it as domestic law, superseding all existing laws on the subject. That covenant includes the right to counsel; the presumption of innocence of the accused; the right to privacy; prohibition of arbitrary arrest; freedom of the press, religion, political expression and assembly, and movement; minority rights; and prohibition of discrimination. Since 1991 specific legislation has further guaranteed freedom of the press and prohibited discrimination in education, language, and employment. Rights of the accused, however, remain undefined pending Armenia's acceptance of international conventions on that subject.

In 1993 several human rights organizations were active in Armenia: the Helsinki Assembly, which represented the international Helsinki Watch; the League of Human Rights; parliament's Committee on Human Rights; a national group called Avangard; and a branch of the international Sakharov Fund.

In 1993 the National Self-Determination Union accused the Ter-Petrosian government of a state terrorism policy that included the assassination of individuals within the union and others opposed to government policy. The most publicized incident was the murder in 1993 of Marius Yuzbashian, a former chief of the Armenian branch of the Committee for State Security (Komitet gosudarstvennoi bezopasnosti—KGB).

The Media

In the Soviet era, the officially sanctioned source of public information was Armenpress, the state news agency assigned to disseminate the propaganda of the CPA. In the post-Soviet years, Armenpress has remained the primary source of information for independent newspapers in Armenia and for periodicals in the diaspora. Under those conditions, the agency has required continued state funding to maintain its information flow to foreign customers, of whom seventeen had reciprocal information supply agreements with Armenpress in early 1994. Meanwhile, the agency has adopted a more neutral position in its reporting.

Early in 1994, the Ministry of Justice reported that twenty-four magazines, nine radio stations, twenty-five press agencies, and 232 newspapers were active. Several national newspapers represent a variety of political viewpoints. *Hayastani Hanrapetutiun* (Republic of Armenia) is the official daily newspaper of the Supreme Soviet, published in Armenian and Russian versions. *Golos Armenii* (The Voice of Armenia), published daily in Russian, is the official organ of the CPA. *Azatamart* (Struggle for Freedom) and *Hazatamart* (Battle for Freedom) are weekly organs of the ARF. *Hazg* (Nation) is published by the Party of Democratic Freedom. Other newspapers include *Grakan Tert* (Literary Paper), published by the Armenian Union of Writers; *Hayk* (Armenia), a publication of the APM; *Ria Taze* (New Way); and *Yerokoian Yerevan* (Evening Erevan). In 1993 thirteen major magazines and journals covered science and technology, politics, art, culture, and economics; the group also included one satirical journal, one journal for teenagers, and one for working women.

Foreign Relations

While it has been engaged in the Nagorno-Karabakh conflict with Azerbaijan, Armenia also has sought international status and security in new bilateral relations and membership in international organizations. In the first years of independence, Armenia became a member of the UN, the IMF, the World Bank, the CSCE, and the CIS. Located in a region that is already unstable, in the early 1990s the three republics of Transcaucasia gained the attention of world leaders because of the potential for a wider war on the northern tier of the Middle Eastern states. The resulting aid and efforts at mediation have had mixed results.

Azerbaijan

Since the outbreak of fighting in 1988, Nagorno-Karabakh has been the principal foreign policy issue for Armenia, creating a huge drain on its financial and human resources. By the end of 1993, estimates of the number killed in the conflict ranged from 3,000 to 10,000. The fighting between Armenians and Azerbaijanis repeatedly has threatened to involve not only other CIS member states but also Turkey and Iran, whose borders have been approached and even crossed during the conflict.

In a speech to the UN in September 1992, Ter-Petrosian stated his government's official position that Armenia had no territorial claims against Azerbaijan, but that the people of Nagorno-Karabakh could not be denied the right of self-determination. Advocating the protection of the region by means of permanent international guarantees, Armenia repeatedly called for cease-fires and negotiations between Azerbaijan and Nagorno-Karabakh, and between Armenia and Azerbaijan, to resolve the issue. In 1992 the Armenian parliament passed a law prohibiting the government from signing any document recognizing Azerbaijani authority over Karabakh. But at that point, Ter-Petrosian resisted advocating Armenian recognition of Karabakh's independence, which would raise yet another obstacle to peace.

The ARF, the party most supportive of the Nagorno-Karabakh government and its army, called for more forceful prosecution of the war and recognition of the independent status of

Karabakh. In early 1993, the ARF began advocating a binding referendum on the status of the region rather than its return to Armenia.

In 1993 the CSCE made repeated but fruitless efforts to maintain cease-fires and to bring the warring parties together for peace talks. Although years of preliminary discussions had finally resolved the details of how a conference would be held, the negotiations of the CSCE's multinational Minsk Group had not resulted in a single meeting by the end of 1993. There were other efforts at peacemaking. A joint meeting of thirty-three states of the North Atlantic Treaty Organization (NATO—see Glossary) and the former Warsaw Pact (see Glossary) expressed its concern, Iran attempted separate mediation between Azerbaijan and Armenia, and Russian and CIS leaders (most notably Russia's President Boris N. Yeltsin) also negotiated brief cease-fires. In 1993 Ter-Petrosian also maintained telephone contact with Azerbaijan's president, Heydar Aliyev.

The situation was complicated by the often unpredictable actions of the government in Nagorno-Karabakh. In December 1991, Nagorno-Karabakh declared itself an independent state, and its armed forces often operated independently of the government of the Republic of Armenia. However, the region and its army remained largely dependent on food, medicine, weapons, and moral support from Armenia, especially from the ARF.

Georgia, Iran, and Turkey

Armenians have long been a significant part of the urban population of Georgia, particularly in Tbilisi. Two districts in southern Georgia are predominantly Armenian. The dictatorial regime of Zviad Gamsakhurdia, which ruled Georgia from late 1990 until early January 1992, was extremely intolerant of all ethnic minorities. More than 70,000 Armenians were caught in the crossfire of the Georgian government's conflict with Abkhazian separatists, which reached crisis proportions in the fall of 1993. In this struggle, extreme Georgian nationalists attempted to drive the Armenian population from the country in order to create a homogeneous Georgia. The crisis in Abkhazia had immediate repercussions for Armenia when fighting resulted in the severing of Georgia's Black Sea railroad, a lifeline from Russia to Armenia. The republic thus was cut off from many supplies, particularly grain. In early 1993, when a natural gas pipeline running through Georgia was repeatedly blown up, the Armenian government sharply demanded that the Georgian leader, Eduard Shevardnadze, make a greater effort to secure the necessary flow of gas to Armenia.

Armenia has had better relations with Iran, although Iran has been worried about the presence of Armenian troops occupying Azerbaijani territory just across its border. Two-thirds of the world's Azerbaijanis live in Iran, and the Tehran government fears that émigrés would spread Azerbaijani nationalism among the Azerbaijani population of northern Iran. Armenian troops have at times been no more than twenty kilometers from the Iranian border. On several occasions, Iran attempted to mediate the Nagorno-Karabakh conflict, but unforeseen actions by the Karabakh forces frustrated these efforts.

Armenia's traditional enemy in the twentieth century has been Turkey. Among outstanding sources of conflict, the most painful and long-lasting has been the Turkish refusal to recognize the deportations and massacres of Ottoman Armenians in 1915 as a deliberate, state-sponsored act of genocide. Many Armenians, particularly those associated with the ARF, aspire to restore Armenian control over the lands of historical Armenia that are now under Turkish sovereignty. Although many Armenian émigrés remain hostile toward Turkey today, the Ter-Petrosian government has made improved relations with Ankara a high priority because of the possibility of opening new supply routes and hard-currency markets for Armenian products.

Although no Armenian politician is willing to retract the demand that the Ottoman genocide of 1915 be acknowledged, those around the Armenian president have resisted raising issues likely to alienate Turkey. In late 1992, when Foreign Minister Raffi Hovannisian spoke about the outstanding differences between Turks and Armenians in a speech in Istanbul, he was swiftly removed from office. On the Nagorno-Karabakh issue, the Turkish government usually has sided with Azerbaijan, particularly during the time of the Azerbaijani Popular Front government in Baku (May 1992–June 1993). Nationalist voices in Turkey have protested Armenian advances against Azerbaijan, and periodically Turkey has prevented Western humanitarian aid from reaching Armenia. Turkish nationalist factions also have accused Armenia of aiding Kurdish rebels in eastern Turkey.

The Commonwealth of Independent States

Increasingly through the early 1990s, the Republic of Armenia's isolation led the government to look for allies beyond Transcaucasia. Ter-Petrosian appealed to foreign governments and to Armenians abroad for material aid to carry the people through the harsh winters. As the rapprochement with Turkey in 1991–92 brought few concrete benefits, Armenia steadily gravitated toward a closer relationship with Russia. Early in 1993, Ter-Petrosian met with Yeltsin in Moscow to discuss deliveries of oil and natural gas to the blockaded republic. The Russian minister of defense, Pavel Grachev, negotiated a brief cease-fire in Nagorno-Karabakh in April. Armenia remained in the ruble zone, the group of countries still using Russian rubles as domestic currency, often in parallel with a new national currency such as Armenia's dram. In 1992 and 1993, large-scale credit payments from the Central Bank of Russia were vital in supporting Armenia's national budget.

Immediately after Armenia declared itself independent, Ter-Petrosian joined in an economic community with seven other republics—but he refused to enter a political union at that point. In December 1991, however, he signed the Alma-Ata Declaration, making Armenia a founding member of the Commonwealth of Independent States (CIS). From that time, Armenia has played an active role in the CIS, signing an accord on military cooperation with Russia, Kazakhstan, Tajikistan, Kyrgyzstan, and Uzbekistan.

In May 1993, Ter-Petrosian announced Armenia's support of a Russo-Turkish-American plan for settlement of the Karabakh conflict. When Aliyev returned to power in June, Ter-Petrosian spoke by telephone directly with the new leader of Azerbaijan, and together they agreed that Azerbaijan and Nagorno-Karabakh must begin direct negotiations. Azerbaijan's entry into the CIS in September 1993 was seen by some as giving Russia a mandate to solve the Karabakh problem. Ter-Petrosian reiterated his conditions for peace: Karabakh was to be recognized as a full party to the negotiations, all blockades were to be ended, and the CSCE-sponsored Minsk Group negotiations were to settle all political and legal questions on the status of Karabakh.

Russia was a logical mediator. Not only did it have military bases and equipment in the region, but Russian troops were still guarding the border between Armenia and Turkey. Russia consistently asserted its hegemonic role in Transcaucasia, opposed the designs of Turkey and Iran in the region, and was even wary of the United States being a mediator in the region without specific Russian invitation or acquiescence. After Yeltsin won a struggle with the Russian parliament in September 1993 and both Georgia and Azerbaijan had joined the CIS, Russia resumed its role as the primary mediator of conflicts in Transcaucasia.

Russia has asserted hegemony in the region in several ways. It has repeatedly claimed the right to protect the major link from Russia to Armenia that passes through conflict-plagued Abkhazia and Georgia. In September 1993, Russia requested a revision of the Conventional Forces in Europe Treaty (CFE Treaty—see Glossary), which had been negotiated between NATO and the Warsaw Pact in 1990, in order to achieve an increase in the number of Russian tanks and heavy weapons in the Caucasus. Although NATO perceived an increased military influence in the formulation of this more assertive Russian policy, Western policy makers recognized that at the end of 1993 Russia was the only power in position to play a meaningful peacekeeping role in the region.

The United States

Independent Armenia enjoys good relations with the United States and the European Union (EU). The United States recognized the Republic of Armenia in December 1991, and a United States embassy opened in Erevan in February 1992. General United States and Armenian strategic interests in common include the promotion of internal democracy, just termination of the Karabakh conflict, and stability in the former Soviet Union that would prevent the resurgence of an authoritarian, imperialist Russia. United States policy toward Armenia must weigh the special relationships of the United States with Russia and NATO ally Turkey. In the first post-Soviet years, the United States has given more aid per capita to Armenia than to any other former Soviet republic. At the same time, the United States has withheld trade privileges from Azerbaijan because of that country's economic blockade of Armenia.

Armenians have been able to influence American policy to a limited degree through the diaspora in the United States, but their interests and those of the United States are not always congruent. Given its special relationship with Turkey, the United States has been reluctant to recognize the events of 1915 as genocide. On several occasions, the United States criti-

Loading butter from United States Department of Agriculture onto Armenian trucks at Zvartnots Airport, near Erevan, after collapse of Soviet Union, February 1992
Courtesy A. James Firth, United States Department of Agriculture

cized Armenian aggression against Azerbaijan outside of Karabakh. Yet both the United States and Russia, as well as the CSCE countries in general, agree that a solution to the Karabakh conflict must be based on recognition of existing borders and the rights of minorities.

In the first winters of the 1990s, many Armenians were on the brink of starvation, and the basic needs of the population were sustained only through foreign aid. In December 1991, the United States Department of Agriculture and the Diocese of the Armenian Church in America arranged for the diocese to distribute food shipments valued at US$15 million in Armenia. Through Operation Provide Hope, the United States government sent food and medical supplies worth over US$6 million to Armenia in the first eight months of 1992. When the

United States Agency for International Development (AID) authorized US$1 million to the American Bar Association for a program to provide legal experts to the member states of the CIS, Armenia became the first country where legislators worked with these legal specialists. The Peace Corps arrived in Erevan in August 1992, followed in the fall by AID and the United States Information Agency (USIA).

National Security

As a nation, Armenia has not had a great tradition of military success, even at the largest extent of the Armenian Empire. In the Soviet period, Armenian troops were thoroughly integrated into the Soviet army, and Armenian plants contributed sophisticated equipment to Soviet arsenals. After independence Armenia profited from some aspects of this close association, and a strong Russian military presence is expected to remain for some time.

Geopolitical Situation

As a small country, Armenia has had an unfavorable geopolitical situation, with no neighbors likely to provide support and security. Lacking an outlet to the sea, Armenia is surrounded by Muslim Turkey and Azerbaijan, both of which generally have been hostile to Armenia's interests; the militant Islamic republic of Iran; and a Georgia torn by civil war. By 1990 Armenia's traditional reliance on Russia had weakened because of internal political conditions—the Karabakh movement had an anti-Russian orientation—and because of the retreat of post-Soviet Russia from military involvement on many fronts.

In the early 1990s, the major external threat to Armenia came from Azerbaijan. A state with twice the population of Armenia, with significant unrecovered oil reserves in the Caspian Sea, and with great potential for securing Western capital for industrial development, Azerbaijan possessed considerable resources with which to fight a long war in Karabakh. In early 1994, the Armenian Army was considered the most combat-ready force in the three states of Transcaucasia. However, experts attributed Armenian combat successes in the conflict in 1992–93 to the political instability in Baku, to regional divisions within Azerbaijan, and to the greater unity and determination of the Armenian forces in Karabakh(see Forming a National Defense Force, ch. 2).

In the years following independence, Armenia saw its future security based on ending the conflict in Nagorno-Karabakh, improving its relations with all its neighbors, and gaining aid and support from the great global powers and organizations— the United States, Russia, the CSCE, and the UN. Once it joined the CIS, Armenia adhered to the organization's security arrangements. In March 1992, Armenia joined Kazakhstan, Kyrgyzstan, and Russia in an agreement on the status of general-purpose forces, and it joined seven other CIS republics in an agreement on the financing, supply, production, and development of military equipment. On May 15, 1992, Armenia, Kazakhstan, Kyrgyzstan, Russia, Tajikistan, and Uzbekistan met in Tashkent and signed the Treaty on Collective Security. According to this pact, former Soviet armed forces were permitted to remain in the signatory republics by mutual agreement. Armenia and several other republics agreed to apportion former Soviet weapons to conform to the CFE Treaty. By that agreement, Armenia was to receive 875 units of heavy matériel (tanks, artillery, aircraft, and helicopters), the same number as Georgia and Azerbaijan.

Armenia's location between two larger states, Russia and Turkey, has long forced it to orient its policies to favor one or the other. Until the late Soviet period, Armenia generally favored its Orthodox neighbor and depended on the Russian or Soviet state for its national security. In 1945 Stalin raised the matter of regaining Armenian territory from Turkey, but the issue quietly expired with the dictator in 1953. After independence was officially proclaimed in 1991, Armenia's member-. ship in the new CIS became a national security issue because it seemingly prolonged Russian occupation. The prevailing view in the early 1990s, however, was that isolation from reliable alliances was the greater threat.

In the decades after World War II, relations between Armenians and Turks degenerated. The Turks became embittered by acts of Armenian terrorism against Turkish citizens in other countries, especially in the 1970s, which served to remind the world of the genocide issue. Starting in the 1980s, Turkey began aspiring to play a major role in European affairs and to exert leadership among the Central Asian Muslim nations that emerged from the Soviet Union in the early 1990s. These foreign policy goals encouraged Turkish ambivalence toward Armenian objectives in Nagorno-Karabakh. However, traditional Turkish nationalism demanded alliance with Muslim

Azerbaijan, and eastern Turkey remained a heavily fortified area after the end of the Cold War—about 50,000 Turkish troops were on the Armenian border in early 1994. In turn, Armenia saw its collective security treaty with the CIS and the presence of Russian troops in Armenia as restraints on the nationalist impulse in Turkish policy making.

The Military

Influenced by the requirements of supporting the forces of Nagorno-Karabakh against Azerbaijan and the long-term objective of military self-reliance, Armenia has worked toward making the Armenian Army a small, well-balanced, combat-ready defense force. Chief architects of the force were General Norat Ter-Grigoriants, a former Soviet deputy chief of staff who became overall commander of the new Armenian Army; Vazgan Sarkisian, named the first minister of defense; and Vazgan Manukian, who replaced Sarkisian in 1992.

As expressed by the military establishment during the planning stage, Armenia's military doctrine called for maintenance of defensive self-sufficiency that would enable its army to repel an attack by forces from Azerbaijan or Turkey, or both. That concept was refuted, however, by radical nationalists who advocated a more aggressive posture, similar to that of the Israeli army in defending a "surrounded" land, of maintaining the armed forces at a high degree of readiness to inflict crippling losses on an enemy within days. Both doctrines emphasized small, highly mobile, well-trained units. The specific outcome of the debate over military doctrine has been concealed as a matter of national security. Although legislation on defense forces called for 1 percent of the population to be in the armed forces, active-duty strength in 1994 was estimated at 20,000, including border troops. By that time, the Ministry of Defense had increased its goal to a standing army of 50,000, to be supplemented in wartime by a reserve call-up.

A top defense priority in 1994 was improving control of the Zangezur region, the vulnerable, far southeastern corridor bordering Iran and flanked by Azerbaijan's Nakhichevan Autonomous Republic and Azerbaijan proper. The program for Zangezur includes new military installations, especially on the Iranian border, as well as a new bridge and a new natural gas pipeline into Iran.

The army and the Ministry of Defense have structures similar to those of their counterparts in the former Soviet Union, except that the highest organizational level of the Armenian forces is a smaller unit, the brigade, rather than the traditional division, to maximize maneuverability. Plans call for brigades of 1,500 to 2,500 troops to be divided into three or four battalions, in the manner of the paramilitary forces of the Karabakh Armenians.

Regular Forces

In 1992 the Ministry of Defense appealed to Armenian officers who had had commissions in the Soviet army to help form the new force to defend their homeland against Azerbaijan and to build a permanent national army. Although substantial special benefits were offered, the new professional officer corps was not staffed as fully as hoped in its first two years. In especially short supply were officer specialists in military organizational development—a critical need in the army's formative stage. In 1994 most Armenian officers still were being trained in Russia; the first 100 Armenian-trained officers were to be commissioned in the spring of 1994. Plans called for officer training to begin in 1995 at a new national military academy.

Eighteen-year-old men constitute the primary pool of conscripts. New trainees generally are not sent into combat positions. The Armenian public was hostile to conscription in the Soviet period; the practice of assigning Armenian recruits to all parts of the Soviet Union prompted large demonstrations in Erevan. That attitude continued in the post-Soviet period. In the first two years of the new force, recruitment fell far short of quotas. The draft of the fall of 1992, for example, produced only 71 percent of the quota, and widespread evasion was reported.

Conscripts generally lack equipment and advanced training, and some units are segregated by social class. Officer elitism and isolation are also problems, chiefly because the first language of many officers is Russian. Desertion rates in 1992–93 were extremely high. In early 1994, the defense establishment considered formalizing the status of the large number of volunteers in the army by introducing a contract service system.

In 1992 the republic established the Babajanian Military Boarding School, which admitted qualified boys aged fourteen to sixteen for training, leading to active military service. By agreement with Russian military institutions, graduates could continue training in Russia at the expense of the Armenian Ministry of Defense. A class of 100 was expected to graduate in

1994. The lack of military training schools is rated as a serious problem. Armenian cadets and junior officers study at military schools in Russia and other CIS states, and senior officers spend two to three years at academies in Russia and Belarus. A military academy for all armed services was in the planning stage in 1994.

The Karabakh Self-Defense Army consists mostly of Armenians from Karabakh or elsewhere in Azerbaijan, plus some volunteers from Armenia and mercenaries who formerly were Soviet officers. The Karabakh forces reportedly are well armed with Kalashnikov rifles, armor, and heavy artillery, a high percentage of which was captured from Azerbaijani forces or obtained from Soviet occupation troops. Significant arms and matériel support also came from Armenia, often at the expense of the regular army. By 1994 the Karabakh Self-Defense Army was building an infrastructure of barracks, training centers, and repair depots. Defeats that Armenians inflicted on Azerbaijan in 1993 were attributed by experts largely to the self-defense forces, although regular Armenian forces also were involved.

The Armenian air defense forces, virtually nonexistent in 1991, were equipped and organized as part of the military reform program of Ter-Grigoriants. Air defense units and the air force each had about 2,000 troops in 1994. The new military aviation program of the air force has been bolstered by the recruitment of Soviet-trained Armenian pilots, and new pilots receive training at the Aviation Training Center, run by the Ministry of Defense. Some modern training aircraft are available at the center. Pilots receive special housing privileges, although their pay is extremely low. Some Soviet-made Mi-8, Mi-9, and Mi-24 helicopters are available to support ground troops, but only one squadron of aircraft was rated combat-ready in 1994. Most of Armenia's fixed-wing aircraft, inherited from the Soviet Union, were unavailable because of poor maintenance.

Reserves

After independence the Soviet-era Volunteer Society for Assistance to the Army, Air Force, and Navy (see Glossary), part of the centralized reserve system of the Soviet army, was renamed the Defense Technical Sports Society. The new system trains personnel for specific military tasks in the Armenian forces, whereas previous training was a general preparation for

Members of Armenian Army parading in Victory Square, Erevan,
Independence Day 1993
Courtesy Azarian Churukian

unknown assignments elsewhere in the Soviet Union. In 1993 the society's schools gave instruction in thirteen military occupational specialties, including tank driving and repair, radio-telegraphy, and artillery and small arms repair.

Like those of the regular military, the facilities of the reserves were cut back sharply at independence. At least nine reserve training facilities, including one technical school, were reassigned within the Ministry of Defense or to another ministry. The Defense Technical Sports Society supports itself by selling military gear and sports vehicles produced in its plants; it has established advisory relations with defense technical societies in other CIS countries.

The Russian Role

After Armenian independence, Russia retained control of the Russian 7th Army in Armenia, which numbered about 23,000 personnel in mid-1992. At that time, the 7th Army included three motorized rifle divisions. In the second half of 1992, substantial parts of two divisions—the 15th Division and the 164th Division—were transferred to Armenian control. The other division remained intact and under full Russian command at Gyumri in early 1994. Meanwhile, Russia completed withdrawal of the four divisions of its 4th Army from Azerbaijan in May 1993. Some Armenian warrant officers were assigned to the division at Gyumri, and the two countries discussed assignment of Armenian recruits to Russian units.

The Russian presence continued in 1994, with an operational command in Erevan providing engineer, communications, logistics, aviation, and training capabilities. Under the

1992 Treaty on Collective Security, which apportioned Soviet weaponry among the former Soviet republics, Armenia was allotted 180 T–72 tanks, 180 BMP–1K armored fighting vehicles, sixty BTR–60 and BTR–70 armored personnel carriers, twenty-five BRM–1K armored fighting vehicles, thirty 9P–138 and 9P–148 guided missiles, and 130 artillery pieces and mortars. An unknown number of weapons systems in the Osa, Strela, Igla, and Shilka classes were also designated for transfer. Much of this equipment was no longer serviceable by the time it was turned over, however.

Internal Security

In the early 1990s, internal security was endangered by growing radical opposition to the moderate domestic and foreign policies of the Ter-Petrosian government. By 1993 a widespread breakdown of law and order in the republic had eroded the authority of the Armenian state.

Shortly after independence, a special internal security force was formed under the Ministry of Internal Affairs, whose special status in the government alarmed many observers in the ensuing years. The original mission of the internal security force was to prevent guerrilla attacks on military installations in the first months of independence. Since that time, this militia also has acted as the sole general (and nominally apolitical) police force. As originally formed, the internal affairs unit had 1,000 troops, including one assault battalion, two motorized patrol battalions, and one armored patrol battalion. Three specialized companies, including a canine unit for drug detection, also were formed. Elements of the former KGB have remained active under Armenian direction. All police agencies are under the Ministry of Internal Affairs.

Border patrols are administered by the Main Administration for the Protection of State Borders. Some of the patrols on the Iranian and Turkish borders are manned by Russian troops, whose presence is partially funded by Armenia. The rest of the border patrols are made up of Armenian troops serving under contract.

In early 1994, Armenia completely reorganized the State Administration for National Security (SANS), the umbrella agency of the Ministry of Internal Affairs that heads all national security activities. All agency activities except border patrols were suspended for three months while staff were reevaluated and an announced focus on intelligence and counterintelligence was introduced. The controversial measure may have been instigated by the assassination of Marius Yuzbashian, a former chief of the Armenian branch of the KGB; SANS had failed to investigate the assassination fully when it occurred, in the fall of 1993.

Experts saw a serious long-term threat to internal security in the independent mercenary Fidain forces that had been trained and expanded by Armenian political parties to fight in Nagorno-Karabakh. The end of the Karabakh conflict would free these combat-hardened forces, which did the bulk of the fighting in Karabakh, for possible guerrilla activity within Armenia on behalf of their respective opposition parties.

Crime

Especially in the chaotic conditions that have existed during the Nagorno-Karabakh conflict, Armenia has suffered steep increases in the gang activity of an organized mafia. Overall crime increased 11.5 percent from 1990 to 1991; then it increased 24.8 percent from 1991 to 1992. "Major" crimes (murder, robbery, armed robbery, rape, and aggravated assault) increased 3 percent from 1991 to 1992. The largest increases in that category were in murder, robbery, and armed robbery. White-collar crime (bribery and fraud) increased about 2 percent in that time, crimes by juveniles increased about 40 percent, and drug-related crimes increased 240 percent. According to one report, 80 percent of crimes committed in Armenia in 1992 were drug related.

In 1992 and 1993, a police campaign temporarily limited the activity of a few large gangs, but gang leaders, whose identities were commonly known in Armenian society, used influence in parliament to stymie the efforts of the Ministry of Internal Affairs. Some deputies in parliament were implicated directly in white-collar crime, and some even had been convicted prior to their election. From 1991 to 1993, six convicts were sentenced to death, but by early 1994 none had been executed.

Prisons

Three major prisons are in operation, at Sovetashen, Artik, and Kosh. Local jurisdictions also have jails. All prisons and jails are under the jurisdiction of the Ministry of Internal Affairs. The Soviet prison system remains intact in Armenia. That system includes two general categories: labor colonies, and prison communities similar to Western prisons. Prison system reforms call for establishment of general and high-security reform schools for teenagers; general and high-security prisons for women; and four grades of prisons for men, from minimum to maximum security. The death penalty is applicable for military crimes, first-degree murder, rape of a minor, treason, espionage, and terrorism.

In 1993 Armenia remained a weak state whose legal system was severely challenged by the activities of regional and family clans, criminal gangs with diverse operations, widespread corruption, and occasional assassinations of political figures. In the absence of a secure rule of law, the stresses of war and material privation, uncertainty about the future, and popular suspicion about the legitimacy of the ruling elites threatened the stability of the new republic.

*　　*　　*

For general historical and cultural narratives on the Armenian nation and people, two books by David Marshall Lang are of special value: *The Armenians: A People in Exile* and *Armenia: Cradle of Civilization.* Ronald G. Suny's *Armenia in the Twentieth Century* covers that period, with an emphasis on social change. The *Economic Profile of Armenia* volume of the United States Department of Commerce's Business Information Service for the Newly Independent States and *Armenia,* an economic review by the International Monetary Fund, provide a picture of Armenia's economy after 1991; the latter source also includes tables on a variety of economic performance indicators in the Soviet and post-Soviet periods.

Current information on Nagorno-Karabakh and conditions in Armenia is provided in the *Monthly Digest of News from Armenia,* published by the Armenian Assembly of America, and the Foreign Broadcast Information Service's *Daily Report: Central Eurasia.* These two publications emphasize political, economic, and national security topics. (For further information and complete citations, see Bibliography.)

Chapter 2. Azerbaijan

Sixth-century water pitcher

Country Profile

Country

Formal Name: Republic of Azerbaijan.

Short Form: Azerbaijan.

Term for Citizens: Azerbaijani(s).

Capital: Baku.

Date of Independence: October 18, 1991.

Geography

Size: Approximately 86,600 square kilometers.

Topography: About half mountainous; surrounded by mountain ranges, most notably Greater Caucasus range to north. Flatlands in center and along Caspian Sea coast.

Climate: Dry, semiarid steppe in center and east, subtropical in southeast, cold at high mountain elevations to north, temperate on Caspian Sea coast.

Society

Population: Mid-1994 estimate 7,684,456; 1994 annual growth rate 1.4 percent. Density in 1994 approximately eighty-eight persons per square kilometer.

Ethnic Groups: Azerbaijanis 82.7 percent, Russians 5.6 percent, Armenians 5.6 percent, and Lezgians (Dagestanis) 3.2 percent, per 1989 census (Armenians and Russians much less in early 1990s).

NOTE—The Country Profile contains updated information as available.

Languages: Azerbaijani 82 percent, Russian 7 percent, and Armenian 5 percent, per 1989 census (Armenian and Russian much less in early 1990s).

Religion: In 1989 Muslim 87 percent (about 70 percent of which Shia), Russian Orthodox 5.6 percent, and Armenian Apostolic 5.6 percent (much less in early 1990s). Many mosques reopened or established after religious restrictions of Soviet period.

Education and Literacy: Compulsory education through eighth grade. In 1970 literacy estimated at 100 percent (ages nine to forty-nine). After 1991 major reform program was begun to modify Soviet system, eliminate ideology, increase use of Azerbaijani language, and reintroduce traditional religious instruction.

Health: Nominally universal health care available but facilities limited, especially after independence. Sanitation, pharmacies, health care delivery, and research and development at relatively low level; medicines and equipment in short supply.

Economy

Gross National Product (GNP): In 1992 estimated at US$18.6 billion, or US$2,480 per capita. Average growth rate 1.9 percent in 1980–91. Production dropped throughout early 1990s because of adjustments to post-Soviet system and because of Nagorno-Karabakh conflict.

Agriculture: Main crops grapes, cotton, tobacco, citrus fruits, and vegetables. Livestock, dairy products, and wine also produced. Slow privatization hinders productivity increase, and production of most crops decreased in early 1990s. Irrigation and other equipment outmoded, although irrigation critical for many crops.

Industry and Mining: Principal industries oil extraction, oil equipment manufacture, petrochemicals, and construction. Besides oil, large natural gas deposits and some iron ore, bauxite, cobalt, and molybdenum. Oil production in decline since 1980s.

Energy: Abundant hydroelectric potential, but most of electric power generated by oil-fired plants. Domestic natural gas production meets 35 percent of domestic needs. Foreign assistance sought to rejuvenate oil extraction industry.

Exports: In 1992 estimated at US$926 million to Commonwealth of Independent States (CIS) nations and US$821 million outside CIS, of which 61 percent refined oil and gas products, 25 percent machinery and metal products, and 7 percent light industrial products (textiles and food products). Largest export markets Russia, Ukraine, Iran, Turkey, and Hungary.

Imports: In 1992 estimated at US$300 million from outside CIS, of which 36 percent machine parts, 21 percent processed foods, and 12 percent nonfood light industrial products. Largest import sources Russia, Turkey, and Ukraine.

Balance of Payments: In 1992 trade surplus approximately US$24 million.

Exchange Rate: Manat, established in mid-1992 at ten rubles to the manat, was used together with ruble until end of 1993, after which manat became sole currency. October 1993 exchange rate US$1=120 manats.

Inflation: Estimated at 1,200 percent for 1993.

Fiscal Year: Calendar year.

Fiscal Policy: State budget consists of central government budget and budgets of sixty-eight local and regional government budgets. Tax system revised in 1992 to improve state income, and budgetary expenditures tightly controlled to minimize budget deficits.

Transportation and Telecommunications

Highways: In 1990 about 36,700 kilometers of roads, of which 31,800 kilometers hard-surface. Generally poorly maintained.

Railroads: 2,090 kilometers of rail line in 1990. Lines connect Baku with Tbilisi, Makhachkala (in Dagestan), and Erevan; rail line in Nakhichevan Autonomous Republic goes to Tabriz (in Iran). Operating costs high because of poor condition of equipment. Service disrupted by Nagorno-Karabakh conflict in early 1990s.

Civil Aviation: Total of thirty-three usable airports, twenty-six with permanent-surface runways. Longest runway at Baku International Airport. National airline, Azerbaijan Airlines, founded in 1992.

Inland Waterways: Most rivers not navigable.

Ports: Baku center of Caspian shipping lines to Iran and Turkmenistan.

Pipelines: In 1994 crude oil pipeline 1,130 kilometers, petroleum products pipeline 630 kilometers, and natural gas pipeline 1,240 kilometers.

Telecommunications: In 1991 total telephone lines 644,000 (nine per 100 persons). Connections to CIS countries by cable and microwave. Connections to other countries through Moscow. International Telecommunications Satellite Organization (Intelsat) station in Baku gives access to 200 countries through Turkey. Turkish and Iranian television stations received through satellite; domestic and Russian broadcasts received locally.

Government and Politics

Government: One autonomous republic, Nakhichevan Autonomous Republic; one autonomous region, Nagorno-Karabakh Autonomous Region (under dispute with Armenia). Fifty-six districts and ten cities under direct central control. Executive branch includes president, elected by direct popular vote, and Council of Ministers, appointed by president with legislative approval; 350-member legislature, Azerbaijani Supreme Soviet, dissolved in May 1992, superseded by fifty-member Melli-Majlis (National Council). Regimes of early 1990s unstable. Adoption of new constitution delayed by political turmoil. Judicial branch remains substantially unchanged from Soviet system, which offered limited rights to those accused.

Politics: Azerbaijani Communist Party, previously only legal party, dissolved formally September 1991 but remained influential and was reconstituted December 1993. Major parties New Azerbaijan Party, led by President Heydar Aliyev; Azerbaijani Popular Front, major opposition party 1990–92; and National Independence Party, major opposition party 1992–94. Several smaller parties influential in coalition politics of Melli-Majlis.

Foreign Relations: Major goal countering worldwide Armenian information campaign on Nagorno-Karabakh. Policy toward Turkey and Russia varies with perception of support and mediation of Nagorno-Karabakh conflict; Aliyev government closer to Russia. Blockade of Armenia brought United States restriction of relations and aid in 1992. Recognized by 120 countries by 1993.

International Agreements and Membership: Member of Commonwealth of Independent States, United Nations, Conference on Security and Cooperation in Europe, International Bank for Reconstruction and Development, and International Monetary Fund.

National Security

Armed Forces: Military affairs overseen by Defense Council reporting to president, not by Ministry of Defense. Armed forces consist of army, air force, air defense forces, navy, and National Guard. In 1994 total of about 56,000 troops (about half of which conscripts), 49,000 of which allocated to ground forces, 3,000 to navy, and 2,000 each to air force and air defense forces. Paramilitary groups extensively used in Nagorno-Karabakh conflict in early 1990s, and volunteers widely sought abroad. All Russian forces withdrawn by 1993. Forced recruitment reported in 1993; discipline poor.

Military Budget: Estimated expenditure in 1992 about 10.5 percent (US$125 million) of state budget.

Internal Security: Border Guards, established in 1992, limited; some Russian troops included. In 1993 major reform of Ministry of Internal Affairs, which controls 20,000 militia troops used as regular police. Customs service unable to prevent smuggling, especially of narcotics.

Figure 8. Azerbaijan, 1994

UNDER THE DOMINATION of the Soviet Union for most of the twentieth century, Azerbaijan began a period of tentative autonomy when the Soviet state collapsed at the end of 1991. A culturally and linguistically Turkic people, the Azerbaijanis have retained a rich cultural heritage despite long periods of Persian and Russian domination. In the 1990s, the newly independent nation still faced strong and contrary religious and political influences from neighbors such as Iran to the south, Turkey to the west, and Russia to the north (see fig. 8). Despite the country's rich oil reserves, Azerbaijan's natural and economic resources and social welfare system have been rated below those of most of the other former Soviet republics. Furthermore, in the early 1990s a long military and diplomatic struggle with neighboring Armenia was sapping resources and distracting the country from the task of devising post-Soviet internal systems and establishing international relations.

Historical Background

The territory of modern Azerbaijan has been subject to myriad invasions, migrations, and cultural and political influences. During most of its history, Azerbaijan was under Persian influence, but as the Persian Empire declined, Russia began a 200-year dominance, some aspects of which have persisted into the 1990s.

Early History

As a crossroads of tribal migration and military campaigns, Azerbaijan underwent a series of invasions and was part of several larger jurisdictions before the beginning of the Christian era.

Persian and Greek Influences

In the ninth century B.C., the seminomadic Scythians settled in areas of what is now Azerbaijan. A century later, the Medes, who were related ethnically to the Persians, established an empire that included southernmost Azerbaijan. In the sixth century B.C., the Archaemenid Persians, under Cyrus the Great, took over the western part of Azerbaijan when they subdued the Assyrian Empire to the west. In 330 B.C., Alexander the Great absorbed the entire Archaemenid Empire into his holdings, leaving Persian satraps to govern as he advanced eastward. According to one account, Atropates, a Persian general in Alexander's command, whose name means "protected by fire," lent his name to the region when Alexander made him its governor. Another legend explains that Azerbaijan's name derives from the Persian words meaning "the land of fire," a reference either to the natural burning of surface oil deposits or to the oil-fueled fires in temples of the once-dominant Zoroastrian religion (see Religion, this ch.).

The Introduction of Islam and the Turkish Language

Between the first and third centuries A.D., the Romans conquered the Scythians and Seleucids, who were among the successor groups to the fragmented empire of Alexander. The Romans annexed the region of present-day Azerbaijan and called the area Albania. As Roman control weakened, the Sassanid Dynasty reestablished Persian control. Between the seventh and eleventh centuries, Arabs controlled Azerbaijan, bringing with them the precepts of Islam. In the mid-eleventh century, Turkic-speaking groups, including the Oghuz tribes and their Seljuk Turkish dynasty, ended Arab control by invading Azerbaijan from Central Asia and asserting political dominance. The Seljuks brought with them the Turkish language and Turkish customs. By the thirteenth century, the basic characteristics of the Azerbaijani nation had been established. Several masterpieces of Azerbaijani architecture and literature were created during the cultural golden age that spanned the eleventh through the thirteenth centuries. Among the most notable cultural monuments of this period are the writings of Nezami Ganjavi and the mausoleum of Momine-Khatun in Nakhichevan (see The Arts, this ch.).

Under the leadership of Hulegu Khan, Mongols invaded Azerbaijan in the early thirteenth century; Hulegu ruled Azerbaijan and Persia from his capital in the Persian city of Tabriz. At the end of the fourteenth century, another Mongol, Timur (also known as Tamerlane), invaded Azerbaijan, at about the time that Azerbaijani rule was reviving under the Shirvan Dynasty. Shirvan shah Ibrahim I ibn Sultan Muhammad briefly accepted Timur as his overlord. (In earlier times, the Shirvan shahs had accepted the suzerainty of Seljuk overlords.) Another extant architectural treasure, the Shirvan shahs' palace in Baku, dates from this period. In the sixteenth century,

*Icheri-Shekher
Fortress, Baku
Courtesy Tatiana
Zagorskaya*

the Azerbaijani Safavid Dynasty took power in Persia. This dynasty fought off efforts by the Ottoman Turks during the eighteenth century to establish control over Azerbaijan; the Safavids could not, however, halt Russian advances into the region.

Within the Russian Empire

Beginning in the early eighteenth century, Russia slowly asserted political domination over the northern part of Azerbaijan, while Persia retained control of southern Azerbaijan. In the nineteenth century, the division between Russian and Persian Azerbaijan was largely determined by two treaties concluded after wars between the two countries. The Treaty of Gulistan (1813) established the Russo-Persian border roughly along the Aras River, and the Treaty of Turkmanchay (1828) awarded Russia the Nakhichevan khanates (along the present-day border between Armenia and Turkey) in the region of the Talish Mountains. The land that is now Azerbaijan was split among three Russian administrative areas—Baku and Elizavetpol provinces and part of Yerevan Province, which also extended into present-day Armenia.

Russian Influences in the Nineteenth Century

In the nineteenth century, Russian influence over daily life in Azerbaijan was less pervasive than that of indigenous religious and political elites and the cultural and intellectual influences of Persia and Turkey. During most of the nineteenth century, the Russian Empire extracted commodities from Azerbaijan and invested little in the economy. However, the exploitation of oil in Azerbaijan at the end of the nineteenth century brought an influx of Russians into Baku, increasing Russian influence and expanding the local economy.

Although ethnic Russians came to dominate the oil business and government administration in the late 1800s, many Azerbaijanis became prominent in particular sectors of oil production, such as oil transport on the Caspian Sea. Armenians also became important as merchants and local officials of the Russian monarchy. The population of Baku increased from about 13,000 in the 1860s to 112,000 in 1897 and 215,000 in 1913, making Baku the largest city in the Caucasus region. At this point, more than one-third of Baku's population consisted of ethnic Russians. In 1905 social tensions erupted in riots and other forms of death and destruction as Azerbaijanis and Armenians struggled for local control and Azerbaijanis resisted Russian sovereignty.

The Spirit of Revolution

The growth of industry and political influences from outside prompted the formation of radical and reformist political organizations at the turn of the century. A leftist party calling itself Himmat, composed mainly of Azerbaijani intellectuals, was formed in 1903–4 to champion Azerbaijani culture and language against Russian and other foreign influences. A small Social Democratic Party (which later split into Bolshevik and Menshevik factions) also existed, but that party was largely dominated by Russians and Armenians. Some members of Himmat broke away and formed the Musavat (Equality party) in 1912. This organization aimed at establishing an independent Azerbaijani state, and its progressive and nationalist slogans gained wide appeal. Himmat's Marxist coloration involved it in wider ideological squabbles in the period leading up to the 1917 Bolshevik Revolution in Russia. After several further splits, the remainder of Himmat was absorbed into the Russian Communist Party (Bolshevik) shortly before Azerbaijan was occupied by the Red Army in 1920.

World War I and Independence

After the Bolshevik Revolution, a mainly Russian and Armenian grouping of Baku Bolsheviks declared a Marxist republic in Azerbaijan. Muslim nationalists separately declared the establishment of the Azerbaijan People's Democratic Republic in May 1918 and formed the "Army of Islam," with substantial help from the Ottoman Turkish army, to defeat the Bolsheviks in Baku. The Army of Islam marched into the capital in September 1918, meeting little resistance from the Bolshevik forces. After some violence against Armenians still residing in the city, the new Azerbaijani government, dominated by the Musavat, moved into its capital. Azerbaijan was occupied by Ottoman Turkish troops until the end of World War I in November 1918. British forces then replaced the defeated Turks and remained in Azerbaijan for most of that country's brief period of independence.

Facing imminent subjugation by the Red Army, Azerbaijan attempted to negotiate a union with Persia, but this effort was rendered moot when the Red Army invaded Azerbaijan in April 1920. Russian leader Vladimir I. Lenin justified the invasion because of the importance of the Baku region's oil to the Bolsheviks, who were still embroiled in a civil war. The Red Army met little resistance from Azerbaijani forces because the Azerbaijanis were heavily involved in suppressing separatism among the Armenians who formed a majority in the Nagorno-Karabakh area of south-central Azerbaijan. In September 1920, Azerbaijan signed a treaty with Russia unifying its military forces, economy, and foreign trade with those of Russia, although the fiction of Azerbaijani political independence was maintained.

Within the Soviet Union

The invasion of 1920 began a seventy-one-year period under total political and economic control of the state that became the Soviet Union in 1922. The borders and formal status of Azerbaijan underwent a period of change and uncertainty in the 1920s and 1930s, and then they remained stable through the end of the Soviet period in 1991.

Determination of Borders and Status

In late 1921, the Russian leadership dictated the creation of a Transcaucasian federated republic, composed of Armenia, Azerbaijan, and Georgia, which in 1922 became part of the newly proclaimed Soviet Union as the Transcaucasian Soviet Federated Socialist Republic (TSFSR). In this large new republic, the three subunits ceded their nominal powers over foreign policy, finances, trade, transportation, and other areas to the unwieldy and artificial authority of the TSFSR. In 1936 the new "Stalin Constitution" abolished the TSFSR, and the three constituent parts were proclaimed separate Soviet republics.

In mid-1920 the Red Army occupied Nakhichevan, an Azerbaijani enclave between Armenia and northwestern Iran. The Red Army declared Nakhichevan a Soviet socialist republic with close ties to Azerbaijan. In early 1921, a referendum confirmed that most of the population of the enclave wanted to be included in Azerbaijan. Turkey also supported this solution. Nakhichevan's close ties to Azerbaijan were confirmed by the Russo-Turkish Treaty of Moscow and the Treaty of Kars among the three Transcaucasian states and Turkey, both signed in 1921.

Lenin and his successor, Joseph V. Stalin, assigned pacification of Transcaucasia and delineation of borders in the region to the Caucasian Bureau of the Russian Communist Party (Bolshevik). In 1924, despite opposition from many Azerbaijani officials, the bureau formally designated Nakhichevan an autonomous republic of Azerbaijan with wide local powers, a status it retains today.

The existence of an Azerbaijani majority population in northern Iran became a pretext for Soviet expansion. In 1938 Soviet authorities expelled Azerbaijanis holding Iranian passports from the republic. During World War II, Soviet forces occupied the northern part of Iran. The occupiers stirred an irredentist movement fronted by the Democratic Party of Azerbaijan, which proclaimed the communist Autonomous Government of Azerbaijan at Tabriz at the end of 1945. The Western powers forced the Soviet Union to withdraw from Iran in 1946. Upon the subsequent collapse of the autonomous government, the Iranian government began harsh suppression of the Azerbaijani culture. From that time until the late 1980s, contacts between Azerbaijanis north and south of the Iranian-Soviet border were severely limited.

Stalin and Post-Stalin Politics

During Stalin's dictatorship in the Soviet Union (1926–53), Azerbaijan suffered, as did other Soviet republics, from forced collectivization and far-reaching purges. Yet during the same period, Azerbaijan also achieved significant gains in industrialization and literacy levels that were impressive in comparison

Sixteenth-century palace of the Sheki khans, Sheki
Courtesy Jay Kempen

with those of other Muslim states of the Middle East at that time.

After Stalin, Moscow's intrusions were less sweeping but nonetheless authoritarian. In 1959 Nikita S. Khrushchev, first secretary of the Communist Party of the Soviet Union (CPSU), moved to purge leaders of the Azerbaijani Communist Party (ACP) because of corruption and nationalist tendencies. Leonid I. Brezhnev, Khrushchev's successor, also removed ACP leaders for nationalist leanings, naming Heydar Aliyev in 1969 as the new ACP leader. In turn, Mikhail S. Gorbachev removed Aliyev in 1987, ostensibly for health reasons, although later Aliyev was accused of corruption.

After Communist Rule

Azerbaijan was strongly affected by the autonomy that spread to most parts of the Soviet Union under Gorbachev's liberalized regime in the late 1980s. After independence was achieved in 1991, conflict with Armenia became chronic, and political stability eluded Azerbaijan in the early years of the 1990s.

Demands for Sovereignty and the Soviet Reaction

In the fall of 1989, the nationalist opposition Azerbaijani Popular Front (APF) led a wave of protest strikes expressing growing political opposition to ACP rule (see Government and Politics, this ch.). Under this pressure, the ACP authorities bowed to opposition demands to legalize the APF and proclaim Azerbaijani sovereignty. In September 1989, the Azerbaijani Supreme Court passed a resolution of sovereignty, among the first such resolutions in the Soviet republics. The resolution proclaimed Azerbaijan's sovereignty over its land, water, and natural resources and its right to secede from the Soviet Union following a popular referendum. The Presidium of the Supreme Soviet, the legislative body of the Soviet Union, declared this resolution invalid in November 1989. Another manifestation of nationalist ferment occurred at the end of 1989, when Azerbaijanis rioted along the Iranian border, destroying border checkpoints and crossing into Iranian provinces that had Azerbaijani majorities. Azerbaijani intellectuals also appealed to the CPSU Politburo for relaxation of border controls between Soviet and Iranian Azerbaijan, comparing the "tragic" separation of the Azerbaijani nation to the divisions of Korea or Vietnam.

Meanwhile, Azerbaijanis unleashed a wave of violence against Armenian residents of Baku and other population centers, causing turmoil that seemed to jeopardize ACP rule. In response, in January 1990 Moscow deployed forces of its Ministry of Internal Affairs (Ministerstvo vnutrennikh del—MVD), Committee for State Security (Komitet gosudarstvennoi bezopasnosti—KGB), and the military in a brutal suppression of these riots. Moscow also began a crackdown on the APF and other opposition forces in Baku and other cities, and Soviet forces cooperated with Iranian authorities to secure the Azerbaijani-Iranian border. These actions further alienated the population from Moscow's rule. Ironically, the Soviet crackdown targeted the large and increasingly vocal Azerbaijani working class. In this process, martial law was declared, and the ACP leader was replaced by Ayaz Mutalibov, a former chairman of the Azerbaijani Council of Ministers. In May 1990, while martial law remained in effect, Mutalibov was elected president by the Azerbaijani Supreme Soviet; elections to the Supreme Soviet were held four months later. The APF, although declared illegal, retained immense popular appeal and visibility.

The Issue of Nagorno-Karabakh

The Soviet Union created the Nagorno-Karabakh Autonomous Region within Azerbaijan in 1924. At that time, more

Memorial to Azerbaijani victims of 1990 Russian invasion, Baku
Courtesy David Dallas, United States Information Agency
Soviet troops sent to quell Azerbaijani nationalist unrest, 1989–90
Courtesy Jay Kempen

than 94 percent of the region's population was Armenian (see fig. 3). (The term Nagorno-Karabakh originates from the Russian for "mountainous Karabakh.") As the Azerbaijani population grew, the Karabakh Armenians chafed under discriminatory rule, and by 1960 hostilities had begun between the two populations of the region.

On February 20, 1988, Armenian deputies to the National Council of Nagorno-Karabakh voted to unify that region with Armenia (see Population and Ethnic Composition, this ch.; Nagorno-Karabakh and Independence, ch. 1). Although Armenia did not formally respond, this act triggered an Azerbaijani massacre of more than 100 Armenians in the city of Sumgait, just north of Baku. A similar attack on Azerbaijanis occurred in the Armenian town of Spitak. Large numbers of refugees left Armenia and Azerbaijan as pogroms began against the minority populations of the respective countries. In the fall of 1989, intensified interethnic conflict in and around Nagorno-Karabakh led Moscow to grant Azerbaijani authorities greater leeway in controlling that region. The Soviet policy backfired, however, when a joint session of the Armenian Supreme Soviet and the National Council of Nagorno-Karabakh proclaimed the unification of Nagorno-Karabakh with Armenia. In mid-January 1990, Azerbaijani protesters in Baku went on a rampage against the remaining Armenians and the ACP. Moscow intervened, sending police troops of the MVD, who violently suppressed the APF and installed Mutalibov as president. The troops reportedly killed 122 Azerbaijanis in quelling the uprising, and Gorbachev denounced the APF for striving to establish an Islamic republic. These events further alienated the Azerbaijani population from Moscow and from ACP rule. In a December 1991 referendum boycotted by local Azerbaijanis, Armenians in Nagorno-Karabakh approved the creation of an independent state. A Supreme Soviet was elected, and Nagorno-Karabakh appealed for world recognition.

Independence

Mutalibov initially supported the August 1991 coup attempted in Moscow against the Gorbachev regime, drawing vehement objections from APF leaders and other political opponents. Once the coup failed, Mutalibov moved quickly to repair local damage and to insulate his rule from Moscow's retribution by announcing his resignation as first secretary of the ACP. These moves by Mutalibov and his supporters were in line with the pro-independence demands of the APF, even though the two groups remained political adversaries. In September 1991, Mutalibov was elected president without electoral opposition but under charges from the APF that the election process was corrupt.

Azerbaijan began the process of achieving formal independence October 18, when the Supreme Soviet passed a law on state independence, ratifying that body's August declaration of independence. Then in December, over 99 percent of voters cast ballots in favor of independence in a referendum on that issue. The constitution was duly amended to reflect the country's new status. Immediately after the law was passed, the Supreme Soviet appealed to the world's nations and the United Nations (UN) for recognition of Azerbaijan. In December Mutalibov signed accords on Azerbaijan's membership in the Commonwealth of Independent States (CIS—see Glossary), a move criticized by many Azerbaijani nationalists who opposed all links to Russia and Armenia. A year later, the Azerbaijani legislature repudiated the signature, rejecting membership in the CIS. Azerbaijan maintained observer status at CIS meetings, however, and it resumed full membership in late 1993.

Political Instability

The intractable conflict in Nagorno-Karabakh contributed to the fall of several governments in newly independent Azerbaijan. After a February 1992 armed attack by Armenians on Azerbaijani residents in Nagorno-Karabakh caused many civilian casualties, Mutalibov was forced by opposition parties to resign as president. The president of Azerbaijan's Supreme Soviet, Yakub Mamedov, became acting president. Mamedov held this position until May 1992, when he in turn was forced from power in the face of continuing military defeats in Nagorno-Karabakh. Mutalibov loyalists in the Supreme Soviet reinstated him as president, but two days later he was forced to flee the country when APF-led crowds stormed the government buildings in Baku. An interim APF government assumed power until previously scheduled presidential elections could be held one month later. APF leader and intellectual Abulfaz Elchibey, who won over 59 percent of the vote in a five-candidate electoral contest, then formed Azerbaijan's first postcommunist government. Elchibey served as president only one year, however, before being forced to flee Baku in mid-June 1993 in the face of an insurrection led by a disgruntled military officer.

Taking advantage of the chaos, Aliyev returned to power, and an election in October 1993 confirmed him as president.

Efforts to Resolve the Nagorno-Karabakh Crisis, 1993

By the end of 1993, the conflict over Nagorno-Karabakh had caused thousands of casualties and created hundreds of thousands of refugees on both sides. In a national address in November 1993, Aliyev stated that 16,000 Azerbaijani troops had died and 22,000 had been injured in nearly six years of fighting. The UN estimated that nearly 1 million refugees and displaced persons were in Azerbaijan at the end of 1993. Mediation was attempted by officials from Russia, Kazakhstan, and Iran, among other countries, as well as by organizations including the UN and the Conference on Security and Cooperation in Europe (CSCE—see Glossary), which began sponsoring peace talks in mid-1992. All negotiations met with little success, however, and several cease-fires broke down. In mid-1993 Aliyev launched efforts to negotiate a solution directly with the Karabakh Armenians, a step Elchibey had refused to take. Aliyev's efforts achieved several relatively long cease-fires within Nagorno-Karabakh, but outside the region Armenians occupied large sections of southwestern Azerbaijan near the Iranian border during offensives in August and October 1993. Iran and Turkey warned the Karabakh Armenians to cease their offensive operations, which threatened to spill over into foreign territory. The Armenians responded by claiming that they were driving back Azerbaijani forces to protect Nagorno-Karabakh from shelling.

In 1993 the UN Security Council called for Armenian forces to cease their attacks on and occupation of a number of Azerbaijani regions. In September 1993, Turkey strengthened its forces along its border with Armenia and issued a warning to Armenia to withdraw its troops from Azerbaijan immediately and unconditionally. At the same time, Iran was conducting military maneuvers near the Nakhichevan Autonomous Republic in a move widely regarded as a warning to Armenia. Iran proposed creation of a twenty-kilometer security zone along the Iranian-Azerbaijani border, where Azerbaijanis would be protected by Iranian firepower. Iran also contributed to the upkeep of camps in southwestern Azerbaijan to house and feed up to 200,000 Azerbaijanis fleeing the fighting.

Fighting continued into early 1994, with Azerbaijani forces reportedly winning some engagements and regaining some territory lost in previous months. In January 1994, Aliyev pledged that in the coming year occupied territory would be liberated and Azerbaijani refugees would return to their homes. At that point, Armenian forces held an estimated 20 percent of Azerbaijan's territory outside Nagorno-Karabakh, including 160 kilometers along the Iranian border.

Physical Environment

Three physical features dominate Azerbaijan: the Caspian Sea, whose shoreline forms a natural boundary to the east; the Greater Caucasus mountain range to the north; and the extensive flatlands at the country's center (see fig. 2). About the size of Portugal or the state of Maine, Azerbaijan has a total land area of approximately 86,600 square kilometers, less than 1 percent of the land area of the former Soviet Union. Of the three Transcaucasian states, Azerbaijan has the greatest land area. Special administrative subdivisions are the Nakhichevan Autonomous Republic, which is separated from the rest of Azerbaijan by a strip of Armenian territory, and the Nagorno-Karabakh Autonomous Region, entirely within Azerbaijan. (The status of Nagorno-Karabakh was under negotiation in 1994.) Located in the region of the southern Caucasus Mountains, Azerbaijan borders the Caspian Sea to the east, Iran to the south, Armenia to the southwest and west, and Georgia and Russia to the north (see fig. 1). A small part of Nakhichevan also borders Turkey to the northwest. The capital of Azerbaijan is the ancient city of Baku, which has the largest and best harbor on the Caspian Sea and has long been the center of the republic's oil industry.

Topography and Drainage

The elevation changes over a relatively short distance from lowlands to highlands; nearly half the country is considered mountainous. Notable physical features are the gently undulating hills of the subtropical southeastern coast, which are covered with tea plantations, orange groves, and lemon groves; numerous mud volcanoes and mineral springs in the ravines of Kobystan Mountain near Baku; and coastal terrain that lies as much as twenty-eight meters below sea level.

Except for its eastern Caspian shoreline and some areas bordering Georgia and Iran, Azerbaijan is ringed by mountains. To the northeast, bordering Russia's Dagestan Autonomous Republic, is the Greater Caucasus range; to the west, bordering

Armenia, is the Lesser Caucasus range. To the extreme southeast, the Talish Mountains form part of the border with Iran. The highest elevations occur in the Greater Caucasus, where Mount Bazar-dyuzi rises 4,740 meters above sea level. Eight large rivers flow down from the Caucasus ranges into the central Kura-Aras lowlands, alluvial flatlands and low delta areas along the seacoast designated by the Azerbaijani name for the Mtkvari River and its main tributary, the Aras. The Mtkvari, the longest river in the Caucasus region, forms a delta and drains into the Caspian a short distance downstream from the confluence with the Aras. The Mingechaur Reservoir, with an area of 605 square kilometers that makes it the largest body of water in Azerbaijan, was formed by damming the Mtkvari in western Azerbaijan. The waters of the reservoir provide hydroelectric power and irrigation to the Kura-Aras plain. Most of the country's rivers are not navigable. About 15 percent of the land in Azerbaijan is arable.

Climate

The climate varies from subtropical and dry in central and eastern Azerbaijan to subtropical and humid in the southeast, temperate along the shores of the Caspian Sea, and cold at the higher mountain elevations. Baku, on the Caspian, enjoys mild weather, averaging 4°C in January and 25°C in July. Because most of Azerbaijan receives scant rainfall—on average 152 to 254 millimeters annually—agricultural areas require irrigation. Heaviest precipitation occurs in the highest elevations of the Caucasus and in the Lenkoran' Lowlands in the far southeast, where the yearly average exceeds 1,000 millimeters.

Environmental Problems

Air and water pollution are widespread and pose great challenges to economic development. Major sources of pollution include oil refineries and chemical and metallurgical industries, which in the early 1990s continued to operate as inefficiently as they had in the Soviet era. Air quality is extremely poor in Baku, the center of oil refining. Some reports have described Baku's air as the most polluted in the former Soviet Union, and other industrial centers suffer similar problems.

The Caspian Sea, including Baku Bay, has been polluted by oil leakages and the dumping of raw or inadequately treated sewage, reducing the yield of caviar and fish. In the Soviet period, Azerbaijan was pressed to use extremely heavy applications of pesticides to improve its output of scarce subtropical crops for the rest of the Soviet Union. Particularly egregious was the continued regular use of the pesticide DDT in the 1970s and 1980s, although that chemical was officially banned in the Soviet Union because of its toxicity to humans. Excessive application of pesticides and chemical fertilizers has caused extensive groundwater pollution and has been linked by Azerbaijani scientists to birth defects and illnesses. Rising water levels in the Caspian Sea, mainly caused by natural factors exacerbated by man-made structures, have reversed a decades-long drying trend and now threaten coastal areas; the average level rose 1.5 meters between 1978 and 1993. Because of the Nagorno-Karabakh conflict, large numbers of trees were felled, roads were built through pristine areas, and large expanses of agricultural land were occupied by military forces.

Like other former Soviet republics, Azerbaijan faces a gigantic environmental cleanup complicated by the economic uncertainties left in the wake of the Moscow-centered planning system. The Committee for the Protection of the Natural Environment is part of the Azerbaijani government, but in the early 1990s it was ineffective at targeting critical applications of limited funds, establishing pollution standards, and monitoring compliance with environmental regulations. Early in 1994, plans called for Azerbaijan to participate in the international Caspian Sea Forum, sponsored by the European Union (EU).

Population and Ethnic Composition

The majority of Azerbaijan's population consists of a single ethnic group whose problems with ethnic minorities have been dominated by the Armenian uprisings in Nagorno-Karabakh. Nevertheless, Azerbaijan includes several other significant ethnic groups. The population of the country is concentrated in a few urban centers and in the most fertile agricultural regions.

Population Characteristics

In mid-1993 the population of Azerbaijan was estimated at 7.6 million. With eighty-eight persons per square kilometer, Azerbaijan is the second most densely populated of the Transcaucasian states; major portions of the populace live in and around the capital of Baku and in the Kura-Aras agricultural area. Baku's population exceeded 1.1 million in the late 1980s, but an influx of war refugees increased that figure to an estimated 1.7 million in 1993. In 1993 the estimated population growth rate of Azerbaijan was 1.5 percent per year. Gyandzha (formerly Kirovabad), in western Azerbaijan, is the second most populous city, with a population of more than 270,000, followed by Sumgait, just north of Baku, with a population of 235,000; figures for both cities are official 1987 estimates. Since that time, Gyandzha and Sumgait, like Baku, have been swollen by war refugees. With 54 percent of Azerbaijanis living in urban areas by 1989, Azerbaijan was one of the most urbanized of the Muslim former Soviet republics. According to the 1989 census, the population of Nagorno-Karabakh was 200,000, of which over 75 percent was ethnically Armenian.

In 1989 life expectancy was sixty-seven years for males and seventy-four years for females. According to legend and to Soviet-era statistics, unusually large numbers of centenarians and other long-lived people live in Nagorno-Karabakh and other areas of Azerbaijan. In 1990 the birth rate was twenty-five per 1,000 population. The fertility rate has declined significantly since 1970, when the average number of births per woman was 4.6. According to Western estimates, the figure was 2.8 in 1990.

In 1987 Azerbaijan's crude death rate was about twelve per 1,000. As in other former Soviet republics, the rate was somewhat higher than in 1970. In Azerbaijan, however, the death rate continued rising through 1992 because of the escalating number of accidents, suicides, and murders; fatalities caused by the conflict with Armenia were also a factor.

According to the 1989 census, about 85 percent of the population was Azerbaijani (5.8 million), 5.8 percent was Russian (392,300), and 5.8 percent was Armenian (390,500). The percentage of Azerbaijanis has increased in recent decades because of a high birth rate and the emigration of Russians and other minorities. Between 1959 and 1989, the Azerbaijani share of the population rose by 16 percent. Since that time, however, growth of the Azerbaijani share of the population has accelerated with the addition of an estimated 200,000 Azerbaijani deportees and refugees from Armenia and the quickening rate of Armenian emigration. About 13 million Azerbaijanis reside in the northern provinces of neighboring Iran. Smaller groups live in Georgia, the Dagestan Autonomous Republic of Russia to Azerbaijan's north, Uzbekistan, Turkmenistan, Kazakhstan, and Ukraine.

The Role of Women

Although religious practice in Azerbaijan is less restrictive of women's activities than in most of the other Muslim countries, vestiges of the traditional female role remain. Particularly in rural communities, women who appear in public unaccompanied, smoke in public, drive automobiles, or visit certain theaters and restaurants are subject to disapproval. Nevertheless, the majority of Azerbaijani women have jobs outside the home, and a few have attained leadership positions. In July 1993, Aliyev appointed surgeon Lala-Shovket Gajiyeva as his state secretary (a position equivalent at that time to vice president), largely because of her outspoken views on Azerbaijani political problems. Gajiyeva was a champion of women's rights and in late 1993 founded a political party critical of Aliyev's policies. In January 1994, she was moved from state secretary to permanent representative to the UN, presumably because of her controversial positions.

Smaller Ethnic Minorities

After the Azerbaijanis, Russians, and Armenians, the next largest group is the Lezgians (Dagestanis), the majority of whom live across the Russian border in Dagestan, but 171,000 of whom resided in northern Azerbaijan in 1989 (see fig. 9). The Lezgians, who are predominantly Sunni (see Glossary) Muslims and speak a separate Caucasian language, have called for greater rights, including the right to maintain contacts with Lezgians in Russia. In October 1992, President Elchibey promised informally that border regulations would be interpreted loosely to assuage these Lezgian concerns.

In 1989 another 262,000 people belonging to ninety other nationalities lived in Azerbaijan. These groups include Avars, Kurds, Talish, and Tats. The Talish in Azerbaijan, estimates of whose numbers varied from the official 1989 census figure of 21,000 to their own estimates of 200,000 to 300,000, are an Iranian people living in southeastern Azerbaijan and contiguous areas of Iran. Like the Lezgians, the Talish have called for greater rights since Azerbaijan became independent.

In 1992 Elchibey attempted to reassure ethnic minorities by issuing an order that the government defend the political, economic, social, and cultural rights and freedoms of non-Azerbaijanis, and by setting up the Consultative Council on Interethnic Relations as part of the presidential apparatus. At

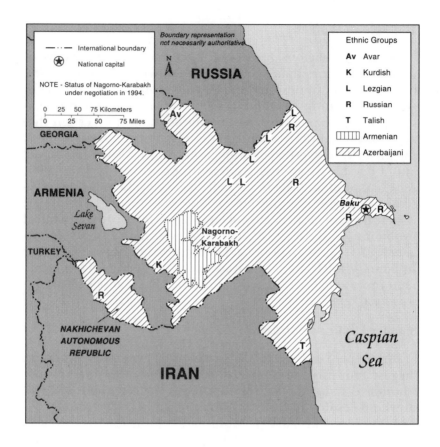

Figure 9. Ethnic Groups in Azerbaijan

no point, however, were Armenians mentioned among the protected ethnic minorities.

Language, Religion, and Culture

Although Azerbaijan's history shows the mark of substantial
religious and cultural influence from Iran, linguistically and
ethnically the country is predominantly Turkic. The republic
was part of the Soviet Union for seventy years, but Russian culture had only an incidental impact.

Language

The official language is Azerbaijani, a Turkic tongue
belonging to the southern branch of the Altaic languages. In

1994 it was estimated that some 82 percent of Azerbaijan's citizens speak Azerbaijani as their first language. In addition, 38 percent of Azerbaijanis speak Russian fluently, reflecting Russian domination of the economy and politics. Although official Soviet figures showed that about 32 percent of Russians living in Azerbaijan spoke Azerbaijani, the Russian population generally was reluctant to learn the local language. Most Armenians living in Nagorno-Karabakh use Russian rather than Azerbaijani as their second language.

The Azerbaijani language is part of the Oghuz, or Western Turkic, group of Turkic languages, together with Anatolian Turkish (spoken in Turkey) and Turkmen (spoken in Turkmenistan). The Oghuz tribes of Central Asia spoke this precursor language between the seventh and eleventh centuries. The three descendent languages share common linguistic features. Dialectical differences between Azerbaijani and Anatolian Turkish have been attributed to Mongolian and Turkic influences. Despite these differences, Anatolian Turkish speakers and Azerbaijanis can often understand one another if they speak carefully. Spoken Azerbaijani includes several dialects. Beginning in the nineteenth century, Russian loanwords (particularly technical terms) and grammatical and lexical structures entered the Azerbaijani language in Russian-controlled Azerbaijan, as did Persian words in Iranian Azerbaijan. The resulting variants remain mutually intelligible, however.

In the immediate pre-Soviet period, literature in Azerbaijan was written in Arabic in several literary forms that by 1900 were giving way to a more vernacular Azerbaijani Turkish form. In 1924 Soviet officials pressured the Azerbaijani government into approving the gradual introduction of a modified Roman alphabet. Scholars have speculated that this decision was aimed at isolating the Muslim peoples from their Islamic culture, thus reducing the threat of nationalist movements. In the late 1930s, however, Soviet authorities reversed their policy and dictated use of the Cyrillic alphabet, which became official in 1940. Turkey's switch to a modified Roman alphabet in 1928 may have prompted Stalin to reinforce Azerbaijan's isolation from dangerous outside influences by switching to Cyrillic. This change also made it easier for Azerbaijanis to learn Russian.

When the Soviet Union disintegrated, the alphabet question arose once again. Iran reportedly advocated use of Arabic as part of a campaign to expand the influence of Shia (see Glossary) Islam in Azerbaijan. Most Azerbaijani intellectuals ultimately rejected switching to Arabic, however, noting that Iran had not allowed proper study of the Azerbaijani language in northern Iran. Instead, the intellectuals preferred a modified Roman alphabet incorporating symbols for unique Azerbaijani language sounds. In December 1991, the legislature approved a gradual return to a "New Roman" alphabet.

Religion

The prophet Zoroaster (Zarathustra), who was born in the seventh century B.C. in what is now Azerbaijan, established a religion focused on the cosmic struggle between a supreme god and an evil spirit. Islam arrived in Azerbaijan with Arab invaders in the seventh century A.D., gradually supplanting Zoroastrianism and Azerbaijani pagan cults. In the seventh and eighth centuries, many Zoroastrians fled Muslim persecution and moved to India, where they became known as Parsis. Until Soviet Bolsheviks ended the practice, Zoroastrian pilgrims from India and Iran traveled to Azerbaijan to worship at sacred sites, including the Surakhany Temple on the Apsheron Peninsula near Baku.

In the sixteenth century, the first shah of the Safavid Dynasty, Ismail I (r. 1486–1524), established Shia Islam as the state religion, although large numbers of Azerbaijanis remained followers of the other branch of Islam, Sunni. The Safavid court was subject to both Turkic (Sunni) and Iranian (Shia) influences, however, which reinforced the dual nature of Azerbaijani religion and culture in that period. As elsewhere in the Muslim world, the two branches of Islam came into conflict in Azerbaijan. Enforcement of Shia Islam as the state religion brought contention between the Safavid rulers of Azerbaijan and the ruling Sunnis of the neighboring Ottoman Empire.

In the nineteenth century, many Sunni Muslims emigrated from Russian-controlled Azerbaijan because of Russia's series of wars with their coreligionists in the Ottoman Empire. Thus, by the late nineteenth century, the Shia population was in the majority in Russian Azerbaijan. Antagonism between the Sunnis and the Shia diminished in the late nineteenth century as Azerbaijani nationalism began to emphasize a common Turkic heritage and opposition to Iranian religious influences. At present, about three-quarters of Azerbaijani Muslims are at least nominally Shia (and 87 percent of the population were Muslim in 1989).

Azerbaijan's next largest official religion is Christianity, represented mainly by Russian Orthodox and Armenian Apostolic groups. Some rural Azerbaijanis retain pre-Islamic shamanist or animist beliefs, such as the sanctity of certain sites and the veneration of certain trees and rocks.

Before Soviet power was established, about 2,000 mosques were active in Azerbaijan. Most mosques were closed in the 1930s, then some were allowed to reopen during World War II. In the 1980s, however, only two large and five smaller mosques held services in Baku, and only eleven others were operating in the rest of the country. Supplementing the officially sanctioned mosques were thousands of private houses of prayer and many secret Islamic sects. Beginning in the late Gorbachev period, and especially after independence, the number of mosques rose dramatically. Many were built with the support of other Islamic countries, such as Iran, Oman, and Saudi Arabia, which also contributed Qurans (Korans) and religious instructors to the new Muslim states. A Muslim seminary has also been established since 1991. As in the other former Soviet Muslim republics, religious observances in Azerbaijan do not follow all the traditional precepts of Islam. For example, drinking wine is permitted, and women are not veiled or segregated.

During World War II, Soviet authorities established the Muslim Spiritual Board of Transcaucasia in Baku as the governing body of Islam in the Caucasus, in effect reviving the nineteenth-century tsarist Muslim Ecclesiastical Board. During the tenures of Brezhnev and Gorbachev, Moscow encouraged Muslim religious leaders in Azerbaijan to visit and host foreign Muslim leaders, with the goal of advertising the freedom of religion and superior living conditions reportedly enjoyed by Muslims under Soviet communism.

In the early 1980s, Allashukur Humatogly Pashazade was appointed sheikh ul-Islam, head of the Muslim board. With the breakup of the Soviet Union, the Muslim board became known as the Supreme Religious Council of the Caucasus Peoples. In late 1993, the sheikh blessed Heydar Aliyev at his swearing-in ceremony as president of Azerbaijan.

The Arts

Azerbaijanis have sought to protect their cultural identity from long-standing outside influences by fostering indigenous forms of artistic and intellectual expression. They proudly point to a number of scientists, philosophers, and literary figures who have built their centuries-old cultural tradition.

Literature and Music

Before the eleventh century, literary influences included the Zoroastrian sacred text, the *Avesta*, Turkish prose-poetry, and oral history recitations (called *dastans*), such as *The Book of Dede Korkut* and *Koroglu*, which contain pre-Islamic elements. Among the classics of medieval times are the *Astronomy* of Abul Hasan Shirvani (written in the eleventh or twelfth century) and *Khamseh*, a collection of five long romantic poems written in Persian by the twelfth-century poet Nezami Ganjavi. Fuzuli (1494–1556) wrote poetry and prose in Turkish, most notably the poem *Laila and Majnun*, the satire *A Book of Complaints*, and the treatise *To the Heights of Conviction*. Fuzuli's works influenced dramatic and operatic productions in the early twentieth century. Shah Ismail I, who was also the first Safavid shah, wrote court poems in Turkish. Fuzuli and Ismail are still read in their original Turkish dialects, which are very similar to modern literary Azerbaijani.

In music an ancient tradition was carried into modern times by *ashugs*, poet-singers who presented ancient songs or verses or improvised new ones, accompanied by a stringed instrument called the *kobuz*. Another early musical form was the *mugam*, a composition of alternating vocal and instrumental segments most strongly associated with the ancient town of Shusha in Nagorno-Karabakh.

Decorative Arts and Crafts

Carpet and textile making, both of which are ancient Azerbaijani crafts, flourished during the medieval period, and Azerbaijani products became well known in Asia and Europe. Azerbaijani carpets and textiles were known for their rich vegetation patterns, depictions from the poetry of Nezami Ganjavi, and traditional themes. Each region produced its own distinctive carpet patterns. Silk production became significant in the eighteenth century. During the Soviet period, carpets, textiles, and silk continued to be made in factories or at home. In medieval times, ornately chased weaponry was another major export. Azerbaijan was also famed for miniature books incorporating elaborate calligraphy and illustrations.

*Man and woman in
traditional costume
Courtesy Embassy of
Azerbaijan,
Washington*

Architecture

Azerbaijani architecture typically combines elements of East and West. Many ancient architectural treasures survive in modern Azerbaijan. These sites include the so-called Maiden Tower in Baku, a rampart that has been dated variously from the pre-Christian era to the twelfth century, and from the top of which, legend says, a distraught medieval maiden flung herself. Among other medieval architectural treasures reflecting the influence of several schools are the Shirvan shahs' palace in Baku, the palace of the Sheki khans in the town of Sheki in north-central Azerbaijan, the Surakhany Temple on the Apsheron Peninsula, a number of bridges spanning the Aras River, and several mausoleums. In the nineteenth and early twentieth centuries, little monumental architecture was created, but distinctive residences were built in Baku and elsewhere. Among the most recent architectural monuments, the Baku subways are noted for their lavish decor.

The Cultural Renaissance

In the second half of the nineteenth century and in the early twentieth century, Azerbaijan underwent a cultural renaissance that drew on the golden age of the eleventh to the thirteenth centuries and other influences. The patronage of the arts and education that characterized this movement was

fueled in part by increasing oil wealth. Azerbaijan's new industrial and commercial elites contributed funds for the establishment of many libraries, schools, hospitals, and charitable
organizations. In the 1880s, philanthropist Haji Zeinal Adibin
Taghiyev built and endowed Baku's first theater.

Artistic flowering in Azerbaijan inspired Turkic Muslims
throughout the Russian Empire and abroad, stimulating
among other phenomena the establishment of theaters and
opera houses that were among the first in the Muslim world.
Tsarist authorities first encouraged, then tolerated, and finally
used intensified Russification against this assertion of artistic
independence.

Several artists played important roles in the renaissance.
Mirza Fath Ali Akhundzade (also called Akhundov; 1812–78), a
playwright and philosopher, influenced the Azerbaijani literary
language by writing in vernacular Azerbaijani Turkish. His
plays, among the first significant theater productions in Azerbaijan, continue to have wide popular appeal as models of
form in the late twentieth century. The composer and poet
Uzeir Hajibeyli (1885–1948) used traditional instruments and
themes in his musical compositions, among which were the
first operas in the Islamic world. The poet and playwright
Husein Javid (1882–1941) wrote in Turkish about historical
themes, most notably the era of Timur.

Under Soviet rule, Azerbaijani cultural expression was cir-
cumscribed and forcibly supplanted by Russian cultural values.
Particularly during Stalin's purges of the 1930s, many Azerbaijani writers and intellectuals were murdered, and ruthless
attempts were made to erase evidence of their lives and work
from historical records. Cultural monuments, libraries,
mosques, and archives were destroyed. The two forcible
changes of alphabet in the 1920s and 1930s further isolated
Azerbaijanis from their literary heritage. Never completely
extinguished during the Soviet period, however, Azerbaijani
culture underwent a modest rebirth during Khrushchev's
relaxation of controls in the 1950s, when many who had been
victims of Stalin's purges were posthumously rehabilitated and
their works republished. In the 1970s and 1980s, another
rebirth occurred when Moscow again loosened cultural restrictions. Under Aliyev's first regime, publication of some mildly
nationalist pieces was allowed, including serialization of Aziza
Jafarzade's historical novel *Baku 1501.*

In the late 1980s, Gorbachev's policy of *glasnost* (see Glossary) energized a major movement among Azerbaijani writers and historians to illuminate "blank pages" in the nation's past, such as Azerbaijani resistance to tsarist and Soviet power and Stalin's crimes against the peoples of the Soviet Union. Reprints of Azerbaijani historical and literary classics became more plentiful, as did political tracts on topics such as Azerbaijani claims to Nagorno-Karabakh.

Education, Health, and Welfare

When the Soviet Union crumbled, Azerbaijan, like other former Soviet republics, was forced to end its reliance upon the uniform, centralized system of social supports that had been administered from Moscow. In the early 1990s, however, Azerbaijan did not have the resources to make large-scale changes in the delivery of educational, health, and welfare services, so the basic Soviet-era structures remained in place.

Education

In the pre-Soviet period, Azerbaijani education included intensive Islamic religious training that commenced in early childhood. Beginning at roughly age five and sometimes continuing until age twenty, children attended *madrasahs*, education institutions affiliated with mosques. In the seventeenth and eighteenth centuries, *madrasahs* were established as separate education institutions in major cities, but the religious component of education remained significant. In 1865 the first technical high school and the first women's high school were opened in Baku. In the late nineteenth century, secular elementary schools for Azerbaijanis began to appear (schools for ethnic Russians had been established earlier), but institutions of higher education and the use of the Azerbaijani language in secondary schools were forbidden in Transcaucasia throughout the tsarist period. The majority of ethnic Azerbaijani children received no education in this period, and the Azerbaijani literacy rate remained very low, especially among women. Few women were allowed to attend school.

In the Soviet era, literacy and average education levels rose dramatically from their very low starting point, despite two changes in the standard alphabet, from Arabic to Roman in the 1920s and from Roman to Cyrillic in the 1930s (see Language, this ch.). According to Soviet data, 100 percent of males and females (ages nine to forty-nine) were literate in 1970.

During the Soviet period, the Azerbaijani education system was based on the standard model imposed by Moscow, which featured state control of all education institutions and heavy doses of Marxist-Leninist ideology at all levels. Since independence, the Azerbaijani system has undergone little structural change. Initial alterations have included the reestablishment of religious education (banned during the Soviet period) and curriculum changes that have reemphasized the use of the Azerbaijani language and have eliminated ideological content. In addition to elementary schools, the education institutions include thousands of preschools, general secondary schools, and vocational schools, including specialized secondary schools and technical schools. Education through the eighth grade is compulsory. At the end of the Soviet period, about 18 percent of instruction was in Russian, but the use of Russian began a steady decline beginning in 1988. A few schools teach in Armenian or Georgian.

Azerbaijan has more than a dozen institutions of higher education, in which enrollment totaled 105,000 in 1991. Because Azerbaijani culture has always included great respect for secular learning, the country traditionally has been an education center for the Muslim peoples of the former Soviet Union. For that reason and because of the role of the oil industry in Azerbaijan's economy, a relatively high percentage of Azerbaijanis have obtained some form of higher education, most notably in scientific and technical subjects. Several vocational institutes train technicians for the oil industry and other primary industries.

The most significant institutions of higher education are the University of Azerbaijan in Baku, the Institute of Petroleum and Chemistry, the Polytechnic Institute, the Pedagogical Institute, the Mirza Fath Ali Akhundzade Pedagogical Institute for Languages, the Azerbaijan Medical Institute, and the Uzeir Hajibeyli Conservatory. Much scientific research, which during the Soviet period dealt mainly with enhancing oil production and refining, is carried out by the Azerbaijani Academy of Sciences, which was established in 1945. The University of Azerbaijan, established in 1919, includes more than a dozen departments, ranging from physics to Oriental studies, and has the largest library in Azerbaijan. The student population numbers more than 11,000, and the faculty over 600. The Institute of Petroleum and Chemistry, established in 1920, has more than 15,000 students and a faculty of about 1,000. The institute

*History class in
elementary school, Sheki
Courtesy Jay Kempen*

trains engineers and scientists in the petrochemical industry,
geology, and related areas.

Health

Azerbaijan's health care system was one of the least effective
in the Soviet republics, and it deteriorated further after independence. On the eve of the breakup of the Soviet Union in
1991, the number of physicians per 1,000 people in Azerbaijan
was about four, the number of hospital beds about ten, and the
number of pharmacists about seven—all figures below the average for the Soviet Union as a whole (see table 2, Appendix).
According to reports, in the late 1980s some 736 hospitals and
clinics were operating in Azerbaijan, but according to Soviet
data some of those were rudimentary facilities with little equipment. Medical facilities also include several dozen sanatoriums
and special children's health facilities. The leading medical
schools in Azerbaijan are the Azerbaijan Medical Institute in
Baku, which trains doctors and pharmacists, and the Institute
for Advanced Training of Physicians. Several research institutes
also conduct medical studies.

After the breakup of the Soviet Union, Azerbaijan's declining economy made it impossible for the Azerbaijani government to provide full support of the health infrastructure.
Shortages of medicines and equipment have occurred, and

some rural clinics have closed. In 1993 a Western report evaluated Azerbaijan's sanitation, pharmacies, medical system, medical industry, and medical research and development as below average, relative to similar services in the other former Soviet republics.

In 1987 the leading causes of death in order of occurrence were cardiovascular disease, cancer, respiratory infection, and accidents. The official 1991 infant mortality rate—twenty-five per 1,000 population—was by far the highest among the Transcaucasian nations. International experts estimated an even higher rate, however, if the standard international definition of infant mortality is used.

Social Welfare

The traditional extended family provides an unofficial support system for family members who are elderly or who are full-time students. The official social safety net nominally ensures at least a subsistence income to all citizens, continuing the practice of the Soviet era. Stated benefits include old-age, disability, and survivor pensions; additional allowances for children and supported family members; sick and maternity leave; temporary disability and unemployment compensation for workers; food subsidies; and tax exemptions for designated social groups. Most of these benefits are financed by extrabudgetary funds; in 1992 more than 4.2 million rubles were transferred from the budget to the State Pension Fund, however.

The actual effect of the social welfare system has differed greatly from its stated goals. During the late Soviet period, Azerbaijanis complained that their social benefits ranked near the bottom among the Soviet republics. The economic dislocations that followed independence eroded those benefits even further. In December 1993, the government estimated that 80 percent of the Azerbaijani population was living below the poverty level, even though about 15 percent of the gross domestic product (GDP—see Glossary) was spent on social security benefits.

The minimum monthly wage is set by presidential decree, but several increases in the minimum wage in 1992–93 failed to keep pace with the high rate of inflation. Retirement pensions, based on years of service and average earnings, also fell behind the cost of living in that period.

In the postcommunist era, government price controls have also been used to ease the transition from the centrally

Dentist's office, Baku
Courtesy Oleg Litvin,
Azerbaijan International

planned economy. In 1992 subsidies were introduced to keep prices low for such items as bread, meat, butter, sugar, cooking oil, local transportation, housing, and medical care (see table 9; table 10, Appendix). At that point, the price-support safety net was expected to absorb at least 7 percent of the projected national budget. At the end of 1993, major increases in bread and fuel prices heightened social tensions and triggered riots because compensation to poor people, students, and refugees was considered inadequate.

The Economy

Azerbaijan possesses fertile agricultural lands, rich industrial resources, including considerable oil reserves, and a relatively developed industrial sector. Utilization of those resources in the Soviet period, however, was subject to the usual distortions of centralized planning. In the early 1990s, economic output declined drastically. The major factors in that decline were the deterioration of trade relations with the other former Soviet republics, the conflict in Nagorno-Karabakh, erosion of consumer buying power, and retention of the ruble alongside the national currency. In 1994 the economy remained heavily dependent on the other former republics of the Soviet Union, especially Russia.

The Work Force

According to Azerbaijani statistics, the work force numbered 2.7 million individuals in 1992. Agriculture was the largest area of employment (34 percent), followed by industry (16 percent) and education and culture (12 percent). In the industrial sector, the oil, chemical, and textile industries were major employers (see table 11, Appendix). In spite of the standard communist proclamation that employment was a right and employment was virtually full, large-scale, chronic unemployment had already emerged in the late 1980s, especially among youth and the growing ranks of refugees and displaced persons (see table 12, Appendix). In 1992 unemployment was still officially characterized as a minor problem, affecting some 200,000 people, but in fact the Azerbaijani government vastly underreported this statistic. Underreporting was facilitated by the practice of keeping workers listed as employees in idled industries. Funds set aside by the government to deal with unemployment proved woefully inadequate. One Western economic agency estimated the 1992 gross national product (GNP—see Glossary) as US$18.6 billion and the average per capita GNP as US$2,480, placing Azerbaijan sixth and eighth in those respective categories among the former Soviet republics.

Economic Dislocations

The general economic dislocations within the Soviet Union in the late Gorbachev period hurt Azerbaijan by weakening interrepublic trade links. After the breakup of the Soviet Union, trade links among the former republics weakened further. Azerbaijani enterprises responded by establishing many new trade ties on an ad hoc basis. Although some moves were made toward a market economy, state ownership of the means of production and state direction of the economy still dominated in early 1994.

Despite the economic turmoil caused in 1992 and 1993 by the demise of the Soviet Union and the conflict in Nagorno-Karabakh, the Azerbaijani economy remained in better condition than those of its neighbors Armenia and Georgia and some of the Central Asian states. According to estimates by Western economists, gross industrial production plunged at least 26 percent in 1992 and 10 percent in 1993.

In 1992 poor weather contributed to a decline in production of important cash crops. Crude oil and refinery produc-

Cultivation of tea in Lenkoran' Lowlands
Courtesy Embassy of Azerbaijan, Washington

tion continued a recent downward spiral, reflecting a lack of infrastructure maintenance and other inputs. Inflation took off in early 1992, when many prices were decontrolled, and accelerated throughout the year, reaching an annual rate of 735 percent by October. Inflation for 1993 was estimated at 1,200 percent, a figure exceeded only by rates for Russia and a few other CIS states. Officials tried unsuccessfully to protect the standard of living from inflation by periodically increasing wage payments and taking other measures. In his New Year's message in January 1994, Aliyev acknowledged that during 1993 Azerbaijan had faced a serious economic crisis that led to further declines in the standard of living, but he promised that 1994 would witness positive changes.

Agriculture

The major agricultural cash crops are grapes, cotton, tobacco, citrus fruits, and vegetables. The first three crops

117

account for over half of all production, and the last two together account for an additional 30 percent. Livestock, dairy products, and wine and spirits are also important farm products (see table 13, Appendix).

In the early 1990s, Azerbaijan's agricultural sector required substantial restructuring if it were to realize its vast potential. Prices for agricultural products did not rise as fast as the cost of inputs; the Soviet-era collective farm system discouraged private initiative; equipment in general and the irrigation system in particular were outdated; modern technology had not been introduced widely; and administration of agricultural programs was ineffective.

Most of Azerbaijan's cultivated lands, which total over 1 million hectares, are irrigated by more than 40,000 kilometers of canals and pipelines. The varied climate allows cultivation of a wide variety of crops, ranging from peaches to almonds and from rice to cotton. In the early 1990s, agricultural production contributed about 30 to 40 percent of Azerbaijan's net material product (NMP—see Glossary), while directly employing about one-third of the labor force and providing a livelihood to about half the country's population. In the early postwar decades, Azerbaijan's major cash crops were cotton and tobacco, but in the 1970s grapes became the most productive crop. An anti-alcohol campaign by Moscow in the mid-1980s contributed to a sharp decline in grape production in the late 1980s. In 1991 grapes accounted for over 20 percent of agricultural production, followed closely by cotton.

Production of virtually all crops declined in the early 1990s. In 1990 work stoppages and anti-Soviet demonstrations contributed to declines in agricultural production. The conflict in Nagorno-Karabakh, the site of about one-third of Azerbaijan's croplands, substantially reduced agricultural production beginning in 1989. In 1992 agriculture's contribution to NMP declined by 22 percent. This drop was attributed mainly to cool weather, which reduced cotton and grape harvests, and to the continuation of the Nagorno-Karabakh conflict. The conflict-induced blockade of the Nakhichevan Autonomous Republic also disrupted agriculture there.

An estimated 1,200 state and cooperative farms are in operation in Azerbaijan, with little actual difference between the rights and privileges of state and cooperative holdings. Small private garden plots, constituting only a fraction of total cultivated land, contribute as much as 20 percent of agricultural production and more than half of livestock production. Private landholders do not have equal access, however, to the inputs, services, and financing that would maximize their output.

The Azerbaijani Ministry of Agriculture and Food runs procurement centers dispersed throughout the country for government purchase of most of the tobacco, cotton, tea, silk, and grapes that are produced. The Ministry of Grain and Bread Products runs similar operations that buy a major portion of grain production. Remaining crops are sold in the private sector.

Industry

During World War II, relocated and expanded factories in Azerbaijan produced steel, electrical motors, and finished weaponry for the Soviet Union's war effort. The canning and textile industries were expanded to process foodstuffs and cotton from Azerbaijan's fields. Azerbaijan's postwar industrial economy was based on those wartime activities. Among the key elements of that base were petrochemical-derived products such as plastics and tires, oil-drilling equipment, and processed foods and textiles (see table 14, Appendix). In 1991 the largest share of Azerbaijan's industrial output was contributed by the food industry, followed by light industry (defined to include synthetic and natural textiles, leather goods, carpets, and furniture), fuels, and machine building. Significant food processing and cotton textile operations are located in Gyandzha in western Azerbaijan, and petrochemical-based industries are clustered near Baku. The city of Sumgait, just north of Baku, is the nation's center for steel, iron, and other metallurgical industries.

The Soviet-era Azerbaijan Oil Machinery Company (Azneftemash) controls virtually all of Azerbaijan's oil equipment industry. Once a major exporter of equipment to the rest of the Soviet Union, Azneftemash has remained dependent since 1991 on imports of parts from the other former Soviet republics. The economic decline and the breakup of the union has disrupted imports and caused an estimated output reduction of 27 percent in the Azerbaijani oil equipment industry in 1992.

Energy

Azerbaijan has ample energy resources, including major hydroelectric generating capacity and offshore oil reserves in

119

the Caspian Sea. Despite what amounts to an overall excess of production capacity, fuel shortages and transport problems disrupted generation in the early 1990s. In 1991 Azerbaijan produced 23 billion kilowatt-hours, but near the end of 1992 the country had produced only 16 billion kilowatt-hours. Electricity is generated at major hydroelectric plants on the Mtkvari, Terter (in western Azerbaijan), and Aras rivers (the last a joint project with Iran). A larger share of power comes from oil-fired electric power plants, however. In the late Soviet period, Azerbaijan's power plants were part of the Joint Transcaucasian Power Grid shared with Armenia and Georgia, but Azerbaijan cut off power to Armenia as a result of the conflict over Nagorno-Karabakh.

Azerbaijan has exported oil and gas to Russia since the late nineteenth century. The birthplace of the oil-refining industry at the beginning of the twentieth century, Azerbaijan was the world's leading producer of petroleum. During World War II, about 70 percent of the Soviet Union's petroleum output came from the small republic. After World War II, when oil output from the Volga-Ural oil fields in Russia increased, Azerbaijan lost its position as a dominant producer of Soviet oil. When the Soviet Union disintegrated, Azerbaijan was producing 60 percent of Soviet oil extraction machinery and spare parts but less than 2 percent of the union's oil.

Azerbaijan's four major offshore oil fields in the Caspian Sea are Gunesli, Cirak, Azeri, and Kepez. In 1992 the Gunesli field accounted for about 60 percent of Azerbaijani oil production. Crude oil production has decreased in recent years, mainly because of a weak global market, well maturity, inadequate investment, and outdated equipment. According to Azerbaijani estimates, for the first seven months of 1993 compared with the same period in 1992, crude oil production declined 7.1 percent, gasoline refining 2.8 percent, and diesel fuel production 19.9 percent. These rates of decline compare favorably, however, with those experienced in the oil production and refining industries of Russia, Turkmenistan, and other former Soviet republics in the early 1990s.

Some oil is shipped by train to Black Sea ports in Russia and Ukraine, and some is shipped by tanker to northern Iran. Pipeline shipment has been slowed by infrastructure problems. One old oil pipeline from Azerbaijan to the Georgian port of Batumi on the Black Sea is inoperable, and the Russian pipeline is unavailable because that line is already at capacity. Azer-

Baku Harbor
Courtesy Azerbaijan International

baijan's oil production is processed at two refineries near Baku. Because domestic oil production has not matched refining capacity in recent years, the refineries also process Kazakh and Russian oil.

Russia, Ukraine, and other former Soviet republics have been involved in contentious negotiations with Azerbaijan over oil payment. Azerbaijan has sought prices close to world market rates for its oil as large payment arrearages have developed with several customer states. Azerbaijanis seek "fair payment" for their oil from Russia, pointing out that during the Soviet period Azerbaijani oil was sold far below market prices to support the Soviet economy.

Azerbaijan has encouraged joint ventures and other agreements with foreign oil firms, and a consortium has been formed with Russia, Kazakhstan, and Oman to build an oil pipeline to Mediterranean, Persian Gulf, or Black Sea ports. In the planning stage, Russia advocated a Black Sea route, whereas Western oil companies, also interested in Azerbaijan's oil, preferred a Mediterranean terminus for a pipeline used in common. In March 1993, Turkey and Azerbaijan agreed on a pipeline traversing Iran, the Nakhichevan Autonomous Republic, and southern Turkey to reach the Mediterranean. In 1993 other negotiations defined terms of exploitation by eight Western oil companies in two Caspian oil fields and established a profit-sharing ratio between Azerbaijan and its partners. In late 1993, Russia's role in the oil industry also increased with the signing of new bilateral agreements.

Azerbaijan has proven natural gas reserves of 2 trillion cubic meters, and a much larger amount is present in association with offshore oil deposits. Although the price of natural gas in Azerbaijan has remained low compared with world prices, in 1991 about half the gas brought to the surface was burned off or vented, while consumption of fuel oil increased. Since 1991 Azerbaijan's production has declined to a level that meets only about 35 percent of domestic needs, which amounted to 17 billion cubic meters per year in 1993. The major sources of natural gas imports are Turkmenistan, Kazakhstan, and Iran. Experts consider that exploitation of untapped natural gas deposits would enhance Azerbaijan's domestic fuel balance and provide substantial export income.

Economic Reform

Azerbaijan's prospects for movement toward a market economy are enhanced by a fairly well-developed infrastructure, an educated labor force, diversity in both agricultural and industrial production, and yet-untapped oil reserves. Obstacles to reform include the rigidity of remaining Soviet economic structures, the Nagorno-Karabakh conflict, continued trade dependence on the other former Soviet republics, insufficient economic expertise to guide the transition, and capital stock that is inefficient and environmentally hazardous.

Price Liberalization

In January 1992, about 70 to 80 percent of producer and consumer prices were decontrolled, although prices for commodities such as gasoline were artificially increased. Further rounds of price liberalization took place in April, September, and December 1992. Because most industries are still monopolies, price-setting is supervised by the Antimonopoly Committee, which approves requests for price increases. Because the state still procures much of Azerbaijan's agricultural production, prices are set by negotiations between the state and producers.

Retail price inflation surged after the first round of price liberalization in January 1992. Thereafter, the monthly rate eased somewhat, averaging about 24 percent during most of 1992. According to official figures, in 1993 average living expenses exceeded income by about 50 percent. The ratio of expenses to income was about the same in Kazakhstan and worse in Armenia and Turkmenistan. Although prices for items such as bread and fuel remained controlled during 1993, in November 1993 the government announced price rises because commodities were being smuggled out of Azerbaijan to be sold elsewhere where prices were higher. By the end of 1993, it was reported that the minimum weekly wage would not even buy one loaf of bread and that hundreds of thousands of refugees in Azerbaijan "simply face starvation," a situation that heightened social and political instability.

Privatization

From the earliest days of Azerbaijan's independence, the country had a vigorous, small-scale private economy whose most urgent need was unambiguous legislation that would legitimize its operations and allow expansion. A privatization law passed in January 1993 was not implemented fully in the year following. Privatization plans envisioned sales, auctions, and joint-stock enterprises. Small retail establishments would be privatized by auction, and medium-sized and large enterprises would be privatized by a combination of auctions and joint-stock programs. Retail establishments were supposed to be privatized fully by the end of 1993, but this goal was not met. Housing was also to be privatized by transferring ownership to the present tenants. At the end of 1993, land redistribution was stalled by disagreement over the choice between private ownership and long-term leaseholding, over optimum terms for either of those arrangements, and over the distribution of agricultural equipment.

The Budget

To lessen the budgetary impact of losing subsidies from the Soviet Union, beginning in 1992 a value-added tax (VAT—see Glossary) and excise taxes were introduced to replace sales and turnover taxes. The new taxes enabled Azerbaijan to maintain only a small state budgetary deficit for 1992 (see table 15, Appendix). The deficit came mainly from increases in wages and from defense and refugee expenses related to the conflict in Nagorno-Karabakh. State-owned enterprises continued to survive on liberal bank credits and interenterprise borrowing, which caused the accumulation of sizable debts. Substantial increases in defense expenditures (from 1.3 percent of GDP in 1991 to 7.6 percent in 1992) drastically reduced expenditures for consumer subsidies in bread and fuels, as well as government investment and other support for enterprises. Increased salaries for civil servants also increased the 1992 deficit.

In mid-1992 Azerbaijan was not receiving enough printed rubles from Moscow to meet wage payments, so it introduced its own currency, the manat (for value of the manat—see Glossary). Because domestic financial transactions still involved Russian banks and because many rubles remained in circulation, the ruble remained as an alternate currency. After ruble notes became more plentiful in late 1992, the manat remained a small fraction of circulating currency. In September 1993, Azerbaijan planned to make the manat the sole national currency, but the weakness of the Azerbaijani monetary and financial systems forced postponement of that move. The manat finally became the sole currency in January 1994.

Banking

Under the Soviet system, Azerbaijani banks were subordinate to central banks in Moscow and elsewhere in Russia. Bank funds were distributed according to a single state plan, and republic banks had little input into the raising or allocation of funds. In early 1992, former Soviet banks were incorporated into the National Bank of Azerbaijan (NBA). The 1992 Law on Banks and Banking Activity and the Law on the National Bank established the NBA as the top level of the new system and commercial banks (state- and privately owned) on the second level. However, in 1993 the system was undermined by poor technology, large unresolved debts among state-owned enterprises, irregular participation by enterprises, and bank delays in transferring funds. The main bank for the exchange of funds among private and state enterprises is the Industrial Investment Joint Stock Commercial Bank.

Foreign Trade

As during the Soviet era, Azerbaijan's economy depends heavily on foreign trade, including commerce with the other former Soviet republics. In the late 1980s, exports and imports averaged about 40 percent of GDP. At that time, Azerbaijan's exports to other Soviet republics averaged 46 percent of GDP and over 90 percent of total exports; its imports from those republics averaged 37 percent of GDP and nearly 80 percent of total imports. In the early 1990s, Azerbaijan's main trading partners in the CIS were Russia, Ukraine, Kazakhstan, and Belarus, in that order.

In the last years of the Soviet Union, Azerbaijan showed a net trade surplus. After a sharp decline in the net trade surplus in 1990, oil sales outside the Soviet Union boosted the surplus in 1991 and 1992. In 1992 Azerbaijan made major gains in hard- currency exports, mainly from selling refined oil products abroad at world prices. Trade with CIS countries, determined by yearly bilateral agreements, declined significantly after 1991. Although products from those countries still dominated Azerbaijan's imports, less than half of exports went to them. Important obstacles were the bypassing of the state order system in the Baltic states and Russia, the high VAT on some items, and the complexity of central-bank credit systems in the transitional period. Trade agreements were negotiated for 1993 with Belarus, Estonia, Kazakhstan, Latvia, Lithuania, Moldova, Russia, Turkmenistan, and Ukraine.

In 1990 Azerbaijan's major trading partners outside the Soviet Union were led by Germany and Poland (see table 16, Appendix). In 1992 Azerbaijan's main non-CIS trading partners were Britain and Iran. According to government statistics for 1993, Azerbaijan had a large trade surplus with Russia, and more than US$60 billion was owed Azerbaijan by customers in Greece, Iran, and Turkey. Through 1993 Turkish enterprises, considered a primary source of new foreign capital, refrained from large-scale investment in Azerbaijan because of concerns about political instability in Baku. Disagreements with Russia and Turkey delayed construction of an oil pipeline that would connect Baku with the Mediterranean through Turkish territory (see Energy, this ch.).

In the early 1990s, increasing numbers of products were sold directly by Azerbaijani enterprises to foreign enterprises without government export licenses, although the inefficient state-managed trade system of the Soviet era remained in place.

In 1993 the Ministry of Foreign Economic Relations monitored all foreign trade and supervised the export of petroleum products and other strategic items. In late 1993, government control was tightened because most private firms were keeping hard-currency foreign-trade earnings outside Azerbaijan.

Transportation and Telecommunications

Azerbaijan's transportation system is extensive for a country of its size and level of economic development. Analysts attribute this advantage to the fact that when Azerbaijan was part of the Soviet Union, its economy was heavily geared to export of petroleum and to transshipment of goods across the Caucasus. The system is burdened by an extensive bureaucracy, however, that makes prompt equipment repair difficult, and the country's economic problems have delayed replacement of aging equipment and facilities.

In 1990 Azerbaijan had 36,700 kilometers of roads, 31,800 kilometers of which were paved. One of the country's two main routes parallels the Caspian Sea coast from Russia to Iran, passing through Baku (see fig. 10). The other, Route M27, leads west out of the capital to the Georgian border. A major branch from this route heads south through Stepanakert, capital of Nagorno-Karabakh. All major towns have a paved road connection with one of the principal routes. An extensive intercity bus service is the primary mode of intercity travel. Maintenance of the system has deteriorated since independence in 1991, however, and one study estimated that 60 percent of the main highways were in bad condition, resulting in excessive wear on vehicles and tires and in poor fuel consumption.

Azerbaijan had 2,090 kilometers of rail lines in 1990, excluding several small industrial lines. Most lines are 1.520-meter broad gauge, and the principal routes are electrified. In the 1990s, the rail system carried the vast majority of the country's freight. As with the highway system, one of the two main lines parallels the Caspian Sea coast from Russia to Iran before heading west to Turkey, and the other closely parallels Route M27 from Baku to the Georgian border. A major spur also parallels the highway to Stepanakert. Another smaller rail line begins just west of Baku and hugs the Iranian border to provide the only rail link to Azerbaijan's Nakhichevan Autonomous Republic, isolated southwest of Armenia. Passenger service from Baku to Erevan has been suspended, and service from Baku to Tbilisi has sometimes been disrupted because of the Nagorno-Karabakh conflict. In 1994 passenger service from Baku to Iran also was halted. Trains making the forty-three-hour trip to Moscow, however, still operate three times daily. The government estimates that 700 kilometers, or about one-third, of the rail system are in such poor condition that reconstruction is necessary. Much of the system has speed restrictions because of the poor condition of the rails.

Baku has a modest subway system with twenty-nine kilometers of heavy-rail lines. The system has eighteen stations and is arranged in two lines that cross in the center of the city. Another seventeen kilometers, under construction in 1994, would add twelve more stations to the system.

In 1992 Azerbaijan had twenty-six airfields with paved surfaces. Baku International Airport, twenty-eight kilometers southwest of the city, is the country's principal airport. The number of international air passengers is higher in Azerbaijan than in Armenia and Georgia, with most air traffic moving between Baku and cities in the former Soviet Union. Besides flights to Russia, Azerbaijan Airlines provides service to Turkey and Iran, and direct flights on foreign carriers are available to Pakistan and Tajikistan.

Although situated on an excellent natural harbor, Baku has not developed into a major international port because of its location on the landlocked Caspian Sea. The port serves mostly as a transshipment point for goods (primarily petroleum products and lumber) crossing the Caspian Sea and destined for places to the west, or for passenger service to ports on the eastern or southern shores of the Caspian Sea. The port has seventeen berths, of which five are dedicated for transport of crude oil and petroleum products, two are used for passengers, and the remaining ten handle timber or other cargo. The port can accommodate ships up to 12,000 tons, and its facilities include portal cranes, tugboats, and equipment for handling petroleum and petroleum products. The port area has 10,000 square meters of covered storage and 28,700 square meters of open storage.

Baku is the center of a major oil- and gas-producing region, and major long-distance pipelines radiate from the region's oil fields to all neighboring areas. Pipelines are generally high-capacity lines and have diameters of either 1,020 or 1,220 millimeters. The main petroleum pipeline pumps crude oil from the onshore and offshore Caspian fields near Baku west across Azerbaijan and Georgia to the Black Sea port of Batumi.

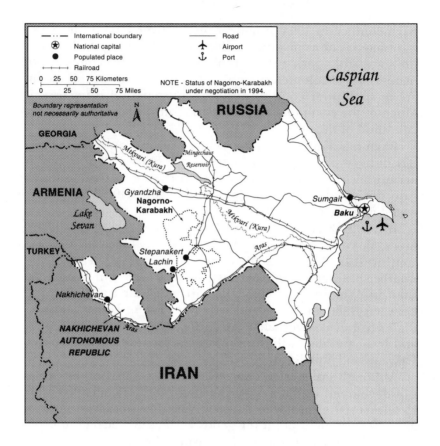

Figure 10. Transportation System of Azerbaijan, 1994

There, the oil is either exported in its crude form or processed at Batumi's refinery. Two natural gas lines parallel the petroleum line as far as Tbilisi, where they turn north across the Caucasus Mountains to join the grid of natural gas pipelines that supply cities throughout Russia and Eastern Europe. A spur extends off these main gas pipelines in western Azerbaijan to deliver gas to Nakhichevan. This spur crosses Armenian territory, however, and in 1994 its status was unclear. Altogether, in 1994 Azerbaijan had 1,130 kilometers of crude oil pipeline, 630 kilometers of pipeline for petroleum products, and 1,240 kilometers of natural gas pipeline.

In 1991 some 644,000 telephone lines were in operation, providing nine telephones per 100 persons. At that time, 200,000 Azerbaijanis were on waiting lists for telephone installation. Azerbaijan's telephone system is connected with other CIS republics by cable and microwave, but connections to non-CIS countries go through Moscow. In 1992 Turkey provided support for installation of an International Telecommunications Satellite Organization (Intelsat) satellite station in Baku, providing access to 200 countries through Turkey. Azerbaijan receives Turkish and Iranian television programming by satellite, and domestic and Russian broadcasts are received locally.

Government and Politics

In the late 1980s, the advent of Gorbachev's policy of *glasnost* in Moscow encouraged vocal opposition to the ruling Azerbaijani Communist Party (ACP). In 1989 the central opposition role went to the Azerbaijani Popular Front (APF), which was able to capture the presidency in the 1992 election. But failure to resolve the disastrous conflict in Nagorno-Karabakh continued to destabilize Azerbaijani regimes throughout the early 1990s. Growing masses of disaffected refugees pressed vociferously for military victory and quickly shifted their support from one leader to another when losses occurred, negating efforts to establish solid political institutions at home or to make concessions that might provide a diplomatic solution to the Nagorno-Karabakh conflict. In 1993 the APF leadership was overthrown, and former communist official Heydar Aliyev was installed as president.

The Appearance of Opposition Parties

The political and social groups that sprang up in Azerbaijan in the late 1980s were initially termed "informal organizations" because they were not yet recognized as legal under Soviet practice. By the end of 1988, about forty such organizations had emerged, many of them focused on nationalism or anti-Armenian issues. The ACP was increasingly regarded as illegitimate by the population, especially after the Soviet army intervened to protect the communist regime in January 1990.

The Azerbaijani Popular Front

Widespread discontent with ACP rule led to the formation of the APF in March 1989 by intellectuals, including journalists and researchers belonging to the Azerbaijani Academy of Sciences. The APF's founding congress in July 1989 elected Abulfaz Elchibey party chairman. The APF characterized itself as an umbrella organization composed of smaller parties and groups and like-minded individuals. A central plank of its program was rejection of self-determination for Nagorno-Karabakh and defense of Azerbaijani territorial integrity. In its initial policy statements, the APF advocated decentralization of economic and political power from Moscow to Baku rather than Azerbaijani independence from the Soviet Union. Nevertheless, the ACP refused to recognize the APF.

Within months of its founding, the APF had hardened its position, launching a series of industrial strikes and rail service disruptions calculated to force recognition by the ACP. By the fall of 1989, the APF was at the forefront of Azerbaijani public opinion on the issue of national sovereignty for Nagorno-Karabakh, and the ACP recognized the APF as an opposition party. The APF used its influence on the Azerbaijani Supreme Soviet, the republic's parliament, in advocating the Law on Sovereignty that was passed in October 1989. In January 1990, APF-led demonstrations against the ACP brought Soviet military intervention. In early 1992, the APF played an important role in organizing demonstrations against then-president Ayaz Mutalibov.

Party Configuration after 1991

Two small parties, the Independent Democratic Party (IDP) and the National Independence Party (NIP), were formed by former members of the APF in early 1992. The IDP was led by Leyla Yunosova, a prominent intellectual who had helped form the APF, and the NIP was led by Etibar Mamedov, a frequent critic of Elchibey's rule and APF domination of the electoral process. Azerbaijani military defeats in March 1993 led Mamedov to call for Elchibey's resignation. Mamedov initially approved Elchibey's ouster by Aliyev and the subsequent referendum on his rule.

The ACP formally disbanded in September 1991 during a wave of popular revulsion against the role it played in supporting the Moscow coup attempted against Gorbachev the previous month. Nevertheless, former leaders and members of the ACP continue to play a role in the family- and patronage-based political system, and Aliyev's faction regained its preeminent position. The ACP was revived formally in December 1993 at a "restorative" congress, after which it reported having 3,000 members. When Aliyev ran for president in 1993, he combined former communists and other minor groups into the New

Azerbaijan Party, which became the governing party when Aliyev was elected.

Under election legislation passed since Aliyev's accession, a party must have at least 1,000 members to be legally registered by the Ministry of Justice. Party membership is forbidden to government officials in agencies of the judiciary, law enforcement, security, border defense, customs, taxation, finance, and the state-run media. The president and members of the clergy are likewise enjoined. Parties are not allowed to accept foreign funding or to establish cells in government agencies. The government has banned parties that reject Azerbaijan's territorial integrity or inflame racial, national, or religious enmity.

Legislative Politics

Parliamentary elections were held in September 1990, under a state of martial law (see After Communist Rule, this ch.). The opposition coalition led by the APF gained only about forty seats in the 350-seat Azerbaijani Supreme Soviet. Communists received the balance of seats in what the APF and others described as fraudulent elections. Most would-be international observers had been expelled from the republic by September. Bowing to massive popular demonstrations calling for the dissolution of the communist-dominated Supreme Soviet and to concerted pressure by the APF and other oppositionists, in November 1991 the Azerbaijani Supreme Soviet voted to establish a fifty-deputy National Council, or Melli-Majlis. This council, a "mini-legislature" that met in continuous session, was divided equally between former communists and the opposition. Because of the Supreme Soviet's complicity in the effort to bring Mutalibov back to power in May 1992, the APF forced the Supreme Soviet to convene, elect APF official Isa Gambarov as acting president, dissolve itself, and cede its power to the Melli-Majlis pending new parliamentary elections.

Having repeatedly postponed the elections, the Melli-Majlis remained the sole legislative authority within Azerbaijan in early 1994. The Melli-Majlis proved generally amenable to Elchibey's policies, but in 1993 the worsening military situation in Nagorno-Karabakh brought increasing criticism. In his first six months as president, Aliyev gained support from the Melli-Majlis for most of his proposals.

The Presidential Election of 1992

The presidential election of June 1992 was the first in more than seventy years not held under communist control. Five candidates were on the ballot, seeking election to a five-year term. The election featured the unprecedented use of television, posters, and other media by multiple candidates to communicate platforms and solicit votes. The candidates included APF leader Elchibey, former parliament speaker Yakub Mamedov, Movement for Democratic Reforms leader and Minister of Justice Ilias Ismailov, National Democratic Group leader Rafik Abdullayev, and Union of Democratic Intelligentsia candidate Nizami Suleymanov. Two other candidates, from the NIP and the APF, withdrew from the race during the campaign. To register, each candidate had to collect at least 20,000 signatures and present them to the Central Electoral Commission. Aliyev was unable to run because of a constitutional provision barring candidates over sixty-five years of age. The government agreed to allow international observers to monitor the election. Etibar Mamedov, Elchibey's main rival in the polls, dropped out of the race a few days before the election, calling for rule by a coalition government and the postponement of balloting until Azerbaijan's state of war with Armenia ended.

Elchibey's election as president signaled a break in communist party dominance of Azerbaijani politics. He received 59.4 percent of more than 3.3 million votes cast. The runner-up, Suleymanov, made a surprise showing of 33 percent of the vote by promising Azerbaijanis instant wealth and victory in Nagorno-Karabakh. No other candidate garnered as much as 5 percent of the vote.

Elchibey had been a student of Arabic philology, a translator, and a college instructor. In 1975 the KGB imprisoned him for two years for anti-Soviet activities. In a postelection address to the nation, he announced a stabilization phase based on the transfer of power to his democratic faction. When that phase ended in 1993, constitutional, economic, and cultural reforms would be implemented, according to this plan. His top domestic policy priorities—creation of a national army and a national currency backed by gold reserves—were seen as necessary elements for national sovereignty. Despite the new president's intentions, the war in Nagorno-Karabakh dominated politics, and Elchibey and his party steadily lost influence and popular appeal because of continual military losses, a worsening economy, political stalemate, and government corruption.

The Coup of June 1993

In June 1993, an unsuccessful government attempt to disarm mutinous paramilitary forces precipitated the fall of Azer-

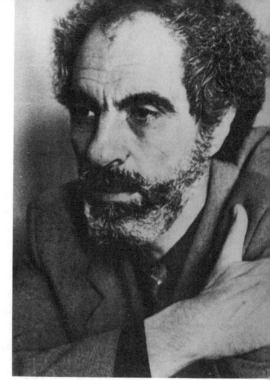

Abulfaz Elchibey, first elected president of Azerbaijan, 1992 Courtesy S. Rasimindir, Azerbaijan International

baijan's fourth government since independence and provided the opportunity for Aliyev's return to power. The erstwhile communist's reappearance was part of a trend in which members of the former elites in various parts of the old Soviet sphere reclaimed authority. Suret Huseynov, a one-time troop commander in Nagorno-Karabakh dismissed by Elchibey, led the paramilitary forces that triggered the president's removal. In support of one of Elchibey's rivals, Huseynov had amassed troops and weaponry (largely obtained from the departing Russian military) in his home territory. He then easily defeated army forces sent to defeat him and precipitated a government crisis by marching toward Baku with several thousand troops.

Huseynov's exploits thoroughly discredited the Elchibey APF government in the minds of most Azerbaijanis. After several top government officials were fired or resigned and after massed demonstrators demanded a change in government, Elchibey endorsed Aliyev's election as chairman of the Melli-Majlis. After a brief attempt to retain the presidency, Elchibey fled Baku in mid-June as Huseynov's forces approached.

Aliyev announced his immediate assumption of power as acting head of state, and within a week a bare quorum of Melli-Majlis legislators, mostly former communist deputies, formally transferred Elchibey's powers to Aliyev until a new president could be elected. Aliyev then replaced Elchibey's ministers and

133

other officials with his own appointees. Huseynov received the post of prime minister. The legislature also granted Huseynov control over the "power" ministries of defense, internal affairs, and security.

In late July 1993, Aliyev convinced the legislature to hold a popular vote of confidence on Elchibey's moribund presidency and an extension of a state of emergency that had existed since April 1993 because of military setbacks. Although the APF boycotted the referendum, more than 90 percent of the electorate reportedly turned out to cast a 97 percent vote of no-confidence in Elchibey's rule. This outcome buttressed Aliyev's position and opened the way for new presidential elections.

In early September 1993, the Melli-Majlis scheduled new presidential elections for October 3, 1993. Removal of the maximum age requirement in the election law allowed Aliyev to run. Aliyev's position was strengthened further in August when paramilitary forces defeated a rebel warlord who had seized several areas of southern Azerbaijan and declared an autonomous republic of Talish-Mugan.

Early in his tenure as acting president, Aliyev stated that his political goals were to prevent civil war, regain territory lost to Armenia during the Nagorno-Karabakh conflict, and ensure the territorial integrity of Azerbaijan. Aliyev claimed that freedom of speech and human rights would be respected in Azerbaijan, although he also called for continuing a state of emergency that would ban political rallies. Huseynov had stated in June that the Azerbaijani government would pursue a negotiated settlement in Nagorno-Karabakh, but, if that failed, a military victory was the goal. He added that the government focus would be on improving the Azerbaijani armed forces, stabilizing the economy, and securing food for the population.

Aliyev and the Presidential Election of October 1993

Aliyev and two minor party candidates ran in presidential elections held in October 1993. Voter turnout was about 90 percent, of which almost 99 percent voted for Aliyev. Many international observers declared the elections biased because no major opposition candidates ran, and reporting by the mass media favored Aliyev and failed to report views of the other candidates or of the APF. Aliyev was sworn in as Azerbaijan's president on October 10.

Aliyev was born in 1923 in Nakhichevan of blue-collar Azerbaijani parents. He crowned a career in Soviet intelligence and counterintelligence services by reaching the post of chairman of the Azerbaijani branch of the KGB in 1967. Appointed first secretary of the ACP Central Committee beginning in 1969, Aliyev purged Azerbaijani nationalists and directed Russification and state economic development activities with notable success through the 1970s. His support of Soviet intervention in Afghanistan in 1979 brought recognition in Moscow and the Order of Lenin from First Secretary Leonid Brezhnev, and in 1982 Aliyev became a full member of the Politburo of the Communist Party of the Soviet Union. From 1982 to 1987, he was also first deputy chairman of the Soviet Council of Ministers.

In 1987 Gorbachev ousted Aliyev from the Politburo and relieved him as party leader in Azerbaijan. Soon after returning to Nakhichevan in 1990, Aliyev was elected overwhelmingly to the Supreme Soviet of the Nakhichevan Autonomous Republic on a nationalist platform. The next year, he resigned his communist party membership. After the failed August 1991 coup in Moscow, he called for total independence for Azerbaijan and denounced Mutalibov, who was then aspiring to the presidency, for supporting the coup. In late 1991, Aliyev built a power base as chairman of the Nakhichevan Supreme Soviet, from which he asserted Nakhichevan's near-total independence from Baku.

The Constitution

The preparation of a new constitution to replace the 1978 document (which had been based on the 1977 Soviet constitution) began in 1992, but adoption has been repeatedly delayed by civil and political turmoil. Pending the adoption of a new constitution, the fundamental document in the early 1990s was the October 18, 1991, Act of Independence, which government authorities have described as the basis for a new constitution. Meanwhile, the provisions of the 1978 constitution are valid if they do not violate or contradict the Act of Independence. The act declares that Azerbaijan is a secular, democratic, and unitary state, with equality of all citizens before the law. Freedoms enshrined in the Universal Declaration of Human Rights and other international human rights documents are upheld, and the right to form political parties is stipulated. The Act of Independence also proclaims Azerbaijan's territorial integrity and its sovereignty over all its territory. In October 1993, the Melli-Majlis revised the existing constitution of 1978, retaining it for the time being. Finally deleted were the document's many references to "Soviet" and "communist" institutions and philosophy.

The Court System

The legal system of Azerbaijan has changed little from the system of the Soviet period. The national Supreme Court serves as a court of appeals; below it are two levels of judicial jurisdiction, the district and municipal courts. These courts, supposedly independent, are not immune to political manipulation, as evidenced by Aliyev's ouster of the chief justice of the Supreme Court in July 1993 because of the judge's support for Elchibey and the APF.

Trials are generally public, and defendants have the right to choose their own attorney, to be present at their own trials, to confront witnesses, to present evidence, and to appeal the verdict. In cases involving national security or sex offenses, a judge may decide to hold a closed trial. Despite the other stipulated rights of the defendant, the presumption of innocence has not been incorporated specifically into the criminal code. Thus the decision of the state prosecutor to bring a case to trial has considerable bearing on the final verdict.

Human Rights and the Media

Ethnic conflict between Armenians and Azerbaijanis has resulted in widespread human rights violations by vigilante groups and local authorities. During the Elchibey period, the minister of internal affairs was replaced after admitting to numerous human rights abuses. Lezgians in Azerbaijan have complained of human rights abuses such as restrictions on educational opportunities in their native language (see Smaller Ethnic Minorities, this ch.). In the early 1990s, Amnesty International and Helsinki Watch cited numerous cases of arbitrary arrest and torture, including incidents that had occurred since Aliyev assumed power in 1993. These organizations and several foreign governments protested against the arrest and beating of hundreds of APF and other political and government officials and raids on APF offices, all after the change of government in mid-1993. At one point, Isa Kamber, a former speaker of the Melli-Majlis, was seized in the legislative chamber and held for two months. In late 1993, other APF officials were reportedly arrested for antigovernment activity, and Aliyev asserted that APF members were plotting an armed uprising against him.

Refugees from Nagorno-Karabakh conflict, summer 1993
Courtesy Oleg Litvin, Azerbaijan International

Based on these and other incidents, in late 1993 the international human rights monitoring group Freedom House downgraded Azerbaijan to the rank of world states adjudged "not free." Nevertheless, Aliyev has proclaimed Azerbaijani adherence to international human rights standards, and in December 1993 he signed the CSCE Paris Accords on democracy and human rights.

News media censorship and other constraints on human rights, tightened after Aliyev came to power, were eased somewhat in September 1993 with the lifting of the national state of emergency. In the face of a growing political crisis in late 1993 caused by heavy military losses, however, many in the Azerbaijani government urged Aliyev to declare another period of emergency rule. Instead, he announced several measures to "tighten public discipline," including curfews and the creation of military tribunals to judge military deserters and draft evaders.

In late November 1993, the legislature refused to pass an Aliyev-backed press bill restricting news media freedom in the name of ensuring national unity. Nevertheless, efforts to restrict the media continued, and passage of a law on military censorship in December 1993 raised concerns among journalists that new restrictions would be imposed on a broad scale. At the end of 1993, the only newspaper publishing house, Azerbaijan, was under government control. The state was able to curtail the supply of printing materials to independent publishers because most of those items came from Russia. Meanwhile, rising prices cut newspaper and magazine subscriptions by over 50 percent in early 1994. Television, the preferred information source for most Azerbaijanis, was controlled by the government, which operated the only national television channel.

Foreign Relations

Azerbaijan carried out some diplomatic activities during its troubled first independence period between 1918 and 1920. In September 1920, newly formed Soviet Azerbaijan signed a treaty with Russia unifying the military forces, the economy, and the foreign trade of the two countries, although the fiction of Azerbaijani autonomy in conducting foreign affairs was maintained. At that time, Azerbaijan established diplomatic relations with six countries, sending diplomatic representatives to Germany and Finland. The Ministry of Foreign Affairs in Moscow initially used Azerbaijani diplomats to increase Soviet influence in the Middle East through missions in Turkey, Iran, and Afghanistan, but most transborder contacts by Azerbaijanis had been eliminated by the 1930s. In the post-World War II period, the Azerbaijani Ministry of Foreign Affairs could issue limited visas for travel to Iran only. Iran also maintained a consulate in Baku.

The Foreign Policy Establishment

After regaining its independence in 1991, Azerbaijan faced reorganization of its minuscule foreign policy establishment. This process involved creating or upgrading various functional and geographical departments within the Ministry of Foreign Affairs, recruiting and training diplomats, and establishing and staffing embassies abroad. Because of the complexity of these tasks, few embassies were established during the first months of independence. Full diplomatic relations, including mutual exchanges of missions, were first established with Turkey, the United States, and Iran.

Post-Soviet Diplomacy

Even before the breakup of the Soviet Union, the Azerbaijani diplomatic establishment had become more active, primarily with the goal of countering a worldwide Armenian information campaign on the Nagorno-Karabakh issue. Initiatives in this policy included establishing contacts with Azerbaijani émigrés living in the United States and reinforcing diplomatic connections with Turkey, Iran, and Israel.

After the breakup of the Soviet Union, most nations moved quickly to recognize Azerbaijan's independence, and several established full diplomatic relations within the first year. The first to do so was Turkey in January 1992. During his presidency, Elchibey stressed close relations with Turkey, which he saw as the best hope for arbitrating an end to the Nagorno-Karabakh conflict. He also endorsed unification of the Azerbaijani populations of his country and northern Iran and, to that end, autonomy for the Iranian Azerbaijanis—a stand that alienated the Iranian government.

During the June 1993 coup, Turkey expressed support for Elchibey, but Aliyev and Turkish authorities subsequently expressed willingness to continue cordial relations. Relations did cool somewhat in the second half of 1993 as Aliyev sought to improve relations with Iran and Russia, which had flagged under Elchibey.

Meanwhile, the failure of arbitration efforts by the Minsk Group, which included Russia, Turkey, and the United States, had frustrated both Armenia and Azerbaijan by mid-1993. The Minsk Group was sponsored by the CSCE, which in the early 1990s undertook arbitration in several Caucasus conflicts under the organization's broad mandate for peacekeeping in Europe (see Threats of Fragmentation, ch. 3). Aliyev's alternative strategies included requesting personal involvement by Russia's President Boris N. Yeltsin, who began six months of shuttle diplomacy among the capitals involved, and initiation of direct talks with Armenian leaders in Nagorno-Karabakh, a step that Elchibey had avoided. Throughout the last half of 1993, the new contacts ran concurrently with formal meetings convened by the Minsk Group to arrange a cease-fire.

To broaden its relations with nations both East and West, Azerbaijan joined a number of international and regional organizations, including the UN, the CSCE, the Organization of the Islamic Conference, the International Monetary Fund (IMF— see Glossary), the European Bank for Reconstruction and Development, and the Black Sea Economic Cooperation Organization. Azerbaijan has observer status in the General Agreement on Tariffs and Trade.

In the early 1990s, the primary criterion governing Azerbaijan's relations with foreign states and organizations was their stance on Azerbaijani sovereignty in Nagorno-Karabakh. Most governments and international organizations formally support the concept of territorial integrity, so this criterion has not restricted most of Azerbaijan's diplomatic efforts. Relations with some states have been affected, however. For example, in 1992 the United States Congress placed restrictions on United States aid to Azerbaijan pending the lifting of the Azerbaijani economic blockade on Armenia and cessation of offensive military actions against Armenia and Nagorno-Karabakh.

In messages and interviews early in his administration, Aliyev asserted that his new government would not alter Azerbaijan's domestic and foreign policies and that his country would seek good relations with all countries, especially its neighbors, including Russia. He criticized the uneven relations that existed between Azerbaijan and Russia during the Elchibey regime. At the same time, Aliyev stressed that he viewed Azerbaijan as an independent state that should never again be "someone's vassal or colony." In the summer of 1993, Aliyev issued a blanket plea to the United States, Turkey, Russia, the UN, and the CSCE to work more resolutely toward settlement of the Nagorno-Karabakh conflict. Later that year, he sought repeal of the Azerbaijan clause of the United States Freedom Support Act, which had been amended in 1992 to prohibit United States government assistance to Azerbaijan.

Relations with Former Soviet Republics

Although Elchibey stressed Azerbaijani independence from Moscow, he signed a friendship treaty with Russia on October 12, 1992, calling for mutual assistance in the case of aggression directed at either party and pledging mutual protection of the rights of the other's resident citizens. Between that time and the coup of 1993, however, Elchibey accused Russia of aiding Armenia in Nagorno-Karabakh, and Russia accused Elchibey of mistreating the Russian minority in Azerbaijan. Relations improved with the return to power of Aliyev, who pledged to uphold and strengthen Azerbaijan's ties to Russia. Russia's official position on Nagorno-Karabakh was strict nonintervention barring an invitation to mediate from both sides; in the Russian view, Azerbaijani territory seized by Armenia was to be returned, however. In early 1994, seizure of property from Russian citizens in Azerbaijan (mostly to house refugees from Nagorno-Karabakh) remained a source of irritation.

Azerbaijan's role in the CIS changed drastically in the early 1990s. After Azerbaijan signed the Alma-Ata Declaration as a founding member of the CIS in December 1991, the legislature voted in October 1992 against ratifying this membership. However, Azerbaijan retained observer status, and its representatives attended some CIS functions. Aliyev's announcement in September 1993 that Azerbaijan would rejoin the CIS brought a heated debate in the legislature, which finally approved membership. Aliyev then signed the CIS charter, its Treaty on Collective Security, and an agreement on economic cooperation. Relations with former Soviet republics in Central Asia also were uneven after independence. Elchibey's advocacy of the overthrow of President Islam Karimov of Uzbekistan caused particular diplomatic problems with that country. In keeping with the policy of rapprochement with the CIS, Aliyev began improving ties with Central Asian leaders in the second half of 1993.

National Security

From the very beginning of its existence as a post-Soviet independent republic, Azerbaijan faced a single compelling national security issue: its enduring struggle with Armenian forces in Nagorno-Karabakh and the surrounding territory. The withdrawal of Russian troops and matériel left an Azerbaijani army ill-equipped and poorly disciplined. Government efforts to build a new national defense force achieved only limited results, and Armenian forces continued to advance into Azerbaijani territory during most of 1993. By the end of that year, the Aliyev regime had bolstered some components of the Azerbaijani military, however.

Forming a National Defense Force

Even before the formal breakup of the Soviet Union at the end of 1991, Azerbaijan had created its own Ministry of

Defense and a Defense Council to advise the president on national security policy. The national armed forces of Azerbaijan were formed by presidential decree in October 1991. Subsequently, the Azerbaijani Supreme Soviet declared that the Soviet 4th Army, which included most of the Soviet troops based in Azerbaijan, would be placed under Azerbaijani jurisdiction. About the same time, the Azerbaijani Supreme Soviet summoned Azerbaijanis serving in the Soviet armed forces outside Azerbaijan to return and serve in their homeland. By the end of 1991, the Supreme Soviet had enacted independently several statutes governing military matters.

Formed in mid-1992, the Azerbaijani navy has about 3,000 personnel in sixteen units from the former Soviet Caspian Flotilla and Border Guards. The navy has five minesweepers, four landing ships, and three patrol boats. The air force has about 2,000 troops, forty-eight combat aircraft, and one helicopter squadron.

According to legislation and a decree both promulgated in 1991, the president serves as the commander in chief of the Azerbaijani armed forces. In this capacity, the president oversees defense and security efforts undertaken by the prime minister and the ministers of defense, internal affairs, and security. Between 1991 and 1993, Azerbaijani presidents exercised this power by ousting several defense ministers because of alleged incompetence. Despite propitious legislation and decrees, however, efforts to field a national army faced many challenges.

In the pre-Soviet period, many Azerbaijanis graduated from Russian military academies, and Azerbaijani regiments of the imperial army were noted for their fighting skill. In the Soviet military system, however, Azerbaijanis were underrepresented in the top ranks of the armed forces, despite the presence of the Higher All Arms Command School and the Caspian High Naval School in Azerbaijan. Many Azerbaijani conscripts were assigned to construction battalions, in which military training was minimal and the troops carried out noncombat duties. Pre-induction military training in most Azerbaijani secondary schools was also reportedly less stringent than in other Soviet republics. For these and other reasons, the Azerbaijanis were not prepared for long-term warfare in Nagorno-Karabakh when independence arrived.

Russian Troop Withdrawal

The continued presence of Russian forces in Azerbaijan

became problematic when Russian troops were alleged to have assisted Armenians in an attack that killed hundreds of civilians in the town of Khodzhaly, in southwestern Azerbaijan, in February 1992. In the face of widespread demands from the political opposition in Baku, components of a 62,000-member Russian force began to withdraw from Azerbaijan almost immediately. Striking a contrast to the protracted withdrawal of Russian troops from the Baltic states, the last Russian unit, the 104th Airborne Division, withdrew from Azerbaijan in May 1993, about a year ahead of the schedule that the two countries had set in 1992.

According to an agreement between Russia and the Transcaucasian states calling for distribution of former Soviet military assets among the participating parties, Azerbaijan would receive most of the matériel of the 4th Army that had been stationed there, together with part of the Caspian Flotilla. The Russians destroyed or removed much of their weaponry upon withdrawing, but a substantial amount was stolen, exchanged, or handed over to Azerbaijani forces. Some Russians answered appeals from Azerbaijani military leaders to serve in the Azerbaijani armed forces. By agreement with Russia, many former members of the Soviet Border Guards also continued their duties under Azerbaijani jurisdiction, with Russian assistance in training and weapons supplies. In January 1994, Russia and Azerbaijan discussed possible use of Russian forces to bolster Azerbaijan's border defenses.

Force Levels and Performance

During the late Soviet period, Azerbaijan had supplied as many as 60,000 conscripts per year to the Soviet armed forces. In August 1992, Elchibey announced projected personnel levels for the Azerbaijani armed forces. His projection called for a force of 30,000 troops by 1996, divided into ground units, air force and air defense units, and a navy. Half of this force would consist of conscripts, half of individuals serving under contract. In 1994 estimated total troop strength had reached 56,000, of which 49,000 were in the army, 3,000 in the navy, 2,000 in the air force, and 2,000 in the air defense forces.

According to training plans, officers would graduate from a revamped Combined Forces Command School (formerly the Baku Higher Arms Command School) and the Caspian High Naval School. The new Azerbaijani armed forces would rely almost exclusively on transferred or purchased Soviet equipment, although Azerbaijani machine industries have the capability to do some manufacturing and repairs. According to most Azerbaijani accounts, defense strategy for the near term is focused on territorial defense, the goals of which are defeating separatism in Nagorno-Karabakh and defending Azerbaijan's borders with Armenia.

Despite Elchibey's ambitious plan, in 1992 and 1993 Azerbaijan was forced to seek military assistance elsewhere. Reportedly, a group of American mercenary advisers arrived in Azerbaijan in 1992, and some Americans were believed still in the country in early 1994. Iranian, Russian, and Turkish officers also were training Azerbaijani forces in the early 1990s. In early 1993, Azerbaijan was able to field no more than a few thousand well-trained troops against Armenia, according to most accounts. In 1993 continued military defeats brought mass desertions.

To meet the need for troops, Azerbaijani authorities encouraged the organization and fielding of up to thirty paramilitary detachments, which in late 1993 were heavily criticized by Aliyev for their lack of military discipline. Aliyev reported to the legislature that these detachments were abandoning positions and weapons to the Armenians without an effort to defend them. About 1,000 former Afghan freedom fighters were hired in 1993, and volunteers from other Muslim countries also reportedly enlisted. In late 1993, the government began forced recruitment of teenagers, who were said to be used in human-wave attacks against Armenian positions.

Supply and Budgeting

Azerbaijan reportedly receives weapons of uncertain origin from various Islamic nations to assist in the struggle to retain Nagorno-Karabakh. In late 1993, the Ministry of Foreign Affairs made an official report to the CSCE on the weapons at Azerbaijan's disposal, fulfilling the requirement of the 1991 Conventional Forces in Europe Treaty (CFE Treaty—see Glossary). According to this report, during 1992 and 1993 Azerbaijan received more than 1,700 weapons—including tanks, armored personnel carriers, aircraft, artillery systems, and helicopters—from Russia and Ukraine, far above the CFE Treaty limits.

According to IMF and Azerbaijani government data, defense expenditures placed a severe burden on the national budget. In 1992 some US$125 million, or 10.5 percent of the total budget, went to defense. The Nagorno-Karabakh conflict also raised expenses for internal security to 4 billion rubles in 1992. By 1994 military expenditures officially reached US$132 million, although unofficial estimates were much higher.

Aliyev's National Security Reform

In November 1993, Aliyev created the Defense Council to provide him direct oversight of military affairs and to curtail the loss of considerable Azerbaijani territory outside Nagorno-Karabakh. The new council, which reports to the president, also strengthened Aliyev's control over military and security affairs, which previously had been directed by Prime Minister Huseynov. At its first meeting, the Defense Council replaced the deputy defense ministers in charge of the Border Guards and the general staff, and the council criticized the Council of Ministers for neglecting urgent defense matters. At the end of 1993, Aliyev continued his criticism of widespread draft evasion, appealing particularly to the 10,000 Afghan war veterans in Azerbaijan to reenlist. Penalties for draft evasion and desertion were tightened. At the same time, Aliyev ordered most officers with desk assignments to be deployed to the front lines.

In 1993 Aliyev attempted to establish better relations with Russian military and political officials by rejoining the CIS and signing CIS agreements on multilateral peacekeeping and mutual security policy. He answered nationalist critics by citing the hope that Russia might coax or coerce Armenia and the Karabakh Armenians into reaching a suitable settlement of the conflict. Some APF members and others denounced these moves as jeopardizing Azerbaijani sovereignty more seriously than did the existing conflict.

In November 1993, the Melli-Majlis approved the Law on Defense, ratifying Aliyev's proposed reforms. Paramilitary forces were officially disbanded, and strenuous efforts were undertaken to increase the size of the military. In early 1994, these measures appeared to help Azerbaijani forces to regain some territory that had been lost in late 1993. These successes were attributed to several factors: Aliyev's success in wooing veterans, including officers, back into military service; increased enlistments and a lower desertion rate; improved morale; a streamlined command system with Aliyev at its head; and training assistance and volunteers from abroad.

Crime and Crime Prevention

In the early 1990s, crime in Azerbaijan generally intensified and expanded to new parts of society. In the confusion of economic reform, white-collar criminals absconded with investment and savings funds entrusted to new and unproven financial institutions, and mass refugee movements and territorial occupation promoted the activities of armed criminal groups. At the same time, law enforcement agencies of the Ministry of Internal Affairs underwent several reorganizations that hindered effective crime prevention.

Narcotics Trade

According to United States and Russian sources, illegal narcotics, including opium, hashish, and marijuana, are assuming a large role in Azerbaijani exports, although official economic indicators do not reflect such commerce. In 1993 the United States Department of State reported that Azerbaijani criminal networks controlled 80 percent of drug distribution in Moscow. Only seven kilograms of narcotics were confiscated by customs officials at border points in 1993, however. According to official Russian sources, in 1993 some 38.6 percent of illegal drugs entering Russia from former Soviet republics came from Azerbaijan, and 82 percent of drug arrests in Moscow were of Azerbaijanis. The Russian government and Armenian authorities have alleged that Azerbaijani government officials are involved in drug trafficking, which they assert helps support Azerbaijani military operations in Nagorno-Karabakh. In 1993 Azerbaijan joined the International Association Against Narcotics Abuse and the Narcobusiness.

Wartime conditions and expanded trade relations also increased other types of smuggling dramatically. Widespread corruption and poor organization in the Azerbaijani customs service fostered customs violations; in one two-month period in 1994, customs officals seized 6,300 Iranian rials, US$23,700, forty truckloads of iron pipe, 1,633 tons of metal, 620 grams of mercury, and batches of military optics equipment.

Crime Prevention Agencies

Azerbaijan established a separate contingent of border troops in 1992, but the demands of the Nagorno-Karabakh conflict have limited staffing. In 1993 liaison was established with the border troop commands of Russia, Kazakhstan, and

Ukraine for cooperative drug control and exchange of methodology. A small officer training program for border troops has been established at the Combined Forces Command School, with the intention of increasing enrollment once the issue of Nagorno-Karabakh is resolved. Long-term plans call for European-style checkpoints after war damage is repaired and official borders are recognized.

In 1993 the Ministry of Internal Affairs underwent a major reform, a significant aspect of which was abolition of its Administration for the Struggle Against Terrorism and Banditry. That agency, nominally the spearhead of national crime prevention, had proven ineffective because of unclear jurisdiction and poor professional performance. Law enforcement cooperation with other CIS countries has been irregular. In restructuring its law enforcement operations, however, the government has consulted the ministries of internal affairs of Georgia, Iran, Kyrgyzstan, Latvia, Russia, and Turkey. In 1993 the Ministry of Internal Affairs sent ninety employees to study law enforcement at education institutions in Russia and Ukraine. Also, contacts were strengthened with the International Criminal Police Organization (Interpol) and the national law enforcement agencies of neighboring countries.

Despite Aliyev's reforms, the delicate state of Azerbaijani national security continued to affect all other aspects of the new nation's activities. Normal foreign relations and trade were blocked by the ramifications of other nations dealing with one side or the other of the Nagorno-Karabakh conflict. But despite the clear need for action, extreme nationalists sharply limited the president's range of options by holding the threat of ouster over his head for any step that might appear to be conciliatory toward the traditional enemy, Armenia.

*   *   *

For historical background on Azerbaijan, the best source is Audrey L. Alstadt's *The Azerbaijani Turks: Power and Identity under Russian Rule.* Earlier sources covering specific historical topics include J.D. Henry's *Baku: An Eventful History* (covering the exploitation of oil in the late nineteenth and early twentieth centuries); *Russian Azerbaijan, 1905–1920: The Shaping of National Identity in a Muslim Community* by Tadeusz Swietochowski (including an introductory chapter covering nineteenth-century Russian rule); Ronald G. Suny's *The Baku Commune, 1917–1918: Class and Nationality in the Russian Revolu-*

tion; and *The Struggle for Transcaucasia, 1917–1921* by Firuz Kazemzadeh. Overviews of nationality issues include Tamara Dragadze's "Azerbaijanis" in *The Nationalities Question in the Soviet Union,* edited by Graham Smith, and Frank Huddle, Jr.'s "Azerbaidzhan and the Azerbaidzhanis" in *Handbook of Major Soviet Nationalities,* edited by Zev Katz. (For further information and complete citations, see Bibliography.)

Chapter 3. Georgia

Religious medallion bearing likeness of Saint George

Country Profile

Country

Formal Name: Republic of Georgia.

Short Name: Georgia.

Term for Citizens: Georgian(s).

Capital: Tbilisi.

Date of Independence: April 9, 1991.

Geography

Size: Approximately 69,875 square kilometers.

Topography: Extremely varied; Greater Caucasus and Lesser Caucasus ranges dominate northern and eastern regions. Many rivers flow through mountain gorges into Black Sea and Caspian Sea. Narrow lowland area along Black Sea. Plains region in east.

Climate: Subtropical, humid along coast. Mountains protect country from northern influences and create temperature zones according to elevation. Eastern plains, isolated from sea, have continental climate. Year-round snow in highest mountains.

Society

Population: Mid-1994 estimate 5,681,025. Annual growth rate 0.81 percent in 1994. Density seventy-nine persons per square kilometer in 1994.

NOTE—The Country Profile contains updated information as available.

Ethnic Groups: In early 1990s, Georgians 70.1 percent, Armenians 8.1 percent, Russians 6.3 percent, Azerbaijanis 5.7 percent, Ossetians 3 percent, and Abkhaz 1.8 percent.

Languages: In 1993 official language, Georgian, spoken by 71 percent of population. Russian spoken by 9 percent, followed by Armenian with 7 percent and Azerbaijani with 6 percent.

Religion: In 1993 Georgian Orthodox 65 percent, Muslim 11 percent, Russian Orthodox 10 percent, and Armenian Apostolic 8 percent.

Education and Literacy: Free and compulsory through secondary school. Previous Soviet system modified to eliminate ideology and strengthen Georgian language and history. Some teaching continues in minority languages. Nineteen institutions of higher learning. Literacy estimated at 100 percent by 1980s.

Health: Universal free health care, among best systems in Soviet period, but under severe stress after 1991. Reform program blocked by civil war and political instability in early 1990s. Facilities overtaxed by refugee and emergency care requirements.

Economy

Gross National Product (GNP): Estimated at US$4.7 billion in 1992, or approximately US$850 per person. Economic growth negative in early 1990s because of destruction of infrastructure, unavailability of inputs, and failure of economic reorganization.

Agriculture: Very productive with irrigation of western lowlands, but efficiency hindered by post-Soviet misallocation of land and materials. Tea and citrus fruits produced in subtropical areas; also grain, sugar beets, fruits, wine, cattle, pigs, and sheep. Over half of cultivated land privatized as of early 1994.

Industry and Mining: Industry heavily dependent on inputs from other members of Commonwealth of Independent States (CIS) and from abroad. Main products semifinished metals, vehicles, textiles, and chemicals. Coal, copper, and manganese principal minerals.

Energy: Scant domestic fuel reserves; 95 percent imported (mostly oil and natural gas) in 1990. Coal output dropped sharply through early 1990s. Hydroelectric potential high, but mainly untapped. Power output does not meet domestic needs.

Exports: Estimated at US$32.6 million in 1992. Major exports citrus fruits, tea, machinery, ferrous and nonferrous metals, and textiles. Main markets Armenia, Azerbaijan, Bulgaria, Czechoslovakia, Germany, Poland, Russia, and Turkey.

Imports: Estimated at US$43.8 million in 1992. Major imports machinery and parts, fuels, transportation equipment, and textiles. Main suppliers Bulgaria, Czechoslovakia, Poland, Russia, and Ukraine.

Balance of Payments: Estimated as US$23.7 million deficit in 1992.

Exchange Rate: Coupon introduced in early 1993. November 1994 exchange rate 1,625,000 coupons per US$1.

Inflation: Estimated in January 1993 at 50 percent per month.

Fiscal Year: Calendar year.

Fiscal Policy: Centralized decision making, but large underground economy limits economic control. Extensive manipulation of tax structure in 1992–93 to shrink large budget deficits. Deficits remained high as revenue estimates fell short. Enterprise privatization slow.

Transportation and Telecommunications

Highways: In 1990 about 35,100 kilometers of roads, of which 31,200 kilometers hard-surface. Four main highways radiate from Tbilisi, roughly in the cardinal directions, to Russia, Azerbaijan, Armenia, and Black Sea. Tbilisi hub of Caucasus region's highway system.

Railroads: 1,421 kilometers of track in 1993. Main links with Russia, Azerbaijan, and Armenia. Substantial disruption in 1992–93 by civil war and fuel shortages. Tbilisi hub of Caucasus region's rail transport.

Civil Aviation: National airline, Orbis, provides direct flights from Tbilisi to some West European cities. Passenger and cargo service limited by fuel shortages in 1991–94. Nineteen of twenty-six airports with permanent-surface runways in 1993; longest runway, at Novoalekseyevka near Tbilisi, about 2,500 meters long.

Inland Waterways: None navigable by commercial shipping.

Ports: Batumi, Poti, and Sukhumi on Black Sea, with international shipping connections to other Black Sea ports and Mediterranean ports.

Pipelines: In 1992 approximately 370 kilometers of pipeline for crude oil, 300 kilometers for refined products, and 440 kilometers for natural gas. Subject to disruption.

Telecommunications: About 672,000 telephone lines in use in 1991, or twelve per 100 persons; long waiting list for installation. International links overland to CIS countries and Turkey; low-capacity satellite earth station in operation. Three television stations and numerous radio stations broadcast in Georgian and Russian.

Government and Politics

Government: Two autonomous republics, Abkhazian Autonomous Republic and Ajarian Autonomous Republic; one autonomous region, South Ossetian Autonomous Region. Strong executive (head of state, who is also chairman of parliament) with extensive emergency powers in civil war period of 1992–93. Cabinet of Ministers selected by head of state; power of prime minister secondary to that of head of state. Unicameral parliament (Supreme Soviet, 225 deputies) elects head of state and has legislative power, but is plagued by disorder and fragmentation. Judicial branch, weak in communist era, under reform in early 1990s.

Politics: Twenty-six parties represented in parliament in 1993, of which most seats held by Peace Bloc, October 11 Bloc, Unity Bloc, Green Party, and National Democratic Party. Shifting coalitions back individual programs. Reform slowed by influence of former communists, who are gradually dispersing. Union of Citizens of Georgia formed in November 1993 to support Eduard Shevardnadze government programs. Shevardnadze remained most popular politician in late 1994.

Foreign Relations: In 1992–94 broad diplomatic campaign to establish relations with CIS nations, other neighbors, and West after isolation created by Zviad Gamsakhurdia government in 1991. Balanced position maintained between warring Armenia and Azerbaijan. Joined CIS in October 1993, after refusing to do so at first, to ensure Russian aid in ending civil war.

International Agreements and Memberships: Member of United Nations, Conference on Security and Cooperation in Europe, International Monetary Fund, European Bank for Reconstruction and Development, and International Bank for Reconstruction and Development.

National Security

Armed Forces: Defense policy made by Council for National Security and Defense, chaired by head of state. Main forces— National Guard (15,000 troops) and paramilitary Rescue Corps (about 1,000 troops formerly known as the Mkhedrioni)—not fully under government control in 1994. Plans call for national force of 20,000 with two-year compulsory service. About 15,000 Russian troops remained in mid-1993, supplemented in fall of 1993 to prevent widening of civil war and to guard borders. In 1993 Georgia joined CIS mutual security agreements.

Major Military Units: Emphasis in early 1990s on establishing national ground forces, with small air force using training aircraft. Most equipment obtained from Soviet (later Russian) occupation forces—both legally, under official 1992 quota agreement, and illegally.

Military Budget: In 1992 estimated at US$23.6 million, or 8.3 percent of budgeted expenditures.

Internal Security: Since 1992 intelligence operations under Information and Intelligence Service, chaired by head of state. Ministry of Internal Affairs combined security agencies in 1993. Government police authority uneven; white-collar and highway crime rampant in some regions.

Figure 11. Georgia, 1994

GEORGIA'S LOCATION AT a major commercial crossroads and among several powerful neighbors has provided both advantages and disadvantages through some twenty-five centuries of history. Georgia comprises regions having distinctive traits. The ethnic, religious, and linguistic characteristics of the country as a unit coalesced to a greater degree than before under Russian rule in the nineteenth century. Then, beneath a veneer of centralized economic and political control imposed during seventy years of Soviet rule, Georgian cultural and social institutions survived, thanks in part to Georgia's relative distance from Moscow. As the republic entered the post-Soviet period in the 1990s, however, the prospects of establishing true national autonomy based on a common heritage remained unclear.

Historical Background

Although Saint George is the country's patron saint, the name *Georgia* derives from the Arabic and Persian words, *Kurj* and *Gurj,* for the country. In 1991 Georgia—called *Sakartvelo* in Georgian and *Gruziia* in Russian—had been part of a Russian or Soviet empire almost continuously since the beginning of the nineteenth century, when most of the regions that constitute modern Georgia accepted Russian annexation in order to gain protection from Persia. Prior to that time, some combination of the territories that make up modern Georgia had been ruled by the Bagratid Dynasty for about 1,000 years, including periods of foreign domination and fragmentation.

Early History

Archaeological evidence indicates a neolithic culture in the area of modern Georgia as early as the fifth millennium B.C. Between that time and the modern era, a number of ethnic groups invaded or migrated into the region, merging with numerous indigenous tribes to form the ethnic base of the modern Georgian people. Throughout history the territory comprising the Georgian state varied considerably in size as foreign forces occupied some regions and as centrally ruled federations controlled others.

Christianity and the Georgian Empire

In the last centuries of the pre-Christian era, Georgia, in the form of the kingdom of Kartli-Iberia, was strongly influenced by Greece to the west and Persia to the east. After the Roman Empire completed its conquest of the Caucasus region in 66 B.C., the kingdom was a Roman client state and ally for some 400 years. In A.D. 330, King Marian III's acceptance of Christianity ultimately tied Georgia to the neighboring Byzantine Empire, which exerted a strong cultural influence for several centuries. Although Arabs captured the capital city of Tbilisi in A.D. 645, Kartli-Iberia retained considerable independence under local Arab rulers. In A.D. 813, the Armenian prince Ashot I became the first of the Bagrationi family to rule Georgia. Ashot's reign began a period of nearly 1,000 years during which the Bagratids, as the house was known, ruled at least part of what is now Georgia.

Western and eastern Georgia were united under Bagrat V (r. 1027–72). In the next century, David IV (called the Builder, r. 1099–1125) initiated the Georgian golden age by driving the Turks from the country and expanding Georgian cultural and political influence southward into Armenia and eastward to the Caspian Sea. That era of unparalleled power and prestige for the Georgian monarchy concluded with the great literary flowering of Queen Tamar's reign (1184–1212). At the end of that period, Georgia was well known in the Christian West (and relied upon as an ally by the Crusaders). Outside the national boundaries, several provinces were dependent to some degree on Georgian power: the Trabzon Empire on the southern shore of the Black Sea, regions in the Caucasus to the north and east, and southern Azerbaijan (see fig. 12).

Occupation and Inclusion in the Russian Empire

The Mongol invasion in 1236 marked the beginning of a century of fragmentation and decline. A brief resurgence of Georgian power in the fourteenth century ended when the Turkic conquerer Timur (Tamerlane) destroyed Tbilisi in 1386. The capture of Constantinople by the Ottoman Turks in 1453 began three centuries of domination by the militant Ottoman and Persian empires, which divided Georgia into spheres of influence in 1553 and subsequently redistributed Georgian territory between them (see fig. 13). By the eighteenth century, however, the Bagratid line again had achieved substantial independence under nominal Persian rule. In this period,

Georgia was threatened more by rebellious Georgian and Persian nobles from within than by the major powers surrounding the country. In 1762 Herekle II was able to unite the east Georgian regions of Kartli and Kakhetia under his independent but tenuous rule. In this period of renewed unity, trade increased and feudal institutions lost influence in Georgia.

In 1773 Herekle began efforts to gain Russian protection from the Turks, who were threatening to retake his kingdom. In this period, Russian troops intermittently occupied parts of Georgia, making the country a pawn in the explosive Russian-Turkish rivalry of the last three decades of the eighteenth century. After the Persians sacked Tbilisi in 1795, Herekle again sought the protection of Orthodox Russia.

Within the Russian Empire

Annexation by the Russian Empire began a new stage of Georgian history, in which security was achieved by linking Georgia more closely than ever with Russia. This subordinate relationship would last nearly two centuries.

Russian Influence in the Nineteenth Century

Because of its weak position, Georgia could not name the terms of protection by the Russian Empire. In 1801 Tsar Alexander I summarily abolished the kingdom of Kartli-Kakhetia, and the heir to the Bagratid throne was forced to abdicate. In the next decade, the Russian Empire gradually annexed Georgia's entire territory. Eastern Georgia (the regions of Kartli and Kakhetia) became part of the Russian Empire in 1801, and western Georgia (Imeretia) was incorporated in 1804. After annexation Russian governors tried to rearrange Georgian feudal society and government according to the Russian model. Russian education and ranks of nobility were introduced, and the Georgian Orthodox Church lost its autocephalous status in 1811. In the second half of the nineteenth century, Russification intensified, as did Georgian rebellions against the process.

Social and Intellectual Developments

By 1850 the social and political position of the Georgian nobility, for centuries the foundation of Georgian society, had deteriorated. A new worker class began to exert social pressure in Georgian population centers. Because the nobility still represented Georgian national interests, its decline meant that the Armenian merchant class, which had been a constructive part

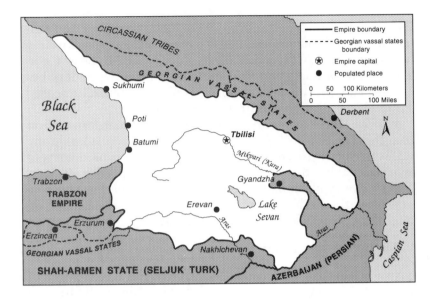

Source: Based on information from Kalistrat Salia, *History of the Georgian Nation*, Paris, 1983, 182–83.

Figure 12. The Georgian Empire of Queen Tamar, ca. 1200

of urban life since the Middle Ages, gained greater economic power within Georgia. At the same time, Russian political hegemony over the Caucasus now went unopposed by Georgians. In response to these conditions, Georgian intellectuals borrowed the thinking of Russian and West European political philosophers, forging a variety of theoretical salvations for Georgian nationalism that had little relation to the changing economic conditions of the Georgian people.

By the end of the nineteenth century, Russia, fearing increased Armenian power in Georgia, asserted direct control over Armenian religious and political institutions. In the first decade of the twentieth century, a full-fledged Georgian national liberation movement was established by Marxist followers of the Russian Social Democrat Party. Marxist precepts fell on fertile soil in Georgia; by 1900 migration from rural areas and the growth of manufacturing had generated a fairly cohesive working class led by a new generation of Georgian intellectuals, who called for elimination of both the Armenian bourgeoisie and the Russian government bureaucracy. The main foe, however, was tsarist autocracy.

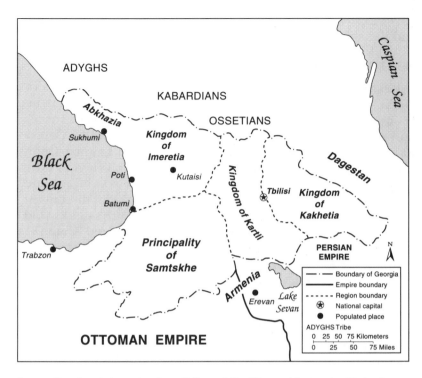

Source: Based on information from Kalistrat Salia, *History of the Georgian Nation,* Paris, 1983, 253.

Figure 13. Georgia in the Sixteenth Century

The Spirit of Revolution

In 1905 a large-scale peasant revolt in western Georgia and general strikes in industrial centers throughout the Caucasus caused Russia to declare martial law. As elsewhere in the Russian Empire, the political reforms of 1905 temporarily eased tensions between the Georgian population and the Russian government. For the next decade, the Georgian revolutionaries of the Social Democrat Party were split between the gradualist Menshevik and the radical Bolshevik factions, and the incidence of strikes and mass demonstrations declined sharply between 1906 and 1917. Mensheviks, however, occupied all the Georgian seats in the first two seatings of the Duma, the Russian parliamentary institution established in 1905. In this period, Joseph V. Stalin (a Georgian who changed his name from Ioseb Jugashvili around 1910) became a leader of Bolshe-

161

vik conspiracies against the Russian government in Georgia and the chief foe of Menshevik leader Noe Zhordania.

World War I and Independence

Because Turkey was a member of the Central Powers in World War I, the Caucasus region became a major battleground in that conflict. In 1915 and 1916, Russian forces pushed southwest into eastern Turkey from bases in the Caucasus, with limited success. As part of the Russian Empire, Georgia officially backed the Allies, although it stood to gain little from victory by either side. By 1916 economic conditions and mass immigration of war refugees had raised social discontent throughout the Caucasus, and the Russian Empire's decade-old experiment with constitutional monarchy was judged a failure.

The revolution of 1917 in Russia intensified the struggle between the Mensheviks and the Bolsheviks in Georgia. In May 1918, Georgia declared its independence under the protection of Germany. Georgia turned toward Germany to prevent opportunistic invasion by the Turks; the move also resulted from Georgians' perception of Germany as the center of European culture. The major European powers recognized Georgia's independence, and in May 1920, Russian leader Vladimir I. Lenin officially followed suit.

To gain peasant support, Zhordania's moderate new Menshevik-dominated government redistributed much of Georgia's remaining aristocratic landholdings to the peasants, eliminating the long-time privileged status of the nobility. The few years of postwar independence were economically disastrous, however, because Georgia did not establish commercial relations with the West, Russia, or its smaller neighbors.

Within the Soviet Union

In seven decades as part of the Soviet Union, Georgia maintained some cultural independence, and Georgian nationalism remained a significant—though at times muted—issue in relations with the Russians. In economic and political terms, however, Georgia was thoroughly integrated into the Soviet system.

The Interwar Years

After independence was declared in 1918, the Georgian Bolsheviks campaigned to undermine the Menshevik leader Zhordania, and in 1921 the Red Army invaded Georgia and forced him to flee. From 1922 until 1936, Georgia was part of a united

Transcaucasian Soviet Federated Socialist Republic (TSFSR) within the Soviet Union. In 1936 the federated republic was split up into Armenia, Azerbaijan, and Georgia, which remained separate Soviet socialist republics of the Soviet Union until the end of 1991.

Although Stalin and Lavrenti Beria, his chief of secret police from 1938 to 1953, were both Georgians, Stalin's regime oppressed Georgians as severely as it oppressed citizens of other Soviet republics. The most notable manifestations of this policy were the execution of 5,000 nobles in 1924 as punishment for a Menshevik revolt and the purge of Georgian intellectuals and artists in 1936–37. Another Georgian Bolshevik, Sergo Ordzhonikidze, played an important role in the early 1920s in bringing Georgia and other Soviet republics into a centralized, Moscow-directed state. Ordzhonikidze later became Stalin's top economic official.

World War II and the Late Stalin Period

Georgia was not invaded in World War II. It contributed more than 500,000 fighters to the Red Army, however, and was a vital source of textiles and munitions. Stalin's successful appeal for patriotic unity eclipsed Georgian nationalism during the war and diffused it in the years following. Restoration of autonomy to the Georgian Orthodox Church in 1943 facilitated this process.

The last two decades of Stalin's rule saw rapid, forced urbanization and industrialization, as well as drastic reductions in illiteracy and the preferential treatment of Georgians at the expense of ethnic minorities in the republic. The full Soviet centralized economic planning structure was in place in Georgia by 1934. Between 1940 and 1958, the republic's industrial output grew by 240 percent. In that time, the influence of traditional village life decreased significantly for a large part of the Georgian population.

Post-Stalin Politics

Upon Stalin's death in 1953, Georgian nationalism revived and resumed its struggle against dictates from the central government in Moscow. In the 1950s, reforms under Soviet leader Nikita S. Khrushchev included the shifting of economic authority from Moscow to republic-level officials, but the Russian Khrushchev's repudiation of Stalin set off a backlash in Georgia. In 1956 hundreds of Georgians were killed when they demonstrated against Khrushchev's policy of de-Stalinization. Long afterward many Stalin monuments and place-names—as well as the museum constructed at Stalin's birthplace in the town of Gori, northwest of Tbilisi—were maintained. Only with Mikhail S. Gorbachev's policy of *glasnost* (see Glossary) in the late 1980s did criticism of Stalin become acceptable and a full account of Stalin's crimes against his fellow Georgians become known in Georgia.

Between 1955 and 1972, Georgian communists used decentralization to become entrenched in political posts and to reduce further the influence of other ethnic groups in Georgia. In addition, enterprising Georgians created factories whose entire output was "off the books" (see The Underground Economy, this ch.). In 1972 the long-standing corruption and economic inefficiency of Georgia's leaders led Moscow to sponsor Eduard Shevardnadze as first secretary of the Georgian Communist Party. Shevardnadze had risen through the ranks of the Communist Youth League (Komsomol) to become a party first secretary at the district level in 1961. From 1964 until 1972, Shevardnadze oversaw the Georgian police from the Ministry of Internal Affairs, where he made a reputation as a competent and incorruptible official.

The First Shevardnadze Period

As party first secretary, Shevardnadze used purges to attack the corruption and chauvinism for which Georgia's elite had become infamous even among the corrupt and chauvinistic republics of the Soviet Union. Meanwhile, a small group of dissident nationalists coalesced around academician Zviad Gamsakhurdia, who stressed the threat that Russification presented to the Georgian national identity. This theme would remain at the center of Georgian-Russian relations into the new era of Georgian independence in the 1990s. Soviet power and Georgian nationalism clashed in 1978 when Moscow ordered revision of the constitutional status of the Georgian language as Georgia's official state language. Bowing to pressure from street demonstrations, Moscow approved Shevardnadze's reinstatement of the constitutional guarantee the same year.

In the 1970s and early 1980s, Shevardnadze successfully walked a narrow line between the demands of Moscow and the Georgians' growing desire for national autonomy. He maintained political and economic control while listening carefully to popular demands and making strategic concessions. Shevardnadze dealt with nationalism and dissent by explaining his policies to hostile audiences and seeking compromise solutions. The most serious ethnic dispute of Shevardnadze's tenure arose in 1978, when leaders of the Abkhazian Autonomous Republic threatened to secede from Georgia, alleging unfair cultural, linguistic, political, and economic restrictions imposed by Tbilisi. Shevardnadze took a series of steps to diffuse the crisis, including an affirmative action program that increased the role of Abkhazian elites in running "their" region, despite the minority status of their group in Abkhazia.

Shevardnadze initiated experiments that foreshadowed the economic and political reforms that Gorbachev later introduced into the central Soviet system. The Abasha economic experiment in agriculture created new incentives for farmers similar to those used in the Hungarian agricultural reform of the time. A reorganization in the seaport of Poti expanded the role of local authorities at the expense of republic and all-union ministries. By 1980 Shevardnadze had raised Georgia's industrial and agricultural production significantly and had dismissed about 300 members of the party's corrupt hierarchy. When Shevardnadze left office in 1985, considerable government corruption remained, however, and Georgia's official economy was still weakened by an extensive illegal "second economy." But his reputation for honesty and political courage earned Shevardnadze great popularity among Georgians, the awarding of the Order of Lenin by the Communist Party of the Soviet Union (CPSU—see Glossary) in 1978, and appointment as minister of foreign affairs of the Soviet Union in 1985.

Patiashvili

Jumber Patiashvili, a nondescript party loyalist, succeeded Shevardnadze as head of the Georgian Communist Party. Under Patiashvili, most of Shevardnadze's initiatives atrophied, and no new policy innovations were undertaken. Patiashvili removed some of Shevardnadze's key appointees, although he could not dismiss his predecessor's many middle-echelon appointees without seriously damaging the party apparatus.

In dealing with dissent, Patiashvili, who distrusted radical and unofficial groups, returned to the usual confrontational strategy of Soviet regional party officials. The party head met major resistance when he backed a plan for a new Transcaucasian railroad that would cut a swath parallel to the Georgian Military Highway in a historic, scenic, and environmentally significant region. In a televised speech, Patiashvili called opponents of the project "enemies of the people"—a phrase used in the 1930s to justify liquidation of Stalin's real and imagined opponents. By isolating opposition groups, Patiashvili forced reformist leaders into underground organizations and confrontational behavior.

After Communist Rule

In Georgia, Gorbachev's simultaneous policies of *glasnost* and continued control energized the forces of nationalism, which pushed the republic out of the central state before the Soviet Union fell apart. The first years of independence were marked by struggle among Georgians for control of the government and by conflict with ethnic minorities seeking to escape the control of Tbilisi.

Nationalism Rises

In April 1989, Soviet troops broke up a peaceful demonstration at the government building in Tbilisi. Under unclear circumstances, twenty Georgians, mostly women and children, were killed. The military authorities and the official media blamed the demonstrators, and opposition leaders were arrested. The Georgian public was outraged. What was afterward referred to as the April Tragedy fundamentally radicalized political life in the republic. Shevardnadze was sent to Georgia to restore calm. He arranged for the replacement of Patiashvili by Givi Gumbaridze, head of the Georgian branch of the Committee for State Security (Komitet gosudarstvennoi bezopasnosti—KGB).

In an atmosphere of renewed nationalist fervor, public opinion surveys indicated that the vast majority of the population was committed to immediate independence from Moscow. Although the communist party was discredited, it continued to control the formal instruments of power. In the months following the April Tragedy, the opposition used strikes and other forms of pressure to undermine communist power and set the stage for de facto separation from the Soviet Union.

The Rise of Gamsakhurdia

Partly as a result of the conspiratorial nature of antigovernment activity prior to 1989, opposition groups tended to be small, tightly knit units organized around prominent individuals. The personal ambitions of opposition leaders prevented

Old salt baths and Narikala Fortress, Tbilisi Courtesy Michael W. Serafin

Old Tbilisi seen from Mtkvari (Kura) River Courtesy Monica O'Keefe, United States Information Agency

167

the emergence of a united front, but Zviad Gamsakhurdia, the most widely honored and recognized of the nationalist dissidents, moved naturally to a position of leadership. The son of Georgia's foremost contemporary novelist, Gamsakhurdia had gained many enemies during the communist years in acrimonious disputes and irreconcilable factional splits.

Opposition pressure resulted in a multiparty election in October 1990. Despite guarantees written into the new law on elections, many prominent opposition parties boycotted the vote, arguing that their groups could not compete fairly and that their participation under existing conditions would only legitimize continuation of Georgia's "colonial status" within the Soviet system.

As an alternative, the opposition parties had held their own election, without government approval, in September 1990. Although the minimum turnout for a valid election was not achieved, the new "legislative" body, called the Georgian National Congress, met and became a center of opposition to the government chosen in the official October election. In the officially sanctioned voting, Gamsakhurdia's Round Table/ Free Georgia coalition won a solid majority in the Supreme Soviet, Georgia's official parliamentary body.

Arguably the most virulently anticommunist politician ever elected in a Soviet republic, Gamsakhurdia was intolerant of all political opposition. He often accused his opposition of treason or involvement with the KGB. The quality of political debate in Georgia was lowered by the exchange of such charges between Gamsakhurdia and opposition leaders such as Gia Chanturia of the National Democratic Party.

After his election, Gamsakhurdia's greatest concern was the armed opposition. Both Gamsakhurdia's Round Table/Free Georgia coalition and some opposition factions in the Georgian National Congress had informal military units, which the previous, communist Supreme Soviet had legalized under pressure from informal groups. The most formidable of these groups were the Mkhedrioni (horsemen), said to number 5,000 men, and the so-called National Guard. The new parliament, dominated by Gamsakhurdia, outlawed such groups and ordered them to surrender their weapons, but the order had no effect. After the elections, independent military groups raided local police stations and Soviet military installations, sometimes adding formidable weaponry to their arsenals. In February 1991, a Soviet army counterattack against Mkhedrioni headquarters had led to the imprisonment of the Mkhedri-oni leader.

Gamsakhurdia moved quickly to assert Georgia's independence from Moscow. He took steps to bring the Georgian KGB and Ministry of Internal Affairs (both overseen until then from Moscow) under his control. Gamsakhurdia refused to attend meetings called by Gorbachev to preserve a working union among the rapidly separating Soviet republics. Gamsakhurdia's communications with the Soviet leader usually took the form of angry telegrams and telephone calls. In May 1991, Gamsakhurdia ended the collection in Georgia of Gorbachev's national sales tax on the grounds that it damaged the Georgian economy. Soon Georgia ceased all payments to Moscow, and the Soviet government took steps to isolate the republic economically.

Rather than consent to participate in Gorbachev's March 1991 referendum on preserving a federation of Soviet republics, Gamsakhurdia organized a separate referendum on Georgian independence. The measure was approved by 98.9 percent of Georgian voters. On April 9, 1991, the second anniversary of the April Tragedy, the Georgian parliament passed a declaration of independence from the Soviet Union. Once the Soviet Union collapsed at the end of 1991, Georgia refused to participate in the formation or subsequent activities of the Commonwealth of Independent States (CIS—see Glossary), the loose confederation of independent republics that succeeded the Soviet Union.

The Struggle for Control

In May 1991, Gamsakhurdia was elected president of Georgia (receiving over 86 percent of the vote) in the first popular presidential election in a Soviet republic. Apparently perceiving the election as a mandate to run Georgia personally, Gamsakhurdia made increasingly erratic policy and personnel decisions in the months that followed, while his attitude toward the opposition became more strident. After intense conflict with Gamsakhurdia, Prime Minister Tengiz Sigua resigned in August 1991.

The August 1991 coup attempt against Gorbachev in Moscow marked a turning point in Georgian as well as in Soviet politics. Gamsakhurdia made it clear that he believed the coup, headed by the Soviet minister of defense and the head of the KGB, was both inevitable and likely to succeed. Accordingly, he ordered Russian president Boris N. Yeltsin's proclamations against the coup removed from the streets of Tbilisi. Gamsakhurdia also ordered the National Guard to turn in its weapons, disband, and integrate itself into the forces of the Ministry of Internal Affairs. Opposition leaders immediately denounced this action as capitulation to the coup. In defiance of Gamsakhurdia, National Guard commander Tengiz Kitovani led most of his troops out of Tbilisi.

The opposition to Gamsakhurdia, now joined in an uneasy coalition behind Sigua and Kitovani, demanded that Gamsakhurdia resign and call new parliamentary elections. Gamsakhurdia refused to compromise, and his troops forcibly dispersed a large opposition rally in Tbilisi in September 1991. Chanturia, whose National Democratic Party was one of the most active opposition groups at that time, was arrested and imprisoned on charges of seeking help from Moscow to overthrow the government.

In the ensuing period, both the government and extraparliamentary opposition intensified the purchase and "liberation" of large quantities of weapons—mostly from Soviet military units stationed in Georgia—including heavy artillery, tanks, helicopter gunships, and armored personnel carriers. On December 22, intense fighting broke out in central Tbilisi after government troops again used force to disperse demonstrators. At this point, the National Guard and the Mkhedrioni besieged Gamsakhurdia and his supporters in the heavily fortified parliament building. Gunfire and artillery severely damaged central Tbilisi, and Gamsakhurdia fled the city in early January 1992 to seek refuge outside Georgia.

The Military Council

A Military Council made up of Sigua, Kitovani, and Mkhedrioni leader Jaba Ioseliani took control after Gamsakhurdia's departure. Shortly thereafter, a Political Consultative Council and a larger State Council were formed to provide more decisive leadership (see Government and Politics, this ch.). In March 1992, Eduard Shevardnadze returned to Georgia at the invitation of the Military Council. Shortly thereafter, Shevardnadze joined Ioseliani, Sigua, and Kitovani to form the State Council Presidium. All four were given the right of veto over State Council decisions.

Gamsakhurdia, despite his absence, continued to enjoy substantial support within Georgia, especially in rural areas and in his home region of Mingrelia in western Georgia. Gamsakhurdia supporters now constituted another extraparliamentary opposition, viewing themselves as victims of an illegal and unconstitutional putsch and refusing to participate in future elections. Based in the neighboring Chechen Autonomous Republic of Russia, Gamsakhurdia continued to play a direct role in Georgian politics, characterizing Shevardnadze as an agent of Moscow in a neocommunist conspiracy against Georgia. In March 1992, Gamsakhurdia convened a parliament in exile in the Chechen city of Groznyy. In 1992 and 1993, his armed supporters prevented the Georgian government from gaining control of parts of western Georgia.

Threats of Fragmentation

The autonomous areas of South Ossetia and Abkhazia added to the problems of Georgia's post-Soviet governments. By 1993 separatist movements in those regions threatened to tear the republic into several sections. Intimations of Russian interference in the ethnic crises also complicated Georgia's relations with its giant neighbor.

South Ossetia

The first major crisis faced by the Gamsakhurdia regime was in the South Ossetian Autonomous Region, which is largely populated by Ossetians, a separate ethnic group speaking a language based on Persian (see Population and Ethnic Composition, this ch.). In December 1990, Gamsakhurdia summarily abolished the region's autonomous status within Georgia in response to its longtime efforts to gain independence. When the South Ossetian regional legislature took its first steps toward secession and union with the North Ossetian Autonomous Republic of Russia, Georgian forces invaded. The resulting conflict lasted throughout 1991, causing thousands of casualties and creating tens of thousands of refugees on both sides of the Georgian-Russian border. Yeltsin mediated a cease-fire in July 1992. A year later, the cease-fire was still in place, enforced by Ossetian and Georgian troops together with six Russian battalions. Representatives of the Conference on Security and Cooperation in Europe (CSCE—see Glossary) attempted mediation, but the two sides remained intractable. In July 1993, the South Ossetian government declared negotiations over and threatened to renew large-scale combat, but the cease-fire held through early 1994.

Church and fortress on Georgian Military Highway at Ananuri
Courtesy Gordon Snider

Abkhazia

In the Abkhazian Autonomous Republic of Georgia, the Abkhazian population, like the Ossetians a distinct ethnic group, feared that the Georgians would eliminate their political autonomy and destroy the Abkhaz as a cultural entity. On one hand, a long history of ill will between the Abkhaz and the Georgians was complicated by the minority status of the Abkhaz within the autonomous republic and by periodic Georgianization campaigns, first by the Soviet and later by the Georgian government. On the other hand, the Georgian majority in Abkhazia resented disproportionate distribution of political and administrative positions to the Abkhaz. Beginning in 1978, Moscow had sought to head off Abkhazian demands for independence by allocating as much as 67 percent of party and government positions to the Abkhaz, although, according to the 1989 census, 2.5 times as many Georgians as Abkhaz lived in Abkhazia.

Tensions in Abkhazia led to open warfare on a much larger scale than in South Ossetia. In July 1992, the Abkhazian Supreme Soviet voted to return to the 1925 constitution, under which Abkhazia was separate from Georgia. In August 1992, a force of the Georgian National Guard was sent to the Abkhazian capital of Sukhumi with orders to protect Georgian rail and road supply lines and to secure the border with Russia. When Abkhazian authorities reacted to this transgression of their self-proclaimed sovereignty, hundreds were killed in fighting between Abkhazian and Georgian forces, and large numbers of refugees fled across the border into Russia or into other parts of Georgia. The Abkhazian government was forced to flee Sukhumi.

For two centuries, the Abkhaz had viewed Russia as a protector of their interests against the Georgians; accordingly, the Georgian incursion of 1992 brought an Abkhazian plea for Russia to intervene and settle the issue. An unknown number of Russian military personnel and volunteers also fought on the side of the Abkhaz, and Shevardnadze accused Yeltsin of intentionally weakening Georgia's national security by supporting separatists. After the failure of three cease-fires, in September 1993 Abkhazian forces besieged and captured Sukhumi and drove the remaining Georgian forces out of Abkhazia. In the fall of 1993, mediation efforts by the United Nations (UN) and Russia were slowed by Georgia's struggle against Gamsakhurdia's forces in Mingrelia, south of Abkhazia. In early 1994, a de facto cease-fire remained in place, with the Inguri River in northwest Georgia serving as the dividing line. Separatist forces made occasional forays into Georgian territory, however.

In September 1993, Gamsakhurdia took advantage of the struggle in Abkhazia to return to Georgia and rally enthusiastic but disorganized Mingrelians against the demoralized Georgian army. Although Gamsakhurdia initially represented his return as a rescue of Georgian forces, he actually included Abkhazian troops in his new advance. Gamsakhurdia's forces took several towns in western Georgia, adding urgency to an appeal by Shevardnadze for Russian military assistance. In mid-October the addition of Russian weapons, supply-line security, and technical assistance turned the tide against Gamsakhurdia and brought a quick end to hostilities on the Mingrelian front (see Foreign Relations, this ch.). His cause apparently lost, Gamsakhurdia committed suicide in January 1994.

Physical Environment

Georgia is a small country of approximately 69,875 square kilometers—about the size of West Virginia. To the north and northeast, Georgia borders the Russian republics of Chechnya, Ingushetia, and North Ossetia (all of which began to seek autonomy from Russia in 1992). Neighbors to the south are Armenia, Azerbaijan, and Turkey. The shoreline of the Black Sea constitutes Georgia's entire western border (see fig. 1).

Topography

Despite its small area, Georgia has one of the most varied topographies of the former Soviet republics (see fig. 2). Georgia lies mostly in the Caucasus Mountains, and its northern boundary is partly defined by the Greater Caucasus range. The Lesser Caucasus range, which runs parallel to the Turkish and Armenian borders, and the Surami and Imereti ranges, which connect the Greater Caucasus and the Lesser Caucasus, create natural barriers that are partly responsible for cultural and linguistic differences among regions. Because of their elevation and a poorly developed transportation infrastructure, many mountain villages are virtually isolated from the outside world during the winter. Earthquakes and landslides in mountainous areas present a significant threat to life and property. Among the most recent natural disasters were massive rock- and mudslides in Ajaria in 1989 that displaced thousands of people in southwestern Georgia, and two earthquakes in 1991 that destroyed several villages in north-central Georgia and South Ossetia.

Georgia has about 25,000 rivers, many of which power small hydroelectric stations. Drainage is into the Black Sea to the west and through Azerbaijan to the Caspian Sea to the east. The largest river is the Mtkvari (formerly known by its Azerbaijani name, Kura, which is still used in Azerbaijan), which flows 1,364 kilometers from northeast Turkey across the plains of eastern Georgia, through the capital, Tbilisi, and into the Caspian Sea. The Rioni River, the largest river in western Georgia, rises in the Greater Caucasus and empties into the Black Sea at the port of Poti. Soviet engineers turned the river lowlands along the Black Sea coast into prime subtropical agricultural land, embanked and straightened many stretches of river, and built an extensive system of canals. Deep mountain gorges form topographical belts within the Greater Caucasus.

Climate

Georgia's climate is affected by subtropical influences from the west and mediterranean influences from the east. The Greater Caucasus range moderates local climate by serving as a barrier against cold air from the north. Warm, moist air from the Black Sea moves easily into the coastal lowlands from the west. Climatic zones are determined by distance from the Black Sea and by altitude. Along the Black Sea coast, from Abkhazia to the Turkish border, and in the region known as the Kolkhida Lowlands inland from the coast, the dominant subtropical climate features high humidity and heavy precipitation (1,000 to 2,000 millimeters per year; the Black Sea port of Batumi receives 2,500 millimeters per year). Several varieties of palm trees grow in these regions, where the midwinter average temperature is 5°C and the midsummer average is 22°C.

The plains of eastern Georgia are shielded from the influence of the Black Sea by mountains that provide a more continental climate. Summer temperatures average 20°C to 24°C, winter temperatures 2°C to 4°C. Humidity is lower, and rainfall averages 500 to 800 millimeters per year. Alpine and highland regions in the east and west, as well as a semiarid region on the Iori Plateau to the southeast, have distinct microclimates.

At higher elevations, precipitation is sometimes twice as heavy as in the eastern plains. In the west, the climate is subtropical to about 650 meters; above that altitude (and to the north and east) is a band of moist and moderately warm weather, then a band of cool and wet conditions. Alpine conditions begin at about 2,100 meters, and above 3,600 meters snow and ice are present year-round.

Environmental Issues

Beginning in the 1980s, Black Sea pollution has greatly harmed Georgia's tourist industry. Inadequate sewage treatment is the main cause of that condition. In Batumi, for example, only 18 percent of wastewater is treated before release into the sea. An estimated 70 percent of surface water contains health-endangering bacteria, to which Georgia's high rate of intestinal disease is attributed.

The war in Abkhazia did substantial damage to the ecological habitats unique to that region. In other respects, experts considered Georgia's environmental problems less serious than those of more industrialized former Soviet republics. Solving Georgia's environmental problems was not a high priority of the national government in the post-Soviet years, however; in 1993 the minister of protection of the environment resigned to protest this inactivity. In January 1994, the Cabinet of Ministers announced a new, interdepartmental environmental monitoring system to centralize separate programs under the direction of the Ministry of Protection of the Environment. The system would include a central environmental and information and research agency. The Green Party used its small contingent in the parliament to press environmental issues in 1993.

Population and Ethnic Composition

Over many centuries, Georgia gained a reputation for tolerance of minority religions and ethnic groups from elsewhere, but the postcommunist era was a time of sharp conflict among groups long considered part of the national fabric. Modern Georgia is populated by several ethnic groups, but by far the most numerous of them is the Georgians. In the early 1990s, the population was increasing slowly, and armed hostilities were causing large-scale emigration from certain regions. The ethnic background of some groups, such as the Abkhaz, was a matter of sharp dispute.

Population Characteristics

According to the Soviet Union's 1989 census, the total population of Georgia was 5.3 million. The estimated population in 1993 was 5.6 million. Between 1979 and 1989, the population grew by 8.5 percent, with growth rates of 16.7 percent among the urban population and 0.3 percent in rural areas. In 1993 the overall growth rate was 0.8 percent. About 55.8 percent of the population was classified as urban; Tbilisi, the capital and largest city, had more than 1.2 million inhabitants in 1989, or approximately 23 percent of the national total. The capital's population grew by 18.1 percent between 1979 and 1989, mainly because of migration from rural areas. Kutaisi, the second largest city, had a population of about 235,000.

In 1991 Georgia's birth rate was seventeen per 1,000 population, its death rate nine per 1,000. Life expectancy was sixty-seven years for males and seventy-five years for females. In 1990 the infant mortality rate was 196 per 10,000 live births. Average family size in 1989 was 4.1, with larger families predominantly located in rural areas. In the 1980s and early 1990s, the Georgian population was aging slowly; the cohort under age nineteen shrank slightly and the cohort over sixty increased slightly as percentages of the entire population during that period. The Georgian and Abkhazian populations were the subjects of substantial international study by anthropologists and gerontologists because of the relatively high number of centenarians among them.

Ethnic Minorities

Regional ethnic distribution is a major cause of the problems Georgia faces along its borders and within its territory (see fig. 14). Russians, who make up the third largest ethnic group in the country (6.7 percent of the total population in 1989), do not constitute a majority in any district. The highest concentration of Russians is in Abkhazia, but the overall dispersion of the Russian population restricts political representation of the Russians' interests.

Azerbaijanis are a majority of the population in the districts of Marneuli and Bolnisi, south of Tbilisi on the Azerbaijan border, while Armenians are a majority in the Akhalkalaki, Ninotsminda, and Dmanisi districts immediately to the west of the Azerbaijani-dominated regions and just north of the Armenian border. Despite the proximity and intermingling of Armenian and Azerbaijani populations in Georgia, in the early 1990s few conflicts in Georgia reflected the hostility of the Armenian and Azerbaijani nations over the territory of Nagorno-Karabakh (see Nagorno-Karabakh and Independence, ch. 1; National Security, ch. 2). Organizations in Georgia representing the interests of the Armenian and Azerbaijani populations had relatively few conflicts with authorities in Tbilisi in the first postcommunist years.

Under Soviet rule, a large part of Georgian territory was divided into autonomous areas that included concentrations of non-Georgian peoples. The largest such region was the Abkhazian Autonomous Soviet Socialist Republic (Abkhazian ASSR); after Georgian independence, it was redesignated the Abkhazian Autonomous Republic. The distribution of territory and the past policies of tsarist and Soviet rule meant that in 1989 the Abkhaz made up only 17.8 percent of the population of the autonomous republic named for them (compared with 44 percent Georgians and 16 percent Russians). The Abkhaz constituted less than 2 percent of the total population of Georgia. Although Georgian was the prevailing language of the region as early as the eighth century A.D., Abkhazia was an autonomous republic of Russia from 1921 until 1930, when it was incorporated into Georgia as an autonomous republic.

In the thirteenth century, Ossetians arrived on the south side of the Caucasus Mountains, in Georgian territory, when the Mongols drove them from what is now the North Ossetian Autonomous Republic of Russia. In 1922 the South Ossetian Autonomous Region was formed within the new Transcaucasian republic of the Soviet Union. The autonomous region was abolished officially by the Georgian government in 1990, then reinstated in 1992. South Ossetia includes many all-Georgian villages, and the Ossetian population is concentrated in the cities of Tskhinvali and Java. Overall, in the 1980s the population in South Ossetia was 66 percent Ossetian and 29 percent Georgian. In 1989 more than 60 percent of the Ossetian population of Georgia lived outside South Ossetia.

The Ajarian Autonomous Soviet Socialist Republic (Ajarian ASSR) in southwest Georgia was redesignated the Ajarian Autonomous Republic in 1992. The existence of that republic reflects the religious and cultural differences that developed when the Ottoman Empire occupied part of Georgia in the sixteenth century and converted the local population to Islam. The Ajarian region was not included in Georgia until the Treaty of Berlin separated it from the Ottoman Empire in 1878. An autonomous republic within Georgia was declared in 1921. Because the Ajarian population is indistinguishable from

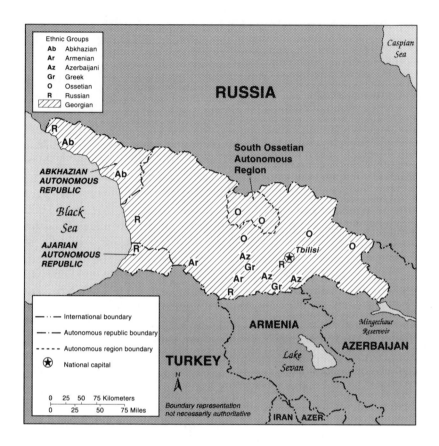

Figure 14. Ethnic Groups in Georgia

the Georgian population in language and belongs to the same ethnic group, it generally considers itself Georgian. Eventually, the term "Ajarian" was dropped from the ethnic categories in the Soviet national census. Thus, in the 1979 census the ethnic breakdown of the region showed about 80 percent Georgians (including Ajars) and 10 percent Russians. Nevertheless, the autonomous republic remains an administrative subdivision of the Republic of Georgia, local elites having fought hard to preserve the special status that this distinction affords them.

The so-called Meskhetian Turks are another potential source of ethnic discord. Forcibly exiled from southern Georgia to Uzbekistan by Stalin during World War II, many of the estimated 200,000 Meskhetian Turks outside Georgia sought to return to their homes in Georgia after 1990. Many Georgians

180

argued that the Meskhetian Turks had lost their links to Georgia and hence had no rights that would justify the large-scale upheaval that resettlement would cause. However, Shevardnadze argued that Georgians had a moral obligation to allow this group to return.

Within the leading ethnic groups, the fastest growth between 1979 and 1989 occurred in the Azerbaijani population and among the Kurds (see Glossary), whose numbers increased by 20 percent and 30 percent, respectively. This trend worried Georgians, even though both groups combined made up less than 7 percent of the republic's population. Over the same period, the dominant Georgians' share of the population increased from 68.8 percent to 70.1 percent. Ethnic shifts after 1989—particularly the emigration of Russians, Ukrainians, and Ossetians—were largely responsible for the Georgians' increased share of the population.

Language, Religion, and Culture

For centuries, Georgia's geographic position has opened it to religious and cultural influences from the West, Persia, Turkey, and Russia. The resultant diversity continues to characterize the cultural and religious life of modern Georgia. However, the Georgian language displays unique qualities that cannot be attributed to any outside influence.

Language

Even more than religion, the issue of language was deeply entwined with political struggles in Georgia under communist rule. As elsewhere, language became a key factor in ethnic self-identification under the uniformity of the communist system. Written in a unique alphabet that began to exhibit distinctions from the Greek alphabet in the fifth century A.D., Georgian is linguistically distant from Turkic and Indo-European languages. In the Soviet period, Georgians fought relentlessly to prevent what they perceived as the encroachment of Russian on their native language. Even the republic's Soviet-era constitutions specified Georgian as the state language. In 1978 Moscow failed to impose a constitutional change giving Russian equal status with Georgian as an official language when Shevardnadze yielded to mass demonstrations against the amendment (see Within the Soviet Union, this ch.). Nevertheless, the Russian language predominated in official documents and communications from the central government. In 1991 the

Gamsakhurdia government reestablished the primacy of Georgian, to the dismay of minorities that did not use the language. In 1993 some 71 percent of the population used Georgian as their first language. Russian was the first language of 9 percent, Armenian of 7 percent, and Azerbaijani of 6 percent.

Religion

The wide variety of peoples inhabiting Georgia has meant a correspondingly rich array of active religions. The dominant religion is Christianity, and the Georgian Orthodox Church is by far the largest church. The conversion of the Georgians in A.D. 330 placed them among the first peoples to accept Christianity. According to tradition, a holy slave woman, who became known as Saint Nino, cured Queen Nana of Iberia of an unknown illness, and King Marian III accepted Christianity when a second miracle occurred during a royal hunting trip. The Georgians' new faith, which replaced Greek pagan and Zoroastrian beliefs, was to place them permanently on the front line of conflict between the Islamic and Christian worlds. As was true elsewhere, the Christian church in Georgia was crucial to the development of a written language, and most of the earliest written works were religious texts. After Georgia was annexed by the Russian Empire, the Russian Orthodox Church took over the Georgian church in 1811. The colorful frescoes and wall paintings typical of Georgian cathedrals were whitewashed by the Russian occupiers.

The Georgian church regained its autonomy only when Russian rule ended in 1918. Neither the Georgian Menshevik government nor the Bolshevik regime that followed considered revitalization of the Georgian church an important goal, however. Soviet rule brought severe purges of the Georgian church hierarchy and constant repression of Orthodox worship. As elsewhere in the Soviet Union, many churches were destroyed or converted into secular buildings. This history of repression encouraged the incorporation of religious identity into the strong nationalist movement in twentieth-century Georgia and the quest of Georgians for religious expression outside the official, government-controlled church. In the late 1960s and early 1970s, opposition leaders, especially Zviad Gamsakhurdia, criticized corruption in the church hierarchy. When Ilia II became the patriarch (catholicos) of the Georgian Orthodox Church in the late 1970s, he brought order and a new morality to church affairs, and Georgian Orthodoxy experienced a revival.

*His Holiness Ilia II,
Patriarch of Mtskheta and
All Georgia, leader of
Georgian Orthodox Church
Courtesy Janet A. Koczak*

In 1988 Moscow permitted the patriarch to begin consecrating and reopening closed churches, and a large-scale restoration process began. In 1993 some 65 percent of Georgians were Georgian Orthodox, 11 percent were Muslim, 10 percent Russian Orthodox, and 8 percent Armenian Apostolic.

Non-Orthodox religions traditionally have received tolerant treatment in Georgia. Jewish communities exist throughout the country, with major concentrations in the two largest cities, Tbilisi and Kutaisi. Azerbaijani groups have practiced Islam in Georgia for centuries, as have the Abkhazian and Ajarian groups concentrated in their respective autonomous republics. The Armenian Apostolic Church, whose doctrine differs in some ways from that of Georgian Orthodoxy, has autocephalous status.

The Arts

In many art forms, Georgia has a tradition spanning millennia. The golden age of the Georgian Empire (early twelfth century to early thirteenth century) was the time of greatest development in many forms, and subsequent centuries of occupation and political domination brought decline or dilution. Folk music and dance, however, remain an important part of Georgia's unique culture, and Georgians have made significant contributions to theater and film in the late twentieth century.

183

Literature

Among literary works written in Georgian, Shota Rustaveli's long poem *The Knight in the Panther Skin* occupies a unique position as the Georgian national epic. Supposedly Rustaveli was a government official during Queen Tamar's reign (1184–1212), late in the golden age. In describing the questing adventures of three hero-knights, the poem includes rich philosophical musings that have become proverbs in Georgian. Even during communist rule, the main street of the Georgian capital was named after Rustaveli.

Architecture

Starting in its earliest days, Georgia developed a unique architectural style that is most visible in religious structures dating as far back as the sixth century A.D. The cupola structure typical of Georgian churches probably was based on circular domestic dwellings that existed as early as 3000 B.C. Roman, Greek, and Syrian architecture also influenced this style. Persian occupation added a new element, and in the nineteenth century Russian domination created a hybrid architectural style visible in many buildings in Tbilisi. The so-called Stalinist architecture of the mid-twentieth century also left its mark on the capital.

Painting, Sculpture, and Metalworking

Like literature, Georgian mural painting reached its zenith during the golden age of the twelfth and thirteenth centuries. Featuring both religious and secular themes, many monuments of this and the later Byzantine- and Persian-influenced periods were destroyed by the Russians in the nineteenth century. Examples of Georgian religious painting remain in some of the old churches. Stone carving and metalworking traditions had developed in antiquity, when Roman and Greek techniques were incorporated. In the golden age, sculpture was applied most often to the outside of buildings. In the twentieth century, several Georgian sculptors have gained international recognition. Among them is Elguja Amasukheli, whose monuments are landmarks in Tbilisi. Metalworking was well established in the Caucasus among the ancestors of the Georgians as early as the Bronze Age (second millennium B.C.). This art form, applied to both religious and secular subjects, declined in the Middle Ages.

Music and Dance

Georgia is known for its rich and unique folk dance and music. The Georgian State Dance Company, founded in the 1940s, has traveled around the world performing spectacular renditions of traditional Georgian dances. Unique in folk-dancing tradition, Georgian male performers dance on their toes without the help of special blocked shoes. Georgian folk music, featuring complex, three-part, polyphonic harmonies, has long been a subject of special interest among musicologists. Men and women sing in separate ensembles with entirely different repertoires. Most Georgian folk songs are peculiar to individual regions of Georgia. The inspiration is most often the church, work in the fields, or special occasions. The Rustavi Choir, formed in 1968, is the best known Georgian group performing a traditional repertoire.

In modern Georgia, folk songs are most frequently sung around the table. The ceremonial dinner (*supra*), a frequent occurrence in Georgian homes, is a highly ritualized event that itself forms a direct link to Georgia's past. On such occasions, rounds of standardized and improvised toasts typically extend long into the night. Georgian cuisine, which includes a variety of delicate sauces and sharp spices, is also an important part of the culture that links the generations. In the Soviet period, the best restaurants in the large cities of other republics were often Georgian.

Film and Theater

In the postwar era, Georgian filmmaking and theater developed an outstanding reputation in the Soviet Union. Several Georgian filmmakers achieved international recognition in this period. Perhaps the single most important film of the *perestroika* (see Glossary) period was Tengiz Abuladze's *Repentance.* This powerful work, which won international acclaim when released in 1987, showed the consequences of Stalin's Great Terror of the 1930s through a depiction of the reign of a fictional local dictator. In 1993, despite chaotic political conditions, Tbilisi hosted the Golden Eagle Film Festival of the Black Sea Basin Countries, Georgia's first international film festival. Georgians also excel in theater. The Tbilisi-based Rustaveli Theater has been acclaimed internationally for its stagings (in Georgian) of the works of William Shakespeare and German dramatist Bertolt Brecht.

Education, Health, and Welfare

In 1992 Georgia retained the basic structure of education, health, and social welfare programs established in the Soviet era, although major reforms were being discussed. Georgia's requests for aid from the West have included technical assistance in streamlining its social welfare system, which heavily burdens the economy and generally fails to help those in greatest need.

Education

In the Soviet era, the Georgian population achieved one of the highest education levels in the Soviet Union. In 1989 some 15.1 percent of adults in Georgia had graduated from a university or completed some other form of higher education. About 57.4 percent had completed secondary school or obtained a specialized secondary education. Georgia also had an extensive network of 230 scientific and research institutes employing more than 70,000 people in 1990. The Soviet system of free and compulsory schooling had eradicated illiteracy by the 1980s, and Georgia had the Soviet Union's highest percentage of residents with a higher or specialized secondary education.

During Soviet rule, the CPSU controlled the operation of the Georgian education system. Theoretically, education was inseparable from politics, and the schools were deemed an important tool in remaking society along Marxist-Leninist lines. Central ministries for primary and secondary education and for higher and specialized education transmitted policy decisions to the ministries in the republics for implementation in local and regional systems. Even at the local level, most administrators were party members. The combination of party organs and government agencies overseeing education at all levels formed a huge bureaucracy that made significant reform impossible. By the mid-1980s, an education crisis was openly recognized everywhere in the Soviet Union.

In the early 1990s, Soviet education institutions were still in place in Georgia, although Soviet-style political propaganda and authoritarian teaching methods gradually disappeared. Most Georgian children attended general school (grades one to eleven), beginning at age seven. In 1988 some 86,400 students were enrolled in Georgia's nineteen institutions of higher learning. Universities are located in Batumi, Kutaisi, Sukhumi, and Tbilisi. In the early 1990s, private education

Elementary school children in English class, Children's Palace, Tbilisi
Courtesy Janet A. Koczak

institutes began to appear. Higher education was provided almost exclusively in Georgian, although 25 percent of general classes were taught in a minority language. Abkhazian and Ossetian children were taught in their native language until fifth grade, when they began instruction in Georgian or Russian.

Health

The Soviet system of health care, which embraced all the republics, included extensive networks of state-run hospitals, clinics, and emergency first aid stations. The huge government health bureaucracy in Moscow set basic policies for the entire country, then transmitted them to the health ministries of the republics. In the republics, programs were set up by regional and local health authorities. The emphasis was on meeting national standards and quotas for patient visits, treatments provided, and hospital beds occupied, with little consideration of regional differences or requirements.

Under this system, the average Georgian would go first to one of the polyclinics serving all the residents of a particular area. In the mid-1980s, polyclinics provided about 90 percent of medical care, offering very basic diagnostic services. In addition, most workplaces had their own clinics, which minimized time lost from work for medical reasons. The hospital system provided more complex diagnosis and treatment, although overcrowding often resulted from the admission of patients with minor complaints. Crowding was exacerbated by official standards requiring hospital treatment of a certain duration for every type of complaint.

The Soviet system placed special emphasis on treatment of women and children; many specialized treatment, diagnostic, and advanced-study centers offered pediatric, obstetric, and gynecological care. Maternity services and prenatal care were readily accessible. Emergency first aid was provided by specialized ambulance teams, most of which had only very basic equipment. Severe cases went to special emergency hospitals because regular hospitals lacked emergency rooms. Although this system worked efficiently in urban centers such as Tbilisi, it did not reach remote areas. Most Georgians cared for elderly family members at home, and nursing care was generally mediocre. Georgian health spas were a vital part of the Soviet Union's well-known sanatorium system, access to which was a privilege of employment in most state enterprises.

When the Soviet Union dissolved, it left a legacy of health problems to the respective republics, which faced the necessity of organizing separate health systems under conditions of scarce resources. By 1990 the Soviet health system had become drastically underfunded, and the incidence of disease and accidents was increased by poor living standards and environmental hazards. Nominally equal availability of medical treatment and materials was undermined by the privileged status of elite groups that had access to the country's best medical facilities. In 1990 the former republics also differed substantially in health conditions and availability of care (see table 2, Appendix). Subsequent membership in the Commonwealth of Independent States, to which Georgia committed itself in late 1993, did not affect this inequality.

According to most standard indicators, in 1991 the health and medical care of the Georgian population were among the best in the Soviet Union. The rate at which tuberculosis was diagnosed, 28.9 cases per 100,000 population in 1990, was third lowest, and Georgia's 140.9 cancer diagnoses per 100,000 population in 1990 was the lowest rate among the Soviet republics. Georgia also led in physicians per capita, with 59.2 per 10,000 population, and in dentists per capita. However, hospital bed availability, 110.7 per 10,000 population in 1990, placed Georgia in the bottom half among Soviet republics, and infant mortality, 15.9 per 1,000 live births in 1990, was at the average for republics outside Central Asia.

Although illegal drugs were available and Georgia increasingly found itself on the international drug-trading route in the early 1990s, the drug culture was confined to a small percentage of the population. The relatively high rate of delinquency among Georgian youth, however, was frequently associated with alcohol abuse.

In 1993 the Republic AIDS and Immunodeficiency Center in Tbilisi reported that sixteen cases of acquired immune deficiency syndrome (AIDS) had been detected; five victims were non-Georgians and were deported. Of the remaining eleven, two had contracted AIDS through drug use and one through a medical procedure. Despite the small number of cases, the AIDS epidemic has caused considerable alarm in the Georgian medical community, which formed a physicians' anti-AIDS association in 1993. The AIDS center, located in a makeshift facility in Tbilisi, conducts AIDS research and oversees testing in twenty-nine laboratories throughout Georgia, stressing efforts among high-risk groups.

As in other former Soviet republics, Georgia began devising health care reform strategies in 1992. Budget expenditures for health increased drastically once the Soviet welfare system collapsed. Theoretical elements of Georgian health reform were compulsory medical insurance, privatization and foreign investment in institutions providing health care, and stronger emphasis on preventive medicine. Little progress was made in the first two years of the reform process, however. In Georgia political instability and civil war have destroyed medical facilities while increasing the need for emergency care and creating a large-scale refugee problem (see Threats of Fragmentation, this ch.).

Social Security

In 1985 some 47 percent of Georgia's budget went to support the food, health, and education needs of the population. Social services included partial payment for maternity leave for up to eighteen months and unpaid maternity leave for up to three years. State pensions were automatic after twenty years of work for women and twenty-five years for men. As inflation rose in the postcommunist era, however, a large percentage of older Georgians continued working because their pensions could not support them. In 1991 the social security fund—supported mainly by a payroll tax—provided pensions for 1.3 million persons. The fund also paid benefits for sick leave and rest homes, as well as allowances for families with young children.

In 1992 subsidies were in place for basic commodities, pensions, unemployment benefits, and allowances for single mothers and children. At that time, a payroll tax of 3 percent was designated to support the national unemployment fund. Deficits in the social security fund were nominally covered by the state budget, but budget shortfalls elsewhere shifted that responsibility to the banking system. In 1992 increased benefit payments and the decision not to increase the payroll tax eroded the financial base of the fund.

The Economy

In the Soviet period, Georgia played an important role in supplying food products and minerals and as a center of tourism for the centralized state economy. However, the republic was also heavily dependent on imports to provide products vital to industrial support. In the post-Soviet years, the Georgian economy suffered a major decline because sources of those products were no longer reliable and because political instability limited the economic reorganization and foreign investment that might support an internationalized, free-market economy. The net material product(NMP—see Glossary) already had declined by 5 percent in 1989 and by 12 percent in 1990, after growing at an annual rate of 6 percent between 1971 and 1985. In late 1993, Shevardnadze reported that industrial production had declined by 60.5 percent in 1993 and that the annual inflation rate had reached 2,000 percent, largely as a result of the economic disruption caused by military conflict within Georgia's borders.

Conditions in the Soviet System

Georgian nationalists contended that Georgia's role in the "division of labor" among Soviet republics was unfairly assigned and that other republics, especially Russia, benefited from the terms of trade set by Moscow. Georgian manganese, for example, went to Soviet steel plants at an extremely low price, and Georgian agricultural goods also sold at very low prices in other republics. At the same time, Georgia paid high prices for machinery and equipment purchased elsewhere in the Soviet Union and in Eastern Europe. Despite Georgia's popularity as a tourist destination, the republic reaped few benefits because most hard-currency earnings from tourism went to Moscow and because Soviet tourists paid little for their state-sponsored "vacation packages." Georgia benefited, however, from energy prices that were far below world market levels.

Despite the ambiguities of official statistics, all evidence indicates that after 1989 Georgia experienced a disastrous drop in industrial output, real income, consumption, capital investment, and virtually every other economic indicator. For example, official statistics showed a decline in national income of 34 percent in 1992 from 1985 levels.

Obstacles to Development

Several noneconomic factors influenced the broad decline of the Georgian economy that began before independence was declared in 1991. National liberation leaders used strikes in 1989 and 1990 to gain political concessions from the communist leadership; a 1990 railroad strike, for instance, paralyzed most of the Georgian economy. In 1991 the Gamsakhurdia government ordered strikes at enterprises subordinated to ministries in Moscow as a protest against Soviet interference in South Ossetia (see Ethnic Minorities, this ch.).

Although combat in Georgia in the period after 1991 left most of the republic unscathed, the economy suffered greatly from military action. Railroad transport between Georgia and Russia was disrupted severely in 1992 and 1993 because most lines from Russia passed through regions of severe political unrest. Georgia's natural gas pipeline to the north entered Russia through South Ossetia and thus was subject to attack during the ethnic war that began in that region in late 1990. In western Georgia, Gamsakhurdia's forces and Abkhazian separatists often stopped trains or blew up bridges in 1992. As a result, supplies could only enter Georgia through the Black Sea ports of Poti and Batumi or over a circuitous route from Russia through Azerbaijan.

In both the Soviet and the post-Soviet periods, conflicts between Georgia and Moscow broke many vital links in the republic's economy. Official 1988 data showed imports to Georgia from other republics of more than 5.2 billion rubles and exports of more than 5.5 billion rubles. As a result of Gamsakhurdia's policies, goods destined for Russia were withheld by Georgian officials. The Soviet leadership, encouraged by conservative provincial leaders in the Russian regions bordering Georgia, responded with their own partial economic blockade of Georgia in late 1990 and 1991. All-union enterprises in Georgia stopped receiving most of their supplies from outside the republic. The strangling of energy resources forced much of Georgian industry to shut down in 1991.

The Underground Economy

Economic statistics for Georgia are difficult to evaluate for both the Soviet era and the post-Soviet period, primarily because of the country's large underground economy. Traditional Georgian familial and clan relations have intensified the economic corruption that infused the entire communist system. Local elites in the communist party joined with underground speculators and entrepreneurs to form an economic mafia. Repeated efforts to eradicate this phenomenon, including an aggressive effort by Shevardnadze in the early 1970s, apparently had little impact. In the postcommunist period, struggles for economic control among competing mafias have been an important part of the political conflict plaguing Georgia.

Wages and Prices

Until 1991 Georgia's price system and inflation rate generally coincided with those of the other Soviet republics. Under central planning, prices of state enterprise products were fixed by direct regulation, fixed markup rates, or negotiation at the wholesale level, with subsequent sanction by state authority. The prices of agricultural products from the private sector fluctuated freely in the Soviet system.

Once it forsook the artificial conditions of the Soviet system, Georgia faced the necessity for major changes in its pricing policy. Following the political upheaval of late 1991, which delayed price adjustments, the Georgian government raised the prices of basic commodities substantially in early 1992, to match adjustments made in most of the other former Soviet republics.

Jewelry-making and gun-repair stand in Tbilisi
Courtesy A. James Firth, United States Department of Agriculture

The price of bread, for example, rose from 0.4 ruble to 4.8 rubles per kilogram. By the end of 1992, all prices except those for bread, fuel, and transportation had been liberalized in order to avoid distortions and shortages. This policy brought steep inflation rates throughout 1993.

Beginning in 1991, a severe shortage of ruble notes restricted enterprises from acquiring enough currency to prevent a significant drop in real wages. In early 1992, public-sector wages were doubled, and every Georgian received an additional 40 rubles per month to compensate for the rising cost of living. Such compensatory increases were far below those in other former Soviet republics, however. In 1992 the Shevardnadze government considered wage indexing or regular adjustment of benefits to the lowest wage groups as a way of improving the public's buying power.

In mid-1993 the majority of Georgians still depended on state enterprises for their salaries, but in most cases some form of private income was necessary to live above the poverty level. Private jobs paid substantially more than state jobs, and the discrepancy grew larger in 1993. For example, in 1993 a secretary in a private company earned the equivalent of US$30 per month, while a state university professor made the equivalent of US$4 per month.

Banking, the Budget, and the Currency

In the spring of 1991, Georgian banks ended their relationship with parent banks in Moscow. The National Bank of Georgia was created in mid-1991 as an independent central national bank; its main function was to ensure the stability of the national currency, and it was not responsible for obligations incurred by the government. The National Bank also assumed all debts of Georgian banks to the state banks in Moscow.

In 1992 the national system included five specialized government commercial banks and sixty private commercial banks. The five government-owned commercial banks provided 95 percent of bank credit going to the economy. They included the Agricultural and Industrial Bank of Georgia, the Housing Bank of Georgia, and the Bank for Industry and Construction, which were the main sources of financing for state enterprises during this period. Private commercial banks, which began operation in 1989, grew rapidly in 1991–92 because of favorable interest rates; new banking laws were passed in 1991 to cover their activity.

Under communist rule, transfers from the Soviet national budget had enabled Georgia to show a budget surplus in most years. When the Soviet contribution of 751 million rubles—over 5 percent of Georgia's gross domestic product (GDP—see Glossary)—became unavailable in 1991, the Georgian government ran a budget deficit estimated at around 2 billion rubles. The destruction of government records during the Tbilisi hostilities of late 1991 left the new government lacking reliable information on which to base financial policy for 1992 and beyond (see After Communist Rule, this ch.).

In 1992 the government assumed an additional 2 billion to 3 billion rubles of unpaid debts from state enterprises, raising the deficit to between 17 and 21 percent of GDP (see table 17, Appendix). By May 1992, when the State Council approved a new tax system, the budget deficit was estimated at 6 billion to

7 billion rubles. The deficit was exacerbated by military expenditures associated with the conflicts in South Ossetia and Abkhazia and by the cost of dealing with natural disasters.

The 1992 budget was restricted by a delay in the broadening of the country's tax base, the cost of assuming defense and security expenses formerly paid by the Soviet Union, the doubling of state wages, and the cost of earthquake relief in the north. When the 1993 budget was proposed, only 11 billion of the prescribed 43.6 billion rubles of expenditures were covered by revenues.

Tax reform in early 1992 added an excise tax on selected luxury items and a flat-rate value-added tax (VAT—see Glossary) on most goods and services, while abolishing the turnover and sales taxes of the communist system. In 1992 tax revenues fell below the expected level, however, because of noncompliance with new tax requirements; a government study showed that 80 percent of businesses underpaid their taxes in 1992.

In early 1993, Georgia remained in the "ruble zone," still using the Russian ruble as the official national currency. Efforts begun in 1991 to establish a separate currency convertible on world markets were frustrated by political and economic instability. Beginning in August 1993, the Central Bank of Russia began withdrawing ruble banknotes; a new unit, designated the coupon (for value of the coupon—see Glossary), became the official national currency after several months of provisional status. Rubles and United States dollars continued to circulate widely, however, especially in large transactions. After the National Bank of Georgia had established weekly exchange rates for two months, the coupon's exchange rate against the United States dollar inflated from 5,569 to 12,629. In September all salaries were doubled, setting off a new round of inflation. By October the rate had reached 42,000 coupons to the dollar.

Industry

In 1990 about 20 percent of Georgia's 1,029 industrial enterprises, including the largest, were directly administered by the central ministries of the Soviet Union. Until 1991 Georgian industry was integrated with the rest of the Soviet economy. About 90 percent of the raw materials used by Georgian light industry came from outside the republic. The Transcaucasian Metallurgical Plant at Rustavi and the Kutaisi Automotive

Works, as well as other centers of heavy industry, depended heavily on commercial agreements with the other Soviet republics. The Rustavi plant, for example, could not operate without importing iron ore, most of which it received (and continues to receive) from Azerbaijan. The Kutaisi works depended on other republics for raw materials, machinery, and spare parts. Georgia contributed significantly to Soviet mineral output, particularly of manganese (a component of steel alloy found in the Chiatura and Kutaisi regions in west-central Georgia) and copper.

In the late 1980s, Georgia's main industrial products were machine tools, prefabricated building structures, cast iron, steel pipe, synthetic ammonia, and silk thread. Georgian refineries also processed gasoline and diesel fuel from imported crude oil. Georgian industry made its largest contributions to the Soviet Union's total industrial production in wool fabric, chemical fibers, rolled ferrous metals, and metal-cutting machine tools (see table 18, Appendix).

Energy Resources

The lack of significant domestic fuel reserves made the Georgian economy extremely dependent on neighboring republics, especially Russia, to meet its energy needs. Under the fuel supply conditions of 1994, only further exploitation of hydroelectric power could enhance energy self-sufficiency. In 1990 over 95 percent of Georgia's fuel was imported. For that reason, the collapse of the Soviet Union in 1991 caused an energy crisis and stimulated a search for alternative suppliers.

The harsh winter of 1991–92 increased fuel demand at a time when supply was especially limited. Oil imports were reduced by the conflict between Armenia and Azerbaijan, cold weather curtailed domestic hydroelectric production, and the price of fuel and energy imports from other former Soviet republics rose drastically because of Georgia's independent political stance and the new economic realities throughout the former union. Beginning in December 1991, industries received only about one-third of the energy needed for full-scale operation, and most operated far below capacity throughout 1992.

Small amounts of oil were discovered in the Samgori region (southern Georgia) in the 1930s and in eastern Georgia in the 1970s, but no oil exploration has occurred in most of the republic. In 1993 some 96 percent of Georgia's oil came from

Hydroelectric station on Georgian Military Highway between Tbilisi and Mtskheta

Azerbaijan and Russia, although new supply agreements had been reached with Iran and Turkey. Oil and gas pipelines connect Georgia with Azerbaijan, Armenia, Russia, and Turkmenistan. Refinery and storage facilities in Batumi receive oil through a long pipeline from Baku in Azerbaijan.

Coal is mined in Abkhazia and near Kutaisi, but between 1976 and 1991 output fell nearly 50 percent, to about 1 million tons. The largest deposits, both of which are in Abkhazia, are estimated to contain 250 million tons and 80 million tons, respectively. Domestic coal provides half the Rustavi plant's needs and fuels some electrical power generation. In 1993 natural gas, nearly all of which was imported, accounted for 44 percent of fuel consumption.

Georgia has substantial hydroelectric potential, only 14 percent of which was in use in 1993 in a network of small hydroelectric stations. In 1993 all but eight of Georgia's seventy-two power stations were hydroelectric, but together they provided only half the republic's energy needs. In the early 1990s, Georgia's total consumption of electrical energy exceeded domestic generation by as much as 30 percent. Georgian planners see further hydroelectric development as the best domestic solution to the country's power shortage.

Agriculture

Georgia's climate and soil have made agriculture one of its most productive economic sectors; the 18 percent of Georgian land that is arable provided 32 percent of the republic's NMP in 1990. In the Soviet period, swampy areas in the west were drained, and arid regions in the east were salvaged by a complex irrigation system, allowing Georgian agriculture to expand production tenfold between 1918 and 1980. Production was hindered in the Soviet period, however, by the misallocation of agricultural land (for example, the assignment of prime grain fields to tea cultivation) and excessive specialization. Georgia's emphasis on labor-intensive crops such as tea and grapes kept the rural work force at an unsatisfactory level of productivity. Some 25 percent of the Georgian work force was engaged in agriculture in 1990; 37 percent had been so engaged in 1970 (see table 19, Appendix). In the spring of 1993, sowing of spring crops was reduced by one-third on state land and by a substantial amount on private land as well because of fuel and equipment shortages. For the first half of 1993, overall agricultural production was 35 percent less than for the same period of 1992.

Land Redistribution

Until the land-privatization program that began in 1992, most Georgian farms were state-run collectives averaging 428 hectares in size. Even under Soviet rule, however, Georgia had a vigorous private agricultural sector. In 1990, according to official statistics, the private sector contributed 46 percent of gross agricultural output, and private productivity averaged about twice that of the state farms (see table 20, Appendix). Under the state system, designated plots were leased to farmers and town dwellers for private crop and livestock raising. As during the Soviet era, more than half of Georgia's meat and milk and nearly half of its eggs came from private producers.

As was the case with enterprise privatization, Gamsakhurdia postponed systematic land reform because he feared that local mafias would dominate the redistribution process. But within weeks of his ouster in early 1992, the new government issued a land reform resolution providing land grants of one-half hectare to individuals with the stipulation that the land be farmed. Commissions were established in each village to inventory land parcels and identify those to be privatized. Limitations were placed on what the new "owners" could do with their land, and would-be private farmers faced serious problems in obtaining seeds, fertilizer, and equipment. By the end of 1993, over half the cultivated land was in private hands. Small plots were given free to city dwellers to relieve the acute food shortage that year.

Crop Distribution

In 1993 about 85 percent of cultivated land, excluding orchards, vineyards, and tea plantations, was dedicated to grains. Within that category, corn grew on 40 percent of the land, and winter wheat on 37 percent. The second most important agricultural product is wine. Georgia has one of the world's oldest and finest winemaking traditions; archaeological findings indicate that wine was being made in Georgia as early as 300 B.C. Some forty major wineries were operating in 1990, and about 500 types of local wines were made. The center of the wine industry is Kakhetia in eastern Georgia. Georgia is also known for the high quality of its mineral waters.

Other important crops are tea, citrus fruits, and noncitrus fruits, which account for 18.3 percent, 7.7 percent, and 8.4 percent of Georgia's agricultural output, respectively. Cultivation of tea and citrus fruits is confined to the western coastal area. Tea accounts for 36 percent of the output of the large food-processing industry, although the quality of Georgian tea dropped perceptibly under Soviet management in the 1970s and 1980s. Animal husbandry, mainly the keeping of cattle, pigs, and sheep, accounts for about 25 percent of Georgia's agricultural output, although high density and low mechanization have hindered efficiency.

Until 1991 other Soviet republics bought 95 percent of Georgia's processed tea, 62 percent of its wine, and 70 percent of its canned goods (see table 21; table 22, Appendix). In turn, Georgia depended on Russia for 75 percent of its grain. One-third of Georgia's meat and 60 percent of its dairy products were supplied from outside the republic. Failure to adjust these relationships contributed to Georgia's food crises in the early 1990s.

Transportation and Telecommunications

Georgia's location makes it an important commercial transit route, and the country inherited a well-developed transportation system when it became independent in 1991. However, lack of money and political unrest have cut into the system's maintenance and allowed it to deteriorate somewhat since independence. Fighting in and around the secessionist Abkhazian Autonomous Republic in the northwest has isolated that area and also has cut some of the principal rail and highway links between Georgia and Russia.

In 1990 Georgia had 35,100 kilometers of roads, 31,200 kilometers of which were paved (see fig. 15). Since the nineteenth century, Tbilisi has been the center of the Caucasus region's highway system, a position reinforced during the Soviet era. The country's four principal highways radiate from Tbilisi roughly in the four cardinal directions. Route M27 extends west from the capital through the broad valley between the country's two main mountain ranges and reaches the Black Sea south of Sukhumi. The highway then turns northwest along the Black Sea to the Russian border. A secondary road, Route A305, branches off Route M27 and carries traffic to the port of Poti. Another secondary road runs south along the Black Sea coast from Poti to the port of Batumi. From Batumi a short spur of about ten kilometers is Georgia's only paved connection with Turkey.

Route A301, more commonly known as the Georgian Military Highway, runs north from Tbilisi across the Greater Caucasus range to Russia. The route was first described by Greek geographers in the first century B.C. and was the only land route north into Russia until the late 1800s. The route contains many hairpin turns and winds through several passes higher than 2,000 meters in elevation before reaching the Russian border. Heavy snows in winter often close the road for short periods. The country's other two main highways connect Tbilisi with the neighboring Transcaucasian countries. Route A310 runs south to Erevan, and Route A302 extends east across a lower portion of the Greater Caucasus range to Azerbaijan. All major routes have regular and frequent bus transport.

Georgia had 1,421 kilometers of rail lines in 1993, excluding several small industrial lines. In the early 1990s, most lines were 1.520-meter broad gauge, and the principal routes were electrified. The tsarist government built the first rail links in the region from Baku on the Caspian Sea through Tbilisi to Poti on the Black Sea in 1883; this route remains the principal rail route of Transcaucasia. Along the Black Sea, a rail route extends from the main east-west line into Russia, and two lines run south from Tbilisi—one to Armenia and the other to Azerbaijan. Spurs link these main routes with smaller towns in Georgia's broad central valley. Principal classification yards and rail repair services are in Batumi and Tbilisi. Most rail lines provide passenger service, but in 1994 international passenger service was limited to the Tbilisi-to-Baku train. Because of fighting in Abkhazia, freight and passenger service to Russia has been suspended, with only the section from Tbilisi to the port of Poti still operative. Service on the Tbilisi-to-Erevan line has also been disrupted because the tracks pass through the area of armed conflict between Armenia and Azerbaijan.

Tbilisi was one of the first cities of the Soviet Union to have a subway system. The system consists of twenty-three kilometers of heavy rail lines, most of which are underground. Three lines with twenty stations radiate from downtown, with extensions either planned or under construction in 1994. The system is heavily used, and trains run at least every four minutes throughout the day. In 1985, the last year of available statistics, 145 million passengers were carried, about the same number of passengers that used Washington, D.C.'s Metrorail system in 1992.

Georgia's principal airport, Novoalekseyevka, is about eighteen kilometers northeast of downtown Tbilisi. With a runway approximately 2,500 meters long, the airport can accommodate airplanes as large as the Russian Tu–154, the Boeing 727, and the McDonnell Douglas DC–9. In 1993 the airport handled about 26,000 tons of freight. Orbis, the new state-run airline, provides service to neighboring countries, flights to several destinations throughout Russia, and direct service to some European capitals. Between 1991 and 1993, fuel shortages severely curtailed air passenger and cargo service, however. Eighteen other airports throughout the country have paved runways, but most are used for minor freight transport.

Georgia's Black Sea ports provide access to the Mediterranean Sea via the Bosporus. Georgia has two principal ports, at Poti and Batumi, and a minor port at Sukhumi. Although Batumi has a natural harbor, Poti's man-made harbor carries more cargo because of that city's rail links to Tbilisi. The port at Poti can handle ships having up to ten meters draught and 30,000 tons in weight. Altogether, nine berths can process as much as 100,000 tons of general cargo, 4 million tons of bulk cargo, and 1 million tons of grain per year. Facilities include tugboats, equipment for unloading tankers, a grain elevator, 22,000 square meters of covered storage area, and 57,000 square meters of open storage area. Direct onloading of containers to rail cars is available. The port primarily handles

Figure 15. Transportation System of Georgia, 1994

imports of general cargo and exports of grain, coal, and ores. Poti is ice-free, but in winter strong west winds can make entry into the port hazardous.

Batumi's natural port is located on a bay just northeast of the city. Eight alongside berths have a total capacity of 100,000 tons of general cargo, 800,000 tons of bulk cargo, and 6 million tons of petroleum products. Facilities include portal cranes, loaders for moving containers onto rail cars, 5,400 square meters of covered storage, and 13,700 square meters of open storage. The port lies at the end of the Transcaucasian pipeline from Baku and is used primarily for the export of petroleum and petroleum products. The port's location provides some protection from the winds that buffet Poti. However, strong winds can cause dangerous currents in the port area, forcing ships to remain offshore until conditions improve.

Sukhumi, capital of the Abkhazian Autonomous Republic, is a small port that handles limited amounts of cargo, passenger ferries, and cruise ships. Imports consist mostly of building materials, and the port handles exports of local agricultural products, mostly fruit. Strong westerly and southwesterly winds make the port virtually unusable for long periods in the autumn and winter. Sukhumi has been unavailable to Georgia since Georgian forces abandoned the city during the conflict of the autumn of 1993.

In 1992 Georgia had 370 kilometers of crude oil pipeline, 300 kilometers of pipeline for refined petroleum products, and 440 kilometers of natural gas pipeline. Batumi is the terminus of a major oil pipeline that transports petroleum from Baku across the Caucasus for export. Two natural gas pipelines roughly parallel the route of the oil pipeline from Baku to Tbilisi before veering north along the Georgian Military Highway to Russia. Pipelines are generally high-capacity lines and have a diameter of either 1,020 or 1,220 millimeters.

Historically, Georgia was an important point on the Silk Road linking China with Europe. Since independence Georgians have discussed resuming this role by turning the republic into a modern transportation and communications hub. Such a plan might also make the republic a "dry Suez" for the transshipment of Iranian oil west across the Caucasus.

In 1991 about 672,000 telephone lines were in use, providing twelve lines per 100 persons. The waiting list for telephone installation was quite long in the early 1990s. Georgia is linked to the CIS countries and Turkey by overland lines, and one low-capacity satellite earth station is in operation. Three television stations, including the independent Iberia Television, and numerous radio stations broadcast in Georgian and Russian.

Economic Reform

Like all the former Soviet republics, Georgia recognized the need to restructure its economic system in the early 1990s, using national economic strengths to accommodate its own needs rather than the needs of central planners in Moscow. The road to reform has been full of obstacles, however: poor political leadership, the economic decline that began in the 1980s, civil war, and a well-established underground economy that is difficult to control.

Price Policy

Gamsakhurdia understood little about economics, and he postponed major economic reforms to avoid weakening his political position. In an effort to maintain popular support, he stabilized fares for public transportation and prices for basic consumer goods in state retail outlets (see table 22, Appendix). In March 1991, a new rationing system bound local residents to neighborhood shops. In April 1991, price controls were imposed in state stores. Price liberalization began only after Gamsakhurdia's departure as president, and it did not cover several basic consumer goods and services. Continued food subsidies were an additional factor contributing to the national budget deficit. In the interest of stimulating competition, a government decree removed restrictions on trade in May 1992, and at the same time taxes were eliminated on goods brought into Georgia. Persistent shortages of bread led the government to introduce ration cards for bread in December 1992. Under these conditions, inflation soared in private markets in 1991–92, although prices remained substantially lower than in Moscow for similar items.

In 1993 wholesale prices increased especially quickly under the influence of falling productivity. In the second half of 1993, the construction industry was hit hard by material cost increases of up to thirty times, although gasoline prices rose only gradually. The prices of heavy engineering and ferrous-metallurgy products rose by three to five times in the second half of 1993.

Enterprise Privatization

Another key element of economic reform, privatization of state enterprises, was stifled under Gamsakhurdia. He feared that the "economic mafia," which already owned a significant share of the nation's wealth, would use that wealth to accumulate state assets. Rapid growth had already occurred in the private retail sector, however, once cooperative enterprises began expanding in 1988. In 1990–91 privately run "commercial shops" began proliferating, often in place of state stores. Typically, these shops offered consumer goods brought from Turkey and resold at very high prices. The Law on Privatization of State Enterprises was adopted in August 1991 to outline general principles, and the Committee on Privatization was established in 1992. Under Shevardnadze, privatization began cautiously in August 1992 when the State Council adopted the

State Program on the Privatization of State Enterprises. The law copied Russia's approach to privatization by providing for several methods, including "popular privatization," consisting of a combination of vouchers distributed to the public and auctions of state enterprises. The country's political crises delayed meaningful measures, however. By 1993 few Georgian industries had been privatized, although large numbers of small enterprises were scheduled for privatization in 1993 and 1994.

Foreign Trade

In the Soviet period, Georgian trade with the world outside the Soviet Union was severely restricted by Moscow's foreign economic policy (see table 23, Appendix). Almost all of Georgian foreign economic activity was conducted by fourteen central enterprises, most of which operated under the direct management of Moscow. Bulgaria, Czechoslovakia, Germany, Japan, and Poland were among the most important of Georgia's trading partners (see table 24, Appendix). Gamsakhurdia, suspicious of businessmen who sought to export Georgian goods, banned all export activity. The Shevardnadze government, however, created conditions for significant improvement of international investment and trade. In May 1992, licensing requirements for import or export activities were dropped except for the import of goods in the military and in medical categories. This change represented a significant expansion of the rights of enterprises to engage in foreign economic activity. Export of twelve commodities, mostly foodstuffs, was still prohibited at the end of 1992. Fees and other restrictions on the registration of joint ventures were removed, and the state tax on all imports was canceled. Import duties ranged from 5 to 55 percent, and export duties from 5 to 90 percent, with an exemption for former Soviet republics; the VAT on exports dropped to 14 percent in late 1992. The National Bank of Georgia imposed a tax of 12 percent on exporters' hard-currency earnings. In early 1993, new trade policies had not led to major increases in foreign trade and investment. Continued political instability, ethnic warfare, and extremely poor transportation and telecommunications facilities continued to discourage foreign investors in 1993.

In the second half of 1993, continued military upheaval did not entirely deter progress in foreign investment. The Renault automobile company of France, the German Tee Kanes tea company, and British and Dutch liquor companies signed contracts in August, and officials of Mitsubishi and an American shipbuilder visited Georgia to assess investment conditions.

Government and Politics

In the late 1980s and the early 1990s, the tone of Georgian political life changed significantly. National elections held in 1989, 1990, and 1992 reflected that change. The nature of governance in newly independent Georgia was most influenced by the personalities of two men, Zviad Gamsakhurdia and Eduard Shevardnadze. But democratic institutions evolved slowly and sporadically in the early 1990s.

Establishing Democratic Institutions

Prior to the 1989 elections, the Georgian Communist Party maintained tight control over the nomination process. Even in 1989, candidates ran unopposed in forty-three of seventy-five races, and elsewhere pairings with opposition candidates were manipulated to guarantee results favoring the party. In Tbilisi grassroots movements succeeded in nominating three candidates to the Georgian Supreme Soviet in 1989. The leaders of these movements were mostly young intellectuals who had not been active dissidents. Many of those figures later joined to form a new political party, Democratic Choice for Georgia, abbreviated as DASi in Georgian. Because of expertise in local political organization, DASi played a leading role in drafting legislation for local and national elections between 1990 and 1992.

The death of the Tbilisi demonstrators in April 1989 led to a major change in the Georgian political atmosphere. Radical nationalists such as Gamsakhurdia were the primary beneficiaries of the national outrage following the April Tragedy. In his role as opposition leader, Gamsakhurdia formed a new political bloc in 1990, the Round Table/Free Georgia coalition.

In 1990 Georgia was the last Soviet republic to hold elections for the republic parliament. Protests and strikes against the election law and the nominating process had led to a six-month postponement of the elections until October 1990. Opposition forces feared that the political realities favored entrenched communist party functionaries and the enterprise and collective farm officials they had put in place. According to reports, about one-third of the 2,300 candidates for the Supreme Soviet fell into this category.

Communist-built secular wedding chapel, Tbilisi
Courtesy Michael W. Serafin

The electoral system adopted in August 1990, which represented a compromise between competing versions put forward by the Patiashvili government and the opposition, created the first truly multiparty elections in the Soviet Union. The new Georgian election law combined district-level, single-mandate, majority elections with a proportional party list system for the republic as a whole; a total of 250 seats would constitute the new parliament. On one hand, the proportional voting system required that a party gain at least 4 percent of the total votes to achieve representation in parliament. On the other hand, candidates with strong local support could win office even if their national totals fell below the 4 percent threshold. When the elections finally were held, widespread fears of violence or communist manipulation (expressed most vocally by Gamsàkhurdia) proved unfounded.

The 1990 Election

The 1990 parliamentary election was a struggle between what remained of the Georgian Communist Party, which still held power at that point, and thirty-one opposition parties constituting the Georgian national movement. The national movement was not completely represented in the official election, however, because many opposition parties organized separate elections to an alternative body called the Georgian National Congress. An important factor in the results was a provision in the election law that forbade members of the communist party to run simultaneously on the ticket of another party. (By contrast, in this interim period other Soviet republics allowed even proponents of radical reform to retain their communist party memberships while representing popular fronts and similar organizations.)

The election decisively rejected the communists and gave a resounding popular mandate to the Round Table/Free Georgia bloc that Gamsakhurdia headed. That coalition captured 54 percent of the proportional vote to gain 155 seats out of the 250 up for election, while the communists gained 64 seats and 30 percent of the proportional vote. Communist strongholds remained in Azerbaijani and Armenian districts of southern Georgia. No other party reached the 4 percent share necessary for representation in the party-list system, and only a handful of candidates from other parties won victories in the individual district races. Boycotts prevented voting in two districts of Abkhazia and in two districts of South Ossetia.

Gamsakhurdia raised initial hopes for compromise in his new government by withdrawing Round Table/Free Georgia candidacies from runoffs against the opposition Popular Front Party in twelve races. That move ensured the election of Popular Front candidates as individuals in those contests; otherwise, the 4 percent rule would have precluded representation for the Popular Front.

The Gamsakhurdia Government

Gamsakhurdia's choice to head the new government, Tengiz Sigua, was almost universally praised. Sigua, formerly director of a metallurgy institute, had been an adroit and evenhanded deputy chairman of the Central Election Commission supervising the 1990 election. The government formed by Gamsakhurdia included many officials who lacked previous government experience. Only one full minister was retained from the communist government, although former deputy ministers were frequently promoted to the top post in ministries concerned with the economy. Initially, the large number of remaining communist deputies formed no organized opposition bloc in the parliament. In fact, the communist party faded rapidly from the scene, and most of its property and publishing facilities were seized. The large, modern facility Shevardnadze had built for the party's Central Committee was taken over by the Cabinet of Ministers. The rapid decline of the communists showed that the major attraction of communist party membership had been the party's position of power; once that power was lost, the number of active communists dropped almost to zero. When the new first secretary of the party ran against Gamsakhurdia for president in 1991, he received less than 2 percent of the vote. After the August 1991 coup in Moscow, Gamsakhurdia banned the communist party, and deputies elected to parliament on the communist ticket were deprived of their seats.

Gamsakhurdia's Ouster and Its Aftermath

A small but vocal parliamentary opposition to Gamsakhurdia began to coalesce after August 1991, particularly after government forces reportedly fired on demonstrators in September. At this time, several of Gamsakhurdia's top supporters in the Round Table/Free Georgia bloc joined forces with the opposition. However, the opposition was unable to convince Gamsakhurdia to call new elections in late 1991. The majority of deputies, most of whom owed their presence in parliament to Gamsakhurdia, supported him to the end. Indeed, a significant number of deputies followed Gamsakhurdia into exile in Chechnya, where they continued to issue resolutions and decrees condemning the "illegal putsch."

In the aftermath of Gamsakhurdia's ouster in January 1992, parliament ceased to function, and an interim Political Consultative Council was formed. Its membership would include representatives of ten political parties, a select group of intellectuals, and several opposition members of parliament. This council was intended to serve as a substitute parliament, although it only had the right to make recommendations. Legislative functions were granted to a new and larger body, the State Council, created in early March 1992. By May 1992, the State Council had sixty-eight members, including representatives of more than thirty political parties and twenty social movements that had opposed Gamsakhurdia. Efforts were also made to bring in representatives of Georgia's ethnic minorities, although no Abkhazian or Ossetian representatives participated in the new council.

Almost immediately after Gamsakhurdia's ouster, Sigua resumed his position as prime minister and created a working group to draft a new election law that would legitimize the next elected government. Immediately after the overthrow of Gamsakhurdia, the new government feared that Gamsakhurdia retained enough support in Georgia to regain power in the next election. As a result, in March the State Council adopted an electoral system based on the single transferable vote. The system would virtually guarantee representation by small parties and make it difficult for a party list headed by one prominent figure to translate a majority of popular votes into parliamentary control.

New Parties and Shevardnadze's Return

After his return to Georgia in March 1992, Shevardnadze constantly stressed the temporary nature of the new power structure and called for elections as soon as possible. But the leadership postponed balloting until October 1992 because it lacked effective political control over many regions of the country and because of factional wrangling over the new election law. Registration of political parties, which had been suspended by Gamsakhurdia in 1991, resumed early in 1992. Among new party registrants was the Democratic Union, a group consisting mostly of former members and officials of the communist party. Claiming a broad mass following, this party had organizations in most regions of the county. Although wooed by the Democratic Union and other parties, Shevardnadze avoided party affiliation in order to maintain his independent position. The parliament that would be elected in October 1992 clearly would be an interim body given the task of writing a new constitution. Accordingly, the term of office was set for three years.

The Election of 1992

After a series of last-minute changes, the electoral system for October 1992 was a compromise combination of single-member districts and proportional voting by party lists. To give regional parties a chance to gain representation, separate party

Burned-out headquarters building of Georgian Communist Party,
Tbilisi, 1992
Courtesy Michael W. Serafin

lists were submitted for each of ten historical regions of Georgia. In a change from the 1990 system, no minimum percentage was set for a party to achieve representation in parliament if the party did sufficiently well regionally to seat candidates. Forty-seven parties and four coalitions registered to participate in the 1992 election. For the first time, the Central Election Commission accepted the registration of every party that submitted an application.

The largest of the electoral alliances, and one of the most controversial, was the Peace Bloc (Mshvidoba). This broad coalition of seven parties ranged from the heavily ex-communist Democratic Union to the Union for the Revival of Ajaria, a party of the conservative Ajarian political elite. Ultimately, the strong programmatic differences among the seven parties would render the Peace Bloc ineffective as a parliamentary faction. The Democratic Union filled as much as 70 percent of the places given the coalition on the party lists. In the 1992 election, the Peace Bloc drew a plurality of votes, thus earning the coalition twenty-nine seats in parliament.

The second most important coalition, the October 11 Bloc, included moderate reform leaders of four parties. Members typically had academic backgrounds with few or no communist connections, and the median age of bloc leaders was about fifteen years less than that of the Democratic Union leadership. The October 11 Bloc won eighteen seats, the second largest number in the 1992 election.

A third coalition, the Unity Bloc (Ertoba), lost two of its four member parties before the election. Many of the leaders of the Liberal-Democratic National Party, one of the two remaining constituent parties of the Unity Bloc, were, like the leaders of the Democratic Union, former communist officials who continued to hold influential posts in the Georgian government and the mass media. Both the Peace Bloc and the Unity Bloc put prominent cultural figures at the top of their electoral lists to gain attention.

Shevardnadze's actions were crucial in building the foundation for the 1992 election. From the time of his return to Georgia, Shevardnadze enjoyed unparalleled respect and recognition. Because of his unique position, the State Council acted to separate Shevardnadze from party politics by creating a potentially powerful new elected post, chairman of parliament, which would also be contested in the October elections. Because no other candidate emerged, Shevardnadze was convinced to forgo partisan politics and grasp this opportunity for national leadership.

The elections took place as scheduled in October 1992 in most regions of the country. International monitors from ten nations reported that, with minor exceptions, the balloting was free and fair. Predictably, Gamsakhurdia declared the results rigged and invalid. Interethnic tensions and Gamsakhurdia's activity forced postponement of elections in nine of the eighty-four administrative districts, located in Abkhazia, South Ossetia, and western Georgia. Voters in those areas were encouraged to travel to adjoining districts, however, to vote in all but the regional races. Together, the nonvoting districts represented 9.1 percent of the registered voters in Georgia. In no voting district did less than 60 percent of eligible voters participate.

An important factor in the high voter turnout was the special ballot for Shevardnadze as chairman of the new parliament; a large number of voters cast ballots only for Shevardnadze and submitted blank or otherwise invalid ballots for the other races. Shevardnadze received an overwhelming endorsement, winning approximately 96 percent of the vote. In all, fifty-one of the ninety-two members of the previous State Council were elected to the new parliament. The four sitting members of the State Council Presidium (Shevardnadze, Ioseliani, Sigua, and Kitovani) also were reelected.

Formation of the Shevardnadze Government

An immediate goal after Shevardnadze's return was to avoid repeating the one-man rule imposed by Gamsakhurdia while keeping a sufficiently tight grip on central power to prevent regional separatism. The newly elected parliament convened for the first time in November 1992. The lack of dominant parties and the large number of independent deputies ensured that Shevardnadze would dominate parliamentary sessions. The precise role of Shevardnadze was not clear at the time of the elections; on November 6, the parliament ratified proposals on this subject in the Law on State Power. Instead of reestablishing the post of president that had been created by—and was still claimed by—Gamsakhurdia, parliament gave Shevardnadze a new title, head of state. In theory, parliament was to elect the holder of this office, although in practice the position was understood to be combined with the popularly elected post of chairman of the parliament. Thus an impasse between the executive and the legislative branches was avoided by giving the same person a top role in both, but the division of power between the branches remained unclear in early 1994.

The Cabinet

The government team selected by Shevardnadze, called the Cabinet of Ministers, was quickly approved by parliament in November 1992. Tengiz Sigua returned as prime minister. Four deputy prime ministers were chosen in November 1992, including Tengiz Kitovani, former head of the National Guard and minister of defense in the new cabinet. In December 1992, the Presidium of the Cabinet of Ministers was created. This body included the prime minister and his deputy prime ministers, as well as the ministers of agriculture, economics, finance, foreign affairs, and state property management.

In December 1992, the Georgian government included eighteen ministries, four state committees, and fifteen departments, which together employed more than 7,600 officials. Many appointees to top government posts, including several ministers, had held positions in the apparatus of the Georgian Communist Party. Although Shevardnadze's early appointments favored his contemporaries and former associates, by late 1993 about half of the positions in the top state administrative apparatus were held by academics. Less than 10 percent were former communists, about 75 percent were under age forty, and more than half came from opposition parties.

In September 1993, the cabinet included the following ministries: agriculture and the food industry; communications; culture; defense; economic reform; education; environment; finance; foreign affairs; health; industry; internal affairs; justice; labor and social security; state property management; and trade and supply. Each of the five deputy prime ministers supervised a group of ministries.

In practice, the Cabinet of Ministers was a major obstacle to reform in 1993. Pro-reform ministers were isolated by the domination of former communists in the Presidium, which stood between Shevardnadze and the administrative machinery of the ministries. In 1993 Shevardnadze himself was reluctant to push hard for the rapid reforms advocated by progressives in parliament. The cabinet was superficially restructured in August 1993, but reformers clamored for a smaller cabinet under direct control of the head of state.

Parliament

In 1993 some twenty-six parties and eleven factions held seats in the new parliament, which continued to be called the Supreme Soviet. The legislative branch's basic powers were outlined in the Law on State Power, an interim law rescinding the strict limits placed on legislative activity by Gamsakhurdia's 1991 constitution. Thus in 1993 the parliament had the power to elect and dismiss the head of state by a two-thirds vote; to nullify laws passed by local or national bodies if they conflicted with national law; to decide questions of war and peace; to reject any candidate for national office proposed by the head of state; and, upon demand of one-fifth of the deputies, to declare a vote of no confidence in the sitting cabinet.

Activity within the legislative body was prescribed by the Temporary Regulation of the Georgian Parliament. The parliament as a whole elected all administrative officials, including a speaker and two deputy speakers. Seventeen specialized commissions examined all bills in their respective fields. The speaker had little power over commission chairs or over deputies in general, and parliament suffered from an inefficient structure, insufficient staff, and poor communications. The two days per week allotted for legislative debate often did not allow full consideration of bills.

The major parliamentary reform factions—the Democrats, the Greens, the Liberals, the National Democrats, and the Republicans—were not able to maintain a coalition to promote reform legislation. Of that group, the National Democrats showed the most internal discipline. Shevardnadze received support from a large group of deputies from single-member districts, aligned with Liberals and Democrats. His radical opposition, a combination of several very small parties, was weakened by disunity, but it frequently was able to obstruct debate. The often disorderly parliamentary debates reduced support among the Georgian public, to whom sessions were widely televised.

In November 1993, Shevardnadze was able to merge three small parties with a breakaway faction of the Republicans to form a new party, the Union of Citizens of Georgia, of which he became chairman. This was a new step for the head of state, who previously had refrained from political identification and had relied on temporary coalitions to support his policies. At the same time, Shevardnadze also sought to include the entire loose parliamentary coalition that had recently supported him, in a concerted effort to normalize government after the Abkhazian crisis abated.

The Chief Executive

The 1992 Law on State Power gave Shevardnadze power beyond the executive functions of presidential office. As chairman of parliament, he had the right to call routine or extraordinary parliamentary sessions, preside over parliamentary deliberations, and propose constitutional changes and legislation. As head of state, Shevardnadze nominated the prime minister, the cabinet, the chairman of the Information and Intelligence Service, and the president of the National Bank of Georgia (although the parliament had the right of approval of these officials).

Without parliamentary approval, the head of state appointed all senior military leaders and provincial officials such as prefects and mayors. Additional power came from his control of the entire system of state administration, and he could form his own administrative apparatus, which had the potential to act as a shadow government beyond the control of any other branch. Key agencies chaired by Shevardnadze in 1993 were the Council for National Security and Defense, the Emergency Economic Council, and the Scientific and Technical Commission, which advised on military and industrial questions.

In response to calls by the opposition for his resignation during the Abkhazian crisis of mid-1993, Shevardnadze requested and received from parliament emergency powers to appoint all ministers except the prime minister and to issue decrees on economic policy without legislative approval. When the Sigua government resigned in August, parliament quickly approved Shevardnadze's nomination of industrialist Otar Patsatsia as prime minister. Although Shevardnadze argued that greater central power was necessary to curb turmoil, his critics saw him setting a precedent for future dictatorship and human rights abuses.

The Judicial System

When Georgia was part of the Soviet Union, the Supreme Court of Georgia was subordinate to the Supreme Court of the Soviet Union, and the rule of law in Georgia, still based largely on the Soviet constitution, included the same limitations on personal rights. Beginning in 1990, the court system of Georgia began a major transition toward establishment of an independent judiciary that would replace the powerless rubber-stamp courts of the Soviet period. The first steps, taken in late 1990, were to forbid Supreme Court judges from holding communist party membership and to remove Supreme Court activities from the supervision of the party. After the overthrow of Gamsakhurdia, the pre-Soviet constitution of 1921 was restored, providing the legal basis for separation of powers and an independent court. Substantial opposition to actual independence was centered in the Cabinet of Ministers, however, some of whose members would lose de facto judicial power.

The Supreme Court

In 1993 the Supreme Court had thirty-nine members, of

whom nine worked on civil cases and thirty on criminal cases. All judges had been elected for ten-year terms in 1990 and 1991. Shevardnadze made no effort to replace judges elected under Gamsakhurdia, although they had been seated under a different constitutional system. The Supreme Court's functions include interpreting laws, trying cases of serious criminal acts and appeals of regional court decisions, and supervising application of the law by other government agencies.

The Procurator General

The postcommunist judicial system has continued the multiple role of the procurator general's office as an agency of investigation, a constitutional court supervising the application of the law, and the institution behind prosecution of crimes in court. In 1993 the procurator general's office retained a semimilitary structure and total authority over the investigation of court cases; judges had no power to reject evidence gained improperly. Advocates of democratization identified abolition of the office of procurator general as essential, with separation of the responsibilities of the procurator general and the courts as a first step.

Prospects for Reform

All parties in Georgia agreed that judicial reform depended on passage of a new constitution delineating the separation of powers. If such a constitution prescribed a strong executive system, the head of state would appoint Supreme Court judges; if a parliamentary system were called for, parliament would make the court appointments. In early 1994, however, the constitution was the subject of prolonged political wrangling that showed no sign of abating. At that point, experts found a second fundamental obstacle to judicial reform in a national psychology that had no experience with democratic institutions and felt most secure with a unitary, identifiable government power. Reform was also required in the training of lawyers and judges, who under the old system entered the profession through the sponsorship of political figures rather than on their own merit.

Regional Courts

Until the Gamsakhurdia period, regional courts were elected by regional party soviets; since 1990 regional courts have been appointed by regional officials. After the beginning of ethnic struggles in South Ossetia and Abkhazia, regional military courts also were established. The head of state appoints military judges, and the Supreme Court reviews military court decisions. The Tbilisi City Court has separate jurisdiction in supervising the observance of laws in the capital city.

The Constitution

Under Gamsakhurdia, Georgia had continued to function under the Soviet-era constitution of 1978, which was based on the 1977 constitution of the Soviet Union. The first postcommunist parliament amended that document extensively. In February 1992, the Georgian National Congress (the alternate parliament elected in 1990) formally designated the Georgian constitution of February 21, 1921, as the effective constitution of Georgia. That declaration received legitimacy from the signatures of Jaba Ioseliani and Tengiz Kitovani, at that time two of the three members of the governing Military Council.

In February 1993, Shevardnadze called for extensive revisions of the 1921 constitution. Characterizing large sections of that document as wholly unacceptable, Shevardnadze proposed forming a constitutional commission to draft a new version by December 1993. According to Shevardnadze's timetable, the draft would be refined by parliament in the spring of 1994 and then submitted for approval by popular referendum in the fall of 1994.

Human Rights

Human rights protection and media freedom have been hindered in postcommunist Georgia by the national government's assumption of central executive power to deal with states of political and military emergency and by the existence of semi-independent military forces. In 1993 the expression of opposition views in the independent media was interrupted by official and unofficial actions against newspapers and broadcasters, despite a stated policy that expression of antigovernment views would be tolerated if not accompanied by violent acts.

Both sides of the Abkhazian conflict claimed widespread interference with civilian human rights by their opponents. Among the charges were abuse of military prisoners, the taking of civilian hostages, and the shelling and blockading of civilian areas. In 1993 the Shevardnadze government began addressing claims of human rights abuses by its military forces and police, particularly against Gamsakhurdia partisans and the Abkhazian population. In January the Parliamentary Commission on Human Rights and Ethnic Minority Affairs formed the Council of Ethnic Minorities, which met with representatives of the Meskhetian Turk exile population to resolve the grievances of that group. At the same time, the Interethnic Congress of the People of Georgia was formed to improve ethnic Georgians' appreciation of minority rights.

Despite the government's efforts, the Abkhazian conflict continued the tension between necessary wartime controls and the need to protect human rights. In June 1993, the international human rights group Helsinki Watch cited Georgia for political persecution, media obstruction, and military abuses of civilian rights, and in October the United States listed human rights progress as a prerequisite for continued economic aid.

The Media

The 1992 Law on the Press nominally reversed the rigorous state censorship of the Soviet and Gamsakhurdia periods and guaranteed freedom of speech. In 1993 Georgian law contained no prohibition of public criticism of the head of state, and Shevardnadze was subjected to accusations and comments from every direction. Three television channels are in operation; one, Ibervision, is run independently. Numerous independent newspapers are published; *Sakartvelos Respublika* (The Georgian Republic) presents the official government view in the daily press.

Despite some liberalization, in 1994 national security remained a rationale for media restriction. During the crisis of September 1993, two pro-Gamsakhurdia newspapers were closed, and the office of an independent weekly was attacked by gunmen. The Free Media Association, an organization composed of eight independent newspapers, blamed a progovernment party for the attack. After his controversial decision in October to join the CIS, Shevardnadze threatened to close hostile newspapers, and no television channel discussed the widespread disagreement with the head of state's CIS initiative.

Foreign Relations

Georgia's long tradition as a crossroads of East-West commerce was interrupted by the trade practices of the Soviet Union and then by Gamsakhurdia's isolationist policy. Although the Shevardnadze government sought to revive the national economy by reinstating ties with both East and West, in 1992 and 1993 domestic turmoil prevented major steps in that direction. In 1993 Shevardnadze traveled widely among the former Soviet republics (Azerbaijan, Kazakhstan, Russia, and Turkmenistan) and elsewhere (Germany, China, and the headquarters of the North Atlantic Treaty Organization in Belgium) to solidify Georgia's international position and to solicit aid. By September, Georgia had diplomatic relations with seventy-eight countries and economic cooperation treaties with sixteen.

The Soviet and Gamsakhurdia Periods

Soviet policy effectively cut traditional commercial and diplomatic links to Turkey, which became a member of the North Atlantic Treaty Organization (NATO—see Glossary) in 1952, and to Iran, a United States ally until the late 1970s. Instead, virtually all transportation and commercial links were directed to Russia and the other Soviet republics. The same redirection occurred with diplomatic ties, which the Ministry of Foreign Affairs of the Soviet Union controlled. Shevardnadze's presence as Soviet foreign minister from 1985 to 1990 provided little direct benefit to Georgia aside from the large number of high-ranking guests who visited the republic in that period. That group included Britain's Prime Minister Margaret Thatcher and United States Secretary of State George Shultz.

Under Gamsakhurdia, Georgia's efforts to break out of the diplomatic isolation of the Soviet period were stymied by the reluctance of the outside world to recognize breakaway republics while the Soviet Union still existed. Romania, which granted recognition in August 1991, was one of the few countries to do so during the Gamsakhurdia period. Several Georgian delegations came to the United States in 1991 in an effort to establish diplomatic ties, but Washington largely ignored those efforts. Given stable internal conditions, the dissolution of the Soviet Union in late 1991 would have released Georgia from its isolation, but by that time the revolt against Gamsakhurdia was in full force. After the violent overthrow of Gamsakhurdia, other governments were reluctant to recognize the legitimacy of his successors. This situation changed in March 1992, when the internationally prominent Shevardnadze returned to Georgia and became chairman of the State Council.

In 1992 and 1993, United States aid to Georgia totaled US$224 million, most of it humanitarian, placing Georgia second in United States aid per capita among the former Soviet republics. In September 1993, Shevardnadze appealed directly to the United States Congress for additional aid. At that time, President William J.Clinton officially backed Shevardnadze's efforts to maintain the territorial integrity of Georgia. Reports of human rights offenses against opposition figures, however, brought United States warnings late in 1993 that continued support depended on the Georgian government's observance of international human rights principles.

The Foreign Policy Establishment

In his role as head of the State Council, Shevardnadze exerted a strong and direct influence on Georgia's foreign policy prior to the 1992 election. The additional post of head of state, which he acquired after the election, gave him the right to conduct negotiations with foreign governments and to sign international treaties and agreements. In the Sigua cabinet, the Ministry of Foreign Affairs was headed by Alexander Chikhvaidze, who had worked previously in the Ministry of Foreign Affairs of the Soviet Union and was serving as Soviet ambassador to the Netherlands at the time of his appointment in Tbilisi. The Council for National Security and Defense was created in late 1992 to formulate strategic and security policy under the chairmanship of the head of state (see National Security, this ch.).

Revived Contacts in 1992

Shevardnadze's diplomatic contacts and personal relationships with many of the world's leaders ended Georgia's international isolation in 1992. In March, Germany became the first Western country to post an ambassador to Georgia; Shevardnadze's close relations with German foreign minister Hans-Dietrich Genscher were a key factor in that decision. Recognition by the United States came in April 1992, and a United States embassy was opened in June 1992. Georgia became the 179th member of the United Nations in July 1992; it was the last of the former Soviet republics to be admitted. By December 1992, six countries had diplomatic missions in Tbilisi: China, Germany, Israel, Russia, Turkey, and the United States. Seventeen other countries began conducting diplomatic affairs with Georgia through their ambassadors to Russia or Ukraine. In August 1993, the United States granted Georgia most-favored-nation status, and the European Community offered technical economic assistance.

Unlike some former Soviet republics such as Armenia, Lithuania, and Ukraine, Georgia lacked a large number of emigrants in the West who could establish links to the outside world once internal conditions made such connections possible. Small groups of Georgian exiles lived in Paris and other European capitals, but they were mostly descended from members of the Social Democratic government that had been forced into exile with the incorporation of Georgia into the Soviet empire in 1921.

The only large group of emigrants that maintained contact with Georgia were Georgian Jews who had taken advantage of the Soviet Union's expansion of Jewish emigration rights in the 1970s and 1980s. Because Jews had lived in Georgia for many centuries and because Georgia had no history of anti-Semitism, many Georgian Jews continued to feel an attachment to Georgia and its culture, language, and people. Largely as a result of these ties, relations between Georgia and Israel flourished on many levels.

Relations with Neighboring Countries

Of particular importance to Georgia's postcommunist foreign policy and national security was the improvement of relations with neighbors on all sides: Armenia, Azerbaijan, Russia, and Turkey. This goal was complicated by a number of ethnic and political issues as well as by historical differences.

Armenia and Azerbaijan

Among the former Soviet republics, the neighboring Transcaucasian nations of Armenia and Azerbaijan have special significance for Georgia. Despite Georgia's obvious cultural and religious affinities with Armenia, relations between Georgia and Muslim Azerbaijan generally have been closer than those with Christian Armenia. Economic and political factors have contributed to this situation. First, Georgian fuel needs make good relations with Azerbaijan vital to the health of the Georgian economy. Second, Georgians have sympathized with Azerbaijan's position in the conflict between Armenia and Azerbaijan over the ethnic Armenian enclave of Nagorno-Karabakh because of similarities to Georgia's internal problems with Abkhazia and South Ossetia. Both countries have cited the principle of "inviolability of state borders" in defending

Eduard Shevardnadze on official visit to the United States with President William J. Clinton, March 1994 Courtesy White House Photo Office

national interests against claims by ethnic minorities (see fig. 3; Nagorno-Karabakh and Independence, ch. 1; After Communist Rule, ch. 2).

In December 1990, Georgia under Gamsakhurdia signed a cooperation agreement with Azerbaijan affecting the economic, scientific, technical, and cultural spheres. In February 1993, Georgia under Shevardnadze concluded a far-reaching treaty of friendship, cooperation, and mutual relations with Azerbaijan, including a mutual security arrangement and assurances that Georgia would not reexport Azerbaijani oil or natural gas to Armenia. In 1993 Azerbaijan exerted some pressure on Georgia to join the blockade of Armenia and to curb incursions by Armenians from Georgian territory into Azerbaijan. The issue of discrimination against the Azerbaijani minority in Georgia, a serious matter during Gamsakhurdia's tenure, was partially resolved under Shevardnadze.

In the early 1990s, Armenia maintained fundamentally good relations with Georgia. The main incentive for this policy was the fact that Azerbaijan's blockade of Armenian transport routes and pipelines meant that routes through Georgia were Armenia's only direct connection with the outside world. Other considerations in the Armenian view were the need to protect the Armenians in Georgia and the need to stem the overflow of violence from Georgian territory. The official ties

223

that Georgia forged with Azerbaijan between 1991 and 1993 strained relations with Armenia, which was in an undeclared state of war with Azerbaijan throughout that period. Nevertheless, Gamsakhurdia signed a treaty with Armenia on principles of cooperation in July 1991, and Shevardnadze signed a friendship treaty with Armenia in May 1993. With the aim of restoring mutually beneficial economic relations in the Transcaucasus, Shevardnadze also attempted (without success) to mediate the Armenian-Azerbaijani conflict in early 1993.

Russia

Of all countries, Georgia's relations with Russia were both the most important and the most ambivalent. Russia (and previously the Soviet Union) was deeply involved at many levels in theconflicts in South Ossetia and Abkhazia, and in 1993 Ajarian leaders also declared Russia the protector of their national interests. Thus Russia seemingly holds the key to a resolution of those conflicts in a way that would avoid the fragmentation of Georgia. Trade ties with Russia, disrupted by Gamsakhurdia's struggle with Gorbachev and by ethnic conflicts on Georgia's borders with Russia, also are critical to reviving the Georgian economy.

Russia recognized Georgia's independence in mid-1992 and appointed an ambassador in October. In 1993 Russia's official position was that a stable, independent Georgia was necessary for security along Russia's southern border. The conditions behind that position were Russia's need for access to the Black Sea, which was endangered by shaky relations with Ukraine, the need for a buffer between Russia and Islamic extremist movements Russia feared in Turkey and Iran, the need to protect the 370,000 ethnic Russians in Georgia, and the refugee influx and violence in the Russian Caucasus caused by turmoil across the mountains in Georgia. Although Shevardnadze was officially well regarded, Russian nationalists, many of them in the Russian army, wished to depose him as punishment for his initial refusal to bring Georgia into the CIS and for his role as the Soviet foreign minister who "lost" the former Soviet republics in 1991.

In pursuing its official goals, Russia offered mediation of Georgia's conflicts with the Abkhazian, Ajarian, and Ossetian minorities, encouraging Georgia to increase the autonomy of those groups for the sake of national stability. At the same time, Russian military policy makers openly declared Georgia's strategic importance to Russian national security. Such statements raised suspicions that, as in 1801 and 1921, Russia would take advantage of Georgia's weakened position and sweep the little republic back into the empire.

Despite the misgivings of his fellow Georgians, in 1993 Shevardnadze pursued talks toward a comprehensive bilateral Georgian-Russian treaty of friendship. Discussions were interrupted by surges of fighting in Abkhazia, however, and relations were cooled by Shevardnadze's claim that Russia was aiding the secessionist campaign that had begun in August.

In September 1993, the fall of Sukhumi to Abkhazian forces signaled the crumbling of the Georgian army, and the return of Gamsakhurdia threatened to split Georgia into several parts. Shevardnadze, recognizing the necessity of outside military help to maintain his government, agreed to join the CIS on terms dictated by Russia in return for protection of government supply lines by Russian troops. Meanwhile, despite denials by the Yeltsin government, an unknown number of Russians still gave "unofficial" military advice and matériel to the Abkhazian forces, which experts believed would not have posed a major threat to Tbilisi without such assistance. Shevardnadze defended CIS membership at home as an absolute necessity for Georgia's survival as well as a stimulant to increased trade with Russia.

Turkey

Despite a history of episodic Turkish invasions, Shevardnadze courted Turkey as an economic and diplomatic partner. Georgians took advantage of the opening of border traffic with Turkey to begin vigorous commercial activities with their nearest "capitalist" neighbor. In 1992 Georgia became a member of the Black Sea Economic Cooperation Organization, which is based in Turkey. In December 1992, Turkey granted Georgia a credit equivalent to US$50 million to purchase wheat and other goods and to stimulate Turkish private investment in the republic. Georgia also signed several diplomatic agreements with Turkey in the early 1990s, including a Georgian pledge to respect existing common borders and official Turkish support of Georgian national integrity against the Abkhazian separatist movement. The issue of reinstatement of exiled Meskhetian Turks eased in 1993 when Georgia established official contacts with that minority (see Human Rights, this ch.).

National Security

Military forces have played a critical role in Georgian politics since 1989. In January 1992, Georgia's president was overthrown by military force, and the Shevardnadze regime relied heavily on the armed forces to stay in power. Warfare in the autonomous regions of South Ossetia and Abkhazia, as well as armed resistance by Gamsakhurdia supporters in western Georgia, have further emphasized the military's major role in national security.

The Military Establishment

Almost from its inception in late 1990, the National Guard became directly involved in Georgian politics. By 1992 repeated human rights offenses against Gamsakhurdia supporters brought calls to change this role. At the same time, the political rivalry between Ioseliani and Kitovani, the leaders of the Mkhedrioni (horsemen) and the National Guard, respectively, became one of the key conflicts in the Georgian government hierarchy, and many political parties continued to retain private armies in the guise of armed bodyguards or security teams. Discipline problems in the ranks of both the National Guard and the Mkhedrioni and their ineffectiveness as fighting forces led the Georgian government to plan for a professional army. In April 1992, the State Council adopted a resolution to form a unified armed force of up to 20,000 soldiers.

At the time the government announced its plans for a professional army, however, neither existing military group had sufficient internal discipline to carry out major restructuring. Efforts to disband the National Guard and Mkhedrioni were delayed by continued violence in western Georgia, by an attempted coup in Tbilisi by Gamsakhurdia supporters, and by the political ambitions of Kitovani and Ioseliani. In May 1992, Kitovani was designated minister of defense in an effort to bring the National Guard under central control. Instead, during the following year Kitovani turned his position into a power center rivaling Shevardnadze's. In May 1993, Shevardnadze induced Kitovani and Ioseliani to resign from their powerful positions on the Council for National Security and Defense, depriving both men of influence over national security policy and enhancing the stature of the head of state.

Shevardnadze complained in early 1993 that a unified army had still not been created. In May the National Guard was abolished as a separate force, and individual distinguished units remained in existence with special guard status. In the second half of 1993, however, outside threats to national security caused Shevardnadze to rely once again on Ioseliani's paramilitary Mkhedrioni, delaying consolidation of a national military force. In September, Shevardnadze's control over the military improved when parliament declared a two-month state of emergency, which had the effect of weakening the Mkhedrioni.

The Russian Presence

The Soviet Union had maintained a substantial military presence in Georgia because the republic bordered Turkey, a member of NATO. The Transcaucasus Military District, which had coordinated Soviet military forces in the three republics of Transcaucasia, was headquartered in Tbilisi. In mid-1993 an estimated 15,000 Russian troops and border guards remained on Georgian territory. Georgia did not press Russian withdrawal as vigorously as did other former republics of the Soviet Union because it did not have enough personnel to patrol its entire border. At the same time, the continued presence of Russian troops energized the Georgian nationalist parties. In the fall of 1993, those groups saw Shevardnadze's call for Russian military assistance, and the significant increase of Russian forces that resulted, as an admission that his national security policy had failed and a sign that the traditional enemy to the north was again threatening.

Draft Policy

The role of Soviet military and internal security forces in the April Tragedy made Georgian connections with those forces a primary target of anticommunist groups. As in other Soviet republics, opposition to the draft became an early focus of opposition activities. Of all the Soviet republics, Georgia had the lowest rate of recruitment in the fall of 1990, approximately 10 percent of eligible citizens. One of the first acts passed by Gamsakhurdia's parliament ended the Soviet military draft on Georgian territory.

In late 1990, Soviet conscription was replaced with the induction of eligible Georgian males into new "special divisions," under the control of the Georgian Ministry of Internal Affairs, for the maintenance of order within the republic. The new body, which became Kitovani's National Guard, was one of the first official non-Soviet military units in what was still the

Soviet Union. Attempts to build a new Georgian national army in 1993 and 1994 were hindered by a very high percentage of draft evasion.

Arms Supply

Relatively little of the military industry of the Soviet Union was located in Georgia. One Tbilisi plant assembled military training aircraft that were the basis of a small Georgian air force. Most weapons obtained by the various armed units operating in Georgia after 1990 apparently were purchased illegally from Soviet (and later Russian) officers and soldiers stationed in the Caucasus. In May 1992, leaders of the CIS set quotas for the transfer of Soviet military equipment to republic armed forces. According to this plan, Georgia was to receive 220 tanks, 220 armored vehicles, 300 artillery pieces, 100 military aircraft, and fifty attack helicopters. Kitovani complained in December 1992 that Georgia had not yet received any of its allotment.

Internal Security

The Georgian internal security agency having the closest ties to Moscow was the Georgian branch of the Committee for State Security (Komitet gosudarstvennoi bezopasnosti—KGB). Beginning in 1990, the anticommunist independence movement exerted direct pressure on the Georgian KGB to accept independence. The first confrontation between Moscow and the Gamsakhurdia government came over appointments to top security posts in the republic. In November 1990, the Georgian parliamentary Commission on Security broke the tradition of Moscow-designated KGB chiefs by naming its own appointee. When Gorbachev threatened dire consequences, Gamsakhurdia simply left the chairmanship vacant but named his candidate first deputy chairman and thus acting chairman. At that point, top Georgian KGB officials voiced support for Gamsakhurdia and protested Gorbachev's interference, signaling a service commitment to Tbilisi rather than to Moscow.

As late as mid-1991, Moscow continued financing activities of the Georgian KGB and provided part of the budget of the Georgian Ministry of Internal Affairs, which ran domestic intelligence and police agencies. Meanwhile, by 1991 the opposition to Gamsakhurdia was accusing the president of using the Georgian KGB to investigate and harass political enemies.

In May 1992, the Georgian KGB, which in the interim had been renamed the Ministry of Security, was formally replaced by the Information and Intelligence Service. The new agency, established on the organizational foundation of the old KGB, was headed by Irakli Batiashvili, a thirty-year-old philosophy scholar who had been a National Democratic Party delegate to the National Congress.

Civilian National Security Organization

In November 1992, the parliament passed a law creating the Council for National Security and Defense. This body was accountable to parliament, but, as head of state and commander in chief of the armed forces, Shevardnadze was council chairman. Shevardnadze named Ioseliani and Kitovani deputy chairmen of the council; Tedo Japaridze, top expert on the United States in the Georgian Ministry of Foreign Affairs, became the chairman's aide. The powers of the council included the right to issue binding decisions on military and security matters.

In May 1993, Shevardnadze disbanded the council to deprive Ioseliani and Kitovani of their government power bases. The council was then reconstituted, with Shevardnadze's chairmanship assuming greater power.

Crime

In the first postcommunist years, levels of crime and civil unrest in Georgia were quite high because of the proximity of the Armenian-Azerbaijani conflict, refugee movement and terrorism resulting from the Abkhazian conflict within Georgia, the gap between official wages and living standards, and the government's lack of police authority in many areas of the country. Crime statistics were unreliable, however, because the extent of law enforcement and reporting varied during 1993. Reported crimes dropped from 1,982 in May to 1,260 in July. In late 1993, however, numerous automobile thefts and kidnappings occurred on Georgian highways, and citizen insecurity prompted the proliferation of private detective agencies.

The natural gas pipeline to Armenia was a frequent target of terrorist bombs in 1993, and several government figures apparently were the targets of unsuccessful bomb attacks. The Mkhedrioni, who often were involved in criminal activity, usually escaped police control because the minister of internal affairs was a Mkhedrioni member. In September, Shevardnadze took personal control of the ministry to bolster police authority.

Long-Term Security

In late 1993, the primary consideration of Georgian national security continued to be the prevention of territorial gains by separatist national movements—a cause for which Russian military assistance was proving indispensable. Longer-term national security, however, would depend on Shevardnadze's ability to reestablish the structures of a viable, unified state: internal and international commercial activity, undisputed sovereignty over the national territory and its populace, and a shift back to government rule by statute rather than by emergency executive powers. In early 1994, all those preconditions remained in doubt, and Shevardnadze's reluctant recourse to Russian military assistance had set a precedent with unknown national security consequences.

* * *

For background on Georgian history, the best basic source is Ronald G. Suny's *The Making of the Georgian Nation.* Earlier histories on the Georgian people were written by David Marshall Lang (*A Modern History of Soviet Georgia* and *The Georgians*) and Kalistrat Salia (*History of the Georgian Nation*). Several scholars have followed contemporary Georgian developments on a regular basis; in addition to the present author, they include Elizabeth Fuller, a writer for the *RFE/RL Research Report*; Stephen Jones, whose journal articles cover political and nationalist issues in the Caucasus; and Robert Parsons of the British Broadcasting Corporation. Human rights issues in Georgia are covered extensively in publications of the United States Congress's Commission on Security and Cooperation in Europe. Useful articles from Russian-language sources are translated in the Foreign Broadcast Information Service's *Daily Report: Soviet Union* (more recently titled *Daily Report: Central Eurasia*). Studies of Georgian culture and history appear occasionally in the *Journal for the Study of Caucasia.* And the *Georgian Chronicle* is a monthly bulletin on current events published by the Caucasian Institute for Peace, Democracy, and Development in Tbilisi. (For further information and complete citations, see Bibliography.)

Appendix

Table 1. Metric Conversion Coefficients and Factors

When you kow	Multiply by	To find
Millimeters	0.04	inches
Centimeters	0.39	inches
Meters	3.3	feet
Kilometers	0.62	miles
Hectares $(10,000 \text{ m}^2)$..................	2.47	acres
Square kilometers	0.39	square miles
Cubic meters	35.3	cubic feet
Liters	0.26	gallons
Kilograms	2.2	pounds
Metric tons	0.98	long tons
....	1.1	short tons
....	2,204.0	pounds
Degrees Celsius (Centigrade)	1.8 and add 32	degrees Fahrenheit

Table 2. *Armenia, Azerbaijan, and Georgia: Selected Health and Health Care Statistics, 1989, 1990, and 1991*

	Armenia	Azerbaijan	Georgia
Disease diagnosis[1]			
Tuberculosis......................	17.6	36.2	28.9
Viral hepatitis.....................	279.0	310.5	226.3
Cancer	223.1	224.9	140.9
Hospital beds[2]	89.4	99.4	110.7
Doctors[2]	42.8	38.9	59.2
Pharmacists[3]	7.0	6.7	14.3
Infant mortality[4].....................	17.1	25.0	15.9

[1] For tuberculosis and cancer, first diagnoses per 100,000 population in 1990; for viral hepatitis, registered cases per 100,000 population in 1989.
[2] Per 10,000 population: in 1990 for Georgia, in 1991 for Armenia and Azerbaijan.
[3] Per 10,000 population in 1989.
[4] Per 1,000 live births: in 1990 for Georgia, in 1991 for Armenia and Azerbaijan.

Source: Based on information from Christopher M. Davis, "Health Care Crisis: The Former Soviet Union," *RFE/RL Research Report* [Munich], 2, No. 40, October 8, 1993, 36.

Table 3. Armenia: Output of Major Industrial Products, 1989, 1990, and 1991

Product	1989	1990	1991
Automobile tires (in thousands)	1,338	1,009	914
Cable (in kilometers)	13,772	8,459	7,746
Canned food (in thousands of cans)	413,119	267,425	181,860
Carpets (in thousands of square meters)	1,585	1,300	947
Cement (in thousands of tons)	1,639	1,466	1,507
Electric energy (in millions of kilowatt-hours). .	12,137	10,377	9,532
Electric engines	736,490	823,295	700,157
Leather shoes (in thousands of pairs)	17,952	18,740	11,340
Natural textile items	90,723	85,473	53,203
Synthetic fibers (in tons)	10,479	9,351	4,050
Synthetic rubber (in tons)	39,150	1,141	10,613
Wine and cognac (in thousands of decaliters) . .	7,104	4,805	4,852

Source: Based on information from International Monetary Fund, *Armenia*, Washington, 1993, 40.

Table 4. Armenia: Durable Consumer Goods, 1989, 1990, and
*1991 (*items per 100 families*)*

Product	1989	1990	1991
Automobiles	33	34	39
Refrigerators	81	81	80
Sewing machines	54	52	50
Tape recorders	42	46	49
Televisions	93	95	93
Washing machines	89	95	96

Source: Based on information from United States, Central Intelligence Agency, *Handbook of
International Economic Statistics, 1993*, Washington, 1993, 73.

Table 5. Armenia: Employment by Economic Activity, 1989–92
(in thousands of people)

Activity	1989	1990	1991	1992[1]
Agriculture	117	115	46	20
Industry	417	398	359	344
Construction	156	167	162	122
Communications	13	13	12	20
Transportation	65	64	69	51
Health and social services	91	90	93	81
Education	143	154	130	152
Science and research and development	52	52	35	30
Other	248	231	231	192
TOTAL	1,302	1,284	1,137	1,012

[1] January to June.

Source: Based on information from International Monetary Fund, *Armenia*, Washington, 1993, 44.

Table 6. Armenia: Annual Per Capita Food Consumption, Selected Years, 1970–90
(in kilograms unless otherwise specified)

Food	1970	1980	1985	1990
Bread	154	140	131	126
Eggs (in units)	94	146	148	163
Fish	4	4	5	8
Meat.....................................	34	47	49	56
Milk and dairy products	328	432	433	446
Potatoes	55	55	65	58
Sugar	26	31	29	39
Vegetable oil	2	3	2	3
Vegetables	101	118	135	132

Source: Based on information from World Bank, *Food and Agricultural Policy Reforms in the Former USSR*, Washington, 1992, 183–84.

Table 7. Armenia: Government Budget, 1991 and 1992[1] (in percentages of GNP)[2]

	1991	1992			
		First Quarter	Second Quarter	Third Quarter	Fourth Quarter[3]
Revenues					
Tax revenues[4]	15.8	10.7	19.6	18.5	15.6
Nontax revenues	10.2	6.0	5.6	5.1	5.3
Total revenues	26.0	16.7	25.2	23.5	20.9
Expenditures					
Current expenditures					
Wages	n.a.[5]	5.6	7.3	6.4	8.9
External interest	n.a.	14.7	9.7	9.3	10.7
Pension and child allowances	n.a.	15.1	13.1	8.9	11.7
Other	n.a.	25.5	7.6	20.0	20.7
Total current expenditures	n.a.	60.9	37.6	44.5	52.1
Capital expenditures	n.a.	4.8	8.7	4.6	5.6
Total expenditures	27.9	65.7	46.4	49.1	57.6
Accrued deficit	– 1.9	– 49.0	– 21.2	– 25.6	– 36.7
Net change in arrears	n.a.	34.1	10.2	11.8	16.5
Cash deficit	– 1.9	– 14.9	– 11.0	– 13.7	– 20.2

[1] Figures may not add to totals because of rounding.
[2] GNP—gross national product.
[3] Projected.
[4] Includes value-added tax; excise, enterprise, and personal income taxes; collection of back taxes; and other taxes.
[5] n.a.—not available.

Source: Based on information from International Monetary Fund, *Armenia*, Washington, 1993, 51.

Table 8. Armenia: Major Trading Partners, 1990

Country	Value[1]		Percentage of Total	
	Exports	Imports	Exports	Imports
Europe	69	585	66.9	66.8
Bulgaria	12	67	11.7	7.6
Britain	3	10	2.9	1.1
Hungary	6	49	5.8	5.6
Italy	4	20	3.9	2.3
Poland	7	84	6.8	9.6
Romania	4	20	3.9	2.3
Germany	11	139	10.7	15.8
Finland	3	22	2.9	2.5
France	3	27	2.9	3.1
Czechoslovakia	9	80	8.7	9.1
Yugoslavia	2	28	1.9	3.2
Asia	11	148	10.3	16.9
India	2	25	1.9	2.9
China	2	24	1.9	2.7
Japan	1	33	1.0	3.8
North America	8	98	7.7	11.2
Cuba	6	51	5.8	5.8
United States	1	32	1.0	3.6

[1] In millions of rubles.

Source: Based on information from World Bank, *Statistical Handbook: States of the Former USSR*, Washington, 1992, 40.

Table 9. *Azerbaijan: Annual Per Capita Food Consumption,*
Selected Years, 1970–90
(in kilograms unless otherwise specified)

Food	1970	1980	1985	1990
Bread	155	160	158	151
Eggs (in units)	90	134	155	143
Fish	3	3	5	5
Meat	26	32	35	34
Milk and dairy products	227	281	293	292
Potatoes	25	25	28	27
Sugar	33	40	37	36
Vegetable oil	2	2	3	3
Vegetables	47	72	62	67

Source: Based on information from World Bank, *Food and Agricultural Policy Reforms in the Former USSR*, Washington, 1992, 183–84.

Table 10. *Azerbaijan: Durable Consumer Goods, 1989, 1990,*
and 1991
(items per 100 families)

Product	1989	1990	1991
Automobiles	16	17	16
Refrigerators	83	83	82
Sewing machines	62	60	58
Tape recorders	36	39	40
Televisions	101	102	101
Washing machines	48	51	52

Source: Based on information from United States, Central Intelligence Agency, *Handbook of International Economic Statistics, 1993*, Washington, 1993, 75.

Table 11.   *Azerbaijan: Employment by Economic Activity, 1989, 1990, and 1991*
(in thousands of people)

Activity	1989	1990	1991
Agriculture	905	914	934
Forestry	6	5	5
Industry	483	469	463
Construction	243	251	248
Transportation and communications	133	143	143
Trade and commercial services	232	230	233
Housing and municipal services	108	99	101
Science and research and development	60	58	60
Education and culture	329	338	341
Health and social welfare	168	170	173
Government	61	62	62
Other	67	71	73
TOTAL[1]	2,794	2,808	2,839

[1] Figures may not add to totals because of rounding.

Source: Based on information from *The Europa World Year Book, 1993*, 1, London, 1993, 442.

Table 12. Azerbaijan: Population and Employment, 1988–91
(in thousands of people)

	1988	1989	1990	1991
Total population	6,963	7,064	7,117	7,175
Urban	3,768	3,829	3,843	3,858
Rural................................	3,195	3,235	3,274	3,317
Total labor force	3,932	3,959	3,977	3,986
Total employed	2,753	2,795	2,808	2,839
In state sector	2,209	2,200	2,173	2,171
In collective farms	304	308	312	325
Self-employed	236	241	260	265
Other	4	46	63	78
Students of working age	325	308	306	307
Employed in households...................	815	721	729	707

Source: Based on information from World Bank, *Azerbaijan: From Crisis to Sustained
Growth*, Washington, 1993, 159.

Table 13. Armenia, Azerbaijan, and Georgia: Share of Total Production of Major Agricultural Commodities in Former Soviet Union by Republic, 1986–90 Average
(in percentages)

Commodity	Armenia	Azerbaijan	Georgia
Citrus fruits	0.0	0.0	96.3
Cotton	0.0	7.7	0.0
Eggs	0.7	1.2	1.0
Fruits and berries	2.0	4.3	6.8
Grains	0.2	0.6	0.3
Grapes	3.1	22.6	11.0
Meat	0.5	0.9	0.9
Milk	0.5	1.0	0.7
Potatoes	0.3	0.3	0.5
Sugar beets	0.1	0.0	0.1
Sunflowers	0.0	0.0	0.1
Vegetables	1.8	3.1	2.0
Wool	0.8	2.3	1.4

Source: Based on information from World Bank, *Food and Agricultural Policy Reforms in the Former USSR*, Washington, 1992, 194.

Table 14. Azerbaijan: Output of Selected Industrial Products, 1989, 1990, and 1991
(in thousands of tons unless otherwise specified)

Product	1989	1990	1991
Aviation fuel	114	89	58
Bitumen	167	146	113
Caustic soda	219	160	171
Diesel oil	4,236	3,899	3,635
Electric energy (in millions of kilowatt-hours)	23,300	23,200	23,300
Fuel oil	7,555	6,686	7,207
Jet kerosene	1,519	1,290	1,205
Lubricants	934	818	763
Motor fuel	1,522	1,479	1,174
Naphtha	550	341	427
Petroleum coke	230	179	161
Steel	696	501	462
Sulfuric acid	768	603	552

Source: Based on information from *The Europa World Year Book, 1993*, 1, London, 1993, 443.

Table 15. *Azerbaijan: Government Budget, 1988–92[1]*
(in percentages of GNP)[2]

	1988	1989	1990	1991	1992
Revenues					
Tax revenues					
Indirect taxes[3]	10.3	10.7	12.5	13.0	20.4
Direct taxes[4]	8.4	7.9	8.6	8.1	8.0
Total tax revenues	18.7	18.6	21.1	21.1	28.4
Nontax revenues	3.5	3.8	5.3	4.4	3.6
Total revenues	22.3	22.3	26.4	25.5	32.0
Expenditures					
National economy[5]	9.5	10.6	15.1	9.9	2.4
Science	0.0	0.4	0.4	0.2	0.5
Education	6.9	6.7	7.7	7.0	10.3
Health	2.3	2.5	2.9	2.9	4.0
Culture and sports	0.1	0.1	0.1	1.0	1.0
Social security	3.0	3.2	4.0	6.6	2.6
Internal security and defense	0.3	0.3	0.5	1.3	7.6
Consumer subsidies	0.0	0.0	0.0	0.0	3.7
Other	1.1	0.7	1.3	1.7	5.6
Total expenditures..............	23.1	24.4	31.9	30.5	37.6
Balance	− 0.9	− 2.0	− 5.5	− 5.0	− 5.6

[1] Figures may not add to totals because of rounding.
[2] GNP—gross national product.
[3] Turnover, sales, excise, and export-import taxes; value-added tax; and duties.
[4] Profit, income, and property taxes.
[5] Investment by budgetary institutions and transfers to the enterprise sector.

Source: Based on information from World Bank, *Azerbaijan: From Crisis to Sustained Growth*, Washington, 1993, 193.

Table 16.   *Azerbaijan: Major Trading Partners, 1990*

Country	Value[1]		Percentage of Total	
	Exports	Imports	Exports	Imports
Europe	286	836	62.7	65.3
Bulgaria	41	92	9.0	7.2
Britain	14	12	3.1	0.9
Hungary	27	60	5.9	4.7
Italy	11	54	2.4	4.2
Poland	26	140	5.7	10.9
Romania	16	30	3.5	2.3
Germany	49	172	10.7	13.4
Finland	10	39	2.2	3.0
France	12	22	2.6	1.7
Czechoslovakia	33	109	7.2	8.5
Yugoslavia.........................	11	53	2.4	4.1
Asia	72	262	15.9	20.5
India	9	57	2.0	4.5
China.............................	8	28	1.9	2.7
Japan	11	53	2.4	4.1
North America	31	131	6.9	10.2
Cuba	26	67	5.7	5.2
United States	4	39	0.9	3.0

[1] In millions of rubles.

Source: Based on information from World Bank, *Statistical Handbook: States of the Former USSR*, Washington, 1992, 68.

Table 17.   Georgia: Government Budget, 1991 and 1992   (in
millions of rubles)

	1991		1992	
	Budget	Actual	Budget	Actual
Revenues				
Tax revenues	3,972	4,631	22,202	15,218
Nontax revenues	1,295	1,567	2,898	3,655
Total revenues	5,267	6,198	25,100	18,873
Expenditures				
National economy[1]	2,979	2,878	11,885	20,815
Social and cultural				
Education and culture[2]	n.a.[2]	1,520	n.a.	8,421
Health and sports	n.a.	812	n.a.	2,996
Social security	n.a.	120	n.a.	34
Science	n.a.	74	n.a.	874
Total social and cultural	2,717	2,526	10,082	12,325
Administration and law enforcement				
State administration	n.a.	124	n.a.	1,288
Internal security and defense.............	n.a.	118	n.a.	5,282
Total administration and law enforcement .	245	242	2,631	6,570
Other	327	276	1,765	2,972
Total expenditures	6,268	5,922	26,363	42,682
Extrabudgetary factors[3]	n.a.	1,000	12,713	-23,320
Interest on foreign debt	0	0	0	21,714
Balance	− 1,001	− 724	− 13,976	− 68,843

[1] Investment by budgetary institutions and transfers to the enterprise sector.
[2] n.a.—not available.
[3] Errors and omissions and extrabudgetary expenditures for social security fund and net lending.

Source: Based on information from World Bank, *Georgia: A Blueprint for Reforms*, Washington, 1993, 120; and *The Europa World Year Book, 1993*, 1, London, 1993, 50.

Table 18. Georgia: Output of Major Industrial Products, 1990,
1991, and 1992
(in thousands of tons unless otherwise specified)

Product	1990	1991	1992[1]
Beer (in thousands of decaliters)	9,477	6,011	3,288
Cigarettes (in millions)	11,200	9,800	5,100
Cotton fabric (in millions of square meters)..........	34	17	13
Diesel fuel	658	495	111
Footwear (in millions of pairs)....................	13	12	3
Heavy oil (mazut)	898	737	189
Machine tools (in units)	1,565	1,417	1,149
Margarine.................................	34	16	2
Motor fuel	399	324	72
Steel	1,316	962	535
Synthetic fibers..............................	32	20	5
Synthetic resins and plastics.....................	40	26	8
Vegetable oil................................	14	7	0.1
Wine (in thousands of decaliters)	16,283	12,166	7,130

[1] Estimated.

Source: Based on information from *The Europa World Year Book, 1993*, 1, London, 1993,
1236; and United States, Central Intelligence Agency, *Handbook of International
Economic Statistics, 1993*, Washington, 1993, 76.

Table 19. *Georgia: Employment by Economic Activity, 1989, 1990,*
and 1991
(in thousands of people)

Activity	1989	1990	1991
Agriculture	656	695	671
Forestry	12	12	11
Industry	537	560	488
Construction	266	281	225
Transportation and communications	123	115	104
Trade and commercial services	267	257	227
Housing and municipal services	123	131	110
Science and research and development	73	73	63
Education and culture	301	310	290
Health, social welfare, and sports	189	184	186
Banking and financial	12	12	12
Government	55	52	48
Other services	86	82	79
TOTAL[1]	2,700	2,763	2,514

[1] Figures may not add to totals because of rounding.

Source: Based on information from *The Europa World Year Book, 1993*, 1, London, 1993,
1235.

Table 20. Georgia: Population and Employment, 1988–91
(in thousands of people)

	1988	1989	1990	1991
Total population	5,396	5,414	5,422	5,421
Males	2,561	2,571	2,579	n.a.[1]
Females	2,835	2,843	2,843	n.a.
Urban	2,989	3,014	3,029	3,024
Rural	2,407	2,400	2,393	2,397
Total employed	2,650	2,635	2,685	2,543
Males employed	n.a.	1,414	n.a.	n.a.
Females employed	n.a.	1,221	n.a.	n.a.
In state sector	2,205	2,148	2,087	1,886
In collective farms	249	218	200	154
Self-employed	177	211	229	356
Other	19	58	169	147

[1] n.a—not available.

Source: Based on information from World Bank, *Georgia: A Blueprint for Reforms*, Washington, 1993, 109–10.

Table 21.   Georgia: Annual Per Capita Food Consumption, Selected Years, 1970–90
(in kilograms unless otherwise specified)

Food	1970	1980	1985	1990
Bread	195	190	190	183
Eggs (in units)	85	135	148	140
Fish	6	8	9	9
Meat	31	43	47	46
Milk and dairy products	235	309	309	289
Potatoes	38	46	49	41
Sugar	35	45	43	39
Vegetable oil	3	5	6	6
Vegetables	51	79	87	82

Source: Based on information from World Bank, *Food and Agricultural Policy Reforms in the Former USSR*, Washington, 1992, 183–84.

Table 22.   Georgia: Durable Consumer Goods, 1989, 1990, and 1991 (items per 100 families)

Product	1988	1989	1990
Automobiles	31	31	34
Refrigerators	95	95	95
Sewing machines	63	63	61
Tape recorders	44	48	52
Televisions	102	106	112
Washing machines	76	81	86

Source: Based on information from United States, Central Intelligence Agency, *Handbook of International Economic Statistics, 1993*, Washington, 1993, 77.

Table 23. Georgia: External Trade, 1988, 1989, and 1990
(in millions of rubles)

	1988	1989	1990
Exports			
Oil and gas	100	68	68
Ferrous metallurgy	375	376	318
Chemical fuels	316	343	339
Machines and processed metals	848	869	804
Nonfood light industrial products	1,275	1,285	1,260
Processed foods	2,438	2,573	2,387
Other industrial products	258	275	310
Agricultural products	280	190	404
Other	11	105	93
Total exports	5,901	6,084	5,983
To other Soviet republics......................	5,508	5,719[1]	5,724
To other countries	393	465[1]	259
Imports			
Oil and gas	413	360	285
Ferrous metallurgy	489	443	430
Nonferrous metallurgy	102	106	97
Chemical fuels	541	544	576
Machines and processed metals	1,533	1,522	1,580
Timber and wood products	248	244	279
Building materials	155	148	117
Nonfood light industrial products..................	1,221	1,287	1,372
Processed foods	1,204	1,142	1,174
Other industrial products........................	212	212	291
Agricultural products	348	358	498
Other	27	103	140

Table 23. *Georgia: External Trade, 1988, 1989, and 1990*
(in millions of rubles)

	1988	1989	1990
Total imports	6,493	6,469	6,839
From other Soviet republics..............	5,218	4,888	4,948
From other countries	1,275	1,581	1,891

[1] As published.

Source: Based on information from *The Europa World Year Book, 1994*, 1, London, 1994, 1237.

Table 24.   *Georgia: Major Trading Partners, 1990*

Country	Value[1]		Percentage of Total	
	Exports	Imports	Exports	Imports
Europe	213	1,687	71.4	71.2
Austria	6	53	2.0	2.2
Bulgaria	32	202	10.7	8.5
Hungary	18	144	6.0	6.1
Italy	13	53	4.4	2.2
Poland	25	256	8.4	10.8
Germany............................	32	420	10.7	17.7
Finland	7	76	2.3	3.2
Czechoslovakia	23	227	7.7	9.6
Yugoslavia	8	64	2.7	2.7
Asia	45	377	15.2	15.9
India	6	48	2.0	2.0
China	6	34	1.9	2.7
Syria...............................	1	76	0.2	3.2
Japan	12	115	4.0	4.9
North America	22	192	7.3	8.1
Cuba...............................	16	114	5.4	4.8
United States	3	37	1.0	1.6

[1] In millions of rubles.

Source: Based on information from World Bank, *Statistical Handbook: States of the Former USSR*, Washington, 1992, 152.

Bibliography

Chapter 1

Aftandilian, Gregory. *Armenia, Vision of a Republic: The Independence Lobby in America.* Boston: Charles River Books, 1981.

Arberry, A.J. (ed.). *Religion in the Middle East, 1.* Cambridge: Cambridge University Press, 1969.

Arlen, Michael. *Passage to Ararat.* New York: Farrar, Straus and Giroux, 1975.

Arpee, Leon. *The Armenian Awakening: A History of the Armenian Church, 1820–1860.* Chicago: University of Chicago Press, 1909.

Aslan, Kevork. *Armenia and the Armenians from the Earliest Times until the Great War (1914).* (Trans., Pierre Crabites.) New York: Macmillan, 1920.

Aspaturian, Vernon V. *The Union Republics in Soviet Diplomacy: A Study of Soviet Federalism in the Service of Soviet Foreign Policy.* Geneva: E. Droz, 1960.

Atamian, Sarkis. *The Armenian Community: The Historical Development of a Social and Ideological Conflict.* New York: Philosophical Library, 1955.

Bardakjian, Kevork B. *The Mekhitarist Contributions to Armenian Culture and Scholarship.* Cambridge: Harvard College Library, 1976.

Bauer-Manndorff, Elisabeth. *Armenia: Past and Present.* Lucerne: Reich Verlag, 1981.

Blackwell, Alice Stone. *Armenian Poetry.* Boston: Atlantic, 1917.

Bournoutian, George A. *Eastern Armenia in the Last Decades of Persian Rule, 1807–1828: A Political and Socioeconomic Study of the Khanate of Erevan on the Eve of the Russian Conquest.* Malibu, California: Undena, 1982.

Braude, Benjamin, and Bernard Lewis. *Christians and Jews in the Ottoman Empire: The Functioning of a Plural Society.* (2 vols.) New York: Holmes and Meier, 1982.

Bryce, James. *Transcaucasia and Ararat.* London: Macmillan, 1896. Reprint. New York: Arno Press, 1970.

Buxton, Noel, and Harold Buxton. *Travels and Politics in Armenia.* London: Murray, 1914.

Chalabian, Antranig. *General Andranik and the Armenian Revolutionary Movement.* Southfield, Michigan: Chalabian, 1988.

Davis, Christopher M. "Health Care Crisis: The Former Soviet Union," *RFE/RL Research Report* [Munich], 2, No. 40, October 8, 1993, 35–43.

Davison, Roderic. "The Armenian Crisis, 1912–1914," *American Historical Review,* 53, No. 3, April 1948, 481–505.

————. *Reform in the Ottoman Empire, 1856–1876.* Princeton: Princeton University Press, 1963.

Dekmejian, R.H. "Soviet-Turkish Relations and Politics in the Armenian SSR," *Soviet Studies,* 19, No. 4, April 1968, 510–25.

de Morgan, Jacques. *History of the Armenian People.* (Trans., Ernest F. Barry.) Boston: Hairenik Press, n.d.

des Pres, Terrence. "On Governing Narratives: The Turkish-Armenian Case," *Yale Review,* 75, Summer 1986, 517–31.

Etmekjian, James. *The French Influence on the Western Armenian Renaissance, 1843–1915.* New York: Twayne, 1964.

Fuller, Elizabeth. "Armenia's Constitutional Debate," *RFE/RL Research Report* [Munich], 3, No. 22, May 27, 1994, 6–9.

————. "Paramilitary Forces Dominate Fighting in Transcaucasus," *RFE/RL Research Report* [Munich], 2, No. 25, June 18, 1993, 74–82.

Gidney, James B. *A Mandate for Armenia.* Kent, Ohio: Kent State University Press, 1967.

Goshgarian, Geoffrey. "Eghishe Charents and the 'Modernization' of Soviet Armenian Literature," *Armenian Review,* 36, No. 1, 1983, 76–88.

Hartunian, Abraham H. *Neither to Laugh Nor to Weep: A Memoir of the Armenian Genocide.* (Trans., Vartan Hartunian.) Boston: Beacon Press, 1968.

Hovannisian, Richard G. *The Armenian Holocaust: A Bibliography Relating to the Deportations, Massacres, and Dispersion of the Armenian People, 1915–1923.* Cambridge, Massachusetts: Armenian Heritage Press, 1978.

————. *The Armenian Republic,* 1 and 2. Berkeley: University of California Press, 1971 and 1982.

————. "Russian Armenia: A Century of Tsarist Rule," *Jahrbücher für Geschichte Osteuropas* [Munich], 19, No. 1, 1971, 31–48.

Hovannisian, Richard G. (ed.). *The Armenian Genocide in Perspective.* New Brunswick, New Jersey: Transaction Books, 1986.

————. *The Armenian Image in History and Literature.* Malibu, California: Undena Press, 1981.

Hovannisian, Richard G., Stanford J. Shaw, and Ezel Kural.

"Forum: The Armenian Question," *International Journal of Middle East Studies*, 11, No. 3, August 1979, 379–400.

International Monetary Fund. *Armenia.* (IMF Economic Reviews, 1/1993.) Washington: 1993.

International Petroleum Encyclopedia, 1992. (Ed., Jim West.) Tulsa: PennWell, 1992.

Jane's World Railways, 1993–94. (Ed., James Abbott.) Alexandria, Virginia: Jane's Information Group, 1993.

Katz, Zev. "The Armenian Church and the WCC: A Personal View," *Ecumenical Review,* 40, July–October 1988, 411–17.

Katz, Zev (ed.). *Handbook of Major Soviet Nationalities.* New York: Free Press, 1975.

Lang, David Marshall. *Armenia: Cradle of Civilization.* London: Allen and Unwin, 1980.

———. *The Armenians: A People in Exile.* London: Allen and Unwin, 1981.

Lang, David Marshall, and Christopher J. Walker. *The Armenians.* (Minority Rights Group Report No. 32.) London: Minority Rights Group, 1976.

Libaridian, Gerard J. *The Karabagh File: Documents and Facts on the Question of Mountainous Karabagh, 1918–1988.* Cambridge, Massachusetts: Zoryan Institute, 1988.

Lloyd's Ports of the World, 1988. (Ed., Paul J. Cuny.) Colchester, United Kingdom: Lloyd's of London, 1988.

Lynch, H.F.B. *Armenia: Travels and Studies.* (2 vols.) Beirut: Khayats, 1965.

Matossian, Mary Kilbourne. *The Impact of Soviet Policies in Armenia.* Leiden, Netherlands: E.J. Brill, 1962.

The Military Balance, 1994–1995. London: Brassey's for International Institute for Strategic Studies, 1994.

Mirak, Robert. "Armenians." Pages 136–49 in Steven Thernstrom (ed.), *Harvard Encyclopedia of American Ethnic Groups.* Cambridge: Harvard University Press, 1980.

Nalbandian, Louise. *The Armenian Revolutionary Movement: The Development of Armenian Political Parties Through the Nineteenth Century.* Berkeley: University of California Press, 1963.

National Democratic Movement in Armenia. *Armenia at the Crossroads: Democracy and Nationhood in the Post-Soviet Era.* Watertown, Massachusetts: Blue Crane, 1991.

Noble, John S., and John King. *USSR: A Travel Survival Kit.* Berkeley, California: Lonely Planet, 1993.

Pipes, Richard. *The Formation of the Soviet Union: Communism and Nationalism, 1917–1923.* New York: Atheneum, 1968.

Rakowska-Harmstone, Teresa. "The Dialectics of Nationalism in the USSR," *Problems of Communism*, 13, No. 3, 1974, 1–22.

Sarkissian, Karekin. "The Armenian Church." Pages 482–520 in A.J. Arberry (ed.), *Religion in the Middle East*, 1. Cambridge: Cambridge University Press, 1969.

Sarkisyanz, Manuel. *A Modern History of Transcaucasian Armenia: Social, Cultural, and Political.* Leiden, Netherlands: E.J. Brill, 1975.

Shaw, Stanford J., and Ezel Kural. *History of the Ottoman Empire and Modern Turkey.* (2 vols.) Cambridge: Cambridge University Press, 1977.

Sheehy, Ann, and Elizabeth Fuller. "Armenia and Armenians in the USSR: Nationality and Language Aspects of the Census of 1979," *Radio Liberty Research Bulletin* [Munich], 24, No. 22, June 13, 1980.

Smith, Anthony D. *The Ethnic Origins of Nations.* Oxford: Blackwell, 1986.

Suny, Ronald G. *Armenia in the Twentieth Century.* Chico, California: Scholars Press, 1983.

————. *The Baku Commune, 1917–1918: Class and Nationality in the Russian Revolution.* Princeton: Princeton University Press, 1972.

————. "Incomplete Revolution: National Movements and the Collapse of the Soviet Empire," *New Left Review*, No. 189, September–October 1991, 111–26.

————. *Looking Toward Ararat: Armenia in Modern History.* Bloomington: Indiana University Press, 1993.

————. "Nationalism and Democracy in Gorbachev's Soviet Union: The Case of Karabagh," *Michigan Quarterly Review*, 28, No. 4, 481–506.

————. "The Revenge of the Past: Socialism and Ethnic Conflict in Transcaucasia," *New Left Review*, No. 184, November–December 1990, 5–34.

Suny, Ronald G. (ed.). *Transcaucasia: Nationalism and Social Change: Essays in the History of Armenia, Azerbaijan, and Georgia.* Ann Arbor: Michigan Slavic Publications, 1983.

Sutton, Peter. "A View of Soviet Armenia," *Contemporary Review*, No. 246, May 4, 1985, 251–54.

Sweeney, Padraic (ed.). *The Transportation Handbook for Russia and the Former Soviet Union.* Arlington, Virginia: ASET/ICI, 1993.

Ter Minassian, Anahide. *Nationalism and Socialism in the Armenian Revolutionary Movement.* Cambridge, Massachusetts:

Zoryan Institute, 1984.

————. *La République d'Arménie.* Paris: Éditions Complexes, 1989.

Thernstrom, Steven (ed.). *Harvard Encyclopedia of American Ethnic Groups.* Cambridge: Harvard University Press, 1980.

Thorossian, H. *Histoire de la littérature arménienne: Des origines jusqu'à nos jours.* Paris: n.p., 1951.

Timofeyev, A. *Motorist's Guide to the Soviet Union.* Moscow: Progress, 1980.

Toynbee, Arnold J. *Armenian Atrocities: The Murder of a Nation.* London: Hodder and Stoughton, 1915.

Tremlett, P.I. (ed.). *Thomas Cook Overseas Timetable.* Thorpe Wood, United Kingdom: Thomas Cook, 1994.

United States. Agency for International Development. Center for International Health Information. *Armenia: USAID Health Profile.* Arlington, Virginia: 1992.

————. Central Intelligence Agency. *Handbook of International Economic Statistics, 1993.* Washington: GPO, 1993.

————. Central Intelligence Agency. *USSR Energy Atlas.* Washington: 1985.

————. Central Intelligence Agency. *The World Factbook, 1994.* Washington: 1994.

————. Department of Commerce. Business Information Service for the Newly Independent States. *Economic Profile of Armenia.* Washington: 1993.

————. Department of State. "Armenia," *U.S. Department of State Dispatch,* 5, May 2, 1994, 255–57.

Walker, Christopher J. "Armenia: A Nation in Asia," *Asian Affairs,* 19, February 1988, 20–35.

————. *Armenia: The Survival of a Nation.* New York: St. Martin's Press, 1980.

Walker, Christopher J. (ed.). *Armenia and Karabagh: The Struggle for Unity.* London: Minority Rights Group, 1991.

Woff, Richard. "The Armed Forces of Armenia," *Jane's Intelligence Review* [London], 6, September 1994, 387–91.

World Bank. *Food and Agricultural Policy Reforms in the Former USSR.* (Studies of Economies in Transformation, Paper No. 1.) Washington: 1992.

————. *Statistical Handbook: States of the Former USSR.* (Studies of Economies in Transformation, Paper No. 3.) Washington: 1992.

(Various issues of the following periodicals were also used in the preparation of this chapter: Armenian Assembly of America, *Monthly Digest of News from Armenia*; and Foreign Broadcast Information Service, *Daily Report: Central Eurasia, FBIS Report: Central Eurasia,* and *JPRS Report: Environmental Issues.*)

Chapter 2

Afandiiev, Rasim. *Folk Art of Azerbaijan.* Baku: Ishyg, 1984.

Akiner, Shirin. *Islamic Peoples of the Soviet Union.* (2d ed.) London: Routledge and Kegan Paul, 1986.

Alstadt, Audrey L. "The Azerbaijani Bourgeoisie and the Cultural-Enlightenment Movement in Baku: First Steps Toward Nationalism." In Ronald G. Suny (ed.), *Transcaucasia: Nationalism and Social Change: Essays in the History of Armenia, Azerbaijan, and Georgia.* Ann Arbor: Michigan Slavic Publications, 1983.

———. *The Azerbaijani Turks: Power and Identity under Russian Rule.* Stanford, California: Hoover Institution Press, 1992.

Apostolou, Andrew, Amberin Zaman, and Naritza Matossian. "Central Asia: New Players in an Old Game," *Middle East,* No. 213, July 1992, 5–10.

Bennigsen, Alexandre, and Marie Broxup. *The Islamic Threat to the Soviet State.* London: Croom Helm, 1983.

Bennigsen, Alexandre, Marie Broxup, and S. Enders Wimbush. *Muslims of the Soviet Empire: A Guide.* Bloomington: Indiana University Press, 1986.

"Dangerous Liaisons in Transcaucasia," *Intelligence Digest,* February 18, 1994, 3–4.

Davis, Christopher M. "Health Care Crisis: The Former Soviet Union," *RFE/RL Research Report* [Munich], 2, No. 40, October 8, 1993, 35–43.

Dragadze, Tamara. "Azerbaijanis." Pages 163–79 in Graham Smith (ed.), *The Nationalities Question in the Soviet Union.* London: Longman, 1990.

The Europa World Year Book, 1993, 1. London: Europa, 1993.

The Europa World Year Book, 1994, 1. London: Europa, 1994.

Fawcett, Louise l'Estrange. *Iran and the Cold War: The Azerbaijan Crisis of 1946.* Cambridge: Cambridge University Press, 1992.

Frelick, Bill. *Faultlines of Nationality Conflict: Refugees and Displaced Persons from Armenia and Azerbaijan.* Washington: U.S. Committee for Refugees, 1994.

Fuller, Elizabeth. "Azerbaijan's June Revolution," *RFE/RL Research Report* [Munich], 2, No. 32, August 13, 1993, 24–29.

———. "Azerbaijan's Relations with Russia and the CIS," *RFE/*

RL Research Report [Munich], 1, No. 43, October 30, 1992, 52–55.

————. "Ethnic Strife Threatens Democratization," *RFE/RL Research Report* [Munich], 2, No. 1, January 1, 1993, 17–24.

————. "The Karabakh Mediation Process: Grachev Versus the CSCE?" *RFE/RL Research Report* [Munich], 3, No. 23, June 10, 1994, 13–17.

————. "Paramilitary Forces Dominate Fighting in Transcaucasus," *RFE/RL Research Report*, 2, No. 25, June 18, 1993, 74–82.

————. "Russia, Turkey, Iran, and the Karabakh Mediation Process," *RFE/RL Research Report* [Munich], 3, No. 8, February 25, 1994, 31–36.

Goble, Paul A. "Coping with the Nagorno-Karabakh Crisis," *Fletcher Forum of World Affairs*, 16, Summer 1992, 19–26.

Golden, Peter. "The Turkic Peoples and Transcaucasia." Pages 45–68 in Ronald G. Suny (ed.), *Transcaucasia: Nationalism and Social Change: Essays in the History of Armenia, Azerbaijan, and Georgia.* Ann Arbor: Michigan Slavic Publications, 1983.

Henry, J.D. *Baku: An Eventful History.* London: Constable, 1905. Reprint. New York: Arno Press, 1977.

Hostler, Charles W. *Turkism and the Soviets.* London: Allen and Unwin, 1957.

Huddle, Frank, Jr. "Azerbaidzhan and the Azerbaidzhanis," Pages 189–210 in Zev Katz (ed.), *Handbook of Major Soviet Nationalities.* New York: Free Press, 1975.

Ibrahimov, Mirza (ed.). *Azerbaijanian Poetry: Classic, Modern, Traditional.* Moscow: Progress, 1969.

International Monetary Fund. *Economic Review: Azerbaijan.* Washington: 1992.

International Petroleum Encyclopedia, 1992. (Ed., Jim West.) Tulsa: PennWell, 1992.

Jane's World Railways, 1993–94. (Ed., James Abbott.) Alexandria, Virginia: Jane's Information Group, 1993.

Katz, Zev (ed.). *Handbook of Major Soviet Nationalities.* New York: Free Press, 1975.

Kazemzadeh, Firuz. *The Struggle for Transcaucasia, 1917–1921.* New York: Philosophical Library, 1951.

Lloyd's Ports of the World, 1988. (Ed., Paul J. Cuny.) Colchester, United Kingdom: Lloyd's of London, 1988.

Maggs, William Ward. "Armenia and Azerbaijan: Looking Toward the Middle East," *Current History*, 92, January 1993, 6–11.

The Military Balance, 1994–1995. London: Brassey's for International Institute for Strategic Studies, 1994.

Nissman, David. "The National Reawakening of Azerbaijan," *World and I,* 7, February 1992, 80–85.

Noble, John S., and John King. *USSR: A Travel Survival Kit.* Berkeley, California: Lonely Planet, 1993.

Pipes, Richard. *The Formation of the Soviet Union: Communism and Nationalism, 1917–1923.* Cambridge: Harvard University Press, 1964.

Richards, Susan. *Epics of Everyday Life: Encounters in a Changing Russia.* New York: Viking Press, 1990.

Saroyan, Mark. "The 'Karabakh Syndrome' and Azerbaijani Politics," *Problems of Communism,* 39, September–October 1990, 14–29.

Sobhani, Sohrab C. "Azerbaijan: A People in Search of Independence," *Global Affairs,* 6, Winter 1991, 40–53.

The Statesman's Year-Book, 1994–1995. (Ed., Brian Hunter.) New York: St. Martin's Press, 1994.

Sturino, John. "Nagorno-Karabakh: The Roots of Conflict," *Surviving Together,* 11, Spring 1993, 10–14.

Suny, Ronald G. *The Baku Commune, 1917–1918: Class and Nationality in the Russian Revolution.* Princeton: Princeton University Press, 1972.

Suny, Ronald G. (ed.). *Transcaucasia: Nationalism and Social Change: Essays in the History of Armenia, Azerbaijan, and Georgia.* Ann Arbor: Michigan Slavic Publications, 1983.

Sweeney, Padraic (ed.). *The Transportation Handbook for Russia and the Former Soviet Union.* Arlington, Virginia: ASET/ICI, 1993.

Swietochowski, Tadeusz. "Azerbaijan: Between Ethnic Conflict and Irredentism," *Armenian Review,* 43, Summer–Autumn 1990, 35–49.

———. "National Consciousness and Political Orientations in Azerbaijan, 1905–1920." Pages 209–38 in Ronald G. Suny (ed.), *Transcaucasia: Nationalism and Social Change: Essays in the History of Armenia, Azerbaijan, and Georgia.* Ann Arbor: Michigan Slavic Publications, 1983.

———. *Russian Azerbaijan, 1905–1920: The Shaping of National Identity in a Muslim Community.* Cambridge: Cambridge University Press, 1985.

Timofeyev, A. *Motorist's Guide to the Soviet Union.* Moscow: Progress, 1980.

Tremlett, P.I. (ed.). *Thomas Cook Overseas Timetable.* Thorpe

Wood, United Kingdom: Thomas Cook, 1994.
United States. Central Intelligence Agency. *Handbook of International Economic Statistics, 1993.* Washington: GPO, 1993.
————. Central Intelligence Agency. *USSR Energy Atlas.* Washington: 1985.
————. Central Intelligence Agency. *The World Factbook, 1994.* Washington: 1994.
Weekes, Richard W. (ed.). *The Muslim Peoples: A World Ethnographic Survey.* (2d ed.) Westport, Connecticut: Greenwood Press, 1984.
World Bank. *Azerbaijan: From Crisis to Sustained Growth.* (A World Bank Country Study.) Washington: 1993.
————. *Food and Agricultural Policy Reforms in the Former USSR.* (Studies of Economies in Transformation, Paper No. 1.) Washington: 1992.
————. *Statistical Handbook: States of the Former USSR.* (Studies of Economies in Transformation, Paper No. 3.) Washington: 1992.
Yefendizade, R.M. *Architecture of Soviet Azerbaijan.* Moscow: Stroiizdat, 1986.

(Various issues of the following periodicals were also used in the preparation of this chapter: Foreign Broadcast Information Service, *Daily Report: Central Eurasia* and *FBIS Report: Central Eurasia.*)

Chapter 3

Benet, Sula. *Abkhazians: The Long-Living People of the Caucasus.* New York: Holt, Rinehart and Winston, 1974.
Bremmer, Ian, and Ray Taras (eds.). *Nations and Politics in the Soviet Successor States.* Cambridge: Cambridge University Press, 1993.
Dale, Catherine. "Turmoil in Abkhazia: Russian Responses," *RFE/RL Research Report* [Munich], 2, No. 34, August 27, 1993, 48–57.
Davis, Christopher M. "Health Care Crisis: The Former Soviet Union," *RFE/RL Research Report* [Munich], 2, No. 40, October 8, 1993, 35–43.
Dragadze, Tamara. "Conflict in the Transcaucasus and the Value of Inventory Control," *Jane's Intelligence Review* [London], 6, No. 2, February 1994, 71–73.
The Europa World Year Book, 1993, 1. London: Europa, 1993.
The Europa World Year Book, 1994, 1. London: Europa, 1994.
Fuller, Elizabeth. "Eduard Shevardnadze's Via Dolorosa," *RFE/*

RL Research Report [Munich], 2, No. 43, October 29, 1993, 17–23.

―――. "Georgia, Abkhazia, and Checheno-Ingushetia," *RFE/ RL Research Report* [Munich], 1, No. 5, February 5, 1992, 3– 7.

―――. "The Georgian Parliamentary Elections," *RFE/RL Research Report* [Munich], 1, No. 47, November 27, 1992, 1– 4.

―――. "Georgia Since Independence: Plus Ça Change . . .," *Current History*, 92, October 1993, 342–46.

―――. "Paramilitary Forces Dominate Fighting in Transcaucasus," *RFE/RL Research Report* [Munich], 2, No. 25, June 18, 1993, 74–82.

Holisky, Dee Ann. "The Rules of the *Supra* or How to Drink in Georgian," *Journal for the Study of Caucasia*, 1, No. 1, 1–20.

International Monetary Fund. *Economic Review: Georgia.* Washington: 1992.

International Petroleum Encyclopedia, 1992. (Ed., Jim West.) Tulsa: PennWell, 1992.

Jane's World Railways, 1993–94. (Ed., James Abbott.) Alexandria, Virginia: Jane's Information Group, 1993.

Jones, Stephen. "The Caucasian Mountain Railway Project: A Victory for *Glasnost*?" *Central Asian Survey*, 8, No. 2, 1989, 47–59.

―――. "A Failed Democratic Transition." Pages 288–310 in Ian Bremmer and Ray Taras (eds.), *Nations and Politics in the Soviet Successor States.* Cambridge: Cambridge University Press, 1993.

―――. "Religion and Nationalism in Soviet Georgia and Armenia." Pages 171–95 in Pedro Ramet (ed.), *Religion and Nationalism in Soviet and East European Politics.* Durham: Duke University Press, 1989.

Katz, Zev (ed.). *Handbook of Major Soviet Nationalities.* New York: Free Press, 1975.

Lang, David Marshall. *The Georgians.* London: Thames and Hudson, 1966.

―――. *A Modern History of Soviet Georgia.* New York: Grove Press, 1962.

Lloyd's Ports of the World, 1988. (Ed., Paul J. Cuny.) Colchester, United Kingdom: Lloyd's of London, 1988.

Mars, Gerald, and Yochanan Altman. "The Cultural Bases of Soviet Georgia's Second Economy," *Soviet Studies*, 35, No. 4, October 1983, 546–60.

The Military Balance, 1994–1995. London: Brassey's for International Institute for Strategic Studies, 1994.

Nichol, James. "Georgia in Transition: Context and Implications for U.S. Interests," *Congressional Research Service Report.* (No. 93794.) Washington: Library of Congress, Congressional Research Service, August 24, 1993.

Noble, John S., and John King. *USSR: A Travel Survival Kit.* Berkeley, California: Lonely Planet, 1993.

Parsons, Robert. "Georgians." Pages 180–96 in Graham Smith (ed.), *The Nationalities Question in the Soviet Union.* New York: Longman, 1990.

Ramet, Pedro (ed.). *Religion and Nationalism in Soviet and East European Politics.* Durham: Duke University Press, 1989.

Rosen, Roger. *The Georgian Republic.* Lincolnwood, Illinois: Passport Books, 1992.

Rustaveli, Shota. *The Knight in the Panther's Skin.* (Trans., Venera Urushadze.) Tbilisi: Sabchota Sakartvelo, 1986.

Salia, Kalistrat. *History of the Georgian Nation.* (Trans., Katharine Vivian.) (2d ed.) Paris: Académie Française, 1983.

Sebag-Montefiore, Simon. "Eduard Shevardnadze," *New York Times Magazine,* December 26, 1993, 16–19.

Shevardnadze, Eduard. *The Future Belongs to Freedom.* New York: Free Press, 1991.

Slider, Darrell. "Crisis and Response in Soviet Nationality Policy: The Case of Abkhazia," *Central Asian Survey,* 4, No. 4, 1985, 51–68.

———. "Party-Sponsored Public Opinion Research in the Soviet Union," *Journal of Politics,* 47, No. 1, February 1985, 209–27.

———. "The Politics of Georgia's Independence," *Problems of Communism,* 40, No. 6, November–December 1991, 63–79.

Smith, Graham (ed.). *The Nationalities Question in the Soviet Union.* New York: Longman, 1990.

The Statesman's Year-Book, 1993–1994. (Ed., Brian Hunter.) New York: St. Martin's Press, 1994.

Suny, Ronald G. *The Making of the Georgian Nation.* Bloomington: Indiana University Press, 1988.

Sweeney, Padraic (ed.). *The Transportation Handbook for Russia and the Former Soviet Union.* Arlington, Virginia: ASET/ICI, 1993.

Timofeyev, A. *Motorist's Guide to the Soviet Union.* Moscow: Progress, 1980.

Tremlett, P.I. (ed.). *Thomas Cook Overseas Timetable.* Thorpe

Wood, United Kingdom: Thomas Cook, 1994.

United States. Central Intelligence Agency. *Handbook of International Economic Statistics, 1993.* Washington: GPO, 1993.

————. Central Intelligence Agency. *USSR Energy Atlas.* Washington: 1985.

————. Central Intelligence Agency. *The World Factbook, 1994.* Washington: 1994.

————. Congress. Commission on Security and Cooperation in Europe. *Human Rights and Democratization in the Newly Independent States of the Former Soviet Union.* Washington: 1993.

————. Department of Commerce. Business Information Service for the Newly Independent States. *Georgia.* Washington: 1993.

World Bank. *Food and Agricultural Policy Reforms in the Former USSR.* (Studies of Economies in Transformation, Paper No. 1.) Washington: 1992.

————. *Georgia: A Blueprint for Reforms.* (A World Bank Country Study.) Washington: 1993.

————. *Statistical Handbook: States of the Former USSR.* (Studies of Economies in Transformation, Paper No. 3.) Washington: 1992.

(Various issues of the following periodicals were also used in the preparation of this chapter: Caucasian Institute for Peace, Democracy, and Development, *Georgian Chronicle* [Tbilisi]; and Foreign Broadcast Information Service, *Daily Report: Soviet Union, Daily Report: Central Eurasia,* and *FBIS Report: Central Eurasia.*)

Glossary

Commonwealth of Independent States (CIS)—Official designation of the former republics of the Soviet Union that remained loosely federated in economic and security matters of common concern after the Soviet Union disbanded as a unified state in 1991. Members in early 1994 were Armenia, Azerbaijan, Belarus, Georgia, Kazakhstan, Kyrgyzstan, Moldova, Russia, Tajikistan, Turkmenistan, Ukraine, and Uzbekistan.

Communist Party of the Soviet Union (CPSU)—The official name of the communist party in the Soviet Union after 1952. Originally the Bolshevik (majority) faction of a pre-revolutionary Russian party, the party was named the Russian Communist Party (Bolshevik) from 1918 until it was renamed in 1952.

Conference on Security and Cooperation in Europe (CSCE)—Originating in Helsinki in 1975, a grouping of all European nations (the only exception, Albania, joined in 1991) that has sponsored joint sessions and consultations on political issues vital to European security.

Conventional Forces in Europe Treaty (CFE Treaty)—An agreement signed in 1990 by the members of the Warsaw Treaty Organization (Warsaw Pact—*q.v.*) and the North Atlantic Treaty Organization (NATO—*q.v.*) to establish parity in conventional weapons between the two organizations from the Atlantic to the Urals. Included a strict system of inspections and information exchange.

coupon—Generic term for bank-issued national currency certificates of Georgia, introduced in early 1993. After introduction, value declined rapidly; in January 1994, the exchange rate was approximately 186,000 coupons per US$1.

dram—National currency of Armenia, officially established for use concurrent with the Russian ruble in November 1993, became single official currency in early 1994. In February 1994, the exchange rate was approximately 15 drams per US$1. A second national unit, the luma (100 to the dram), was introduced in February 1994.

glasnost—Russian term, literally meaning "openness." Applied in the Soviet Union beginning in the mid-1980s to official permission for public discussion of issues and public access to information. Identified with the tenure of Mikhail S. Gorbachev as leader of the Soviet Union.

gross domestic product (GDP)—The total value of goods and services produced exclusively within a nation's domestic economy, in contrast to the gross national product (*q.v.*). Normally computed over one-year periods.

gross national product (GNP)—The total value of goods and services produced within a country's borders and the income received from abroad by residents, minus payments remitted abroad by nonresidents. Normally computed over one-year periods.

International Monetary Fund (IMF)—Established in 1945, a specialized agency affiliated with the United Nations and responsible for stabilizing international exchange rates and payments. Its main business is providing loans to its members when they experience balance of payments difficulties.

Kurds—A mainly Muslim people speaking an Indo-European language similar to Persian. Kurds constitute significant minorities in Iran, Iraq, and Turkey, with smaller groups in Armenia and Syria. Despite international proposals in response to minority persecution, never united in a single state.

manat—National currency of Azerbaijan. Introduced in mid-1992 for use concurrent with the ruble; became sole official currency in January 1994. Classified in 1994 as a "soft" currency, hence nonconvertible.

millet—In the Ottoman Empire, the policy for governance of non-Muslim minorities. The system created autonomous communities ruled by religious leaders responsible to the central government.

net material product (NMP)—In countries having centrally planned economies, the official measure of the value of goods and services produced within the country. Roughly equivalent to the gross national product (*q.v.*), NMP is based on constant prices and does not account for depreciation.

North Atlantic Treaty Organization (NATO)—During the postwar period until the dissolution of the Soviet Union in 1991, the primary collective defense agreement of the Western powers against the military presence of the Warsaw Pact (*q.v.*) nations in Europe. Founded 1949. Its military and administrative structure remained intact after 1991, but early in 1994 the Partnership for Peace proposed phased membership to all East European nations and many former republics of the Soviet Union.

perestroika—Russian term meaning "restructuring." Applied in the late 1980s to an official Soviet program of revitalization of the Communist Party of the Soviet Union (CPSU—*q.v.*), the economy, and the society by adjusting economic, social, and political mechanisms in the central planning system. Identified with the tenure of Mikhail S. Gorbachev as leader of the Soviet Union.

Shia—The smaller of the great two divisions of Islam, supporting the claims of Ali to leadership of the Muslim community, in opposition to the Sunni (*q.v.*) view of succession to Muslim leadership—the issue causing the central schism within Islam.

Sunni—The larger of the two fundamental divisions of Islam, opposed to the Shia (*q.v.*) on the issue of succession of Muslim leadership.

value-added tax (VAT)—A tax applied to the additional value created at a given stage of production and calculated as a percentage of the difference between the product value at that stage and the cost of all materials and services purchased or introduced as inputs.

Volunteer Society for Assistance to the Army, Air Force, and Navy (DOSAAF)—In the Soviet national defense system, the agency responsible for paramilitary training of youth and reserve components.

Warsaw Pact—Informal name for the Warsaw Treaty Organization, a mutual defense organization founded in 1955. Included the Soviet Union, Albania (which withdrew in 1968), Bulgaria, Czechoslovakia, the German Democratic Republic (East Germany), Hungary, Poland, and Romania. The Warsaw Pact enabled the Soviet Union to station troops in the countries of Eastern Europe to oppose the forces of the North Atlantic Treaty Organization (NATO—*q.v.*). The pact was the basis for the invasions of Hungary (1956) and Czechoslovakia (1968). Disbanded in July 1991.

World Bank—Informal name for a group of four affiliated international institutions: the International Bank for Reconstruction and Development (IBRD); the International Development Association(IDA); the International

Finance Corporation (IFC); and the Multilateral Investment Guarantee Agency (MIGA). The four institutions are owned by the governments of the countries that subscribe their capital for credit and investment in developing countries; each institution has a specialized agenda for aiding economic growth in target countries. To participate in the World Bank group, member states must first belong to the International Monetary Fund (IMF—*q.v.*).

Index

Abdullayev, Rafik, 132

Abkhazian Autonomous Republic, 165, 174–75; Abkhaz in, 179; cease-fire in, xxviii, xlv, xlix, 175; elections in, 208, 212; ethnic groups in, 179, 218; Georgians in, liii, 179; language in, 179, 187; matériel for, 225; military advisers in, 225; mining in, 196; peace talks, liv–lv; Russians in, 179; Russian support for, 174, 224; separatist movement in, xxv, xxvii, xliii, 171; war in, xxvii–xxviii, liii, 65, 174, 177, 195, 200, 201, 216, 218–19, 224, 225

Abkhaz people, 174; in Abkhazia, 179; ethnic background of, 177; life spans of, 178

Abovian, Khachatur, 37

Abuladze, Tengiz, 185

ACP. See Azerbaijani Communist Party

acquired immune deficiency syndrome (AIDS): in Armenia, 41; in Georgia, 189

Act of Independence (1991) (Azerbaijan), xxxviii, 135

Administration for the Struggle Against Terrorism and Banditry (Azerbaijan), 147

administrative districts: of Armenia, 61

Adoian, Vosdanik. See Gorky, Arshile

Afghanistan: Azerbaijan's relations with, 138

agricultural production: in Armenia, 42, 44; in Azerbaijan, xxxvii, 116–17, 118; in Georgia, 165, 198; as percentage of net material product, 118; under Soviet Union, 42, 198

agricultural products (see also under individual crops): of Armenia, 45; of Azerbaijan, 99, 117–18; citrus fruit, 99, 117–18, 199; cotton, 117–18, 119; distribution of, 199; export of, 199; of Georgia, 191, 198–99; grain, 199; grapes, 117–18, 119, 198; import of, 199; prices for, 118, 191; tea, 99, 119, 198, 199

agriculture: in Armenia, 42, 44–45; in Azerbaijan, xxxvii, 91, 115, 116, 117–19, 122; collectivized, xxv, 92; diversity in, 122; employment in, 51, 116; in Georgia, 165, 191, 198–99; privatization in, xxv, 198; problems in, 199; reform in, 165; women in, 45; work force in, 44

Agriculture and Industrial Bank of Georgia, 194

AID. See United States Agency for International Development

AIDS. See acquired immune deficiency syndrome

air force. See under armed forces

airports: in Armenia, 55–56; in Azerbaijan, 127; in Georgia, 201

Aivazovsky, Ivan, 37

Ajarian Autonomous Republic, 179–80

Akhundov. See Akhundzade, Mirza Fath Ali

Akhundzade, Mirza Fath Ali (Akhundov), 110

Akstafa River valley, 26

Alaverdy Metallurgical Plant: pollution caused by, 29

alcohol abuse, 189

Aleksandropol'. See Gyumri

Alexander the Great, 87–88

Alexander I, 159

Aliyev, Heydar: as Azerbaijani Communist Party leader, 93, 135; background of, 134–35; platform of, 134; as president, xxxi, xxxiii, xxxix, lii, liii, 65, 98, 107, 129, 134; removed from power, 93, 135; returned to power, xxxvii, xxxviii, 25, 133–34, 135

Alma-Ata Declaration (1991), 67, 141

Amasukheli, Elguja, 184

American Bar Association, 70

American Telephone and Telegraph Company, 56

American University of Armenia, 50

Amnesty International, 136

Anatolia: ancient peoples in, 9; Arme-

Contributors

Glenn E. Curtis is Senior Research Analyst for Eastern Europe and Central Eurasia in the Federal Research Division, Library of Congress.

James Nichol is a specialist in the Caucasus and Central Asia for the Congressional Research Service, Library of Congress.

Darrell Slider is Associate Professor in the Department of Government and International Affairs, University of South Florida.

Ronald G. Suny is Professor of History and holder of the Armenia Chair at the University of Michigan.

Published Country Studies

(Area Handbook Series)

550–65	Afghanistan	550–52	Ecuador
550–98	Albania	550–43	Egypt
550–44	Algeria	550–150	El Salvador
550–59	Angola	550–28	Ethiopia
550–73	Argentina	550–167	Finland
550–111	Armenia, Azerbaijan, and Georgia	550–173	Germany, East
550–169	Australia	550–155	Germany, Fed. Rep. of
550–176	Austria	550–153	Ghana
550–175	Bangladesh	550–87	Greece
550–170	Belgium	550–78	Guatemala
550–66	Bolivia	550–174	Guinea
550–20	Brazil	550–82	Guyana and Belize
550–168	Bulgaria	550–151	Honduras
550–61	Burma	550–165	Hungary
550–50	Cambodia	550–21	India
550–166	Cameroon	550–154	Indian Ocean
550–159	Chad	550–39	Indonesia
550–77	Chile	550–68	Iran
550–60	China	550–31	Iraq
550–26	Colombia	550–25	Israel
550–33	Commonwealth Caribbean, Islands of the	550–182	Italy
550–91	Congo	550–30	Japan
550–90	Costa Rica	550–34	Jordan
550–69	Côte d'Ivoire (Ivory Coast)	550–56	Kenya
550–152	Cuba	550–81	Korea, North
550–22	Cyprus	550–41	Korea, South
550–158	Czechoslovakia	550–58	Laos
550–36	Dominican Republic and Haiti	550–24	Lebanon

550–38	Liberia	550–180	Sierra Leone
550–85	Libya	550–184	Singapore
550–172	Malawi	550–86	Somalia
550–45	Malaysia	550–93	South Africa
550–161	Mauritania	550–95	Soviet Union
550–79	Mexico	550–179	Spain
550–76	Mongolia	550–96	Sri Lanka
550–49	Morocco	550–27	Sudan
550–64	Mozambique	550–47	Syria
550–35	Nepal and Bhutan	550–62	Tanzania
550–88	Nicaragua	550–53	Thailand
550–157	Nigeria	550–89	Tunisia
550–94	Oceania	550–80	Turkey
550–48	Pakistan	550–74	Uganda
550–46	Panama	550–97	Uruguay
550–156	Paraguay	550–71	Venezuela
550–185	Persian Gulf States	550–32	Vietnam
550–42	Peru	550–183	Yemens, The
550–72	Philippines	550–99	Yugoslavia
550–162	Poland	550–67	Zaire
550–181	Portugal	550–75	Zambia
550–160	Romania	550–171	Zimbabwe
550–37	Rwanda and Burundi		
550–51	Saudi Arabia		
550–70	Senegal